Lennox & Freda

How love came in, I do not know,
Whether by th' eye, or ear, or no;
Or whether with the soul it came,
At first, infused with the same;
Whether in part 'tis here or there,
Or, like the soul, whole everywhere.
This troubles me; but I as well
As any other, this can tell;
That when from hence she does depart,
The outlet then is from the heart.

Of Love: A Sonnet
ROBERT HERRICK (1591–1674)

The composer Lennox Berkeley set these lines to music in 1933, the last year of his long apprenticeship in Paris with Nadia Boulanger. Three years were to pass before he met, and later shared a house with, Benjamin Britten, six before Britten left him for Peter Pears (and America), and eleven before Lennox met Freda. The song was published by Boosey & Hawkes in 1936, and first recorded by Britten and Pears in 1956.

Lennox & Freda

TONY SCOTLAND

For [illegible]
With best wishes
Tony Scotland
27.ii.2011

MICHAEL RUSSELL

First published in Great Britain 2010
by Michael Russell (Publishing) Ltd
Wilby Hall, Wilby, Norwich NR16 2JP

Page makeup in Sabon by Waveney Typesetters
Wymondham, Norfolk
Printed in Great Britain by the MPG Books Group
Bodmin and King's Lynn

ISBN 978-0-85955-319-3

A grant from the RVW Trust helped towards
publication of this book

FOR FREDA

IN MEMORY OF LENNOX

Contents

List of Illustrations and Permissions

NB: Unless otherwise indicated all the images are the property of Lady Berkeley and the Lennox Berkeley Estate, and used with their permission and that of the Britten–Pears Foundation, where the Berkeley Family Papers are on permanent loan.

SECTION 1

The author and publisher are grateful for permission to use these photographs. Every reasonable effort has been made to trace copyright owners. We apologise to those whom we have been unable to locate, or have inadvertently omitted, and would ask them to make contact with the publisher, who will be pleased to insert an appropriate acknowledgement in any subsequent printing or edition of this book.

Sources and Acknowledgements

This book has drawn on a number of previously untapped sources, particularly the extensive collection of unpublished letters, diaries and miscellaneous papers, books, memorabilia, photos and drawings connected with Sir Lennox Berkeley and his family, which have been assembled and preserved by his widow Lady (Freda) Berkeley to form the Berkeley Family Papers, now on permanent loan at the Britten–Pears Library, Aldeburgh, Suffolk (and used by permission of Lady Berkeley and the Lennox Berkeley Estate, and the Trustees of © the Britten–Pears Foundation).

Other significant sources are: letters between Lennox Berkeley and Benjamin Britten, and their friends and associates including Wulff Scherchen, whose letters, recollections and poems are preserved as the John Woolford Papers at the Britten–Pears Library (used by permission of © the Britten–Pears Foundation, and of John Woolford, who has also allowed me to quote from email letters he wrote to me in 2008), Peter Dickinson's biography, *The Music of Lennox Berkeley* (2nd edition, Woodbridge, The Boydell Press, 2003), an essential reference work for anyone interested in Berkeley's life and music, together with Dickinson's own research material, including an important collection of taped interviews (many of them with subjects now no longer living), which he most generously made available for publication; Roger Nichols's notes and interviews and detailed chronology (for a proposed life of Berkeley), and his knowledge as a specialist in early-twentieth-century French music, to all of which he was kind enough to give me unlimited access, and permission to use; letters from Berkeley to his publisher in the archives of Chester Music (used with permission of Lady Berkeley and the Lennox Berkeley Estate, and Chester Music Ltd); letters, memoranda and other papers relating to Berkeley's years with the BBC, at the BBC Written Archives Centre, Caversham, Reading (used with the Centre's permission); Richard Thompson's archive of Burra family papers (including Peter Burra's correspondence with Berkeley, Britten, Pears and E. M. Forster, etc), and his own unpublished essays illuminating the rich seams to be mined there (in particular his detailed accounts of the death of Peter Burra, and the related events preceding and following it), all of which is used with the kind permission of Dr Richard Thompson and the Burra–Moody Archive; the original diaries and letters of James Lees-Milne, to which I was allowed privileged access (and generous permission to use) by his literary executor, editor and biographer, Michael Bloch, who has been unstinting in sharing his research material and scholarship; a collection of 127 letters which Berkeley wrote to Nadia Boulanger, 1928–79, most of them in French, which forms part of the Fonds spécialisé Nadia Boulanger NLa 54/210–369, in the Département de la musique, Bibliothèque nationale de France in Paris (and which I have been allowed to use by permission of Lady Berkeley and the Lennox Berkeley Estate, the Bibliothèque nationale de France, and the Fondation internationale Nadia et Lili Boulanger).

The following manuscripts have also been a valuable resource: Howard Davies's collection of unpublished writings by the late David Ponsonby (used by permission of Ponsonby's niece Tanya Lawrence), together with Davies's helpful observations about Berkeley's social circle in London during the war; nineteen letters from Berkeley to the pianist Hélène Kahn-Casella, now acquired for the Berkeley Family Papers, on permanent loan at the Britten–Pears Library, Aldeburgh (and used by permission of Lady Berkeley and the Lennox Berkeley Estate, and © the Britten–Pears Foundation); eight further letters from Berkeley to Kahn-Casella, together with letters from Berkeley to James Lees-Milne and Alan Pryce-Jones, at the Beinecke Rare Book and Manuscript Library, Yale University (and used with their permission and that of Lady Berkeley and the Lennox Berkeley Estate); nineteen letters from Berkeley (and one from his mother, Mrs Hastings Berkeley) to Somerset Maugham's secretary and companion Alan Searle, in the W. Somerset Maugham Collection at the Howard Gotlieb Archival Research Center at Boston University (to the existence of which I was alerted by Maugham's biographer, Lady Selina Hastings, and for the use of which I am grateful to Lady Berkeley and the Lennox Berkeley Estate, and the Director of the Howard Gotlieb Archival Research Center at Boston University); the handwritten memoirs of his years as a student and friend of both Berkeley and Nadia Boulanger by the composer, novelist and painter Richard Stoker (used with permission); correspondence between Berkeley and Patric L. Dickinson (then a schoolboy, now Norroy and Ulster King of Arms), which Patric Dickinson, Lady Berkeley and the Lennox Berkeley Estate have allowed me to use.

Of the books I have consulted, those permanently on my desk have included: Stewart Craggs's published research into the sources of Berkeley's life, career and compositions, *Lennox Berkeley: A Source Book* (Aldershot, Ashgate, 2000); Joan Redding's list of Berkeley's works (for *A Descriptive List of the Musical Manuscripts of Sir Lennox Berkeley* [MSc. Library Science Thesis, University of North Carolina at Chapel Hill, 1988], published by Chester Music); the comprehensive edition in four volumes (so far) of Britten's letters and diaries (meticulously edited and notated by Donald Mitchell, Philip Reed and, latterly, Mervyn Cooke): *Letters from a Life: Selected Letters and Diaries of Benjamin Britten* vol. i, 1930–39, vol. ii, 1939–45 (Faber & Faber, 1991); vol. iii, 1946–51 (Faber & Faber, 2004); vol. iv, 1952–57 (Woodbridge, The Boydell Press, in association with The Britten–Pears Foundation, 2008), and the biography of Britten by the late Humphrey Carpenter, *Benjamin Britten: A Biography* (Faber & Faber, 1992), from both of which sources Faber have allowed me to use extracts; and John Bridcut's *Britten's Children* (Faber & Faber, 2006), based on the TV documentary film he made for the BBC in 2004, from which I have been allowed to quote by permission of John Bridcut and Faber.

I have also drawn on the late Richard D. E. Burton's monograph *Francis Poulenc* (Bath, Absolute Press, 2002) which explores the links between homosexuality, Catholicism and modernism in inter-war France; Michael Burn's autobiography, *Turned towards the Sun* (Norwich, Michael Russell, 2003), which covers, amongst much else, a recognizable tussle between Catholicism, homosexuality and marriage; an interview which C. B. Cox, Allan Young and Michael Schmidt conducted with Lennox Berkeley for the magazine *Poetry Nation* in 1974 (used by permission of © *Poetry Nation Review* [formerly *Poetry Nation*], 1974); the autobiography of the composer Humphrey Searle, *Quadrille with a Raven – Memoirs*, published on the Web at http://www.musicweb-international.com/searle/titlepg.htm (and used by permission of Fiona Searle, and of MusicWeb); Graham Johnson's lectures on the music of Benjamin Britten, *Britten, Voice & Piano* (Aldershot, the Guildhall School of Music & Drama and Ashgate Publishing, 2003), and our many conversations on the subject of

Berkeley and Britten; and Dolf Mootham's table of changing money values, based on inflation figures from the Central Statistical Office, which Jonathan Gathorne-Hardy helpfully provides at the start of his autobiography, *Half an Arch* (Timewell Press, 2004).

Copyright material, not already mentioned above, is quoted by permission of: Edward Mendelson, on behalf of © the Estate of W. H. Auden (for quotations from Auden's unpublished letters); King's College, Cambridge, and The Society of Authors as agent for the Provost and Scholars of King's College, Cambridge (for letters from Peter Burra to Edward Dent, and E. M. Forster to Christopher Isherwood, in the Papers of Edward Dent at King's College Library); Lilly Library, Indiana University, Bloomington, Indiana (for extracts from letters from Berkeley to Desmond Shawe-Taylor in the Desmond Shawe-Taylor Papers at the Lilly Library); A. P. Watt Ltd, on behalf of The Royal Literary Fund, (for an extract from a letter from Somerset Maugham to Alan Searle); David Higham Associates (for the use of extracts by Dylan Thomas, John Davenport and Constantine FitzGibbon from *The Death of the King's Canary*, Hutchinson, 1976); and the Harry Ransom Humanities Research Center at the University of Texas at Austin (for a copy of a letter from Terence Greenidge to Charles Linck); the late Rt. Hon. Michael Foot, and the Hyman Kreitman Research Centre at Tate Britain (for the use of extracts from letters written by Jill Craigie to Paul Nash); the Britten–Pears Library (for the use of extracts from the letters of Barbara Britten); Sally Schweitzer (for permission to quote from the letters of her mother Beth Welford née Britten), and Bridget Kitley (for the use of extracts from the letters of her mother Enid Slater).

Every effort has been made to trace holders of other copyright material, and I very much regret any inadvertent omissions; these can be rectifed in future editions.

Additionally I have carried out my own, original research into the Berkeley, Drummond de Melfort, Harris and Bernstein family histories; and, over the course of thirty-six years, I have had many dozens of conversations with Freda Berkeley, the more substantial of them preserved on tape.

So my chief debt of gratitude is to Freda, who has encouraged and endorsed the writing of this book, wholeheartedly and unconditionally, from the beginning, allowing me total freedom to tell the story as I wanted (and letting me see, and use, her intimate wartime diary); and to

Michael, Julian and Nicholas Berkeley, who have most generously trusted me to write their father's life, despite some disquiet, which I too share, about the inevitable invasion of a very private man's privacy.

In addition to those mentioned above, the following have been kind enough to provide me with material, information, leads, ideas, or practical help: the late Anne Dowager Marchioness of Aberdeen, the late Leo Abse and Ania Abse, John-Mark Ainsley, Anda Anastasescu, the late Michael Annals, Giselle Bähr, Robin Baird-Smith, Dame Janet Baker, Louise Bangay and James Rowsell, Ariane Bankes, the late Frith Banbury, Charles Berkeley, Rowan Berkeley, Richard Bernas, Lewis and Ernestine Bernstein, Edward Blakeman, David Carter, Harvey Chalmers, Hugh Cobbe, Hugues Cuénod, the late Lady Darwin, Natalie Davenport, Patric L. Dickinson, Jessica Douglas-Home, Harry Ellis, Dr John Evans, Joe de Freitas, Elizabeth Gibson, Jacqueline E. Gill, Robin Golding, the Countess of Gowrie, Edmund Gray, Paul Guinery, the late Lady Dorothy Heber-Percy, the late Richard Hickox, Roger Highfield, Jo Hill, Penny Hoare, Lord Hutchinson of Lullington and the late Lady Hutchinson, Angela Huth, Allan Clive Jones, Francis King, Claire Launchbury, Tony Leech, Helen Leneman, Donald Macleod, Sir John Manduell, Belinda Matthews, Andrew C. Mayes, Jane Norman, Anthony Nunney, the late Patrick O'Connor, the late Ann Orbach, Judge Aron Owen, Peter Parker, Nicholas Parkhouse, the late Burnet Pavitt, Fr Terry Phipps, Godfrey Pilkington, Hector Pilkington, Robert Ponsonby, Thomas Ponsonby, Aveva Price, Oliver and Meredith Ramsbotham, the late Fr Cormac Rigby, Deirdre Rigby, Nick Robinson, Dr Barbara Schwepcke, David and Annie Scotland, Edward Scotland, Lady Spender, Joy Stibbe, Astrid Sweetenham, Chris Taylor, Tay Cheng-Jim, Roy Teed, Alexander Titov, the late Patrick Trevor-Roper, Zoë Waldie, Christopher J. Walker, Kathleen Walker (co-founder, the Lennox Berkeley Society), Stephen Walsh, William Whitehead, David Wordsworth, the late Dr William Wynne Willson and Lady Young.

For professional assistance I am indebted to: the staff of the Britten–Pears Library with whom I have been constantly in touch for a decade, especially Chris Grogan, Director of Collections and Heritage (and his predecessor as Librarian, Jennifer Doctor), the Archives Assistants Pam Wheeler and Anne Surfling, who took care to check my typescript and advised about the text, the Librarian Nick Clark, Andrew Plant and Judith Ratcliffe; James Rushton, Managing Director, Chester Music Ltd., and his staff, especially Kate Johnson, Victoria

Small and, though he has now left the company, David Smith, for all their generous help with my enquiries over more than a decade; Jacquie Kavanagh, Archivist, and Trish Hayes, Archives Researcher, BBC Written Archives Centre, Caversham; Catherine Massip, Directrice, and Elisabeth Vilatte, Département de la musique, Bibliothèque nationale de France, Paris; Sean D. Noel, Associate Director, Howard Gotlieb Archival Research Center, Boston University; Kathleen Dickson and Roger Young, British Film Institute, London; Rupert Cornwell and Nicolas Bell, Music Collections, The British Library; Judith Curthoys, Archivist, Christ Church, Oxford; Robin Houghton, The Dragon School, Oxford; Pam Weatherley, Archivist, St George's School, Harpenden; Richard Morgan, Archivist, Glamorgan Record Office, Cardiff; J. S. Rayner, Archivist, Gresham's School, Holt, Norfolk; Colin J. Gibson, Gwent Record Office, Cwmbrân; Toby Barnard, Archivist, Hertford College, Oxford; Sue Hodson, Curator of Literary Manuscripts, and Gayle M. Richardson, Library Assistant, The Huntingdon Library, San Marino, California; Erika Dowell, Public Services Librarian, The Lilly Library, Indiana University; John Howard Wilson, Editor, *Evelyn Waugh Newsletter and Studies*, and Assistant Professor, English Department, Lock Haven University of Pennsylvania; Inez Lynn, Librarian (and her predecessors Alan Bell and Douglas Matthews), and the unfailingly helpful and friendly staff at the London Library; Michael Stansfield, Archivist, Merton College, Oxford (and his successor, Julian Reid); Gina L. B. Minks, Special Collections Librarian, McFarlin Library, University of Tulsa; Sandra Grace, Reference Library, Newport, Monmouthshire; Louis-Gilles Pairault, Conservateur du patrimoine, Directeur des Archives, Mairie de Nice; Eluned Hallas, Administrator, Oxford Preservation Trust, St Ebbes, Oxford; Simon Blundell, Secretary's Office, Reform Club, London; Sue Whyte, Archive Assistant, Royal Opera House Archives, Covent Garden; Richard Crampton, Archivist, St Edmund Hall, Oxford; Mrs J. Mitchener, St Joseph's College, Beulah Hill, London SE19; A. Sword, H. M. Coroner's Court, St Pancras; Richard Workman, Associate Librarian, Tara Wenger, Research Librarian, and L. Christine Amos, Harry Ransom Humanities Research Center, The University of Texas at Austin; Janet Birkett, Theatre Museum, London; Sheila Markham, Librarian, The Travellers' Club, London; Clare Hopkins, Archivist, Trinity College, Oxford; Ellen Doon, Alan Pryce-Jones Papers, and Graham Sherriff, Beinecke Rare Book and Manuscript Library, Yale

University; Suzanne Eggleston Lovejoy, Assistant Music Librarian for Public Services, Irving S. Gilmore Library, Yale University.

I also want to record my thanks for assistance given by the Librarians, Archivists and Reading Room staffs of: British Architectural Library, Royal Institute of British Architects, London; British Library Newspaper Library, Colindale; Camden Local Studies and Archives Centre, London; Companies House, Cardiff; Aaron Copland Collection (of letters and miscellaneous writings etc), by permission of the Aaron Copland Fund for Music, online at The Library of Congress (http://memory.loc.gov/ammem/achtml); Family Records Centre, London; the Hyman Kreitman Research Centre at Tate Britain, London; *Jewish Chronicle*, London; Special Collections Division, Lauinger Library, Georgetown University; Leicester Probate Registry; National Army Museum, Chelsea; Powys County Archives, Llandrindod Wells; Probate Search Rooms, High Holborn, London; Public Record Office, Kew; George Charles Grantley Fitzhardinge Berkeley Papers, Rush Rhees Library, University of Rochester, New York; National Library of Wales, Aberystwyth; City of Westminster Archives Centre, London; Westminster Central Reference Library, London.

I am particularly grateful to Michael Russell for his comprehensive help and to Barrie Fairhead of Waveney Typesetters for dealing so skilfully and patiently with a barrage of late corrections.

And finally I owe an enormous debt to my friends Julian Berkeley, Michael and Deborah Berkeley, Michael Bloch, Howard Davies, the late Jill Day Lewis, Peter Dickinson, Lady Selina Hastings, John Holmstrom, Sir Michael Howard, Roger Nichols, Richard Thompson, Petroc Trelawny and, especially, Adam Bager, for reading my early drafts, and for their corrections, suggestions and encouragement. The book has gained immeasurably from their wise advice, so kindly given; any remaining mistakes, omissions or misinterpretations are mine.

Abbreviations

BB	Benjamin Britten.
BBCWAC	BBC Written Archives Centre (Caversham Park, Reading, Berkshire RG4 8TZ).
BFP	Berkeley Family Papers at the Britten–Pears Library (Aldeburgh, Suffolk IP15 5PY).
B–MA	Burra–Moody Archive (Dr R. D. Thompson, Egham, Surrey TW20 0RL).
BPL	Britten–Pears Library.
CMA	Chester Music Archives (Chester Music Ltd., 14–15 Berners Street, London W1T 3LJ).
DPM	David Ponsonby Manuscripts ('War Memoir', 'Nadia Boulanger', 'Ravel, etc.' and other unpublished papers) in the possession of Howard Davies.
FB	Freda Berkeley née Bernstein.
FSNB	Fonds spécialisé Nadia Boulanger, Département de la musique, Bibliothèque nationale de France, Paris.
HC	Humphrey Carpenter, *Benjamin Britten: A Biography*, London, Faber & Faber, 1992.
JWP	John Woolford Papers at the Britten–Pears Library.
LB	Lennox Berkeley.
LFAL	Donald Mitchell and Philip Reed (eds), *Letters from a Life*, volumes 1 and 2, and (with Mervyn Cooke), volume 3, London, Faber & Faber, 1991 and 2004; and volume 4, Woodbridge, The Boydell Press, in association with The Britten–Pears Foundation, 2008.
MB	Michael Berkeley.
MBA	Michael Berkeley Archives, Britten–Pears Library.
MLB	Peter Dickinson, *The Music of Lennox Berkeley*, 2nd edn., Woodbridge, The Boydell Press, 2003.
NB	Nadia Boulanger.
PB	Peter Burra.
PD	Peter Dickinson.

Abbreviations

PDA	Peter Dickinson Archives (Aldeburgh, Suffolk IP1 5QD).
RN	Roger Nichols.
RNA	Roger Nichols Archives (Kington, Herefordshire HR5 3BA).
SRC	Stewart R. Craggs, *Lennox Berkeley: A Source Book*, Aldershot, Ashgate, 2000.
TS	Tony Scotland.
WS	Wulff Scherchen (later John Woolford).

Dramatis Personae

AN ALPHABETICAL LIST OF THE PRINCIPAL CHARACTERS

Aline	Lennox's mother, Aline Carla Berkeley (1863–1935), second daughter of James and Gerhardine Harris.
Alan	Lennox's friend 1933–5, Alan Searle (?1910–85), Somerset Maugham's secretary and companion at Cap Ferrat from 1944 till Maugham's death in 1965.
Barbara	Benjamin Britten's unmarried elder sister, Edith Barbara Britten (1902–82).
Ben	Lennox's friend and collaborator, the composer Edward Benjamin, Baron Britten of Aldeburgh (1913–76).
Beth	Ben Britten's second sister, Charlotte Elizabeth Britten (1909–89), wife of Christopher [Kit] Welford (1911–73).
Cécile	Lennox's paternal grandmother, Cécile, Countess of Berkeley (1832–1914), daughter of Edouard Drummond, comte de Melfort, by his wife Maria Naysmith, and wife, successively, of Admiral Sir Fleetwood Pellew (divorced 1859) and Captain George Lennox Rawdon Berkeley, later 7th Earl of Berkeley.
Claude	Lennox's first cousin, Claude Berkeley (died *c.* 1976), only son of Ernest and Nelly Berkeley.
David	Lennox's Oxford contemporary and fellow pupil of Nadia Boulanger in Paris, the pianist, composer, watercolourist and Resistance fighter David Brabazon Ponsonby (1901–86).
Ernest	Lennox's uncle, Sir Ernest Berkeley (1857–1932), second son of George and Cécile Berkeley, and husband of Lennox's Aunt Nelly née Harris.

Freda — Lennox's wife, Elizabeth Freda (born 1923), only child of Isaac and Grace Bernstein.

George — Lennox's paternal grandfather, George Lennox Rawdon, 7th Earl of Berkeley (1827–88), husband of Cécile, Lady Pellew née Drummond.

Geraldine — (aka Gerry), Lennox's unmarried sister, Geraldine Margaret Berkeley (1897–1988).

Gerhardine — Lennox's maternal grandmother, Gerhardine, Lady Harris (*c.* 1839–1912), daughter of Ferdinand Wilhelm, Freiherr von Gall, by his wife (and cousin) Leonore, Freein von Gall, and wife of Sir James Harris.

Grace — Freda's mother, Grace Amy Bernstein (1893–1926), youngest daugher of Frederick Charles Nunney by his wife Blanch Allen, and wife of Isaac Bernstein.

Hans — One of Freda's admirers, the art historian Hans Gronau (1904–51), head of Old Masters department at Sotheby's, and husband of the art historian Carmen Joachim von Wogau (died 1999).

Hastings — Lennox's father, Captain Hastings George FitzHardinge Berkeley, RN (1855–1934), eldest son of George and Cécile Berkeley and husband of Aline née Harris.

Hedli — Benjamin Britten's friend, the singer and actress Hedli Anderson (1907–90), wife of Louis MacNeice (1907–63).

Igor — Lennox's friend and fellow pupil of Nadia Boulanger in Paris, the conductor and composer Igor Markevitch (1912–83).

Isaac — Freda's father, Isaac Bernstein (1869–1928), second son of (Hyman) Joseph Bernstein (*c.* 1841–1912) by his wife Fradel (1832–1909), and husband of Grace Amy Nunney.

James — Lennox's maternal grandfather, Sir James Charles Harris (1831–1904), son of Commander J. Harris, RN, by his wife Harriet Bird, and husband of Gerhardine, Freiin von Gall.

John Davenport — Lennox's friend (and host at the Malting House,

Marshfield near Bath, 1939–40), the writer and critic John Davenport (1908–66), husband of Clement (later wife of William Glock).

John Greenidge Lennox's lifelong friend, the architect John Theodore Waterman Greenidge (1899–1953).

José Lennox's friend in Paris in the 1930s, N. José Raffalli (died *c.* 1941).

Julian Lennox and Freda's second son, Julian Lennox Berkeley (born 1950).

Kate Lennox's aunt by marriage, Kate, Countess of Berkeley (1854–98), youngest daughter of William Farries Brand, widow of Arthur Herbert Jackson and first wife of Randal, Earl of Berkeley.

Lennox [aka Coss], the composer Sir Lennox Berkeley (1903–89), only son of Hastings and Aline Berkeley, and husband of Freda née Bernstein.

Ma'moiselle See *Nadia*.

Michael Lennox and Freda's eldest son, the composer Michael FitzHardinge Berkeley (born 1948).

Molly Lennox's aunt by marriage, Mary Emlen, Countess of Berkeley (*c.* 1884– 1975), daughter of John and Mary Lowell of Boston, Massachusetts, divorced wife of Frank Lloyd of Philadelphia, and second wife of Randal, Earl of Berkeley.

Nadia Lennox's composition teacher in Paris 1926–33, lifelong friend and inspiration, the celebrated teacher, conductor and recreator of early and baroque music, Nadia Boulanger (1887–1979).

Nelly Lennox's double aunt, Leonore (Nelly) Magdalen Berkeley (1868–1929), amateur pianist and composer, wife of Sir Ernest Berkeley (younger brother of Hastings), and elder sister of Aline, Mrs Hastings Berkeley née Harris.

Nicholas Lennox and Freda's youngest son, Nicholas Eadnoth Berkeley (born 1956).

Peter Burra A friend of Lennox, Ben Britten and Peter Pears, the writer and critic Peter James Salkeld Burra (1909–37). [Not to be confused with his distant cousin, the painter Edward Burra (1905–76).]

Peter Fraser	Lennox's wartime friend, Peter (Raymond Laurance) Fraser (1920–76).
Peter Pears	Benjamin Britten's lifelong friend and companion, the tenor Sir Peter (Neville Luard) Pears (1910–86).
Randal	Lennox's uncle, the scientist Randal Thomas Mowbray, eighth and last Earl of Berkeley (1865–1942), third son of George and Cécile Berkeley, husband of, successively, Kate Jackson née Brand, and Molly Lloyd née Lowell.
Sybil	Lennox's godmother Sybil Deane Jackson (1877–1976), unmarried daughter of Arthur and Kate Jackson, and stepdaughter and companion of Randal, Earl of Berkeley.
Vally	The tomcat at the Old Mill, Snape (died August 1939).
Vere	Lennox's Oxford flatmate and lifelong friend (and Freda's employer at Sotheby's, 1946–7), Charles Vere Pilkington (1905–83), son of Charles Carlisle Pilkington by his wife Emilia née Lloyd, and husband of Honor Philipps, daughter of 1st Lord Kylsant. An accomplished amateur harpsichordist and collector of old keyboard instruments, Pilkington was a director of Sotheby's 1927–58, and Chairman 1953–8.
Vonnie	Lennox's first cousin, Helen Yvonne Berkeley (1899–*c.* 1984), unmarried only daughter of Ernest and Nelly Berkeley.
Widow, The	Lennox's Oxford contemporary and lifelong friend, the conservationist, historian and former Bright Young Thing, John Davies Knatchbull Lloyd (1900–78), Mayor of Montgomery 1932–8, High Sheriff of Montgomeryshire 1940; brother of Wyndham.
William	Lennox's friend, the critic and music administrator, William (later Sir William) Glock (1908–2000), second husband of Clement Davenport.
Winnie	Lennox's friend and patron, Winnaretta Eugénie, princesse Edmond de Polignac (1865–1943), daughter of Isaac Merritt Singer, and wife of prince Edmond de Polignac.

Wystan — Lennox's friend and Oxford contemporary, the poet W. H. Auden (1907–73).

Wulff — Benjamin Britten's young friend and musical inspiration Wulff Scherchen – later John Woolford – (born 1920), son of the German conductor Hermann Scherchen by his wife Gustel.

A skeleton pedigree of LENNOX BERKELEY*'s family*

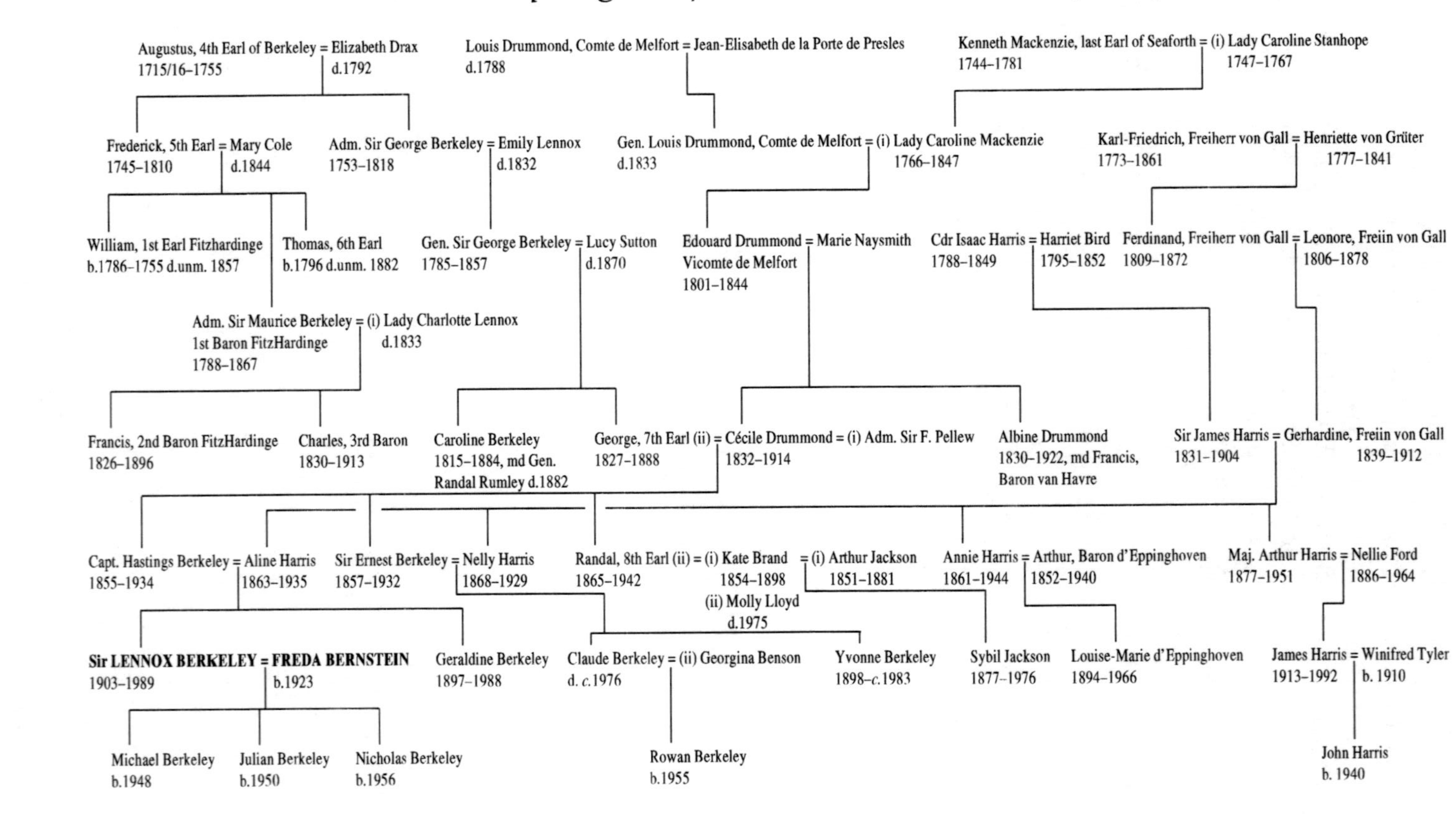

A skeleton pedigree of FREDA BERNSTEIN*'s family*

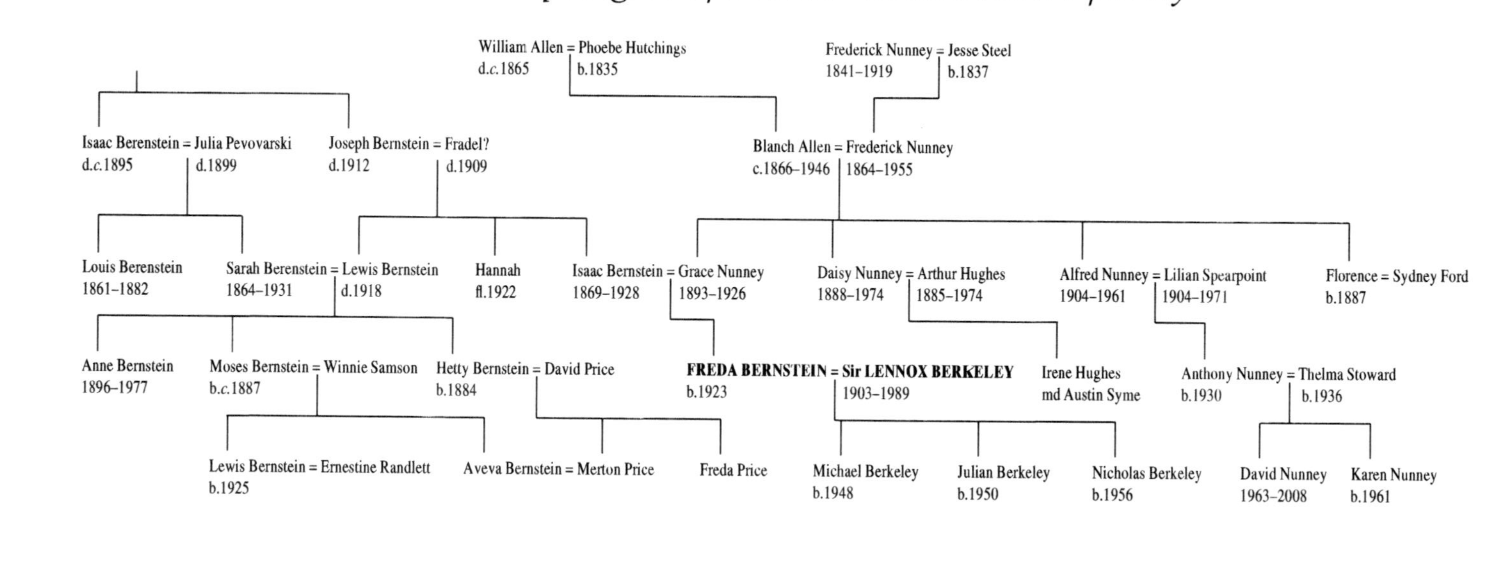

Preface

This is the story of an artist's struggle to find his orientation and his faith, in a morass of family feuds, two world wars and changing social values, and of the remarkable woman who helped him. It is not an orthodox biography of either of them. It dwells instead on the ways their lives converged and coalesced, and the background against which this happened, and it ends with the marriage which brought them the confidence to fulfil their potential.

It has been difficult to write about the composer Lennox Berkeley, because he was such a shadowy figure – private, modest and absorbed in his own interior world. I lived with the Berkeleys, as part of the family, for most of the last decade of Lennox's life, yet he remains an elusive, though lovable, figure. In one sense he was all he seemed: sweet, shy and gentle, with beautiful manners, an attractive, gravelly voice, and a quiet chuckle. In appearance he was as Continental as his ancestry and upbringing: elegantly informal, and immacutely groomed. He was also absent-minded and indecisive, but he may have exaggerated these characteristics as a screen behind which he could retreat into his inner life – for this was where his reality lay.

Lennox was never happier than at home with his family and his dog Prince, working in the seclusion of his study, teaching composition students and entertaining (and playing duets with) friends. His day was strictly ordered, but there was always time for visitors, and no one who crossed the Berkeleys' threshold will forget the warmth of the welcome and the pervading sense of security.

There should be less need to explain Freda, who is as transparent as Lennox was opaque, but though she may seem an open book – to the point, indeed, of recklessness – there are hidden wells of strength and determination that played as crucial a part in winning Lennox as her understanding and generosity. A kind heart, and almost supernatural sympathy and a great emotional need of her own have made her, as Jim Lees-Milne observed in 1971, 'universally beloved'. The same qualities still bring new, young friends and admirers in the middle of her eighth decade.

Preface

Since this book is about the making of 'Lennox and Freda', those who knew them later are not included amongst the friends pictured within. Some, alas, are no longer with us anyway, but many still are and I hope they will understand their absence from this story.

A word about nomenclature. First, proper names. My subjects are 'Lennox' and 'Freda', and, for the sake of consistency, I have called others whom I never knew by a Christian name I should not have presumed to use otherwise: in particular, Lennox's intimate friend 'Ben' (Britten), his revered teacher 'Nadia' (Boulanger), Ben's young friend 'Wulff' (Scherchen) and the writers 'Wystan' (Auden) and 'Christopher' (Isherwood). Secondly, that tricky little adjective 'gay'. Throughout the book I have chosen this now neutral epithet in preference to the less anachronistic, but somehow clinical and even disapproving, 'homosexual'. After some uncertainty, I decided that what was good enough for Dominic Hibberd in his masterly biography of Wilfred Owen (born 1893) was good enough for me in my story about Lennox Berkeley (born ten years later). In neither case is the three-letter word the *mot juste*, if only because the love of man for man (and, of course, woman for woman) did not need, and would not have dared to make a public claim for, its own special word in those more innocent (yet proscriptive) times; but at least it is less un-*juste* than any of the alternatives, which include an expression used about Lennox by a distant cousin, 'a Left Bank lad'.

Finally, the music. Lennox himself held that his work was entirely distinct from his life, that it was not possible to draw parallels between them, but the evidence does not always support this. And certainly if you want to know what the man was like you have only to listen to the music – any of it, for it is all distinctive and idiosyncratic, but particularly the songs, the piano pieces, and the liturgical settings. Hardly a Sunday passes without one of his Masses or anthems performed in one or more of our great cathedrals (for a diary of Berkeley music, and more, visit the Lennox Berkeley Society at www.lennoxberkeley.org.uk). As an introduction listen to the merry *Serenade*, then try the *Six* (contrasting) *Preludes* for piano, followed by the profoundly beautiful *Four Poems of St Teresa of Avila*. Listen carefully, and twice. You will want to hear more.

Baughurst, June 2010 TONY SCOTLAND

1
Berkeley, Britten and Burra, Barcelona, 1936

Benjamin Britten's journey was the bumpiest. He flew in by seaplane,[1] landing in the harbour near the Estació Maritima, where he was met by friends who drove him up the Ramblas to his hotel, the Falcón, on the Plaça del Teatro.

Lennox Berkeley came, more conventionally, by train: around the Mediterranean coast, from his late mother's now empty villa at Cap Ferrat. He picked up a taxi outside the Estació de França and cut across the south-west corner of the Old City till he reached the Falcón later that same afternoon.

The next morning, Saturday 18 April 1936, Peter Burra flew in from Madrid,[2] and he too made for the Falcón.

They had never met before, these three young Englishmen – two composers and a writer – but they knew of one another's reputations, had friends in common, and shared at least three interests: music, literature and young men (though the refinements of their attraction to the latter were subtly different). Furthermore, they were all the adored sons of over-protective mothers. For each of these clever, thoughtful, ambitious young men, the fourteenth festival of the International Society for Contemporary Music, in a Barcelona on the verge of civil war, amidst what Burra described as 'a tottering Europe',[3] was to be a crossroads – not least because of the determining friendships they formed with, and through, one another.

Burra, then twenty-six – sandy-haired and fine-boned, ex-Lancing and Christ Church, Oxford – was a writer and critic who had already made his mark as a biographer, with studies of Van Gogh and Virginia Woolf, and such a perceptive article on the novels of E. M. Forster that Forster himself described Burra as 'the best critic of his generation'.[4] Later in 1936 Burra was to publish a life of Wordsworth that is still admired today, [5] and by the following year he was reviewing fiction for the *Spectator*. He was also a keen amateur musician who played the violin and sang. Now he was on his first foreign assignment as a special correspondent of *The Times*, with a brief to review the concerts and write about the festival. He intended to use the opportunity to see at first hand, in the epicentre of Spanish revolutionary politics, the simmering discontent which had caused the dramatic downfall of the President of the Second Republic the previous week, and was to lead to Civil War within three months.

In the event the official festival hotel, the Falcón, was to prove a propitious base for observing the Republicans' struggle: by the end of the year, when Barcelona was 'a revolutionary city, a city of posters and slogans, of collectivized shops and gutted churches',[6] the Falcón had been requisitioned by the British anti-Fascists who had joined the International Brigades to fight against the Royalists and their Nazi supporters; in 1937 it was converted into a rest and recuperation centre for soldiers of POUM, the Workers' Party of Marxist Unification, on leave from the front; and the following year, when POUM was declared illegal, the secret police arrested the entire complement of the Falcón, and turned the hotel into a prison. The idea of sharing quarters with soldiers might have appealed to the passionate Burra, who was romantically drawn to fit young men of action and tested his sexuality by risk-taking, both in and out of bed. If he himself was sensitive, intellectual and gay, his idols were rugged, audacious and straight, and the confusion of these contradictions was one of the causes of a looming personal crisis.*

At twenty-three, Britten was the baby of the trio, frizzy-haired, buttoned-up, still 'a prep school boy who adored maths and cricket'[7] and clung to a hearty slang of 'beastly nice', 'simply topping' and 'absolutely ripping'.[8] A dentist's son from East Anglia, he had already won a reputation for 'cleverness' that was not a compliment in the England of the 1930s.[9] He had a natural genius for composition, a leaning to the Left that was emotionally pacifist and intellectually Communist – and an almost unhealthy fixation on a controlling mother. Mrs Britten's ambition for her prodigy was Olympian in its presumption: she intended that he should be the fourth B in the panoply of composers that began with Bach, Beethoven and Brahms[10] (coincidentally these had been the teenage Britten's favourite composers). And, against all odds, he was on the way to getting there. Since entering the Royal

* BB hints at the problem in his diary for 14 March 1937: 'A first rate brain, that was at the moment in great difficulties' (LFAL, p. 479).

College of Music five and a half years earlier he had had at least nine public performances of his work (some of them broadcast on the BBC), and had signed an exclusive publishing contract with Boosey & Hawkes. He was 'house composer' and director of music at Rupert Doone's experimental Group Theatre,* and he had also begun an association with the GPO Film Unit, writing incidental music for documentaries.

Through the Film Unit he had met, the previous summer, the poet W. H. Auden, under whose spell he had fallen politically, if not (despite Auden's siren efforts) sexually. Barely a month before Barcelona, Auden had written a poem called 'Night Covers up the Rigid Land', which not only declares his love but also recognizes he has not a hope. Its dedication to Britten seems to suggest that he is the second person singular to whom the lines are specifically addressed: 'You love your life and I love you, / So I must lie alone.'[11]

Britten's apparent rejection of his seasoned suitor was not entirely personal: it was also, as the wise Auden well knew, a fear of flesh in general. And in the course of the coming year Auden was to work hard at trying to 'unfreeze his younger colleague into a state of emotional responsiveness'.† He was not unsuccessful, though Barcelona, via Burra, Lancing and the old boys' network, was to guide Britten's love in quite a different direction.

Ten years Britten's senior, Lennox Berkeley was smoothly good-looking and elegantly dressed, with all the social graces, but this sophisticated exterior masked a profound lack of confidence in himself and his music. Like Britten and Auden, Berkeley had been, for a short time, at the ultra-progressive Gresham's School, Holt; and, like Burra, and with Auden, at the ultra-permissive Oxford. Unlike both, he was also a patrician – the scion of a family of earls, admirals and masters of

*Burra's twin sister Helen was to marry a founder member of the Group Theatre, the actor John Moody, the following year.

†This is the telling phrase, and part of the compelling thesis, of a former student of Britten, the accompanist and musicologist Graham Johnson: 'When he first met Auden, Britten was, in physical terms, still almost certainly a virgin: "cold", "frozen" or "suspended" are common descriptions of his attitude to love and sex at this point in his life. Auden seems to have taken it upon himself to "unfreeze" his younger colleague into a state of emotional responsiveness'(Graham Johnson, *Britten, Voice & Piano – Lectures on the Vocal Music of Benjamin Britten*, p. 145.)

hounds who had dominated the West of England since the Conquest; with direct links, on the female side, to the crowned heads of Europe, and to the sibling Earls of Perth and Melfort who had virtually ruled Scotland at the end of the seventeenth century. Like Britten and Auden, Berkeley was homosexual, but unlike them he was also Catholic, a convert who had gone over in Paris in 1929, inspired by his revered teacher, the devout Nadia Boulanger.

Attracted initially by the Latin liturgy (which he had first encountered in its musical form as Gregorian chant at the otherwise un-Catholic Gresham's),[12] Lennox had gone on to develop such a deep religious sense that he had thought of becoming a priest a year or two after his conversion.[13] What held him back was the usual conundrum of how to reconcile spirituality and sexual freedom. He knew he was homosexual, and he enjoyed gay life, in the discreet way of his class and of the times, but he was not entirely at ease with its physical expression, which was anathema to a Church that regards any sexual coupling outside marriage as a sin. The 'world of the senses' might be 'great fun', he wrote to a friend, but it was not 'the real world'.[14] The real world, for Lennox, was the world of the spirit.

At a still sexually-segregated Oxford, in the *Brideshead* years of teddy-bears and posing Blanches, homosexuality had been not only *à la mode* but even *de rigueur*, so that it had hardly been possible, as the poet Louis MacNeice later maintained, for an intelligent man not to be homosexual.[15] Lennox had shared rooms, and possibly more, with his Christ Church friend Vere Pilkington, and later, in Paris, he had shared a house, and probably more, with his boyhood friend, the architect and painter John Greenidge. From about 1929 till about 1933 he lived with a young Corsican called José Raffalli, a clever, artistic, managing young man of the epicene kind to which Lennox was serially drawn, to the dismay of his family, who would have been even more distressed if they had known that the two men were lovers. And for the last three years, while living it up with the international set that gathered around Somerset Maugham on Cap Ferrat, he had had an extended affair with another graceful young man, a doe-like Cockney clerk called Alan Searle. Now that the affair was over, it must have come as a shock to Lennox to see the likeness of Alan Searle replicated in Benjamin Britten: the same wavy hair and soft curling lips, the same long face and lissom figure. Britten's boyishness had a strong appeal for Lennox, though not all his friends saw it: the diarist James Lees-Milne, recalling his first meeting with Britten six years later, thought 'what a plain, abstracted, dim-looking man' he was – even if he did feel 'an affinity unexpressed'.[16]

Lennox's father had died without ever knowing that Lennox was homosexual, and now his mother, who must have known, had gone too. Lennox was alone, homeless, aimless and unhappy. His circle was almost entirely gay – it could hardly have been otherwise for a young artist in the cauldron of rebellious creativity that made Paris such a magnet in the 1920s and '30s. Anglo-Saxons were attracted by the city's relative cheapness, its *laissez-faire* attitudes and openness to new ideas. His special friends were gay, or at least bisexual – Francis Poulenc, John Greenidge, David Ponsonby (a contemporary at Oxford who had preceded him to Paris to study under Boulanger), Vere Pilkington (another Oxford friend), and the teenage prodigy Igor Markevitch (Boulanger's star pupil and Diaghilev's last lover, who this very week of mid-April 1936, in a bizarre twist to the story, was in Budapest marrying Nijinsky's daughter Kyra).

The conflict between a faith he felt very profoundly indeed and a sexual orientation to which that faith was hostile had already caused him much soul-searching in Paris. On the one hand he had been studying composition with the ascetic Boulanger and taking instruction at the Carmelite Chapel of Sacré Coeur, on the other he lived with a man, moved in a gay circle that included Ravel and Poulenc, and frequented nightclubs like Le Boeuf sur le Toit (which may not have been exclusively gay, but did not discourage men dancing together), and it was difficult to see how the two could co-exist. The battle lines of a moral dilemma that he still had not resolved were soon to form again, and this time more dangerously than ever.

But for the moment Lennox's mind was focused elsewhere: on his still unfinished oratorio *Jonah* (for which the BBC was pressing him), and, more importantly, on the loss of his French-born mother, Aline, his beloved 'Maman'. She had died at Cap Ferrat (in the villa that bore the name of Lennox's French ancestors, the comtes de Melfort), just after Christmas, following months of terrible suffering that had been horrible to watch.[17] (Aline suffered from crippling arthritis and had been confined to a bath chair for some years, never complaining, always cheerful, despite the constant pain.)

The death of Aline drew Lennox even closer to Nadia Boulanger, for whom death played a major part in life. Since the loss of her younger sister Lili (on 15 March 1918, aged only twenty-four) she had worn mourning black (and would continue to do so till the end of her life), and she marked the anniversaries of the deaths of Lili and of their Russian mother Raïssa, with a month of Masses and memorials every March. Lennox shared this reverence for the dead, and the certainty of eventual reunion. Faith, in his view, was all – faith and the understanding and affection of true friends; without those such sadness was insupportable. 'We both live a little in another world,' he wrote to Nadia Boulanger, 'invisible but quite real.'[18] The older he got, he told her a few years later, the more he realized that the spiritual life was all that mattered: it held everything that was beautiful.[19]

With new friends to make, new music to hear, and the *sardana* to dance, Barcelona would offer both a welcome diversion and an entreé to a wider world. That Lennox was able to enjoy these attractions despite the political tensions which were so soon to explode into war is partly because as a foreigner, and a singularly apolitical one at that, he did not really notice them. He was also, of course, preoccupied with his mourning and his music, the novelties of a country he had never visited before, and the unfamiliarity of the Spanish language.

The three men were physically similar – slim and slightly-built, coxes rather than oarsmen – but their personalities and backgrounds were distinctively different. Britten, curly-headed and dimple-cheeked, was impish with 'the bright face of a little animal';[20] the sandy-haired Burra 'exhaled ... *joie de vivre* but he combined it with a notable unselfishness',[21] had a genius for making 'first-rate friends'[22] and was generally held to be 'a darling of the 1st rank'[23]; and the pipe-smoking Berkeley was modest, quiet and charming, a little vague and indecisive, a lot mixed up, and more impressionable than was good for him at the age of thirty-three. But a mischievous twinkle in the eye suggested an appreciation of life's oddities.

Berkeley seems to have cast the young Britten in the role of idol even before meeting him. Discovering that the reality was so pleasing, and so extraordinarily like Alan Searle, only increased his interest. Writing, nine years later, to congratulate Britten on the success of the opera *Peter Grimes,* Berkeley said he had known, with a very profound certainty, that Britten was destined for great things when he first saw a very early composition before they became friends.[24] And some forty years later, in a diary item recalling the Barcelona festival, Lennox wrote that he was deeply impressed by Britten's sheer musical ability and immense knowledge of music. He had felt certain that here was a composer of really exciting potential. He could claim, therefore, to be one of the earliest Britten fans, for Britten was then very little known, 'and among those who knew him few realized his true capabilities or believed in him as strongly as I did'.[25] Lennox clung to this faith, and remained proud of it, till the end of his life.

The two men were brought together, in the hotel, on their first day in Barcelona, by the President of the ISCM, the English musicologist Edward Dent (Professor of Music at Cambridge, and unofficial leader of an international 'homintern' of gay artists). It is unlikely that Lennox would have been able to resist the temptation to speak of his admiration. Doubtless Britten, a well-brought-up boy, returned the compliment, since we know from his diaries that he had heard the older composer's *Petite Suite*, for the unusual combination of oboe and cello, at a recital in the Grotrian Hall in London in 1931, and thought it 'v. interesting'.[26]* As Old Greshamians and fellow composers they must have compared notes about the influential Director of Music at Gresham's, Walter Greatorex – or 'Gog', as he was called at school. Lennox was a great admirer, not least because of Gog's love of plainsong, but Britten, who took his music lessons privately (with Frank Bridge and Harold Samuel), could not abide the man, partly because Gog was so scornful of his schoolboy compositions,[27] and partly because of Gog's piano technique (which Britten regarded as 'absolutely lacking in sanity').[28]

Berkeley and Britten met Burra, if not at lunch on the day he arrived, then at the formal opening of the festival in the grand old Palace of the *Generalitat*, the Catalan parliament, that same Saturday evening. And it was not long before Berkeley and Burra discovered they had not only Oxford in common, but a circle of Twenties 'prancers' and aesthetes including Brian Howard and the ubiquitous John ('the Widow') Lloyd, to whom Burra had been introduced by John Bryson, his tutor at Christ Church. Burra had spent some time in Germany with Bryson in 1932,[29] and had made some young friends who were to cause him and his circle a great deal of trouble the following year: at least two of them were

*The critics had approved too. 'There is a pleasing wit in Mr Berkeley's work', the *Daily Telegraph* had said – 'much more successful than one would at first have thought possible [for these two instruments together], and always held one's attention' (*Daily Telegraph* 18 March 1931).

members of the *Hitlerjugend*, and possibly Nazi spies too.[30] In Barcelona he was to meet two more dubious young Germans.

The festival introductions were done by no less a figure than the Catalan hero Lluis Companys, President of the *Generalitat*, who had just been released from prison (but was soon to be executed by Franco). Professor Dent, determined not to be drawn into the hornets' nest of Catalan politics, made a speech in which he rebuked those countries which had refused Barcelona's invitation to the festival 'for reasons other than musical'. Music, he said pointedly, should be 'free of everything but itself'; in a world suffering from 'the sickness of exaggerated nationalism', it was important to remember that the ISCM delegates were in Barcelona 'simply as musicians, concerned with nothing but that'.[31]

It made good copy for Burra, who told his readers back home, not without relishing the irony, that the *Generalitat* took absolutely no notice and proceeded instead 'to express their own new-born nationalism with quite especial fervour'.[32] As the delegates filed out of the parliament beneath a fifteenth-century relief of Sant Jordi, the Catalan saint, and crossed the courtyard of orange trees, they were waylaid by a choir singing Catalan folksongs. Then, descending into the main square of the old city, they were introduced to the holy grail of Catalan nationalism, the public dance known as the *sardana*. And it bowled them all over.

The *sardana* is so complicated and so laden with significance that one English enthusiast had recently devoted an entire book to it.[33] Elsewhere the same writer, John Langdon Davies, claims that it is not just a folk-dance but the symbol of national consciousness: 'the *sardana* is Catalonia.'[34] Anyone can dance it – and everyone does (even St Teresa of Avila, who is reputed to have made her nuns join in)[35] – but only a Catalan can dance it properly, because it is 'an arithmetical puzzle'.[36] Professor Dent was captivated, and said so effusively: the *sardana* would remain an unforgettable memory of Barcelona, 'a rite and a symbol, a dance of international friendship, in serene contemplation of the horizons of the future'.[37] Burra was confused: nationalism was meant to be the devil incarnate, yet here they were in its thrall. He turned to compromise for a solution. 'The common paradox remains', he wrote, 'that nationalism, which has been the most deadening spirit in politics, is the most vital one in art.'[38]

The *sardana* became quite a *leitmotif* of the festival, not only at organized events on the first and last days but popping up unexpectedly all over Barcelona. Britten loved it: '... great dancing', he wrote to the young Welsh composer Grace Williams, 'the whole town turns out to dance Sardanas on the slightest provocation! Oh – this native music!'[39] It made such a powerful impression on Lennox that, nearly half a century later, he confessed it had almost overshadowed everything else he saw and heard that week:

> ... a small band mainly of wind instruments would set itself up in a square or even a street corner and the passers-by would join hands in a circle. The steps were quite complicated but people all seemed to know them. At a particular moment ... the dance changed from a gentle tapping of the feet to a vehement stamping ... The precision with which this happened was tremendously exciting. It was moving too to see an obvious businessman lay down his case and umbrella and join hands with people of a quite different status. The thought of the tragedy that was so soon to engulf the whole country gives an added poignancy to one's recollection of such scenes, but they remain as vivid in my memory as anything that took place in the Festival itself.[40]

It is revealing that Lennox should have been surprised by the sight of the middle classes holding hands with working people. Possibly it was the first time he had actually seen southern *égalité* in practice, perhaps he was even a little excited by the romantic possibilities it offered. It must have touched him, or he would not have mentioned it all those years later. The radical Britten, tutored by Auden, would have seen this same little vignette as evidence of real change, the fulfilment of the Thirties dream as described by Julian Symons: 'the feeling among young people ... that we were moving into some deeply significant new social and political condition'.[41] Britten was to try hard to implant these ideas in Lennox's more conservative mind in the months ahead. And he made some progress. By the time the Civil War had started, and Auden, Stephen Spender and George Orwell were restless to go off and fight for the Republicans, Lennox was cautiously supporting the cause, despite its anti-Catholicism. It was too awful about Spain, he wrote to Peter Burra in August: 'naturally one wants the [left-wing, Popular Front] government to win, but why must the Communists [one of the Popular Front's many factions] kill all those poor wretched nuns who do nothing but good, and bust all the churches!'[42]

On the afternoon of the last day the three Englishmen took the funicular up the mountain that rises over Barcelona from the side of the port, for an organized performance of folk dancing in the huge, half-wild park known as Montjuïc. The views from there are so spectacular that Hercules is said to have chosen Montjuïc as the best spot to sit and admire his handiwork after building Barcelona during the ninth of his Twelve Labours. Lennox and Benjamin were tremendously excited by the Catalan melodies accompanying the dancers that afternoon, and Ben, according to Lennox's later recollection, 'producing old envelopes and various pieces of paper from his pockets, wrote them down', having earlier tried to find some sheet music of the *sardanas* in a Barcelona music shop, but without success.[43] (In a tribute to Britten on television on 5 December 1976, the day after he died, Lennox recalled a slightly different version of the story: that Ben had jotted down the melody of 'a man singing in a café'.[44]) Those sketches were to bring the two composers closer together in the months that followed. But for now Peter Burra, not Benjamin Britten, was the honey-pot of the trio; both Lennox, who was four years older, and Ben, four years younger, seem to have fallen a little in love with him.

After the folk-dancing at Montjuïc, the three new friends had supper together in a restaurant in the Sant Gervasi district, and Peter scribbled a letter to his mother at home in England about 'the loveliest folk dancing performance we've ever seen; indescribably fascinating.'[45]

Lennox's assertion that the *sardana* remained his most vivid memory of the festival is quite a claim, since the Festival also included the premiere of one of the most influential works of the twentieth century, Berg's *Violin Concerto*. Ben described this as 'just shattering';[46] Lennox was captivated by 'the sheer beauty of the sound and the passionate but wonderfully disciplined character of the music';[47] and Peter said it dominated everything else.[48] Also on the festival programme were Berg's *Three Wozzeck Fragments*, and Bartok's *String Quartet No. 5* (which Lennox found 'difficult').[49]

The first of the two English works was Britten's *Suite for Violin and Piano* ('highly effective' according to Berkeley),[50] which Ben himself played with his friend the Spanish virtuoso Antonio Brosa. Ben told his mother all about it when he got back to his desk in the hotel: 'My darling,' he wrote, 'the concert went very well – Toni played like a God, & tho' I was very nervous nothing went wrong in my part! It went down surprisingly well, considering the kind of music it was up against [Walter Piston, Egon Wellesz and Bartok] & we were re-called three times.'[51]

Lennox's contribution was the neo-classical *Overture for Chamber Orchestra*, which had been given its world premiere at the ISCM Festival in Czechoslovakia in September 1935, and its UK premiere at the Proms the following month, when the critics found it 'dry', 'drab' and 'noisy'.[52] Peter thought it was 'delightfully written with some dazzling orchestration', breaking into moments of 'sheer lyrical beauty'. He reported that it received a brilliant performance from the Madrid Symphony Orchestra with Lennox himself conducting.[53] Characteristically Lennox himself decided he did not like it and later suppressed it. 'I can't remember a note of it today' he wrote in his diary some forty years later.[54]

Lennox's piece was performed in one of the most fantastic examples of over-the-top architecture in the world, the Palau de la Música Catalana. The architect – Lluís Domènech i Montaner – spent the years 1905–8 encrusting every inch of the inside with figures of marble, mosaic, glass, stone, scrap-iron and concrete: naked muses poking out of the back of the stage, horses galloping through the side of the hall, stained glass in the ceiling. Peter said it was all so 'purely irrelevant' that it resembled nothing so much as a 'surrealist game of Consequences'.[55] And it was vastly too extravagant for Lennox's refined taste: in a letter to Peter three months later, when Barcelona was at war, he expressed the hope, in jest, that the Palau de Mùsica would be burned down: it would, he said, 'atone for much'.[56]*

Burra noted in his London reports that though Berkeley and Britten were representing Britain, 'neither was interested in being English'.[57] That is putting it mildly: in fact they had both consciously rejected Englishness – the philistinism, the suspicion of anything modern (like the new music from Europe, which was 'perceived as something specifically pernicious'),[58] and the idea that it was somehow abnormal to be an artist. It rankled with Lennox that the English musical establishment regarded clever technicians such as Britten as necessarily superficial and that there was something not quite gentlemanly about the professional musician. These, he said, were 'curious aberrations to which the English mind is particularly prone'.[59] Only six months earlier a London critic had dismissed Lennox's *Overture* with the comment, 'The breakaway school to which it belongs is now a dwindling by-path on which

*It was spared, restored in the 1980s and is now one of the city's biggest attractions, with tours every half an hour – and there is even a new 600-seat concert hall, the Petit Palau, built 11 metres below the square outside it.

the art of music is turning its back.'[60] But Peter Burra judged that the work of Britten and Berkeley 'had its roots in genuine individual character'. And, with the zeal of the young socialist, he hoped that their Englishness might express itself sooner or later 'in attachment to some social or moral interest'.[61] The composer Richard Stoker, who was a student of Berkeley (and of Boulanger) and knew Britten well, believes that both composers consciously sought cosmopolitan influences 'to get some new blood into British music'. In his view, their Englishness, like that of the great English composers of the sixteenth and seventeenth centuries, is balanced by 'a breath of fresh air from across the Channel', which makes their music more English, not less. And one day, Stoker believes, their work will seem as English as Elgar's.[62]

The social if not moral interests of the delegates were as much attended to by the Barcelona Festival organizers as their music. On the Sunday the three young Englishman were directed up to Montjuïc to watch a motorcycle rally – this must have been Peter's idea – but the event turned to disaster when one of the bikes left the track and killed a spectator near where they were standing. 'Noises of people screaming hysterically,' Ben recorded in his diary, 'police whistles and roar of machines'.[63]

On the penultimate day there was an excursion to the mountain-top basilica of the Benedictine monastery at Montserrat, perched on 'incredible fingers of stone',[64] for a concert, in semi-darkness, of old church music, including a canon by Victoria sung by the monks and boys of the famous Escalonia choir school. Lennox, for whom this ought to have been a specially significant experience – because of his faith, his attraction to monastic life and his love of the Latin Mass – has left no record of the visit. Yet he was so excited by the same hard-edged quality of the boys' voices at Westminster Cathedral half a century later that he was inspired to write his first liturgical settings specially for it.*

*Malcolm Williamson, Master of the Queen's Music from 1975 till his death in 2003, described this distinctive sound as 'sharp, almost nasal', as opposed to 'the Anglican hoot' (Interview with Peter Dickinson 22 Feb 1991, PDA.) It was first introduced to Britain by Sir Richard Terry, first organist of Westminster Cathedral 1901–24, and has remained a characteristic of the Westminster Cathedral Choir ever since George Malcolm restored it during his time as Master of the Music there 1947–59. Under Malcolm and two of his successors, David Hill and James O'Donnell, the choir has made several records of Masses by Victoria and other masters of the Spanish Renaissance.

Ben, though no longer a church-going Christian,[65] confided to his diary that it was 'a heavenly spot ... the sensuous beauty of darkness and incense ... It is difficult not to believe in the supernatural when in a place like this.'[66] He too was affected by the raw physicality of the voices of the Escalonia trebles – the energy of boys 'fighting it out in the playground'[67] – and when Lennox introduced him to the same sound at Westminster Cathedral two decades later he was inspired to write his *Missa Brevis*.

There was also an outing to the fishing village of Sitges. And given Sitges's reputation, even then, 'outing' it may well have been. Lennox, Peter and Ben were driven there in an open sports car by the colourful opera producer J. B. (Jack) Gordon (of the gin family) who was talent-scouting in Barcelona for Sadler's Wells Opera – and doubtless talent-scouting no less diligently on the beach at Sitges too.* Peter was captivated: 'There are such lovely little bathing places everywhere here', he wrote to his mother, 'where you can live incredibly cheaply if you could find someone nice to do it with.'[68] And that's just what he did, for another month after the festival, at a cost of 62 pesetas a week (then £1.66)† including laundry.[69]

If Sitges did not tip them the wink of their own shared sexuality – in those innocent, pre-Wolfenden days when gay still meant jolly, and men could be sent to prison for sleeping together in their own beds at home – then the Barrio Chino will have left them in no doubt. The name means literally 'Chinese Quarter', but no one seems to know why, since, as one English resident recorded: 'I have seen many things [in the Barrio Chino] but not a Chinaman.'[70] The painter Edward Burra (a distant cousin of Peter) had visited Barcelona in 1935 and made straight for the Chino – as his female companion recalled fifty years later: 'Ed loved the tiny stages where nudes in diamanté jock straps pranced and sang in piercing voices. One night we heard a high Bloomsbury voice pipe from the row behind us, "So much beyooteh in such a sordid little place". This became one of Ed's favourite sayings.'[71]

The French writer Jean Genêt was working as a young rent boy in

*Jack Gordon was the Sadler's Wells producer responsible for repertory and casting (LFAL, p. 424). BB may have met him at the Royal College of Music, where Gordon produced the opera *Christmas Rose* by Armstrong Gibbs five years earlier (LFAL, p. 220).

†'226 pts, about £6' (BB, Diary, 27 November 1936, BPL).

the Barrio Chino at this very time, and later recorded his erotic adventures in *The Thief's Journal*. He describes the Chino as 'a multitude of dark, dirty, narrow streets' in a stinking neighbourhood. It was 'a kind of haunt thronged less with Spaniards than with foreigners all of them down-and-out bums'. One of these foreign bums was Genêt himself, a 'louse' drawn there by the money, dressed sometimes in a jonquil-yellow silk shirt and worn-out rope-soled sandals, sometimes in a skirt, bodice, mantilla and fan. During his brief period as a *transformista*, Genêt worked at *La Criolla,* the most celebrated cabaret club of the time, earning three pesetas a night giving his clients quick *flautes* before robbing them.[72]

It was this club, at No. 10 Calle Cid (now a block of flats)[73] in the very heart of the Chino that Lennox, Ben and Peter visited on the night of 22 April. Ben is the only one of the three who has left a record of the occasion, describing it in his diary as his '1st & not particularly pleasant experience' of the kind of activity the Chino specialized in. He, and the others too, liked the dancing – 'mostly males – & dressed as females ... But my god the sordidity – & the sexual temptations of every kind at each corner.'[74] Ben was still very buttoned up about sex. But Lennox would not have been shocked – he was not shockable anyway – and the 'natural and attractive petulance' that was said to be a feature of Barcelona boys[75] would have suited him perfectly. Peter seems to have been even more actively engaged. When Lennox was back in Paris a fortnight after the Chino expedition, he wrote to Peter to check that he was 'being a good boy', and not being 'a wicked thing and spending all night in the Barrio Chino'. In a PS, Lennox sent his love to 'Hans and to Rodriguez'.[76] 'Hans' appears to have been Hans Raab, who had been part of the German contingent at the festival, along with a young man called 'Willi'. Peter had made friends with both, but their connections with the Nazis were to cause him some serious problems back home in England later in the year.

Lennox adored his week in Barcelona: he told Peter that he had hardly ever enjoyed himself more.[77] His instant rapport with Peter and Ben was matched by their feelings for him. Peter thought Lennox was 'an enchanting young composer',[78] and Ben found him 'a very delightful person, with sound ideas & music'.[79] No wonder Lennox was suddenly lost without them – particularly the fair-haired Peter. 'I've been missing you horribly,' he wrote from a hotel in Madrid, where he stayed for a couple of nights on his way back to Paris, 'and feeling very lonely and depressed. I suppose it's reaction ...'[80] Rashly he had invited Peter to stay in Paris on his way home to England, but when Peter, quite understandably, tried to take him up on the offer, Lennox retreated – not because he was any less keen to see his new friend again, but because his former lover, now no more than his flatmate, José Raffalli, had put his Corsican foot down and refused to allow Lennox to entertain a rival. Peter thought it was Lennox being indecisive, but it was actually Lennox being pushed around by the young man who had helped him to become a Catholic in 1929 and had had a hold over him ever since. Finally Lennox – under orders, one senses – had to spell it out: 'I'm afraid', he wrote to Peter, 'it's impossible for me to put you up. I share this flat with a French friend (the same with whom I lived when I was studying here) and there is only just room for two and no possibility of squeezing anybody else in.'[81] Peter got the message this time, and returned home by sea, having agreed to join Lennox in London in June for the premiere of his new oratorio, *Jonah*, in the Concert Hall of Broadcasting House. But the first-night plan never quite worked out: when the jealous José got to hear about it, he made Lennox offer a compromise that favoured the Corsican.

Before he left Barcelona, Peter wrote home to say the festival had been terrific fun and he had made lots of new friends, 'especially Lennox Berkeley who is having a work done and is adorable. Will you be singing in his *Jonah* next month?' And he added, almost as an afterthought, 'Benjamin Britten is a very good person too.'[82] The recipient of this letter was a young tenor who had been a close friend at Lancing, and with whom he was now sharing a cottage in Berkshire. To Burra he was Luard Pears, but history would soon know him better as the singer Peter [Neville Luard] Pears. As yet neither Ben nor Lennox had ever heard of him.

2
The Berkeleys

Lennox was brought up in ignorance of a dark family secret. Today the details would be almost too commonplace to bother to hide, but in the old world before the Great War they constituted the greatest shame. Though Lennox was not aware of it at the time, he realized, when looking back, that a cloud had hung over the family throughout his childhood. Born and raised in its shadow, he was affected profoundly and permanently – not only by the events themselves but also by the attitudes of those around him. An awareness of some unspoken shame so pervaded his youth that he was often ill, for no apparent reason. Though his health improved as he got older, he never overcame a chronic lack of confidence and an inability to make decisions. As an adult he disguised these shortcomings with charm and a chuckle; and in old age they were easily ascribed to absent-mindedness. But beneath the surface, for all his life, Lennox suffered from an acute sense of 'not being good enough'. This feeling of unworthiness found a natural home in the Catholic Church, in the same way as his deepest feelings found a natural outlet in music. But the cloud of the past, and the shadow of disapproval which he felt it cast over him, never quite lost its power to disturb him, even when, in middle age, his life took a surprising new turn and he found, at last, peace and understanding.

Lennox's parents were good, quiet, enlightened people who led blameless lives. Hastings Berkeley was a captain in the Navy, an independent thinker who wrote a handful of learned books on obscure subjects: the mystical language of mathematics, British trade policy in the 1880s, and a study of European manners from a Japanese perspective.[1] He was also a passionate cyclist and a music-lover with a large collection of pianola rolls. Lennox's mother, Aline Harris, possessed all the virtues – she was, in Lennox's own words, 'most frightfully good ... unselfish, generous, modest and good-natured'.[2] She was also 'exceptionally intelligent', a devout High Anglican and a fair singer. She inherited the gentle charm, sweetness of character, unaffected courtesy and artistic gifts – possibly, too, the asthma – of her father, the popular British Consul in Nice (and an outstanding watercolourist).* From her mother, a spoiled and egotistical Württembergisch baroness who liked to be the centre of attention, she inherited little but an imposing presence. Nor did she share the snobbish prejudices of both her parents: her mother once confessed that her 'German pride ... revolted rather against the idea of making my friends in ... the merchant set',[3] and her father made no secret of despising the *nouveaux riches* who flocked to Nice with the advent of the railways.[4]

Hastings and Aline met at a consular party in Nice when she was a schoolgirl of twelve and he a midshipman of twenty. They married sixteen years later, and remained in love for the rest of their lives, signing their letters 'W. G.' (Weenie Girl) and 'W. B.' (Weenie Boy), or, sometimes, ''Quirrel' and 'Little Boy Blue'.

The family skeleton was not theirs, but they were its victims. And Aline's parents were not to blame either: the rich Anglo-Irish Harrises and the artistic but *versnobt* von Galls of Württemberg may have assumed airs but in morals they were beyond reproach. The scandal was a Berkeley one, and it happened two generations back from Lennox. Nor was it the first time that this ancient family had been eclipsed by disgrace. In fact the Berkeleys of Berkeley Castle had been so often in trouble, in a recorded history stretching back to the Conqueror, and had so often bounced back against the odds, that their devoted chronicler, John Smyth, was moved to write, in the reign of James I, that 'The mercy of the Almighty takes this family by the chin and keeps the head from drowning.'[5]

The shame was of the usual 'caddish' kind: sex and money – too much of one, not enough of the other. Lennox seems never to have known about his grandfather's bankruptcy (since that's how far the money problem went), and he did not hear about the sexual irregularities – adultery, elopement, illegitimacy – till he was grown up. When it all came out at last, he began to understand that his parents had chosen to live quietly and unobtrusively in order to protect the good name of Hastings's mother, Cécile, Countess of Berkeley.

Hastings had adored his mother and, in Lennox's words, he was determined that 'the family situation should not be known and her somewhat unconventional life be frowned upon'. Lennox admired his

*For a fuller account of Sir James Harris see Appendix 5, pp. 458–9.

father for this delicacy of feeling, and though he acknowledged that Hastings was by nature 'very modest and retiring and probably undervalued himself',[6] he always felt sad that his father was omitted from Berkeley family histories, as though he had never existed.

Lennox had little time for his Berkeley ancestors. Indeed he once suggested that the good blood of the Harrises had been contaminated by the bad of the Berkeleys. Writing in 1946 he said there were so many 'good people' on the Harris side of his family that it made him feel 'a veritable monster'. But he had the excuse, he said, that his 'less desirable tendencies' came from the Berkeleys, 'most of whom seem even more dissolute and badly-behaved than was usual among people of their position, and that's saying a good deal.'[7]*

The lady whose life had been 'somewhat unconventional', Lennox's grandmother, Cécile née Drummond, was the daughter of Edouard, vicomte de Melfort, whose ancestor, John Drummond, had followed James II into exile in France.[8] Edouard was the bastard son of General Louis Drummond, comte de Melfort, by Lady Caroline Mackenzie – of another Scots family of Jacobite sympathizers. His parents had been unable to marry till late in life because Louis was already married to Caroline's Irish cousin Lady Caroline Barry, a fast and foul-mouthed Regency minx widely known as 'Lady Billingsgate'. Cécile, who inherited the Drummonds' disregard of convention, was said to be 'beautiful, fascinating, small and dainty, but full of character',[9] her third son, Randal, spoke of her having a 'first-class reasoning mind',[10] and Randal's stepdaughter said she was 'gaiety itself'.[11] Not surprisingly Cécile was snapped up the moment she made her *début* in the cut-throat marriage market of European high society. The successful bidder was a hard-bitten English admiral called Sir Fleetwood Pellew (younger brother of Pownoll Bastard Pellew, 2nd Viscount Exmouth). Quite apart from his reputation for cruelty,[12] Sir Fleetwoood was hardly an ideal match: Cécile was a young beauty of eighteen, while he was a battle-scarred widower of sixty-one.

They were married in Brussels in February 1851 and lived together in England and on the Continent till the end of 1852.[13] To her intense relief – and to the alarm of the lower decks – Admiral Pellew was then

*An eighteenth-century Berkeley coat of arms sporting two cavemen wielding bludgeons does little to dispel the image of brutality associated with the castle.

posted to Hong Kong as Commander-in-Chief, East Indies and China station.

Southern China was at this time in the grip of the Taiping Rebellion, led by a religious fanatic called Hong Xiu-quan, a sandy-bearded, blue-eyed schoolmaster, who believed he was the younger brother of Jesus Christ and that he had been called by God his father to destroy the Qing dynasty and replace it with his own Heavenly Kingdom of Great Peace. In March 1853 the rebels captured Nanking, the medieval capital of China, and murdered all 40,000 Manchu residents by burning, stabbing or drowning. The Heavenly King then put on a jewelled crown decorated with a cockerel, a duck and a tiger, had himself carried into the captured city on a golden palanquin, and set up shop in a palace built by the Ming Emperors. Abandoning himself to the varied pleasures of 30 wives, 100 concubines and 64 pageboys, he relinquished the day-to-day administration of the Heavenly Kingdom to his Deputy King, a former charcoal-burner who claimed to be the Holy Ghost.

The British, no less than the Empress Dowager herself, greatly feared the rebels who were strongest in the maritime province of Guangdong, where so many British trading interests were based, and Admiral Pellew's brief was 'to be ready to fly to Canton' to protect the British if needed.[14] It was a return to home in some ways, since he had served in China at the start of his career, when he took part in the destruction of the Dutch fleet which had led to the capture of Java in 1811.[15] It was there, as a commander aged, astonishingly, only seventeen, that Fleetwood Pellew had made a name for bravery and efficiency. He had also picked up what the poet and naval historian Sir Henry Newbolt called 'such an unfortunate reputation for brutality towards his crew' that the Admiralty had had difficulty finding him another command because no one wanted to serve under him.[16]

In the circumstances, Cécile's doctors decided it would be imprudent for her to accompany her husband to China, so she returned to Brussels to stay with her mother. Still young and beautiful, and with a passionate nature which the widowed vicomtesse de Melfort was too weak to check, Cécile was bound to fall in love – and bound, perhaps, to choose the wrong man a second time. In cosmopolitan Brussels, which, since Waterloo, had offered more diversions than even London, both things happened. Her beau was a young captain in the 35th Regiment of Foot, the Royal Sussex, then based in the new Belgian capital. His name was

George Berkeley,* and he was twenty-six. His father was also his commanding officer: General Sir George Berkeley, former Surveyor-General of the Ordnance and Conservative MP for Devonport. His mother Lucy was an heiress: the elder daughter of Sir Thomas Sutton, first and last baronet, of Molesey in Surrey.

There are no photographs or portraits or even descriptions surviving to give us an idea of what George looked like,[17] but the good looks of his three fair sons are unlikely to have sprung only from their dark-haired mother. One of George's daughters-in-law described him (though she never met him) as 'daredevil but enchanting'.[18] If Cécile had not been married already, and if her lover had not been more deeply flawed than Cécile was then in a position to know, George Berkeley might have made a perfect husband.

It is unclear how the affair progressed, but it cannot have gone far under the watchful eye of George's father, General Berkeley, and the less effective though very present deterrent of Cécile's mother. In the spring of 1853 George learned that the 35th was bound for a long posting in Bengal in the autumn. Guessing that he would lose his prize if they were parted, he resigned his commission and left the Army (though his departure was recorded as 'retirement').[19] In the battle for Cécile, it was a wise move. For just before Christmas 1853 some extraordinary news filtered back to Brussels from London: there had been trouble in Hong Kong, and Vice-Admiral Pellew was on his way home – presumably, amongst other things, to reclaim his wife.

The rumour was confirmed by a paragraph in *The Times* three days after Christmas. According to a correspondent in Hong Kong, a mutiny had broken out aboard Admiral Pellew's flagship, HMS *Winchester*.

*In his will (dated 5 March 1884) the 7th earl identifies himself as George Rawdon Lennox Berkeley, and in his uncle General Rumley's will (dated 1884) he is also George Lennox Rawdon, but in the baptismal certificate of his eldest son Hastings (1 December 1855), in his own death certificate (29 August 1888) and burial registration (30 August 1888), in the *Army Lists* and in *The Times*'s reports of his bankruptcy proceedings he is given as George Lennox Rawdon Berkeley. There is some evidence that he was known as Lennox: *The Times*, 1 July 1882 (reporting the alleged death of the 6th Earl), and the marriage certificate of his third son Randal (1887) both record him as Lennox Rawdon Berkeley, and in his eldest son Hastings's death certificate (1934) he is named as Lennox Berkeley. For the purposes of the present work he is George Berkeley.

The men had been cooped up in their hot ship, with no shore leave for a year and a half, and when they presented their grievances to the admiral in the form of a petition, he was so outraged by their impertinence that he ordered the ship to put to sea. But the crew had had enough of Pellew's tyranny and set up 'a great howling & whistling' in the lower decks. The drum was beat to quarters, and when some of the men refused to come on deck, 'the officers were ordered to compel them at the point of the sword', and in doing so several were severely wounded.[20] The Admiralty decided that three alleged mutinies on one officer's record was enough, and issued a summary recall.

By the summer of 1854 Admiral Pellew was back in London, and summoned to the Admiralty Board for a dressing-down – by, amongst other Lords Commissioner, Rear-Admiral Sir Maurice Berkeley, who just happened to be the second of the illegitimate sons of the 5th Earl of Berkeley, and a cousin of the wife-stealing George. Pellew was not formally punished, beyond the ignominy of his recall from duty, but he remained 'beached' for the rest of his service (though, through sheer longevity, he was promoted to full admiral before his retirement).

The moment he was out of the Admiralty building, disgrace notwithstanding, Admiral Pellew sent a message to Brussels instructing Cécile to meet him at a spa in Germany. There he doubtless hoped that, in the embrace of his young bride, and with the stimulus of the curative waters, he might forget the recent past, recover some of his youthful vitality – and perhaps generate a boy Pellew to claim one day the Exmouth title.

Cécile did as she was told, but the reunion was short-lived, and dramatic. At the beginning of October she had had enough of bullying admirals. Yielding to the passionate blood of the Melforts and drawing on the audacity of the Drummonds, she sent a message to George Berkeley – and together they eloped. With the law and public opinion at their backs, the lovers fled, like so many other illicit couples of the mid-nineteenth century, to Second Empire Paris – than which, declaimed Thomas Carlyle, there had never been 'a more corrupt, abominable city'; Paris, in the view of the dyspeptic historian of the French Revolution, was 'nothing but a brothel'.[21] It was a perfect hideout for runaway lovers. Cécile and George found themselves an apartment in the Batignolles, near the cemetery of Montmartre, sharing a tenement with the Tivoli public baths,[22]and there they dug in.

One of the first things Cécile did on reaching Paris was to write to her husband, to try to explain herself. She told him she thought it was better to brave the opinion of the world than to deceive him under his own roof. She had 'endeavoured to overcome her attachment to Capt Berkeley' and believed that if she had been 'less left alone' she might have had some protection against her feelings. She concluded by suggesting that the admiral should take steps to obtain a divorce so that she might cease to bear his name and have an opportunity of rehabilitating herself. On receiving these letters, dated 8 and 11 October 1854, the admiral broke off all relations, and applied for an ecclesiastical separation. He could have sued for divorce, but held back – partly, he claimed, out of consideration for Cécile and her family, and partly for the purely practical reason that it might have been difficult to serve the necessary papers on George, who was never in England long enough to receive them. Perhaps, too, he was anxious to spare himself the indignity of a public trial, since the world has a way of laughing at elderly cuckolds. Furthermore – and this must be the crux of it, given the admiral's vicious reputation – there is a suggestion that Cécile was ready to give evidence of physical assault: her granddaughter Yvonne Berkeley claims, in an unpublished (and, it has to be said, often unreliable) memoir, that he 'ill-treated' Cécile and that she could no longer bear his 'brutalities'.[23] Even Admiral Pellew will have realized that a naval officer associated with three mutinies was unlikely to win much sympathy in a divorce court.

By the winter of 1855 George and Cécile were the parents of an illegitimate son, Hastings George FitzHardinge Berkeley (Lennox's father), born in Paris on 12 November. Eighteen months later they produced a second son, Ernest. Admiral Pellew's Continental spies watched and listened and despatched the news back to their employer in Devonshire. Fearing that his wife might present her misbegotten Berkeley boys as Pellews, with a claim on his fortune and, possibly even, on the Exmouth title, Admiral Pellew decided to go to law, and in 1859 he entered a petition in the Divorce Court. In a short hearing on 8 July he won his case, and the marriage was dissolved. All England read of the scandal in *The Times* the next day.

For all the dishonour, George and Cécile, who had now moved back to Brussels, were free to marry at last – and, to make quite sure it was done properly, they performed the ceremony twice: once according to the rites of the Church of England in a service conducted by the Chaplain at the British Vice Consulate in Brussels on 26 July 1859, and again six months later when, in the same place, the Consul himself married them by licence.

They may now have been man and wife, and doubly so, but no amount of marrying after the event could legitimize their first two children. It could, and did, however, ensure the legitimacy of any future issue. And when, at the end of January 1865, a third son, Randal, was born in Brussels, he became his father's first and only legal heir. As things then stood this did not amount to much, since George Berkeley had turned out to be a chronic and reckless spendthrift, his losses probably occurring at the gambling tables. With no income of his own, he spent whatever resources his wife was able to beg from the Drummonds and her rich and sympathetic in-laws. And he spent so wildly that in the spring of 1872 he went bankrupt with debts of more than £14,000[24] (the equivalent of at least a million pounds today).

Long aware of George's problem, the Berkeley family, wisely and generously, had taken steps at an early stage to protect and provide for any putative wife and children for whom he might one day become responsible. In 1854, at the time of the elopement, his father General Berkeley had made a will leaving a legacy of £3,000 not to the unreliable George himself but to 'any woman who might become [George's] widow'.[25] The following year George's brother Colonel Charles Berkeley made a similar will leaving Cécile an annuity of £500 on the same exclusive terms. And in 1884, on the death of George's brother-in-law, General Randal Rumley, it turned out that his will too had craftily bypassed the black sheep, leaving instead a fortune of £13,500 to be divided equally between George's three sons, Hastings, Ernest and Randal.[26] By these means George's considerable inheritance was saved from sequestration by the London Bankruptcy Court.

The unfortunate creditors may have lost out, but so, directly, had George. Hoping that George's late mother, the heiress Lucy, Lady Berkeley, might have left him something which they could divide between them, as a sop at least, the creditors applied to the court for an adjournment of his bankruptcy proceedings in July 1872. But, whether by accident or design, Lady Berkeley confounded them all by leaving no will. When the complications of her estate were finally unravelled it turned out that her effects were worth no more than £450, all of which went, eventually, to the Mr Fowler she had married on the death of General Berkeley. The Trustee in Bankruptcy did have one success, though. Under the will of his brother-in-law General Rumley, George was left a quantity of 'souvenirs', including family portraits by Romney and Gainsborough, war medals won by his father, grandfather and great-grandfather, and a set of 106 silver spoons and forks. But when George went down to Wiltshire to collect his booty from the Rumleys' executors at Chilton Lodge, Hungerford, he was met by officers of the court who promptly confiscated the lot. A couple of months later, in February 1885, the Rumley property was sold without reserve by Phillips of Bond Street – and reported, in detail, in *The Times*, thus rubbing salt into the family's still open wounds. The report does not name the sum raised but it does show that the crayon portrait by Gainsborough fetched nearly 22 guineas. This cannot have made many inroads into George's huge debts, and he remained an undischarged bankrupt for the rest of his life.

The human cost of all his indiscretions, so well publicized by the press, was that George was forced to live abroad like a fugitive, sustained by remittances from the Berkeleys and the Drummonds. His double shame may have been regarded as little more than piquant on the Continent, but at home it was a stigma. The French did not applaud it, but, being more sophisticated, they did not moralize. For Cécile, of course, France was not exile at all, but home. Nevertheless, her total dependence on family generosity, and the need to lie somewhat low, hurt her pride.

For her three boys it caused, according to the American who was to marry one of them, 'a sad childhood'. George Berkeley 'had done so many things that he should not have done' that they were forced to live 'in a very dingy and outcast way on the French Riviera'. From her privileged perspective as a Boston aristocrat whose social and financial security had never been in doubt, Molly, Countess of Berkeley, second wife of Randal, writing a century later, imagined the deprived Berkeley boys 'walking around looking in shop windows. No tennis or games or gang of young friends.'[27] But in reality their childhood was restricted rather than blighted by their father's bankruptcy, and they lived perfectly comfortably, but with their heads down.

Destined for careers in the services, like their father and both grandfathers, the three brothers were educated in France (in Randal's case at a *lycée* in Fontainebleau) till they were eleven, then sent to England to board at Burney's Royal Academy for naval and military pupils in Gosport. Life there was as tough as at any other Victorian public school where homesick little boys, torn from their mothers, were reconstructed as chivalrous knights of the British Empire, bristling with manliness and moral righteousness, through a process of games-playing and evangelicalism known as Muscular Christianity. Thomas Hughes spread the word in his prototype of the public school novel *Tom Brown's School Days*. At its heart lay the notion of self-sacrifice and the ideal of the Christian Gentleman – or what the writer Peter Parker has vividly described as 'passing the ball in a game of rugger and allowing the other fellow to score the try'.[28] Sport, the Classics, Chapel and Corps were the means used, and terror licked the victims into shape: terror of failure, terror of being different and terror of the cane and other instruments of punishment applied not only by the staff but also by prefects and fag-masters. Burney's Academy was distinguished for two tortures, both reserved for the exclusive use of senior boys, or 'bull-dogs'. One was holding a boy's 'back and breech as near to a hot fire as his clothes would bear without burning'. The other involved threading a jagged disk of slate on a loop of string, coiling the string tight, then releasing it, spinning at speed, against a boy's upturned palm till the flesh was ripped. One victim recorded that this 'terrible bullying' left a 'long white cicatrice' on his right hand.[29] It was not the ideal place for a boy who was as passionately fond of music as Hastings.

After two years of Burney's discipline Hastings, the eldest Berkeley boy, and – ten years later – Randal, the youngest, passed into the Royal Naval College at Dartmouth to train as officers aboard the over-crowded and insanitary wooden hulk *Britannia*, in the isolated estuary of the Dart, away from what the Royal Navy still refers to today as 'the distractive temptations of naval ports like Portsmouth and Plymouth'.[30] The middle boy, Ernest, chose the Army and went on to Sandhurst.

If the bankruptcy was something that their parents learned to live with, illegitimacy was more difficult. It would not have been absolutely necessary – nor appropriate since they were so young – to tell Hastings and Ernest the truth about their birth till the arrival of Randal. And even then George and Cécile might have felt it was wiser to keep quiet. After all, George was not only bankrupt but several removes from the line of succession to the earldom of Berkeley and the Castle, which anyway had been in dispute ever since the death of his great-uncle Frederick, the 5th earl, in 1810.[31]

As the third son of the only son of a second son, it had never occurred to George that the coronet might one day be his, but, as a succession of potential heirs was disqualified by illegitimacy, bachelordom or infertility, when the 6th Earl of Berkeley died on 27 August 1882 (aged eighty-six, at his house at Cranford in Middlesex),* Lennox's grandfather, George Berkeley, aged fifty-five, bankrupt, wife-stealer and outlaw, suddenly found himself elevated to the peerage as the 7th Earl of Berkeley.† And George's third – and only legitimate – son, Randal, succeeded, as his legal heir, to the courtesy title of Viscount Dursley, thus publicly exposing the passed-over elder brothers as illegitimate. This must have caused quite a *bouleversement* within the family. Till then Randal had been the idolized baby brother, handsome, strong, fearless and good at all games. But he was also, and perhaps inevitably as the spoiled darling of a doting family, selfish, argumentative and impatient of authority. His instructors at Darmouth described him, with grudging admiration, as 'wild as a hawk', and put it down to his 'having been left to go his own way in his early days'.[32] The consequence was that he flew off the handle whenever he was crossed. Years later his second wife Molly said that 'Berkeley was always throwing things around rooms and out of windows'.[33] Now he was Viscount Dursley, heir to one of the oldest and grandest families in England and one of the richest fortunes in Europe, and it is unlikely that his title did anything to curb either his temper or his arrogance.

No one knows what George felt about it all, or even where he was at the time: there is a sense, but only that, that he may not have shared in his sons' upbringing, that, in fact, he lived apart from the family, indulging at a safe distance the vices that had so depleted his fortune. What is clear is that Cécile's chief concern was for her two elder sons, suddenly rejected by English society and swept aside in the wake of Randal's good fortune; nor, judging from letters she wrote later, could she trust her youngest son to look after their interests in the future. Indeed Cécile may have guessed that Randal would abuse his privileged position by bullying his elder brothers.[34] Molly Berkeley later wrote that she thought 'the change from a lonely childhood into great wealth, bringing with it the deference with which the world then treated him, made him the misanthrope he became'.[35] Particularly to his unfortunate brothers. Years later, when a friend, commenting on Sir William Orpen's portrait of Randal as Master of the Berkeley Hounds, told

*All that remains now are some of the out-houses with a clock in a wall, visible from the M4, to the south, near Heathrow Airport.

†For fuller details of the history of the Berkeley Peerage Case, see Appendix 3.

Randal he thought it made him look contemptuous, Randal replied, 'But I am contemptuous. Don't you know it?'[36] The writer L. P. Hartley, who knew him well, wrote that Randal 'kept the world at arm's length ... A scientist and an aristocrat, he was protected by a two-fold remoteness, and the outside world ... hardly existed for him.'[37] His obituary in *The Times* confirmed that he 'found little pleasure in ordinary society'. Molly seemed proud of the fact that he 'had no time for humanity. [He] just said, "I loathe humanity!" And let it go at that.'[38] But, in her brash American way, Molly knew how to handle Randal, and his money.

Just six years after inheriting the earldom, George the bankrupt died – and Randal, as his father's only legitimate son, became 8th Earl of Berkeley. The death occurred in London, at Brown's Hotel in Dover Street, Piccadilly, on 27 August 1888, and the funeral followed four days later at West Molesey, Surrey. The causes of death were given as disease of the heart and kidneys. He was sixty-one. By his will, drawn up four years earlier, George left nothing at all to his heir ('my Infant [i.e. legally minor] son Viscount Dursley'), presumably because he knew that Randal would, in due course, inherit the earth. To Hastings and Ernest, 'my two sons of my present wife' (an attempt, perhaps, to clarify their parentage), he left his residuary estate to be divided between them equally. Alas, it was not much of a gift: his gross estate at probate, in November 1888, was found to amount to exactly £56. 16s. 2d.

Hastings and Ernest were bailed out by their mother, now managing comfortably on the generous annuities and legacies which had been carefully routed directly to her by the Berkeley family. She lived in a smart villa at Carabacel in Nice, from where, like the rest of the *beau monde*, she retreated northwards the moment the sun came out and the mistral whipped up. She spent the summer and autumn with her sister, Albine, Baroness van Havre, at Fontainebleau, before heading south again in January for the Nice season.

By the time of his successful claim for the earldom in 1891, Randal was twenty-six. Four years earlier, tired of service discipline, he had resigned from the Navy as a lieutenant, in order to study geology and crystallography. Such a career move must have surprised his former instructors at Dartmouth, who had not noticed that he was particularly clever, or even much interested in learning – but he had been converted to the thrills of chemistry by a naval chaplain later on. He was now working towards the research into osmotic pressure which was to remain a passion for the rest of his life – and which would lead to his being elected a Fellow of the Royal Society in 1908.

There had been another reason for leaving the Navy: marriage. The new Countess of Berkeley, the beautiful daughter of a salesman in Manchester,[39] was the widow of a promising young composer called Arthur Herbert Jackson, who had died in 1881 of tubercular meningitis, aged only twenty-nine,[40] shortly after being appointed Professor of Harmony and Composition at the Royal Academy of Music in London. 'The death of Mr Arthur Herbert Jackson', reported the *Musical Times*, 'has thrown quite a gloom over the Royal Academy of Music ... Mr Jackson was more than a student of promise, for he had already given to the world some important compositions ... He had, shortly before his death, finished a cantata called "Jason and the Golden Fleece" and ... we need scarcely say how bright a future has been suddenly blighted. Mr Jackson was held in high estimation by all who knew him [who] can amply attest how modestly and unassumingly he received the many proofs of success which he had so fairly won.'[41] His widow, Kate, known as Kitty, was also a musician, a professional singer,[42] and their daughter, Sybil – eight at the time of her mother's second marriage in 1887 – was already showing promise as both singer and pianist.

For a few years, till the peerage case in 1891,* the Randal Berkeleys and Sybil lived together in a *ménage à quatre* with Hastings, still a bachelor in his mid-thirties, in South Kensington. At Randal's insistence, the house was fitted with the new electric light. Hastings felt this was unnecessarily extravagant and was not at all sure it would work, but Randal 'is very wilful &, in fact, rather crazy on this point so he has had his way'.[43] Hastings referred to his brother and the countess as 'the Kittys'. Quite often Randal was away 'geologising'; quite often Kitty was ill (heart trouble, it later turned out), [44] or shopping.

Hastings, had also left the Navy by now: frail, thin and prone to illness ('my old enemy "tummy"'),[45] he had been invalided out, with the rank of commander, in 1886. He was now working as a director of a Cornish mining company based in the City. He did not like the job, and diverted himself with academic study and music – and dreams of Nice and the Consul's pretty daughter, Aline, with whom he used to walk over the top of the Vinaigrier (the mountain above the Consul's villa, Les Rochers) along a path strewn with pine needles, overlooking the sea.[46]

*For a fuller account of the case see Appendix 3, pp. 452–5.

In 1890 Hastings proposed to his 'Weenie Girl', Aline Harris. 'What a good and true and tender woman you are ... what a treasure I have found,' he wrote two months earlier. It was rare luck, he said, in a slightly less felicitous metaphor, that he had singled out 'this jewel from the rubbish which lay about it'.[47]

Hastings's lack of financial prospects, as the illegitimate son of a bankrupt, seems to have been something of a problem at the start of his engagement. His annual income was about £900 (£70,000 in current values) – nearly ten times as much as the average stipend of a country parson in England that year.* But he felt obliged to warn Aline that he was 'a comparatively poor man'. Nevertheless he was confident that 'with common prudence we ought to get on very comfortably'.[48] In a letter about bridesmaids' presents, he warned that it was 'no use having any false pride about these matters & trying to do things grandly with rather exiguous means'. (Aline had proposed that they should give the girls silver hairbrushes engraved with their interlaced initials, but Hastings pointed out, a little tactlessly, that he had taken advice from Kitty who had ruled that 'it was now a little out of fashion to put the initials on', [49] so they settled instead on simple moonstone brooches.)

A panic on the London and New York stock exchanges in November 1890 hit his securities, reducing his income to £850, and for a week or two he was seriously worried that James Harris might withdraw Aline's hand. But she was soon able to reassure him that her father was 'really pleased and happy about our engagement', and a relieved Hastings reported back to Nice that the good news was 'like little gleams of sunshine in rather gloomy weather'.[50]

The wedding took place on 27 January 1891 in the larger of the two churches serving the English community in Nice, Holy Trinity, Place Alziary. It was a grand occasion for the six or seven thousand British visitors who lived in Nice during the winter: the marriage of a daughter of their Consul to the eldest son of the Dowager Countess of Berkeley, conducted by the Bishop of Gibraltar, Dr Charles Sandford, heading a triumvirate of clergy, in the presence of Prince and Princess Albert of

*That same year the author's maternal great-grandfathers, the Revd James Dunn, then Vicar of St John the Baptist, Bathwick, and the Revd Sydney Boyd, then Vicar of St Giles, Norwich, earned, respectively, £155 and £76, and the benefice of his great-great-grandfather, the Revd Robert Dunn, Rector of Huntsham in Devon, was valued at £122 (*Crockford's Clerical Directory,* 1890).

Monaco. The bridesmaids were Aline's younger sister Nelly, soon to be her sister-in-law too, and Mlle Rose d'Elchingen (later Duchess of Lanza Branciforte and Princess di Trabia) daughter of the Duchess of Rivoli. Others in this Gilbert and Sullivan cast list included Nicolas Wilhelm, Prince of Nassau, and Marie, Dowager Countess of Caithness and Duchess of Medina Pomár.[51]

As the couple stood together at the altar, the guests sang that warhorse of the Victorian wedding, Keble's religiose hymn *The Voice That Breathed o'er Eden*, in a new setting by Aline's friend G. S. Aspinall, who wrote at the foot of the score, 'Composed expressly for and dedicated to Miss Aline Harris on the occasion of her marriage with Captain Berkeley.' (Actually he was still then Commander Berkeley, but it was a generous error on his wedding day.)

Calling on the 'awful Father, to give away this bride', the ultra-correct Harrises must have trembled as they heard the rattling skeletons of the Berkeleys. Mrs Harris was a formidable Württembergische baroness, haughty, severe and censorious. Her husband, though easier, warmer and altogether more likeable, was still acutely conscious of Victorian proprieties, of his own responsibility as Her Britannic Majesty's Consul to ensure that they were upheld in the Queen's favourite French resort, and of the difficulties he faced in a rapidly changing world. Seven years earlier he had published a pamphlet deploring Nice's social decline, and blaming the railway connection with Paris and the growth of gambling in neighbouring Monaco. Up to then, he wrote, Nice had been Europe's centre of fashion and celebrity, 'where you'd recognize many well-known people', where well-bred visitors could conduct themselves with simplicity and grace, picnicking in the countryside and enjoying the fine art of conversation. Now it had become *vulgarisée*. The gentry went to Cannes, while money – and worse – came to Nice. 'I do not want to say, thank God, that there are not still many respectable people in Nice,' wrote the Consul, holding his nose, 'but it is also true that you see here quite a number of captains of industry, people of both sexes of more or less blemished reputation, people who affect titles to which they have no right, hiding their true, sad selves.'[52]*

*Harris would have been appalled by the further decline of Nice in the twentieth century. In the preface to his 1994 volume of diaries, James Lees-Milne describes the Riviera coast as 'that resort of good-timers dubbed "the septic belt"' (James Lees-Milne, *A Mingled Measure*, p. vii).

Since his daughter's mother-in-law, Lady Berkeley, was indisputably a person of blemished reputation, for all that she was universally loved, it is difficult to believe that the Consul and his wife did not have some misgivings about marrying their family into hers. They had already given away their eldest daughter, Annie, to an illegitimate son of Leopold I, King of the Belgians. And before the century was out they were to lose a third daughter, Nelly (a musician who had studied composition in Paris), to another illegitimate son, Hastings' younger brother Ernest.*

But with French sophistication the guests brushed aside these technicalities as they mounted their carriages for the wedding party at Les Rochers, the Harrises' villa on Mont Alban in the hills to the east of Nice, off the old road to Villefranche (the famous Route de la Grande-Corniche, described by Baedeker as one of the most beautiful roads in Europe).

After the usual lengthy wedding tour, Hastings took his wife back to England, first to a cottage in Hindhead and then to a house at Winslow in Buckinghamshire, close to his old naval friend, Captain Sir Edmund Verney at Claydon. There in 1897 their first child was born – a girl named Geraldine in honour of her maternal grandmother, now Lady Harris (James having been knighted in 1896 by a Queen grateful for all his attentions during her annual holidays in Nice).

Meanwhile the Kittys, now the Earl and Countess of Berkeley, but still lacking their castle, had moved out of the South Kensington house in 1893 (making way for the Nursing Sisters of St John the Divine) and bought a large new red-brick house called Wootton Heath at Boars Hill, which was then 'an island ... of Scotch firs, bracken and gorse',[53] on the ridge of the Cumnor Hills south-west of Oxford, and full of artistic and literary associations.

It is unlikely that Randal will have been swayed by either poetry or painting. For him the attractions will have been the healthy air (he had just had double pneumonia, and Boars Hill was famous for its dry and

*Ernest left the Army soon after joining up and enrolled in the Consular Service in Africa, rising to become Consul-General in Tunis – and a knight. The Ernest Berkeleys' marriage was not a success: Nelly fought a losing battle with ill-health and homesickness for Nice, while Ernest fought a losing battle with his roving eye (unpublished memoirs of Yvonne Berkeley, *c.* 1970s, BFP).

bracing climate*), the proximity to Oxford, the scope for improvements and additions, and the space for a golf course (also recommended for his chest). The house at Wootton Heath, originally called Bores Hill Heath, had been built a decade earlier for the President of Trinity College, Oxford, the Revd Henry Woods.[54] Determined that it should be worthy of an earl, Randal decided it needed a banqueting hall with a tower, three lodges and a 'ceremonial drive' – not to mention a sunken Italian garden, a concrete swimming pool hidden in the woods, private gas and water pumps and an electricity generator – and he gave the job to Sir Ernest George, one of the last architects of English stately homes before the new Estate Duty virtually brought the business to a close.

Sir Ernest had designed country houses at Batsford, Crathorne, Motcombe, North Mimms and West Dean - and the Royal Academy of Music in London (where Kate may have met him, when her first husband was teaching there).

Randal, who fancied himself as a Renaissance man, designed and made many of the fixtures and fittings himself, including the stained glass windows which he emblazoned with the Berkeley arms, and the lead gutters on which he embossed capital Bs.[55] And when at last it was all done, Randal called his grand but dotty hotchpotch of a house Foxcombe,† after the rise it sat on. To the locals – who may have been mocking his pretensions, since he does not seem to have been popular (and once said to a neighbour pushing a pram: 'How suburban can one be!')[56] – the house was always known as 'Berkeley Castle'. In order to stop the residential development of Boars Hill, Randal bought up all the remaining building sites along the main road – and hung on to them till 1927, when, safely ensconced in the real Berkeley Castle, he sold the entire estate, which was then broken up and sold on for housing.[57]

Before Foxcombe was quite complete the Kittys learned that they were now only one old man away from possession of the castle and the

*The author's great-great-great-uncle, Sir Henry Acland, Regius Professor of Medicine at Oxford, and physician to Edward VII, used to tell his patients that the air on Boars Hill was 'the best in the three kingdoms'.

†In the 1901 Census (RG13/1130/82/2/11, National Archives) Foxcombe is listed as Foxcombe House; at or just after its sale by Lord Berkeley in 1928 it was called Foxcombe Hall; in 1934 when occupied by Ripon Theological College, it was renamed Ripon Hall, and on its resale to the Open University in 1975, it was once again called Foxcombe Hall, the name by which it is still known today.

Berkeley estates, following the death in 1896 of Randal's kinsman Francis Lord FitzHardinge, an unsuccessful Dairy Shorthorn breeder. But the new proprietor, Charles, 3rd (and last) Lord FitzHardinge, was to live another twenty years, and Kitty, though twenty-five years Randal's junior, never survived to become chatelaine of Berkeley. In 1898, at the age of only forty-three, after five years of decline, she died of diseases of the heart, lungs and kidneys, leaving Randal a widower in sole charge of her nineteen-year-old daughter Sybil Jackson.

Since Lady Berkeley had borne no Berkeley children, and the heir to the title – Randal's great-uncle Grenville Berkeley – had died in 1896, without sons, the question of providing a baby Viscount Dursley to inherit and continue the Berkeley earldom must have weighed heavily at this time. Randal was still only thirty-three and could easily have married again, but he chose not to; at least not immediately. It was to be another twenty-six years before he remarried – and his bride this time was a patrician American divorcée, Molly Lloyd, a Lowell from Boston.

Till then his stepdaughter Sybil was to play the part of his constant companion and hostess. Some said she filled an even more intimate role. A Boars Hill neighbour claimed that Lord Berkeley and Miss Jackson 'went all over Europe, trying to get married but nobody would do it – it's not on: the Table of Affinities and so on.'[58] Her domestic duties were so onerous – and probably (judging by the enthusiasm conveyed by her scrapbooks and letters) pleasurable – that she had to abandon her dream of becoming a professional musician, though she was talented enough to have been taken on as a student of singing by the great tenor Jean de Reszke and as a student of the piano by Carlo Albanesi.[59] According to a newspaper interview at the end of her life, her musical career came to an end because she was working so hard that she collapsed under the strain.[60] According to a friend of Lennox, she was hysterical, and, though 'the last word in civilisation', she was undependable and erratic and eventually converted to Catholicism – because 'they looked after the old better'.[61] Occasionally she sang at dinner parties where 'her beautiful voice and rare gift for music' left a lasting impression on those guests who were not as obsessed with golf and osmotic pressures as the 8th Earl of Berkeley.[62] And soon she was to have a little step-cousin and godson to whom she could pass on her love of music.

In 1899 Hastings and Aline considered taking a house in Headington near Oxford, but discovered that the chances were not promising: 'the district is just now very much run after', Hastings told Aline, 'and there never comes anything to be let which is not instantly snapped up'.[63] For a while they stayed with Randal and Sybil at Foxcombe, and in the summer of 1902 they rented a house called Sunnymead in the newly expanding North Oxford. (There is no sign of it now, though the area surrounding it, just north of Summertown, still bears its name.) The following January they were back in France: Hastings (with his 'bikey', nicknamed Greyhound, and missing 'my Weenie badly') settled his mother into a new apartment in Paris, while Aline and the 'teeny one' (Gerry) stayed with the Harrises in Nice. By now it was clear that another teeny one was on the way, and Hastings was soon back in England, staying at Foxcombe with his brother and making preparations for the new arrival in the family's very first own house. A mile to the east of Foxcombe, at the end of Hamel's lane, it was a three-storey, seven-bedroom Arts and Crafts house called Melfort Cottage, in honour of Hastings's beloved 'Mammie', Cécile née Drummond (de Melfort).[64]

Both brothers must have considered the gossip likely to arise from their living in such close proximity. 'If Captain Berkeley is the elder brother,' neighbours might have whispered, 'then why isn't he the earl?' But Hastings was generally thought to be the younger brother. Since he was ten years the senior – and, as a sick man, he looked it – the story that he was younger must have been put about by Randal to protect himself from wagging tongues, and the gentle Hastings would have been happy to go along with it, to protect the memory of their mother.

Melfort Cottage was not quite ready in time for the birth, and when the new baby arrived on Tuesday 12 May 1903, the Hastings Berkeleys were lodging in a rented house called Sunningwell Plain, on the other side of what is now Foxcombe Road, a few minutes due east of Foxcombe Hall, on the edge of the heathland that was about to become Randal's new golf course.

It was a difficult birth, and the baby boy was small and sickly, but his mother was confident that, as a 'Tuesday's child', he would at least be 'full of grace'. He was given the names Lennox (after his imprudent grandfather, who was himself named after *his* great-great-grandfather, Charles Lennox, 2nd Duke of Richmond) and Randal (after his prickly uncle, who had been named in honour of *his* uncle, General Randal Rumley). But the little Berkeley was soon known in the family as 'Coss', which was the closest he himself could get, when he started to talk, to the sound of the name 'Lennox'. For Hastings this may have seemed an ironic self-identification: 'coss' is the x factor in an equation, an unknown quantity, and for the rest of his life, the sweet but enigmatic Lennox was to remain exactly that.

3
The Bernsteins

Freda's family were English Protestant working-class on the mother's side, and, on the father's side, 'Russians' from South Wales. Neither White nor Red, nor even, strictly speaking, Russian, the Bernsteins were poor Jews from Lithuania and Poland. As political subjects of the Tsar, they formed part of a colossal exodus of refugees, more than two million in number, on the run from Russian persecution. Under Catherine the Great, who had added both Poland and Lithuania to the Russian empire, Jews had been forced to live in the ghettoes of a Pale of Settlement, which incorporated most of Poland and Crimea. Within the Pale they had been subjected to further crippling restrictions: no more than ten per cent of them were allowed into secondary and higher education, all were banned from practising certain professions, and they were not allowed to serve on their local councils. Alexander II, the so-called Tsar Liberator who freed the serfs, slowed down the process of Jewish suppression, but in 1881 he was assassinated, the Jews were wrongly blamed and a wave of anti-Jewish pogroms swept through southern Russian. The new Tsar, Alexander III, held the Jews themselves responsible for the violence and introduced further repressive measures known as the Temporary Regulations (which remained in force for more than thirty years). Russians must never forget, he said, that it was the Jews who 'crucified our Master and shed his precious blood'.[1]

Jewish emigrations which had started as a trickle in the mid-1830s became a stream in the wake of the riots and the persecutions that followed, rising to a flood in the first decade of the twentieth century when widespread anti-Semitism throughout the Russian empire provoked even bloodier pogroms.

Ninety per cent of all Russia's Jewish emigrants sailed away to the 'Goldene Medine', the golden land of America. Of those who chose to start new lives in Britain, the Lithuanians favoured South Wales, drawn by stories of the opportunities in the steelworks and coalmines of the Welsh valleys, where Lithuanian timber was used for pit props,[2] and encouraged by reports that every Welsh home had a bible open on the kitchen table.[3] Possibly as many as 2,000 East European Jews emigrated to South Wales. There were three ways west (before the Kiel Canal was ready for traffic in 1895): the long but door-to-door route, in steerage with the timber, all the way from Riga, down the Baltic, up through the winding channels of the Scandinavian islands to the North Sea, south to the English Channel, and up the Bristol Channel to Cardiff; or the quicker route by land to Hamburg, and either straight across the North Sea to Hull or Newcastle, or over the top of Scotland in an American-bound ship, which would put in at Edinburgh and Liverpool before continuing across the Atlantic. Those who took the Hamburg options peddled and hawked their way down to Cardiff – perhaps via London, where the Jewish Temporary Shelter provided beds, food, clothing and holy books for prayer. In Cardiff the emigrants made for the local Jewish Board of Guardians, which placed them in safe-houses in the towns growing up around the booming coal and mineral fields.

Some of the refugees were skilled industrial workers who were able to find jobs in the mines at Dowlais, Penydarren, Cyfarthfa and Pentrebach. But most were artisans who had to scratch a living as travelling packmen, trudging up and down the mining valleys selling door to door. 'Anything wanting?' was their familiar cry [4] – till they had made enough money to start their own businesses from supplying the miners and their families with hob-nailed boots, moleskin trousers and grey woollen shirts, furniture, curtains, picture frames, window panes, cheap jewellery, cash on tick, and betting slips.

It was a grim and lonely life, with few rewards for the pioneers themselves, but in the hybrid population of Highland Scots, West Countrymen, Geordies, Irish, Italians and Spanish, the migrant Jews were less conspicuous than they had been at home. In Catholic Poland, ruled by Orthodox Mother Russia, they had been regarded, in the words of an emigrant tinker's descendant, as 'the lowest form of life – lower even than pigs – like garbage'.[5] But the Noncomformist Welsh 'esteemed the Jews as "People of the Book", and very often had a special regard for them',[6] (though they were not so tolerant of the Irish, who undercut their jobs in the mines – and stole their women). The Welsh also shared with the Jews an unfamiliarity with English, the language of the mines. But they had more than this in common: both were 'deeply religious, addicted to rhetoric, and convinced of the value of education in the advancement of their children'.[7] That the Welsh called their places of worship after Hebrew place names from the Old Testament – Zion, Ebenezer, Bethel – forged a further link between the two communities.

But life for the Jews in the valleys was not entirely free of prejudice, and in 1903 inter-racial fighting broke out, first at the Dowlais Iron Works, then in the streets of Merthyr Tydfil. The trouble is thought to have been caused by poor Jewish immigrants accepting low wages which undercut the Irish labourers and forced them out of work. Things got so bad that many Jews were assisted to migrate to Canada, while others actually returned home to Eastern Europe. In September that year the *Jewish Chronicle* published an article, signed by I. Raffalovitch, of Synagogue Chambers, Merthyr, urging Jewish workers not to be 'allured' by the prospect of jobs at Dowlais, and warning them that if they insisted on coming they would have to bear the consequences themselves.

The veteran Labour politician, reformer, lawyer and writer the late Leo Abse, himself a descendant of Jewish emigrants to South Wales, pointed out that they were a mixed bag, the early settler Jews of the Welsh valleys. Very many of them, particularly the 'Polaks' (Polish Jews), possessed the 'vice of the Jews ... gambling', but not 'their virtue ... respect for learning'. In Abse's view, 'Escaping from the imposed ghettoes of the Czar to a self-imposed ghetto in Wales, playing cards was their only recreation – as it had been in Poland. Yet a small group ... devoted all their scanty leisure ... to learning ... the highly-developed Jewish religious culture based for millennia on close study of text.'[8]

Some of those who did break free of 'the ghettoes of the synagogue and the pawnshop'[9] made names for themselves well beyond the valleys: for example, the chemist and industrialist Dr Ludwig Mond, founder of Clydach Refinery and father of the 1st Baron Melchett; the entrepreneur Harry Sherman, founder of the football pools empire; the Labour politician and solicitor Lewis (later 1st Baron) Silkin, two of whose sons became privy councillors and government ministers; Ernest and Charles Pearl, pioneers of cinema advertising; and the solicitor and cinema owner Rudolf Abse, father of the psychoanalyst Wilfred, Leo himself, and the poet Dannie.

Joseph Bernstein was no such high-flier, but, as a 'Litvak' (a Lithuanian Jew), he considered himself shrewder, more cultured, less insular than most of the Polish Jews. When he and his wife Fradel, and their sons Lewis and Isaac – young men in their twenties – arrived from

Kaunas, in what was then Russian Poland (now Lithuania),* in about 1870, they had a ready-made family to join.[10] Joseph's brother Isaac had emigrated to the Welsh valleys in the late 1850s, when he was in his twenties, and, slowly bettering himself, had risen from itinerant tinkering around Merthyr Tydfil to respectability, if not prosperity, as a clothes dealer – first in Bedwellty, twelve miles to the south-east, and then, three miles up the road in Tredegar, at premises in Commercial Road (later known as Commercial Street). But in August 1880 this brother had suddenly died, worn out at the age of only fifty-five. Since then the shop had been run by Isaac's Polish widow, Julia, with their sickly son and two daughters. In prospect, the arrival of Joseph and Fradel and their two sturdy sons from the Bernsteins's home *shtetl* may have seemed a blessing: Uncle Joseph had been in the *schmatte* business all his life, so he was familiar with every aspect of the rag trade, the boys were intelligent and would be able to help in the shop, and Aunt Fradel could keep house for them all.

But in reality there was neither room for them above the shop, nor business enough to support them. While Fradel found a place to rent in a terrace of miners' cottages nearby, Joseph was forced to hawk jewellery around the valleys. His pieces were probably amber trinkets, since the name Bernstein comes from the Hebrew *burshtin*, which means amber – often known as 'Lithuanian gold'. It is likely that the Bernsteins came originally from the Baltic coast – perhaps the Jewish settlement of Palanga in Zamet – where most of the world's amber was extracted, then travelled inland to Kaunas to sell the amber, and, in later generations, turned to the clothing business.[11]

In Tredegar, Joseph's elder son Lewis moved in with his aunt Julia and his cousins above the shop in Commercial Road, and set up as a glazier. The younger son Isaac – a clever and ambitious nineteen-year-old – bought himself an apprenticeship as a draper, and went to live and work four miles away, with a well-to-do Jewish family called Fine, who owned an outfitter's and pawnbroker's in Merchant Street, Pontlottyn (now Rhymney).

The South Wales mines, off which they all lived, formed one of the

*They came from Raseiniai, aka Rasein, Rossiena, Rossieny – and, in Isaac Bernstein's will of 3 August 1922, 'Rosiane' – then a town of about 6,000 people, in the south-eastern foothills of the Zemaitija highland in the Kaunas (aka Kovno) province, about 100 miles W.N.W. of Vilnius, the capital of Lithuania.

major industrial centres of the world at the time and must have seemed tremendously exciting to the new arrivals from agricultural Lithuania (where three and a half million peasants, working in serfdom, raised cattle and bees, or gathered and processed raw amber, for absentee landlords in Poland and Germany). But it was not a healthy place, this hectic, sulphurous, rain-battered mountain valley, with its clattering pithead wheel-towers, spitting furnaces, smoke-belching chimney stacks, slag heaps and jerry-built slums. Tuberculosis was rife, and Merthyr Tydfil in particular was frequently swept by epidemics of cholera. According to an undated article in the *Jewish Telegraph*, Merthyr by the turn of the nineteenth century was characterized by 'the smell of sulphur and a sense of urgency, steel hawsers and pools of tar, clouds of black smoke from tall stacks, hissing steam, shrill whistles, loud hooters and showers of sparks from scores of furnaces – never-ending clamour'.[12]

Not surprisingly the Bernsteins were soon affected by disease. During the summer of 1882 Julia's sickly son caught smallpox, suffering with terrible eruptions for seven days before he died, aged only twenty. In need of a new manager, the widowed mother tempted her nephew Lewis, the glazier, back to the shop by offering the hand of her daughter Sarah. The marriage took place at No. 4 in June 1883. That the bride and groom were first cousins was no problem for the Bernsteins. Such marriages were not only permitted under *halacha*, but were the rule rather than the exception in many poor Jewish families which could not afford dowries, and wanted to keep what little property they had within the family.[13] But it may have been a problem for chapel-minded Tredegar, which is perhaps why Sarah always spelled her maiden name Berenstein or even Beirnstein, while Lewis used Bernstein – to convince a suspicious, gentile community that their cousinhood was decently remote.

Lewis's good fortune was the widow's too, since she now had a good manager tied to the shop, a secure future for the business, one daughter married off, and the prospect of lots of little Bernsteins to look after her in old age. By 1901 Lewis and Sarah had produced six boys and five girls, but Julia never lived to see the last two of her grandsons. In 1899, aged sixty-six, she died of 'natural decay', and joined her husband and son in the bleakly beautiful Jewish graveyard at Cefn Coed y Cymmer, on the Brecon road two miles from Merthyr. The graveyard was opened in 1872, the same year in which work started on the fairytale synagogue in Merthyr that is still standing in the centre of town, at the top end of, ironically, Church Street. But it is no longer a synagogue. By the 1920s, with the iron works closed and the market for coal diminishing, the mortgage was still unpaid and the dwindling Jewish community was beginning to find it a burden to maintain the building. Nevertheless worship continued till 1983 when the community could not even muster the minyan, the quorum of ten adult Jews required for public prayers. The trustees were in a bind: without a quorum they could not hold services, without services they were not eligible for a grant from the Welsh Development Agency and without a grant they could not keep the place going. So they sold up – to a Christian group – for £6,000; the silver fetched another £12,000. The new owners got an immediate, substantial grant from the Agency and sold on to a fitness centre within a year.[14]

Even without Julia Bernstein, the clothing business flourished, so that in about 1891 Lewis and Sarah were able to open a bigger outfitter's – with a pawnbroker's at the back – at 27 (later still, 28 and 29) Bridge Street, Tredegar. To keep the supply of cloth within the family, Lewis established his parents Joseph and Fradel as drapers in the same street, at No. 7. Meanwhile they retained the original shop in Commercial Road. It was a prosperous business and they were able to afford both a housemaid and a nurse for the toddlers. Nine years older than Joseph, Fradel Bernstein soon began to fail and in the winter of 1909 she caught bronchitis and died, aged sixty-five.

Then came the Riot. It happened in August 1911, during a period of national unrest – rail strikes, union troubles, economic tension – when 'underlying currents of anti-Semitism, fanned by the Welsh Baptists', broke out in violence against the Jews in Tredegar.[15] According to *The Times*, a wild mob, which started as '200 disorderly young men' and increased to 'several thousands', rampaged through the town centre in the middle of the night, smashing the windows and looting the contents of all the shops owned by Jews – eighteen shops in all.[16] Not a single Jew was hurt, but 'the intervening police put 15 of the mob into hospital'.[17]

The Times held the Left responsible. The troubles had been caused, a special correspondent suggested, by 'a spirit of indiscipline run riot, prompted neither by want nor deep class feelings', but by 'the present insubordinate doctrines preached by the half-baked intelligences which are the mouthpieces of socialism'.[18] Some blamed the Tredegar Jews themselves, for monopolizing the furniture, clothing and jewellery trades, for charging unnecessarily high prices, for renting out inferior property, and for forcing their tenants to buy furniture on hire purchase. Leo Abse did not discount the 'tension in existence in labour relations that year', but in his view the real villains were the 'disreputable' Jews of Tredegar – the '*schleppers*' – who were 'notorious as tough pawnbrokers, money lenders or minor Rachmans'. His wealthy grandfather, descended, he claimed, from an ancient line of Phoenician Jews, regarded them as 'loan sharks'.[19] Even the great Jewish philanthropist Lord (Nathan) Rothschild is supposed to have said of the Tredegar Jews, 'They are a bad lot and probably deserve what they are getting.'[20]

They were not all bad, and the worthy ones – among them the Samuels, Harrises and Broders, the Wolfsons, Rosenbaums, Fines and the Litvak Bernsteins – were well-respected in the town. The morning after the riot, the Liberal agent for the local parliamentary constituency, Mr Ebenezer Thomas, took his daughter Marie, then aged thirteen, on a tour of the town to inspect the damage and sympathize with the victims. In Bridge Street they called on the Bernsteins, who had had both their shops broken into and robbed. In the parlour they found Joseph Bernstein, 'a rather large, elderly man', sitting 'in deep sorrow surrounded by members of his family' and muttering in bewilderment, 'I never thought Tredegar would do this to me. I am Tredegar!'[21] The teenage girl who recorded Joseph's lament, Marie Thomas – or Mrs Davies, as she later became – was a firm believer in the contribution of the Jews to Tredegar. 'Now', she wrote in 1987, 'there are no Jewish families, no Synagogue, no Jewish culture in Tredegar, and, I believe, Tredegar is the poorer for that.'[22]

Young Isaac Bernstein, by then a substantial landlord, lost nothing in the riot, but his friends in Rhymney, the Fines, who owned much property in the area, suffered heavy losses. The local council awarded the Tredegar Bernsteins £231. 8s. 1d. in compensation for damage and losses, which provided for considerable improvements to the premises. A neighbouring trader who was just as generously compensated – another Lithuanian – is reported to have said, 'They were not rioters, they were angels!'[23]

Not long after the riot, old Joseph Bernstein had a heart attack and died. Nine months later, in November 1918, his elder son Lewis followed him, leaving (after a year's delay, because he never made a will and his affairs took some time to resolve) the substantial inheritance of £6,067 (about a quarter of a million pounds by today's values). The sole beneficiary was his son Moses, who now took over the clothing businesses in Bridge Street and Commercial Road.* Moses's sister Anne, who ran her own draper's shop at 36 Castle Street, stayed on, despite the troubles, and was still there in 1975, when she told the *Jewish Chronicle* that she 'couldn't live anywhere else' – although she admitted that she missed seeing a Jewish face, and, to keep in touch, she had the *Jewish Chronicle* delivered every Friday.[24]

Isaac had not wasted a moment of his apprenticeship at Tobias Fine & Co. He had learned not only the outfitting trade but the rudiments of business itself. He had also mastered English, unlike the majority of the Jewish emigrants who spoke only Welsh, and, thanks to the 2,000 volumes in the workmen's library in Merchant Street – and possibly with the help of the local schoolmaster David Jones, who was 'on intimate terms' with him 'for upwards of six years' during this period [25] – he had acquired an excellent basic education as well. In particular, like many of the more enterprising South Wales Jews (including his own great-nephew Lewis Bernstein, who became a barrister), Isaac seems to have acquired a keen, legal turn of mind – analytical and disciplined, with an attention to detail.

By the time Isaac Bernstein was thirty-two, the Fines, recognizing his ability, had promoted him to manager of their drapery department. Two years later he applied for naturalization as a British subject, stating that he intended to settle permanently in Great Britain, that he desired the full rights of a British citizen (partly so that he could own freehold property), and that he hoped to stand for election to the local council. His application was supported by the written references of four local traders who knew him well – all of them grocers, and at least three of them gentiles – and of Mr Jones the schoolmaster. In forwarding the application to the Home Office, the Chief Constable of Cardiff, Lionel Lindsay, reported that all the referees were of good character and that the applicant himself was of 'very good character and respectability'.[26]

*Administration of the Estate of Lewis Bernstein, outfitter, who died at 27 Bridge Street, Tredegar, on 28 November 1918 was granted one year and one day later to his son Moses (aka Moss) Bernstein, outfitter, of the same address (Leicester Probate Sub Registry.)

Isaac Bernstein became a British subject on 12 June 1903. And just in time, because only eighteen months later the Aliens Act made it very much more difficult for Jewish refugees to enter Britain. Officially the act was intended to repel 'undesirable aliens', defined as paupers, lunatics, vagrants and prostitutes, but the unofficial targets were Jewish immigrants from Eastern Europe.

There is no evidence that Isaac did ever stand for election as a councillor – unlike his distinguished friend and mentor Israel Fine, who was a councillor in Rhymney for many years and a justice of the peace.[27] But there is evidence that he soon took other advantage of his rights as a naturalized Briton. By 1910 he was the owner of no fewer than twelve residences in Plantation Road, Pontlottyn, all of them occupied by gentiles, while he himself was living in a smart new house in a terrace built by, and named after, the Fines. It must have been a profitable enterprise because he raised sufficient money to set up his own business in St John's Road, Newport, where he was operating as an outfitter by 1919.[28] And not long afterwards, identifying a new market, he opened a boot dealer's on Cardiff docks, catching the trade as it came and went between the mines and the outside world. By 1921 he was able to buy even more valuable property: numbers 180, 182 and 184 Chepstow Road, Newport. He himself moved to the middle house, let No. 180 and ran a branch of his boot shop at 184 (a shrewd move, since the tenants either side of the Bernstein properties – at 178 and 186 – were makers of boots).

Isaac Bernstein was now a merchant of considerable means. He had also reached his fifties, without having married – a serious black mark for a Jewish man. According to the *Shulchan Aruch*, the code of Hebrew law, it is a duty to marry – preferably at eighteen – and to go forth and multiply. No family letters, papers, diaries or photos have survived to explain why he had never married (or indeed anything else about Isaac or any of his Bernstein relations, apart from the barest facts of their existence).

Early in 1922 Isaac seems to have stopped to consider his predicament. Perhaps responding to the economic decline (that would lead to a worldwide slump in 1929), he decided to retire from active business. Tired of the incessant quarrelling and intolerance of the 'shabby pawnbroker hierarchy'[29] in which he had been raised, he made the momentous decision to abandon his family and his Welsh roots, and move to London. Such 'disappearances' were not uncommon among the more resourceful and broad-minded of the Welsh Jews. To put his affairs in order, he resolved to make a will, and, following an instinct that warned him never to skimp on important things, he made an appointment with the smartest law firm in London at the time, Lewis & Lewis, of Ely Place. Then, leaving the business in the hands of his friend Samuel Wolfson, he took the train to the big city.

4
Lennox, Schooldays I

Lennox used to recall – with a hint of regret, as though he would have preferred a more settled home life – that the Berkeleys were always moving when he was little.[1] And indeed his parents did flit restlessly between an often-changing base of their own, in or around Oxford, and their parents' houses in France.

Sometimes Lennox and his sister Geraldine stayed behind with their mother, while Hastings went off on his own, usually with his precious 'bikey', to look after his sick mother Cécile; sometimes Aline took the children, when she went to visit her elderly father at the villa Les Rochers, leaving Hastings at home to supervise the garden and to work on his books. And on these trips Aline and the children would occasionally take the carriage along the Grande Corniche – or the steamer from Nice – to Menton (Mentone as it was still then called) to visit Aline's sister Annie d'Eppinghoven and Annie's pretty daughter Louise-Marie ('Lison'), who, though nine years older than Lennox, liked to play with him, since she had no brothers or sisters of her own.

When they could, they all went to France together – and on these occasions 'bikey' was a tandem (Aline being something of a New Woman). Having parked the children with one or other of the mothers-in-law, Hastings and Aline mounted the tandem – he in front with the map, she behind with the picnic – and set off to explore the Alpes Maritimes. Their favourite excursion was southwest along the Mediterranean coast to the former Roman naval port of Fréjus, then up through the Estrelles, the thickly wooded hills above Cannes – once the haunt of the Robin Hood of Provence, Gaspard de Besse – and into the rustic hinterland of the Var.*

*LB, who wrote an orchestral suite, now lost, called *Estérel* (offered as a 'novelty' for the 1945 season of Promenade Concerts in London (SRC 72), inherited his parents' love of the Midi, despite the bitter Mistral that batters it in

The death of Aline's father, Sir James Harris, in November 1904, and of her mother in February 1912, changed but did not halt these trips to the Riviera. On the death of Hastings's Aunt Albine, Baroness van Havre, six years earlier, they had inherited a second French base at Fontainebleau, fully furnished and fully staffed. Aunt Albine's death had also brought a little windfall. 'Having put away rather more money than we supposed', she had been able to leave Hastings and his brother Ernest about £2,800 each. Randal seems to have been overlooked in Aunt Albine's bequest, presumably because Mme la baronne knew by then that he could count on the Berkeley trusts.[2]

Shortly after her sister's death, and mindful of her own mortality, Cécile wrote a note, which she attached to her will, urging Randal to do his duty by Hastings and Ernest, who stood to lose a quarter of their incomes on her death. She also recommended to his charity her two faithful servants Désirée and her sister Alice and their family (Alice was barely fit for service now, and the pair had to support a poor old mother and two other sisters who were 'incapable of work from usure & ill health'[3]). She does not seem to have pressed the matter at the time: indeed it is possible that Randal had broken off relations with his mother, since her note to him, written on black-edged paper (mourning her sister Albine), explains

> These few lines are written to you in case I should not be able from one cause or another, to see & speak to you ... I know, my dearest Son, your high feelings of duty & justice & I feel sure you will always help & protect your brothers ... My blessing & love will always remain with you, I feel it so & I pray earnestly that God will bless & guard you, & give you light! Your loving Mother Cécile Berkeley.[4]

Whatever the explanation, it is clear that she could not bring herself to upset Randal by pressing her elder sons' claims in person. When the

---

winter and spring. His 'dream-house', he told his diary, would lie between the village of Le Buis-les-Baronnies, in the Drôme, and the Rhone valley to the west: 'it's rural, not much built over, mountainous with lovely views, and there are acres of vines and olive groves – olive trees I love, and I would have to be somewhere where there are some' (LB, Diary 30 April 1972, BFP).

Hastings Berkeleys took Frinton Hall* in the exclusive new resort of Frinton-on-Sea on the north-east Essex coast for three months of golf and tennis and sea bathing in the summer of 1911, they begged Cécile to come and join them, but she refused. They could not understand why – till Hastings went to stay with her in Nice the following January and discovered she had been afraid it might compromise her relationship with Randal, who by then had fallen out with Hastings.[5]

Meanwhile, in about 1897 Randal had moved into Foxcombe with his wife Kate (who was to die the following year, aged only forty-three[6]) and her nineteen-year-old daughter Sybil Jackson. It was now such a stately home (albeit an architectural jumble) that Randal's niece Yvonne, daughter of Lennox's uncle Ernest (the British Consul in Tunis), was overawed when she went to stay there in 1915. 'Its grandeur and servants rather scared me,' she wrote in an unpublished memoir. 'I was used to Arab servants, but the English ones were a little frightening, they were so very correct.'[7] (And so numerous: seven in 1911.) She was delighted with the beautiful gardens, in particular the flowering rhododendrons and the water lilies on the lake, but she did not mention the fourteen gardeners, or the woods of Corsican pine which later generations were to deplore for darkening the landscape and obscuring the famous views.

During the first year at Foxcombe Randal travelled in to Balliol College every morning for lectures by Sir Henry Miers, Professor of Mineralogy. He had enrolled as an undergraduate, at the advanced age of thirty-two, and was, according to Miers, an active and clear thinker, eager to learn but intolerant of criticism. This intolerance was the undoing of his brief career as an Oxford student. When the University refused to allow him to keep term as an undergraduate while continuing to live at Foxcombe, on the reasonable grounds that his residence there broke the rule requiring students to live within one and a half miles of the university, Randal stormed off, never to return.[8] Oxford was the loser. Randal had intended to build the university a new research laboratory, but instead he built one for himself, at home – in the oldest part of the Foxcombe complex, an early-nineteenth-century stone milking parlour with a thatched roof (which he replaced with

*Frinton Hall was a large house, at the top of Connaught Avenue, just behind St Mary's Church, with unbroken views across the esplanade to the sea; it has long since been demolished for residential development.

tiles).[9] And there, with a hand-picked team of scientists, he worked on his experiments in physical chemistry – first on an improved method of determining the density of crystals, then on osmotic pressures – till the outbreak of war in 1914. He lived, according to the chemical engineer Brigadier-General Sir Harold Hartley, 'an almost monastic life, absorbed in research – and golf', which he played every afternoon, and soon became a scratch player.[10]

Despite having weak wrists, golf was an abiding passion – about which he was to write a typically obsessive and dogmatic book years later.* It was also, as far as can be gathered, the cause of a rift between Randal and his brother Hastings, who was now a Boars Hill neighbour, having built Melfort Cottage in Hamel's Lane, to the east of Foxcombe Hall. The quarrel involved the nine-hole golf course which Randal had laid out in 1904, on land immediately below Foxcombe, on the other side of what is now Berkeley Road, between Tommy's Heath and Yatscombe Copse. This new course replaced an earlier 'Golfing Course' and pavilion further down the hill towards North Hinksey. Designed to ensure that Randal always won, the new course incorporated the 'novel principles' which he had developed by laboriously calculating the dynamics of every possible shot in the game. Randal played there every afternoon, his caddie carrying a mysterious bundle of canes, which were 'used for marking out new bunkers which sprang up most unexpectedly where his own practice shots never landed the ball, but sagaciously placed for the discomfiture of his visiting opponents'.[11] In 1927 Lord Berkeley sold this land – amounting to 64 acres - to a group of speculative builders, on the understanding that it would remain a golf course. The following year, perhaps as a public relations exercise, since their development of Boars Hill had made them unpopular locally, they sold it on to the Oxford Preservation Trust for £11,000.[12]

It seems that Hastings – while still renting Sunningwell Plain on the eastern boundary of the new golf course – wanted to pull down, or even just reduce a little, the high and close-boarded wooden fence which surrounded the links, and blocked the famous views of

***Sound golf by applying principles to practice* was written for 'goats' (average players) and describes 'the simplest ways of playing different shots [including the pinch and the poached egg] evolved by studying each as a problem in dynamics' (Hartley, *Obituary Notice*, p. 178).

Oxford.* It was a typical neighbours' dispute, but Randal was not used to resistance, and would not tolerate it. Worse, it resulted in a tyrannous act of revenge. Ignoring Cécile's wishes, Randal refused to have any more to do with Hastings, and eventually he cut both Hastings and Ernest and all four of his nephews and nieces, his only close relations, entirely out of his will. That he was capable of over-reacting to a trifle with such impulsive finality was due to those qualities of character which the writer L. P. Hartley, who knew him as an old man, described as 'capriciousness' and 'inflexible determination', 'single-mindedness' and 'inscrutability'. With Lord Berkeley, he wrote, 'to wish was to decide, and to decide was to act; he had the courage of his impulses and ... almost unlimited means of gratifying them.' Everything had to be done the best way, but the best way had to be his way too.[13]

If golf and science occupied Randal during the day, music played a large part in the life of Foxcombe in the evenings. His stepdaughter Sybil, continuing the practice of her late mother, gave regular *soirées*, at which she sang at the piano, or accompanied visiting musicians. These occasions, together with his mother playing the little German piano (which she sold in 1916 for £12),[14] provided Lennox with his first experiences of live music. Nearly seventy years later Sybil Jackson recalled visiting the Hastings Berkeleys at Melfort Cottage in 1906, and singing Schubert *Lieder* to Lennox, who was then 'a tiny little chap' of three. 'I can remember him standing there absolutely motionless, watching and listening. It was the first time I noticed he was at all musical ... He always asked ... when I went to the house – would I sing?'[15] Lennox's Aunt Nelly – his mother's younger sister, who had studied composition in Paris – wrote some salon pieces for voice and piano, which he remembered her singing when he was on holiday at Les Rochers; and when he was older, he used to accompany her.

By 1907, when he was four and attending the Woodside kindergarten school at Boars Hill,[16] Lennox was 'growing quite a big boy and

*This information, fragmentary and unclear as it is, was conveyed to FB by Randal's second wife, Molly Berkeley. In fact the fence was sawn down to about three or four feet high when the land was sold to the Oxford Preservation Trust; and this reduced fence remained in place until the early 1970s (Aldiss, ed, *A Boars Hill Anthology*, p. 35).

... very sensible and good',[17] but he was prone to head colds, which often laid him low for long periods, and during these he would lie in bed (in his room at Melfort Cottage looking out over the long wild garden towards distant Radley, down by the Thames) listening to the mechanical music which was such a feature of his childhood. Almost as soon as it was patented in America in 1897, Hastings had bought a pianola, and Lennox recalled hearing, at a very early age, rolls of all kinds of music, in particular Beethoven sonatas and keyboard arrangements of concertos. Like other little boys, he could not resist pressing on the pedals and running his fingers along the keys while 'watching fascinated as the perforated roll unfolded'.[18] Hastings was 'passionately fond of music' though he was not a musician, having never had the time to learn an instrument, and his energetic peddling of the pianola provided Lennox's first real awareness of music as a child, and 'certainly woke something in me'.[19]

Despite all this music at home, it was not till 1911, when he was eight, that Lennox started having piano lessons – at the Dragon School in Oxford, or Lynam's as it was then called. And he does not seem to have shown much active interest in music till about 1914. A letter from his father, in Nice, in January 1913 – mentioning Lennox and music for the first time in his correspondence – warns Aline, back home in Oxford, that if she catches 'Cossie' shirking his piano practice, she is to remind him that his lessons will be stopped unless he pulls his socks up.[20]

Lynam's was intended to be his moral suspenders. He had begun there in April 1911, and though his elder sister Geraldine was a boarder at her school – St Helen's, Abingdon (newly founded to provide a Christian education for girls) – it was decided that Lennox should be a day-boy, because of his chronic ill-health. Lynam's was chosen partly because it was so close to their new house in North Oxford, and partly because of its radical views on education.

The school had been founded by a group of dons in 1877 as the Oxford Preparatory School ('for the Sons of Gentlemen'),[21] but it had since adopted the name of its pioneering headmaster C. C. 'Skipper' Lynam, whose unconventional philosophy that boys should be happy, positive and independent struck a chord with parents of an advanced and liberal turn of mind. Lennox might have benefited if he had been healthier, but that first winter, 1911/12, he was so out of sorts that Hastings took 'the dear little fellow' to a doctor for a thorough check-up. It transpired that there was not much the matter, though indeed he was a little fellow – now aged nine, he was only four foot three-and-a-half and weighed four stone four.[22] The doctor, however, was 'positive that he is quite sound and free from any organic trouble'.[23] So they persevered with Lynam's, and a resident French nurse.

The new house the Berkeleys had moved into was one of the finest in North Oxford: a seven-bedroomed, whitewashed villa, with a coach house, set in its own little park at the top end of the Woodstock Road, near what's now the Wolvercote roundabout on the A40. Number 304, known as The Lodge (upgraded to 'Summertown Villa' when offered for sale in 2003),* looks like a Regency rectory, but in fact it was not built till the 1840s (despite the '1862' carved into the ornate lintel over the front door.) [24] In 1911 Hastings paid £3,250 for it, including lease and fixtures;[25] by 2001 its value had risen to £3.6 million.[26] Lennox rediscovered the place in the summer of 1968 while 'wandering round my old haunts in North Oxford', and records in his diary that he 'managed to get a good view of our old house' and was 'able to indulge in an orgy of nostalgia'. Having never taken much notice of the architecture before, he realized now that it was 'really a rather pretty Victorian building with a nicely proportioned verandah looking on to the garden'.[27] In fact the iron-latticed verandah, linking conservatories on either side of the front of the house, is quite exceptionally fine, and a perfect foil to the classicism of the rest of the front elevation, which rises to a plain parapet with an exquisite moulded cornice beneath and a decorated roundel centrally placed above. To see the house, romantically derelict, through the pair of Wellingtonia trees that stand at the end of the terraced part of the garden is to wonder why the Berkeleys ever left it – and it is interesting that the London house that Lennox eventually settled in, 8 Warwick Avenue, is strikingly similar.

It is clear enough why the Berkeleys wanted to buy No. 304. Apart from its elegance and the charm of its rambling country garden, it was only a stone's throw from Lynam's. Even so it was a bit too far for Lennox to walk to school every day (all the way down to the bottom of the long Woodstock Road, then across the Banbury Road to Bardwell

*From sale particulars published by Knight Frank, Oxford, March 2003. The asking price then was £2.25 million for the house, coachhouse and ¾ acre of a garden that must once have comprised at least five times that much. Part of the original plot was sold in 1954 to form Bishop Kirk Place; the remainder of the land has been retained for possible future development.

Road on the banks of the Cherwell), so he used to cycle instead. He remembered till the end of his life the perils of dodging the horse-drawn trams that hurtled up and down the Banbury Road.[28]

The plan was that Lynam's should prepare the boy for entry to the Royal Naval College at Osborne, the feeder school for Dartmouth, from where he would follow his father into the Navy. But he was such 'a goose about arithmetic' – one of the prerequisites for entry – that his exasperated father had to resort to some modern psychology. As a subscriber to *Mind*, the quarterly review of psychology and philosophy edited by the Cambridge philosopher G. F. Stout, Hastings believed in the theory that 'ideas seek to act themselves out'.[29] In a letter to Aline from Nice in January 1912 he explained to her how to put this idea into practice,

> Give the dear little lad my love and tell him ... if he goes on steadily, honestly *trying* & not *shirking* the work he will find that he will get on quite well enough to please me. If he says to himself *every day*: I want to go to Osborne, & I cant go to Osborne unless I know Arithmetic, then he will also say to himself: I *will* learn arithmetic, & I shall pretend to like it even if I don't, just because I've made up my mind that I will go to Osborne; and then I shall have a good laugh at Daddy, who says he does not think I shall ever get to Osborne.[30]

With a child of Lennox's temperament and 'deficiency of determination', Aline would have to work hard at firing his imagination, Hastings warned, and she would need to be persistent so the idea became familiar, and the will trained by that familiarity.[31]

It was a brave effort but it did not work, and they soon had to give up the idea of the Navy. Lennox would not have got in anyway, because of his poor health and his colour-blindness – a specialist had discovered the only colour he could see was yellow. Hastings must have been disappointed, not only because of his own naval links but also because of his love of maths. He was – as usual – philosophical: since Lennox 'would probably not be particularly suited for the service it matters less than it might have otherwise'.[32]

Hastings was nothing if not an independent thinker. Divining that his only son needed some distance from home – and from feminine cosseting – he scouted around for a small, experimental school that could be trusted to give an unusual boy a better chance of developing his full potential. And he found what he was looking for. From radical Lynam's, where Lennox was such a reluctant learner, it was decided to move him to the prep school of an even more progressive institution. It lay 186 miles from Oxford in the market town of Holt in North Norfolk, and its name was Gresham's.

5
Lennox, Schooldays II

In the summer of 1914 Gresham's was a school on the up.[1] As war loomed in Europe and Hastings feared for the safety of his family, the remoteness of Norfolk and the rising reputation of Gresham's must have combined to persuade him in its favour. Within weeks of the outbreak of war, eleven-year-old Lennox and his tuck box were stowed on to a Great Western Railway train at Oxford station for the cross-country adventure to Holt via Paddington, Liverpool Street and Norwich. It must have been as much of a wrench for Hastings and Aline themselves as it was for poor little Lennox who had never spent a night away from home on his own before.

There had been some talk in 1913 of sending the boy to Rugby, where the reformer A. E. David was busy demolishing Arnold's principles of 'muscular Christianity', as immortalized in *Tom Brown's School Days*, in which the hero metamorphoses from a shy and homesick little chap into a robust and manly rugger-player. In its place David was attempting to introduce a new way of thinking that was based less on the houses and teams of the public school system than on the individuals within them. This represented a revolution in public school thinking, and it would have appealed strongly to a victim of Burney's Academy. Hastings may also have been influenced in favour of the Rugby option by the fact that one of Lennox's fellow-pupils at Lynam's, John Greenidge (who lived with his grandmother Alice Lucy further down the Woodstock Road), was now a pupil there. But Rugby seems to have said no to Lennox.[2] That Gresham's was just as unconventionally liberal was more than a consolation. That the costs involved were less than half may have settled the matter: Gresham's fees were a very reasonable £48 a year, against Rugby's pricey £119. 10s.; Eton itself was only £6 more.[3]

The essence of the Gresham's experiment, under its progressive headmaster George Howson, was brain over brawn. Howson hated the cult of games and the hero-worshipping of athletes, which were both so prevalent in British public schools at the time (and remained so for half a century); he even forbade his boys from cheering at football matches. But he positively encouraged work, particularly self-motivated work (for which purpose a fine library bequeathed to the school by its sixteenth-century founder, Sir John Gresham, Lord Mayor of London, proved invaluable to generations of Gresham's bookworms[4]). And if self-motivation failed, there was a master-boy ratio of one to ten to give a personal fillip to the learning process.[5]

Boys could make friends freely (i.e. across year and house barriers),* in marked contrast to the isolation system which had been introduced to prevent 'unnatural relationships'. They could also roam wherever they chose, since there were virtually no school bounds, so long as they got back in time for evening prayers; and the grounds alone would have taken some exploring – forty acres of playing fields amidst sixty acres of woodland.[6] Unlike most other public schools, every boy had the use of a shared study, and slept in a private cubicle; there were no dormitories.

Furthermore, and most avant-garde of all, there was no corporal punishment. Instead, in pursuit of character-building, Howson introduced a controversial system of self-regulation, under which each boy promised on his honour not to swear, not to smoke and not to practise, talk about or allow any sort of 'beastliness'. If a boy broke any of his promises he was honour-bound to confess to his housemaster, who, instead of reaching for his cane, would try to help. The objective was pure Boy Scouts: 'High heart, high speech, high deeds'.[7] Whether it worked in practice is debatable. The writer Jonathan Gathorne-Hardy argues that Howson's honour system produced 'an extremely repressed community founded on guilt and fear – fear of informers, fear of "sin", guilt about breaking promises'.[8] W. H. Auden, who was at Gresham's a few years after Lennox (and a few years before Benjamin Britten), claimed that the consequence of suppressed emotions, particularly sexual ones, was that, like all things that are shut up, they 'go bad on you'. Still referring specifically to Gresham's, he said that no one had ever devised a 'more potent engine for turning [boys] into neurotic

*In practice this did not happen because, as Kemeys Bagnall-Oakeley explained in a letter to RN, 11 May 1989, 'In the days before interschool matches, house matches were the thing and the resulting rivalry made it impossible to have friends in another house' (RNA).

innocents, for perpetuating those very faults of character which it was intended to cure'. And, in a final shot at his old school, the poet who was to rush to the aid of the republicans in the Spanish Civil War, said the best reason he had for opposing Fascism was that 'at school I lived in a Fascist state'.[9]

Britten, who arrived at Gresham's nine years after Howson's death, thought the honour system was a disaster, judging by his experience of the prevalence of 'Atrocious bullying ... vulgarity & swearing'. There was not any point running a disciplinary system based on honour, he wrote in his diary, when the boys did not have any. Small and weak boys were turned into 'sour & bitter boys, & ruined for life'.[10]

It had been different with the charismatic Howson still at the helm – and nothing but German guns at the end of it all. In those four grim years, many if not most boys at Gresham's regarded the place as more than school – it was home, a place where soldier Old Boys, on leave from the Front, could and did, sometimes five or six at a time, return for a rest in the peace and safety of Howson's private wing at Gresham's.[11]

There is no record of Lennox's response to the honour system, though he was closer to its creator than many boys, since, after moving to the senior school from its prep, he joined School House, whose housemaster was Howson himself (which is why the house was then more usually called 'Headmaster's' – and later 'Howson's'). Lennox's early departure from Gresham's – he left in 1918 at the age of only fifteen – was the result of poor health, though he was not happy at school and would have been glad of any excuse to get home.

The absence of any surviving letters between him and home may suggest that they were too depressing to preserve. Since Aline assiduously saved all Hastings's letters from the time of their courtship in the Eighties up to the end of the First World War, it is inconceivable that she would not also have kept her beloved only son's letters. Perhaps when he cleared the house at Cap Ferrat on Aline's death in 1935, Lennox destroyed them all.

Later in life Lennox never spoke of his schooldays, but it was generally felt that he had been utterly miserable at boarding school: insecure, overwhelmed, nervous, ill, longing every moment of every day to get back home, and wondering what on earth induced his parents ever to abandon him to such a hell of tormenting boys and mocking masters, rugger, plunge baths and lumpy custard.

Music would have been a compensation, even though Gresham's was not then known for its interest in any of the arts. According to the poet and novelist John Pudney (a contemporary of the spy Donald Maclean – and of Auden, who fell in love with Pudney), the school placed 'great emphasis upon science, none whatever on classics or English', and was not 'in any sense dedicated to the arts'.[12]

It was the kindly presence of Walter Greatorex, Director of Music from 1911 to 1936, that made all the difference. 'Gog' was a giant of a man with a head that was bald on top with crinkled curls at the back, and he made a strongly positive impression on most of his pupils (even if it was only for his 'advanced' tastes in music – he was keen on Scriabin).[13] Auden remembered him with special affection: 'As a musician he was in the first rank ... As a person he was what the ideal schoolmaster should be, ready to be a friend and not a beak ... without at the same time making any demands for himself in return ...' The existence of Walter Greatorex alone, Auden said, would be reason enough to recall his schooldays with pleasure.[14] And Stephen Spender, who was also at Gresham's prep school for a time, hailed 'Gog' as 'a great king' who had 'come down among us'.[15] We do not know precisely what Lennox thought, but we can read admiration, respect and affection into the body language of an old snapshot showing Lennox, hands in jacket pockets, in conversation with a boater-hatted Greatorex by the bike sheds at the junior school in about 1916.

Benjamin Britten seems to have been alone in disliking Walter Greatorex. A boy at Gresham's ten years after Lennox, when 'Gog' was still in charge of music, he wrote in his diary in 1930: 'how ever the man got the job here I cannot imagine. His idea of rhythm, logic, tone, or the music is absolutely lacking in sanity.' Three months later he twisted the knife even further in: 'I really can't be bothered about him any longer. He ought to have retired 50 years ago or better never have tried to teach music ever.'[16]

A former chorister at King's, Cambridge, Greatorex took pride in the school choir. Lennox was soon enlisted as a treble,[17] and must have been something of a favourite because, when he went up to Howson's in the senior school, it was his job to help choose and accompany the hymn at evening prayers. Diplomatically his list included 'Woodlands', the hymn written by Greatorex – and named after the Gresham's house he was attached to. The boy who shared hymn duties with Lennox was Roy Daniell and he recalled that they always selected hymns suitable for singing in unison, and played them 'at a quick lusty pace'.[18] The hymn that Lennox liked best was 'The day thou gavest, Lord, is ended' to the tune 'St Clement'. He was told that he should not like it because it was 'too mellifluous', but in 1977 it was still his favourite.[19] (Queen Victoria liked it too, and chose it as her official jubilee hymn in 1897.)

Among the service books in use in chapel (both the old one, and the new, free-standing chapel consecrated in Lennox's second year) was *A Manual of Plainsong for Divine Service containing ... The Psalter noted to Gregorian tones.* It had been introduced by Greatorex's predecessor in 1902, and Greatorex firmly held to the tradition throughout his time.[20] This is likely to have been Lennox's first introduction to plainchant, and, though the Manual was a distinctly Protestant (albeit High Church) instructor, applying the principles of plainsong to Anglican texts in English translation, it may have sown the seeds of that love of the Latin liturgy that played such an important part in his later conversion to Catholicism. His passion for plainchant was sufficiently known amongst his friends at Oxford later on that one of them gave him, as a twenty-first birthday present in 1924, a copy of *The Elements of Plainsong*, published by the Plainsong and Mediaeval Music Society.

French was the only other subject Lennox was good at, and he helped some of his friends with their French prep.[21] At Gresham's junior school, if not even earlier at Lynam's, he had taken the 'lamentable decision' to study French rather than continue with Latin or start Greek, simply because he knew French already. And he always regretted that he had been 'so lazy at school': indeed he admitted in 1962 that he was deeply ashamed of having abandoned the classics, since he was later strongly drawn to Greek and Roman literature and felt that he 'could have taken pleasure in a great deal of it'.[22] Meanwhile, and perhaps inevitably, he excelled at French, and on Speech Day 1916 his pre-eminence was rewarded, when a hero of the Indian Mutiny, Field Marshal Sir Evelyn Wood, VC, presented him with the second form French prize. A cinch for a boy who was bilingual.

Both Lennox's parents were bilingual too – Aline's English even betrayed 'a very slightly foreign accent' (which Hastings claimed never to have noticed).[23] The flavour of the accent is not revealed, but if it had been tinged with German – after all Aline's mother was a baroness from Württemberg, and never lost *her* German accent (or wanted to) – and if

Aline met other boys when she visited Lennox at Gresham's,* the acute ear of a vicious schoolboy might well have picked up the idea that Berkeley was a Hun, and – this being wartime, and boys being boys – such a dangerous rumour could have led to bullying. Never mind that the King himself had German blood and that Kaiser Bill was his first cousin.

Bullying was quite a problem at Gresham's during the First World War, because of deficient supervision by a reduced and 'pretty inadequate' staff.[24] (There were no such things, in that war, as 'reserved occupations'; if there had been, more young men would have been encouraged to stay at home and teach, and a higher standard of education would have been maintained.) For defence the boys at the junior school used to go about in pairs. Lennox's other half was a boy called Kemeys Bagnall-Oakeley, who once had to defend him – against, of all things, taunts of being a swank.[25] In the hothouse world of prep school this is as off-limits as being a swot or a goody-goody. It is very hard indeed to think of Lennox boasting, but perhaps he had been forced to admit that his grandfather was an earl.

There is, however, one area of his life where he might have been tempted to show off a bit. Two of his contemporaries remember his distinctive style at the piano. Richard Higham never forgot hearing Lennox practise Bach 'on a horrid little upright piano ... with great confidence ... for the best part of an hour'.[26] Bagnall-Oakeley recalled that Lennox was not the best pianist at the junior school but he was, surprisingly, the most flamboyant: 'he raised his hands high over the keys during rests, and if he had to play a high note with his left hand he crossed his arms with an extravagant gesture.' It was exuberance rather than exhibitionism, Bagnall-Oakeley hastened to add, for fear of seeming to suggest that the little Lennox was a Liberace in the making.[27] Lennox's piano-playing, even in private, continued to involve florid crossings of hands when the music called for it, but always 'with a naughty look in his eye, as though he were relishing the need for a show of dexterity – enjoying the physical game of it'. This was a characteristic that was to remain typical of Lennox. Years later, when Goldie the eagle escaped from the aviary at London Zoo, Lennox was highly amused to hear the bird's keeper admonishing Goldie for being 'very,

*The Rt. Revd John Daly, Bishop, successively, of Accra, Korea, and Taejon, writing to RN, 7 July 1989, reveals that Mrs Berkeley did visit occasionally and 'seemed to me rather special', RNA.

very naughty'. He himself would thereafter use the same expression, with a knowing smile, whenever he came across a chord or a phrase that was *un peu risqué*: delicious but a bit fruity, like a Poulenc harmony.*

Lennox was also a kind boy, according to Higham, and a good conversationalist with bags of charm.[28] Bagnall-Oakeley recalled, with mixed feelings, an example of Lennox's conspicuously compassionate nature. After releasing a prized Bath White butterfly from a breeding cage (in an insect collectors' shed called, in all innocence, 'The Buggery'), Lennox casually confessed to Bagnall-Oakeley: 'Oh by the way, there was a white butterfly fluttering itself to pieces in your bug box – so I let it go, poor thing.'[29] Lennox loved animals, which may be why he later chose, for his baptism as a Catholic, the name of François, after Francis of Assisi, the patron saint of animals. And he especially loved dogs. Many years on, he was to witness the shocking death of his beloved Labrador, Black Prince, who was run over by two vehicles in succession, outside his house in Little Venice. The incident so affected him that he wrote a motet, setting the Marian prayer 'Hail Holy Queen', dedicated to 'B.P. 6 iii 70'.

The rest of Lennox's school work showed 'Little or no improvement', according to a half-term report for the Michaelmas term of 1916. This was not news to Hastings, who commented to Aline, in a mood of resigned despair: 'Always the Stereo Typed remarks to which we have been now for so long accustomed.'[30]

By now Commander Hastings was back in naval uniform. Though very nearly sixty, and in poor health, he had rejoined the Navy as a retired volunteer, a month into Lennox's first term. After a little while at sea – aboard HMS *Colleen* in Irish waters – he was appointed officer in charge of trawlers in the Auxiliary Mine-Sweeping Patrol at Larne Harbour in Northern Ireland, and stayed there, in the same post, for the rest of the war. His letters home to Aline suggest that he did not have much to do, apart from walking, smoking his pipe after dinner (which, one night, consisted of a 'fine large young hare shot by Lieut. Bayne'), and reporting the news (and gossip) of the base – 'changes at Admiralty: Jellicoe to be 1st Sea Lord, Beatty to command Grand Fleet'

*MB, in conversation with TS, 20 September 2005, and again 13 October 2005, when MB cited as an example LB's *Six Preludes*, which 'obviously enjoy making the hands swap over'.

(November 1916), the bolting of a wife who had 'gone wrong', the dismissal of a drunken bar manager at his hotel billet and the arrival of a new Commodore 'with a ring of fluffy white hair ... rather a nonentity' (February 1917).[31] Earlier in the war Hastings had thought of applying for a better post in Dublin, but by the autumn of 1916 he was writing to Aline in the Woodstock Road: 'I am so well and comfortable here that I hesitate over taking the risk of being sent somewhere else.'[32]

Hastings was not fit. To appease his troublesome stomach, he lived on what he called '"slops" and bismuth powder'. He weighed only eight stone eight, and was following a strict regimen of 'matutinal cold plunges, now followed – even in the coldest weather – by the rubbing exercises ...' and these he had to get through as quickly as possible because 'this poor thin body of mine won't stand much cooling down ...'.[33] Hastings confessed that he felt himself 'almost daily growing old and fagged, though well'. He longed to be finished with the war and reunited with his 'Sweet Weenie'.[34] Meanwhile he 'hung on' her letters, and became dispirited and disinclined to reply when they were delayed by even a day. Of his son Hastings has almost nothing to say during his Larne exile in the last two years of the war.

For her part Aline was busy looking after miscellaneous Harris relations who came to stay at 304 and would not go, and the perennial problem – worse in wartime – of finding and keeping servants. Hastings, though the other side of the water, remained master of the house. He rebuked his 'little 'Quirrel' for her softness towards those guests who outstayed their welcome, hoping there was no 'lurking idea' of their taking up permanent residence. ('If there is I hope you will hold out against it: 304 is not a lodging house or a hotel and you will never keep any servants if there is too much work for them to do.'[35]) He instructed her that when it got cold she was to buy some cheap Russian oil for the lamps in the conservatories.[36] And he reminded her to 'Vaseline the bright parts of the tandem and pump up the tyres'.[37] To this last letter of November 1916 he added bleakly, 'Some of us begin to think that this wretched business will not be over next year.' Nor was it: the war still had another 104 weeks to run.

Nobody could have prayed harder for an end to the fighting than Howson of Gresham's, who was devastated by the loss of his boys on the muddy fields of Flanders – and by the destruction of 'ideals which he had devoted his life to building up'.[38] In those four years the school sent five hundred boys to fight – and lost no fewer than one hundred of them, plus a young master. And this in a school which, in 1914, at the start of the war, had numbered only 250 boys. The shock was such that Howson died two months after the Armistice – killed by the war 'as straightly and surely as if he had fallen at the front'.[39] His funeral was held in the chapel that had meant so much to him, and he was buried beside it; the oak stalls inside and an oak screen bear, in memory, the carved names of himself and the boys he lost.

Howson once confessed that he found it hard to sleep in his comfortable bed, feeling it ought to be a trench. This sense of guilt – exacerbated by bitterness – spread through the staff to the boys themselves. Though games had always been low on the agenda, by Christmas 1914 they had dropped below Corps. Even then, with Lord Kitchener's finger commanding every young man to do his duty, Gresham's boys were not obliged to join the Officers' Training Corps. But they did have to take part in rifle practice and learn about musketry and signals, and they were expected to maintain certain military standards, as a sarcastic officer reminded them in the pages of *The Gresham*: 'We may be straining after gnats when we insist that ... lack of and too much attention to the hair is unsoldierly.'[40] He might have been addressing Cadet Berkeley whose own springy locks remained unmanaged, till the fashion of the Thirties oiled them down and slicked them back.

In 1915 the war actually came to North Norfolk. It happened on a wintry night in January, just after term had started. Two Zeppelin airships, on course for the Humber, got lost in the fog, and hovered over Sheringham, a few miles to the north of Gresham's; locals claimed they were so low they could see the faces of the helmeted pilots peering down trying to establish where they were. Lennox's housemaster in the junior school, Dallas Wynne Willson,* recalled that 'At about eight o'clock they came over us at Holt, and we put out all lights. The little boys in my boarding house [Lennox among them] were on the whole more excited than alarmed.' Mr Wynne Willson's six-year-old daughter may have been nearer the truth when she wrote that everyone 'was very fritened several boys were crying'. After all they were witnessing the

*It is a nice coincidence that Dallas Wynne Willson's great-nephew the late Dr William Wynne Willson was a stalwart of the Lennox Berkeley Society, the designer of its first website, and editor of some of LB's piano music published by the Society. See: http://www.lennoxberkeley.org.uk and www.musicwww.co.uk.

very first bombs ever dropped on British soil, and the huge Zeppelins must have been terrifying. Two or three small bombs fell on a nearby farm. No one was hurt, but some sheep and a turkey were hit. Next morning the boys rushed out to investigate, but found nothing more alarming than 'six small craters in a turnip field', which they proceeded to excavate for relics. Great Yarmouth and King's Lynn were less lucky: four people, including a woman and a child, were killed in raids there that same night.[41]

In the summer the Germans sent their Zeppelin bombers to London for the first time, and Lennox's cousin, Yvonne Berkeley, then seventeen, happened to witness the first raid on 1 June. (She was on her way to Geneva, for treatment for rheumatism, after a short stay at Foxcombe with Uncle Randal.) Her astonishment at the phenomenon of the Zeppelins, vividly recalled in her memoirs, gives some idea of what Lennox and the other boys at Gresham's must have felt that night in January when they watched their version of what Yvonne called 'a frightful drama right over my head'.

> ... one morning my bath was interrupted by a Zeppelin visit ... Hurriedly dressed, I watched things dropping from the great cigar to the cries of fury from the streets. Then came the wonder of wonders: tiny little flies [?aircraft of the Royal Flying Corps] appeared and dashed about round the cigar, there were faint firing sounds; suddenly great shouts went up, one [British] flyer was aiming straight for the monster, and disappeared inside it, while flames began to appear. The flames spread all over the huge thing, and little black shapes [of German airmen] began falling from it, to the howls of joy from the streets. I have never been able to forget that the people of London on that occasion, when the flaming thing fell on Hampstead Heath, behaved like savage beasts fighting each other furiously for souvenirs from the burnt out frame-work.[42]

On 11 November 1918 it was all over. That very morning the post office in Holt pinned up a telegram confirming that the Allies had signed an armistice with Germany. At midday the headmaster summoned the whole school and broke the news of peace. He also announced a half-holiday. The OTC celebrated with a modest *feu de joie*, during which the jubilant cadet officers fired blanks over the playing fields. The remaining menfolk of Holt – those too young or too old to have fought – could not contain themselves and raced round Mr Wynne Willson's beloved cricket ground on motor bikes. But at Gresham's it was impossible to forget the terrible cost of peace.

Whatever the carnage and the honour system and homesickness may have done to Lennox's psyche, the gently undulating landscape of North Norfolk made such a positive impression on his romantic imagination that it is hard to believe his time at Gresham's was all that bad. Years later, he was still so powerfully drawn to the atmosphere of the chalk downs of the East Anglian Heights, and the wild and windswept marshlands that spread along the coast beneath them, that he bought a cottage, aptly called Coldblow, on the coast at Morston, only six miles from Holt.

By Christmas 1918 he was safely home in Oxford, reunited with his mother and sister and a father who was now Captain Berkeley, RN (Rtd – for the second and last time). Gratifying though it may have been to have that additional ring of gold braid on his cuffs, it did not help much in solving all the domestic problems that had been accumulating at home during the war.

First, there was the aftermath of the death in 1914 of his eighty-two-year-old mother, Cécile Lady Berkeley, at a hydrotherapy clinic at St Didier in the Vaucluse hills,[43] where she had been receiving treatment for a chronic heart condition. On her deathbed she had expressed the wish that she might be buried in the same grave as her sister, Albine van Havre, in Fontainebleau. But because of the imminence of war it had been impossible to carry out her wishes, and reluctantly the family had had to arrange interment, in their absence, at the chateau where she died. To move her remains to Fontainebleau would involve complicated permissions for the exhumation and re-burial, and expensive transport arrangements; not to mention time. Nevertheless Hastings would gladly have done it for his beloved Mammie. In the event his brother Ernest oversaw the re-burial, with the help of Lady Berkeley's maid Alice, over the course of three days in January 1922.[44]

Then there were Cécile's bequests to her servants, which Hastings, the senior executor, had been unable to pay because the £10,000 his mother had been forever expecting from the Berkeley Settled Estates had never materialized, and she had died leaving an estate worth no more than £634. 14s.7d. net.[45] But Hastings still felt it a moral duty to carry out his mother's wishes, and he would when he could.

Next there was the continuing problem of the Harrises' empty villa Les Rochers. Though Aline's mother, Lady Harris, had died two years before the war, the family had still not resolved the future of the property. There had been talk of letting the house, and selling off some of the land for development, and indeed two speculative syndicates were interested, but nothing had yet been done.[46]

Finally there was the outstanding £10,000 (worth at least half a million pounds at today's values). Under the terms of a settlement drawn up in 1888 – as his father, George the 7th Earl, lay dying – Randal had undertaken to pay this sum to his mother or her executors when he came into possession of Berkeley Castle and its estates. He was as eager for his birthright as they for their inheritance, but the owner of the castle, Charles 3rd Lord FitzHardinge, remembering the humiliation of his defeat in the 1891 peerage case, was no less determined to live on. It was not till 1916, just before Christmas, that the old man died – at Berkeley Castle, aged eighty-six – the last survivor of the illegitimate line from the 5th Earl. Though he had been married, he had had no children, and so the political barony of FitzHardinge died with him. By a settlement of 1858 the Castle and 23,000 acres of prime farmland in Gloucestershire and Middlesex and the FitzHardinge Estate in Mayfair automatically passed to Randal; and, by the 1888 settlement, Randal inherited the obligation to pay Cécile's executors – Hastings and Ernest – their £10,000. The trouble was that old Lord FitzHardinge had never liked young Randal, and when his will was proved in 1917 it turned out that he had left all his money – a total of nearly £434,000 – to thirty-eight beneficiaries (including a superintendent of the Metropolitan Police, one Creswell Wells, who received £1,000) but conspicuously excluding his legal heir, Randal.[47] All he left the foreign Berkeley who had triumphed in the courtroom battle for the earldom were the contents of the castle and of Cranford House plus the 'guns rifles and pistols and garden tools also guns traps coops netting and other implements in the custody of Keepers and Decoymen ... and ... my pack of Foxhounds and other dogs and kennel utensils'. This was a calculated snub, since Randal was no countryman: indeed he had never ridden a horse in his life, let alone to hounds. (Yet, to the surprise of many, though not of those who knew how much he enjoyed a challenge, he was very soon to take up both horsemanship and hunting, and to play his part as Master of the Berkeley.)

Meanwhile traps, coops and netting would not go very far towards raising the £10,000 his elder brothers had waited for so long and patiently. And till it was met he was obliged, by the deed he had signed in 1888, to pay them an income of 4% of the capital. It is a measure of the bad blood that now existed between them that Hastings could have written (to Aline, from Larne, in 1916): 'I think it hardly possible that R[andal] would repudiate the liability altogether, but I do not feel equally assured that some endeavour will not be made to whittle it down.'[48]

Randal was in a fix. And the £10,000 was the least of it. He was faced with colossal succession duties (about £1m then – or £52m today), he owed money that he had borrowed in the mistaken expectation of Lord FitzHardinge's fortune,[49] and, to cap it all, he and Sybil had just moved out of Foxcombe and into the castle, where their living expenses were much higher. Randal took drastic action. He gave some of the Berkeley tenants notice to quit, and warned the others to expect rent rises of up to 60%. With a war still on, this was a foolish miscalculation, and in Parliament in April 1918 the Liberal MP for Gloucester (Thornbury), Athelstan Rendall, accused the earl of 'a form of profiteering' – than which, in 1918, nothing could have been baser. Randal, cornered, broke the cardinal rule of landowning: he decided to sell – and on a reckless scale. In May 1919 he disposed of twenty acres of the FitzHardinge estate in Mayfair, including most of Berkeley Square and Berkeley Street, with Audley, Hill, Charles, John, Bruton, Waverton, Queen and Stratton Streets, and Bruton Place. The buyer was the multimillionaire philanthropist Sir Marcus Samuel (later Viscount Bearsted), founder of Shell and a former Lord Mayor of London. The price was not made public at the time, but Randal's obituary twenty-two years later revealed that it was about £2m – a snip for one of the grandest estates in London. [50] Not content with this, three months later Randal sold 7,656 acres of Berkeley land in Gloucestershire to the Welsh colliers and shipowners, Cory Brothers & Co., for £300,000, and in 1927 he sold the 593-acre Foxcombe estate at Boars Hill to a syndicate of local businessmen, the Berkeley Estates Company, in which he himself held shares, and which wasted no time in breaking up the estate and re-selling it piecemeal for building.[51] The Earl of Berkeley was now a very rich man indeed, and though his elder brothers, Hastings and Ernest, were not destitute by any means, they must have felt the injustice of his disproportionate wealth – not to mention the imprudence of his reckless disposal of the Berkeley birthright.

Meanwhile, there was Lennox – now school-less at the age of fifteen and a half, and ill again. His poor health was characterized by lassitude, general weakness and a susceptibility to coughs and colds and all the other ailments of childhood, but he does not seem to have been suffering from any specific complaint. For nine months he was confined to the Woodstock Road with a tutor, while Hastings scouted around for the right school for the rest of his education. At last he found it – in the rapidly expanding dormitory town of Harpenden, sixty miles east of Oxford: St George's, Harpenden, a co-educational, independent boarding school for the children of 'unconventional, intellectual and articulate parents'.[52] St George's had been founded twelve years earlier by a Cumberland parson called the Revd Cecil Grant, a socialist who believed passionately in the Montessori principles of spontaneous expression and freedom from restraint. Hastings heard of it through a friend in Boars Hill, Dorothy Matthews, who was headmistress of the Montessori School in Harpenden. The idea was that boys and girls should live together in an atmosphere closely related to family life and based on Christian principles. Though deeply pious, Grant, the founder, had little time for Christian dogma and devoted his sermons to expositions of the philosophies of Kant and Hegel. For Hastings, an agnostic liberal with a lively interest in philosophy, this was just the ticket. Lennox would be taught to think for himself in an environment that was as *en famille* as school could get in 1919, with other boys – and girls – from the ages of three to eighteen. That the school also possessed a strong music department (though no proper music buildings) and a swimming pool also weighed in its favour.

Lennox started at St George's, Harpenden, in the autumn of 1919. We know very little about his time there, except that he took part in various concerts, including one in October 1920 in which he played piano arrangements of selections from *Messiah*, that he was awarded a certificate for scripture, that he once came third in the long jump, and that in March 1921 he won a prize for a piano piece he had composed in France the previous summer. And one intriguing nugget, indicative of both confidence and piety: on 2 November 1920, Lennox took part in a school debate, seconding the proposition 'That all is vanity'. According to the Debating Society records, he drew attention to the common sin of pride and argued that it often led to crime. Since the climax of his speech was the refrain from Ecclesiastes, he may have made the common mistake of assuming 'vanity of vanities' meant conceit rather than futility. But perhaps he did not want to depress his young listeners with the pessimism of the Preacher's real message.

At the end of that spring term in 1921, shortly after his eighteenth birthday, Lennox left St. George's (having engraved his name, with a penknife, on the lid of his classroom desk).* There are no records to indicate whether he had already taken his Higher Certificate exam (without which he would not have been qualified to go on to university), or whether he crammed for it privately afterwards. At all events, since he had chosen Oxford, he would have needed to brush up on his prep-school Latin. The subjects he elected to study were French, Old French and Philology, and his college was Merton. There does not seem to be any obvious reason for the choice of Merton, but Hastings never took educational decisions lightly. As Merton enjoyed a reputation for philosophy in general, and idealist views in particular – earned chiefly by two leading members of *Mind*, F. H. Bradley (famous for his pluralistic approach to philosophy) and his disciple Harold Joachim, Wykeham Professor of Logic, and proponent of the coherence theory of truth – it is possible that Lennox was frog-marched there by his father and his headmaster, Mr Grant, both of whom would have read Bradley's *Truth and Reality* and Joachim's *The Nature of Truth*, and shared the same devotion to Hegel's system of realism. That the Warden of Merton, Thomas Bowman, was a mathematician and Joachim an accomplished musician (and nephew of the legendary violinist Joseph Joachim) must also have helped. Not that any of this would have cut much ice with Lennox. But Merton's small size (154 undergraduates in the year he went up), its antiquity (founded 1264), its relative unfashionableness (according to his contemporary, the poet Louis MacNeice, it 'contained comparatively few public school boys and still fewer "intellectuals"')[53] – all this would have appealed to Lennox's modesty and conservatism and that lack of class consciousness which singled him out both then and later.

*Twenty-six years later, a young music student called Celia Davies (later to become Music Director of the Graff Orchestra of England, and Trustee and Artistic Director of Peckleton Arts, Leicestershire) recognized LB's 'deeply incised' name, while examining the other schoolboy carvings on her desk at St George's, Harpenden, and, having confirmed that it was indeed the work of a composer who by then was something of a celebrity, added her own initials nearby, more modestly scratched with a compass point. In 1949 Celia Davies left St. George's and went to study at the Royal Academy of Music in London, where LB was a professor of composition (email Celia Davies to TS, 25 June 2007).

It was not till October 1922 that he matriculated at Merton. Meanwhile Hastings and Aline had come into their Berkeley inheritance at last, and decided to return to France for good. When they found a buyer for 304 Woodstock Road they settled Lennox in rooms in a terrace cottage 100 yards from the college,* then said goodbye to Oxford for the last time, and retired to the South of France – first to a house called Mezzo Monte in the medieval village of Roquebrune, isolated on a steep precipice 1,000 feet above the Mediterranean coast between Monaco and Mentone, and then to Les Anthémis, on the Boulevard Edouard VII in one of the Riviera's most attractive villages, Beaulieu-sur-mer, nearer Nice.

Once he had passed his School Certificate and prepared for his Oxford entrance exam, Lennox seems to have joined his parents for the best part of a 'gap year', taking with him two favourite books, Romain Rolland's life of Beethoven and the *Oxford Book of French Verse*, together with Vaughan Williams's settings of R. L. Stevenson's *Songs of Travel.* Inspired by Rolland's vision of the artist as a realist, a seeker of truth, drawing in 'through every pore the all-puissant breath of life',[54] he set off for Roquebrune as free and unworldly as Stevenson's Vagabond, seeking neither wealth nor hope, neither love nor friendship, but 'the heaven above, / And the road below me'.[55]

Reunited in his beloved Alpes Maritimes with his ageing and ailing parents, he must have heaved a sigh of relief at their escape from Randal's caprices – and his own escape from boarding school – and settled down for a happy year in the sun and the olive trees, after the chaos of the First World War.

From now on, France, where Hastings and Aline had been born and raised, was to be the Berkeleys's permanent home. In the winter they lived in country houses at, successively, Roquebrune, Beaulieu, Falicon and Cap Ferrat – with the Mediterranean to swim in, hills to explore, and opera, ballet and concerts in Monte Carlo and Nice; in the summer they retreated north to Aunt Albine van Havre's house in the cool of the forest of Fontainebleau.

*No. 13 Merton Street (overlooking the beautiful college gardens and the meadows beyond the old city wall) is the address at the top of a sheet of paper on which Lennox wrote to St George's School, Harpenden, applying for membership of the Old Georgian Association in 1921.

6
Freda Bernstein, London, 1923

The first thing that Isaac Bernstein had to do when he arrived in London, that summer of 1922, was to find somewhere to stay. It is likely that on his occasional previous visits, like so many other out-of-town Jewish businessmen, he booked in at the grand old First Avenue Hotel in High Holborn ('one of the oldest of London's premier caravanserai', according to its own flowery advertising;[1] bombed during the Second World War, the hotel was demolished immediately afterwards, and the site is now the home of the Principal Registry of the Family Division Probate Department.) This time planning a longer visit, he chose instead a boarding house. His business associates back in Newport, the boot dealer Samuel Wolfson and the boot maker Sidney Fry, had recommended an establishment they had found satisfactory on their own recent trips to London, so he took a cab to Swiss Cottage and went to inspect rooms at 6 Adamson Road, owned by Mrs 'Florrie' Boas. Satisfied, he moved straight in. And when the dinner gong was rung he realized he had made the right decision. The menu was exactly to his taste, the cooking likewise. When after a few days it was clear that his initial impression had been correct and the cuisine was consistently good, he asked Mrs Boas to present his compliments to the cook.

In no time the cook was smartened up, shown into the dining room and introduced to the prosperous Jewish guest. She turned out to be a tall, straight-backed, square-jawed, striking young woman called Grace Nunney. She was twenty-eight, single, and one of the ten children of a master plasterer in Queen's Park. Though Grace was a complete stranger who was not even Jewish, Isaac seems to have fallen in love at first sight. He was fifty-four and old by the standards of the day, but he was rich and cut a fine figure, so it is not so very surprising that a poor working girl, anxious to avoid lifelong maidenhood, should have been grateful for his attentions. Besides she had always been attracted to Jewish people.[2] But why a clever and cautious Jewish businessman, protective of a fortune he had worked so hard to amass, should suddenly, at the end of his life, propose a marriage that was both alien to his faith and unprofitable is a mystery.

At Paddington Register Office on 2 August 1922 the couple were married, in the presence of the bride's parents, Frederick and Blanch Nunney. The consequences back home in Wales were immediate, final and terrible. Isaac's nephew and namesake, head of the family in Isaac senior's absence, was a deeply conservative Jew, who responded in the traditional way. Marrying out of the faith was strictly taboo – on the practical grounds that any children born of such a union were likely to be lost to Judaism – and a betrayal of family values, and in particular of all those persecuted Bernsteins in 'Russia' who had died for their faith. So Isaac Bernstein junior and his brothers and sisters did what Orthodox Jews had always done when a family member 'married out': they went into mourning.* This involved draping photos of Isaac, and all other pictures and mirrors, with white sheets, ripping their shirts, linking arms and squatting on stools. For a week they were required to 'sit *shiva*', with their feet bare, their bodies unwashed, reciting the *kadish* three times a day, and eating uncut fruit and kosher cakes brought to the house by friends. When the mourning period was over, they ate hard-boiled eggs, bread and lentils – to indicate that, despite the 'death', life went on.

The Bernsteins of Tredegar felt the shame of Isaac's marriage so profoundly that they could not bring themselves to admit what really happened – instead they seem to have put it around that he had died in a drowning accident on the Day of Atonement.† Of course they were

*This, and the revelation of Isaac Bernstein's response to the birth of his first and only child, was conveyed to FB – to her great astonishment – at 8 Warwick Avenue, London, W2, in 1976, in the presence of TS, by FB's cousin Mrs Irene Hughes née Nunney, a former dancer then visiting the UK from her home in Toronto. Mrs Hughes never knew either of FB's parents, but gathered this information from the Nunney family. She first met FB when she came over from Canada for a holiday when both cousins were little girls.

†This information – concerning 'a single brother' of 'Moses Bernstein (a married man) who had a gentleman's outfitters in Commercial Street' – was kindly provided by Judge Aron Owen (born in Tredegar in 1919) in a letter to Julian Berkeley, 28 March 1995. Isaac was actually Moses's uncle, but a small boy, even one destined to be a judge, might easily have confused the details. Or the drowned man might indeed have been a brother of Moses, who had five brothers.

also bitterly disappointed, since a young wife was likely to divert Isaac's fortune away from the family – and by now there were eleven nephews and nieces, and a tribe of great-nephews and great-nieces, all in need of a rich uncle's patronage.

There is no way of knowing how Isaac felt about being killed off by his family, but, since he had been independent enough to marry out of the faith, he is likely to have been strong enough to deal with the consequences. If he had not already broken with his faith before he left Wales, he did so now. In the will which he drew up at Lewis & Lewis's offices on the day after his marriage, he inserted the sentence, 'I desire that my body shall be cremated, and that no religious ceremony shall be held over my body'. Not for him the solace of burial with his father and mother beneath a Jewish tombstone in that outpost of the Promised Land on a Welsh hillside at Merthyr Tydfil.

But he did his duty by his family and his former faith, leaving £500 (about £15,000 today) to his sister Hannah* who was still living in Raseiniai, £500 to his favourite niece Annie Bernstein, who was running a drapery business at 36 Castle Street, Tredegar, and £100 to each of her seven surviving brothers and sisters. He also left £100 each to the Hebraic Congregations at Tredegar and Newport, and a further £100 towards the upkeep of the Jewish graveyard at Merthyr. And in the event of the failure of a trust which he set up for the benefit of any putative children of his union with Grace Nunney (or, failing that, for his niece Hetty Price née Bernstein and her daughter Freda), he instructed that the residue of his estate should go to the Jewish Hospital and Orphan Asylum of West Norwood Road, London. Isaac appointed the Public Trustee, a government legal office, as the sole executor and trustee of his will.

According to the will, he was 'now residing at 6 Adamson Road', with Mrs Boas (and, presumably, a new cook). Yet only seven weeks later he was living at the First Avenue Hotel, where, on 25 September, he added a curious codicil to his will, instructing that the tax-free annuity of £300 payable to Grace on his death, for as long as she remained his widow, was to be dependent on a significant condition: that she

*The will refers to 'Mrs Hannah Madelowitz', but this is probably a transliteration error. It is more likely that the surname was Mendelovicz or Mendelovich. There was a David Mendelovich (son of Schloma), a retired soldier, living in Raseiniai, Kaunas province in 1885 (JewishGen.org).

should lead 'a chaste respectable life'. (Considerately he absolved his trustee from the impossible responsibility of ensuring that this condition was carried out.) The wording seems to suggest that something had happened since the marriage in August. Perhaps Isaac had discovered that Grace was 'fast'. Maybe, even in that short time, he had caught her out in an affair – or learned that she had had affairs before she met him. No one who knew the facts survives to tell, but Grace's sister Daisy Hughes remembered visiting the Bernsteins at home soon after their marriage and discovering to her surprise that they lived 'entirely separate lives'.[3]

If Isaac had moved to the hotel on his own, then it might be reasonably guessed that there had been a row and a temporary break. But it is really more likely that the newly-weds moved to the hotel for the wedding night (and possibly for a short honeymoon), intending to return to Adamson Road (which is why Isaac gave that as his address for the will), that they liked the smart hotel with its 'homely and refined atmosphere', its palms and lifts and 'famous French chef' – not to mention its newly-renovated 'sanitary system'[4] – and that they stayed on there till they could find a house of their own.

Quite soon, but not improperly so, Mrs Bernstein discovered that she was pregnant, and, with plenty of time before her lying-in, the couple moved into a new house at 613 Finchley Road, two thirds of the way up one of north London's longest roads, in the improving suburb of Child's Hill. Sixty years earlier, with the opening of the Child's Hill (now Cricklewood) railway station, the area had become over-populated and was described as a 'very low' place, with cock-fighting, drunkenness, and vice. By 1903 it was still considered a 'disgrace to civilisation'.[5] But the arrival, a decade later, of motor buses, trams and the tube at Golders Green began to transform the area into the middle-class suburb which it was to become when, in 1927, the Hendon Way swallowed up the remaining farmland to the north and blurred Child's Hill's boundaries with those of Golders Green. The Bernsteins' house was part of the Burgess Park estate which was completed by the beginning of the First World War, and included at least two Arts and Crafts houses designed by Charles Voysey.[6] Number 613 lay between Platt's Lane and Burgess Park, on the west side of Finchley Road, a few hundred yards from the wide open spaces of Hampstead Cemetery. It was 'a nice comfortable-sized house' called The Pines (because of a group of them in the front garden), with modern cane furniture, lots of light (despite the trees) and French windows leading on to a long garden.

On the first floor of this house, on 25 May 1923, Grace Bernstein gave birth to her first – and only – child. Since he had been laid to rest by his family in South Wales, Isaac must have reconciled himself to the idea that no issue of his could ever join the Chosen. Indeed he may even have felt, like the Ukrainian brother Leon in Bernice Rubens's novel *Brothers*, that marrying out was the only way for a Jew to survive, since remaining in the faith would have meant surrendering his sons to the Czar under the system of *rekrutschina* which required all Jewish boys between the ages of twelve and twenty-five to serve in the Russian Army. [7]

But it did matter very much indeed that the child should be a boy, to inherit the boot business. When Isaac was called upstairs to see his baby, he was not just disappointed, he was devastated. Turning his back on his new family, he ran downstairs, and tore out all the wiring that connected the newly-installed electric lights.[8] Life for Isaac Bernstein would never be the same. His child was not a boy, but a girl. To appease him, Grace called the baby Freda, after her husband's Lithuanian mother, Fradel.

7
Berkeley, Auden and Waugh, Oxford, 1923–5

On the very day that Freda was born, Lennox was sitting on the Isis in a peaked cap and a striped blazer, facing eight strapping young men in a rowing shell at the start of the Eights Week bumping races. Just past his twentieth birthday, and in his second term at Oxford, he was playing a new role as cox of the Merton 2nd VIII.

Lennox was not by nature a sportsman, but his slight frame – 8 stone 13 lb that term[1] – and his sense of rhythm were ideal for the helmsman of a racing eight. And even if his voice was not quite as loud as a cox's should be, it was clear and deep. According to another Merton rowing man of the period, Reginald Ellison, Lennox possessed other qualities that recommended him as a cox: 'cool assessment of district, authority over the crew, ability to ignore all the noise and turmoil from the river bank, steering a straight course throughout'.[2] Ellison conceded that Lennox's way of exercising his authority was somewhat on the polite side ('Would you kindly row a little faster?')[3] but it must have been effective, because the Merton 2nd VIII bumped Trinity College that day, and all their opponents on every other day of the regatta. These successes would not have been possible unless Lennox as cox had been able 'to motivate and inspire eight men almost twice his size to get that superhuman bit more from each of them'. It takes, as the mother of the coxswain of the Oxford crew that won the 2006 Boat Race pointed out in a letter to *The Spectator*, 'ambition, determination, and almost monastic dedication'.[4] That same year (in which Oxford had won the Boat Race for the first time in a decade) Lennox coxed the Merton Clinker-built IV to a victory in the Oxford University Boat Club Clinker Fours, trouncing Worcester by two lengths – and winning for himself promotion to the 1st VIII for the 1924 season.

As a college cox, Lennox would have been safe at the Bump supper 'orgies' that were such a feature of Eights Week, but he would not have enjoyed all the drinking and aggression. An aesthete at heart, a modest one, not an athlete at all, he might otherwise have been as vulnerable as an early Christian on these Roman holidays: like his Magdalen friend, the 'lean, dark and singular' Henry Yorke (soon to become the novelist Henry Green).[5] Yorke was a particular target of the hearties because of his friendship with Evelyn Waugh and the aesthetes. He knew the dangers, and took precautions. On Bump supper nights he used to make sure he got back to college just before the gate was closed – to avoid the rowdy rowing men and their supporters ('ninety-five out of every hundred in the college') who would be on the rampage for aesthetes to beat up. He took care to get drunk 'so, if they did come, it would not hurt too much', but the alcohol did not dull the fear:

> ... there was the difficulty of reaching my rooms unseen and then the wait far into the night with every now and then a rush of them through the cloisters, that awful screaming they affected when in motion imitating the cry when the fox is viewed, that sense curiously of remorse which comes over one who thinks he is to be hunted, the regret, despair and feeling sick the coward has.[6]

Sport – let alone violence – was *terra incognita* for Lennox, and the physical discipline and training involved would have been especially hard for someone used to neither. Not surprisingly he gave up rowing after the 1924 season. But, on the evidence of the team photos preserved in the Merton College library, his work on the river may have done him good. In the 1923 group he is still a schoolboy: sitting cross-legged on the ground, dwarfed by the swollen calves of four much larger men, he looks a trifle anxious. A year later, and half a stone heavier, he is much more confident, and, though he has not gone as far as Tom Driberg (who responded to the mood of Twenties Oxford with a pair of bright green flannel bags with bottoms two feet wide*), he has acknowledged the prevailing dandyism with romantically mussed hair, a pastel-shaded shantung tie (plus gold pin) and a fashionable *hauteur*. He seems to have been trying for a look that captured the new Oxford disdain for authority, but it does not quite come off and he ends up

*He was soon de-bagged by some hearties, presumably just as he had hoped. His trousers were then cut into strips and hung in the Junior Common Room at Christ Church, 'like hunting trophies' (Francis Wheen, *Tom Driberg: His Life and Indiscretions*, p. 37).

looking simply Etonian – though *hauteur* was no more in his nature than press-ups.

Striking attitudes has always been part of growing up, but it was paramount at Oxford during the 'wild bright time'[7] of the early Twenties when the 'children of the sun',* aping the arbiters of the new aestheticism, Harold Acton and Brian Howard, turned themselves into peacocks, villains or *ingénus*. All the strutting and the rutting, all the young men's tongues stuck down other young men's throats,[8] all the bunfights, boozing and vomiting, all the larks and practical jokes that Evelyn Waugh either invented or promoted, revelled in and recorded so vividly in the opening chapters of *Brideshead Revisited*, were nothing but a dazzling spreading of wings by the nestlings who could not go to war in 1914–18 and had never been allowed to forget it. While the war was on, they had been made to feel guilty; when it was all over and the survivors had returned, wounded and wiser, these younger men had felt themselves to be inadequate, even useless. As a reaction to the moustachioed heroes who 'were interested in cricket and thought it cissy to like art', they developed a habit of cynicism, self-mockery and frivolity, talking nonsense, running down their friends and never being serious about their work.[9] If not actually effeminate they were mostly girlish: that was 'the sort of boy which has grown up since the war',[10] either androgynous or bisexual – and if they were not they pretended to be.[11] Collectively they formed what Waugh's elder brother Alec called a generation 'with a chip on its shoulder, rebellious and self-distrustful';[12] he himself had seen front-line action in a machine-gun unit at Passchendaele while Evelyn was still in his first year at Lancing.

How they spread their wings. According to Lennox's Merton friend Billy ('Cracky') Clonmore, an Anglo-Irish nobleman obsessed with the Church, 'pranks' and handsome young men, Oxford was a 'whirl of Uranian antics in which the streets are thronged with scented sirs'.[13] (His own favourite sir was not scented at all: Peter Rodd was as pretty as Rimbaud but a heterosexual man-of-action who provided the model

*In *Children of the Sun: A Narrative of Decadence in England after 1918(* New York, Basic Books, 1976), Martin Green analyses the aestheticism of Harold Acton and Brian Howard, who 'cultivated alternative styles of young manhood – the dandy, the rogue and the naif', and their influence on a whole generation of Oxford men. The book moved Acton 'to a near apoplexy of rage' (Stannard, *Evelyn Waugh*, vol. i, p. 80).

for Waugh's Basil Seal.[14] For love of this unresponsive lady-killer, who later married Nancy Mitford, the acrobatic and essentially pious Lord Clonmore won a reputation as a reckless roof-climber and picker-of-fights.[15]) For another Merton man, the 'defiantly poetic'[16] Louis MacNeice (who arrived the term after Lennox had left), the Oxford of the Twenties was a period of 'deliberate decadence', in which 'the air was full of the pansy phrase "my dear"'. If you had brains, MacNeice recalled, you slept with men and drank cocktails; if you had brawn you slept with girls and drank beer. As McNeice was both intelligent and decidedly 'normal' – despite his aesthetic principles, Oxford bags and exotic ties – he himself drank regardless.[17] Waugh's drinking companion and co-conspirator, Terence Greenidge (brother of Lennox's lifelong friend John), wrote an entire book on the mores of this decadent Oxford, reaching the conclusion that whilst 'Queer deeds may occasionally get done among those who come from over-emancipated Public Schools ... the majority of us favour that vague Romanticism which may be likened to a warm, misty July morning.' But Greenidge held it against this matutinal Romanticism that it produced bad lovers – and mass-produced effeminacy. 'Go down the High or the Cornmarket', he wrote in his extraordinary book, *Degenerate Oxford?* (published by Waugh's father), and

> You will observe several of them with their locks shining in the sun through a rather unnecessarily liberal application of grease and with their faces subtly adorned by the art which seeks to improve upon nature ... They will be wearing rather brightly coloured coats, cut short and very tight in the waist, their grey flannel trousers will be of a conspicuous ... hue and flowing loosely, their feet will be shod with gay suede shoes. They will speak with artificial voices of a somewhat high timbre, also they will walk with a mincing gait.[18]

Greenidge argued that the sporting types who shouted at these swishing queens, '"You filthy aesthetes, you adore men"' were not so wide of the mark, since Romanticism was the admiration of the beautiful, and young men *in statu pupillari* were indisputably beautiful: their faces smooth, their bodies possessing 'all the magnificence of straight lines ... slender and strong ... like poplar trees'. But nothing would change it: as an old colonel of his acquaintance used to say, 'You won't stop Romanticism till you stop young men being beautiful.'[19]

Waugh's level-headed biographer Martin Stannard makes the important point – missed by Martin Green – that all this posing was not an end in itself, but a conscious mockery of the even greater poses of conformity, affectation and sentiment. What really mattered to the bright young things was to entertain.[20] As Henry Yorke put it, '... one did things to startle.'[21] But it was not all pose, this brief burst of fantasy that interrupted 'the old, pleasant, unique but mainly humdrum place' that Oxford always had been – and would be once more, come Autumn 1926.[22] Despite the prancing, it was still, as Waugh himself observed on first arriving, 'Mayonnaise and punts and cider cup all day long'.[23] And, to a Fresher like the poet C. Day Lewis, who went up to Wadham in the term that Lennox entered Merton, it was 'a dream-like life', in which the Warden called you Mister, you had a room – or even two – all your own, a 'scout' to clean, and unaccustomed time and space at your disposal: 'this was the strangest illusion, the short eight-week term proving far more capacious than a three-month term at school.'[24]

Lennox matriculated at Merton in the Michaelmas (Autumn) term of 1922, with thirty-one other freshmen, including Graeme Galbraith, a hearty Wykehamist who became bow of the Clinker IV (and later a solicitor), and two conspicuously aesthetic Etonians, the beautiful Rudolph Messel (subversive, over-sexed and passionate about Wagner[25]), and the provocative Robert Byron who looked like the old Queen Victoria, wore loud tweeds, a deer-stalker, yellow gloves and horn-rimmed pince-nez and spoke with a pretend cockney accent.[26]

For the first two years of Oxford, Lennox, like all other undergraduates, was obliged to live in college and to vacate his rooms in Merton Street, which, though overlooking the college gardens and a stone's throw from the gate, were not Merton property and could not be considered 'in'. His day would have passed pretty much according to the timetable Robert Byron sent his doting mother in January 1923: 'Roll-call 5 to 8 – bath after or before. Breakfast by fire 8.45. May or may not be lecture from 10 to 12. Lunch at 1.15 ... may or may not be an hour's tutorial in the evening. Dine in hall at 7.30 – or dine out. Cinema or orgy afterwards. Gates shut at 12.'[27] But in Lennox's case, for 'Cinema or orgy' read Music, his 'obsession' while at Oxford.[28]

He was supposed to be studying French, Old French and Philology, and indeed he did read French – lots of it, especially medieval poetry and modern novels – but by his own admission his forays into French literature were not entirely *à propos*. He was doing too much musically to concentrate on more academic matters.[29] So when he opened a French book it was likely to be something by Gide, whom he much admired, 'perhaps because he was alleged to have a pernicious influence on youth', or by Huysmans – *À rebours*, for example, whose hot-house aestheticism he then thought '"decadent" and therefore interesting'.[30] It is easy to imagine the frustrated artist in the young Lennox identifying with Huysmans's restless hero, the duc des Esseintes (Huysmans himself), who is bored with the reality of everyday life and seeks escape in some rarefied imaginings of perfume, paintings, circus acrobats, medieval Latin and music. And no less easy to recognize the embryo Catholic responding to des Esseintes's prayer: 'Have pity, Lord, on a Christian who doubts; I am an unbeliever who tries to believe.'[31]

In his last year at Oxford Lennox discovered a new French-language author, Julian Green, whose later, dark and guilt-ridden novels, 'pervaded by an atmosphere of unease, and even anguish', were distinguished, Lennox felt, by compassion, restraint and spareness[32] – qualities he prized highly. Green was also to explore, indirectly in his fiction and directly in his nineteen volumes of diaries, the conflict between his homosexuality and his religious and moral convictions – not to mention his preoccupation with madness and death.* Unlike the 'conventional figures' of Proust, Lennox once wrote that he would like to have met some of Green's characters, or even some of Simenon's; but Proust, with his 'unsympathetic attitude to humanity', was 'so preoccupied with trivialities' that Lennox was repelled: 'The motivations of his characters', he wrote in his diary, towards the end of his life, 'are described with infinite subtlety, but they themselves are boring (one would surely run a mile rather than actually encounter the princesse de Guermantes or M. de Charlus).'[33]

It is no coincidence that the work of all three of Lennox's favourite writers is concerned, one way and another, with the search for religion. Huysmans eventually converted to Catholicism (and devoted his last book, *En route*, to a description of his sense of triumph in the victory of faith). Gide never quite made the leap to Rome but was always hankering after salvation, and Green who did convert (first at fifteen, and

*The diaries, to which LB constantly returned, also reveal Green's fascination with, and fear of, death. With Green's approval TS assembled and read some of these entries from the diaries for 1928-39 at LB's Requiem Mass, 20 March 1990.

again, in the Pauline sense, much later) nearly lost his faith under attack from Gide – but, when he had re-found it, his Catholicism survived to become the bedrock of his existence.[34] All three wrote at length about their tussles with the flesh – Gide and Green specifically from the gay perspective. At a time when he was considering conversion to Catholicism himself, as a man who would have been unable in the Oxford of the mid-Twenties to avoid the realization that he was gay too, Lennox found such writing compelling.

By an odd chance, the man whose books were to become Lennox's preferred religious reading, Mgr Ronald Knox, arrived in Oxford to start what turned out to be a thirteen-year term as Catholic chaplain just as Lennox was leaving. This wise, witty and holy priest, himself a convert from Anglicanism, was widely regarded as a great unraveller of spiritual conundrums. Waugh, whose admiration was unbounded, wrote the official biography which brought Knox's work to an even larger audience. Knox for him was both saint and genius: '... the boon companion of a generation of legendary heroes; the writer of effortless felicity and versatility; the priest ... who was always the 'special preacher' on great occasions ... the man whose exquisite politeness put everyone at his ease; the translator who brought the Vulgate to life ...'[35] Who knows how Lennox's life might have changed if he and Knox had not passed one another like ships at night that autumn of 1926.

Lennox had always been an avid reader. Apart from French literature his list at Oxford included two of the works on every undergraduate's shelves at the time, *The Waste Land* and *Time and Western Man*, together with Bridges's anthology, *The Spirit of Man*. Long before Oxford, Lennox had been reading poetry for pleasure. Now he began to see it as a source of song texts. For expert guidance he sought the advice of the Professor of Poetry who happened to be a Fellow of Merton, H. W. Garrod, the widely-loved classics tutor. Garrod was himself a poet, whose verse was described by his obituarist in *The Times* as 'perfectly sweet melodies for gracious thoughts and fancies'.[36] Their author thought his poetry was Victorian (like himself), that it improved as it went on, and, that though it had no public, the people he liked best liked it – and that might explain why he liked them best.[37]

Since Lennox was part of Garrod's charmed circle, he was probably an admirer of the 'romantic dreams and delicate idolatries' that characterize Garrod's verse.[38] He respected Garrod's authoritative views on old French poetry, of which the sage of Merton was an expert translator (later used by the BBC).[39] It may have been through Garrod that Lennox discovered the texts by Ronsard, du Bellay and Charles d'Orléans which he set as songs and performed at the Oxford University Musical Club and Union.[40] His setting of the du Bellay pastoral *d'un Vanneur de blé aux vents* (dedicated to John Greenidge, and published by OUP in 1927 as *The Thresher*) was described by the pianist and critic Gordon Bryan as a 'charming trifle': if Berkeley had pursued 'this vein of unaffected melody he would have won considerably more renown than he actually has', Bryan wrote in 1929.[41] The song was first performed at the OUMCU in 1926 by the future Poet Laureate, C. Day Lewis, who had a 'ravishing light tenor singing voice'; since he also had 'music in his bones',[42] it was significant that he should have valued *The Thresher* as 'one of the most musical pieces of song writing produced during our period'.[43] But Berkeley's two Auden settings which Day Lewis sang in that same concert were a bit of a disaster. Day Lewis recalled that he limped through the first one – about a coach-load of trippers – and stalled irretrievably in the second, which was received 'with a sustained outburst of silence'.[44]

It was Auden who persuaded Berkeley to allow Day Lewis to sing these three new songs, after Auden had tried out his Wadham friend in some more standard fare.[45] Auden had a piano in his rooms at Christ Church, on which he thumped his way through the forty-eight preludes and fugues by Bach – 'the <u>only</u> composer'.[46] According to Day Lewis, his playing was 'loud, confident, but wonderfully inaccurate'.[47]

Auden must have approved of Berkeley's two settings of his poems because, that same year, he presented Lennox with his own, personal copy of *Oxford Poetry 1926*, edited by Charles Plumb and himself. He can have been confident that Lennox, the composer of new music, would approve of the editors' intention 'to pacify, if not to content' both progressives and reactionaries. 'If', argues the unmistakable voice of Auden in the Preface, 'it is a natural preference to inhabit a room with casements opening upon Fairyland, one at least of them should open upon the Waste Land.'[48] T. S. Eliot, whose controversial poem was by then four years old, was not represented in the new collection, since he had never been an undergraduate at Oxford (though he spent some time at Merton in 1914, when he was officially a student at Harvard[49]). The volume included three poems by Auden himself, four by Cecil Day-Lewis [*sic*], and, amongst thirteen others, one by Tom

Driberg. In one of Auden's contributions, 'Cinders', a 'dissolute man' sees 'a phallic symbol in a cypress tree', wonders whether he dares to drink from the stream of 'sweet lust' and, deciding that he can, he

> Forsakes phlegmatic company of stars
> For pressure of strange knees at cinemas.
>
> But, after sporting thus a little, he
> Turns back to lyric, tired of lechery[50]

There is absolutely nothing to prove it, but this seems to convey something of the state of mildly experienced innocence which Lennox himself may have reached, but not yet passed, at Oxford – unlike the less than virginal poet, who was already sleeping with Christopher Isherwood.[51] Inside the front of the book Auden crossed out his own name at the top of the blank page and wrote below it: 'To Lennox with love Wystan. Auden' [*sic* – with the surname added, as though Lennox might have forgotten who Wystan was].

Despite the affectionate inscription, Berkeley and Auden were never close, but they kept in touch, meeting occasionally, and in 1957, when he had returned to Oxford as Professor of Poetry (and an American citizen), Auden wrote to say he would be 'honored and delighted' if Berkeley cared to set any of his poems, adding generously: 'Please treat the words simply as raw material and change or cut anything as you feel inclined. It is impertinent, I know, for me, to venture a suggestion, but I would like you to glance at a song called *Nocturne* 2 ("Shield of Achilles") ... since it was written consciously as something to be set ...'[52]

Lennox felt differently about what worked with music and what did not, though he would have been just as diffident about saying so, and in the event he set, not 'Nocturne 2', but 'Lauds' from *The Shield of Achilles*, using it as the opening song of his *Five Poems of W. H. Auden*, first performed in New York in 1959. When, in the Sixties, he set some poems by Laurie Lee, he wondered, in his diary, how poets could ever tolerate 'having their work freely interpreted, pulled about, the prosody destroyed and sometimes the meaning obscured by a composer'. And yet he felt that a composer could occasionally 're-create the atmosphere of a poem and even (though this is almost impossible with great poetry) add something to it'.[53]

Lennox had a gift for what his Merton contemporary J. F. Waterhouse called a 'naturally intimate ... association of music with words', and these early poetry settings, in Waterhouse's opinion, were among the best of Lennox's undergraduate compositions. Only one was published while Lennox was still at Oxford, and the others have long since been lost. But they left such a deep and lasting impression in the mind of John Waterhouse that he claimed nearly thirty years later, when he was music critic of the *Birmingham Post*, that he could still quote extensively from at least four of them. Furthermore, he said he had never been able to read Keats's 'La belle dame sans merci' 'without continually recalling Mr Berkeley's vocal line'.[54] It was to Waterhouse whom Lennox dedicated a high-spirited, virtuoso piano piece called simply *Toccata*, which he wrote in 1925. The piece was given its first performance at the OUMCU on 6 March 1926.[55] The previous month Lennox had been the dedicatee of an unnamed and highly avant-garde piano piece, signed 'William Arthur, Oxford Feb 19th 1926',[56] with a cover cartoon showing Lennox with an extravagant quiff of hair, eyes raised in astonishment, and a bow tie in his mouth. (It is possible that 'William Arthur' is a play on the first five letters of the name Waterhouse.)

Apart from poetry, Professor Garrod's other passion was the company of young men, 'whom he equally loved and teased with an outrageously impish tongue.'[57] They loved him in return, and it is easy to see why. Photos show Garrod in a trilby (hiding a bald, round head), with spectacles, dimples and a playful smile, a cigar in his hand and a terrier at his feet. A Mertonian of Lennox's generation, Stephen 'Gamesmanship' Potter once described Garrod as an 'evil old oyster' – but he was probably cross that on that particular occasion in 1939 Garrod was 'itching to get on to the handsome don he favours'.[58] To everyone else Garrod was gentle, courteous and kind and always ready to entertain, help and inspire any surprise callers with conversation that was sometimes deliberately paradoxical or wantonly challenging and always tender-hearted.[59] One of his last classics pupils, Sir George Mallaby, recalled that he was both clever – cleverer even than the Balliol dons who had taught him – and curiously absent-minded. 'Do you like your tea hot or cold?' he would ask 'in a high quavering sing-song, his voice often fading away into little more than a whisper'.[60] Lennox, usually miles away himself, would have enjoyed these quirks, and must have made a charming and appreciative acolyte – decorative too, with his big dark soulful eyes and winning smile, his floppy hair and slender figure. No wonder Professor Garrod invited him to Sicily, first class, for the New Year's holiday in 1925. David Nicol Smith, then Reader in English and later Professor of English Literature, was asked to come along too. 'We mean to stay one week,' Garrod told him. 'If you like, we'll travel second.'[61] Nicol Smith did not join them, so presumably they held to their original plan to travel first. First or second, Lennox's gain would have been great, for what Garrod taught was 'a love of learning and a love of style'.[62]

Style had always been important to Lennox – part, indeed, of his character; learning was rapidly becoming so. Neither was then in plentiful supply at Merton – even in the Senior Common Room. According to MacNeice, who was not one of Garrod's young men, the dons were a positive 'Walpurgisnacht' of grotesques, who hid from the world behind their cigar smoke, and read detective stories when no one was looking. 'They lived in a parlour up a winding stair and caught little facts like flies in webs of generalisation ... Some of them had never been adult ... Some of them had never been male.'[63] Chief witch was the Warden himself, Thomas Bowman, a stingy, reclusive mathematician, who had been there since 1903 – to the increasing disadvantage of the college – and showed no sign of resigning. (He was finally pushed out by the Fellows in 1935.) Lennox's lawyer friend Reginald Ellison remembered Warden Bowman as 'a complete old crab – a strong negative influence, who refused all requests on principle'.[64]

After the Merton Freshmen of Michaelmas 1922 had signed the college register on 16 October, Lennox and Messel – press-ganged, perhaps, by Galbraith the sportsman – signed up for the college dining club, haunt of the Merton hearties. The Myrmidons, as they called themselves, dined twice a term – sherry in a member's rooms, dinner at the Mitre or the Clarendon or the Criterion, then dessert back in college. Not much seems to have happened apart from multiple toasts and curious parlour games, of which the following entry from the club's minutes for 28 November 1925 gives a flavour: '... the President's guest *again* winning much money by guessing the number of leaves on the pineapple *exactly*.'[65] (Lennox, who was neither a drinker nor a gambler, had resigned by then.) For naughtiness the Myrmidons Club was not a patch on the Hypocrites Club ('Gentleman may prance but not dance'[66]), where Waugh & his 'Hertford underworld'[67] did all their carousing (before it was closed down because the members were thought to bite one another when drunk[68]). In Waugh's view, there was 'nothing like the aesthetic pleasure of being drunk': indeed it was the 'greatest thing Oxford had to teach'.[69]

Drinking for drinking's sake was not at all to Lennox's taste. But he may have found it hard to say no when the Greenidges urged him to come along to the Hypocrites' wake at the Spread Eagle pub in Thame in the summer of 1924. As it was also the twenty-first birthday party of the club's last president Lord Elmley, everyone was there, and the champagne flowed freely. For the fifty guests Elmley provided sixty bottles, placed at nine-inch intervals down the middle of a forty-foot table. John Fothergill, the notoriously prickly innkeeper, remembered it as one of the best parties of his entire time at the Spread Eagle. And he was not easy to please: the Basil Fawlty of his day, he took such pleasure insulting his guests that Waugh used to go there just for the sport. Fothergill made a habit of jotting down in his diary odd little notes about the guests, concentrating on the prettiest, the tallest, the oddest and the grandest. Of the Hypocrites' swansong he noted that the guests included Elmley himself in a purple dress suit; David Plunket Greene, six foot nine, in white flannels and a thin white vest; Robert Byron, 'shrouded in lace trimmings'; the Greenidges of course ('pleasantly quite mad'); and Rudolph Messel ('the vainest ... of the lot'). Harold Acton made a speech in his 'Big Ben-like voice'. If Lennox did not go then, he certainly dined at the Spread Eagle on another occasion because he signed his name, at about the five foot eight mark, on Fothergill's 'Heights on the Wall'. Perhaps, like so many other undergraduates who came of age at the Spread Eagle, he took his friends to a birthday dinner there on 12 May 1924. His would have been a more discreet affair than the Hypocrites' last and biggest party, which ended in a bacchanale of dancing, fondly recalled by Innkeeper Fothergill in an image of 'wild goats and animals leaping in the air'. The Spread Eagle, said the gay Scottish actor, Ernest Thesiger, was a lunatic asylum.[70]

Dining with the tamer Myrmidons brought Lennox into close contact with Messel, and through Messel with the erratic but lovable Clonmore who was the conduit to important friendships with a new set of sophisticated Christ Church men. These new friends were quite as unconventional – if not as wantonly so – as Waugh, Byron and Terence Greenidge, but they did not shout it from the rooftops. Though close to the joint founts of aestheticism, Harold Acton and Brian Howard, with whom most of them had been at Eton, they kept their distance from its rowdier excesses. That is largely why Lennox was drawn to them. They included the budding archaeologist David Talbot Rice, 'who seemed to live a life of carefree pleasure but was secretly studious';[71] an amateur pianist, Edward Sackville-West ('a frail, elegant little figure, who went out with a stick and a muffler',[72] and became a novelist and radio dramatist); a pianist and aspiring composer, later turned painter and writer, David Ponsonby, then struggling to persuade his parents to allow him to pursue a career in music; and W. H. Auden. Christ Church also offered Robert Gathorne-Hardy (Eton too), who first studied medicine, then took a degree in law and became a writer, botanist and private press printer; and a career soldier, John Codrington, who had served, as a teenager, on the Western front and was now up at Oxford for a year, before rejoining the Coldstream Guards – in later life, he became a garden designer and lent his name to a variety of the plant least like him, the perennial wallflower.

Lennox had two other special friends at Oxford. One was his boyhood companion John Greenidge,[73] architect, painter and amateur pianist, whom Lennox valued for his steadiness (he once told a mutual friend that John was 'very contented and restful'[74]). The other was a flamboyant prankster and wit (later a historian, and pillar of the Establishment), John Davies Knatchbull Lloyd. James Lees-Milne quotes a couplet that J. D. K. Lloyd composed about an 'old painted (but nice) queen', a mutual friend called Headley Hope-Nicholson: 'H is for Headley, the pride of Old Place, /What he earned from his bottom he spent on his face.'[75] Lloyd was universally known as 'the Widow' – a nickname which came not from his hair-line or his married status but from an English shaving preparation called 'Lloyd's Euxesis' ('A delightful cream ... for Shaving Without Soap, Water or Brush ... in one-half the ordinary time.'[76]) John Lloyd discovered the eponymous euxesis while still a boy at Winchester, by which time an improved formula was being produced by the inventor's elderly widow, Aimee Lloyd, at her works in Spur Street, off Leicester Square. A curious and precocious youth with exotic habits, Lloyd was fascinated as much by the bizarre name of the cream as by its smelly stickiness, and he used to order tubes by the boxful, even before he needed to shave, so that he could squeeze out gobs of what he called 'the Widow Lloyd's Euxesis' into the upturned palms of his blindfolded fags, challenging them to guess what it was. The ritual came to be known as 'the Euxesis', and the sacerdotal Lloyd became the Widow.

Actually both Johns – Greenidge and Lloyd – had left Oxford before Lennox went up: Greenidge had been at St Edmund Hall, but dropped out in 1920 to study architecture at University College, London; the Widow graduated from Trinity two years later, with a degree in history. But both still haunted Oxford throughout the mid-Twenties. Unlike their younger contemporaries, they had been soldiers in the war, and were eager to catch up with the year of youth that each had lost. (Greenidge had left Rugby in March 1917, aged nearly eighteen, and had gone straight into the Royal Garrison Artillery as a second lieutenant, training with heavy guns at the Royal Military Academy, Woolwich, for the last year of the war; Lloyd had left Winchester early in 1918 and had gone up to Trinity 'on military service as a cadet'.[77]) John Greenidge was now working in London as an architectural assistant in the private practice in Russell Square of his professor at University College, A. E. (later Sir Albert) Richardson, and occupying a studio flat in Ormond Chambers, a seventeenth-century house in Great Ormond Street, Bloomsbury. The Widow had inherited from his uncle an estate called Castell Forwyn in Montgomeryshire, and, whilst deciding what to do about it, was living around the corner from John Greenidge in an elegant flat at 3 Queen Square (now the home of the publishers Faber & Faber).

For John the attractions of Oxford were his friends and OUDS, the theatre society in which he and his brother Terence could experiment with plays and films, as directors, actors and designers. For the Widow, the chief draw was the infamous drinking club he himself had helped to found in rooms below a small flat he had taken at 31 St Aldate's. There he and his fellow Hypocrites used to swill beer and make as much racket as possible, dancing to jazz records or reciting verse in unison, dressing up, skipping and making love, surrounded by what Anthony Powell remembered as 'subtly pornographic frescoes' of men wrestling, painted on brown paper by Robert Byron.[78]

But perhaps Lennox's closest friend at Oxford – certainly in his last year, when he shared rooms with him – was Vere Pilkington, sleek, fun-loving and witty. Vere was a born organizer – in later years he became Chairman of Sotheby's – a keen motorist and pilot, and he knew how to make Lennox laugh. But his chief attraction for Lennox was that he was an enthusiastic and accomplished musician, who played the harpsichord (to professional standards) and took a scholarly interest in early music.[78]

Apart from the gregarious Vere and the wild Widow, most of Lennox's friends shared a dislike of the riotous party scene. Like Lennox they were not really 'joiners',* preferring instead more intimate gatherings on their own; Auden was such a loner that he was said to live in 'hermit-like seclusion' at Christ Church.[80] What all shared without exception was a love of music. And, the unwaveringly straight Talbot Rice apart, they were, in the Eton argot of the Twenties, 'homo' to a man (though Vere was later to marry the divorced wife of his incorrigibly un-heterosexual Christ Church friend Gavin Henderson, later Lord Faringdon – after Henderson's ill-judged marriage, engineered by his mother, had broken down in a matter of weeks). Talbot Rice seems to have been one of the few Oxford men in the Twenties who ever had anything to do with women. In 1927 he proposed to the clever Russian 'undergraduette' Tamara Abelson (though he had never till then kissed her). They married in Paris later that year, and Lennox was one of the few guests.[81] Each of these friends was to reappear in Lennox's life.

Lennox may have been an intimate of John Greenidge's, but he had little to do with John's extravagantly unconventional brother Terence[82] – till a silent film brought them together in his second year. Evelyn Waugh wrote the script; Waugh and Terence produced it, and, with John Greenidge and John Sutro, found the £20 to back it; all of them, with other Oxford friends, acted in it; and Lennox provided the musical accompaniment. The film, called *The Scarlet Woman – an Ecclesiastical Melodrama*, is a comic fantasy about a papal conspiracy to restore Catholicism to contemporary England by exploiting the bisexuality of the Prince of Wales. The objective of the Vatican is nothing if not radical: 'All the leading Protestants of the country ... are to be cut down without remorse or pity.'[83] It is a modern Gunpowder Plot, plus sex and booze, written in the satirical vein of *Decline and Fall* and shot in a parody of D. W. Griffith's style of 'episodic narrative with sudden shifts of scene' and all the American movie director's pioneering techniques of close-ups, long shots, flashbacks and fade-outs.[84]

John Greenidge plays the bowler-hatted prince who is converted first to Sodom and then to Rome. Waugh, in a wonky white wig, is the sinister and Catholic Dean of Balliol who corrupts him. Sutro plays the crafty fixer Cardinal Montefiasco, while Waugh's brother Alec is the

*'L not a joiner, but v. friendly' (Beatrice Playne, niece of LB's friend Gladys Bryans, interviewed by RN, in Malvern, 4 December 1986, RNA).

Cardinal's drunken mother who is having an affair with the Pope (played by a Catholic Guards officer under an assumed name). Terence does the Irish Jesuit who steals the King's signet ring to finance the plot, and the young Elsa Lanchester, then a dancer, was roped in (for free lunches) to play the drug-crazed Evangelical cabaret singer with whom the Prince falls in love. The plot is foiled when the singer's Protestant scruples get the better of her, and she warns the King, who executes the Prince, the Dean and the Cardinal with spiked cocktails.

A clever but complicated narrative, the exposition on screen is so unclear that none of Waugh's biographers seem able to agree on the story-line. Since it is silent, the only clues are the captions – together with a lot of hysterical over-acting: leering, lurching and touching up, rolling of eyes, pulling of corks and hammy stroking of stuck-on beards. The whole exercise is so silly and self-indulgent that it is really quite difficult to believe that those Children of the Sun were not, after all, just spoiled scholarship boys. *The Isis*, the undergraduate paper, threw itself into the spirit of the thing: 'truly a masterpiece', raved its reviewer John Fernald (later a distinguished director) after the first night in the rooms of the OUDS on 23 November 1925: 'may Hollywood tremble.'* Oxford anyway rolled in the aisles, because Oxford was the audience it was made for.

Even Roman Catholic Oxford approved. The distinguished Jesuit Fr Cyril Martindale, Master of Campion College, hearing rumours of a new (and possibly blasphemous) student film, asked for a private showing for the Newman Club – and 'laughed till his tears flowed'.[85] He then added his own joke by giving *The Scarlet Woman* the Vatican's grade-two seal of approval, *Nihil obstat* (literally 'Nothing to be objected to'), which John Greenidge promptly shot as the new opening caption.

The Scarlet Woman was an in-joke, a student rag poking fun at the real-life Dean of Balliol, F. F. 'Sligger' Urquhart, gay and Catholic, who

*(John Fernald, president, OUDS, 'Mr Greenidge's Films', *The Isis*, 2 December 1925.) The other of the Greenidge films which Fernald reviewed was *Bar Sinister*, in which John Greenidge played the Hero and David Talbot Rice the Sheriff (see also JDK Lloyd Photo Album 2 (1923–28) Llyfr Ffoto Album 153, National Library of Wales). The following summer John Fernald himself joined the fun, filming *Next Gentleman, Please*, with the same cast of players and technicians, plus Rudolph Messel and the testy John Fothergill, at the Spread Eagle, Thame, and the Bushey studios (JDK Lloyd Photo Album 2 (1923–28) Llyfr Ffoto Album 153, National Library of Wales).

had had the temerity to close down the Hypocrites Club – and to steal one of Waugh's pretty favourites, the fair-haired and brilliant Richard Pares (steering him away from 'contamination' and towards a double First and a Fellowship at All Souls[86]). The film is as full of hidden allusions to the actors as it is to the characters they play. The joke is seeing Waugh who was 'usually and offensively drunk' at Oxford [87] playing the sober Sligger who drinks barley-water,[88] the zany and light-fingered Terence Greenidge playing the zany and light-fingered Jesuit, the gay John Greenidge as a bisexual Prince of Wales, the Jewish John Sutro dressed up as a cardinal, and Waugh's bald brother Alec in drag as the Cardinal's drunken mother. The locations are part of the joke: the Waugh family home in the Jewish suburb of Golders Green is the Catholic Dean's 'vacation haunt', the gay cruising grounds of Hampstead Heath provide the setting for the Jesuit's pursuit of the cabaret singer. And, in a gesture designed to appeal to the boozy Hypocrites, each character has his own alcoholic leitmotif, or 'favourite sport' as *The Isis* put it: the Pope and his girlfriend, the Cardinal's old mother, are never without their whisky, the Cardinal himself drinks cognac and the King's tipple is gin. The Dean is condemned to seltzer, and the cabaret singer sniffs cocaine.

Waugh conceived the project in July 1924. Filming started that same month, and a week or two later he and his brother and Elsa Lanchester went round to John Greenidge's flat in Great Ormond Street for a showing of the scenes Terence had shot so far. Waugh decided that he was already 'quite disgusted with the badness of the film' and regretted the fiver he had invested in it.[89] The following month he and his friend Alastair Graham escaped to Ireland, while the Greenidge brothers and a party of OUDS friends went to Lundy Island to make some more films, including *The Lighthouse Keeper* and *Bar Sinister*.[90] There was a further, very drunken screening of more of *The Scarlet Woman* in Oxford in November 1924; Waugh later remembered little of the occasion, except that he got a sword from somewhere, got into Balliol somehow and was got out again by being lowered from a window. In his autobiography he recalls that it happened on his last night as an undergraduate, at a party in Patrick Balfour's rooms in Balliol, and that it was Balfour himself who lowered him on a rope into the street in the small hours of the morning to climb back into his own college. Years later, as Lord Kinross, Balfour wrote that he had no recollection of the episode – 'But it has the ring of truth.'[91]

It is difficult to imagine Lennox there too that night, though it is no less difficult to imagine how he could have conceived the music without seeing the film at some time before the first official showing the following year. Nothing whatsoever is known of the music he provided, though he must have made notes about characters and situations and timings, then improvised on the night. The *Isis* review does not mention the music. Thirty-six years later Terence Greenidge recorded simply that 'the film had a glorious First Night at the Oxford University Dramatic Society in 1925, Lennox Berkeley in charge of the musical accompaniment'.[92]

If nothing else the experience gave Lennox an appetite for film music which he was to exploit with half a dozen scores in the Forties and Fifties, and though the outrageous *The Scarlet Woman* might have disqualified him, one of these later films, *The Sword of the Spirit*, was a propaganda documentary for British Catholics during the Second World War. But by then, 1942, Lennox had become a Catholic himself; so had Waugh, Billy Clonmore, Henry Yorke, Christopher Sykes, Christopher Hollis and John Greenidge.

Religion may have been a negligible factor during the madcap years of the mid-Twenties, but, as the Archdeacon explains to Bradshaw in Alec Waugh's novel *Island in the Sun*: 'within a few years many of my contemporaries [at Oxford] had come to feel the need for authority and guidance.'[93] Those who did not embrace the Red Flag of Communism chose instead the Scarlet Woman of Rome.

8
Lennox, Oxford, 1925–6

Lennox was already thinking of Rome while still at Oxford. Unlike John Greenidge (and even, for a while, Terence) and many other Protestant undergraduates in the mid-Twenties, including the Marxist Tom Driberg, who were attracted to the rituals of Anglo-Catholicism – the sanctus bells, the thuribles and candles, the vestments and the mystery of Latin – Lennox was specifically attracted to the liturgy, and, at that time, particularly the chant. Even before Oxford he made a habit of attending the Church of England service of Matins with his mother, who used to jot down the subjects of the sermons in her notebook. At the university, falling naturally under the influence of the Tractarian Movement, Lennox explored the High Church end of Anglicanism with John Greenidge (who gave him a copy of the *Anglo-Catholic Prayer Book* in 1929, and himself converted to Rome at about the same time), and with Billy Clonmore, who, for all his wild oats, was an ardent Anglican while at Oxford, but of the Low persuasion. In a typical volte-face, after coming down in 1925, Clonmore suddenly swung High and went to work at an Anglo-Catholic mission in a working-class parish in the East End of London, and then became a Catholic.

In February 1923 another of Lennox's friends, Leonard Williams, thought him sufficiently serious a Christian to deserve a copy of *The Treasury of Devotion – A Manual of Prayers for General & Daily Use* edited by the Revd T. T. Carter. A leading Anglo-Catholic of the turn of the century, Father Carter was rector of Clewer Parish Church in Somerset, to which he introduced such extravagantly High Church practices (facing east across the altar, mingling water with the wine, placing a cross on the altar, using processions, candles and choral communion) that his bishop was held to account for 'papistical practices'. The Bishop of Oxford, though against the practices himself, stood firm for Carter and won, whereupon Carter honourably resigned his living and went to live at the House of Mercy for fallen women, which he had founded at Clewer. Lennox must have found the High tone of these prayers helpful since he bought a further copy to give to his mother that autumn.

The following year he seems to have moved significantly closer to Rome when he acquired a copy of *Catholic Prayers for Church of England People*,[1] which spells out unequivocally the Catholic doctrine that 'The Holy Eucharist ... is verily and indeed the Body and Blood, the Soul and the Divinity of Jesus Christ, under the form of bread and wine ... He is really present to be adored upon the Altar ... the bread and wine become the Body and Blood of Jesus Christ.' To have accepted this unfathomable mystery would have been tantamount to thinking like a Catholic already.

That summer of 1924, with his new prayer book in his pocket, Lennox went to Italy for the first time – to Florence and Assisi – with a priest at the forefront of the Anglo-Catholic mission in East London, Fr Frank Thorne, curate of the Anglo-Catholic 'cathedral' of All Souls, Clapton Park.* It was Billy Clonmore who brought them together. The visit to Assisi, which left a lasting impression on Lennox, may have been responsible for his choosing François as his baptismal name when he converted five years later. It was undoubtedly responsible for his giving his mother, in 1926, a copy of Chesterton's *St Francis of Assisi*, to which he was so attached that he removed it from the library at his parents' house in Cap Ferrat, after Aline's death in 1935; it is now in the possession of his son Julian. (Lennox's agnostic father seems also to have been drawn to Assisi and to St Francis. Photographs in a family album include a monochrome reproduction of Luca della Robbia's famous statue of St Francis in the Basilica of Santa Maria degli Angeli, which, coincidentally, bears an extraordinary likeness to Lennox – not just in the shape of the head and the fine features but in the modesty, sadness and resignation of the expression.)

Returning to England on his own, after spending a week with his parents in a hotel on the lake of Annecy, Lennox paid a visit to Chartres. Overawed by the magnificence of the two-spired Gothic

*From Christ Church, Oxford, Fr Thorne had joined up, as a commissioned officer, to fight in the First World War, during which he was wounded and awarded the MC. In 1925 he joined the Universities' Mission to Central Africa, became Bishop of Nyasaland, and died, a bachelor still, and a member of Morden College, Blackheath, in 1981 (Obituary, *The Times*, 23 September 1981).

cathedral, he bought Huysmans's *La Cathédrale*,* and climbed down into the darkness of the crypt, where the hero of the book, yearning for the return of an age of faith, decides to become a Benedictine monk. Listening to the Gregorian chant of the afternoon office, in the chapel of Notre Dame de Sousterre, Lennox must have pondered on Huysmans's theory that the Renaissance had destroyed the mysticism of religious devotion, and that the only remaining place to realize 'the poetic dream of life' was in the peace and seclusion of the cloister.[2] In principle Lennox would have agreed. In practice, the monastic life did not work for Huysmans; nor would it, Lennox knew, for him.

But, in his twenty-first year, he was immersed in the poetry of Baudelaire, Mallarmé and Verlaine, and what Wilfred Owen's biographer, Dominic Hibberd, has called 'the secret autonomous world of the imagination, where the supreme task was to capture beauty in pure form'.[3] His attraction to the principles of the 'Decadents' and the 'Symbolists', combined with his longing for the Church of Rome, made him particularly responsive to Huysmans's *Décadence* – not only its morbid tastes, unconventional behaviour and aesthetic temperament, but also its religious message of 'vicarious suffering' or 'mystical substitution'. Huysmans believed that the contemporary world was lost to Satan and that if the people of France would not pray and suffer for Christ, then it was the duty of the remaining Catholics to do it for them.[4] No sooner had Lennox arrived back in Oxford than he called at Blackwell's to find the poems of the *Décadents'* English disciple Arthur Symons. This collection, first published in 1901, had become so hugely popular that it had run through eight reprints by 1924, despite the violent disapproval of the *Pall Mall Gazette*, which regarded Symons as 'a very dirty-minded man' whose mind was 'reflected in the puddle of his bad verses'. Lennox loved them, finding a congenial Frenchness in their eroticism and intensity. Years later when he had the idea of setting some of the poems of St Teresa of Avila, it was Symons's translation, remembered from that old Heinemann volume, that he used to convey the ecstasy of St Teresa's 'mystic marriage' with God.†

*LB's copy of a 1923 edition of *La Cathédrale* is signed and dated 'Chartres 14 August 1924'.

†LB's *Four Poems of St Teresa of Avila* for contralto and string orchestra, written in 1947 and dedicated to John Greenidge, was first performed by Kathleen Ferrier and the Goldsbrough String Orchestra at Broadcasting House in London on 4 April 1948.

All his life Lennox was drawn to the mysticism that lies at the heart of Catholicism, and on his twentieth birthday, in 1923, David Talbot Rice gave him Thomas à Kempis's *The Imitation of Christ.* For more than five centuries this 'manual' of Catholic mysticism has inspired believers, helping them in the impossible quest for perfection, and teaching them about the inner life and contemplation. The so-called 'Gloomy Dean' of St Paul's, W.R. Inge, once described it 'an idealized picture of monastic piety'.[5] Just what Lennox was looking for: if he was not cut out to be a monk, and he was not, he could at least develop and discipline his inner life as a layman. (In 1937 he spent Christmas at the Benedictine Abbey at Solesmes, which was then at the centre of the revival of Gregorian chant, and right into his marriage he used to go on retreat at the Benedictine Abbey of Prinknash near Painswick in Gloucestershire. Indeed it was often said in the family that he should have been a monk, since he felt happiest in monastic seclusion, and that it would not be all that surprising if one day he took his Missal off to Prinknash for the rest of his life.)

During all this period of what was surely a laying of the groundwork for his conversion, he only once seems to have attended the Roman Mass to see and hear the liturgy at work. In his mother's diary there is an entry against 30 August 1925 that records that she and Lennox attended 'service' – she cannot quite bring herself to use the papistical word 'Mass' – at Westminster Cathedral. Whatever Aline's doctrinal reservations may have been, it is inconceivable that she could have failed to feel the tremendous spiritual power of that grand Byzantine building (opened for worship in the year of Lennox's birth). For his part, though he left no record of the visit, witnessing the Catholic Mass that day must have been a significant milestone for Lennox on his path to Rome. We know there were musical repercussions, since he subsequently bought a copy of the Westminster Cathedral Choir's early acoustic recording of two Masses by Palestrina, *Papae Marcelli* and *Aeterna Christi munera* (and recommended it to his mother).[6] Thirty-five years later, when he had found not only his faith but his place within his new Church, he paid his respects to Westminster Cathedral with two fine settings of the Mass written specially for the voices of its boys' choir. (Two of his own sons, Michael and Julian, were then choristers at Westminster Cathedral, and they became so closely involved with the cathedral that whenever the poet John Betjeman came to dinner at Warwick Avenue he would say to one or other of them, 'Tell me, how is Bentley's glorious basilica.'[7])

At Merton, daily attendance at Morning Prayer was obligatory for undergraduates in their first two years. The thirteenth-century Chapel comprises just the choir and transepts of what would have been a veritable cathedral if the plans of the founder Walter de Merton, Bishop of Rochester, had been fully carried out and the nave built. As Lennox began his spiritual journey to Rome during these years at Oxford, he must often have thought how beautiful the classical liturgy of the Roman Catholic Church would have sounded when chanted by the monks of Merton in this same Chapel before the Reformation. Little did he know then that the Catholic reformers of the Second Vatican Council, forty years on, would cast out the Church's 'immutable' liturgy, in the interests of modernization; that he himself would take part in the campaign for its restoration; that seventeen years after his death the old Tridentine Rite would return to Merton College Chapel, after an absence of more than 450 years, for three days of Masses and Divine Offices, in Latin to Gregorian Chant, during the 11th Colloquium of the International Centre for Liturgical Studies;* and that in 2007 Pope Benedict XVI would restore the ancient form of the Mass.[8] The initiative of 2006 was consolidated in 2007 and 2008 by week-long seminars at Merton organized by the Latin Mass Society to train more than a hundred priests in the traditional liturgy.

Even with his eyes still then unopened to the visual arts, Lennox cannot have failed to admire the beautiful tracery of the Chapel's stone windows, the original stained glass of the Catherine Wheel window over the altar, and the wooden screen designed by Wren. Nor will he have missed the pipe organ, partly because of its odd position outside the Chapel, and partly because of the thick soup of sound it must then have produced. A small two-manual instrument, it stood beneath the fine squat tower, facing the screen, producing a flood of diapason tone that lacked any brilliance whatsoever, because its stops were all either unison (piano pitch) or an octave higher.†

*The Colloquium took place at Merton College from 13–16 September 2006 (See *CIEL UK Chronicle*, Newsletter of the Friends of CIEL UK, Issue Number 25, December 2006, www.CIEL-UK.org).

†Julian Berkeley's interpretation of the specifications in W. L. Sumner, 'Some Oxford Organs', *The Organ* vol. xxvi no. 104 April 1947, pp. 162–3.

Lennox would not have been able to play the Merton organ that first term, because it was closed for major reconstruction. Instead he cycled round to New College Chapel where he took lessons for a while with the resident organist, the mild and modest W. H. (later Sir William) Harris, who fed him a diet of Bach which was to prove invaluable later. Harris was also a busy choral conductor responsible for many interesting concerts at Oxford including a historic performance of Monteverdi's *Orfeo* in Lennox's last year, thus arming Lennox for further French forays into the forgotten music of the Venetian courts with Nadia Boulanger later in the Twenties.

The conversion of the Merton organ's action from clunky old mechanical to modern pneumatic (an 'improvement' he may not have approved of, and which could not have corrected the basic inadequacies of the instrument) began in March 1923. The work was done at a cost of £1,770 by the Liverpool firm that had built it in the first place, Rushworth & Dreaper, and to keep an ear on progress the college hired one of the most distinguished organists of the day, Henry Ley, of Christ Church Cathedral. When the Trinity (summer) term started on 4 April, Dr Ley was still buried in pipes, and it was not long before Lennox introduced himself. It turned out that they had Gog in common – Walter Greatorex, the music master who had taught them both, Lennox at Gresham's and Ley at Uppingham before the war. Lennox was enchanted with Henry Ley, as everyone was, and soon he was taking lessons with him, not on the completed organ at Merton, which still sounded as muddy as ever, but high up on the Willis in Christ Church.[9] Dr Ley's playing of Bach in those lessons provided one of Lennox's earliest experiences of live music, after years of listening to his father's recorded piano rolls.

Lennox was not a natural organist, any more than he was a natural pianist, but that did not matter: he was learning about music from one of the most inspiring teachers of the early twentieth century. Not just Bach, and not just organ music, but all the other gods in Henry Ley's pantheon: Haydn, Mozart, Beethoven, Schubert and Brahms – and, for a time, Rheinberger.[10]

Both agreed that much as they adored Bach they hated Wagner, who represented to them the epitome of romanticism, the enemy of progress. Like all composers of his generation, Lennox was strongly influenced by the early works of Stravinsky, especially the raw, pulsating ballet scores,[11] and he was keen to spread the word. John Codrington, one of his Christ Church friends, remembered being introduced to the music of Stravinsky with gramophone records of *Petrushka* (already fourteen years old), when Lennox was living with Vere Pilkington in rooms in King Edward Street in 1925.[12] They followed the 78s with the Russian edition of the score which Lennox had recently bought.*

Lennox was also much influenced in these Oxford days by French music of the turn of the century. It was the 'clarity, order and emotional climate' that appealed; and a subtlety and delicacy that he could not find in any other music of the period. The *fin-de-siècle* French composers shared a harmonic language, which he also detected in the music of his contemporary Francis Poulenc (soon to become a close friend) – and it was this harmonic language that Lennox felt he himself could use, in his own music, in his own way.[13]

His new teacher had a passion for Debussy. 'I have gone mad on him,' Ley had written some years earlier to a childhood friend who played the violin. 'He is a genuine artist and not a fraud like Strauss or Elgar – his scale consists of whole tones and his whole aim is to paint a picture.'[14] Lennox was enthusiastic about Debussy too: the music 'seemed to speak to a different part of one's sensibility'.[15]

Ravel had an even more significant impact on Lennox. He thought the 'deeply poetic' *Introduction and Allegro* was 'as effective a piece of writing for the harp as has ever been contrived'. He found these pieces so intoxicating that he was 'immediately and completely subjugated'. Their precision, tenderness and nostalgia, and their subtlety of feeling, seemed to realize something he had never heard in music before, and 'it opened up a new, if somewhat unreal, world in which only the most exquisite feelings had any part'.[16] He was also especially fond of *Daphnis et Chloé* – particularly the opening of the second suite which he judged to be 'one of the loveliest sounds that a composer has ever devised'.[17] But the work that meant most was *La Valse*, bitter-sweet and full of paradoxes, its 'sumptuous climaxes' betraying 'a certain emptiness', the delirium of the ending 'nearer despair than gaiety'.[18] Much later Lennox said he felt sure that the sensuous charm and vapid glitter that characterize the waltz touched Ravel at some deep psychological level, 'for he was a man to whom the finer shades of feeling made a greater appeal than the most powerful emotions'.[19]

*LB also bought at Oxford this year Arthur Bliss's *Conversation* for chamber ensemble and Lord Berners's *3 Valses Bourgeoises* for piano duet.

In 1925 Lennox actually met his hero, when Ravel came over to London for talks with Mrs Elizabeth Sprague Coolidge, the American music patron who had commissioned his still-unfinished song cycle, *Chansons madécasses*. Ravel was staying with friends of Lennox's god mother Sybil Jackson, the Swedish soprano Louise Alvar and her husband Charles Copeley Harding, a rich Birmingham businessman, in their large house at 14 Holland Park. The short dark composer and the tall blonde singer had often toured together in America and Europe, and Madame Alvar-Harding was familiar with Ravel's social idiosyncracies.[20] What she needed was an attractive young man to interpret for him (because Ravel spoke no English), to entertain him on outings in her yellow Rolls-Royce, and to organize his appoinments. Sybil Jackson proposed Lennox, who was not only charming and bilingual but a composer too (thought singularly unsuited to secretarial work).

As he packed his bag for London, Lennox had a very clear image of the man he was going to meet: 'someone of exceptionally rarefied mind and heart, an ethereal being ... above the grosser habits of ordinary mortals'. So it was a little disillusioning to discover instead 'a benevolent gnome' who was so thoroughly 'down-to-earth' that he chain-smoked acrid *caporal bleu*, army-issue cigarettes with a strong, pungent smell.[21] All the same Lennox had the feeling that his original expectations matched the real, interior Ravel, which lay carefully hidden beneath a veneer that was part childlike simplicity and part sophisticated man-of-the-world. Though affectionate by nature, Ravel 'hated anything too demonstrative and always remained slightly aloof'. Lennox could not help being a touch awe-struck, although Ravel, never one to play the star, tried to put him at his ease. (Thc Italian conductor Massimo Freccia, who was similarly intimidated by his first meeting with Ravel a year or two later, failed to see in the man the personification of his music. As far as he was concerned the 'thin little man, with grey hair, reddish complexion and sharp pointed nose', far from being a dreamy poet, was frigid, bitter and sarcastic.[22])

Perhaps because Ravel hated being lionized (and at this point in his life always was), he seems to have been a devil to manage – easily diverted, no idea of punctuality, picking at his food, reluctant to leave the table after eating (because he wanted to go on chatting), reluctant to go to bed (because he could not sleep) and most reluctant to get up in the morning.[23] But Lennox charmed the unpredictable Frenchman into best behaviour, ensuring that he was on time for all his engagements, including the Hardings' celebrated salons, which attracted such luminaries as Elgar, Ida Rubinstein and Sir Henry Wood – and the young conductor Anthony Bernard, whom Lennox was to meet again.

Lennox was aware, even in those early days, that his reticence often lost him important opportunities. (Years later he wrote of his regret at failing to get to know the celebrated Maurice Bowra, who was a Fellow and tutor at Wadham in Lennox's day, and was later immortalized as Mr Samgrass in *Brideshead Revisited*. 'Had I been more forthcoming as an undergraduate, I could have, but I was too undeveloped ...'.[24]) He was determined not to make the same mistake with Ravel. Eager to show the great man some of his own music, but nervous about its inadequacies, he plucked up his courage that weekend in 1925 and produced some early compositions (that he later blushed to think of). They included the *March* he had just written for Vere Pilkington, and he played them on the Hardings' piano 'with trembling fingers'.[25] Ravel was kind and encouraging, probably recognizing something of himself in Lennox's characteristic bitter-sweet harmonies.[26] Nothing was wrong with the music's harmonic sense, he said – but the technique was unsound. Ravel was a stickler for technique, which he himself had studied for close on fourteen years at the Paris Conservatoire, and he never tired of insisting that young composers should have the whole method of musical composition at their fingertips: without it, he said, they could not show whether they had any talent or not.[27]

It was not news to Lennox that his music lacked technique[28] – but he did not know what to do about it. Was it possible that Ravel himself might teach him? He had a faint hope, and dared to voice it – but Ravel said no, he no longer took pupils[29] (although he had taught Vaughan Williams before the war – and, thanks to what the 1928 edition of *Grove* calls Ravel's 'suppleness of mind', V. W. had returned to England 'with his powers of expression clarified'[30]). There was only one other possibility: the genius of the rue Ballu in Paris, the centre of a salon that attracted Stravinsky, Roussel, Milhaud, Honegger, Poulenc and Auric; a teacher so brilliant and dedicated that she was already a legend yet still in her thirties – Nadia Boulanger. When the time came, once Lennox had left Oxford, if he was still set on a career in music, Ravel promised to bring them together. This was a generous offer – Lennox cannot have known how generous, since Ravel and Boulanger had barely spoken for twelve years, following a misunderstanding at the time of her sister Lili's victory in the Prix de Rome in 1913. (Noticing that Ravel had failed to write to congratulate Lili, and overlooking what everyone knew about Ravel – that he was a notoriously lax correspondent – Nadia Boulanger informed him, with extraordinary tactlessness, that his 'breach of good manners should be corrected'. In his reply, Ravel pointed out, first of all, that it was by then too late, and secondly that he was sure Lili would forgive him. Relations between the two were never the same again, Ravel resenting Boulanger's interference, Boulanger smarting at her failure to correct his bad manners.[31])

Since first hearing his father's pianola rolls, Lennox had felt instinctively drawn to music.[32] Since starting at Oxford he himself had felt the urge to write his own music. Now he knew that composing was his vocation. 'I felt it was the one thing I could do, or stood a chance of getting anywhere with,' he said, half a century later [33] – 'as I didn't seem to be much good at anything else.'[34] And for the rest of his time at Oxford, to the almost complete neglect of his French studies, he devoted himself to music: going to concerts, operas and ballets, listening to records, reading scores, playing the piano and the organ – and composing. His parents loved music too and his mother, at least, was happy he had decided to become a composer;[35] his father, though a freethinker – and 'a musician *manqué*'[36] – seems to have been less keen, if only for practical reasons.

During his three years at Oxford Lennox wrote more than seventeen works – mostly songs and keyboard pieces. Converted to the early music revival as much by his own conservative instincts as by the examples of his organ teachers Ley and Harris (and of the university Professor of Music, Sir Hugh Allen, a Schütz specialist), he wrote several pieces for Vere Pilkington to play on the harpsichord.*

While still a boy at Eton, Vere had attended a recital given by the charismatic harpsichordist Violet Gordon Woodhouse, and had been so profoundly impressed by both her technique and her musical understanding that he begged her to give him lessons, even though he knew she had always made a point of refusing to teach. For Vere she made an exception – he was the first of only two pupils she ever took on – and he emerged as 'one of the best amateur musicians of his day'; for the rest of

* *March* ('To Vere Pilkington', 1924), *Mr Pilkington's Toye* ('From Lennox and John [Greenidge] Christmass [*sic*] 1926'), untitled piece 'For Vere, Boreham [near Chelmsford, home of Vere Pilkington's parents] 29th December 1927', 'Capriccio' ('To Vere Pilkington') from *Three Pieces for Piano* (1935), 5-movement *Suite for the Harpsichord* ('To Vere Pilkington, Paris May-June 1930').

his life he remained a devotee of the harpsichord and its repertoire – and for the rest of Mrs Gordon Woodhouse's life, of her. [37] (In April 1945 Lennox heard Mrs Woodhouse – presumably not for the first time – playing the clavichord after a dinner party at Alvilde Chaplin's house in London. Another guest there that night, the civil servant and scholar Sir Edward Marsh, was 'rather disappointed because tho' I stood not more than a foot away from the instrument I heard no more than if she'd been a fly buzzing in the next room.'[38])

On his twenty-first birthday, on 1 January 1926, Vere was given a harpsichord by his father,[39] and it is likely that on this instrument he played *Mr Pilkington's Toye*, which Lennox wrote for him in the autumn of 1926. The music is pretend-Scarlatti, the title a play on the sort of caprices which Elizabethan composers wrote for the virginal. The cover of the autograph score at the British Library is decorated with a line drawing of an early Georgian dancing gentleman, in a tricorn hat over a long curly wig, with a beauty spot on his left cheek, a lace handkerchief in his gloved right hand, and the ribbon of the Order of the Garter on his well-turned left leg. At the bottom of the page is the inscription 'from Lennox & John Christmass [*sic*] 1926',[40] so presumably the artist was John Greenidge, with whom Lennox was then staying in Paris. In the Oxford rooms which Lennox shared with Vere, he and Vere played together Lennox's *Two Dances* for piano duet (now lost); they may even have been the musicians who gave the first public performance at the University Musical Club in March 1925.

But Lennox's early output was not confined to small-scale works. In 1925 he went to a lunchtime concert in Oxford to hear Ravel's *Le Tombeau de Couperin* performed by the London Chamber Orchestra and its enterprising young conductor Anthony Bernard, then making a name for himself with his interpretations of twentieth-century French music. Knowing that Bernard was always scouting for new talent, Lennox invited him back to his rooms, gave him tea and produced the score of his first orchestral work, *Introduction and Dance*. When Bernard expressed his admiration for the 'busy and effective harp part', Lennox said he had learned to write for the harp by listening to records of Ravel. Then he popped the question he had not quite dared ask Ravel, 'Do you think I am good enough to be a composer?'[41] Touched and impressed – as much by Lennox's diffidence as by his talent – Bernard answered by promising to play the new work at a concert in London in April 1926. This was Lennox's first public exposure outside Oxford – and the public was much larger than he could possibly have hoped, since the concert was broadcast on the radio: the first chamber music to be relayed live by the BBC. Lennox's new piece joined an enterprising programme: Vaughan Williams's *Songs from 'Hugh the Drover'* and Ernest Bloch's *Concerto Grosso*, neither of which had been heard in Britain before.[42]

Lennox might now consider himself a *bona fide* composer, but he still needed technical help. Whom did Anthony Bernard think he should go to? The answer was the same, and as spontaneous, as Ravel's had been: Nadia Boulanger. Bernard even suggested that he and Lennox should go to Paris together, so that he could introduce the younger man to Ma'moiselle.[43]

Come the end of the academic year 1926, Lennox, ruefully, sat for his Finals. And, as he expected, he did very poorly indeed, taking a Fourth Class degree, thus ending what he himself later described as an 'utterly undistinguished' career at Oxford. This was almost worse than being sent down, which had been Robert Byron's fate the previous November (after precipitating a riot in the Cornmarket by calling a mob of undergraduates 'girl men'[44]). Lennox was not alone at the bottom of the class lists: even Harold Acton, self-styled 'scourge of the Philistines' and one of the most brilliant undergraduates of Lennox's generation at Oxford, limped home with a shaming Fourth.* But, as William Boyd's fictional Oxford undergraduate Logan Mountstuart says of his unexpected Third in History a year later: 'Look at Waugh, look at Connolly, look at Isherwood ...: it would seem almost *de rigueur* to take a bad degree in order to make your way' as an artist.[45] (According to Alexander Waugh, his grandfather's poor Third was due to 'a cocktail of drunkenness, lassitude, and raw, adolescent rebellion'.[46])

Oxford had served its purpose. Lennox now knew he wanted to be a composer and a Catholic. He knew too – who could have emerged innocent from Oxford in the Twenties? – that his feelings for his friends John Greenidge and Vere Pilkington and probably David Talbot Rice too, went beyond the 'normal'. He did not know how to resolve the paradoxes thrown up by his newly-discovered self-knowledge, but he knew where he would not be able to resolve them: in buttoned-up, backward-looking, disapproving England, where gay relationships,

*RN points out that 'Taking a 4th was, in fact, quite a delicate balancing act and thus, in its own way, rather distinguished' (RN to TS, email, 5 September 2007).

even in private, were to remain illegal till 1967. If buggery was no longer punishable by death, as it had been under a law of 1553, all homosexual activity between men, in private as well as in public, had been outlawed under the Labouchere amendment of 1885, and remained punishable by up to two years in prison, with or without hard labour, until the Wolfenden Report's recommendations brought a change in the law. Lennox had matured sufficiently to see clearly where he ought to go next – and how to make the decision that would get him there.

Throughout his Oxford career he had returned regularly to France to see his family, but there is no record that he ever visited his uncle Randal only sixty-three miles away at Berkeley Castle. For Randal war was war, even if the cause was a hedge across a private golf course and the enemy his own blood brother Hastings. Once you crossed Lord Berkeley, you and your entire family were never forgiven. When Randal married his Bostonian divorcée Molly Emlen Lloyd, in the Castle chapel in November 1924, neither Lennox nor his parents were invited. The only family Randal tolerated were his distant cousins from Spetchley in Worcestershire and his stepdaughter and displaced mistress Sybil Jackson, who had to travel alone from her new 'dower house' in Boars Hill. The other guests were neighbours and fast friends from abroad.

It cannot have been easy for Sybil Jackson. On the morning that Randal had proposed to Molly Lloyd at Berkeley Castle, earlier that autumn, Sybil was upstairs having a bath. Banging on the door, Randal had told her to get some clothes on because he was going to marry again and she would have to move out. Within six weeks Sybil had been ejected from the Castle and installed in Foxcombe Cottage, a new house at Boars Hill earmarked for her retirement (on the north side of the Ridgeway, a short distance from what was now called Foxcombe Hall). If she had been unable to see her godson while she was mistress of the Castle, she was now only too glad of his visits to her lonely cottage – though it is likely that she entertained him not with music-making but with bitter memories of Randal Berkeley and the Castle.

For six years Randal had been working as his own architect on the restoration of the much-neglected Castle, ripping the ivy off the old walls and repairing them with liquid cement, unearthing every fragment of the original masonry and timber and putting it back in its old position. And when he could not find the original door, window or panelling, he scoured England, France and Italy for suitable replacements. The work was to continue till 1930, when Berkeley Castle was revealed as 'one of the most beautiful medieval homes in England' – even if purists sniffed at some of the improvements.[47]

No sooner had Molly acquired her coronet that winter of 1924 than she prised Randal from his beloved Castle and carried him off on an endless round of trips to Europe and America, where he played golf and she bought property: in California, a house overlooking a golf course; in Rome, a villa; a palazzo in Venice (with a private complement of gondoliers in the Berkeley livery of green-and-yellow striped waistcoats and brass buttons engraved with the Berkeley arms[48]); and what Molly called 'other such gadgets'.[49] Though born a Boston Lowell ('the Lowells speak only to the Cabots and the Cabots speak only to God'), she claimed years later that she had been strapped for cash at the time of her re-marriage.* She was not strapped for the grand manner to go with her new station, nor the grand dimensions. Already plump, she was, according to Edith Sitwell, 'every cubic inch a Countess'.[50] (In later years she was said to behave 'like a Queen', with a style that was 'very straight from the shoulder'.[51]) With access to Randal's cheque book, she was able to ensure that he was every inch her idea of an Earl, by ordering, for example, a Rolls landaulette, painted yellow with green wheels, and fitted up like a Pope-mobile, with an armchair on a raised platform in the open back, so he could cruise around the estate with his head and shoulders sticking out of the top, spying for poachers and trespassers with his field glasses.[52]

Still there was money and Randal developed a taste for spending it on travel. 'Where do you want to go now, darling?' he asked his inexhaustible Molly – 'and off we would start,' she records in her memoirs: 'Egypt three times, the Dalmatian coast, Austria, Hungary, Germany, Algeria and Tunisia.'[53] With them went Randal's devoted chauffeur-valet Lowe, who was taught to walk a few steps behind his master, 'with the palms of his hands out of respect turned backwards'.[54] Molly claimed to love her earl – or 'Dear Old Camembert' as she called him; and he loved her friends: in fact that seems to be why he married her. 'Fill the house with your friends,' he said. 'I haven't any.'[55] He must

*Lady Berkeley admitted that 'I was so broke before I married Berkeley that I had ... to hock two very fine diamond and sapphire rings' (Molly Berkeley, *Beaded Bubbles*, p. 58).

have expected her to fill the nursery too, judging by his will of 1936 which leaves the Castle to 'my first or only son if and when he attains the age of twenty four years' and gives annuities to 'each of my younger sons and to each of my daughters'. This must have been wishful thinking, since his countess was then fifty-two.

If Lennox and his parents were not welcome at Berkeley Castle, it is clear they would not have liked it much anyway, either before the second marriage – when Randal and Sybil entertained Edwardian rakes in Edwardian luxury – or afterwards when Molly painted everything, even the castle rubbish bins, in the Berkeley colours of yellow with green stripes.[56] Besides, Hastings and Aline were now happily settled in the South of France, on a rocky ridge at Falicon above Nice, in a large country house, which they had bought for themselves and their children and for Ernest and Nelly Berkeley and their two children. Lennox was about to join them for the rest of the summer of 1926, and considering settling in France for good. What was the point of staying in England? The English hated anything new, regarded individuality with suspicion and considered it faintly abnormal to be an artist.[57] In France painting and music mattered above all else; in England, they were dead. Lennox's Christ Church friend David Ponsonby had gone to study music in Paris the previous year and had sent back vivid accounts of the flourishing music scene there. Though audiences, he found, were snobbish and prejudiced, the French, being a particularly intelligent race, understood that 'creation in art requires conscious and constantly-renewed calls on the imagination'. Paris was 'a kind of laboratory of art', where a foreigner would blossom and find recognition. The flame of Paris, said David, was positively quickening.[58] Lennox's godmother Sybil Jackson confirmed this: she had studied piano and singing in Paris a quarter of a century earlier, and had never lost her love of the city or her memory of its magic.

The city exercised a similar attraction for four of the composers in Lennox's family history who studied, or supervised performances of their works, in Paris: his Harris aunt, Nelly Berkeley; his step great-uncle, Arthur Jackson; his Berkeley great-great-great aunt, Elizabeth, Margravine of Brandenburg-Ansbach (dramatist and composer of songs, incidental music and an opera);[59] and his Drummond first cousin twice-removed, Marie-Caroline, baronne Durand de Fontmagne (whose grand opera *Bianca Torella*, based on a poem by Paul-Armand Silvestre, was staged at the Théâtre Lyrique in 1907).

Whether or not he was aware of these musical precedents within his own family, Lennox did not need any persuading. He had always known that Paris was the place to be. Your money went further, you could live with whomever you wished without being arrested, Catholicism was still a potent force, and, yes, the arts were seething with the new ideas of Stravinsky, Diaghilev, Cocteau and Gide. Intellectually Paris was the capital of the world, as Harold Acton claimed.[60] To have chosen to study in France rather than in Germany may have seemed perverse for a young English composer in 1926, but Lennox had a hunch that Paris would be the perfect place for him. Besides, his friend John Greenidge was now working there as a stage designer, and had invited him to share his flat near Sacré Coeur.

Years later Lennox said that it was not just the cultural ferment of the place, the *laissez-faire* attitude and the cuisine that drew him across the Channel, but the very air of Paris was an inspiration: you could breathe more freely there.[61] 'The people are not really as nice as the English,' he wrote on another occasion, 'and yet there is something about the country as a whole that attaches me deeply and for ever to it. Perhaps one likes the French for being so unashamedly down to earth and at the same time so much more lively than we are.'[62]

For Lennox, with as much cockerel in his blood as lion, France was home. Little did he realize that he would find there not only a music teacher, but a spiritual guide who was to become one of the most significant influences in his life.

9
Freda,
London, 1926

At The Pines in the Finchley Road that same autumn of 1926, Freda Bernstein, aged three and a half, was alone with her nanny. Her mother was mysteriously absent. No one explained that she was seriously ill, and had been taken away for special care. The trouble had started with an upper respiratory infection which deteriorated into a high fever, with pains in the chest and breathing difficulties. When Grace Bernstein's skin turned blue it was clear she had pneumonia. The doctor ordered complete bed rest and professional care, and recommended Mrs Rhoda Maddison's nursing home in Broadhurst Gardens, a mile down the road near the Finchley Road tube station. Fortunately Isaac could afford it. But the prognosis for Grace was not good.

At the eleventh hour the nanny must have revealed to Freda that her mother was not well, because Freda has a vague memory of being taken to Broadhurst Gardens 'to say goodbye'. This was 1926: pneumonia was as lethal as some cancers still are today. Though Alexander Fleming was already working on antibiotic experiments at St Mary's Hospital, Paddington, it was to be another two years before he discovered penicillin – and about fifteen years before penicillin came into production. Meanwhile pneumonia was untreatable, and usually fatal.

On 10 October 1926 Grace was fighting for breath, but as it was a Sunday no doctor could be found, so the matron called the duty chemist instead. By the time Mr Sandelson arrived, the patient's heart had already stopped beating, and there was nothing he could do but certify death.

There is some suggestion emerging from these bare facts (and from the undercurrents of family memories) that Grace's susceptibility to the virus arose from general debility, and that this may have been caused by depression, brought on, perhaps, by neglect. It is possible to deduce from Isaac Bernstein's hysterical response to Freda's birth in 1923 that he was unstable, and it is likely that this got worse rather than better. It is significant that Grace was attended on her deathbed not by her husband but by her father Frederick Charles Nunney, and that it was he and not Isaac who registered the death.

The funeral service took place in the more southern of the 'Gothic' chapels of the Hampstead Cemetery, barely a quarter of a mile from the Bernsteins' house in Finchley Road. Despite Isaac's wishes for his own funeral, as expressed in the will he drew up just before his marriage three years earlier, the service was conducted according to the Church of England's Order for the Burial of the Dead. Afterwards the plumed horses of Messrs Hurry's funeral carriage conveyed the coffin to the consecrated ground south of the main avenue of the cemetery, where Grace Bernstein's body was laid to rest beneath a plain granite cross bearing the words:

GRACE AMY
WIFE OF ISAAC BERNSTEIN
DIED 15TH OCTOBER 1926
AGED 34 YEARS

Actually she died on 10 October and she was 33 (having been born at 126 Lancefield Street, Queen's Park, on 25 September 1893). As a memento each member of the congregation was given a small, black, leather-bound volume containing, in sixteen gilt-edged pages, every word of the funeral service from the revised prayer book of 1662, retaining Archbishop Cranmer's beautiful English.

From then on, Isaac, who was now nearly fifty-eight (and looked much older), became more and more of a recluse. He locked himself in his study – working, perhaps, on his Welsh rent books, or maybe looking through memorabilia of his late wife whom he had loved, it was said, very much more than the evidence suggests.[1] There does not seem to have been much contact between him and his motherless daughter, who was left to the care of her nanny – the only servant now allowed in the house. One of Freda's clearest early memories is of being out with the nanny in the Finchley Road, and seeing a tan-coloured dog run over by a bus – an experience which brought on 'terrible nightmares and screaming fits'. In another, even more disturbing nightmare, which still recurs in her old age, she sees 'a hand coming down on top of me, a man's hand, on my face'. Despite repeated questioning on many different occasions, Freda has been unable to explain the origin of this violent image. Is it connected with her father's rage that she was not a boy, or a symbol of her fear that her father did not love her? Could it be more sinister – an indication, perhaps, of molestation? The questions have to be asked, but Freda has no answers. 'It could be any of those things,' she says, 'who knows?'

By the winter of 1927 Isaac Bernstein had become so withdrawn that he had his meals alone in his study, collecting a tray left by the nanny outside the door, and returning it there, empty, a little later. For the rest of the time his door remained not only locked, but bolted and even barred.[2] Shortly after Christmas 1927 he seems to have fallen ill. Freda, who slept in the nanny's room next door to Isaac's study, remembers hearing him call out something that sounded like 'Goodbye', or it could have been, she says, 'Tired'.[3] On Monday 9 January 1928 after a weekend of uncollected meals, the nanny was so concerned that she broke all the rules and knocked on the master's door. When she got no reply she banged a little harder, then called out. But there was no response and she could hear no sounds of any kind through the door, so she sent for the police.

Breaking into Isaac's study was not easy. Freda recalls a constable sitting her up on his shoulder and asking where her daddy kept his spare keys. But there were not any: the only keys were with Isaac on the other side of the study door. And anyway keys would not have drawn the bolt and released the bars. In the end the police had to cut a panel out of the door. They found Isaac dead in his bed.[4] At first it was thought he had committed suicide, but a post mortem established that he had died of a) heart failure, b) toxaemia, and c) lobar pneumonia. Nevertheless the talk of suicide continued, and to investigate the circumstances an inquest was held in Hampstead the following Saturday. The court records have long since disappeared, but the local paper reported a few brief facts that emerged at the hearing: that Bernstein was a wealthy man who owned property in Cardiff, where he at one time carried on a store at the docks, and that he had lived the life of a 'recluse' since his wife's death. But an unnamed witness – possibly the nanny, since no one else ever saw him – is quoted as saying that he 'seemed to enjoy his lonely life'. The coroner, Sir Walter Schröder, recorded a verdict of 'death from natural causes'.[5]

Isaac Bernstein was cremated and his ashes were buried in his wife's grave at Hampstead Cemetery,[6] with no religious ceremony whatever, according to the specific terms of his will of 1922. (The inscription added to the tombstone gives his age as 65, and the death certificate says 'about 65', but he was actually only 59.) The will was proved on 4 April. After the named beneficiaries and funeral expenses had been paid, Freda stood to inherit £23,370.14s.11d. net (about a million pounds today).* To care for his only child, now nearly five, and her Welsh fortune, Isaac had appointed as guardian not the Bernstein relatives who had cut him out of their lives, nor his Nunney in-laws, but his executor, the Public Trustee. Under an Act of 1906, the Trustee was appointed by the Lord Chancellor to represent children in legal proceedings, to protect their welfare and rights, and to administer estates and trusts, 'where there is no other suitable person or agency willing or able to act'.[7] Since at least one of the Nunney aunts had expressed a willingness to adopt Freda, the Public Trustee must have ruled out these alternatives as unsuitable. Instead Freda was sent to live with her elderly grandparents, Fred and Blanch Nunney, in a terraced house in the working-class suburb of Queen's Park.

*Will of Isaac Bernstein, dated 3 August 1922, proved 4 April 1928. With the birth of FB, Isaac's niece Hetty Price, and his great-niece Freda Price, were dispossessed of their inheritance as his residuary legatees. Yet Freda Price's cousin Lewis Bernstein told TS in a telephone conversation, 11 April 2006, that, as a child, Freda Price had inherited a large sum of money from an unknown relative.

10
Berkeley and Boulanger, Paris, 1926–8

Nadia Boulanger's rambling apartment was in a dark and austere building near the fork of the narrow, noisy streets of Ballu and Vingtimille, in the heart of the red-light district of Montmartre. Three blocks north-west lay the disreputable place Blanche and the low life of the Moulin Rouge; a little further west was the notorious place Pigalle, haunt of prostitutes of both sexes; linking the two was the place de Clichy, where female transvestites and lesbians danced together at La Souris; and immediately to the south, the rue de Clichy specialized in rent-boys. 'I like to live where everything is happening around me,' she used to say.[1]

The sanctum where she gave her lessons was a typical late-nineteenth-century salon, large and homely, with flowery cornices going a little grey, quantities of potted plants and bouquets in vases, signed photographs on every available surface, and a glass door covered in pleated yellow silk leading to a dining room. The furniture, which had been modern thirty years earlier – light-wooded, elongated, and curvy, with inlaid tulip designs – was dominated by three large keyboard instruments: two grand pianos and a full-size, two-manual Mutin-Cavaillé-Coll organ, with a pedal-board. On the chimney-piece stood a marble bust of her younger sister Lili, the gifted composer whose death at the age of twenty-five had been so traumatic for Nadia that she wore black for the rest of her life.

One morning in the autumn of 1926 Lennox left the flat he had taken near the site of Berlioz's old house in the rue du Mont Cenis, below the magnificent basilica of Sacré Coeur, and crossed the place Pigalle to the Clichy quarter to meet Nadia Boulanger for the first time. Arriving at 36 rue Ballu, he climbed into the tiny, wrought-iron cage of the ancient lift, which slowly rose 'with alarming shuddering and creakings' to the fourth floor.[2] He was met by Katya, the old Russian maid, who showed him into the waiting room, where the great teacher, stern but smiling, was expecting him. Nadia was thirty-nine, and already a legend; Lennox was a very young twenty-three. 'Bonjour Bairkelé,' she said, as she shook him by the hand, and led him through to the salon – into a new life that was 'strangely exhilarating'.[3]

Meeting Nadia Boulanger – 'a very nice, severe person' – was 'a little frightening', according to the tenor Hugues Cuénod, who joined the Boulanger singers in 1933.* Cuénod recalled that she was always 'severely dressed in black with grey, parted hair', the archetype of an '*institutrice* of a good girls' school'.[4] Lennox himself has left only the briefest record of his first meeting with Nadia, though in the course of his long life he wrote more about her than about any other individual. Perhaps he felt a personal description was unimportant, or intrusive – or even redundant, since other pens had already, and so comprehensively, covered the ground. But as those others include Winnaretta, princesse de Polignac, the Singer sewing machine heiress and music patron, who exclaimed of Ma'moiselle, 'What a profile! This is one of the muses', the poet Alliette Audra who observed no less loftily that Nadia's 'tread was that of the Victory of Samothrace',[5] and the American composer Virgil Thomson who gushed about a 'tall, soft-haired brunette still luscious to the eye',[6] a plain English description might be helpful. Lennox's Oxford friend David Ponsonby, who studied harmony and counterpoint with Nadia from 1925 till the mid-Thirties, provided a vivid cameo in a long essay about Nadia and her methods, which has never been published.

> My first vision of Nadia was entering a hall of the École normale ... She swept forward, a strong impressive figure, her pale face animated in speech addressed to a group of students who were following ... her well-filled music-case under her left arm and a long veil of deep mourning falling from her small black hat.[7]

According to David, she was slim, with an oval face, pale skin, a noble brow and a strong chin. Her hair was dark, her hands long-fingered and well cared for, and her eyes almost alarmingly intelligent:

> Those eyes seem to reveal the surpassing rapidity of her perceptions and as she fixes them on a speaker one feels that she has read more than his thoughts, supplemented them with deductions and

*Cuénod is immortalized as the high tenor in NB's pioneering recordings of Monteverdi.

analogies, and lifted the whole matter in hand on to the plane of universal interest, long before he has finished his sentence.[8]

Apart from the black hat, her usual dress included a black coat and skirt – long, full and impeccably cut – with a blouse of fine fabric (to which was pinned a small gold watch), rimless pince-nez and low-heeled shoes (for playing the organ). She stood and sat with a ramrod back and walked with a somewhat stiff gait, as a result of baby training when she had been 'swaddled tightly and tied to chairs to force her to develop good posture'.[9] With her spectacles and her chignon, she had 'the appearance proper to a "maiden lady teacher of music"',[10] but David Ponsonby observed that her fondness for fine textures and rare perfumes softened any hint of austerity.[11]

Lennox cannot have failed to be as impressed by his first glimpse of the formidable Nadia Boulanger, as hundreds of others before and after him. For her part, Nadia was taken by him – by his good looks, charm, modesty and his good breeding, a quality to which she was always acutely susceptible. Breeding, she believed, was 'discipline practised over several generations'. She once said, in a curiously snobbish analogy, that if she 'invited her charlady to luncheon and she proceeded to eat fried potatoes with her fingers, I should be disgusted', but 'Lennox could consume the whole dish in this way and I should never even notice it'.[12] Having been *bien élevé*, Lennox was permitted such a freedom, under Nadia's code, because for generations the Berkeleys had bent themselves to the counterpoint of good manners[13] – while the charlady, who had known no such discipline, could not finger the chips without being accused of *mauvais goût*.

Sitting by the piano at the window overlooking the rue Ballu, Lennox showed Nadia some of his compositions, which he later described as 'very tentative and immature'. She saw at once that he had an original talent, combined with an acutely musical ear and a natural sense of harmonic structure, which meant that he could instinctively dissect chords, but she could also see that he had no technique. Many years later Lennox himself acknowledged that this early work was 'slipshod', and, at best, 'of very uneven quality'.[14] What he needed, Nadia said, was a strict course of traditional exercises in counterpoint and fugue.[15] Politely but firmly she explained that until he had reached some degree of proficiency in purely technical matters his own compositions were unlikely to prove of much value.[16] A composer had to be, first and foremost, a proficient workman – only then could he write what he liked and realize what ideas he had. Artistic freedom could only come from drudgery. In the same way as a man had to lose his life in order to find it, so a composer had to lose his originality and personality in order to find them. The Nadia method was threefold: first a study of the form and orchestration of the great masters, then musical exercises, and finally an analysis of the student's own compositions.[17]

On the strict understanding that Lennox would refrain from writing music for a whole year, Nadia agreed to take him on as a pupil, both privately and in group classes at home in the rue Ballu and at the École normale de musique (the private music college which the pianist Alfred Cortot and his partner Auguste Mangeot had established in *belle époque* buildings at the Centre Malesherbes). Despite the tough conditions – 'a most appalling state of affairs ... for a young composer who's longing to write music and get his music played'[18] – Lennox was 'very pleased and somewhat astonished' that she had accepted him.[19] He left the rue Ballu as elated as David Ponsonby when he had emerged from his first lesson a year earlier, 'filled with a feeling that life was a hundred times more worth living than I had ever thought till then, that every second was precious ...'.[20]

Lennox does not seem to have stuck quite to the letter of his agreement, since the record shows that he actually wrote at least seven new works in that first year. He cannot have been hoping to keep them secret from Ma'moiselle because most were given public performances – at least two of them in Paris. But he felt it did not matter so long as they were not submitted as course work. Much later he disowned them as juvenilia. Apart from a couple of early songs, the first works he was happy to claim, he said in 1974, were not written till the late 1930s.[21]

One of the first things he wrote on arrival in Paris was a set of five songs, *Tombeaux*, to poems by Jean Cocteau, and these show a marked change from the few surviving examples of his Oxford music. He had reached France at the end of a period of what he later saw as 'an entirely new artistic theory' in music, and these songs seem to be celebrating 'the return to simplicity, the avoidance of the romantic and the picturesque', as preached by Cocteau himself and practised in music by the eccentric Erik Satie and others of the group of composers known as Les Six.[22] But there is more to it than that: the simplicity, the clarity and the restraint of Les Six were achieved by a self-mocking nihilism that was designed to *épater les bourgeois*. Like the undergraduates of the *Brideshead*

Oxford from which Lennox had just come, Les Six were naughty boys cocking a snook at the middle-class conventions of the old world before the war. At Oxford that had meant green flannel bags with bottoms two feet wide, posing, strutting, getting drunk and kissing men. In Paris, in new music, it meant irony, mockery, silliness, even vulgarity – anything that would banish the allusive vagueness of Debussy, the poetic delicacy of Fauré, and all German music (except Bach), and chip away at sentiment. The movement did not last long, largely because it was not a movement at all; and, having made its point, the six composers drifted apart to pursue their own careers. Lennox caught the tail-end, and the *Tombeaux* represent his vigorous response to the cause, and a clear (and surprising) understanding of Cocteau's black humour.

The five 'tombs' in the set are those of Sappho, Socrates, a stream, Narcissus and Don Juan. They were originally intended for voice and piano, and in this form were given their first performance by Charles Sautelet, with Lennox himself accompanying, at a concert promoted by the 'elitist' *Société musicale indépendante* in the Salle Gaveau on 1 June 1927.[23] And they must have gone down well, because Lennox made an orchestral version which the BBC broadcast in England in the spring of 1929.[24] The copyist's manuscript (bound and dated 'Paris 1926'),* is illustrated with an undistinguished drawing in black ink, probably by John Greenidge.

Although Lennox had been attracted to Paris because it was the centre of modern art generally, rather than the centre of any particular school,[25] his Cocteau songs are clearly influenced by the atmosphere of Les Six – in particular by Poulenc's bitonality (the simultaneous use of two or more different keys).[26] Detractors may have found Les Six 'niggling, charming art-for-art-sakers' – as Arthur Bliss did, twenty years later (in fact he was so disapproving that he could barely resist condemning them as 'collaborationists'[27]) – but Lennox responded eagerly to their 'engaging simplicity, freshness and tunefulness'.[28] His *Tombeaux* owe quite a lot to Cocteau too. Like Cocteau's poems (and drawings, novels and films), but unlike the essentially straightforward Lennox himself, the settings are studiedly anti-Romantic, enigmatic and theatrical.

There is no record that Lennox ever actually met *le prince frivole* –

*Preserved as LOAN 101.92b, with other Berkeley MS scores, at the British Library.

let alone slept with him (though their mutual friend, the English artist Eardley Knollys, who, years later, did, dismissed the experience as 'not much fun, too intricate'[29]). But it is unlikely that Lennox did not meet Cocteau, since one of his favourite clubs was Cocteau's (and Picasso's and Poulenc's, the de Polignacs', the de Noailles', Gide's, Ravel's and Coco Chanel's – the meeting-place of *le Tout-Paris*, in fact). It was called Le Boeuf sur le Toit (The Ox on the Roof), after the circus ballet which Cocteau had created to a Latin-American 'Cinema-Symphony' by Darius Milhaud, who had borrowed the surrealist title from a popular song he had heard while working as a diplomat in Brazil. Le Boeuf was 'un bar-dancing' (and later a restaurant too) in the rue Boissy d'Anglas near the place de la Madeleine. Here, according to the painter and stage designer Jean Hugo, was 'the crossroad of destinies, the cradle of loves, the matrix of disputes, the navel of Paris'.[30] The loves were mostly of the Greek kind, which, Hugo said, 'was no stranger to the natives' of Le Boeuf, who even had their own expression for gay cruising, 'faire la promenade'.[31]

Although it was the fashionable place for the *avant-garde* in Paris during the jazz years, Le Boeuf could not have looked more bourgeois from the outside: two windows discreetly half-curtained, with potted geraniums on the sills. Inside were about ten tables, with a Pleyel piano and a bar along the back. The side walls were decorated with pale cloth coverings, and on one there was a large canvas by the Dadaist painter Francis Picabia – a work called *l'Oeil cacodylate*,* showing one of Picabia's diseased eyes, after treatment with cacodyl, a foul-smelling compound of arsenic and methyl; the rest of the canvas was filled in with the signatures and graffiti of the artist's friends (Cocteau signed 'couronne de mélancolie', i.e. 'crown' – or, in the gay slang of the Twenties, 'anus' – 'of melancholy').[32] While the clients drank 'champagne for luxury, whiskey for style, or the white wines of Alsace', and ate 'thin sandwiches or thick *foie gras en croûte*',[33] the virtuoso house-pianists Jean Wiéner and Clément Doucet played jazz and dance music or their own dazzling arrangements (or send-ups) of the classics – music of the kind Francis Poulenc used to call *délicieuse mauvaise*.[34] Wiéner, who graduated from the Paris Conservatoire with Poulenc and Jacques Février, had played the piano in the first Paris performance, in 1922, of

* *l'Oeil cacodylate* by Francis Picabia can now be seen at the Centre Pompidou in Paris.

Schoenberg's song cycle *Pierrot Lunaire* (conducted by Milhaud);[35] he also recorded *St Louis Blues* on a harpsichord. The Belgian Doucet invented a cross between a harmonium and a piano and called it an *orphéal*. Their novelty piano duo – with Doucet playing the top line – was much admired by the night-owls of Le Boeuf, particularly Cocteau who had first spotted them, and such *habitués* as Artur Rubinstein and Pablo Casals. Their repertoire ranged from *Bye Bye Blackbird* and *The Man I Love* to arrangements of Chopin (a fantasy called *Chopinata*), Wagner (a wicked *Liebestod*, re-named *Isoldina*), and even Bach (the opening *Sinfonia* from the *Cantata No. 29*). They also played Satie and Milhaud, and Doucet's own pastiche on the bar itself, *La Vache dans la Cave* (The Cow in the Cellar).[36]

Through the rue Ballu, Lennox soon made friends with the 'young hornets' of Paris music:[37] Georges Auric, Arthur Honegger, Milhaud and Poulenc, together with the Ukrainian-Italian composer Igor Markevitch (then still in his early teens), the pianist and composer Soulima Stravinsky (younger son of Igor), and the Americans Aaron Copland and Roy Harris.[38] Most of them were regulars at Le Boeuf, but it was probably Maurice Ravel who introduced Lennox.[39]

A chronic insomniac looking for any excuse to avoid bed,[40] Ravel spent a large part of most nights in the bars, cafés and clubs of the place Pigalle and the other pleasure centres of Montmartre. After a concert he used to collect Lennox, sometimes with another student or composer, and march the group off to Le Boeuf, or its sister club, Le Grand Écart in the rue Fromentin, or one of the big cafés in the St Lazare district, where they would talk about the music they had heard.[41] Lennox and his friends would listen to Ravel telling stories, which had 'the same elegance, richness, and clarity as his compositions',[42] and in a gently ironic tone recognizable from his music.[43] But the running was very much Ravel's. His last student Manuel Rosenthal recalled years later that the convention of the time was for the master to open a conversation, and if he did not and there was silence, then there was silence.[44] Ravel liked to prolong these evenings by taking his young companions on to a nightclub, where there would often be some virtuoso jazz playing, but he 'paid no attention whatever' to the music; all he wanted was a lively background against which he could hold forth. According to his friends, he was fascinated by the young gay men who danced with one another, although he never danced himself. 'Ravel loved it', Lennox recalled, 'and would remain until the early hours when he would at last walk back to his hotel at a leisurely pace.'[45] (This was before he moved into an apartment in his brother Édouard's house in the suburb of Levallois-Perret. As his country house at Montfort l'Amaury was thirty miles away in the Ile-de-France, he used to keep a room permanently reserved at the modest Hôtel d'Athènes near the Opéra.[46])

Sometimes Lennox joined Ravel at the concerts that preceded these nocturnal excursions. Once David Ponsonby bumped into them, strolling arm-in-arm, in the interval of a concert at the Salle Pleyel. Lennox was wearing 'a pretty mauve shirt rather frayed, with hair rather long and untidy for those days'. Introducing his fellow student to Ravel, Lennox suggested they should all meet for supper afterwards in the corner café on the place des Ternes. David arrived a little late, and found Lennox and a couple of other young friends listening to the famous composer.

> Ravel was 'holding forth' on the subject of people thinking that he and Debussy had been responsible for the *same* 'revolution' in harmony, and he was explaining the great differences between his own harmonic inventions and those of Debussy. At one point, he wound up a speech with the words: 'Il faut toujours être de mauvaise foi en art [In art, you've got to be dishonest], n'est-ce-pas, Monsieur?' (turning to me). Terrified and uncomprehending, I replied, with bated breath: 'Oui, maître.' Since then I have often thought of this statement, and it seems to me to be the whole explanation of art.[47]

Years later Lennox wondered why Ravel, who had been in his fifties when he and Lennox were clubbing in Paris, had not found 'more entertaining company' than himself and his callow chums from the rue Ballu, and he concluded the reason was that Ravel was 'bored by the world he had already conquered, and preferred to be with young musicians however humble'.[48] In fact, Lennox's company must have been exactly what Ravel wanted: an attractive and attentive young man, quiet, thoughtful and civilized, a French-speaking fellow composer who chuckled at his jokes, lapped up his theories and made absolutely no demands of him. A perfect match they made, according to a friend of Lennox: both like elves, but Ravel the more extrovert – sparkling, cerebral and heady – while Lennox was dreamy and contemplative.[49] It helped too that Lennox was attuned to Ravel's psyche – he knew instinctively that the older man had 'an intense inner life that was very private', and, since he himself had an inner life too (though of a more strictly religious kind), he respected Ravel's and kept his distance.

Those evenings cannot have been easy, however, because Ravel was so full of contradictions: reserved yet gregarious; devoted but never really close;[50] childlike yet sophisticated;[51] open and friendly, even affectionate, but pretending to be cold and detached.[52] Photos show an immediate and obvious paradox in his very face – between the smile that seems to linger on those thin, disdainful lips and a fear that lurks in the eyes. Lennox did not know Ravel intimately. Few people did – he was a man who 'fought shy of close relationships'[53] – and Lennox was aware of 'a barrier that one knew must not be crossed'.[54] Though Ravel had many friends, no one seemed able to pass beyond this barrier: 'he was never known', Lennox wrote later, 'to have any intimate relationship with either woman or man.'[55] Berkeley was not the only friend who found this puzzling, considering 'the extreme tenderness and often passionate feelings in his music'[56] – for example, the 'romantic, not to say erotic' moment in the first song of the *Chansons madécasses* when 'the Madegascan youth waits in voluptuous expectation'.[57] Lennox speculated that Ravel's 'real tastes' may have been in conflict with his 'ethical standards', or that he feared losing some of 'that great self-control and poise'.[58] In other words, that he was, perhaps, gay, as has often been suggested – though never proved; or that he took comfort from the place Pigalle's *filles de joie*, whose company he was said to enjoy (according to Vaughan Williams, amongst others).[59]

The musicologist Roger Nichols, an authority on French music generally and Ravel in particular, quotes a French Freudian who showed that one of the characteristics of Ravel's facial type (*retracté de la base*) was a 'virtual absence of sexual appetite', and Gerald Larner, quoting the pianist Marguerite Long, writes about the composer's horror of licentiousness. Nichols reveals that Ravel had the highest regard for precision (in language and in thought), rating it as a sign of civilization. Perhaps he regarded intimate relationships, whether sexual or romantic, as behavioural imprecisions that fell far short of civilized standards.[60] The closest Ravel himself ever got to discussing the matter was in a letter to Hélène Kahn-Casella, ex-wife of the Italian composer Alfredo Casella, to whom he confided: '... we are not made for marriage, we artists. We are rarely normal ...'[61] For all that – and perhaps because of it – Lennox thought Ravel 'one of the most fascinating and endearing characters that I ever had the good fortune to know'.[62] It is surely more than coincidence that the next composer to captivate him so intensely was Benjamin Britten, who shared with Ravel both genius and sexual repression. Since the nature of their repression involved an emotional under-development that left both in a state of suspended childhood (behaving like children, enjoying childish things – games and teasing – and loving the company of children), perhaps it was the child in Lennox – that is to say, the playful, the trusting and the biddable – that drew them to him; and perhaps it was the parent in him that was so touched by them.

The music which Lennox and Ravel heard in the clubs was usually either American jazz or Parisian *musette*: dance music borrowed from the Manouche gypsies – for example, the *toupie* (spinning steps, to waltz rhythms), the *musette* tango and *musette boléro* (*chassé* steps), and the saucy *Java*, in which the man had to clasp his partner's bottom. The jazz was played by such virtuosi as the guitarist Django Reinhardt, the violinist Stéphane Grappelli and the trumpeter Philippe Brun, the *musettes* by orchestras comprising one or two accordions, with piano, violin and/or clarinet or saxophone, and banjo. If Ravel really was not listening, then it must have been by osmosis that these sounds and rhythms were absorbed into some of his own work: directly, in his sonatas for violin and for cello, and indirectly, in the opera *l'Enfant et les Sortilèges*, the two piano concertos and *Boléro*. Lennox was not immune to their influence either. His 1927 *Sonatine* for solo violin (now lost), had a tango movement, and his *Prélude, Intermezzo et Finale* of the same year features a central blues. Five years later Lennox wrote an untitled ballet which incorporated a *Java* section (scored for oboe or clarinet, with trumpet, saxophone and bassoon) and an *Andante*, which is virtually a blues. But, as Peter Dickinson points out in a fascinating analysis of these jazz elements, Lennox used jazz as no more than a 'subtle inflection in his musical idiom', as can be heard in Dickinson's piano arrangements of these two movements (and a third, *les Amoureux*).[63]

It was through Ravel that so many of Lennox's early works were performed by the *Société musicale indépendante* (which Ravel and Charles Koechlin had founded in 1909, specifically to promote new music). Nadia was on the committee, and Lennox was on close terms with the SMI's assistant Secretary-General, Mme Kahn-Casella. We know, from his letters to her, that she sent him tickets, and even scores, lent books, suggested performing artists for his new works and gave him dinner, so it is not unlikely that she encouraged the programming of his music too.[64] These three important influences must have played a large part in securing for Lennox such a distinguished list of performers for his new works in Paris in the late Twenties and early Thirties. They include Jane Bathori, the French mezzo-soprano who sang so much of the music of Les Six (*Tombeaux*, Paris, 1928) and Jeanne Dusseau, the Glasgow-born Canadian soprano who created Ninette in Prokofiev's *The Love for Three Oranges* in 1921 (*Tombeaux*, London, 1931), Walter Straram (*Suite for Orchestra*, 1928), the Polish pianist Jan Smeterlin, who specialized in the music of Chopin and Szymanowski (*Three Piano Pieces*, 1929), Robert Soetans* and Jacques Février (*Violin Sonata No. 2*, 1933). And it is a measure of the cosmopolitanism that had attracted Lennox to Paris that the SMI was so eager to introduce such a lot of foreign music in the Twenties – not only by himself, but by Lord Berners, Sorabji, Szymanowski, Hindemith, de Falla, and the American composers Thomson, Copland and Piston.[65]

These same powerful friends at the SMI are likely to have been the go-betweens who brought Lennox together with the guitarist Andrés Segovia. We do not know precisely when it happened, but towards the end of the Twenties Lennox wrote a set of *Quatre pièces pour la guitare* specifically for Segovia, who had made a legendary début in Paris in 1924 and had been a favourite there ever since. Lennox first heard Segovia playing at a concert in Paris in November 1926[66] – we know he was in Paris then, because he raced back from a weekend in Bournemouth with Gordon Bryan to attend a Honegger concert at about the same time – possibly a performance of a concert version of his incidental music *Le Roi David*, which had been presented as an oratorio for the first time in Rome in March 1926.[67]

Like everyone else in Paris, Lennox was excited by the young Spaniard's artistry and virtuosity,[68] and, since he knew that Segovia made a point of including new music in his recitals – Roussel, Rodrigo, de Falla had all written specially for him – he must have felt encouraged to offer something himself. The four pieces he wrote (and dedicated *à Señor Andrés Segovia*) not only show his flair for melody, and those bitter-sweet harmonies that Poulenc liked so much, but also a natural

*'Soetans' may be 'Soëtens'.The first sonata was also launched at an SMI concert, on 4 May 1932 (RN, email to TS, 5 September 2007).

understanding of the guitar, which, till Segovia's trail-blazing arrival in the concert hall, had been locked in the world of folk and popular traditional music. They also betray traces of the jazz, blues and popular music which Lennox was hearing in Paris at the time, and they give a hint of the qualities which were to come to their maturity in Lennox's later pieces for the English virtuoso Julian Bream (the *Sonatina*, *Theme and Variations*, *Songs of the Half-light* and the *Guitar Concerto*), which form one of the most important individual contributions to the guitar repertoire by any composer of the twentieth century.[69] There is no record that Segovia ever played his Berkeley pieces publicly, but he kept them safely in his archive at Linares in Spain, where the Italian guitarist Angelo Gilardino discovered them in 2001.* We're able to guess 1928 as the date of their composition, because Julian Bream, to whom the Berkeley *Sonatina* and *Concerto* are dedicated, remembers that Lennox passed on to him in 1974 a number of scores which Segovia had given to him in 1928 'for consultation' – presumably in connection with the *Quatre pièces*.[70]

It was at an SMI concert – at the Salle des Agriculteurs, in January 1928 – that Lennox's *Prélude, Intermezzo et Final* for flute, violin, viola and piano was given its French premiere (having been played in London in 1927). Reviewing the new work in *Le Ménestrel*, Joseph Baruzi welcomed a composer whose work was 'both muscular and dense', and capable one day of 'intense evocation and vigorous distillation' (whatever that might mean). Was he mistaken, Baruzi wondered rhetorically, in detecting signs of future greatness?[71]

At the rue Ballu Lennox was still on a tight leash, and his private work – as opposed to his course work – was a reaction against Nadia's fierce discipline. A year on she would positively encourage this independence, laughing at Lennox's occasional 'clumsiness', as she called his technical lapses.[72] She was all for boldness and a sense of adventure in original work. Though she had very decided ideas about what contemporary music should be like, she could 'divine what one was trying to do and draw it out of one, unerringly pointing out weak spots, and suggesting alternatives'.[73]

But for Lennox artistic freedom was still a few months off. For the

* Angelo Gilardino and Luigi Biscaldi edited the newly-discovered works, and they were published by Edizioni Musicali Bèrben in 2002, with a facsimile of the autograph score and introductions by PD and Angelo Gilardino and a note by MB.

time being it was still all technical exercises, and these were very strict indeed. Nadia Boulanger's biographer and former pupil Alan Kendall has written that she was 'capable of being hard, even cruel' to students who showed any lack of commitment. She felt strongly that if one freely chose to do something then one should do it as well as possible, regardless of the hardships involved.[74] Lennox was soon made aware of his 'abysmal incompetence'.[75] No technical shortcomings were tolerated. His work was returned with crossings-out and underlinings, and each exercise containing mistakes had to be done again. Once he found the bewildering marginal note, 'Very musical, but forbidden'. Lennox thought it sad that anything musical should be forbidden, but he accepted it philosophically, believing, like Nadia – and the parallel applies not only to their shared love of music, but to their shared faith – that there was no point in voluntarily submitting oneself to a discipline if one was not prepared to abide by the rules.[76] Besides he recognized, as the poet Paul Valéry wrote on a photograph which he presented to Nadia in 1928, that her strictness was the source of the enthusiasm she inspired.[77]

Looking back years later, Lennox concluded that Nadia's means of teaching composition may have been the traditional ones of analysis, counterpoint and fugue, but it was the atmosphere she radiated that produced such an effect.[78] Aaron Copland, who was a Boulanger student at the American Conservatory at Fontainebleau earlier in the Twenties, said that 'half the trick' of her teaching was the sense her students felt of being in the presence of a remarkable musical personality. In such circumstances, the student 'imbibes things – attitudes, reflections, principles, knowledge'.[79]

To David Ponsonby, Nadia was nothing less than a symbol of eternity. He learned from her that 'beauty is the only really enduring thing we know', and that the natural rhythm of life – 'that unending pulsation in which the seasons, the days, our very breaths succeed one another in an ever forward movement' – was a vital ingredient in art. Without rhythm, art was lifeless.[80] One of the most important elements in her teaching, he wrote, was an understanding of the breadth of conception in the works of the masters. She was forever telling her students, 'Prenons les grandes lignes' (Let's take the broad outlines).[81] Copland remembered these *grandes lignes* too. In notes he jotted down in the Fifties, he recalled '... the long line – The sense of flow and continuity ... inevitability in construction ... the whole piece as an entirety –

all contained in that phrase.' Nadia's teaching, he wrote, was French in its emphasis on clarity and proportion, but un-French in its insatiable curiosity.[82]

Order was another of Ma'moiselle's rallying cries – order, in the sense of the divine order of things. But any sort of order was better than none: 'Il faut un ordre', she would tell her students, as she pointed out stylistic inconsistencies, lapses of order, in their own chosen musical language (for, as David Ponsonby records, she was careful not to impose any particular language, least of all her own). And to show just how perfectly obvious her principles were, she would pepper her 'deep, patient yet rapid speech' with frequent, and utterly characteristic, exclamations of 'Mais naturellement', accented on the first syllable (which, to a Frenchman, is as quirky as 'But naturally', accented on the final syllable).[83] Under such a godlike *précepteuse*, it was very difficult indeed for a student to hand in a piece of music that was not up to scratch. Lennox said he felt 'an almost moral obligation ... to do his best'[84] for a teacher who spent twenty hours of every twenty-four giving of her best.[85]

Ponsonby's memoir is full of references to Nadia's extraordinary stamina. As a companion she was 'like a being ... on a different dimension,' he wrote, and very few people were able to keep up with her. In May 1931 David and his sister Odeyne, a painter, together with Lennox, accompanied Nadia to the Exposition Coloniale Internationale de Paris, the festival celebrating France's status as the most extensive colonial empire in the world. The culmination of twenty-five years' planning, it took place on a huge site of 500 acres surrounding lac Daumesnil in the bois de Vincennes. Nadia insisted that they must visit everything, from replicas of the temple of Angkor Wat and George Washington's house at Mount Vernon to the Danish diorama showing Greenland 'Esquimeaux' and their dog trains. They ate pilaf from Morocco, drank cocoa from Guadeloupe and listened to gamelan music from Bali.* A narrow-gauge railway delivered them to most of the pavilions, but there was still a marathon of walking, 'Nadia leading with her Victory of Samothrace step in full play, the others soon

*Poulenc was so impressed by Balinese gamelan music, when he first heard it at the same exhibition, that he added 'a bizarre tinkly passage', inspired by it, at the end of the first movement of his *Concerto for Two Pianos* the following year (B. Ivry, *Francis Poulenc*, p. 82).

dragging rather listlessly behind'. The exhibition closed at midnight and Nadia maintained a commentary that was 'brilliant and all-embracing till the last minute'. When next morning, at a lesson, the exhausted David expressed the hope that his teacher was not too tired, 'she appeared very much surprised by the idea'.[86]

The lessons were by no means confined to music. David recalled that the range of Nadia's topics could include Plato, Proust, the Farnese Palace, medicine, politics or behaviour in general. She might even touch on such personal matters as the care of teeth or nails. Yet the pupil went home feeling 'a better musician, a wiser man and a harder worker – for she imparts ... a sense of the brevity of time allowed to us by life and the amount to be done in it.'[87]

One of the things Nadia insisted on was a thorough knowledge of the masters, and during most of Lennox's time at the rue Ballu, she would devote her public classes on Wednesday afternoon to the study of work which the pupils had previously analysed by themselves: a Beethoven piano sonata or string quartet, perhaps, some early polyphonic music, Stravinsky's *Les Noces*, works by Debussy or Ravel – and the Bach cantatas.[88] (Nadia believed that all composers worthy of the name should be able to compose a cantata a week, just as Bach had done.)[89] With as many as fifty pupils and friends squeezed into the salon, two of them playing part of Bach's orchestral score at one piano, Nadia herself playing the rest at the other, members of her distinguished vocal ensemble singing the solos and the remainder of the class joining in the choruses, it cannot have been easy to manage these sessions, but Nadia was in complete control. 'Her brain was so quick and her intuition so acute that she seemed to behave like two or three people at a time, playing, say, a piano version reduced from an orchestral score at sight with one hand, conducting with the other, singing a text and interrupting herself continually to comment on the music, to translate the text or to give a short sharp piece of morality to some pupil she had sensed was not paying attention ... .'[90]

For David, Nadia's conception of Bach was 'something very near the sublime'. Her profoundly religious nature with its 'vision of things divinely ordained in a majestic sequence', together with 'the serenity of an accepted faith and the sweetness of death as its ultimate goal', connected very directly with the greatest moments of Bach's music.[91] Her students' performances of Bach, according to Lennox, were not always of the same celestial order: 'We sang and played with great fervour and considerable innaccuracy, and we would hear through the music her voice [from the organ] saying "Qu'est ce qu'il vous arrive là-bas? J'entends des choses étranges!" [What's happening down there? I hear strange things].'[92]

Before the class started Ma'moiselle used to give a short talk on each movement, and Lennox remembered not only that her technical analysis was always illuminating, but that she spoke about the inner significance of the music in a way that seemed positively inspired. 'We were often left deeply moved,' he said. 'I don't think anyone who attended these classes can ever forget them.' For Lennox they remained among the most significant musical experiences of his life.[93]

At the end of the Wednesday afternoon classes, Nadia's mother, Mme Boulanger, a pious Russian *grande dame* enveloped in black veils, would throw open the glass doors to reveal a long table laden with cakes: 'a dream of chocolate, caramel and Chantilly cream flavoured with rhum'.[94] This was the sumptuous hospitality of old Russia. Here, David realized, was the true spirit of 36 rue Ballu: it might be Ma'moiselle's home, but it was Madame's house.

There were no cakes at Nadia's analysis classes at the École normale, where some twenty pupils gathered to dissect a Passion of Schütz or a cantata of Bach, in an austere atmosphere dictated by the 'almost Jansenist rigour' of Ma'moiselle's artistic principles and her 'taste for moderation, discipline and economy'.[95] Most of the pupils were adults – 'sometimes mature to the point of over-ripe'. But one was a bold boy in shorts, the Ukrainian prodigy Igor Markevitch, son of a Kiev aristocrat. In the autumn of 1927, when he joined the class, he was just fifteen, vivacious, noisy and ambitious. Nadia who had as much of a weakness for the *haut monde* as a respect for musical talent, made a special pet of him, to the resentment of some of her other students.[96] Though Igor grew to love and respect his teacher very deeply, and to credit her with all his success, he called her, behind her back, by a variety of cheeky nicknames, including La Générale, Le Pince-nez and Gottes Will (God's Will). One day, before class, young Igor posted himself in the corridor to keep an eye out for Ma'moiselle's arrival. The moment he saw her turn the corner of the stairs, he raced back into the classroom and announced to his fellow students in a stage whisper, 'Gottes Will kommt [God's Will's coming].' Then while Nadia dictated an exercise, Igor sang, under his breath, a spoof Bach chorale, 'Gottes Will, muss ich sterben? [God's Will, must I die?]'. Ma'moiselle pretended not to hear, and the students bit their lips so as not to smile.[97]

Lennox, who sat with Igor in the 'naughty back row',[98] liked the boy well enough to spend part of the summer of 1928 with him and his family at their 'dacha' below La Tour de Peilz near Vevey on the Lake of Geneva. (Photographs in Lennox's albums show the two young men outside the Villa Maria, and on the beach, Igor Markevitch looking older than sixteen, which may be why Lennox's later recollections refer to Igor as being 'about 19' when they first met in Paris in 1927.)[99] Three years later he hailed Markevitch's new *Concerto Grosso* as an astonishingly precocious work that took the breath away with the brilliance of its orchestration, the untiring vitality of its rhythms and 'the almost diabolical cleverness of its counterpoint'. But, he said, it was more exhilarating than moving, and 'one is a little doubtful whether Markevitch is capable of real depth of feeling'.[100] In 1972, when they met again in Monaco, where Lennox was judging the Prince Pierre Music Prize and Markevitch guest-conducting the Monte Carlo Philharmonic Orchestra, Lennox noted in his diary that he was 'never really fond' of the younger man, though he admitted to being 'strangely moved' to see him again after so long. As a performer he was calm, dignified and authoritative, and his conducting showed perfect taste. As a man he had an immense and disturbing charm, with 'something that fascinates and even subjugates one'.[101]

This must have been the quality that captivated the impresario Serge Diaghilev when they met in 1928. In a way Lennox was responsible, for it was he who introduced the boy to the Ballets russes at a soirée in the Théâtre Sarah-Bernhardt in the spring of that year.[102] Igor was so *bouleversé* by this first glimpse of the ballet world that for months afterwards he plotted with a friend in the company, Alexandrine Troussevitch, for an introduction to Diaghilev himself, in the hopes of getting taken up and commissioned to write a ballet. Two days after Christmas Alexandrine fixed it. Lennox was not present – he was spending the holiday with Vere Pilkington's family in England – but he knew the ways of the Ballets russes (and the atmosphere of Byzantine intrigue that surrounded Diaghilev's court) so he would have recognized Igor's first impression of the flamboyant despot on the stage of the Paris Opéra: 'His slightly passé elegance and his sheer bulk thickened the air around him, and his approach – with furs, monocle, opera glasses, white silk scarf, cane, gloves and the friends and secretaries who bustled around him – was as slow and sedate as the docking of a steamship ...'[103]

And Lennox would not have been surprised by the steamer's derisive hoot as Alexandrine introduced the tender composer. Diaghilev was fifty-six and one of the most famous and powerful artistic figures in the world; Igor, slight and faunlike, and clutching part of his first symphony, was still only fifteen.

> 'Is that your protégé?' asked Diaghilev, as he stared across me into the distance. 'He doesn't look old enough to be out of his nursery.' And without waiting for a reply, he said in Russian, while watching some scenery being lowered in a cloud of dust, 'Get him to bring his music to the Grand Hotel tomorrow at five.' ... I thanked him for his invitation which had given me the chance to see the ballets on the programme for the first night, 'I hope that it will not be the last', he replied with an icy courtesy, smiling into his 'possum fur collar ... .[104]

Igor duly reported at the hotel with his music – and was commissioned to write not only a ballet (*l'Habit du roi*), but a piano concerto. The *quid pro quo*, whether he liked it or not, was that he should replace Nijinsky as Diaghilev's intimate companion. But not for long, because by March Diaghilev was dead. In the circumstances, Igor was lucky the meeting happened at all. For this was the sad and traumatic occasion on which *Petrushka* was being staged specially for Nijinsky, the creator of its title role, in the vain hope that seeing it again, with his old partner Tamara Karsavina as the Ballerina, might trip his mind back into reality. But it could not: Nijinsky had been diagnosed as a paranoid schizophrenic in 1917, and no treatment had been able to help him. He never recovered his sanity, but lived on till 1950, surviving Diaghilev by twenty-one years.

With no one able or willing to take over Diaghilev's company, Markevitch's new ballet, which had been all set for production (with a scenario by Boris Kochno, based on the Hans Andersen fairytale, choreography by Serge Lifar and designs by Picasso) had to be abandoned.*

*Some of the music found its way into Markevitch's *Cantata* (1930), with a new text specially written by Cocteau, and some of the choreography was salvaged for Lifar's *Le Roi Nu* (1936), to the score by Jean Françaix (which was re-used by the Vic-Wells Ballet in 1938).

But the boy's name was made – though he was soon to abandon composing in favour of conducting; and, perhaps out of gratitude to his displaced predecessor, he went on to marry Nijinsky's daughter and to name their son Vaslav, in his memory.

Lennox had always loved the ballet and had often seen Diaghilev's dancers – not only in Paris, but in London and in Monte Carlo, near where his parents were now living. And with Ravel and Poulenc he occasionally met Diaghilev himself. He was much more than an impresario, he recalled later – a man of taste whose understanding of music and painting enabled him to stir the imagination of composers and artists, 'and to draw out of them what he felt was there'.[105] Lennox got to know Diaghilev's leading character dancer Leon Woizikovsky (who had been one of the athletic boys in rowing costumes in Poulenc's jazzy ballet *Les Biches*), and in 1932, when Woizikovsky helped to form the Ballets russes de Monte Carlo, he asked Lennox to write a new ballet for him. But the project never seems to have reached the stage. All that survived was a copy of a manuscript score dated 'Paris: May/June 1932', but with no title (though it may have been called *Les Amoureux*); there are seventeen movements, including the jazzy ones mentioned earlier in this chapter, and others with references to 'Camelot' and 'Bistot'.[106]

Meanwhile, under the influence of Les Six, Lennox continued to write light music that sounded like ballet music. In September 1929 he conducted the Henry Wood Symphony Orchestra in a performance of his four-movement *Suite for Orchestra** at the Proms in the Queen's Hall in London, and *The Times* paid him the back-handed compliment of dubbing the work 'Cheerful Nights at the Russian Ballet'. This was exactly the kind of thing, the paper said, which Parisians found ravishing one week – and forgot the next. 'Neat and captivating' as some of the music was, *The Times* felt that Berkeley had not quite found himself and would probably do well to shake off the company of Paris for a while, and even the influence of Ravel. 'One may perhaps express a hope of his emancipation without impertinence, for one feels convinced that there are elements of originality in this artist which need only to be set free to yield us as individual a new composer as he is already a fanciful and accomplished one.'[107]

*It had already been performed in Paris at the Salle Pleyel, under Walter Straram, on 16 February 1928 (MLB, p. 12); the full score of this work was found in Novello's hire library in 1987 (*ibid.*, pp. 13 and 14).

Six weeks earlier the orchestral *Suite* had been given its British premiere in a radio broadcast on the BBC conducted by Ernest Ansermet. Whilst it was a coup to have been taken up by the BBC, it was not hugely profitable, as Lennox's correspondence file in the BBC archives shows. After the broadcast of the orchestral version of his *Tombeaux* in March 1929, he wrote to the Music Department, with, surely, his tongue in his cheek:

> I hope you will not think me very indiscrete [*sic*] in asking whether it is the custom of the B.B.C. to pay a fee to composers whose works they broadcast? – I have in mind the performance of my 'Tombeaux' for voice and orchestra which was broadcast from London last month, and have been wondering whether one could hope for any material encouragement on such occasions.[108]

A week later, a reply came back from Kenneth Wright, a producer in the Music Department (later Deputy Director of Music):

> We do not normally have to pay fees to composers for manuscript works [...] We can however see no particular objection to your claim and we are therefore arranging for a nominal payment of £1. 10s. 0d. from which we have to deduct income tax at the rate of 4/- in the £ ... and assume that this will be satisfactory.[109]

Lennox was in no position to argue. But the issue was not over. Six weeks later the BBC broadcast his orchestral *Suite*. Lennox was delighted and grateful, and again wondered if the BBC might be good enough to pay him: 'I hate to keep bothering you for money – but I am in rather low water financially! – and composers never seem to get paid, unless they insist or beg.'[110]

This produced another nominal £1. 10s. – apparently, this time, without the tax deducted.[111] And after the Proms performance of the *Suite*, for which he had had to travel to London, Lennox put in a request for travelling expenses as well as fee.[112] The BBC refused both, but told him the work itself might qualify for a performance fee, if he was not a member of the Performing Right Society.[113] Presumably he was not, because he received a third 'nominal' £1. 10s. four days later.[114]

Composing was all very well, but even if you were lucky enough to get your music performed, you could not reckon on making your fortune, nor could you count on generosity from the critics. *The Times* might think he should give the dangerous sirens of Paris and Ravel a wide berth, but Lennox continued to plough his own furrow. Paris was his ideal, and Ravel his dear friend and mentor.

If anything he was seeing even more of Ravel now than before. In the summer of 1928 he took the train out to Montfort-l'Amaury, on the edge of the forest of Rambouillet, south-west of Paris, to spend the weekend at Ravel's quaint Gothic house, under its Basque-style conical tower overlooking the wooded countryside of Yvelines. Like everything else about Ravel, Le Belvédère was peculiar. Built on a hillside, its front door led straight into the top of the house, so that you had to go down an outside staircase to get to the bottom. All the rooms were scaled down to Ravel's diminutive size, and stuffed full of mechanical toys and ornaments, ingenious but not beautiful. Lennox particularly remembered a ship at sea, under a glass dome, with a handle to make the waves go up and down and the ship to roll. But he liked best the Siamese cats, of which there were many. Ravel 'observed them with immense interest', he said, 'and worried greatly about their relationships with one another.' [115]

In the autumn of 1928 the two men travelled to England together, staying in London with their mutual friends, the Hardings of Holland Park. Ravel was supervising a concert of his own works promoted by Gordon Bryan at the Aeolian Hall in Bond Street, and Lennox was attending the premiere, at a British Music Society concert in London, of his new *Suite for Oboe and Cello*, played by Helen Gaskell and John Barbirolli. Since Ravel could speak only three words of English – 'one', 'two' and 'pencil'[116] – and since his social time-keeping was famously wayward, Bryan (the mastermind of the trip) asked Lennox to repeat the role of interpreter and minder which he had played on Ravel's 1925 and 1926 visits, and to enlist as assistant nursemaid his equally bilingual cousin, Claude Berkeley, then an undergraduate at Cambridge. Between the three of them, they managed to get Ravel to rehearsals, lunches and parties, 'more or less on time, though it was all extremely exhausting'.[117] Photographs in the Hardings's garden, taken by Bryan, who specialized in composer portraits,[118] show the two young Berkeleys, eager as pups, dancing attendance on the little man, who sits cross-legged and puckish, in a light grey suit of the latest cut, chain-smoking Caporal Bleu with chubby, square-tipped fingers.*

*We know he was the photographer because one of the photos taken at the time (which LB kept) is published in N. Demuth, *Ravel*, with a credit to Gordon Bryan.

The Ravel concert, which included the British premiere of his *Sonata for Violin and Piano*, was such a draw that the hall filled to overflowing and many fans had to be turned away.[119] The Berkeley suite was no less of a success in its own modest way: 'a little work of great charm', which disguised its feelings, one review said, with a reticence and 'a worldly grace' that were 'very engaging'.[120] The skill, clarity and craftsmanship of its writing would have gratified Ravel, who used to impress on Lennox that even though a composer could not alter his basic inspirational gifts, he could nevertheless show them to ever-increasing advantage if he concentrated on the development of technique.[121]

The chief purpose of the trip was a pilgrimage to Oxford on 23 October, for Ravel to receive an honorary doctorate. Though he had what his friend Roland-Manuel called 'a Baudelairean horror of decorations'[122] – and notoriously refused the Légion d'honneur – he was happy to accept a D. Mus. (*honoris causa*) from Oxford. Gordon Bryan records that Ravel was fascinated by the details of the ceremony, and particularly by the 'gay pink silk robe which had to be hired for the occasion' (and shortened to fit him); he longed to take it back to Paris with him, but it had to be returned to the shop. The investiture took place at a solemn ceremony in the Sheldonian Theatre, with the Public Orator, A. B. Poynton, delivering an encomium in academic Latin. Ravel listened 'with a quizzical expression on his face', then asked for a written translation.[123] He was greatly tickled to learn that he was 'the ornament and darling of his most agreeable fatherland ... a charming artist, who persuades all cultured people that Pan is not dead and that even now Mount Helicon is green.' Afterwards Gordon Bryan and his musicians repeated their Aeolian programme in Oxford Town Hall, in the presence of Dr Ravel. *The Times*, reporting the event the following day (and relishing all the Latin, which it quoted without translation), observed wryly that the all-Ravel programme 'aroused a great deal of interest in musical Oxford, whose taste is, speaking generally, conservative and Teutonic'.[124]

Lennox, who had left England to escape from those very things, must have smiled when he read the paper in his guest room at Merton the next morning.*

*Half a century later he smiled again at the memories revived by the flowery Latin and the pink gown when he too received an honorary music degree at Oxford on 6 June 1970.

11

Berkeley and Ravel, Paris, 1928–33

No sooner had Lennox and Ravel returned from Oxford than it was time for the premiere run of Ravel's latest work, *Boléro*, in its original version for ballet, at the Paris Opéra. Ravel himself could not attend the opening night on 22 November 1928, because he was in Spain on a concert tour. However he was back in Paris in time for the last night, and invited Lennox to join him in his private box, with his young Oxford friends, the archaeologist David Talbot Rice, and the Russian-born writer and art historian Tamara Abelson, who were now living in Paris, where they had married a year earlier.

Ida Rubinstein, the rich Russian-born dancer, actress and impresario who commissioned the new work, had asked for a Spanish ballet based on six of the pieces in Albéniz's piano suite *Iberia*. It was to be called *Fandango*, and she herself would be the star. But after starting work on the orchestration, Ravel discovered that another composer had already acquired the arrangement rights, so he abandoned *Iberia* and created an original piece based on the castanet rhythms of the *bolero*. In Rubinstein's scenario, choreographed by Bronislava Nijinska (sister of Vaslav), and designed by Alexandre Benois, a Spanish girl dancer climbs on to a huge table in a smoky bar and begins to sway seductively to the rhythm of the music. Four handsome young men leap up to join her, stamping and clapping, while a dozen others sit at tables, pounding out the beat with their fists. Urged on, the dancer increases her tempo, whipping the men's admiration to lust. As the climax approaches, knives are drawn – but fighting is averted, and by the last chord the bar is empty. Ravel did not entirely approve of this plot, which he regarded as too 'picturesque'[1]. He had in mind something more 'industrial', set in a factory – like, for example, his family's engineering works.[2] His idea was that the roar of heavy machinery should provide the background for a scenario in which factory workers dance out the story of a bullfighter killed by a jealous rival. (It was staged like this at the Opéra in

1941, with choreography by Serge Lifar and designs by Ravel's friend Léon Leyritz.)

With its throbbing rhythm, repetitive melody and steady crescendo, *Boléro* can easily be heard as a 'musical metaphor for the sexual act', an expression of his 'secret and probably unconsummated' homosexual yearnings,[3] but Ravel never gave any indication that this was his intention, or even that he was aware of any such interpretation. The one thing that he was absolutely adamant about was that the rhythm should remain mechanically constant throughout, neither accelerating nor slowing down. He was furious when Toscanini came to Paris in 1930 and played it twice as fast as the metronome marking, and added insult to injury by increasing the tempo at the end. When Ravel complained, Toscanini told him he did not know anything about his own music: the Toscanini way, the Italian maestro insisted, was the only way to make *Boléro* work.[4] Whether sped up to the authentic tempo of a Spanish *bolero*, or taken with Ravel's clockwork precision, *Boléro* soon became quite phenomenally popular, the piano version selling out as soon as it was published. It is now reckoned to be one of the most frequently-played pieces of classical music ever written, and the royalties on this one work alone are estimated to have amounted to more than £40m.[5]

Lennox left no record of the performance he saw, but, writing in his diary many years later, he indicated that he preferred Ravel's earlier works. *Boléro*, he felt, was a wonderful idea brilliantly executed, but such a method of composing was 'too arbitrary to lead anywhere', and 'its final paroxysm so calculated that it can thrill only once'.[6]

It thrilled on the first night, which marked not only the premiere of *Boléro*, but the launch of *Les ballets Ida Rubinstein*, and the introduction of two other new scores. First on the programme was Honegger's *Les noces d'Amour et de Psyché*, which arranged Bach for full symphony orchestra, then came Milhaud's arrangement of Liszt's recreation of Schubert waltzes, *Les soirées de Vienne*;[7] *Boléro* was last.

Tamara Talbot Rice recalled something of the excitement of the last night in her autobiography. In particular she remembered that Ravel had not joined them in the box till the moment the curtain was going up on his ballet at the very end of the evening. He was immaculately dressed in tails, and, to her surprise, he was not nervous but excited. It was only afterwards, when the fans who had surged on to the stage to mob Ida Rubinstein had been returned to the auditorium, and the tumultuous applause had at last died down, that they learned why

Ravel had been so late – and so uncharacteristically exhilarated. 'Still struggling to control his mirth, he explained that the train bringing him to Paris running late, he had changed into evening clothes in one of its lavatories. Seldom, he thought, could a composer have dressed for one of his first nights in quite such unexalted surroundings.'[8]

For this complicated manoeuvre, adjusting braces, laces and bow tie in a tiny space bucketing on a railway line, it must have helped that Ravel was so small – barely five foot three in his stockinged feet; and the escapade appealed to his childlike nature. But the operation will have been lengthy, for he was quite the dandy: no longer, perhaps, the *gandin* of his youth, but still the 'impeccable and style-conscious dresser', studiously matching his costume to the occasion.[9] And no less carefully choosing the venue. Outside the Opéra Ravel called a cab and took Lennox and his friends to Le Boeuf sur le Toit, a couple of minutes westwards, to mull over his unexpected triumph in his favourite corner.

When Lennox could decently get a word in edgeways, he probably passed on some backstage gossip from two young English dancers he had made friends with. One was Cocteau's ex-lover Rupert Doone, who was a soloist in the Rubinstein company (but gave up dancing two years later to help found the Group Theatre of London, for which he directed various productions involving Auden, Isherwood and Britten). The other was Frederick Ashton, who had joined Ida Rubinstein at the beginning of August, and spent his first few weeks in Paris in Lennox's flat in Montmartre, while Lennox was on the Riviera with his parents. (Lennox also knew the conductor of *Boléro*, Walter Straram, who had conducted his *Suite* the previous February, with the Straram Orchestra, which he regarded as 'perhaps the best in Paris at the moment'; no conductor in Paris, Lennox wrote gratefully in 1933, 'has done more for young and unknown composers'.[10])

According to Ashton, the reclusive Mme Rubinstein used to take class separately from the company, but when it was necessary to 'piece things together', her chauffeur would drive her to the rehearsal hall, then roll out a red carpet so she could walk to the door like a star.[11] For some of the *Boléro* rehearsals the dancers were summoned to Rubinstein's elegant house in the place des États-Unis, and told to put on clean white shirts and white socks. Before entering the Bakst-designed interiors, each boy was handed a bottle of eau de cologne, because Ida Rubinstein could not bear the smell of sweat. White-gloved and richly clad in furs she walked herself through her part, while the mystified dancers just watched, feeling they were nothing less than a ballet 'run by an Electress of a Palatinate for her own amusement'. At the end of the rehearsal a footman passed round a plate of *petits fours.* [12]

Though Rubinstein was remote, enigmatic and dictatorial, Ashton admitted she had 'style and dignity and immaculate manners'. He was mesmerized by her tall slim figure, dark russet hair and heavy-lidded eyes, even if he did not have the highest regard for her actual dancing – or her false teeth, which once dropped out while she was taking an arabesque in *Les Sylphides.*[13] For the rest of his life he dined out on his Ida Rubinstein impression, tottering around like a 'sick ostrich', with 'curiously hunched shoulders and spread, bent knees', throwing back his head, fluttering his eyes and 'making little moues'.[14]

Ashton's English friend, the dancer (and, later, designer) William Chappell, was also in that opening production of *Boléro* – at least for the first night.[15] He and the painter Edward Burra had travelled up to Paris after a sailor-spotting holiday with some lesbian friends on the Mediterranean at Toulon.

The flat which Ashton borrowed that summer (at the suggestion of the Widow Lloyd, who was having an affair with Billy Chappell) – and in search of which Chappell and Edward Burra plunged '40 miles into Old Montmartre (the heart of the Apache quarter you know)'[16] – was not actually Lennox's at all. It belonged to John Greenidge, who had found it when he first went to Paris in 1926 to study theatre design, and shared it with Lennox from early 1928 when Lennox moved out of Mont Cenis. The new flat was in the cobbled rue du Ruisseau, just beyond the Cimetière de Saint-Vincent and the Métro station Lamarck-Caulaincourt, on the upper floor of a little lodging house at No. 4, next door to a *pâtisserie.* The Widow Lloyd, who visited John Greenidge there in 1927, just before Lennox moved in, took some photographs of the outside of the house, and pasted them into his album with the ironic caption, 'Pavilon [*sic*] Henri IV'.[17] Since this was the name of the hunting lodge at Fontainebleau where Henri of Navarre is supposed to have conducted a secret affair, he may have been suggesting that John and Lennox were similarly entwined; or he could have been making a coded reference to their growing attraction to the Catholic Church, Henri having been the famously tolerant leader of the French Protestants who converted to Catholicism and introduced the Edict of Nantes which protected the Huguenots. (It is unlikely to have referred to the famous nineteenth-century restaurant of that name, run by the chef who invented Béarnaise sauce, because neither John nor Lennox could so much as boil an egg.)

From the photographs, both inside and out, 4 rue du Ruisseau looks spacious, plainly elegant and attractive, and John and Lennox, who could have afforded better if they had wanted to move, were justly proud of their home. Ashton, however, found it 'gloomy, damp and run down'[18] – maybe because he was missing company in general and his mother's in particular. In fact he was so homesick that he sometimes went downstairs to talk to the concierge, 'an extraordinary old creature with a riddled face'.[19]

For all the time that Lennox and John shared the flat in rue du Ruisseau, Lennox kept on – and probably let out – his original rooms at 19 rue du Mont Cenis, and in the autumn of 1929, when John returned to London to resume his practice as an architect, in his studio flat in Great Ormond Street, Bloomsbury, Lennox moved back to Mont Cenis, announcing that this was 'now my permanent address'.[20]

Lennox was later to join John Greenidge at 28 Ormond Chambers, at the east end of Great Ormond Street, surrounded by the Young Communist League, the National Minority Movement and Miss Italia Conti's School of Dancing,[21] and there they both remained till they were bombed out during the war. Great Ormond Street was quite a haven for Oxford men: the Widow Lloyd had had a flat in Norton Chambers since about 1925, Tom Driberg had moved there in 1927, and the novelist Anthony Powell joined the Ormond set in 1934, in a house at the other end of the road, opposite the children's hospital.[22] (Cedric Morris and Lett Haines, fellow artists and former Paris friends, though not Oxford men, lived at No. 32 till they left in the 1930s to found their painting school in East Anglia.) Lennox knew and liked them all, but his quiet reserve and sense of privacy were at variance with their flamboyance and outrageousness, and he was never more than a fringe member of the circle. If Burra, Chappell, Ashton and co. were camp queens who preferred the Dandyism of Montparnasse on the left bank, Lennox and his friends were straight queens who felt more at home in gritty Montmartre on the right.

Tamara Talbot Rice, who saw a lot of Lennox and John in 1928, claimed that they were not living in Montmartre at all, but in Montparnasse – 'in an enchanting little house rented from the painter [Jean] Lurçat, who had decorated it with abstract and cubist murals'.[23] Actually this was never their home, but John's studio. He needed the extra space to design and construct sets and costumes for the theatre and the cinema – and Lurçat let him use it while he himself was travelling abroad for a year. The house at No. 3 Villa Seurat was part of an ultra-modern complex of artists' villas newly built by Lurçat's brother, the Communist architect André Lurçat, in a charming lane in the Montsouris *quartier*. (The murals which Tamara Talbot Rice remembered were the fruits of a new venture by Jean Lurçat, who was better known as a tapestry designer, but wall painting never brought him the same satisfaction and in 1931 he resumed tapestry-making.)

It seems likely that Lennox and John were lovers during these early years in Paris. If so, the shy and inexperienced Lennox was probably seduced by the older and more worldly John (who may himself have been seduced by the seasoned, charming and irresistibly persuasive Widow Lloyd; as well as sharing a flat in London, the two Johns had been on holiday together to Chambéry in the spring of 1926, and they had spent that summer at the Spread Eagle inn at Thame, and the Bushey studios, making films with Terence Greenidge, David Talbot Rice, Rudolph Messel, John Fernald and others.)[24] Lennox kept in his scrapbook some photos showing John Greenidge and himself together in the Ruisseau flat in January 1928, and these suggest an intimacy that is closer than 'flatmates'. It is only a suggestion, a feeling, but somehow John's body language gives an impression of ownership, even somewhat anxious, ownership of Lennox, while Lennox's gives an impression of willing dependency. John (four years older than Lennox) poses in a silk dressing gown; Lennox, in polo-neck sweater, holds his pipe, leans slightly in towards John (who shows recognition of the gesture) and seems lost in a dream. The same look – and sweater and pipe – feature in an oil portrait of Lennox which John himself had painted in the Mont Cenis flat in 1926. Lennox is sitting at a table, with his pipe in his right hand and his arms folded on a sheet of handwritten music (two staves, so it must be piano music – perhaps the *Toccata* which he had written at Negron the previous autumn). At his right elbow are his spectacles, and his pipe bowl is to his left.* Behind and to the right is a

*Kathleen Walker suggests that the pipe was an aid to concentration. It is not the smoking that focuses the mind, she writes (as the widow of a pipe-smoker), but 'the fiddling about with tobacco, tamping down and fying out with a dwile' - a Norfolk expression that means, Mrs Walker explains, 'to clean out with a clout' (email Kathleen Walker to TS, 13 October 2005).

theatrically-draped curtain, bearing the signature 'Greenidge 1926' and to the left of the picture is a view through a window of some Paris posters of the day, including no fewer than four for a bank in which the word 'CREDIT' seems to shout for attention. (Perhaps John thought Lennox's music deserved more 'credit' than it was getting.) Lennox is staring directly in front of him, with a faraway look in his eye: young, hopeful, vulnerable, even a little sad.

At about the time that John Greenidge returned to London – and maybe precipitating his departure – José Raffalli came into Lennox's life. Almost nothing is known about him, except that he was Corsican, and a little younger than Lennox. Photographs show a short, smooth-skinned, slightly-built figure, with something foxy about him. He has short black hair smoothed back from a widow's peak to reveal a high wide brow, with a small shapely mouth and pale, compelling eyes. It is easy to imagine he was vain, demanding and tricky. A few brief references in letters between Lennox, Benjamin Britten and Peter Burra, some years later, suggest a man of lower social status, with a forceful personality. Neither Ben nor Peter seems to have shown any sort of interest in him, though both met him. Lennox fell very much under José's spell – and the Berkeleys, who met him when Lennox brought him down to the South of France in the summer, were not happy about the relationship. According to Lennox's aunt Nellie Harris, 'the Berkeleys couldn't stand him: they thought he was taking Lennox for a ride'. Apart from believing that he was generally a bad influence, their particular worry was that he might be a drain on Lennox's financial resources.[25] But Lennox was strongly drawn to José: he liked epicene young men and, undomesticated himself, he needed a practical hand at home. It was soon after 1930 that José moved into the Mont Cenis flat, organizing Lennox's life, doing the shopping and cooking, hanging the pictures, moving the furniture, screening Lennox's friends. José was musical but not a musician[26] – though he may have played the piano a little, since Lennox later dedicated to him his set of *Five Short Pieces*. The affair seems to have lost its intimacy by 1932, when Lennox left Nadia and went to live in Cap Ferrat with his parents, but by then Lennox had installed José in a new flat, at 1 Cité Chaptal, just around the corner from the rue Ballu, and there he stayed, with and without Lennox, but still financially dependent on him, and still good friends, till he was called up as the Germans advanced on Paris in 1940. The regiment he joined was part of the *Défense Passive*, a sort of civil defence force set up to protect Paris from fires and looting, and to engage in occasionally unpassive guerrilla operations like the sabotaging of German vehicles. It may not have been the front line, but it was more patriotic than fleeing south as many Parisians did in June 1940, and it must have impressed those members of Lennox's family who had dismissed José as effete.

With the Talbot Rices, who were based in Paris for three years, Lennox and John dined together as much as once a week, went to art exhibitions and on outings to the country. One of their favourite destinations was the forest of Fontainebleau. Wherever they went they talked, and the subjects ranged, Tamara remembered, from the landscape paintings of the Barbizon school (the nineteenth-century landscape artists who lived in the village of that name in the Forest of Fontainebleau) to the wit of Satie and the one-act operettas like Ibert's *Angélique* that were so popular at Madame Bériza's theatre in the Champs-Elysées.[27]

Lennox had other reasons for visiting Fontainebleau: Nadia taught at the American Conservatory there, and his parents had a holiday house in the neighbourhood. To escape from the heat and hordes of Nice, the Hastings Berkeleys took a succession of houses – the first, on the edge of the forest at Veneux-les-Sablons, where the Seine meets the Loing, the second at Moret, further up the Loing, the river much painted by Monet, Renoir and Sisley. They had known and loved the woods and rivers of the *département* of Seine-et-Marne ever since the early days of their marriage when they used to stay at Fontainebleau with Hastings's aunt Albine van Havre. Lennox often went to see them there, donning his plus-fours and his Fair Isle stockings, sometimes taking John with him. Photos from the late Twenties show them posing with the frail old parents: bearded Hastings, thin as a rake and wearing a Homburg; Aline, gentle and sad, in a fur-shouldered coat; John unsmiling and detached; Lennox boylike and nervous; and occasionally Lennox's sister Geraldine, plump and maidenly in her home-made clothes. (If Geraldine seems to play a shadowy role in this book, it is because her place in Lennox's life was indeed shadowy: eccentric and gullible but firmly independent, she went her own way – until the family could ignore her strange behaviour no longer.)

Even given the formality of the times, it is a curious feature of these old Berkeley photos that the subjects look so stiff and grim. They seem to bear no relationship to one another: Hastings and Aline do not look married, Lennox shows no sign of being their son, nor Geraldine their daughter, and John could be anyone's friend – or nobody's. The figures do not touch, or even look at, anyone else; there is no sign of parental pride or filial fondness – indeed there is little sign of any interest whatsoever, let alone the adoration that Lennox was known to have felt for his mother. They all seem to be leading entirely separate lives, and possibly rather sad ones. Perhaps Lennox's relationship with his father was more strained than he later admitted, and these group photos were a trial for them all. Or perhaps the Russian cook was a disaster and they all had permanent indigestion.

Not far from Moret was the village of Grez-sur-Loing, home since 1899 of Frederick Delius, now aged, blind and paralysed. Lennox admired Delius's incidental music to Flecker's play *Hassan*,[28] and when his friend Gordon Bryan proposed a visit in the summer of 1927, he eagerly accepted the chance of meeting such an important figure in English music. Nor was Delius the only luminary there that day, since there were two other composers staying with him at Grez: Henry Balfour Gardiner (composer of such very English works as the evening hymn, *Te lucis ante terminum*, and *Shepherd Fennel's Dance*) and the Australian composer Percy Grainger, together with Grainger's girlfriend Ella Ström, the Swedish poet he was to marry the following year in a spectacular stage-managed wedding in the Hollywood Bowl (with 20,000 people watching, and an orchestra playing his latest work, *To a Nordic Princess*).

Though only just in his thirties, Gordon Bryan seems to have known everyone in music in the late Twenties. On another occasion in 1927 he invited Lennox down to his house in Bournemouth to meet the South African-born composer Victor Hely-Hutchinson (later Director of Music at the BBC); and on one of many trips to Scandinavia he had got to know Sibelius. The Grez visit must have come about because Bryan was, or had once been, a pupil of Percy Grainger.[29]

On a hot day in the middle of August the two young men drove down through the great barrier of woodland south-west of Paris to the medieval village of Grez-sur-Loing, where Delius lived in a rambling old house with a walled garden. Eric Fenby, the young Yorkshireman who was to arrive at Grez the following year to act as Delius's amanuensis, has left a vivid description of his first glimpse of the elderly composer: 'gaunt, deathly pale, his classical head proud and erect', looking like a Roman cardinal.[30] For Lennox's visit, the old man was dressed in summer whites, with a straw hat and dark glasses, and sitting in a bath chair. There are no written records of the visit, but Lennox's photo album contains photos (by Gordon Bryan) which convey something of the happy atmosphere of the day.* These show Delius in his chair, by the garden wall, with his head turned towards the young male nurse, Wolf Karge, who is reading to him; Grainger, in a dark three-piece suit, talking to Delius outside the French windows; Balfour Gardiner, sprawling in a wicker chair with his leg in the air, curly-headed Grainger behind him, laughing, and pretty Ella sitting on the grass in front of them both, under a big floppy hat with a fringe; and Grainger with both Ella and Mrs Delius.

Balfour Gardiner had given up composing by then. He had a theory that at a certain age a man ceased to be musical, and, at fifty, he felt that he had reached that age; besides he was disenchanted by the changes in musical life since the war, and gloomy about the future. Now he spent his time planting trees and keeping pigs on his estate on the Shaftesbury Downs (two acres of which he was to leave to the nation), and generously helping young composers whom he judged to be on the right track.[31] The brilliant Grainger had even more pet theories than Balfour Gardiner – Delius, who was especially fond of him, thought he was positively 'bunged up' with them.[32] Balfour Gardiner would not have been able to resist letting off steam about modern musical life in general, and doubtless Lennox was encouraged to let off some of his steam about the English scene in particular: its chronic conservatism, its 'regrettable lack of interest in the newer developments of art'.[33]

Gordon Bryan played a prominent part in the promotion of Lennox's early work – and a prominent part in evaluating it too. He seems to have heard his first Berkeley at the concert in the New Chenil Galleries in London in the spring of 1926 when Anthony Bernard conducted his London Chamber Orchestra in the *Introduction and Dance*: Bryan described it as 'a brief but effective little work' (though Lennox had disowned it by 1929).[34] In 1927 he and his Aeolian Players gave the world premiere in London (repeated in Oxford) of the *Prélude, Intermezzo et Final* which Lennox had written in Paris and Veneux that summer (and dedicated to Bryan). And in 1928 Bryan programmed the *Sonatine pour*

*The album does not attribute the pictures to Bryan, but one of them is reproduced in Arthur Hutchings, *Delius*, and credited on p. ix as being taken by Gordon Bryan.

Clarinette et Piano in his chamber music series at the Aeolian Hall, when he himself played the piano part, with Frederick Thurston playing the clarinet.[35] (Six years later the *Sonatina* was scheduled for a London performance, but the score got lost in the post, and the clarinettist decided to play Bax's new *Sonata* twice instead.[36]) An unidentified review (from a musical paper), signed only 'F. B.', accused Lennox of having 'caught some of the Parisian tricks fashionable at the present moment' – in particular, Poulenc's way of creating a double tonality.[37]

The musical establishment back home did not approve of these French experiments, or Lennox's interest in them. Even Gordon Bryan, friend, interpreter and advocate, had his doubts about the value of Lennox's total immersion in the new music of Paris, and he did not hesitate to express them. In an article in the *Monthly Musical Record* in 1929 he noted Lennox's debt to Hindemith in three new sonatinas (for violin, clarinet and piano, and piano). Whilst these works were part of a 'steady output of increasing importance' which Berkeley had produced in the three years since his arrival in Paris, they betrayed a 'narrowing [of] his outlook into what may be styled anti-diatonicism' – and the reason was clear: too much exposure to contemporary music. What Berkeley needed now, Bryan believed, was a strict diet of the classics. After six months of this, his work would show 'considerably more originality than he has, as yet, allowed himself to attain'.[38] (Bryan himself had recently given up composing for arranging, and was now immersed in the Domenico Scarlatti sonatas which he was to quarry for a whole series of orchestral concertos – in the hopes, perhaps, of achieving an originality of his own.[39])

This well-meant but harsh, and public, criticism from a friend and fellow musician must have stung. Perhaps there was even a falling-out, because Berkeley does not feature in any more of Bryan's London concerts. It may be significant that the piece Lennox produced after the publication of the Bryan article, the *Suite for Flute, Oboe, Violin, Viola and Cello*, was written under the pseudonym John Dursley (John, by association with Greenidge, perhaps; Dursley from a courtesy title of the Berkeleys). Did Lennox now feel the name of Berkeley was so blackened by association with the new music of Paris that the only way to ensure a fair hearing was to pretend to be someone else? If he did, he changed his mind back again: on the manuscript score which he gave to Nadia (and which her executors returned to the family on her death) he crossed out, or overlaid, all the John Dursleys and replaced them with

Lennox Berkeleys. But the shaft of Bryan's message – that Lennox needed to return to the classics – may have struck home, because the five movements of this new suite are written in 'baroque and earlier stylisations'.[40]

Apart from Ravel, the contemporaries who left their mark on Lennox's early music are easy to trace both from the music itself and from the series of eighteen reports from Paris, which he wrote for the *Monthly Musical Record* from 1929 to 1934,* (and which gave him privileged access to new music's front line during those brilliant and creative years). These composers (and Lennox's favourite works by them) include: Hindemith (the cantata *Die Serenaden* and the *Klaviermusik* Pt 1, both of which Lennox bought in Paris in 1927), Honegger (*Rugby* and the *Cello Concerto*), Martinu (chamber works), Poulenc (*Le Bal masqué*, *Mouvements perpétuels* and *Concert Champêtre*, which he heard Wanda Landowska playing, with Pierre Monteux conducting, in Paris in 1929), and Ravel (*String Quartet in F*, orchestral suite *Ma Mère l'Oye*, *La Valse* and the *Septet for String Quartet, Harp, Flute and Clarinet*). He also admired the 'very strong and personal' later work of Albert Roussel, which deserved to be better known abroad. The *Suite in F* of 1926 was 'particularly fine and vigorous' and his setting of the *80th Psalm* was 'interesting but rather complicated'.[41] But the greatest influence on Lennox, as on all other composers of his generation, was Stravinsky.

Lennox became friends with Stravinsky's son, Soulima, the composer and pianist who was a fellow pupil at the rue Ballu. In 1934, when Stravinsky moved his wife Katya and his mother up to Paris from their house in Nice, Lennox got to know the whole family. They had a large flat by the President's palace in the rue du Faubourg-St-Honoré, and sometimes Lennox was invited to dinner, amidst the practical old furniture and modern paintings with which Stravinsky liked to surround himself – and the clouds of smoke that rose from his daily ration of forty bad French cigarettes. Lennox was introduced to the fine claret which Stravinsky bought by the barrel in Bordeaux, and treated to what a reporter a couple of years later called 'the drawing room charm of the verbal virtuoso'.[42]

On one occasion Stravinsky asked Lennox to play some of his piano music, but Lennox was so awestruck that he forgot to register the

*Examined in greater detail in MLB, pp. 18–20.

verdict. He did, however, remember that Stravinsky was kind, well-mannered, elegant – and 'terrified of his mother' Anna Kirillovna Stravinskaya.[43] He was courteous to all, 'though he held very definite opinions about everything and could be devastatingly critical of what he didn't like'.[44] Lennox was relieved to discover that Stravinsky, though 'intensely purposeful',[45] was no different from ordinary composers in finding it impossibly difficult to get started on a piece. He would wander round the flat, checking the windows and the boilers, looking for any excuse to delay the moment when he would have to face the 'bureaucratically neat' desk, where he somehow managed to compose for three hours every morning.[46] Lennox knew the feeling well, and, as he often told his students years later, he had to force himself to sit at his desk and do a bit of a scoring to get his mind into gear; the rest, he discovered, would flow from there.[47]

Lennox loved everything Stravinsky wrote – till he rejected tonality for serialism. In particular he admired the constant experimentation – the 'boldly striking out afresh' with each new work.[48] And he was grateful for the lead which Stravinsky gave in steering music back to classicism – 'setting his face against all sensuous and sentimental appeals' and making music for 'pure aesthetic feeling only'.[49] Lennox liked his music plain. In March 1933 he heard Stravinsky and Samuel Dushkin playing the *Duo Concertant* (twice – so that people would have a better chance of getting to know it), and loved it, as he told Nadia Boulanger, 'It's truly a masterpiece – how can one find the music of Stravinsky cold?! It's certainly spare, but properly shorn of all that does not come from the heart.'[50] Lennox did not comment on the other violin-and-piano pieces in that night's all-Stravinsky programme in the Concert Hall of Broadcasting House: the *Suite on Themes of Pergolesi* and five transcriptions from the opera *The Nightingale*, and the ballets *Firebird* and *Petrushka*.[51]

Another important influence on Lennox in those Paris days was Arthur Honegger, the German-Swiss composer brought up in France, whose music showed a respect for technique, a fondness for the counterpoint of Bach and a hint of the Romanticism which Les Six were supposed to be dead against, moderated by the economy they actively encouraged. In 1924, while he was still at Oxford, Lennox had bought the score of Honegger's orchestral tone poem *Pacific 231*,[52] which describes a journey of the steam locomotive of that name, and in his first report for the *Monthly Musical Record*, he referred to the second orchestral tone poem, *Rugby*, as 'a masterpiece'. Although the work makes no attempt to imitate the sounds of a rugby match, Lennox wrote, 'the general atmosphere of exhilaration, speed and physical energy is reproduced with wonderful vividness and power'.[53] Honegger was essentially more serious than other members of Les Six, and when Ida Rubinstein (who had almost as great a knack for creating artistic partnerships as Diaghilev) introduced him to the poet, playwright and diplomat Paul Claudel, he got caught up in the Christian revival in France, producing, amongst other large-scale religious works, his stage oratorio, *Jeanne d'Arc au bûcher*.

Francis Poulenc, who was even more profoundly affected by the Catholic revival of the 1930s, was a much closer friend of Lennox, both then and for the rest of his life. Though Poulenc was not a student of Boulanger's – and could not have been: the two were poles apart – it was the rue Ballu where he and Lennox first met. Turning a blind eye to the 'dissolute *boulevardier*' side of Poulenc, Boulanger had invited 'the neo-classicist and mystic' side to one of her Wednesdays, and their mutual respect turned to friendship.[54] Poulenc even sought Boulanger's musical advice, and was given 'constructive criticism and praise'.[55] Through one of the singers in Boulanger's madrigal group, Marie-Blanche, comtesse Jean de Polignac, Poulenc angled for a commission from the comtesse's formidable aunt, Winnaretta, princesse Edmond de Polignac, which eventually produced the *Concerto for Two Pianos* and the *Organ Concerto*.

The music critic Claude Rostand identified the two sides of Poulenc as '*moine*' (monk) and '*voyou*' (guttersnipe),[56] and, since few composers have worn their hearts on their musical sleeves to the extent that Poulenc did, both monk and guttersnipe are there for all to hear in his music.[57] Lennox regretted years later that Poulenc was so easily dismissed 'as a composer of frivolities, fashionable in the 1920s', when he had written such remarkably intense religious music – the *Litanies à la Vierge Noir*, for example, the *Mass*, the *Four Motets*, the *Stabat Mater* – and more than 150 songs. Lennox thought that Poulenc was at his best in the songs. Their prevailing mood of nostalgia, he said, was unique in music: 'Poulenc ... evolved a technique of song-writing that is quite his own, based on his melodic gift and skill in writing for the piano, his very individual harmony, and understanding of how to set words.'[58]

Lennox thought it also helped that Poulenc was an excellent pianist, because he had been able to make the accompaniments 'exceptionally interesting and effective'.[59] Poulenc's music, Lennox believed, was music for pleasure. He was a natural, rather than an intellectual, composer, with a spontaneity that was positively refreshing, and his work was instantly recognizable because of his personal use of a basically traditional harmony: a gorgeous diatonic harmony that is often described as bittersweet. As a man, Lennox said, Poulenc had a very strong personality, and an irresistible charm and humour which turned some of the most unpromising situations into fun. He had a capacity for warm friendship, and was notably loyal to colleagues: once he was convinced of a fellow composer's talent and integrity he would support him through thick and thin.[60] He also possessed an easy confidence. Lennox felt there was a basic optimism in him that must have sprung from his faith – the deep Catholic faith that came from his Aveyron roots and was revived and enhanced by the pilgrimage to Notre Dame de Rocamadour in August 1936, which brought him back to the Church and directly inspired his *Litanies*. It was this religious sense, coupled with an innate modesty, that led him to direct that there should be no music at his funeral – especially none of his – except the Gregorian Chant which was still then part of the traditional liturgy of the Catholic Church. (In the event, the funeral, in the church of Saint Sulpice in Paris on 2 February 1963, did contain more music than just the plainchant: some Bach played on the organ by Marcel Dupré.)

Lennox had been wrestling with the problems of religious faith at Oxford. In Paris his spiritual journey reached its climax, as he finally made the decision to convert, and prepared for his reception into the Roman Catholic Church. It was not a dramatic conversion, like that of some of his friends and acquaintances in the Cocteau circle – Satie, for example, or the gay writer and thinker Julian Green, or the gay and Jewish poet Max Jacob, or Cocteau himself – who were processed (largely unsuccessfully) by the 'conversion machine' of the philosopher Jacques Maritain and his wife at Meudon. The Maritains' grand strategy was the 'rechristianizing' of France's intellectual and artistic *élite*.[61] Lennox's regeneration, like Lennox himself, was private, quiet, slow and profound.

12
Freda, London, 1928–30

Try as they might, the old Nunneys were not ideal foster parents for their granddaughter Freda Bernstein, a sturdy and spirited little girl of four and a half. Though still only in their sixties, Fred and Blanch were both frail and worn out after a lifetime of hard work and bringing up no fewer than ten children of their own. In addition Blanch had a problem with her legs and found it difficult to get about. Financially it could have been a help for them if the Public Trustee had been fairer in providing for Freda's upkeep, but the reality was that the Public Trustee interpreted Isaac's will to the disfavour of the Nunneys. 'My father must have thought', says Freda, 'that as they were poor they'd probably lay into some of my money – which wouldn't have been the case.' The Public Trustee was no more generous to Freda herself. Though her cousins and friends in Queen's Park knew her as 'the Heiress', she was not even allowed any pocket money for sweets.[1]

There is some evidence, though it is not at all clear why, that the Nunneys disguised Freda's parentage, passing her off as Fred's niece. Their grandson Anthony Nunney (Alfred's only son), who got to know Freda well when she stayed with his family for a short time during the war, was not aware till he met her again sixty-three years later that she was actually his first cousin. Although he knew of the existence of Isaac Bernstein (and recalled seeing an 'impressive' photo of Isaac in his grandparents' house), he never knew that Bernstein had been married to someone called Grace Amy Nunney – or that this Grace was his father's sister. Both Anthony Nunney and Freda were astonished, even disturbed, when in 2006 they discovered this mysterious gap in his knowledge of the family history, but, rather than face the perils of exploring the cause, they were content to put it down to their grandparents' constant fear of a claim on Freda's inheritance by her Bernstein relatives in South Wales.[2] This was undoubtedly why the Nunneys kept quiet about the Bernsteins, but it does not explain why they were equally secretive about their own Grace. It is possible that Fred and Blanch Nunney were ashamed of Grace – either because she married Isaac Bernstein against their wishes, or because they believed she had deceived him into marriage by failing to reveal some unpalatable truth about her life up to then. There is nothing to support either conjecture, but there is evidence (from Freda) that her grandparents withheld information about her father and his Bernstein relations, and (from Anthony Nunney) that they withheld information about Freda's mother. Furthermore, it is significant that Freda has never seen any photographs of herself with either of her parents, or of them with one another, or any at all of her father and other members of the Bernstein family. It is impossible that such pictures did not exist, and difficult to believe that when the Public Trustee came to dispose of the Bernstein house in the Finchley Road that its staff did not offer any family photographs to the Nunneys, so the orphaned child would have some memento of her parents. Perhaps, though, in his deluded final years, Isaac Bernstein himself destroyed all his photos.

Unaware of the family politics, Freda was happy living with her grandparents in their large, empty, old-fashioned, working-class house at 126 Lancefield Street. It was part of an estate of tightly-packed terraced houses built by the United Land Company in the late 1870s specifically for churchgoing artisans, clerks, policemen and railwaymen. The first tenant of Number 126 had been Freda's great-grandfather, Frederick James Nunney. Born at Burford in the Cotswolds in 1841, Frederick James was at least the fourth generation of a family of builders, slaters and plasterers, which moved from Burford to Paddington in the early 1830s. Before his twenty-second birthday, Frederick James sailed to America with a view to emigrating, but, failing to find work, he had returned to his parents' house in Cirencester Street, Paddington (by the High Church St Mary Magdalene's, just south of the Grand Junction Canal). And in 1863, having set up on his own as a builder's plasterer in Windsor Place, Paddington,* he married Jesse Margaret Steele, daughter of a carriage-builder in Fitzroy Square. Their first son, Frederick Charles Nunney (Freda's grandfather), was born at 3 Windsor Place in 1864, and by the time he had come of age, the family and the business had moved to 126 Lancefield Street, where

*Windsor Place no longer exists, but was within the parish of Holy Trinity Church, Bishop's [Bridge] Road, W2.

Frederick James himself did all the internal plasterwork, including the ceiling decorations, and possibly the external stucco work. In 1886 Frederick Charles married Blanch [*sic*] Allen, daughter of a butler who ran his own victualling business in the covered market in Oxford, and in 1919, on the death of his father, he inherited the plastering business and the tenancy of 126.

By the time Freda went to live with her grandparents, Frederick Charles had long since retired from plastering. Freda remembers him as gentle, artistic, humorous and kind – 'a darling'. She did not know then, but her cousin Anthony Nunney told her in 2006, that 'Fred' had once been a music hall 'song and dance man', and an athlete – a runner with the Queen's Park Harriers.[3] Blanch was musical and taught the piano. Sometimes Freda was sent over the road to the pub to put a bet on a horse, and on these occasions she would take a jug to fill a pint of mild-and-bitter. Sometimes Grandfather Nunney would take her to the market in Kilburn Lane, and as a treat on Sundays he would walk her up the road to hear the band in Queen's Park, scene of his early successes as a runner.

For all her happy memories of her Nunney grandparents, Freda remembers 126 Lancefield Street as a lonely house with no electricity. She used to have to wash in a tin hip-bath in front of the kitchen stove (where Blanch cooked the Sunday joint on a vertical spit called a 'jack'); the lavatory was in a shed in the back garden; and there was a glass-roofed workshop where the plastering equipment lay idle. To help cover their running costs, the Nunneys took in a lodger, an elderly spinster called Miss Fiedler, who lived in a room half way up the stairs. Freda thought she was a witch. But Miss Fiedler was nothing by comparison with Freda's own personal phantoms, which terrified her to such an extent that she used to creep out of bed at night and settle down on the landing at the top of the stairs. 'I sort of sat on the floor and leant against the banisters. I didn't like being alone.' (Fear of being left alone has stayed with her into old age, so that to this day Freda still sleeps with the light and the radio on – often the television too, and likes nothing better than to hear the sounds of her neighbours late at night.)

Haunted by frightening visions of stifling hands, run-over dogs and elderly witches, it is not surprising that Freda became chronically afraid of the dark, and a persistent bed-wetter. In the rough streets of north Paddington, and, in particular, at school at the Paddington and Maida

Vale High in Elgin Avenue, she also picked up a cockney accent, some 'coarse habits' and a rich vocabulary which ran to 'lewd jokes'. A snap of a seaside outing at about this time shows a delightfully ill-assorted trio on a bench at Herne Bay in Kent: Grandfather Fred in a cloth cap and co-respondent shoes, Granny Blanch with a parasol, a clutch bag and wrinkled stockings, and Freda, a wild and sturdy-legged little girl with gappy teeth and thick fair plaits – grubby plimsolls on her feet, a bandage around one ankle, and a stick of rock in her hand. Herne Bay was where this colourful trio always went in the summer, staying in St George's Terrace overlooking the sea, at a boarding house run by Mrs Marie Russell. Blanch Nunney had been a childhood friend of Mrs Russell – and of Matilda Wood, later to achieve fame as the Queen of the Music Hall, Marie Lloyd. Blanch and Mrs Russell and Fred knew all the old songs, and Freda, herself tone deaf, recalled the three of them – Blanch at the piano – belting out some of Marie Lloyd's sauciest songs, 'The Boy I Love Is up in the Gallery', 'Oh Mr Porter' and 'A Little of What You Fancy Does You Good'. Mrs Russell could not do enough for her boarders, and Freda has fond memories of her holidays there, and of her friendship with Mrs Russell's 'larky' twin daughters, Tommy and Gladys, both a bit older – and considerably more experienced in what she calls 'pranks' ('they always had a lot of young men in tow, you know'[4]). The young men seem to have been foreign students who had come over to learn English, and were lodging at Mrs Russell's – playing all the latest dance tunes on her wind-up gramophone.[5]

After a couple of years the Nunneys decided they could no longer manage their high-spirited granddaughter. The Public Trustee had already reached the same conclusion, following a succession of negative reports by the welfare officer who visited Freda in Queen's Park every few months. A change of scene was prescribed, and in 1930 Freda was sent away to boarding school in Berkshire – to St Helen's, Abingdon, a Christian school 'for girls who would have to earn their own living', run by the High Anglican Wantage Sisters, in association with the smarter and better-known St Mary's, Wantage ('for débutantes').[6] (By coincidence St Mary's was the school Lennox's sister Geraldine attended up to the outbreak of the First World War.)

Mrs Joy Stibbe, then Joy Thornton, the daughter of a parson, arrived at St Helen's in the same term as Freda and recalls none of the undercurrents in Freda's life at the time – no nightmares, no bed-wetting, no screaming. She remembers only a happy, uncomplicated, approachable child, full of fun, with lots of personality, strong white teeth and flyaway curls. Never cross and never critical, she always had a kindly smile for everyone. In the classroom Freda was not backward, on the sports field she was not conspicuously forward. Though half Jewish, she took to the High Church practices of the Sisters' daily Evensong as naturally as any of the other girls. 'We were all believers, of course,' said Mrs Stibbe, 'but of the accepting kind – we didn't question.' Freda was known to be an orphan, but that did not mark her out as an oddity, since there were 'at least four girls from Russia – you know, refugees'. Nor did her name mark her out, even though 'there was a certain mystique about her: she was different'.[7]

13
Lennox, Paris, 1929–33

Lennox felt different too – at least in England. By nature a Frenchman, he was not at ease with Anglo-Saxon music, he lived with another man and he was about to convert to Roman Catholicism. Furthermore, he actually thought about things. One of the subjects that most occupied his mind was faith.

To Lennox, then and for the rest of his life, a belief in something other than human reason was fundamentally important. In his view, true religion was less to do with the power of reason than with faith. Writing about Frances Partridge's wartime diaries, *A Pacifist War*, just after the book had come out in 1978, he was exasperated by so much reasoning, and recorded in his diary, 'Lord (as Pepys would say) how depressing the rationalist philosophy is. How can one function in life on the belief that human reason is sufficient, when there is so much that it is quite unable to explain. Unbelief raises as many difficulties as does belief.'[1]

Like Cardinal Newman, Lennox had no problem with faith, but, initially, every problem identifying where the true Church was to be found – until he realized, like Newman, that if you did not have 'an interior and unreasoned conviction of the existence of God', then you were an agnostic, and that if you did (as both he and Newman did) then you were bound, sooner or later, to become a Roman Catholic.[2] There were no half measures. Evelyn Waugh, grappling with the same issues at the same time, took the same view. It seemed to him natural, even inevitable, that someone should want to become a Catholic – the only surprise was that more did not. Conversion, wrote Waugh, was like climbing out of 'a Looking-glass world, where everything is an absurd caricature, into the real world God made'. Then began 'the delicious process of exploring it limitlessly'.[3] (Curiously Waugh was actually in Paris, and staying with their mutual friends, the Talbot Rices, while Lennox was becoming a Catholic. Hearing of the break-up of Waugh's first marriage, Tamara had invited him over to help him recover – and to protect him from an American heiress who was in hot pursuit.)[4]

13 Lennox, Paris, 1929–33

In a diary entry of 1975 Lennox gave a clue as to how he came to Catholicism. Deploring the loss of the Latin Mass in the Vatican reforms, he revealed that for many people – the implication being that he was among them – it was the liturgy that had first brought them to an understanding of the Catholic Faith.[5] He realized that the Latin liturgy was not what Christianity was about, but its beauty was important – in its relation to 'the mysterious side of religion ... the numinous side that is beyond'.* He 'thought a good deal' about faith, and 'read a good deal', and came to the conclusion that the Roman Catholic Church was 'nearer the truth than anything else'.[6] Writing on the same subject in 1971, Lennox gave a further hint about the reasons for his conversion: 'the immutability of the Church's doctrine and liturgy was one of the points that, in those days, was much stressed in the course of a prospective convert's instruction.'[7] Like Waugh, he revered the Catholic Church 'not because it is established or an institution', but 'because it is true': unchanging and unchangeable, faithful to its beginnings.[8] To uphold its absolute authority as the Church established by God, Catholicism requires of the faithful a rigorous discipline, including unquestioning obedience, and the understanding that obedience to the Church is obedience to God. One of Lennox's reasons for converting was the attraction of this rigid ethical and institutional framework. He may have welcomed the Church's inflexible rules as safety railings in the constant struggle to keep to the path. (The Jacobite genes he inherited from the Drummonds and Mackenzies may also have affected his decision.)

His parents seem to have expressed no objection to his conversion – indeed his mother was an Anglo-Catholic who had actively assisted his quest for Rome. His father was an agnostic,[9] who had an intellectual preference for Protestantism on the grounds that it did not distract from business, and avoided 'blind obedience to authority' and 'the dominance of a priestly caste'. If it were possible, he argued in one of his books, to construct a religion 'free from dogma concerning the unknowable, the Protestant religion, by its natural tendency to protest and dissent ... will afford us the easiest path to that very desirable end'.[10] Like many Protestants, Hastings Berkeley was what Waugh called an 'ultimate introvert, fashioning a God to justify human behaviour'.[11]

Lennox was received into the Roman Church on 16 October 1929 in

*See Appendix 1, pp. 446–8.

the chapel of the Carmelite Convent of Sacré Coeur in Montmartre, adjacent to the basilica, by his spiritual adviser, Fr Louis Maillet, the convent's chaplain, who had supervised his instruction.[12] The conditions of his reception – as with all adults seeking to join the Catholic Church – were the knowledge and profession of the Catholic faith, and the resolve to live in accordance with it. After carefully examining his sincerity and steadfastness, the instructing priest would have had to apply to the Archbishop of Paris for authority to absolve him from excommunication and so receive him into the Church. Baptism was the next stage – by Fr Maillet, in the presence of witnesses – after which Lennox would have made his confession and received sacramental absolution.

He took the Catholic name of François, and that is the only forename used on the certificate, which he signed, simply, 'Berkeley' (not because he considered himself the rightful heir to the title but because he could not decide whether, as a newly-baptized Catholic, he was now Lennox or François).* His chosen saint was the animal-loving monk of Assisi, who had been Lennox's age when he turned to a life of asceticism and mysticism, drawn by what he felt to be the joyousness of religion and a love of nature.[13] This same St Francis was also Aline Berkeley's favourite saint.

Just after his conversion Lennox seems to have made the acquaintance of a distinguished prelate whose saintly example left its mark on his religious life. He was wandering around Sacré Coeur one morning when he was approached by an old priest and asked if he would serve Mass. Though Lennox did not realize at the time, this was none other than the Archbishop of Paris, Cardinal Jean Verdier, who was visiting the Carmelite nuns at their convent at Sacré Coeur, in his capacity as Superior of the Carmelite Seminary at St Sulpice.[14] Lennox served Mass for Cardinal Verdier then and regularly afterwards – and as he remembered this so fondly many years later, it is possible that the cardinal's well-known qualities of humility and goodness may have inspired Lennox to take his conversion even further.

When the composer and teacher Richard Stoker was studying with Nadia Boulanger in 1962, he attended one of her evenings at the rue Ballu, with Igor Markevitch's wife Kyra (daughter of Nijinsky), the

*LB's second son Julian, who has inherited his father's love of the old Latin Mass, is now the owner of the Latin/French daily Missal which LB inscribed with his full Catholic name and the date of his reception into the Church.

American composer Virgil Thomson, and the Turkish Ambassador to France. According to Stoker's recollection, Thomson revealed that at some time between the end of 1930 and the end of 1932 Lennox had thought of becoming a priest. Stoker is unable to remember Boulanger's reaction – but he does recall that they all thought Lennox would have made a good priest, in those still firmly traditionalist days before the reforms of the Second Vatican Council.[15]

There are no surviving diary entries or letters or any other written or spoken material confirming that Lennox ever considered a vocation, but in his diary in 1968 he recorded a Sunday lunchtime conversation with his friends Michael Astor and Natasha and Stephen Spender at Astor's house, Bruern Abbey in Oxfordshire, and this perhaps illuminates Lennox's thoughts about the priesthood. They were talking about the poet and translator Peter Levi, who had been born into a Jewish family which had converted to Catholicism, had later become a Jesuit priest, and had died a married man. This led to a discussion about why people enter religious orders and the priesthood, and Lennox felt they all missed the point: 'Every sort of reason including escape, security, having decisions made for one etc – was advanced, but nobody mentioned the perfectly straightforward reason which is that a man may do so simply because he has a very strong religious sense and believes he has a vocation.'[16]

Lennox felt it was unfair to assume that just because Peter Levi was 'not wholly occupied with religion' or because Fr Dominique de Grunne had 'an intense social life' they must have gone into religion from some ulterior motive. A man did not have to be a saint, he held, to become a priest. (Actually both Levi and de Grunne ultimately abandoned the priesthood, if not the Church.)

By his own reckoning Lennox came to the Catholic Church by 'macabre paths'* – though quite what he meant is hard to fathom: perhaps that it had involved an intense struggle with his homosexuality.

*The composer Malcom Williamson, former Master of the Queen's Music, recalled, in a taped interview with PD, 22 Feb 1991, that he had first met LB at a gathering of the Catholic Musicians' Guild on 21 Nov 1953 when the composer Edmund Rubbra (who had converted to Rome in 1948) had made a speech in which he said he had come to the Church 'through very devious and macabre paths,' and LB, the next to speak, had said, 'I came to the Catholic Church through even more macabre paths'. The interview does not reveal what these paths were.

It has always been assumed that Nadia Boulanger, devout and forceful, must have influenced his decision to convert. Her example was certainly an inspiration, but she was not one of the four witnesses at his baptism, and David Ponsonby, who knew her well (and was not a Catholic himself – or much of an Anglican*) has made it clear that her influence would have gone no further, if even that far. 'Herself the most devout of Catholics, she would never encourage anyone to adopt a religion other than that to which he was born, being of the opinion that people do things much better that they have been accustomed to do from their earliest youth or better still for generations. She thought the thinking and heart-searching entailed by a change of faith a waste of time.'[17]

In other words, Nadia might even have discouraged the Anglican Lennox from going over to Rome. This view was supported by another former pupil of Nadia's (and of Lennox's), the composer Malcolm Williamson, Master of the Queen's Music, and himself a Catholic convert. When Peter Dickinson put it to him that Lennox's conversion might have had something to do with Nadia Boulanger, Williamson replied, loud and clear: 'Fiddlesticks! It would not have mattered if she'd been a Mohammedan, he'd still have become a Catholic.'[18]

Since Lennox was very impressionable as a young man, and was, all his life, cautious and collected, it is inconceivable that he would have converted to Catholicism as a sudden grand gesture. He seems to have been flirting with Anglo-Catholicism, but there is no indication that he was preparing to convert, and he never wrote directly about his conversion. His admirers always think of him as a spiritual man and refer to his faith as being a profound part of his life, and so he was and it was, but, like everything else of value, his faith was very slow to grow. Moved by Nadia's Catholic goodness and steadfastness and discipline, discovering through her the sacred music of the baroque, living close to Sacré Coeur into whose dark and mysterious interior he must have been tempted to venture during Mass on occasions, and intoxicated by the Latin chanting and the Tridentine Rite that were then standard fare in the Catholic liturgy, Lennox was ripe for conversion. It is not impossible that he was encouraged by his lover, 'N. José Raffalli', whose

*DP was not, however, an unbeliever. As his friend and editor Howard Davies rightly points out, ' He was a student of music, of Bach; how can one keep religion (the Christian religion) out of that?' (Letter to TS, 21 February 2006).

signature appears on the baptismal certificate, as one of the four witnesses; none of the other three is recognizable as a familiar friend, or even acquaintance, of Lennox.

Yet José was part of the other side of the conflict with which Lennox must have been engaged then (and was undoubtedly engaged later): the old tussle, common to religious people of all faiths, between spirituality and sexuality. The problem was particularly acute for gay men within a Church that regarded the practice of their sexuality as alien to the sanctity of marriage, and therefore evil.

The Church is still unremittingly hostile. In July 2003 the Congregation for the Doctrine of the Faith, acting in the name of Pope John Paul II, declared that 'homosexual acts go against the natural moral law'. Those who suffered from this 'anomaly' should be 'accepted with respect, compassion and sensitivity', but the physical expression of their tendencies was seriously depraved, intrinsically disordered and a sin gravely contrary to chastity. The document was drawn up and signed by Joseph, Cardinal Ratzinger, now Pope Benedict XVI, then Pope John-Paul's ultra-conservative adviser on doctrine – the so-called 'Panzerkardinal', who supported a return of the Latin Mass, to which Lennox was so devoted.

Lennox reveals – but only very obliquely – something of his own feelings about the Catholic conflict of God versus sex in a diary entry for 1978, when he referred to the novel he was then reading, Graham Greene's *The Heart of the Matter*:

> He [Greene] quotes [the French Catholic poet Charles] Péguy on the title page – 'Le pécheur est au coeur même de la chrétienté. Nul n'est aussi compétent que le pécheur en matière de chrétienté. Nul, si ce n'est le saint.' ['The sinner is at the very heart of Christianity. No one is better qualified in its affairs. Except, perhaps, the saint.'] I have always thought of this as a paradox, which indeed it is, but a deep truth underlies it, and nowhere can it be more perfectly illustrated than here. Greene has a great understanding of the Christian faith as taught by the Catholic Church, particularly of that part of it that is most misunderstood by those outside it – the whole matter of sin, of repentance, confession, of stupid or unworthy priests and bad Catholics who nevertheless cling to such shreds of belief as they can. The principal character in the book is finally crushed and driven to suicide by being unable to reconcile divine love with human love.'[19]

This was Lennox's problem too, as indeed it was Poulenc's and Cocteau's and that of many of the post-French-Catholic-Revival converts in Paris in the Twenties and Thirties. Maritain's advice to these men was spiritual. He urged them to follow a life of prayer and meditation in order to convert the heart. Once the heart had changed, the rest would follow, with the aid of grace and the sacraments. But this approach involved cutting out all homosexual activity, and not all Maritain's converts were prepared to commit themselves to a life of celibacy. Some tried and failed and left the Church, others – the writer Julian Green, for example – stayed in, at the price of 'self-lacerating guilt, perpetual evasiveness and spiritual anguish'.[20] Lennox, who had joined because of the rules, attempted to reconcile his personal dilemma by doing his best to obey them. There was in his nature a streak of submission to authority which made this easier. As the years passed he found that 'there are cases where the only sensible solution [to problems arising from the Church's rules] involves breaking with strict observance',[21] but he remained truly Catholic at heart, growing in devotion, even if he could never feel truly accepted as a Catholic so long as he remained a practising gay man. Jacques Maritain once said that a convert was 'a man whom God has turned inside out like a glove'.[22] In Lennox's case the glove was to take a long time turning.

Nothing moved fast in Lennox's life. It was not till the summer of 1932, nearly six years after he had started his studies at the rue Ballu, that he realized he had to begin to wean himself from his teacher. It was not good for him to continue sitting at her feet; the time had come to stand on his own. Nadia had taught him technique, now he had to put this at the disposal of his musical ideas and become a full-time, professional composer.

In a letter, a little later, he reiterated what he had often said before, and would continue saying till the end of his life, 'I can never tell you what your influence has been, not only on my music but on my life.'[23]

So what exactly was this influence? How had six years' intensive study with Nadia Boulanger affected Lennox's music and life? As far as music is concerned, he had learned a 'lifelong love and respect for counterpoint',[24] 'taste, style, good musical manners',[25] 'self-criticism' and how to create the greatest effect with the fewest notes.[26] Perhaps this economy of style was the most important lesson of all: the musicologist Roger Nichols, who has made a close study of Berkeley and his work, thinks so: '... there's no fluff. There are no bits lying around.

It's all absolutely economical – absolutely pared down. And every note tells.'[27]

The Boulanger influence on Lennox generally was to do with modesty, discretion, dedication, respect for the past, hard work, and an understanding of the shortness, and therefore the urgency, of human life. They also shared an absolute belief in traditional Catholic values, and Lennox drew tremendous inspiration from Boulanger's example of a Christian leading a righteous life in preparation for death (and eternal life). But they shared more than this: without speaking about it, but instinctively feeling it, they were both preoccupied with death, to a degree that seems, to the non-Catholic, not far from morbid. Nadia Boulanger showed it by devoting the whole of March every year to remembering her beloved sister and mother, and by refusing to allow the natural healing of time to remove the pain of her original grief, so that the rue Ballu in March was like a mausoleum, with visitors talking in whispers and walking on tiptoe, as the teacher sat at her piano, with tears streaming down her cheeks. She also made a point of attending funerals, whether she knew the deceased or not, weeping as if they had been her close friends, and sending letters of condolence to their survivors on the anniversaries of their deaths.[28] Lennox revealed his feelings for death in his settings of sacred texts on the theme of ecstatic death, and in his devotion to the memory of his mother on the anniversary of her death, when he and Nadia would exchange letters revelling in misery and mortification.

Even while his mother was alive, Lennox regarded Nadia Boulanger as a surrogate mother. To all her students, but particularly to the gay men (including Lennox, Aaron Copland, Igor Markevitch, David Ponsonby), she was a mother figure: strong, controlling, protective – and essentially feminine. Copland writes that 'she possessed an almost old-fashioned womanliness'.[29] Many of her students of both sexes were a little in love with her.

Despite her strict Catholicism, Boulanger had a *laissez-faire* attitude to sexual matters, insisting only on absolute discretion. According to her biographer, Léonie Rosenstiel, many of her gay students were open with her about their sexual preferences and 'her acceptance of them was certainly not due to ignorance of their proclivities'.[30] Rosenstiel even speculates that Boulanger 'could not actively condemn in others a tendency she felt within herself'.[31] It is highly unlikely that the secretive Lennox ever discussed his private life with her, but no less unlikely that she was not aware of most of what he could have told her. Her students, after all, were her children – and it is clear from her correspondence with Lennox that he was a special pet, a friend with whom she had an unspoken understanding that went very deep indeed.

It was a wrench to detach himself from the rue Ballu, but Lennox knew he must – if only because his ailing parents needed him at home in the south of France. But he was to return to Paris as often as he could, to see Boulanger, Ravel, Poulenc, José and his other friends, and to take part in various postgraduate courses which Boulanger organized from time to time. So, at the end of June 1932, he packed his things, left José in charge of the flat in Mont Cenis, and headed south to join Hastings and Aline on their estate overlooking the bay of Nice, the Domaine du Rayet at Falicon. His mother, still crippled with arthritis, was no better, but 'so courageous and gay, as if there wasn't anything wrong'.[32] There is no mention of his father: there rarely was – till after he had died.

In July Lennox caught an infectious feverish disease that may have been malaria but was more probably typhoid. For the rest of that month and most of August he was confined to bed, but the devoted attention of the Russian servants, combined with constant sunshine and fresh air, visits from friends, and the olive oil from the Berkeleys' groves on the rocky land around the house, nursed him back to health, and by September, though weak and easily tired, he was composing again. He wanted to write something for Nadia, who had just been made a chevalier of the Légion d'honneur, and he settled on a second violin sonata.* He told Mme Kahn-Casella that he was 'reasonably happy with it', and he hoped it would be performed by Stravinsky's violinist, the self-effacing Samuel Dushkin, in Paris in the winter.[33] Nadia saw the music for the first time in the autumn, and her approval, he told her, gave him 'profound joy': 'You know that your praise counts more for me than anything ... If I wrote you a hundred sonatas I could never repay the debt I owe you.'[34]

Dushkin was known to be interested in the new sonata, but he was not in Paris, so Lennox asked Viola Mitchell to play it instead.[35] This plan seems to have fallen through too, and when, the following spring of 1933, there was still no violinist available to play the new piece, Nadia recruited Robert Soetans, for whom Prokofiev had written his second concerto.[36]

*The first had been dedicated to Gladys Bryans, and was probably first performed at an SMI concert in Paris in May 1932 (RN, email to TS, 5 September 2007).

Lennox had already decided to offer the piano part to Jacques Février, having heard him (and Poulenc) playing Poulenc's *Concerto for Two Pianos and Orchestra* in London in February – after which he had taken them both to dinner at the Reform Club. By May it was fixed, and on 14 June 1933, at an SMI concert in the École normale in Paris, Lennox's *Sonata for Violin and Piano No. 2* was at last introduced to the public by Soetans and Février. A review in the Paris edition of the *New York Herald* described Lennox – the 'neveu de Lord Berkeley' – as 'a composer of great talent', whose new work had 'won a lively success'.[37] Among the friends supporting Lennox that night were Mme Kahn-Casella, and possibly the Polish composer Karol Szymanowski, who was visiting Paris for a performance of his own *Symphonie Concertante*, and had told Lennox how much he was looking forward to hearing his work.[38] (The following year Lennox met the Hungarian violinist József Szigeti with some friends in the South of France, and Szigeti 'promised to have a look at' the sonata, but nothing seems to have come of his interest.*)

Lennox's mother was not able to hear the new piece because she was confined to bed, at home in the Alpes Maritimes, suffering from worsening arthritis and bronchitis. The big house at Falicon might have wonderful views – south to the Mediterranean, north to the Bald Mountain of Aspremont – but the climate was not maritime enough. Her doctors advised her to move down to the coast; the sodium and iodine in the sea air would ease the pain of her aching joints, and the warmer, more temperate, climate would help her chest trouble. Aline did not need much persuading: a few years earlier she had bought a plot of land on the tip of Cap Ferrat, the beautiful promontory that juts out from the coast between Nice and Monte Carlo, and enjoys the best climate in the whole of Europe. It is not clear what Aline intended to do with her land, since it was not big enough to build on.† But in 1933

*The meeting took place at the home of Edith, comtesse Gautier-Vignal in Beaulieu-sur-mer (LB to Alan Searle, undated (Summer 1934), W. Somerset Maugham Collection, Howard Gotlieb Archival Research Center, Boston University).

†It is believed that to this day the heirs of LB may still own this small, hatchet-shaped plot, directly overlooking the sea, on the cliffs at the southern tip of Cap Ferrat, with access to the Avenue de la Corniche. Letters from the British Consul in Nice, Mrs Pauline Challoner, solicitor, of 11 rue Paradis, to FB, 18 April 1995 and 16 January 1996 (BFP), examine Aline Berkeley's complicated purchases of property at Falicon and St Jean-Cap Ferrat in the 1920s and '30s, but without satisfactorily resolving what happened to any of them.

her agents found another plot, further back from the Cap itself, on the Avenue centrale, which runs from the Corniche to the village of St Jean-Cap Ferrat. There she built the villa where she and Hastings were to spend their remaining days. They named this last house, as they had named their first house on Boar's Hill thirty years earlier, in memory of the paternal ancestors of Hastings's mother, the comtes de Melfort. There are no surviving photos of the Villa Melfort, or even a description of it. All we know is that it was staffed by the Russian servants from Falicon, and contained two grand pianos.

The new place must have been extremely expensive, because Cap Ferrat had become one of the smartest parts of the South of France – ever since the death of King Leopold II of the Belgians who had bought up most of the Cap, with the proceeds of his Congo Free State, and established separate households for himself, his teenage mistress, Blanche Delacroix, and his Catholic chaplain. By 1933 the king had been dead for nearly a quarter of a century, but his mistress (whom he married a few days before his death, and was now styled the baronne de Vaughan) was still alive and a frequent visitor to Cap Ferrat. The Berkeleys' other neighbours were no less exotic: they included Queen Victoria's favourite son, Arthur, Duke of Connaught, and his American mistress Lady Leslie; the 'bewitching' and 'dangerously mischievous' Singer heiress Mrs Reginald ('Daisy') Fellowes (widow of the bisexual prince Jean de Broglie);[39] the handsome and music-loving comte Jean de Polignac; the bisexual Violet Trefusis; the much-married Australian beauty, Enid, Countess of Kenmare;[40] and, in a Venetian palazzo with seven ornamental gardens (and thirty-four gardeners in sailor suits), baronne Béatrice Ephrussi de Rothschild. Aline Berkeley's elder sister Annie who married a half-brother of Leopold II, baron Arthur d'Eppinghoven, had a house not far away, in Menton (and royal cousins still living on Cap Ferrat), and it was she who helped Aline to wrest the precious piece of land from the king's heirs.

For all his love of France, and the south in particular, Lennox would have preferred his parents to retire to England – possibly to Devon or Cornwall: '... I love the Cap and like the life here, but I would rather live in England. It is only because I don't think Mother could stand the English climate that we are here ... '[41]

The healing sun and the sea were potent attractions, but Cap Ferrat had a specific appeal for Lennox.

14
Lennox and Alan, Cap Ferrat, 1933–6

The Berkeleys' new villa on Cap Ferrat was only five minutes' walk from a large, square, white house that had become one of the most celebrated literary and social salons of the time. Set in twelve acres, the Villa Mauresque stood on the side of a hill above the Cap itself, with a wide view of the Mediterranean – Nice on the right, the mass of the Estérel hills away in the distance. King Leopold built it in 1906 for his chaplain, who had spent much of his life in North Africa, so he gave it an arabic appearance with keyhole windows, domes and minarets, and named it Villa Mauresque – the Moorish villa. The house was now occupied by Somerset Maugham who bought it in 1926 – cheaply, he claimed, because it was so ugly. The first thing he did was to strip away what he called all the 'Moorish nonsense and Renaissance exuberance', revealing a plain two-storey house with a flat roof and long green shutters, built around an interior courtyard with arches. He whitewashed the walls, inside and out, and filled the rooms with books and pictures, and friends.[1] He then added an Arab touch of his own: on the white pilaster gateposts he etched in red the mystical Moorish sign which he used as a colophon on his books – a pictorial symbol of the hand of Fatima warding off the evil eye.

Maugham shared the house with his entertaining but increasingly alcoholic boyfriend (officially his secretary), Gerald Haxton – a dissolute young American he had met when they were both driving ambulances for the Red Cross in Flanders during the First World War. Given to mercurial mood swings 'from manic gaiety to angry outbursts' (against Maugham 'for keeping him in gilded detention'[2]), Haxton still had a vitality that was magnetically attractive – particularly to women. Men were not so comfortable with him – some found him 'unpleasant', others even 'evil'.[3] One young English visitor claimed there was such 'an aura of corruption' about him that he actually 'stank'.[4] Maugham and Haxton – and a herd of dachshunds all named after characters in

Wagner operas – were looked after by thirteen servants and gardeners, including a Swiss butler, an Italian footman and a French chauffeur.[5]

Much as he liked England, Willie Maugham had never felt at home there. 'To me', he wrote in one of his volumes of autobiography, 'England has been a country where I had obligations that I did not want to fulfil.'[6] It was also a country where he could not live with Haxton, who had been deported from Britain, as an undesirable alien, in 1919 – possibly as a result of a homosexual offence in 1913, more likely because of spying activities. Maugham had been brought up in France – till he was orphaned at the age of ten and sent to school in England. In France, he felt – like Lennox – free: free to write, free to live openly with Haxton (though he never admitted they were lovers), free to entertain on a lavish scale. All *le beau monde* visited the Mauresque – writers, royalty, film stars, politicians, and any good-looking young man smart enough to sing for his supper. No one declined an invitation – or ever arrived late. Maugham's stylish generosity was legendary, but, as his biographer Frederic Raphael has noted, 'he himself ate sparsely of the lotus he offered others'.[7]

Lennox had already met Maugham and Haxton in Paris, where they kept a flat and occasionally visited the Select, an all-night gay *café terrasse* (popular with American writers and the ballet crowd) on the boulevard du Montparnasse. It is likely too that, with so many young friends in common – Patrick Balfour, Raymond Mortimer, Alan Pryce-Jones, Edward Sackville-West – Lennox had already visited the Mauresque, while staying with his parents at Falicon. At all events it was natural that when the Berkeleys moved into the Villa Melfort in July 1933, Maugham should invite them all to a luncheon party. By then Lennox was thirty, Maugham nearly sixty and Haxton just past forty.

The Berkeleys' Russian chauffeur Igor motored them up a curved gravel drive through groves of orange, lemon and banana trees to a broad terrace in front of the house. Maugham came out to meet them and guided them through terraces of oleanders and camellias to a large swimming pool hewn from the rock and fed by water that gushed from a marble mask by Bernini. In a little cave at the back, shaded from the sun, Haxton hovered around the drinks table while a footman mixed the cocktails. After one of Haxton's favourites – 'mother's ruin' or a 'sidecar' – Lennox and his parents made their way along a grass path that meandered under pine trees to a terrace set for lunch. There they found themselves in the midst of what the Irish writer and feminist

'George Egerton' called 'a queer, gossipy, cliquey community all emulating one another's gardens and expenses', and enjoying 'perfect unfussed service'. It was, she said, the '*raffinement de luxe*'.[8] The luxuries often included an ice-cream which the chef made from the avocados grown on trees Maugham had imported from California. These were the first avocado trees ever seen in France, and guests were so impressed that Maugham was encouraged to sell the pears in the local market.[9]

Only later, as he got to know his hosts better, was Lennox exposed to what a young English visitor of the period, the writer Beverley Nichols, called 'the rows, the intrigues, the bitchiness' that contributed to an 'awful atmosphere of tension', and the 'dark and misshapen' shadows cast by the presence of Gerald Haxton.[10] But even then, Lennox, who saw the good in everybody, may not have noticed the chill of the undercurrents.

On this first visit, the hosts of the Mauresque made a special effort to charm their new neighbours, and the Berkeleys enjoyed the attention. A few weeks later Aline returned the invitation, and Maugham and Haxton came to the Villa Melfort, bringing with them a svelte young man who was to brighten Lennox's life for the next two years – and Maugham's till his death: a Cockney typist, sweet and doll-like, called Alan Searle.

Jealous tongues later claimed that Alan was a rent-boy[11] who had been discarded by Lytton Strachey, that he was 'unctuous and money-grubbing', a 'house-broken, tail-wagging, pet-like little man'.[12] It is clear from the Maugham literature and surviving letters to, from and about Alan, that he was insecure, ambitious, indiscreet, muddle-headed and not a little self-pitying. He may never have been a rent boy, but he certainly set his cap at rich older men, sometimes enjoying their favours concurrently. Lennox never paid much attention to past form. He was content, simply, to admire the dark, wavy hair, the Bronzino features, and the 'soft feminine charm'; that Alan was also gentle, sensitive and kind counted for even more. Lennox was not quite alone in appreciating Alan's finer points. Beverley Nichols, writing about him ten years later (by which time Haxton had died and Alan was installed in his place at the Mauresque), thought he was 'something of a saint', who combined the roles of court jester, male nurse, secretary and comforter-in-chief: he was, wrote Nichols, 'an influence for sanity, for dignity, and for moderation'.[13]

Lennox found the combination of angel and doe quite irresistible, and Alan Searle was soon 'Alan darling'. A year after their first meeting, when Lennox was thirty-one and Alan twenty-four,* Lennox wrote to tell him, 'I love you and shall always love you, and it is more than just the ordinary thing.'[14] His letters to Alan, so full of love, often contain apologies for being 'silly' or 'romantic'. In one, Lennox admits that he is 'an incorrigible sentimentalist – always have been, and I don't seem to grow out of it.'[15] The fact is that Alan was nice-looking, sweet, and affectionate, and his letters, and their occasional meetings in London and France, transformed Lennox's life at this frustrating turning-point, when he had finished his studies and longed to plunge into the English musical scene, but could not leave the South of France because of his elderly parents.

Soon after their first meeting, they exchanged photographs. Lennox sent one of himself which he quite liked but his mother thought was awful – she said it made him look 'like a hairdresser's assistant'.[16] Alan sent one back that Lennox said he was 'crazy about': it was 'a wonderful likeness, and just your adorable self.'[17]

What Lennox probably did not know (and possibly would not have minded anyway) was that Alan had at least one other ardent admirer at this time: Guy Little,'an elderly gent in Chelsea',† who, by his own admission, was 'in a state of perpetual adoration'.[18] From the beginning of 1934 until the middle of 1949 – long past the date at which Lennox's brief affair had ended – Little wrote at least sixty-one love letters to Alan. From these we know that he thought of himself as a 'dull lover,'[19] and Alan as 'the darlingest pet in the world'.[20] Alan signed one of his letters as your 'starry eyed little friend'.[21] He owed the older man, amongst other kindnesses, his job as an unofficial visitor at Wormwood Scrubs Prison.[22]

Old parties, no less than the still young Lennox, were particularly susceptible to Alan's seductive charms. His delicate vulnerability kindled their protective instincts, his prettiness appealed to their

*Bryan Connon's *Somerset Maugham and the Maugham Dynasty* and his article on Maugham in the *Oxford Dictionary of National Biography*, 2004, give 1905 as Searle's birth date, but Maugham's biographer Selina Hastings feels 1910 is more likely. (The 1911 census records a one-year-old Alan Charles Searle living with his father Charles James, a bank clerk aged thirty, and mother Lilian Charlotte, aged thirty-one, at 5 Verdant Lane, Catford.)

†Possibly a solicitor, Little lived at 33 Tite Street, in a house full of artists.

aesthetic instincts (and, in the case of the old boys, to something a great deal earthier), and they were all immensely flattered by his tender and devoted attentions, whether in person or in beautifully penned letters. Not all Alan's elderly admirers were men. Lennox's mother was so smitten that Lennox, jokingly, described her relationship with Alan as a 'flirtation'.[23] At Christmas 1933 she sent the young man a postcard that spelled out the warmth of her maternal feelings, 'Dearest Alan, ... I can't tell you all the lovely things I would like to give you in this coming year. I & Lennox are both very devoted to you & hope to see you often & often. Your very loving old friend Aline C. Berkeley.'[24]

Maugham first met Alan at a stag dinner in London in 1928, just after he had bought the Mauresque. Alan was then about eighteen and working as a typist for the Discharged Prisoners' Aid Society; Maugham was fifty-four and one of the richest and most celebrated writers in the world. As planned by the host, an antique dealer called Tritton, Maugham fell for Alan instantly. Sensing a biddability and loyalty that were, one day, to prove mutually useful, he invited him to Cap Ferrat for a holiday, there and then. The young man consulted his mother, with whom he was living in Bermondsey, and she, smelling a rat, strongly advised him not to go. But Alan was determined, defied her and went anyway.

The affair that followed was long and complicated, because of the need for secrecy. The two met mostly in London, where Maugham had appointed Alan as his London secretary and installed him in a flat of his own. But they also met at Maugham's own flats in London and (when Haxton was not there) in Paris. However much Maugham might have wanted Alan with him permanently at the Cap, it was impossible – not so much because Alan had psoriasis and could not bear the Riviera sun, but, more importantly, because the hearty American frightened the shy young Englishman.

Haxton, by this time, was becoming increasingly difficult – drinking too much and making scenes. But he could still 'charm the birds from the trees', and Maugham was 'always enraptured'.[25] It was not till after Haxton's death, in an alcoholics' ward in New York in 1944, that Maugham, still grieving, was able to install Alan as his secretary at Cap Ferrat. The two remained together there from 1946 till Maugham's death in 1965.

It says much for Maugham that he not only tolerated Lennox's strong feelings for Alan Searle (and, presumably, Little's too), but even, perhaps, encouraged them. 'Willie ... asked whether I had heard from you,' Lennox wrote to Alan on Christmas Eve, 1934, adding, 'I feel that he understands.'[26] And doubtless Maugham did understand, which is why he was content to let Lennox love on, since Alan, he knew, was never seriously engaged – any more than Lennox really was.

They saw one another no more than two or three times a year, but corresponded frequently. In the two years of their relationship Lennox wrote dozens of letters to Alan. The nineteen that survive are full of puppy love, gossip and fun – quite unlike any of Lennox's other letters. It is clear that he was having a wonderful time at the Cap, playing golf and tennis in the afternoon and bridge in the evenings, going to parties, and making new friends.

Among these new friends were two gay young Englishmen who had been inseparable since meeting at Cambridge. One was George 'Dadie' Rylands, who was, according to Lennox, 'very blonde' [*sic*] and 'terribly high-brow'; he was also 'dean of King's (and Queen of Queens)'. The other, eight years Rylands's junior, was Arthur Marshall, who 'didn't say much, but looked quite nice and played tennis magnificently'.[27] Rylands went on to become one of the greatest Shakespeare scholars of the century, and Marshall, who was then teaching at his old school, Oundle, was soon to blossom as the comic writer of skits involving larky public schoolgirls and butch headmistresses ('There's ever such a dainty hellebore by your left plimsoll, Cynthia.')[28] Lennox does not go into this, though both men were to remain on the fringes of his life. In January 1935 Maugham and Haxton took Marshall and Rylands to a concert in Monte Carlo and asked Lennox to join them; to his delight, they heard 'a magnificent cellist called [Gregor] Piatigorsky'.[29]

Through the Mauresque network Lennox also got to know Osbert Sitwell, then at the start of a career of intellectual skirmishes – against philistines, and in support of 'compulsory Freedom everywhere, the suppression of Public Opinion ... and the rationing of brains', in the interests of 'true democracy'.[30] He dined with Sitwell and his decorative boyfriend David Horner at the Mauresque in the autumn of 1935, and liked them so much he invited them to lunch with his mother a few days later. At previous encounters Lennox had found Sitwell frightening – not surprisingly, since Sitwell told malicious stories and stared at people 'as though committing some defect to memory, for subsequent use'.[31] But now Lennox thought he was 'as amiable as he could be' –

and newly thin, having been slimming hard at the thermal resort of Brides les Bains (which Lennox later translated for Alan as 'Brides-in-the-Bath').[32] Aline, who seems to have had a weakness for the sort of aesthetic boys her son liked, must have been bowled over by Horner's pretty blond curls, delicate head and slender figure – a look described by Sitwell as 'orchidaceous'.[33]

One of the most amusing parties Lennox attended at the Mauresque was at Christmas 1934 when Maugham's resident guests included H. G. Wells and his Russian mistress, Moura, Baroness Budberg,[34] formerly wife of a Tsarist diplomat, and mistress, successively, of the British agent Robert Bruce Lockhart, who nearly toppled the Bolshevik government, and the revolutionary writer Maxim Gorky. (Budberg told Maugham that the reason she liked old Wells, then nearly seventy, was 'because he smells of honey'.[35]) The guests were asked for 8.30, and Lennox would not have been alone in taking care to arrive punctually. He was unaware at the time that while the footman was mixing him a dry martini in the drawing room, his neighbour and friend Mrs Emily Borie Sherfesee – a stout American heiress, in black, with pearls – was sitting on the lavatory, in a nearby bathroom, staring in astonishment at an old man having a bath. Taken short by her incontinence, Mrs Sherfesee had rushed in without knocking. Neither party knew what to do next – till the American rose from her seat with a dignified bow, tidied her hair and returned to the salon. At a quarter to nine, when the same old man, now looking pink, made his entrance, Maugham took him over to meet Mrs Sherfesee.

'Emily, my dear, I don't believe you know Mr W-W-Wells.'

'On the contrary', she replied. 'I think we've met before.'[36]

Also there that night was the novelist G. B. Stern, just finishing the penultimate novel in her 'Matriarch' series, *Shining and Free*. 'Peter' Stern was one of Maugham's closest female friends – 'blessed among women', he called her.[37] She had a gift for drawing people out, and, according to Lennox, she kept the guests in gales of laughter that night.[38]

Quite often a party at the Mauresque would go on to Monte Carlo or Nice, Mougins or Beaulieu-sur-Mer. On one of these merry excursions Lennox was all but ravished by Haxton and a lusty older admirer, as he enjoyed telling Alan Searle afterwards:

> [Yesterday] evening I was bidden to dinner at Mauresque — we had a lovely dinner out on the terrace. There were two other men,

> rather elderly queers whose names I didn't catch. Willy [*sic*] was charming as he always is ... After dinner I played the piano (very badly) and finally Gerald and I and one of the afore-mentioned gentlemen went in the car to Beaulieu. On the way they both suddenly became rather cave-mannish and started banging me about. I didn't care about that much. I mean it does rather depend on who the cave-men are, doesn't it dear? And anyhow two against one is not fair. We went to a café at Beaulieu, where we were joined by Edie Gautier-Vignal [step-mother of Proust's 'nocturnal companion' comte Louis Gautier-Vignal, and sister of the novelist Sydney Schiff[39]] and Marie de Marwicz, and there was much screaming and giggling. After that we went back. The other man started with us but when we got back he was no longer there. I hope he didn't fall out of the car, by that time I fear I was rather tipsy and I don't remember very clearly what happened, mercifully perhaps ...[40]

This shows clearly not only that Lennox was having a gay time, but also that he was entirely comfortable about it. There is none of the guilt, the sense of unworthiness, the religious angst that fill his letters to Nadia Boulanger. It also seems to suggest that Haxton had taken a shine to Lennox – though that's no compliment, since Haxton was not choosy about the trousers he lunged at. In 1934 Haxton pressed Lennox to join him on a trip to Vienna in the autumn. Not only was Lennox planning to be in London then, with Alan, but he was also worried about the unspoken *quid pro quo*, so he said no[41] – whereupon Haxton took instead the American gossip-columnist Elsa Maxwell (the original 'hostess with the mostest').[42]

Haxton must have had a very curious idea of Lennox's psychology. Apart from pouncing on him, he also provided him with the scenario for a ballet (which Lennox thought might make 'something quite amusing'[43]), and an improving book, St John Ervine's two-volume biography of General Booth of the Salvation Army. Lennox told Alan he assumed that Haxton had lent him the Booth for the good of his soul: 'It is terribly long, but gets a hold on one – one cannot help admiring people like that tremendously, and they make one feel such a worm. I suppose one ought to think more about the state of one's soul, and other people's; but high-minded people are often so unattractive – and anyhow, I never seem to be able to make up my mind about anything.'[44]

Lennox was not the only one of his circle to benefit from Maugham's famously generous hospitality. His friend Vere Pilkington, staying with his parents at Menton, was invited to the Mauresque quite as much as Lennox was. Vere used to pilot himself over from London to Nice, in what Lennox called one of his 'beastly flying machines' (Lennox himself had never been up in a plane, and had no wish to).[45] In some ways Vere Pilkington made the greater hit at the Mauresque, since his tennis was so good ('which is what they're always looking for', wrote Lennox, whose own game, he admitted glumly, 'gets worse and worse'[46]). Lennox's golf was no better, and the prospect of playing with Maugham at Cagnes in January 1935 filled him with foreboding: 'I am rather terrified because I play so badly, however I am now the proud possessor of five clubs, a very efficient looking bag, and lots of balls so I shall just hope for the best. Besides your opponent doesn't generally mind if you play badly at golf, and short of actually hitting him in the eye with a ball, which I shall at all costs try to avoid, nothing very disastrous can happen.'[47]

When not at the Mauresque the two Oxford friends would motor, cycle or walk in the Estérel hills, swim in the sea or in Mrs Sherfesee's pool (despite the doctor's warning against, it, because Lennox had a twinge of rheumatism in one arm [48]), or play a round of golf on their own, on the course in the pine woods near the Cap. In the mornings Lennox composed, and in the evenings he and Vere would drive to Monte Carlo for a concert or to see René Blum's new ballet company, dine with friends, or stay at home and play duets.

Late in the summer of 1934 they went to Mougins for tennis and dinner with Maugham's friend Bill Burton, who wanted them to drive on afterwards to Cannes for further partying. But Lennox, pining for Alan, was leading 'rather an austere life' and, 'feeling very virtuous', refused to join them for what he claimed was no more than 'sheer debauchery'.[49] Instead he drove home alone, leaving Vere and Bill Burton to their 'pretty riotous time', which made Vere sick for the next two days. It was usually Vere who organized the entertainments, and indeed everything else: he was the perfect companion, knew how to tickle Lennox's sense of humour, and solved all the practical problems.[50] Furthermore he was a first-rate keyboard player, so there was lots of two-piano playing at the Villa Melfort, as Lennox told Alan: '... it is marvellous to have somebody to do music with. We have got all the *Brandenburg Concertos* arranged for two pianos – they are such wonderful things one can never get tired of them. I like the slow movements the best, they are extraordinarily moving, and I think as near perfection as anyone has ever got in any art.'[51]

Alan Searle played the piano too, and Lennox expressed his fondness by writing a piece for him.[52] Since, like Alan's other admirers, Lennox seems to have regarded him as something of an infant – one of his letters is actually signed, 'All my love, dear child' – it is not surprising the piece is a cradle song or *Berceuse*.* Lennox told Alan he had been able to write 'with more facility than usual lately,' and the credit was largely Alan's, 'because being in love makes one do it better'.[53] He wrote another piano piece at the same time – a *Capriccio* – and dedicated that to Vere Pilkington.[54] Maugham took an interest in the new pieces and promised to do all he could to try to promote them. 'It is too sweet of Willie to do so much to help,' Lennox wrote to Alan Searle, 'he has been such an angel to me altogether, and has made my life here much happier and more interesting than it would have been.'[55] Maugham was well aware that Lennox had what he called 'a thin time', stuck at home with his sick mother, and his composing, and that 'he looks forwards to visits from his friends very eagerly', so he did what he could to cheer him up with visits and parties and outings.[56]

Maugham and Lennox shared more than mere social pleasures. There was, perhaps surprisingly, esctatic mysticism as well – for Maugham, whilst professing a 'sturdy agnosticism', was deeply interested in religion.[57] The year the Berkeleys moved to Cap Ferrat and Lennox was thrown into the Mauresque set, Maugham travelled south to gather material for a second book about Spain. In this new book, *Don Fernando: or Variations on Some Spanish Themes*, Maugham tells the story of one of Lennox's favourite religious writers, St Teresa of Avila, who ran away at the age of seven to seek martyrdom among the Moors, underwent a religious experience at the age of forty, which led to a series of spiritual ecstasies, wrote some of the most vivid religious writings in Christian literature, and later became mother superior of the Carmelites. Maugham discusses the autobiographical accounts of her spiritual life, with its moments of ecstasy and depression, her attempts to reform the Carmelites, and her descriptions of the life of prayer from

*Marked 'Allegretto', the *Berceuse* had been composed by the autumn of 1934 (Letter LB to Alan Searle, undated [September 1934] , Somerset Maugham Archive, Howard Gotlieb Archival Research Center, Boston University).

meditation to the so-called 'mystic marriage' (the state which she herself claimed eventually to have reached).

Since Maugham had finished the new book by Christmas 1934, at the time of the party with Wells and Budberg, Stern and the Cambridge pair, and as the latter spent hours discussing with Maugham and Lennox 'writing style, language and literature',[58] it is entirely possible they also touched on the contents of *Don Fernando*. Maugham knew quite a lot about Lennox from Alan Searle, and he would have wanted to draw out Lennox on the subject of the Catholic mystics – and about his conversion in Paris. But there is no actual evidence that they talked about any such things: indeed a serious conversation *à deux* would have been difficult on any subject since Lennox was so diffident and Maugham so tortured by his stammer.

Lennox did raise the subject of religion with Alan, though. Just after that same Christmas party, Alan wrote a confused and emotional letter to Lennox to say he was in a terrible muddle, thought he must be ill, and wondered if he ought to see a psychiatrist. Lennox's reply was no less clumsy, largely because he was embarrassed about its religious nature – but it bears the stamp of real conviction: he clearly needed to say what he said, come what may. For this reason the letter throws a valuable light on his own faith, and the struggle that continued to torment him, deep down, as a homosexual Catholic.

> Judging from what you say I shd think that you must be very much in need of more of an interior life such as religion gives people. If you were a catholic I should advise you to go and see a priest – in fact there's no reason why you shouldn't even though you are not one, because I am sure it is your soul that is ill rather than your body. I am not a particularly religious person myself, but I do believe in it – and if I behave nohow [*sic*] from time to time, it is because I am very weak and never can resist temptation. But at the bottom of my heart I believe it to be wrong, though I don't think it is terribly serious. The world of the senses is great fun, but it is not the real world ... if you were a catholic, and able to go to confession you would be able to pray all right, and that would do you more good than all the psycho-analists in the world.[59]

Behaving 'nohow' is such an un-Lennox-like expression that it will strike the reader as a misreading, but several pairs of eyes have checked the text of the original letter, and all agree that, however untypical, the word is indeed 'nohow'. Lennox must have been using a slang expression, possibly a mockery of Gerald Haxton's American English, which he knew Alan would understand – and might even chuckle over. What he actually meant was, 'if I behave badly', and in the context of 'resisting temptation' and the 'world of the senses', the particular kind of bad behaviour is obviously sexual. The moment he had written it, Lennox regretted it – not enough to rewrite the letter (because, after all, it expressed his deeply-held beliefs) – but he needed to cover his tracks, in case this unaccustomed burst of religion should scare his friend away; so he added, 'For heaven's sake forgive this sermon and tear up this ridiculous letter, only I love you so much that I can't help saying what I really feel at the risk of appearing grotesque to you.'[60]

He longed to take Alan in his arms, he said, to hear his voice and feel his touch. But that was impossible, given the distance that separated them, so he proposed instead that Alan should consult wise old John Greenidge. It is unlikely that Alan would have done any such thing, since what he was seeking was an emotional, not a rational, response to his self-pity. He wanted just the kind of passionate response Lennox in fact provided, even if the religious solution could not quite work for him.

For Lennox, the whole of his time in France before the war was 'a sort of formative period'. Everything he did was 'part of a natural eclecticism', moving towards what he wanted to do.[61] Precisely what this was became clearer when his father died in 1934. The Russian chauffeur Igor Ermakhov found old Captain Berkeley slumped in his chair in the drawing room of the Villa Melfort, after luncheon on Saturday 17 February. He was seventy-eight. A few days later he was buried with the remains of his brother Sir Ernest (who had died in 1932) in the English cemetery in Nice (now part of the Cimétière de Sainte Marguerite, on the heights to the west of the town).[62]

Freed of the responsibility of looking after his father, Lennox now felt able to return to London and carve out a place for himself in English musical life, even though it meant leaving his beloved Maman. Nadia had discovered and stimulated his talent, it was now up to him to fulfil her Nietzschian motto: 'To become oneself'.[63] When Elgar died, six days after his father's death, Lennox recognized the end of the movement of modern English musical reaction, and took it as sign that he had made the right decision. He would see what English music offered, nearly a decade after he had left Oxford for France, show them what he had learned in Paris, and continue with his musical experiments. He was fortunate to have some money of his own, which meant that he did not, in his own words, 'have to get a job right away'.[64] And in the two and a half years since he left Nadia, he had composed quite a little body of show-pieces – 'so as to be able to do my stuff in London'.[65] These included the *Sonata for Piano and Violin No. 2*, a *Polka for Two Pianos*, the two piano pieces dedicated to Searle and Pilkington, the sketches for his Haxton ballet, and the first draft of an oratorio, *Jonah*. Nothing else he had written since Oxford was worth anything, he decided – and jettisoned the lot.

He was convinced that his music would have a better chance if he did not live abroad, and that he needed to write something 'rather important', if he was to make any impact.[66] He was also aware of the value of powerful allies in dropping his name in the right places. Thanks to his friend the composer Lord Berners, who had given him an introduction to the London music publishers J. & W. Chester, two of his new pieces had already been published – the *Sonata for Piano and Violin No. 2*, which was now his Opus 1 (dedicated 'À Mademoiselle Nadia Boulanger'[67]), and the *Polka*.

It was about this time that Lennox turned to opera, possibly in his search for the something rather important. His friend, the writer and critic Alan Pryce-Jones, sketched a plot based on ideas they had jointly conceived. Lennox thought the plot was 'an excellent one to build something on', and that it gave 'ample scope for all the things that we thought of – polkas etc'. He envisaged an opening scene incorporating 'a grand finale to an opera in the Italian style', and he imagined them having 'such fun with an Italian tenor!'[68] But the idea came to nothing – though the two men were to collaborate on an opera a decade later.

Chester's launched their new composer with a little fanfare in the spring of 1934, describing the *Violin Sonata* as 'strikingly vital' and the *Polka* as 'brilliant'.[69] But Lennox knew that he would have to use his address book if he was going to get these works performed – as he revealed in a letter to Alan a few months before his trip to London in October 1934:

> I do hope that I shall be able to get some music played in London soon – the trouble is that I am quite unknown outside the musical profession which makes it very difficult. It is certainly most important to be known by the right kind of people. Conductors won't

> bother about one unless one is talked about by the right kind of people, otherwise you are simply one amongst a score of young composers who are said to have talent. Willie Walton for instance got there almost entirely through the Sitwells. So I must try and do something in that line when I come to London – a terrifying thought here where one has forgotten the existence of suits and collars and ties.[70]

A few weeks later Lennox wrote to Alan to say that Osbert Sitwell had told him to telephone when he got to London, and to go and see him. 'I think', said Lennox, 'he could be very useful to me, don't you?'[71]

As the time for his departure drew nearer, Lennox became increasingly anxious: not only about having to dress up again in 'all kinds of utterly improbable things like collars and ties and hats', after nearly six months of casual clothes,[72] but also about Alan's expectations of him – he was fearful that Alan would find he had made a mistake 'and will think me an awful old drab'.[73]

In his eagerness to see Alan again, he spent no more than a few hours in Paris before catching the last train to London, and, though it arrived at ten to eleven at night, he could not resist going straight to Alan's flat, where he was soon reassured that he was not an awful old drab. Lennox was hoping that Alan had kept the weekend free so that 'we can see each other rather a lot'. He even hoped he might be able to stay at Alan's, rather than with John Greenidge in Great Ormond Street. It seems unlikely that Alan would have allowed this, since his flat, after all, belonged to Maugham, nor is it likely that he would have been able to give Lennox the whole weekend, with so many other admirers to keep happy. Lennox, however, was grateful for whatever crumbs he was offered, and wrote or telephoned when he was not actually seeing Alan. 'You know that I love you', he wrote in one, 'and that you are the most precious being in the world to me.'[74]

As well as being a charmer, Alan was also a networker – and generous with his contacts. It was he who introduced Lennox, during that same autumn trip of 1934, to the pianist Harriet Cohen, mistress of the composer Arnold Bax. Lennox was touched that Cohen appreciated Alan so much – though her interest was less focused on the faun than on the prison worker. Indeed she believed, like Beverley Nichols, that Alan was a sort of saint. Years later she published a memoir in which she expressed the conviction that he was the prototype for Larry

Darrell in Maugham's 1944 novel, *The Razor's Edge* – about a worldly young American traveller converted to the holy life by a visit to India.[75] Warming to her enthusiasm for his friend, Lennox showed her the *Berceuse* he had written for Alan, and offered to write another piece for her.

Lennox was disappointed by what he saw of music in Britain. It was, he said years later, 'more restricted, more limited to fewer composers' than he had known in France. But there were 'some interesting things' – by Vaughan Williams, William Walton, Constant Lambert, Arnold Bax and Arthur Bliss.[76] He did not really try to enter this narrow stage – not because he did not think it any good, but because he could not find any composer with whom he had any real affinity.[77]

He did hear some exciting and original music in London during his two months there that autumn – but it was not British. And he shared it with Alan Searle.[78] On 28 November the two young men went to the Queen's Hall to hear Stravinsky conducting the British premiere of his Sophoclean melodrama *Perséphone*. Lennox had already heard this work in Paris during its stage production by the Ida Rubinstein company in April (which had prompted him to invest in a copy of the piano score the following month). Quite apart from the music, which he greatly admired, Lennox was also deeply interested in the libretto by André Gide. Like the Orthodox Stravinsky, the Protestant Gide was fascinated by Catholicism, and both men were intellectually involved for a time with the Catholic proselytizer Jacques Maritain, whose work had influenced Lennox's own decision to convert in 1929.

In the Greek myth on which the piece is based, Persephone is abducted by the god of the dead, while picking flowers in Sicily, then dispatched to Hades as queen of the underworld. In Gide's version of the story, Persephone volunteers to go down to the underworld, as an act of self-sacrifice, thus introducing the Christian idea of atonement.

The original, staged, version was written for Ida Rubinstein, who created the choreography, danced the part and, simultaneously, narrated it. In the concert version for London, Madame Rubinstein confined herself to narrating the text from a position immediately beside Stravinsky. Also taking part were a tenor, two choirs (one of them for boys) and a large orchestra.

Lennox loved the spareness of the work – in one of his *Monthly Musical Record* reports from Paris earlier in the year, he had described it as austere, restrained and 'ruthlessly stripped' of orchestral effects and purple patches.[79] But the *Times* critic hated it, bitterly regretting that Stravinsky should have 'outgrown' his ballet music of twenty-five years earlier – 'when the ballet was really Russian, and Russia was still beguiled by fairy tales'. It was, wrote the critic, a 'severe' product of Stravinsky's 'present day disillusionment', with the text delivered in 'a curiously disjointed, ejaculatory fashion', so that 'one wonders why the BBC should go to so much trouble and expense to give this lopsided presentation of a work from which so little can be gleaned.'[80] After the concert, which also included Stravinsky playing the piano part in his *Capriccio* ('a triumph of dryness' – *The Times*[81]), Lennox took Alan backstage to meet the composer.

As things turned out, Lennox was able to congratulate Stravinsky a second time, when he found himself travelling back to Paris on the same train a day or two later. From Paris, Lennox wrote to Alan to say that in consequence the journey had been 'much less dismal' than it would otherwise have been, because Stravinsky had been 'quite charming', and invited him back to his carriage to join himself, his friend 'Samsky' Dushkin, and his 'girl-friend' (later, his second wife), the dancer Vera de Bosset (wife of the ballet designer Sergei Soudeikin):

> [Stravinsky] was in a very gay mood, insisted on my dining with him in the Wagon restaurant, and drank quantities of red wine, after which they played bridge until we got to Paris. He was very pleased with the London concert, and thought that it was a very good performance – of course he had a very bad press, but he always does now and though it makes him rather sad, he is getting used to it – besides he is so certain that he is right, and that the time will come when people will appreciate his later style, which all except a very few so much dislike at present. Anyhow he is a most delightful man, whatever one thinks of him as a composer.[82]

Lennox told Alan than he still had moments of 'wanting you terribly, and not wanting anybody but you'. He was going to miss him in Cap Ferrat, but he had to be there, at home, because of his mother. 'Good bye Alan darling – you are so much in my thoughts, I wish I could think of you less, and yet somehow I cannot wish that I could love you less, because it has been worth it. Give my love to Willie.'[83]

Before leaving Paris, Lennox paid a visit to the photographer who had taken some pictures of him two years earlier, and ordered a print for Alan, as a memento. He thought it showed him looking 'nice and clean, if rather foolish',[84] but Alan was welcome to burn it if he thought it was awful. Lennox also bought some new golf clubs, then caught the train south to Nice, to practise his swing, before Maugham arrived from London. It was not going to be easy, back at the Cap, alone at the Villa Melfort with his sick mother and the ghost of his father. And he was not looking forward to a Mauresque without Alan, whose occasional visits had added 'such wonderful and romantic associations' to the villa's own natural beauties.[85]

When he reached Cap Ferrat, Lennox found a letter from Alan, reaffirming his love. 'Such a wonderful letter,' he wrote in reply, 'I can hardly believe that it is real and that I am not dreaming.'[86] Reassured that his feelings were fully reciprocated, Lennox resigned himself to a lonely separation for the next four months, and started composing again. By Christmas he had finished a new piece, a short *Overture for Chamber Orchestra*, and in January 1935 he learned that it had been chosen 'to represent English modernism' at the Carlsbad Festival in Czechoslovakia, where it was to be given its premiere in September.[87]

By then he had also finished his new piano piece for Harriet Cohen, an *Étude* [88] (which she described as 'charming'[89]). He added this to Searle's *Berceuse* and Pilkington's *Capriccio*, in that order, and the group was published as *Three Pieces for Piano*. The following summer, thanks largely to the influence of Willie Maugham, Harriet Cohen gave the first public performances – at the Contemporary Music Centre in London, in June (when she played the *Etude* alone), and on the BBC a month later (when she broadcast the entire set, in a concert with the clarinettist Frederick Thurston[90]).

Meanwhile, in the spring of 1935, Lennox returned to London, for a second attempt at making a name for himself, and to see Alan. And at this point the correspondence with Alan suddenly stops. Since there are no subsequent references to Alan in any of Lennox's other letters or diaries, it seems likely that the affair came to an abrupt end. It is possible that Maugham had called his London secretary to order, or that Guy Little had got to hear of the existence of a rival and had warned him off, but it is really more likely, judging by the letters that have survived, that Alan, never very seriously committed to Lennox, lost interest. Lennox must have been very upset, but he cannot have been surprised: the relationship could never have gone anywhere – and perhaps neither of them had ever wanted it to.

The break with Alan did not stop him working. On the contrary.

When he got back to Cap Ferrat, Lennox put his mind again to the 'rather important' piece he needed for his launch in London, and returned to the oratorio *Jonah*, which he had started in 1933 (and which may now have absorbed something of Lennox's response to Stravinsky's choral writing in *Perséphone*). He also sketched out a string quartet, and revised his orchestral *Overture*.

In September 1935 Lennox travelled to Czechoslovakia for the premiere of the *Overture*, and the following month he was back in London to conduct the BBC Symphony Orchestra in the work's British premiere at the Proms. It was not a success. His peers on the ISCM's selection board – they included the English conductor and champion of new music, Edward Clark, and the German conductor Hermann Scherchen – may have rated the work highly, but the critics were almost unanimously hostile, even vicious. According to them, the new work was 'jazzy and dry jazz too',[91] 'singularly drab – sad little tunes against a plodding accompaniment',[92] 'a naïve but unlikeable expression of youthful high spirits in the calculated-whimsical style',[93] and 'more noises than tunes'.[94] The *Evening News* revived some of the old jingoism that Lennox had heard so many times before – and which had propelled him to France in the first place. The new work, the paper said, was not 'representative of English music' – the 'break-away school' to which it belonged was now 'a dwindling by-path on which the art of music is turning its back'.[95]

A fortnight after the *Overture* was played at the Proms, Lennox's two-piano *Polka* was given its first performance in Bristol. This did not fare much better – with one local critic dismissing it as 'grotesquely gay'.[96]

Roundly rejected and deeply discouraged, Lennox limped back to Cap Ferrat. This was hardly the grand launch he had hoped for. But it says much for his resilience and determination that he was able to bury his disappointment – indeed, his hurt – in hard work, completing, in a matter of weeks, the *Quartet for Strings* (the first of three). The work is in four movements, which move from fierce drama, through mystery and agitation, to 'an enigmatically reposeful conclusion'.[97] Lennox had better luck with this work. The Brussels-based Pro Arte Quartet – then one of the most distinguished quartets in the world – took up the new piece and gave the first performance in Cowdray Hall in November. Though reluctant to abandon his mother, Lennox travelled to London for the occasion, and reported that the work had been 'marvellously played'.[98] The programme also included Bartok's *Quartet No. 5* and Milhaud's *Quartet No. 2*. *The Times* wrote that the Milhaud 'showed up the prentice-hand' in Lennox's quartet – but that Lennox's writing was nevertheless 'fresh and vigorous'.[99]Another critic said it 'showed the young composer getting his teeth into his medium and beginning to worry it into shape',[100] a third that it was, on the whole, 'sane, robust and well-wrought'.[101] This was better than the response to the *Overture*, but it hardly added up to the recognition he had hoped for.

On the very same night as the premiere of Lennox's quartet, his old friends Vere Pilkington and David Ponsonby were themselves appearing on the concert platform in another part of London, in a concert of music by Bach and Handel conducted by Arnold Goldsbrough. A review in *The Times* took the unusual step of pointing out that the concert was given 'from the simple motive of a love of music ... without thought of profit or publicity or personal aggrandisement'.[102] After some cantatas by Bach, sung by Isobel Baillie, Pilkington and Ponsonby came on to play the same composer's *Concerto for Two Harpsichords in C Major*.

As a result of this clash of engagements, Pilkington and Ponsonby missed the début of Lennox's quartet, but they were able to hear the Pro Arte playing it again in a live broadcast on the BBC on the 9th.[103] They, too, repeated their Bach, twice more, but Lennox could not catch either performance because he had to get home to look after his mother.

On 9 December, back in Cap Ferrat, Lennox and Aline heard his quartet on the wireless. The broadcast meant a great deal to Aline, not only because it indicated that her son had made his mark as a composer at last, but also because she had never heard any of his music played really well.[104]

This proved to be 'one of Maman's last joys'.[105] Just eight days later she died. Though she had been ill with cancer for so long and must, at the end, have welcomed death – Lennox was heartbroken. He told his aunt Annie, Baroness d'Eppinghoven, how it happened:

> I shd like you to know that she didn't suffer at the end – as soon as it was certain that the end was near, the doctor ordered injections to help her to sleep peacefully and avoid pain. For the last 48 hours she lay asleep most of the time and only semi-conscious, gradually her breathing got fainter until it just ceased without any struggle or difficulty. She certainly suffered far less during the last week than she had for months. It was really the general break-up

> and poisoning of the whole system that brought about her death, but it was really a happy release if ever there were one. Poor darling, she had suffered so terribly it was heartrending to see – but now we must not be sad as she is surely reaping the reward of her patience and courage.[106]

The parting was 'a cruel thing to bear',[107] and for some days he lacked the courage to go on. His sister Gerry came to help for a week, then a friend, Gertrude Ford (sister-in-law of his uncle Arthur Harris) moved in to look after him, and for a while the Arthur Harrises themselves were there too. Lennox was so overwrought that he was unable to face the practical tasks of winding up his mother's affairs, selling the Villa Melfort and moving back to England. (In fact he kept the villa on till at least 1938,[108] and when at last he did sell the place, it was never registered properly.*)

Lennox told Nadia he was glad that his mother's soul had been liberated from a body that caused her such bitter suffering, and he knew he ought to rejoice in her deliverance – but could not:

> I try to get used to this absence, but I know that till I die I'll miss her every day ... it's not necessary that I should grieve so much because for her it's infinitely better – she was suffering more and more – it was so horrible, and now her soul has been liberated from a body that made her suffer so cruelly. So I mustn't be too sad, because there's an element of 'self pity', as we say in English, in that, and I feel that I ought to rejoice in this deliverance.[109]

It was now that his faith came to the rescue. He could not doubt for a single moment that her soul lived, and that one day he would be able to rejoin her – because that's what he wanted more than anything in the world. 'What's so strange is that I feel her influence on me is deeper now than when she was alive, that I must try to be worthy of her ... and I am so little worthy of her ... what I do is no more than a shadow of what I'd like to do – it's so difficult!'[110]

*This should have been done by his lawyer, in the form of an 'Attestation Immobilière après décès' registered at the Land Registry, but in 1995 Pauline Challoner, a lawyer in Nice, discovered there was no record. 'Had she [Mrs Berkeley] died elsewhere, it would be understandable that the estate in France may have been forgotten; but she lived and died in Nice and therefore it is most unusual that her estate not be wound up' (Mrs Challoner to FB 28 April 1995, BFP).

He told Nadia he was thinking of her all the time. The death of his 'Maman' had drawn him even closer to her, since they both lived a little 'in another world, invisible but quite real'.[111]

For all the strength of his faith in the invisible world, Lennox was close to despair in this one. Sorrowing, broken and alone, he had lost, in only two years, his father, his lover and now his mother. And the public acceptance of his music that he so much longed for seemed as elusive as ever. Not even the prospect of a further performance of his *Overture* at the ISCM Festival in Barcelona in three months' time could brighten his horizon.

15
Freda, Boarding School, 1930–9

Freda remembers very little of her early years at St Helen's School, Abingdon – except that she enjoyed games and lessons (especially English and history), that she was 'hopeless at sums', and 'really wasn't musical'. She distinctly recalls that she was fond of snails (because they were 'slow and soft – and no one else liked them'), and that she converted some old shoe-boxes into a multi-ward snail hospital where she could look after the wounded snails, which the other girls brought in for treatment.[1]

But no one looked after Freda, who may have seemed happy and uncomplicated but was actually nervous, insecure, and tormented by recurring nightmares. 'I was terrified of the dark, terrified of being left alone, terrified of traffic – I was frightened of everything, and used to wake up screaming in the night.' When her bed-wetting got worse, the school decided that she had been packed off to board too early and should return home for a year to grow out of it. But where was home, now that the Public Trustee had decided that Lancefield Street was unsuitable? It was left to the school to decide, and, in consultation with the Public Trustee, the principal, Sister Theodora Hilary, made arrangements for Freda to live in the lonely village of Aldworth on the chalk downs twenty miles south-east of St Helen's, as a paying guest of the impoverished vicar, the Revd Arthur Watson, and his wife. The Watsons had no fewer than six girls of their own at St Helen's (and a further four boys at school elsewhere) and, to help with all the school fees, they took in other children as paying guests – mostly the offspring of parents serving abroad. Such a large and youthful household, Sister Theodora thought, would provide the bracing environment that Freda needed. But it was not the right place for a London girl with emotional problems – and not only because it was cold and dark and altogether 'too rough and tumble'.

The overworked Mrs Watson was not really able to manage ten of her own children and up to four additional child boarders, including this new girl who needed special attention. Instead of helping to exorcize Freda's demons, she added to them by persecuting her, and regularly smacking her, on the bare bottom, 'for seemingly not very big misdemeanours', including wet beds (which only, of course, got wetter). But Freda, though frightened, was not resentful: in fact, she thought it was all her own fault. Looking back now, she says that Mrs Watson had 'some very good points to her', but probably resented the extra work that Freda's problems caused. 'I think, you know, if you have ten children and no money you inevitably get rather worked up and worn out.' Mr Watson must have heard Freda's occasional screams, but he was a quiet, studious man who 'lived on a higher plane', and never got around to asking what was going on. The other children knew. Several of them have made contact with Freda since then, expressing regret about the past, and in 2005 the youngest, Stephen Watson, of Duncan, British Columbia, invited Freda to a family reunion at Aldworth in June that year, adding, 'I hope and pray that your life with our family was not too much of a trial ...'[2] Freda was touched by the letter, and grateful to all the Watson children for their kind thoughts, but she preferred not to return to Aldworth.[3]

A welfare officer from the Public Trustee, Miss Harris, called at the vicarage three times that long year to check that all was well. Freda could have made a complaint about the punishments, but she did not. 'It was, sort of, difficult to explain – you know.' So the smacking went on; and the bed-wetting (and the nervousness that lay at its root) got much worse.

Throughout that year at Aldworth Freda did her lessons with the younger Watsons in the vicarage dining room, under the tutelage of 'Jilly' Gillette, a governess who lived in a cottage down by the cowshed. When at last the year was up she was glad to get back to school and her friends and organized games – and away from her tormentor.

Her life now took on a certain predictable regularity: school during term-time, the crowded vicarage during the holidays, Herne Bay for a fortnight in the summer, and Lancefield Street for Christmas. Except one year when there was an epidemic of mumps and Freda and her friend Ann Leeper* had to stay at school for Christmas. Freda remembers

*Ann Leeper was the daughter of Sir Reginald Leeper (1888-1968), architect of the British Council, who was then Head of the Foreign Office Press Department, and was later to become Ambassador to the Court of the King of the Hellenes during the post-war Greek Civil War. In 1950 he published a book about the Greek

little of it all, except that it was then that she acquired her beloved Milly Miles, a doll with golden curls. Christmas with the Nunneys has remained a happy memory: with a turkey roasting on the 'jack', and the uncles and aunts and cousins gathered around the piano in the parlour while Fred and Blanch led the singing of all the old ballads and music hall songs they had learned from Marie Lloyd. On Christmas morning there was a stocking hanging at the end of her bed with nuts and a tangerine, and everywhere decorations and lights – even the market stalls in Kilburn Lane were ablaze with gas lamps. For Freda, up from the country, Christmas in London was fairyland. But though her kind old grandparents did all they could, with no money, she used to feel a bit deprived when she got back to school and heard about the other girls' presents.[4] The irony was that Freda herself had more money than the rest of them put together, only it was all in trust for later.

Old copies of the *St Helen's School Magazine* mark the passing years with occasional events. For example, in the autumn term of 1935 Freda joined the school outing to The Mohammedan Court (whatever that might have been); on All Saints Day she went to the Regal Cinema to see *The Scarlet Pimpernel*, and afterwards to a White Dance (for which special permission had been given, for the very first time, for the girls to wear coloured frocks); and as a member of the junior netball team Freda will have shared in the disappointment at the loss of the away match against Greycotes – and in the chagrin of a public rebuke to the players for being 'far too slow in accommodating themselves to the grass court'.[5]

But that same year, 1935, brought a big change 'at home', another major move in Freda's life. Mr Watson resigned the living of Aldworth in favour of a better parish, with a larger stipend, at Ufford, between Peterborough and Stamford, and Freda (and Milly Miles) were rehoused in a rectory at Harvington near Evesham. The new foster parents were the Revd Horace Boultbee, a former missionary in Australia, and his wife. Freda was much happier with 'Pop' and 'Ma' and their smaller family of four daughters: Fay, who was a friend from St Helen's, Joy, Pam and Esmé.

Crisis called *When Greek Meets Greek*. Ann Leeper married Donald Orbach, became a psychotherapist involved with older people and attitudes to death, about which she wrote at least two books, and died in 2003, leaving a son, David.

In the summer of 1936 Freda was among the first of the St Helen's girls to use the new school swimming pool – previously they had to walk all the way through Abingdon to get to a bathing spot in the Thames. She also had her first poem published. It was called 'If'. If it were possible to go back in time, she would like to 'rove the seas with Drake so bold' and 'search for lands not found as yet / and hunt for ivory, pearls and gold'.

> And I would go to London town
> And watch fair ladies going in
> To where there sat in velvet gown
> A fair queen, waiting for a king.

But then she banishes romance: it was far better, her poem decided, to 'think of happiness / And of the joys of present day'.[6]

That Christmas a gloom fell on the school as the headmistress gathered the girls together and announced that King Edward VIII had abdicated. She did not go into details but the possibility that the country was on the verge of revolution so unnerved some of the girls that they burst into tears. Freda and Ann Leeper, more knowing that the rest, had seen it coming. At the carol service a few days later they expressed their feelings in a reworking of an old favourite. 'Hark the herald angels sing, Mrs Simpson stole our king.'[7]

The following spring – on, as it happened, Lennox's thirty-fourth birthday – Edward VIII's younger brother Albert was crowned king as George VI, and the whole school had three days' *exeat*. This left Freda and a handful of other homeless girls in a more or less empty school, enjoying 'quite a holiday spirit, all rules being generally relaxed'. That same term Freda and Ann, encouraged by their success at the carol service, collaborated on a new poem called 'Wishes', which included the innocent lines, 'Imagine the feeling of pleasure I'd get / If at tennis my balls would go over the net.'[8] And each year Freda progressed through the grades of the Elocution exams, until in 1939 she reached Grade VI. And became a prefect. (And got a crush on the matron, Miss Carter.)

When Freda was seventeen, her schooling came to an end at last. Summer 1940 could not have been a worse time to emerge from her cocoon. France had fallen to the Nazis, the Battle of Britain was at its peak and the Blitz had brought the war into the streets of London. The Public Trustee had planned that Freda should go on to a finishing school in Switzerland. That was now impossible. Instead it was decided that she should continue to do what St Helen's girls were bred to do: learn how to earn her own living. So she was enrolled in a smart secretarial college run by, and named after, Miss Kerr-Sander. In peace time the college used to occupy a house in Stratton Street, on the former Berkeley estate in Mayfair. When war broke out, the college was evacuated to the Elizabethan manor house of Stanway near Broadway in the Cotswolds, home of the Earl of Wemyss and March. There Freda spent three terms learning how to be a secretary, and on 30 July 1941, as the Germans entered Ukraine and the Japanese landed in Indo China, she graduated with 120 words a minute in shorthand and 55 wpm in typewriting, 'Fair' in book-keeping and simple accounts, and 'a good clear style and descriptive talent' in journalism.

Thus armed for commercial life, Freda Bernstein caught the train home to Pop and Ma Boultbee and the girls at Harvington – and applied for a job with a pig farmer.

1a Pietro Fabris, *Kenneth Lord Fortrose At Home in Naples, 1770. Concert Party.* Fortrose (Lennox's great-great-great grandfather) back view, centre; Wolfgang and Leopold Mozart at keyboards rear left.

1b Jean Laurent Mosnier, *Lady Caroline Mackenzie* (Lennox's great-great-grandmother, later Comtesse de Melfort)

1c Cécile Berkeley, née Drummond de Melfort (Lennox's grandmother), later Countess of Berkeley, *c.* 1872

2a Sir James Harris (Lennox's grandfather), 1901, when consul at Nice

2b His wife Gerhardine, (Lennox's grandmother), *c.* 1900

2c Randal, Viscount Dursley (Lennox's uncle), later 8th Earl of Berkeley, in Bermuda, *c.* 1886

2d Kate Jackson, née Brand (Lennox's aunt), later Countess of Berkeley, *c.* 1886

3a Aline Harris (later Mrs Hastings Berkeley, Lennox's mother), left, and her siblings, Nelly, Arthur and Annie, Nice, *c.* 1889

3b Lennox and his cousin Louise-Marie ('Lison') d'Eppinghoven, Menton, 1906

3c Lennox and his terrier, Tip, Boars Hill, *c.* 1908

3d School House, Gresham's, 1918: Lennox front row right

4a Lennox, Oxford, 1926

4b W. H. Auden, Oxford, 1926

4c John Greenidge (left) as the Prince of Wales, Evelyn Waugh as the Dean of Balliol, in the OUDS film *The Scarlet Woman*, 1925

4d David Ponsonby (holding hat) at a family wedding *c.* 1924

5a Maurice Ravel and Lennox, London 1925 or 1926

5b Lennox, centre, with his father, Captain Hastings Berkeley, and godmother, Sybil Jackson, outside her house, Foxcombe Cottage, Boars Hill, *c.* 1923

5c John Greenidge in the dicky, Michael Dugdale, Alan Pryce-Jones and Vere Pilkington (at the wheel)

6a Lennox at upper window, 4 rue du Ruisseau, Paris, 1928

6b José Raffalli, Paris, *c.* 1928

6d John Greenidge and Lennox, 4 rue du Ruisseau, Paris, 1928

7a Nadia Boulanger at her Cavaillé-Coll organ, 36 rue Ballu, Paris, late 1920s

7b John Greenidge, *Lennox Berkeley, Paris, 1926*

7c Lennox with his sister Geraldine and their parents at Domaine du Rayet, Falicon, 1930s

8a Widow Lloyd and Vere Pilkington, Fawley, 1926

8b Georges Auric and Francis Poulenc, Monte Carlo, *c.* 1927

8c Igor Markevitch, Lake Geneva, 1928

16
Lennox and Ben, Cornwall, 1936

Barcelona not only brightened but broadened Lennox's horizon. He was gratified by the Madrid Symphony Orchestra's 'brilliant performance' of his neo-classical *Overture for Chamber Orchestra*, excited to hear Alban Berg's new masterpiece, the *Violin Concerto*, and exhilarated by dancing the *sardana* and listening to the Catalan melodies on Montjuïc. And, most significantly of all, he made two important new young friends, the composer Benjamin Britten and the writer and critic Peter Burra.

Back in Paris in May 1936, after a brief stay in Madrid, following the festival in Barcelona, Lennox set to work on preparations for the premiere in London of his first major choral work, the oratorio *Jonah*. He had completed it in 1933,[1] while still a student of Nadia Boulanger, and had spent another two years revising it. The second version finished, Lennox dedicated it to the memory of his mother and father. The first performance was to be given by the BBC Chorus and Orchestra in the Concert Hall of Broadcasting House on 19 June 1936, and broadcast live on the BBC. This was Lennox's biggest and most public work so far, and he had high hopes that it might make his name. His publishers J. & W. Chester were equally optimistic. Berkeley, they claimed, had been 'under observation' by musicians ever since his piano music had revealed the 'lines of genius that were amplified by his orchestral *Overture*'. The new oratorio, one of the most notable choral works of its time, offered 'a welcome proof that much of the future of great music is still within England's reach'.[2] No new work could have received a more promising fanfare.

Lennox's *Jonah* is a setting (for tenor and baritone, mixed chorus, boys' voices and orchestra) of the first part of the Bible story. It stops at the point when 'the fish ... vomited out Jonah upon the dry land' – with some words of praise from Psalm 139 forming a chorus at the end. So it never gets to the moral of the story, the part that might have been expected to appeal to a newly-converted Catholic composer: that repentance wins forgiveness – even for the sinners of Nineveh, whom Jonah is bidden to condemn for their habitual, but unnamed, vice. Instead Lennox's setting concentrates on the first two verses, which tell the familiar tale of the storm, the shipwreck and Jonah's swallowing by the whale. He uses the psalm for the final chorus in which the boys sing of God's absolute protection, in heaven and in hell, in the lightness of the morning and the darkness of the night. But Lennox, usually a stickler for the integrity of his texts, miscopied the words, writing 'Whither then shall I go then [*sic*] from thy presence and whither shall I go then from thy presence?' instead of 'Whither shall I go from thy spirit? Or whither shall I flee from thy presence?' And throughout the work he keeps repeating even the least interesting phrases of the text, so the momentum of the story is lost.

Before he reached London in late May, Lennox was in a maelstrom of printer's proofs and pre-rehearsal problems: who should conduct, Adrian Boult or Ernest Ansermet ('amazingly good at modern works'),[3] and which boys should sing the final chorus? In the end the conductor was neither Boult (musical director of the BBC) nor Ansermet (founder-conductor of the Orchestre de la Suisse Romande), but the intolerant and hot-headed Clarence Raybould (assistant conductor of the BBC Symphony Orchestra) – who was to stab both Lennox and Ben in their backs a few years on. The final chorus was a knottier problem. Lennox was insistent that it should be sung by boys, but the London County Council refused to give permission – perhaps because they were afraid it would keep the boys up too late at night. In despair, Lennox told the BBC that if he had known the LCC had what he called this 'choirboy complex' he would have recast the final chorus; as it was, the ending would now be spoiled.[4] Actually it was not. In a compromise solution, Sadler's Wells's principal soprano Joan Cross sang the boys' part – and Lennox was delighted. 'Cross is absolute heaven,' he wrote after a rehearsal on 15 June; 'when I heard her sing in the last chorus, I didn't mind about the absence of the choir-boys, which is saying quite a lot!'[5]

Lennox had to wrestle with another, entirely private, and very typical, dilemma: whom should he take to the premiere as his companion – José Raffalli, his former lover and dependent (and possessive) friend, or Peter Burra, his new friend and possible future lover? He had promised, when they parted in Barcelona, to take the latter, but he knew José would be furious. Having just spent an idyllic weekend with Peter,* during which they seem to have discovered that they had more in common than music and books, Lennox was keener than ever that Peter should be there for the new work. He was also very anxious that he should like it, and gave him a proof copy of the full score, signed and inscribed, so he could read it in advance.† On saying good-bye to Peter, Lennox was surprised to discover that he had suddenly found the key to the start of a projected symphony,‡ and this seems to have reinforced his feeling that Peter was a very special new friend. But how was he to get him to Broadcasting House, without offending José ? Lennox reached a diplomatic solution: both young men would go to the concert, but only José would sit beside the composer. 'I do hope that you don't think I am being horrible about Friday evening,' Lennox wrote to Peter, 'but you know the reason, and I think that it will be better if we first meet after the concert and go somewhere together.'[6]

As things turned out Lennox must have wished that neither had come. Most of the critics hated it, and the huge audience listening at home could not hear it properly because the broadcast was ruined by a freak storm.[7] But one important 'critic', his other new friend from Barcelona, Ben Britten, 'enjoyed it a lot', despite the atmospherics – which were so bad in Frinton-on-Sea (where he was staying with his mother) that he was afraid they would be electrocuted by the radio aerial.[8] Nevertheless Ben was able to judge that *Jonah* had 'some really good things in it'. In his diary, on the night of the broadcast, he wrote that it was to the work's advantage that it showed the influence of Stravinsky, but the harmony was 'extremely personal' and the choral writing 'extremely beautiful – especially at the end'.[9] In a letter to Lennox, Ben made the point that it was 'emotionally dramatic rather than eventfully descriptive'[10] – an observation which Lennox took as a

*It is unclear whether this was at Burra's rented cottage in Berkshire or at LB's flat in Great Ormond Street, London, but wherever it was LB was 'terribly happy the whole time' (LB to PB, undated but probably 15 June 1936, B–MA).

†Long after Burra's death in 1937, this inscribed copy was sold privately (email Dr Richard Thompson to TS, 28 February 2006).

‡LB did not start serious work on his *Symphony No. 1* till March 1941 when he was staying with his Uncle Randal at Berkeley Castle; it was first performed at the Proms in July 1943.

compliment. In his reply, he said that he had deliberately allowed only enough description 'to make a décor for the real business' (the musical argument). He was quite pleased with the actual performance, although he felt things were 'a bit ragged in places'. The chorus was excellent but lacked 'quite enough attack', the piano part was full of mistakes and Raybould had been 'an efficient and lively conductor if not an inspiring one'. As far as the writing was concerned, Lennox was 'by no means satisfied with it', but thought it was 'the right kind of music'.[11] By this he seems to have meant that dissonant harmonies now had the upper hand, whereas his earlier music, influenced by the 'clarity, order and emotional climate' of his favourite French composers (Ravel, Fauré, Françaix, Poulenc),[12] had been what Basil Douglas called warm, cheerful and sensitive.

Douglas was then working for the BBC (though he went on to become a music administrator and, later, an artists' agent). He had met Lennox for the first time three days earlier, over lunch at the flat in Charlotte Street, just behind Broadcasting House, which he shared with Peter Pears and a BBC conductor, Trevor Harvey. Afterwards he noted in his diary, 'liked him [Lennox] much better than I thought I would'.[13] It was rehearsals of *Jonah* that brought them together, and it was clear that Douglas did not much like the music. He happened to be in the engineering control room at Broadcasting House on the night of the *Jonah* broadcast, and in his diary later he wrote,'*Jonah*, by Lennox Berkeley, first performance. Clarence Raybould conducted, very stiffly ... I don't think there is very much to the work, but there are original touches in the choral writing here and there. A lot of it is frankly boring.'[14]

Many years later Douglas said he had been surprised by the change in Lennox's musical language and believed it was a deliberate attempt to shake off his reputation as a 'very charming sort of salon composer'. If it was, it backfired badly, because Lennox's music was immediately seen as *avant-garde* while he himself 'came under suspicion' by the grey-suited arbiters of the musical establishment. Douglas speculated that Nadia Boulanger might have been responsible.[15] An unidentified music critic of *The Times* was in no doubt that Ma'moiselle was the culprit. In a brutally frank review of Lennox's music years later, this anonymous critic wrote that *Jonah* had revealed the full effect of the 'Stravinskian desiccation' to which Lennox had been subjected by his famous French teacher; her influence had nearly wrecked his chances as a composer and it had taken him years to get over it and to find himself.[16] (Perhaps Lennox agreed, because he later withdrew *Jonah*, telling his biographer Peter Dickinson in 1972 that he did not think he had been able to speak with his own voice in such a large-scale work, and he was not interested in it any more.[17])

Whether Ben saw Lennox's new asperity as the 'right kind of music' is another matter. He certainly did not care for the methods of the teacher it was supposed to have come from: indeed he is said to have 'profoundly distrusted the "school" of composition which he felt to be the result of her [Boulanger's] influence'. It was his belief that a good teacher should discover and draw out a pupil's individuality, and never impose his or her own aesthetic.[18] And in his view Nadia Boulanger had 'ruined Lennox' with all her musical 'chi-chi'.[19]

Curiously enough, given her voracious appetite for new music, Boulanger had neither seen nor heard a note of Ben's music by 1936, according to Lennox, but she was interested, and when *Our Hunting Fathers* was published she asked him to lend her a copy.[20] Her opinion is not recorded, but she did not care for Ben's Rimbaud cycle, *Les Illuminations*, when Lennox showed her a proof in Paris in 1940, as Lennox told Ben in a letter at the time:

> I couldn't get Nadia to be very keen – she doesn't seem to take to your music easily. We had a terrific argument about it. She much admired the String writing, but thinks that you haven't found your real musical language yet – she doesn't feel that the harmony is sufficiently personal. I can see what she means, but it doesn't worry me so much – in fact I definitely disagree. I suspect that it's a temperamental thing really.[21]

Ten years younger than Lennox, Ben was light years older in terms of musical confidence. He had already found his composing voice, knew how to use it – and knew he had to use it: what was the point of being a composer if your music was not you? Lennox had not yet learned this lesson, or if he had he had not yet acquired sufficient confidence to apply it. His music still lacked any powerful sense of individuality; emotional commitment was not strongly evident either, and though a defining musical personality was to come, largely through Ben's influence, it was never more assertive than a heartbeat. Music, for Lennox, was essentially something private, a means of communicating with his maker rather than stirring an audience. And when it does seem about to stir, Lennox often pulls back to some elegant classical formula, as though drama or emotion were unsafe. The presence of Nadia at his elbow is almost palpable.

Lennox never forgot his debt to Nadia Boulanger – for her example of self-criticism, economy (achieving maximum effect with the minimum number of notes) and self-discipline.[22] And for her 'infinitely precious' trust and encouragement. 'I find more and more', he told her in 1937, 'that music is a horribly difficult thing. You support me in this struggle, as in the other battles of life.'[23] Lennox knew that Ben disapproved of his distinguished teacher, and he may have sensed that this would be a valuable counterweight to the effects of his six years at what fellow students called the 'Boulangerie'. He envied the younger man's superb craftsmanship, his 'technical adroitness and instrumental wizardry'.[24] As Peter Dickinson has observed, 'Everything he [Lennox] had been struggling to acquire technically for over a decade Britten seemed to possess already.'[25]

But Ben was very much less confident outside the staves of his own musical world. He 'still looked and felt like an adolescent', and 'though astonishingly gifted, and already immensely knowledgeable within his vocation, was relatively untutored in nearly everything else'.[26] At about this time, his credentials were put to the test in both love and politics. From his mentor Auden he had received what seems to be a passionate declaration of love in a poem dedicated to him, 'Night Covers up the Rigid Land' (though Donald Mitchell is at pains to warn against the danger of interpreting this poem too autobiographically,[27] and the critic John Fuller 'is not at all certain ... that it is addressed to Britten himself').[28] When an old school friend, John Pounder, wrote to say that, like so many other idealistic young men who were looking to Russia as an alternative means of ordering the world economy, he had recently joined the Communist Party, Ben noted approvingly: 'I am very glad you have taken the plunge. Very courageous.'[29] Which sounds somehow more dutiful than heartfelt. To Wystan Ben said nothing, and, though in the habit of setting his verses, he did not put the new lines to music for another eighteen months.

Ben himself had not yet taken the plunge into either love or the Party. In love he was still a public school sixth-former enjoying romantic crushes on pretty 'juniors' (Piers Dunkerley, then aged fifteen – and later to become a Royal Marine Commando – was his current passion), and intellectual crushes on clever 'prefect' figures (like Wystan

Auden).* In politics he was, at this time, as we know from Barcelona, left-of-centre: sympathetic to Communism, opposed to Fascism, anti-Establishment and all for peace. By mid-1936 he was brimming with ideas about politics and longing to talk, not, just then, to Wystan, whose cleverness alarmed him as much as it excited him, but to an admirer who would listen sympathetically and uncritically. Auden, according to the pianist Graham Johnson, made Britten feel inadequate, 'wrong-footed by the poet's intelligence and his conversation which sometimes resembled an overwhelming monologue'.[30] Britten himself said at this time that he wished he could 'conquer this appalling inferiority complex that I always have when with vital brains like his [Auden's]'.[31]

Lennox would have seemed an ideal substitute because he could play Ben to Ben's Wystan – and there is nothing like reversing the roles to get into the characters. Besides there were some telling connections: Lennox had known Wystan at Oxford (and had been the very first composer to set his verse to music), and, like Wystan and Ben himself, had been to school at Gresham's. It also helped that Lennox so clearly admired the musical prodigy from Lowestoft: 'The rest of us are all children compared to you,' he was to write to Ben a few years later. Nor was his admiration confined to Ben's music – and no one warmed to adoration more than Ben (or kicked so hard against it when that adoration got too intense). But if Ben sought a mother substitute in Lennox, as he seems to have sought in all his important relationships,[32] he was soon to find out that he had misread the signs; for that's what Lennox needed too. (But the following year Lennox was to liken himself to Ben's mother,[33] and to show how perverse human psychology can be, he was to tell Freda that she reminded him of his own mother.[34])

While Lennox was in London reading Peter Burra's biography of Wordsworth and the score of Berg's opera *Wozzeck* (which he thought 'very beautiful, though I get rather tired of the thickness of the harmony and the continual jumping of the major 7th interval which is a mannerism shared by all the atonal school'[35]), Ben arranged to rent what he called a 'hut' in Cornwall for the rest of the summer. It was not going to

*Donald Mitchell develops this theory in LFAL, p. 18, and Graham Johnson explores the relationship with Auden in his revealing sixth lecture in Johnson, Graham, *Britten, Voice & Piano - Lectures on the Vocal Music of Benjamin Britten.*

be cheap – '£1 per week for hut, 12/6 for woman [who cleaned and cooked], & goodness knows what for food'[36] – but it would be worth it, to be able to work 'with absolutely no interruptions'.[37] He took with him his new piece, a setting for soprano and symphony orchestra of Auden's animal parable *Our Hunting Fathers* (due for performance at the Norwich Festival in September), the scores of some Mahler symphonies and Beethoven late quartets, Forster's *A Passage to India* (recommended by Burra)[38] and a dose of Karl Marx (prescribed by Auden).[39] And in the week in which Civil War broke out in Spain, he invited Lennox to come and join him.

At this time – mid July – Lennox was staying in Gloucestershire with his elderly musical admirer Gladys Bryans.* He was working on his *Five Short Pieces* for piano and wrestling with problems in a piece for choir and orchestra.† The truth is that Lennox's mind was full of *Our Hunting Fathers*, which Ben had played through for him on the piano in London a week earlier. Lennox had been deeply impressed – 'far the most important thing he has done'[40] – so he leapt at the chance to see more of a composer whose talent and technical proficiency he admired so much. 'Your letter', he wrote to Ben, 'made me feel how much I wanted really to take the opportunity of spending a little time with you and being able to talk over many things that we want to talk about.'[41] So he said yes and set off.

The 'hut' was at Crantock near Newquay, in the grounds of a house called Quarryfield, a few hundred yards from the rocky coast of the Atlantic. Lennox arrived on the evening of 25 July, and the two friends went straight down to the sea for a swim before dinner – and a walk and a talk afterwards. Doubtless their subjects included Spain, since Ben had been so upset by the news the day before about 'fascists lining up all the little Popular Front boys against a wall & putting machine

*Gladys Sophia Bryans (died 6 January 1951), of Rudge House, Painswick, Glos, the spinster aunt of the Playne brewing family of Minchinhampton (hence FB's later, temporary, nickname for LB: Minchinhampton, or just Minch).

†The choral and orchestral piece was *Deux Poèmes de Pindar*, dedicated to princesse Edmond de Polignac; LB finally got it finished, and it was given its first performance at a concert in the Queen's Hall, London, on 24 November 1936, by the Oriana Madrigal Society Choir and the London Symphony Orchestra conducted by Nadia Boulanger, making her debut in Britain (LB to PB 16 July 1936, B–MA).

guns on them' that he had sketched a funeral march in their memory.[42] And Ben may have pointed the finger at the Catholic Church. In a letter to Ben later in the year Lennox agreed that the Catholic Church was very much to blame for the Civil War, but, he added prophetically, '... I suppose it is no concern of ours – it's their muddle and their tragedy – we may have ours soon enough.'[43]

It was seven years since Lennox had converted to Catholicism. Not surprisingly he believed passionately that some sort of Christian faith was essential: how could one function in life believing in human reason alone, when there was so much that reason could not explain? For Lennox, believing the Church's teaching, even if he failed to live up to it, was 'an immense happiness'. This did not mean that he did not have doubts and difficulties, but he was convinced that we should be resigned to the fact that 'our understanding, in this life, is limited, and that disbelief involves just as many intellectual difficulties as any religion known to me'.[44] Perhaps he even tried to interest Ben in Catholicism – though it would have been unlike Lennox to proselytize. The younger man's Low Church upbringing – and temporary disenchantment with conventional Christianity – would not seem to have provided fertile soil, yet Ben did believe that 'there is in every man the spirit of God'.* Significantly, someone at some point in 1936 gave Ben an English Missal, which he went so far as to sign,† even though he did not consider himself a Christian at this time.[45] The fact that this book subsequently fell into the hands of Lennox suggests that he himself may have been the donor and that Ben, on deciding that Catholicism was not for him, returned it. At all events, by January 1937 Ben was noting in his diary, 'it wouldn't take much to turn me R. C.'[46] But it has to be admitted that he was responding less to his new Missal than to another new addition to his library, Firbank's richly decadent novel, *Concerning the Eccentricities of Cardinal Pirelli* – which ends, fatally, with the mad cardinal streaking around a cathedral in pursuit of a coquettish choirboy called the Chicklet. Ben thought it '... brilliantly amusing ... the stuffy sensual atmosphere of these Sanctuaries moves me a lot ... They are so incredibly peaceful, so absolutely divorced from realities.'[47]

*The opening of BB's submission to the Tribunal for the Registration of Conscientious Objectors, 4 May 1942 (LFAL, p. 1046)].
†This *Small Missal* (Burns & Oates, 1936), signed 'Benjamin Britten', is preserved in BFP.

But before exploring Chicklets and the Church, there were more immediately pressing matters, such as the dangers of sea bathing at Crantock. Ben warned that there had been 'umpteen tragedies' because of dangerous currents – Augustus John's son, Henry, had been drowned while staying at Quarryfield the previous summer*[48] – and he advised that it was unsafe to 'go in deeper than one's penis'.[49] Despite this curiously particular constraint, they swam and sunbathed whenever it was fine ('a strange occurrence for Crantock as the weather is as treacherous as ever'[50]). Ben, who loved surfing on the wild Atlantic breakers, was becoming 'the complete surfist',[51] staying in for hours and coming out 'solidified with cold'.[52] Lennox was so taken with the new sport that when he was in Jersey the following month he sought out a surfing beach in order to perfect his technique.[53]

Ben had colonized a bit of Crantock beach for bathing stark naked: 'the sheer sensual extasy [*sic*] of it,' he wrote in his diary. 'Utter bliss!'[54] But with Lennox he would not allow himself anything quite so Dionysian: they lay together on the beach only 'partly naked'.[55] This fondness for cold bathing (and, in the winter, cold baths) was almost a fetish with Ben. The librettist and director of several of his operas, Eric Crozier, recalled that in the 1940s Ben used to swim four or five times a day in summer and quite often last thing at night too – and frequently with nothing on. 'One had to be perpetually plunging into the water, not for the physical pleasure it was supposed to give, but as if it were a kind of moral code one had to obey.'[56] Lennox, who loved swimming, would not have gone that far, but he believed that sea-bathing 'does one good both morally and physically'.[57]

They wanted to play tennis but could not find a court, so they went for long walks instead, though Ben the socialist was irritated by the amount of trespassing they had to do in order to avoid Keep Out signs on private land: 'Oh this capitalist system!' he complained in his diary.[58]

When it was raining they stayed in, working, writing letters and reading. Lennox was thoroughly enjoying Forster's *A Passage to India*, while Ben was persevering with his Marx, which he found 'hard going but edifying'.[59] Lennox had never read any Marx but was familiar with the general drift, and told Ben: '... though I feel a certain amount of sympathy with Communist ideas as an economic thing, I can't help thinking

*For a fuller account of the tragedy see Holroyd, *Augustus John*, vol. ii, pp. 167–8 .

that it is based on the most unattractive of all philosophies. I don't think I could ever accept such a materialistic conception, it seems to me to rob humanity of many of its best qualities and to put in their place a sort of self-sufficiency that is generally a very unpleasant thing ... .'[60]

From Russian Communism their conversation may have moved back again to Spanish fascism and the Civil War – and the revolution in Barcelona the previous week when the workers defeated the army. What had happened to that gaudy concert hall? Would the militia have taken over the Hotel Falcón? And were the people still dancing the *sardana*? By some such route the two friends will have returned to that sunny afternoon with Peter Burra on Montjuïc when they were so stirred by the Catalan melodies accompanying the *sardana* dancing display and Ben had jotted down the notes on an old envelope. Exhilarated all over again, the two composers there and then agreed to collaborate on converting those notes into an orchestral suite of Catalan dances.

With *Mont Juic* thus happily conceived, Lennox and Ben put their heads together to work on their most recent pieces. Lennox was 'helping me alot [*sic*] with Our Hunting Fs,'[61] Ben noted. (Lennox thought the work was both exciting and very beautiful, and likely to 'make rather a sensation'.[62]) And Ben was helping Lennox with his new piano pieces. The two composers had very different ways of working. Ben 'thought first of each new composition in terms of forms' which gestated in his mind, often at night or on a walk, and only when he had planned a piece did he sit down and write it, at a desk, never a piano – though he did use the keyboard to 'play through what he'd just written to hear the shape'.[63] Lennox would start with a clear idea of the general 'feeling' he wanted to convey, then he would search for the right notes at the piano;[64] he called this process 'the strumming-through' school of composition.[65] (In later life he was still relying on the piano and regretting that he could not write a bar of music without it. In this respect he was like Stravinsky, though the Russian stuffed a blanket in his upright, in order to muffle the sound.[66] All they both required of a working piano was that it should convey some sense of the pitch.)* Either way, a

*MB makes the point that Stravinsky's reliance on the piano as a compositional aid can be detected in many of his works, including *The Rite of Spring*, where the famous accented and repeated chords of E flat and E major, played simultaneously, lie precisely under the fingers. RN notes that Stravinsky's studio piano in Los Angeles was out of tune, like Dutilleux's piano in Paris still is today (RN email to TS, 5 September 2007).

piano was essential, and Lennox managed to find one in the village, but it was such a poor instrument that 'the effect of *Our Hunting Fathers* and Lennox's new organ & piano pieces is beyond description',[67] so they used their eyes and minds to bring their scores to life, which came naturally to Ben but was a painful discipline for Lennox; then they dissected them together.

This comparing of notes, common to all young artists, is especially useful to young composers, who, as Aaron Copland has observed, can 'learn more from the attentive eye and sensitive ear of a fellow craftsman than from almost any other source'. Recalling, years later, his own rapport with Ben in 1938, Copland noted that long before a composer was afforded the luxury of hearing his own orchestration in actual sound there was the possibility that a young colleague would, as it were, hear it for him. 'Peering at the same four measures of orchestral score for fifteen minutes, carefully weighing the pros and cons of instrumental balance while you wait with bated breath, your composer friend is likely to come up with some completely unexpected judgement such as you never would have thought of yourself.'[68]

Lennox would have discovered just the same excitement exchanging ideas with his new-found composer-friend – though he felt it easier to accept criticism than to dish it out. More's the pity, perhaps, since, in their discussions about *Our Hunting Fathers* he might have been able to advise Ben to simplify the writing. The text was devised by Auden as a protest against the international political situation (German troops entering the Rhineland, the rise of the Popular front in France, the annexation of Abyssinia by Italy). It took the form of what Humphrey Carpenter calls 'a parable of man's relations to the animal kingdom',[69] opening and closing with poems by Auden himself, 'The Creatures' and 'Our Hunting Fathers'. The verses are unusually obscure, but there is no denying the underlying Communism: the epilogue actually quotes Lenin, 'To hunger, work illegally and be anonymous'. The county audience at the premiere in Norwich in September was to find it pretty hard going, and Lennox was not entirely surprised: 'I like it immensely,' he told Peter Burra afterwards, 'but I admit that it wouldn't be easy to follow at first hearing, and Auden's words, beautiful as they are, don't make it any easier to understand for the uninitiated.'[70] (There seems to be some evidence that Lennox changed his mind about the work later in his life.)

As a counterpoint to the serious business of scrutinizing their own scores, there was Laughing at the Masters. Lennox had brought with him the scores of new symphonies by Walton (No 1 in B Flat) and Vaughan Williams (No 4 in F Minor) and, like naughty schoolboys, the two composers spent what Ben called 'hysterical evenings pulling them to pieces – the amateurishness and clumsiness of the Williams – the "gitters" [presumably 'jitters', i.e. nervousness] of the fate-ridden Walton – & the over-pretentiousness of both – & *abominable* scoring.' Ben acknowledged that both these works were superior to most contemporary English music, but he found it difficult to resist knocking them when so much was ascribed to them.[71] (Nevertheless when he met Walton the following year he felt the same crippling awe as Wystan inspired in him: '... he is so obviously the head prefect of English music, whereas I'm the promising young new boy,' he wrote.[72]) Lennox felt the same about the English musical scene generally, which was much more limited than the French, and dominated by Vaughan Williams, Walton and Lambert – but there was not a single composer in England with whom he had any real affinity.[73] That is why the friendship with Ben meant so much.

Ben was delighted to find that Lennox agreed with him on most points '& it is nice to discuss things we don't agree on!'[74] One of these was pacifism, about which Lennox subsequently recalled they had 'great arguments ... but I don't know what conclusions we reached – almost certainly opposite ones!'[75] Both men were basically pacifist, but while Ben was uncompromising in his opposition to war, Lennox was more pragmatic, recognizing that there were occasions when confrontation was inevitable and even desirable, in order to crush a ruthless oppressor.

Another area of disagreement was sex – as they discovered when they continued their talk at night, in bed. Ben noted, teasingly, in his diary 'how intimate one becomes when the lights are out!'[76] The intimacies must have remained spoken only, as the next day's diary suggests some kind of physical resistance by Ben: 'I am very attached to him [Lennox], even after this short time. In spite of his avowed sexual weakness for young men of my age & form – he is considerate & open, & we have come to an agreement on that subject.'[77]

Talking will have done them both good. Ben had not yet committed himself to his sexuality – he was fascinated and excited but repelled and fearful. He had not even reached any real emotional acceptance of his sexuality (Wystan and his friends thought he was positively backward in this respect[78]), and he badly needed to talk about it. Lennox, by comparison, was something of an old hand, but he would have found talking about it difficult, even unnecessary. He must have made, or at least suggested, a sexual approach which Ben disliked. The agreement they reached on the subject was at Ben's bidding and seems to have been a formula along the lines of 'I like you very much – but not in that way': in other words, no bed. After all, Ben's weakness, however suppressed it may have remained, was for boys – and Lennox was an old man of thirty-three. Lennox accepted Ben's terms because he could not refuse without losing what he (and Wystan) wanted even more, the *ami particulier*-cum-artistic collaborator; like Wystan, he dreamed of 'an equals' meeting'.[79] But it did not stop either of them wishing the relationship could be complete.

Britten's tastes need some explaining. His editor and close friend Donald Mitchell sees the relationship with Piers Dunkerley (whom Britten first met when he was twenty-one and Dunkerley only thirteen) as 'a model example of Britten's schoolboy relationships'. These, he argues, were friendships 'in which he could play the role of counsellor and proxy father ... and which at the same time embodied a kind of idealized senior-junior boy comradeship, an extension of the hierarchies and friendships of school.'[80] But this may be a little disingenuous, since anyone who has ever been to public school will know that 'senior-junior boy comradeship', particularly in those days when the system was still defiantly all-male, by no means precluded sex. Dr Mitchell is, however, aware of the 'guilty tension ... between children as necessary adjuncts ... and as objects of desire'.[81]

To put the record straight, there is, in all the Britten biographical literature, no evidence of any physical relationship with boys (despite an alleged claim by his thirteen-year-old choirboy friend, Harry Morris, that Britten made what Morris took to be a sexual approach – but was probably only a hug or a goodnight kiss – while the two were on holiday in Cornwall in 1937[82]). In a review of the third volume of the annotated letters of Britten (which contains an essay by Donald Mitchell largely on the subject of Britten's boy relationships),[83] the writer and critic Rupert Christiansen points out, quite simply, that Britten 'liked playing with boys', because 'he maintained within himself his own boyishness and drew inspiration from it'.[84] This view is amplified by the documentary film maker John Bridcut, who made a close study of Britten's friendships with adolescent boys for his TV film, *Britten's Children*, and the subsequent book based upon it. Bridcut believes that 'the inner man in Britten' felt himself to be thirteen 'throughout his life' and that he needed to have a thirteen-year-old 'favourite of the moment' because it was 'an essential part of his creativity, and of his knowledge and understanding of himself.'[85] Bridcut makes the further point that Britten's removal from Gresham's (and from 'the comforting rhythms of school and the companionship of schoolboys') at the age of only sixteen, in order to specialize at the Royal College of Music, left him 'unconsciously hunting for those three missing scholastic years' for the rest of his life.[86] But this does not quite explain Britten's obsession with thirteen-year-old boys, nor his summary execution of these friendships the moment the voice broke,[87] and it does not explore the important roles of class and power. There was a sexual element in Britten's feelings for boys, but he held it firmly in check, and, as the biographer Peter Parker has pointed out, 'the resulting tension fed into the work', inspiring what he describes as 'wonderful, complex and exhilarating' music – which is why Britten's relationships with boys are of such interest to the rest of us.[88]

There is a sense from the letters and diary jottings about Lennox's week with Ben in Cornwall that his host was proud of his catch. Ben was a dentist's son, brilliant and successful, but callow, gauche and conscious of the university experience he had missed, while Lennox was sophisticated, bilingual, well-connected, rich, the polished product of Oxford and six years of intensive schooling under Nadia in Paris. Ben's social milieu was an uneasy mix of the outrageous (Wystan and his gang), the intellectually rigorous (his teacher Frank Bridge) and the cosy (the Brittens back home in Lowestoft). Lennox's, by comparison, was distinctly grand: encompassing both Montmartre and the Faubourg St Germain – and extending from Ravel, Stravinsky and Diaghilev's Ballets russes to the Almanach de Gotha and Berkeley Castle. Social differences, though never discussed, still mattered in the years beween the wars, and even music might not have been enough to bring them together. (It may have helped – if either had been sufficiently tasteless to have raised the subject – that they shared the shadow of illegitimacy: Lennox's father, and Ben's maternal grandfather.) The snob in Ben was conscious that he had bagged a *rara avis*, and he wrote to his mother boasting that Lennox Berkeley – 'he of that noble ancestry', as he later called him[89] – had altered his plans specially to come and stay with him in a hut in Cornwall.[90]

It had been a happy and stimulating and important six days in both their lives. So it was, as Ben recorded, 'a very sorrying farewell' when Lennox left on 30 July. 'He is an awful dear,' wrote Ben, 'very intelligent & kind.'[91] Of Ben, Lennox said he was 'a charming creature and I am devoted to him. I have certainly never met another musician with whom I felt so much in sympathy.'[92] Nor was he ever to meet another musician who would have such an overwhelming influence on him. Britten's music was to trigger a 'tremendous imaginative release',[93] which would reveal Lennox's vocation for choral and vocal writing. And Ben's personal charms were to trigger a similarly potent emotional release.

After seeing Lennox off to London from Newquay station, Ben went home alone, worked and dined and worked again, and, with no one in the hut to talk to, took himself to an early bed, telling his diary that he was feeling 'quite lonely'.[94] But, with his new little friend Derek (the four-year-old son of his cleaning lady), to play with in the morning, his doting mother coming down from Frinton in the evening,[95] ping-pong with young Dunkerley ('a first rate kid'[96]) to look forward to in the school holidays, his publisher waiting to give him dinner at the Café de Paris, and Wystan (and Wystan's school friend Christopher Isherwood) eager to broaden his horizons, Ben's solitude was only temporary.

The really lonely one was Lennox. He had no parents; an odd and awkward sister Geraldine, a vegetarian Christian who gave away all her money to a religious sect;[97] an enormously rich but spiteful uncle – Randal, the earl – who refused to have anything to do with him; emotional feelings that clashed with his religious beliefs; and a temperamental flatmate. Was it too much to hope that Ben might turn out to be the ideal friend, who would fit all the pieces of Lennox's jigsaw together at last?

17
Lennox, London and Paris, 1937

Revived by his intimate week with Ben in Cornwall in August 1936, Lennox felt ready to face France and the ghosts of his childhood. Flying for the first time in his life, he began his pilgrimage at St Saviour in Jersey, at the home of his favourite uncle, Arthur Harris. His well-meaning Aunt Nellie Harris was eager that he should meet some nice girls, and he was soon launched on a lively social round. Lennox told Ben he was having a grand time, with lots of tennis and surfing, cocktail parties and dances. For all its aggressive heterosexuality, he was 'really coming through it very well', and even managing to do a little work. His *String Quartet*, first performed in 1935, needed a little buffing up for publication, and he had made some sketches for a symphony (which was to take another six years to complete).[1]

From the bourgeois formality of Jersey, Lennox went on to the Riviera to spend September in the empty Villa Melfort at Cap Ferrat. His intention may have been to sell the house and wrap up his other interests in the South of France; if it was, he never quite completed it. Instead he played tennis and golf and went to parties with Maugham and whatever young men happened to be staying at the Villa Mauresque. Within a month he had had enough, and returned, not to London and his new life, but to Paris, José Raffalli and his old life.

Paris, he wrote to Peter Burra, was a good place for work, and he planned to 'settle in for a bit'. He had once thought of taking a house in the country, in England, but now he had given up the idea. After all he already had the flat in Paris, another in London – at 28 Great Ormond Street, which he shared with John Greenidge – and the use of Domaine du Rayet, the country house at Falicon which he and his sister Geraldine shared with their cousins Claude and Yvonne. And anyway, he told Burra, 'I can't face the idea of living alone', which was the prospect that faced him in London because John was away. In Paris, at his piano at 1 Cité Chaptal, he was working on 'various things which I hope will bear some result in due course'.[2] One of these was the collection of *Five Short* [piano] *Pieces* dedicated to José. The other was a setting for percussion, piano and strings of two hymns to athletes by the Greek poet Pindar, which he was writing for the princesse de Polignac. The Pindar pieces were milestones for Lennox. Everything he had written till then 'was part of a natural eclecticism'; now, thanks largely to Ben, he felt freer to be himself – freer, at any rate, to move towards what he wanted to be.[3] But of course he owed a debt to the princesse too, and acknowledged it to Nadia a few years later. Mme de Polignac, he said, was 'the perfect patron', like the Rasumovskys and the Esterházys – but unlike those undiscriminating patrons of music history who 'merely obeyed a convention and occasionally, rather to their embarrassment, found themselves landed with a genius!'[4]

The idea was that Nadia and her ensemble would take the two Pindar settings, *Deux Poèmes*, to London in November and play them at a concert in the French Embassy, in the presence of the princesse. But who was to play the piano part? Lennox regarded himself as 'a pretty catastrophic pianist', so he asked Ben if he would help out – for love, since there was no fee.[5] Ben was not terribly keen – he was too busy living it up with his generous publisher and patron Ralph Hawkes: swanning around in a chauffeur-driven Hispano Suiza, going to see *Der Rosenkavalier* at Covent Garden, dining at the Café de Paris and dancing to the music of Ambrose and his Orchestra at the Mayfair Hotel ('Lap of luxury,' the socialist Ben confessed to his diary, 'and I admit I enjoy it'[6]). With some reluctance, he did, however, agree to play for Lennox – but in the event he never had to, for the concert was cancelled.[7] This worked very much to Lennox's advantage, because Nadia was able to persuade Princess Winnie, as they all called her, to allow the new work to be added to the much more important concert she was giving with her singers and the London Symphony Orchestra at the Queen's Hall on the 24th.[8] But Ben could not make the new date because he was working to an immovable deadline for the completion of his film score, *Love from a Stranger*;[9] the same commitment prevented his attending Robert and Dorothy Mayer's luncheon party for Nadia at the Ritz at the beginning of the week and a cosy supper at the Café Royal that same night with Lennox and Edward Dent, Professor of Music at Cambridge.[10] After spending hours looking for a deputy (and further time complaining about it), Ben finally produced the admirable Millicent Silver.*

It was a curious programme: Berkeley's *Deux Poèmes*, followed by Schütz's dramatic *Resurrection* (with newly-composed instrumental parts by Boulanger, who had even added brass to the vocal lines[11]) and finally a performance of Fauré's *Requiem*, which had not been heard in England for half a century. No woman had ever conducted a London orchestra before, and the audience responded with 'thunderous applause'. They had heard Boulanger talking about her methods on the wireless the previous week – in English, coached by 'Professor' Berkeley, who listened in at home and wrote the next day to congratulate her on a performance which was 'parfaitement claire et comprehensible'[12] – and they hailed her now as a great interpreter of music. The following day the *Morning Post* concurred, adding that her conducting was 'an essay in restraint, in delicate tones'; and in the *Sunday Times*, Ernest Newman wrote that he could recall few performances of major works that had been so completely satisfactory. It was less of a success for Ma'moiselle's star pupil, in the view of *The Times*: 'The chief thing which a teacher of composition can do is to discipline the pupil to write that which he really means, and that she seems to have done in this case ... Whether what the composer wants to say is what any given audience wants to hear is not the concern of the teacher ...'[13] The review added that if the audience failed to be moved by it, the performance was not at fault.†

The same acid critic even wondered if it had really been the LSO that Boulanger conducted, since that orchestra was supposed to have been in the pit at Covent Garden on the same night.[14] (He knew perfectly well that the orchestra had fleshed itself out with deputies, as orchestras have always done, but he could not resist a further dig.)

*(BB, Diary, 20 November 1936, BPL.) Millicent Silver's husband, the flautist John Francis, commissioned LB's *Flute Concerto* and gave its first performance with the BBC Symphony Orchestra conducted by Malcolm Sargent on 29 July 1953. Their daughter Sarah, the oboist, took part in the first broadcast performance of LB's *Petite Suite* and his *Trio for Flute, Oboe and Piano* in 1988, and their other daughter Hannah, then a harpist but later a soprano, commissioned LB's *Nocturne* for harp in 1967.

†By Christmas LB had completed a third Pindar setting which Boulanger conducted with the other two hymns at a concert in Paris (possibly at the rue Ballu) on Boxing Day 1936. At LB's request she invited José Raffalli (LB to NB, translated from French, 18 December 1936, FSNB).

Lennox was as disappointed by the reception of his Pindar settings as Ben had been when his Auden settings failed to make themselves properly understood in Norwich a couple of months earlier. What they both needed was a diversion. After Nadia and the princesse and their musicians had returned to France, to plan the recording of that famous pioneer album of Monteverdi (with the sweet high tenor of Hugues Cuénod, and Nadia accompanying on a piano), the two bloodied young composers decided to organize a reunion lunch with Peter Burra in London on 29 November. They chose as their meeting place Castano's Restaurant in Soho, whose sympathetic atmosphere drew many other artists and intellectuals including the Widow Lloyd, Constant Lambert and dancers from Sadler's Wells. It was six months since the three friends had last got together, and though Lennox (chaperoned by José) had visited the cottage which Burra shared with his schoolfriend, the singer Peter Pears, in the Berkshire village of Bucklebury, Ben had not been there (nor had he met Pears yet). Work, the good life and the attentions of both Wystan and Lennox had claimed Ben's summer and autumn.

The Spanish Civil War was still very much on all their minds. Only four days earlier Hitler and Mussolini had recognized General Franco as Caudillo of the Nationalist state, but the Republican government was still fighting on (and in fact held out for another two and a half years). What worried Ben was that Wystan was thinking of going out to Spain to assist the Republic. Still very young and easily dazzled, Ben was at this time very much under Wystan's spell and not all his friends thought the influence was benign. The wise Marjorie Fass, who had got close to Ben through the Bridges, believed that 'sober unshockable' friends like the Bridges were better for him than 'meeting brilliant people who are not brilliant in <u>his</u> sphere, but their own, & so make a mutual admiration society'. (This is much the same point as Wystan himself was to make to Ben in a letter from America in 1942 which all but broke their friendship: that Ben should resist the temptation to make things easy for himself by building 'a warm nest of love'.[15]) Marjorie Fass thought that Christopher Isherwood's 'adolescent "smartness" & his unwise interest in prostitutes male & female' was tiresome.[16] But Ben thought Christopher was 'a grand person; unaffected, extremely amusing & devastatingly intelligent'.[17] As for Wystan, 'court poet to the Left',[18] Ben thought he was 'the most charming, most vital, genuine & important person' he knew, and if the Spanish rebels were to take his life it would be 'a bloody atrocity'.[19]

Within a week Wystan confirmed that he had volunteered for the International Brigades, and that he would be leaving for Spain after Christmas. Ben tried to dissuade him by pointing out that the world would gain more by his continuing to write than the Spanish government would gain by his fighting for them (an argument Lennox was to use when trying to dissuade Ben from returning from America to fight in 1940), 'but no one can make W. H. A. alter his mind'.[20] Wystan left for Spain on 12 January 1937 but never actually fought. Refused permission to serve as a stretcher bearer, he worked in radio propaganda for a while, then visited the Aragon front and returned to London unscathed on 4 March.[21]

The three friends cannot have failed to exchange views about the King and Mrs Simpson, the love affair which was the talk of London that autumn of 1936 (though it was not yet the 'Colossal sensation'[22] which it was to become when the press broke the news, four days later, that Edward VIII was actually hoping to marry her). In a letter to Ben at the time of the Coronation of Edward VIII's younger brother as George VI the following May, Lennox expressed the view that it was a good thing to have a king, 'but I do dislike all the nonsense and hypocrisy connected with it'.[23] Ben was all for Mrs Simpson: writing in his diary, on the day of the Abdication Bill debate in the House of Commons, he thought a divorced American would make an excellent and democratic queen who would be good for Anglo-American relations. But he guessed that the politicians 'wanted to get rid of a King with too much personality & any little excuse sufficed'.[24] Like the rest of Britain, Ben followed the events of the abdication crisis on his wireless, especially the King's farewell speech: 'really a most moving affair', he wrote, culminating in 'a terrifying "God save the King" that made one shiver in ones shoes'.[25]

The conversation that lunchtime may also have touched on the private lives of the three young men themselves, and the emotional tensions of a complicated triangular relationship: Lennox still drawn to Peter Burra but really wanting Ben, Ben basking in Lennox's adoration and also drawn to Peter but still unable to accept his own real nature, and Peter fond of both but wrestling with his own sexual demons which excluded both his composer friends (and involved an admiration of sportsmen, daredevils and action men, and a dislike of what he thought himself to be). They were all discreet by nature, and sensitive to the prevailing hostility to homosexuality, so their wariness was not as unnatural as it might seem to us today. 'Very pleasant' was the guarded comment about their meeting which Ben allowed himself in his diary that night, 'and they are dears'.[26] Equally valued 'dears' at that moment, but the dynamics were to shift in the following three months – and, come the spring, Ben was to meet his first 'darling'.

On the day that Wystan left England for Spain, Ben, 'feeling very sore',[27] also left the country – with two young musical friends (the writer – and later Britten librettist – Ronald Duncan, whom he had met in Cornwall the previous summer, and the music critic Henry Boys, a friend from RCM days). The three young men were bound for Paris for four days of sightseeing, which began, accidentally, in a brothel. They had intended to go to the Folies Bergère, but when they arrived it was too early for the performance, so the doorman escorted them to 'another little show' in a large house nearby. Ben admitted in his diary that they were fools to go, 'but a mixture of ignorance & curiosity made us follow'. He was not amused: '20 nude females, fat, hairy, unprepossessing; smelling of vile cheap scent, & walking round the room in couples to a gramophone. It is revolting – appalling that such a noble thing as sex should be so degraded. We are given cheap champagne, but decide that we've had enough & to the disgust of the fat proprietress, take a hasty departure – it cost us 100 F too.'[28]

After this 'disgusting little exhibition', they were in no mood for the Folies but went anyway and found it little better: 'just chocolate box pornography,' Ben said. Furthermore the much-vaunted black entertainer Josephine Baker was 'as old as the hills', and quite unable to dance, sing or act.[29] So they left in the interval, and found their way to the safer attractions of Notre Dame, which was indeed 'a sight for sore eyes'. The following day they went to look for Oscar Wilde's grave, but could not find it because they were in the wrong cemetery. And when, in desperation, they followed the tourist trail to the Eiffel Tower they found that shut. But at least they were able to get into the Louvre, and the Opéra (for *Fidelio*). Lennox was in Paris for the last day of Ben's visit, preparing for a concert of motets by himself, Markevitch, Copland, Françaix and other Boulanger students, but, curiously, the two friends do not seem to have met.

On his return to London, Lennox met Peter Burra, to whom he gave, that January of 1937, a signed copy [30] of one of the first fruits of a new, though not exclusive, publishing deal with Boosey & Hawkes: a charming little song for soprano or tenor, called *How Love Came In*.

Dating from about 1933,* at the start of his relationship with Alan Searle, it sets a ten-line sonnet by the seventeenth-century English poet Robert Herrick. The poem wonders about the source of love – does it come in through the eyes or the ears, or with the soul? Of one thing it is sure: when love goes out, it is the heart that hurts. Lennox knew that Peter Pears, who was acutely sensitive to words and to feelings, would appreciate the subtlety and the wisdom of these graceful lines, and it is possible that Peter even sang it with him, privately at home in London or in Berkshire. Like Lennox himself, the music is private, diffident and delicately allusive (almost to the point of naughtiness), but under its fine skin lies hard muscle – and this is the wonderful surprise to be discovered in so much of Lennox's music. Ben liked this song too, and in 1955 he accompanied Peter Pears in a successful recording of it.†

There were problems awaiting Ben when he got back to London. His sister, Beth, who shared his flat in the Finchley Road was laid up with a bad case of 'flu, which quickly turned to pneumonia, and Mrs Britten, who came up to London to nurse her, almost immediately fell ill too. So then did Ben. By the time Ben was better, Mrs Britten was much worse. Worried, tired and weak, her 'flu degenerated into bronchial pneumonia, and on the last day of January, after a delirious night, she had a heart attack and died. 'I lose', Ben wrote in his diary, 'the grandest mother a person could possible have ... Nothing one can do eases the terrible ache that one feels – O God Almighty.'[31]

Lennox understood only too well, but hesitated to express to the distraught Ben feelings which he freely poured out to Nadia Boulanger. She had recently marked the first anniversary of his own mother's death with a sympathetic letter (and was to continue writing to Lennox on subsequent anniversaries of Aline's death till the end of her life in 1979). In his reply, a little over three weeks before Ben's mother died, Lennox wrote about his continuing sense of loss for his mother. His sentiments were couched in language similar to Ben's, but were overlaid with a spirituality which they did not share: '... when one has understood the grandeur of the love of a mother anything else seems so

*The exact date is unknown. A review by Andrew Porter in *The Gramophone*, July 1956, suggests 'about 1933'. Stewart Craggs, *Lennox Berkeley*, opts for 1935. The song was published by Boosey & Hawkes in 1936.

†First released on Decca LW 5241 in 1956, re-released, in stereo, on Eclipse ECS 545 in 1970.

trivial by comparison, and only things of the spirit are of any importance ... I think of living for Maman as much as when she was with me, if not more; it's a thought that frightens me a little, but it's the only thought that gives me the wish to live.'[32]

Mrs Britten's death was as bitter a blow for Ben as Mrs Berkeley's had been for Lennox, but it seems to have had the same effect of releasing him from an emotional straitjacket. Ben's childhood friend Basil Reeve actually went so far as to suggest that it was only now that Ben's life could begin.[33] But first Ben had to resolve the question of his sexual identity. Early in March he had lunch in London with David Green, an architectural student from Lowestoft, with whom he had shared lodgings during his college days. During a frank and intimate discussion, Green urged Ben to 'decide something' about his sexual life. His point made its mark because Ben wrote it up in his diary that night, confirming to himself that a decision was indeed necessary.[34]

Spurred on by this and the need to ease the 'awful ache' of his mother's death, [35] Ben went to stay with Peter Burra at Foxhold, on Bucklebury Common, not far from Reading.* (Burra's house-mate Peter Pears, whom Ben still had not met, was absent at the time: he was in London at the flat in Charlotte Street which he shared with his two friends from Oxford and the BBC Trevor Harvey and Basil Douglas.) Ben and Peter Burra played squash – new to Ben, who loved it – and piano and violin ('swapping parts & making the most extraordinary noise'[36]). They also went for long walks, and talked till late, in a re-run of the Cornish holiday with Lennox. And Ben discovered 'a kindred spirit in thousands of ways (one way in particular)'.[37] This typically coy admission presumably means that in the sympathetic ambience of Foxhold their affection for one another carried them off to bed, since they cannot have failed to pick up signs of their shared homosexuality in Barcelona a year earlier. On this new level of intimacy they were able to exchange further secrets. It was then that Peter told Ben he was attracted to rough, tough, risk-taking youths (bikers, athletes, pilots),

*The cottage was rented cheaply from kind, rich friends, Louis and Mary Behrend – Socialists, Fabians and patrons of Stanley Spencer, Lytton Strachey and Henry Lamb. The Behrends had taken Burra under their wing following the publication of his biography of Van Gogh, and Foxhold was intended to provide a peaceful environment for him to work on his study of Wordsworth (R. Thompson, *The Burra–Moody Archive*, unpublished MS, 2002, B–MA).

and that he had been reading Freud to try to resolve his angst about his sexuality. Peter Pears's biographer Christopher Headington implied that Burra's problems were so great that he actually consulted a psychoanalyst, [38] but the Burra scholar Richard Thompson thinks this is unlikely.[39] Dr Thompson, who owns Burra's annotated copy of Freud's *The Interpretation of Dreams*, believes Peter simply told Ben that he was '"consulting Freud", which isn't', he points out, 'the same thing as lying on the couch'. Peter did, however, speak of a need to prove his manhood and to be accepted as 'normal'.[40]

But it was not these fears and anxieties which lay at the root of the 'great difficulties' Peter was facing at the time.[41] It was something altogether more insidious and threatening. A young German staying with him at Foxhold in July – 'Willi', one of the two young Germans Peter had met at the ISCM Festival in Barcelona in 1936 – had turned out to be a Nazi spy. This not only put him in a difficult situation, since he himself was a committed anti-Fascist, and Willi was his friend – probably his lover – but his wider circle was implicated too. His admirer E. M. Forster was so concerned about the possible consequences that he undertook to talk to Peter and to warn him that he was putting himself in real danger by continuing his association with Willi. Reporting back to Christopher Isherwood at the end of January 1937, Forster said his mission had not been conspicuously successful, since Peter 'clings to the numerous friendly references' which Willi had made about their mutual friends. He thought Peter was bored with Willi and wanted to 'terminate the visit', but he guessed that it was 'boredom with ecstatic interruptions'.[42] By the end of February Peter was convinced that Willi was 'beyond all reasonable doubt a Nazi agent'.[43] Extensive enquiries among their mutual friends in London, Berlin and Barcelona had led him to the inescapable conclusion that Willi had been sent to Britain to compile a list of prominent British homosexuals, as targets of the Third Reich.[44] In a letter to his mentor Edward Dent, president of the ISCM (and Professor of Music at Cambridge), Burra reported that their other young German friend Hans Raab had 'quite furiously' denied that Willi was working for the Nazis. But this, he wrote, proved only that 'Hans must be very innocent'. The whole episode and 'the pursuit of its ramifications has driven me quite crazy,' he wrote, 'and of course brought everybody else under suspicion. It is evident that one must be extremely careful.' Although Willi was back in Germany 'for the time being, and I think I'm free of him for a bit',

Burra asked Dent to destroy his letter, just to be on the safe side.[45] They were all getting jittery.

Peter discussed some of this with Ben at Foxhold in March. In return for these confidences, Ben spoke more freely than usual about his own life. As a result of this new closeness, Peter Burra was promoted in Ben's estimation from a mere 'dear' to 'one of the world's dears'.[46] In fact Ben was so taken with both Peter and the country around Bucklebury that he made up his mind to spend the £2,000 his mother had left him on buying a cottage nearby.[47]

One of the consequences of Ben's new sense of liberation was that he felt able to open up a little more to Lennox. On 24 March they dined together at the Reform Club, which Lennox (following his father's footsteps) had recently joined, and afterwards they walked home to John Greenidge's flat in Bloomsbury, where Lennox was now living. They talked till one, and Ben later recorded in his diary, 'I am very fond of him – he is a charming creature & I feel a very good composer – but so far no more than "fond".'[48] So far. Lennox was going to have to work a bit harder.

In April Lennox invited Ben to stay with his musical friend, and passionate admirer, Gladys Bryans, an old-school spinster – correct, conventional and possessive – who lived in a handsome villa in the mellow-stone wool town of Painswick, on the scarp edge of the Cotswolds above Gloucester. There they enjoyed intimate walks and talks, with tennis, sightseeing and music-making (Ben playing his viola, Lennox the piano). At a dinner party on the 8th (for which Ben had been warned to bring a dinner-jacket), a niece of their hostess sang some Fauré songs, and Ben improvised a little canon. Also present that night was the song-writer C. W. Orr*(dismissed in Ben's diary as 'a musician of some slight note'), who lived in a cottage by the church.[49]

Together for a whole week, Lennox and Ben were able to make real progress on the Spanish suite they were writing from their memory of the Catalan dances they had heard in Barcelona. This now included a lament for the Civil War (including a solo for the saxophone, which

*Charles Wilfred Orr (1893-1976) wrote 35 songs, 24 of which are settings of Housman, with whose poetry he became besotted after the First World War. He was said to have grown 'increasingly bitter at the neglect of his songs' (Andrew Green, sleevenote,'A. E. Housman *A Shropshire Lad*', *Hyperion English Song Series*, CDD22044).

may have been inspired by Berg's pioneering use of the saxophone in the *Violin Concerto* played in Barcelona). Writing to Peter Burra, with an invitation to come and join them in Painswick for a day – which does not seem to have been taken up – Lennox reported that the collaboration was going well 'and we haven't fought over it (or anything else) so far'.[50] Later the two composers swore a solemn oath never to divulge who wrote which of the four movements,[51] but Ben's diary nearly gives the game away: 'He [Lennox] has sketched two movements which we discuss fully & alter accordingly, & then while I sketch a third (having settled form etc) he makes out a rough score of the first. Everything goes very amicably & tho' of course we don't agree on everything at once I feel the final arrangements are satisfactory. Certainly the music seems nice.'[52]

In a letter to Ben after the first performance in January 1938, Lennox refers to 'our orchestration' and 'your two pieces' (which, typically, he considers 'more effective than mine'[53]), and later in 1938 he writes again to Ben to say 'the last movement is terrific orchestration and betrays the master hand!'[54] It seems likely – as Lennox confided to Peter Dickinson – that the first and second movements were mostly Lennox's and the last two mostly Ben's.[55] But for the rest of their lives the two composers continued to assert publicly what the music itself suggests and Lennox's introduction to the 1979 pocket score spells out – that they had both been so involved in all the movements that it would be 'difficult to disentangle which of us had thought first of any particular feature'. And anyway they decided, early on, that they would prefer to 'leave the music to speak for itself'.[56] It was a bit of a game – to create an air of mystery,[57] though thumbprints of both composers are recognizable in all four movements.[58]

The week at Painswick gave Lennox and Ben a chance to build on the intimacy they had established in Cornwall. By the end of it – and after a 'long & deep conversation with Lennox' on the 11th – Ben decided that he was 'very, very fond of him'. But there were sexual incompatibilities which no amount of fondness could overcome, for the diary entry adds: 'it is a comfort that we can arrange sexual matters to at least <u>my</u> satisfaction.'[59] The compromise, whatever it involved, may have been a comfort for Ben, who did not really 'fancy' Lennox, and was not attracted to adult males anyway, but it must have been inhibiting for Lennox, who was very strongly drawn to Ben. At least, however, it was an advance on the situation in July, when sex of any kind seems to have been forbidden. It is more than a coincidence that this relaxation of the rules followed a conversation Ben had had with his brother, Robert, the previous week. It happened in Frinton while the two young Brittens were clearing up their mother's things. According to Ben's diary, he told his brother about what he called his 'queerness' and was surprised to find that, despite his 'obstinate conservativism', Robert was not shocked and had 'even helped with sympathy and advice'.[60] This confession could never have happened while Mrs Britten was alive, and represents a major change in Ben's life.

The two composers returned to London the following day, and over the next fortnight they met frequently – to work on the score of the suite, to lunch and dine together, to talk, to listen to a broadcast of a mediocre performance of *Otello* (Beecham conducting), to attend rehearsals of Ben's incidental music for a BBC drama feature *King Arthur* (about which Ben recorded 'all comes off like hell so there's nothing to worry about'), and to play tennis (Ben boasting in his diary that he had dazzled in one game with 'a glorious brilliant patch'). They were getting on so well that they decided to pool their resources and buy a country cottage where they could live and work together. For Ben this was a question of little more than convenience and companionship; for Lennox it was tinged with the highest hopes of very much more. Peter Burra had told them of a farmhouse near Bucklebury which was available and they agreed to go down and look at it early in May.[61] But they were never to see it.

Many of Peter's friends knew he was excited by speed and masculine pursuits – by motor bikes, aeroplanes and Lawrence of Arabia (who was himself so obsessed with acceleration that he used to race his Brough bike beside planes taking off[62]). They knew too that he admired the physical prowess of tough young men, that he sought to emulate them to some extent; and probably desired them too. He respected 'men of action' like Auden, Spender and Orwell who were fighting for the Republican cause in Spain. He himself wanted to learn to fly, and he even dreamt of becoming an airman in André Malraux's International Squadron.[63] When Peter bought a BSA early in 1937, Ben wrote to say, 'How goes the motor-bike? I hope your ecstasies are continuing.' Peter's Oxford friend Simon Nowell-Smith, then assistant editor of *The Times Literary Supplement*, warned him to take care, and to remember what happened to Lawrence (who died after fracturing his skull in a motor cycle accident in Dorset in 1935.) Peter's reply was typically romantic, and horribly prophetic: death on a motor bike or in an aeroplane was, he said, 'a good way to die'.[64]

On the afternoon of 27 April, after lunch at Foxhold with Peter Pears, who was staying for rehearsals of the Beethoven *Missa Solemnis*, in which he was performing in Oxford later that week,[65] Peter Burra had a date at the Reading Aero Club in Woodley. He was meeting his young friend and neighbour Alleyn Anderson for a joy-ride in a Miles Hawk Major monoplane. Anderson, who had been to school at Stowe, was a daredevil pilot known locally as 'Crackie', because of his aerial antics over the village (and because he had once taken a potshot with his airgun at a couple of villagers on bicycles).[66] A gifted linguist and keen flyer, he had been determined to join the RAF, but was rejected on the grounds of poor sight (his thick spectacles had been the cause of 'desperate bullying' at Stowe). This had left him feeling 'bitter, bitter', according to his sister.[67] Although he was only nineteen, Anderson had already clocked up 200 hours' flying time, and Peter, who had often flown with him before, had 'great trust in him as a pilot'.[68] But Anderson had limited experience flying monoplanes and he was surprised that the Miles M-2 low-wing planes (built by Phillips & Powis at Woodley four years earlier) needed the whole length of the runway to lift off. Once airborne, he found the engine response unexpectedly sluggish: instead of the usual maximum speed of 120 mph he could not get it to exceed 108 mph. (By a strange coincidence this is the very speed T.E. Lawrence reached when racing against aircraft.[69]) Anderson assumed that this was due to the aerodynamic drag of the blind flying-hood which was folded behind Burra in the rear cockpit, but as 'others had flown it', with the hood in this position, he decided it must be all right.[70]

Their destination was Bucklebury, so they could get a good aerial view of the places where they lived. When they got to the Common, Anderson dropped the plane to 300 ft and dipped a wing over Foxhold. In the garden below, Peter Pears waved as they flew over. Anderson then made for his own cottage, Tomlins, before swinging round again to inspect a nearby field, where he had often landed a biplane. He claimed later that he had no intention of attempting a landing this time, as he realized he would never get out again, since he was uncertain about the length of the take-off area for a monoplane. Eyewitnesses claimed, however, that it was clear that he was planning to land.

As he was preparing to make a final turn down-wind of the field, the throttle suddenly jammed and the plane started to spin out of control. He fought to try to right it, but failed, and the plane ploughed into a wood, losing its wings of plywood-covered spruce, as it ripped through the heavy branches of the trees with a thunderous crash. A deathly hush then descended on the crash scene. By a miracle Anderson himself managed to scramble free, as petrol began to leak on to the hot engine and into the fuselage. For some minutes he lay dazed, then, hearing the sound of approaching rescuers, he shouted, 'Get him [Burra] out'. But it was too late. Still strapped into the crumpled rear cockpit, it was obvious to the farm workers who came to the rescue that Peter Burra was dead. The force of the impact had broken his neck. They carried Anderson to safety on the back of a five-bar gate, and in Newbury Hospital later he was found to have incurred nothing worse than cuts and bruises.[71]

At an inquest a month later, Anderson attributed the cause of the crash to 'lack of air speed caused by drag of the hood over the rear cockpit and the closing of the throttle due to engine vibrations'. It is hard not to wonder whether a more experienced pilot would have turned back after finding the engine so unresponsive; and hard to avoid the conclusion that young 'Crackie' was in fact trying to bring the plane down in the field near his home, and lost control in the process. Richard Thompson, who has carried out a meticulous examination of all the evidence of the crash (including weather conditions at the time), believes that the two men were indeed intending to land in the field near Tomlins, and that the accident was caused by a combination of Anderson's lack of experience flying monoplanes and a miscalculation of the windspeed required to make the final turn over High Wood, Midgham.[72] This never came out at the inquest, nor were questions asked about the discrepancies between the stories of Anderson and of the eyewitnesses. The Borough Coroner Mr S.V. Pinniger recorded a verdict of Accidental Death.[73]* The Lloyds List entry for the crash states unequivocally: 'Crash near Buckleberry [*sic*], Berks. P. Burra killed, pilot Anderson (a youth of 19) attempted to land near his home.'[74]

*Alleyn Anderson served in Egypt during the Second World War, which left him partially disabled. He died in the early 1990s, in Putney, London (Dr Thompson, in a telephone conversation with TS, 17 February 2006, and an email to TS, 27 February 2006).

Peter Burra's sudden death at the age of only twenty-seven came as a huge shock to all who knew him, and a loss not only to them but – as Joe Ackerley, literary editor of *The Listener*, put it – 'to civilized thought generally ... We simply couldn't afford to lose him.'[75] For Peter himself, death may have come as a release, since he once wrote that death was the same as life – 'only just a cessation of its activities'.[76]

Ben heard the news from a friend who had read it in the evening paper the day it happened: 'Go to bed feeling desparate [*sic*] as I've just heard that dear old Peter Burra has been killed flying ... with one of his 'tough' friends. He was a darling of the 1st rank, & ... has been very close & dear to me. A first rate brain that was at the moment in great difficulties – tho' this is far too terrible a solution for them ... This is a bloody world.'[77]

The funeral took place in Bucklebury Cemetery, at the western end of Bucklebury Common, on a warm spring morning two days later. Peter Pears, who was staying with friends nearby, rode over on his motorbike. Lennox and Ben took the train from London. The *Times* music critic Frank Howes and his wife drove down by car. Jack Gordon, Peter Burra's opera producer friend, sent flowers. Peter's patrons and admirers, the Behrends, drove over from their house at Burghclere, bringing with them the parson, Canon R.S. Medlicott, who conducted the service. The coffin was carried away from Foxhold under a black-tasselled canopy on a black farm wagon drawn by two Shetland ponies with black plumes. The service was brief and simple – just Psalm 121, 'I will lift up mine eyes', and some readings from Wordsworth, ending with the climax of the 'Ode on Intimations of Immortality'. Then, in a shady corner of the burial ground, the coffin was lowered into the grave, the edges of which had been decorated with sprays of young green birch leaves, tufts of wild cherry and yellow roses, arranged by the pilot's widowed mother, Audrey Anderson.[78]

Lennox thought the funeral had been 'one of the most heartrending things I have ever known'. It had left him in such a 'sterile condition' that he could not work. Peter's death, he told Ben in a letter from Brussels a week after the funeral, was a tragedy that made him 'cling desperately to such religious faith as I have', and he urged Ben to reconsider 'all that', since it mattered 'so terribly'.[79] The latest news from Spain did not ease his mind: on the very day of the accident in Bucklebury, German bombers, supporting the rebels, had destroyed the Basque town of Guernica. Lennox, for all his pacifism, newly stoked by Ben, was not alone in wondering what lay ahead for Europe if Nazism remained unchecked.

Peter Pears had the toughest time of Burra's death. As the only friend on the spot, he had to deal with the hospital, the coroner, the undertaker and the press, as well as informing the Burra and Anderson families and friends of both. On top of all that he was also preparing for his concert with the New English Singers in Oxford on the very night of the funeral. But there was another, no less sensitive, problem worrying him, and after the midday service in the churchyard, he raised the subject with Lennox and Ben, as the three young men walked back across the Common to Foxhold. Peter Pears barely knew either of them (though he had met Ben at lunch in the London flat on 6 March,[80] and was familiar with Lennox's piano music), so he found it difficult to say what he had to say. The fact was that in the cottage there were some photos and letters and other papers that might possibly incriminate Peter Burra's gay circle, including all three of them, and several others more distinguished than they.

By our standards today it is almost inconceivable that anyone should have been concerned about some affectionate letters, a few photos of young men in bathing trunks (among them the Widow Lloyd), and veiled hints in diaries.[81] But Pears was not being paranoid. Gay men in pre-war Britain lived in constant fear of exposure – and of what Professor Robert Stradling has called 'the sordid cycle of blackmail, arrest, court proceedings, newspaper stories, fines and jail which had become an occasional purgation ritual of "society" since the Wilde case'.[82] If Burra's private papers were to fall into the wrong hands they could, at the least, create a scandal or lead to blackmail, and, at the worst, result in prosecution under the 1885 Criminal Law Amendment Act (which was to continue to prey on gay men till the Wolfenden Report changed the law in the 1960s). But there was much more at stake even than this. If his young German friend, Willi, really had been compiling a sort of gay hit-list for the Nazis, the danger was very grave for a large number of their friends.

Peter Pears and Ben discussed the matter with Basil Douglas in London the next evening (Lennox by then was on his way to Brussels). Ben was 'very concerned', having perhaps the most to lose, since he had confessed his secrets to Peter Burra during his Foxhold weekend only six weeks earlier, and probably wrote letters on the subject. Accordingly Ben offered to go through Burra's papers with Peter Pears and, in

Pears's later recollection, to 'get them ready, as it were, for anything the family wanted to do with them';[83] in other words, to spirit the offending items out of the cottage while the Burra family were away in Dorset.[84] And this is just what Ben and Peter did on 7 May, having travelled down by train the previous night and ridden over to Foxhold on Peter's motorbike. They spent the entire day 'sorting out letters, photos & other personalities [presumably personal effects] preparatory to the big clear up to take place soon'.[85] Ben's diary does not suggest they did any more than 'sort out', but Richard Thompson believes that they actually removed or destroyed material they were worried about. At all events, he says, they left the place 'eerily tidy', so that when Mrs Burra and her daughter Nell arrived for their 'big clear up' the following day they never guessed what had happened.*

This covert episode was to have lasting repercussions on the lives of both Britten and Pears, if only by bringing them close together for the first time. But, after returning to London, clinging to Peter's waist on the motorbike for the drive to Reading Station where they caught the train up to Paddington, Ben jotted in his diary nothing more revealing than 'Peter Pears is a dear & a very sympathetic person'.[86]

Ben was still keen to find a place where he and Lennox could live and work together in the country. Practical as ever, he bought a car to make the house-hunting easier. Having seen in London, on the day after Peter Burra's funeral, an exhibition of paintings by John Constable, he longed to live in Constable's romantic Suffolk.[87] Lennox was 'terribly keen' on the house idea: 'I think it will be a grand arrangement,' he wrote, 'if you can put up with me.' But he was careful to insist that the place should be big enough for them both to work without hearing each other, because he would be 'absolutely paralysed' if he thought that Ben could hear him 'banging away at one bar for hours on end and trying to find the next one, and it would without doubt drive you out of your mind too'. Lennox was wise to forewarn Ben of his working practices, since his habit of making endless rough copies of each passage involved endless repetitions at the piano. Explaining this years later,

*Among the sensitive material which Dr Thompson claims BB and PP removed were some photos now in the safe-keeping of the BPL. Dr Thompson speculates that they may also have destroyed some of Burra's correspondence with Anthony Howard, Tony Bower, Christopher Harris and his brother Robert (the actor), the Widow Lloyd, Francis Watson, Jack and Noel Blakiston and Douglas Cooper (R. Thompson, 'Air Smash', unpublished MS, 2002, B–MA).

Lennox wrote in his diary that he never seemed to 'get anything right the first time',[88] and indeed his neighbours in Warwick Avenue years later, Heywood and Lady Anne Hill, remembered hearing through the wall the sound of Lennox at his piano in the study playing the same phrase over and over again.[89]

From Brussels, where he was staying with his d'Eppinghoven relations and doing very little beyond reading the score of Verdi's *Otello* ('which is quite amazing ... its full-bloodedness makes ones one feel that one's own efforts are very pale indeed'[90]), Lennox went on to Paris. There he found a letter from Ben to say that he was working on a piano concerto which he wanted to dedicate to Lennox. Writing back immediately, Lennox said he was excited about the new work, proud to be its dedicatee (if that is what Ben really wanted) – and felt he almost deserved it as Ben's greatest admirer. (Lennox returned the compliment the following year by dedicating to Ben his *Introduction and Allegro for Two Pianos and Orchestra.*) Ben must have shown promising signs of a certain reciprocation of Lennox's affectionate feelings, because Lennox ended the letter, 'I miss you a lot too – but it gives me something very nice to look forward to when I get back. Best love and write again soon Lennox.'[91] Things continued to look up the following week when Lennox returned to London for a few days and entertained Ben to tea. Ben wrote in his diary that Lennox seemed as pleased to see him as he was to see Lennox – 'quite considerably that is'.[92]

By late June Ben thought he had found the right house for them to share – a disused mill in the Suffolk village of Snape, on a hillock upriver from Aldeburgh. It would need a lot of work, he told Lennox, but it seemed to have possibilities, with a grand view over the Alde marshes and the Maltings, and plenty of its own land.[93] But when they went to see it together on 8 July Ben thought it looked much less impressive, and seemed 'noisy & messy'.[94] Nevertheless he made an offer, and by August the mill was his – wholly his, Lennox being just a tenant. Unlike Lennox, who had a private income, Ben had no capital, beyond the money his mother had left him, and his earned income was entirely unpredictable. The purchase of the house used up all his resources, and the subsequent building works ran him into overdraft at the bank. But when the house was ready for occupation, Lennox's rent would help to pay that off, and though the running costs were to be high – with a full-time housekeeper and gardener – these could at least be shared.[95]

The property comprised the two-floored, brick-based circular mill with a row of three small cottages behind. The idea was to remove the timber superstructure of the mill building, and the sails, and to convert what was left into two circular rooms for Ben himself, the proprietor: a studio on the ground floor, and a bedroom above it. One of the cottages was to be thrown into a single room as a studio for Lennox, the tenant; another was converted into two bedrooms (one for Lennox, the other for guests); and the third was to be a dining-cum-living room. The mill was then to be joined to the rest by a single-storey weatherboarded boilerhouse containing bathrooms and the central heating system.

The alterations and additions were designed and overseen, for nothing, by the architect father of Kit Welford, fiancé of Ben's sister Beth. But Ben had to pay the builders, and the conversion work from redundant windmill to dwelling was extensive – and lengthy: it was to be April 1938 before the house became habitable. Meanwhile Ben spent the weekends at the Welfords' house in Peasenhall, and the rest of the week with Beth at the flat in the Finchley Road. Lennox continued to flit between the flats he shared with John Greenidge in Great Ormond Street and with José Raffalli in Paris, and the Berkeleys' country house at Falicon in the Alpes Maritimes.

Ben was delighted to be sharing the mill with Lennox. 'He is a dear', he wrote in his diary on 28 July, '& I'm glad I'm going to live with him.' But Lennox was not his only dear – nor was he to be Ben's only living companion. Early in September 1937 Ben decided to look for a flat in London to share with Peter Pears, with whom he had been playing tennis, dining out and going to concerts – and he used precisely the same formula, word for word, to record this decision in his diary: Peter was 'a dear – & I'm glad I'm going to live with him'.[96] Lennox did not know Peter very well, though he thought him charming and admired his singing.[97] It never crossed his mind that Peter might one day replace him.

Potentially far more threatening to Lennox, whether he knew it then or not, was Ben's weakness for 'thin-as-a-board juveniles'.[98] This was 'a part of Britten beyond the reach' of his relationships with adults.[99] The first boy favourite in Ben's life had been Piers Dunkerley, now nearly seventeen and still at Bloxham School, Banbury. There had also been Harry Morris, the 'splendid little boy'[100] Ben had taken on holiday to Cornwall in August (though after two weeks he found he had had a slight over-dose'[101]), a twelve-year-old Basque refugee called Andoni Barrutia (who was to feature in Ben's life only slightly longer, before the boy got bored and the housekeeper fed up), and a teenage German poet he had met in Italy in 1934 and was soon to see again.

Ben may still have been hiding from his true nature, but at least he was no longer a stranger to sex, having spent a summer night in the steam, deep underground, at the Savoy Turkish Baths in Jermyn Street, with Christopher Isherwood as guide, pimp and referee. 'Very pleasant sensations,' Ben recorded, in some surprise, 'completely sensuous, but very healthy. It is extraordinary to find one's resistance to anything gradually weakening ... couldn't sleep a wink on the hard beds, in the perpetual restlessness of the surroundings.'[102]

The choice of Jermyn Street as the catalyst for Ben's coming out was Christopher's idea, but the need to come out at all had been urged by Wystan for months, not only privately, but publicly – starting with two poems in March 1936 both specifically addressed to Ben, 'Night Covers Up the Rigid Land', and 'Underneath the Abject Willow'. This second poem was, in Graham Johnson's vivid simile, like 'a message left under Britten's pillow, the advice of a friend to "lighten up" and "*carpe diem*" ... be who you are and enjoy it.'[103] It is also a very direct invitation to Ben to give himself to love – perhaps to Wystan's love – and so to life itself.

> Coldest love will warm to action,
> Walk then, come,
> No longer numb,
> Into your satisfaction.[104]

Ben cannot have enjoyed being described as 'cold' and 'numb' and seems never to have accepted the invitation into what was more likely to have been Wystan's satisfaction than his own. Perhaps, though, he did accept the general advice, because he made songs of both these highly personal poems the following year. He also set six more Auden texts, including 'Now the Leaves are Falling Fast', which spells out the reasons for Wystan's (and later Ben's own) rejection of Europe (its sexual hypocrisy and the advance of the 'fascist "trolls"'[105]), and the openly erotic (but pre-Britten) 'To Lie Flat on the Back with the Knees Flexed'. Ben assembled the first five of these settings in the cycle *On This Island*, which was first performed, privately, by Peter and Ben for Lennox and Christopher Isherwood after dinner in Ben's new (and temporary) flat at 33 Upper Park Road, NW3, on 15 October. According to Ben's diary, 'Peter sings them well – if he studies he will be a very good singer. He's certainly one of the nicest people I know, but frightfully reticent.' He noted that Lennox and Christopher were 'considerably pleased [by the songs] – as I admit I am'.[106]

The first public performance was given by Sophie Wyss (the Swiss soprano who had sung *Our Hunting Fathers*) with Ben accompanying – in a BBC broadcast from the Concert Hall of Broadcasting House, London, on 19 November 1937. Lennox was there – and also at the party afterwards, with William Walton – and wrote to Ben the next morning to say not only that he had loved the songs ('such real and natural music') but that he too had 'got bitten with Wystan's poems', and was working on another setting. Since Lennox was the very first composer ever to set Auden – while they were both undergraduates at Oxford – it was hardly necessary to add 'I promise not to do any more!', as though he were treading on Ben's toes, but that was Lennox. No less typical was his self-deprecating rider, 'Not that it matters – they are not as good as yours.'[107]

Perhaps, however, Lennox did need to explain himself, because the two love poems he proceeded to set – 'Night Covers Up the Rigid Land' and 'Lay Your Sleeping Head, My Love' – were the intimate ones associated with Ben. The first is dedicated to, and perhaps about, Ben; and though it is debatable whether the second, the lullaby, is specifically addressed to Ben, it is significant that Wystan wrote it out for him (on the flyleaf of the vocal score of *Our Hunting Fathers*) when they met for what could have been the last time, before Wystan's departure for Spain and the civil war January in 1937.[108] Furthermore Ben himself had already set the first of these two poems.

From the outside of this complicated little triangle, and at the distance of more than sixty years, Lennox's annexing of these personal verses might smack of intrusion – like barging into someone's bedroom. If it had been anyone else but Lennox it would be worth a guess that he was cocking a snook at Wystan ('Your words have failed to win him – let's see what my music can do!'), or, like the lover carving his beloved's name on a tree trunk, proclaiming, as publicly (if obliquely) as Wystan, his feelings for Ben. But, in the case of 'Night Covers', the love is acknowledged to be unattainable. The words, as Graham Johnson has pointed out, are words of mourning for a love that is not possible:[109] 'You love your life and I love you, / So I must lie alone.'[110] Besides, barging in, cocking snooks and issuing proclamations are so uncharacteristic of Lennox that perhaps, after all, the simplest explanation is the right one: that the poems were now in the public domain, so he – and they – saw them not as expressions of personal feelings but as art open to all comers.

Lennox loved setting words (particularly Auden's words: he made beautiful settings of five more Auden poems twenty-one years later),[111] but he concentrated less on the meaning of the words than on the atmosphere they created. He believed that when a composer set a poem he had 'in a way to destroy one side of that poem in order to re-create it in another form ... in another language, translated, re-made'.[112] Auden understood this, since he was later to give Lennox *carte blanche* to 'treat the words simply as raw material and change or cut anything as you feel inclined'.[113] That is not to say that Lennox did not recognize the particular relevance of the Auden poems to Ben, but publication had de-personalized them, and Lennox was responding simply to their mood. And anyway, he was firmly of the opinion that the 'time & period at which a piece is written is irrelevant' – in other words, that a composer's music bears no relationship to the circumstances of his life.[114]

We do not know what Ben thought of Lennox's settings of 'Night Covers Up the Rigid Land' and 'Lay Your Sleeping Head, My Love' (which are dedicated to him), but we do know that he never much cared for other composers treading on his heels,[115] and in these particular circumstances who could have blamed him? Perhaps it is significant that they were not publicly performed in his lifetime. The Berkeley setting of 'Night Covers' was given its first outing just after Ben's death, in a broadcast performance, in February 1977, by the mezzo-soprano Meriel Dickinson, who has done so much to promote Lennox's songs, and her brother Peter – pianist, composer, teacher, broadcaster and biographer. Professor Dickinson provides a fascinating analysis of Lennox's settings of these two Auden songs in his comprehensive study of Lennox's work.[116]

Meanwhile there had been other musical developments. On the day between the death of Peter and the funeral, in a feverish spurt of activity before Lennox went abroad to Brussels, he and Ben, 'tho feeling desparate [*sic*]', had finished composing the Spanish suite and had taken it around to Ben's publisher Ralph Hawkes, who was 'very pleased indeed'.[117] They agreed to call it *Mont Juic – Suite of Catalan Dances for Orchestra* (under which title, and with the names of its composers in order of seniority, it was published by Boosey & Hawkes in 1938). And in tribute to the friend with whom they had first heard the dances in Barcelona in the spring of 1936, they decided to dedicate the new work to the memory of Peter Burra.

Mont Juic was scored and ready for copying by Christmas and first performed on 8 January 1938 as part of a concert of light music broadcast live by the BBC Orchestra (Section C) conducted by Joseph Lewis, senior staff conductor at the BBC. (This was not quite the send-off the republican Burra had had in mind for the Berkeley/Britten *sardanas*. He had suggested in the summer of 1936 that his patrons 'Bow' and Mary Behrend should 'light a candle to the annihilation of Franco by offering a performance of the work in Queen's Hall on the day of victory' – and he had added, in a letter to Ben, 'That should appeal to Lennox! ... Viva la Republica.'[118]) But the BBC broadcast reached many thousands more listeners than even the Queen's Hall could hold – among them Lennox himself, who tuned in to the broadcast at home in Paris. Though poor transmission obscured the soft passages and made it difficult to judge the success of the orchestration,[119] he felt that 'a reasonably homogeneous Suite emerged'.[120] Ben, who was present at the concert in Broadcasting House, recorded in his diary a laconic 'Comes off OK'. This is the one thing that Lennox had been in absolutely no doubt about. Working at such close quarters with Ben he already knew his friend's 'extraordinary flair for "what comes off" in actual performance, and his readiness to subordinate other considerations to it'.[121]

Lennox was not without his own extraordinary flair (for subtle harmonies, for elegant phrasing) but he was always ready to minimize his accomplishments in maximizing those of others, particularly Ben – and this was as bad for Lennox, who did not get as much encouragement as he deserved, as it was for Ben, who got, perhaps, too much. In September 1937, after hearing a BBC broadcast of a religious feature called *The Company of Heaven*, for which Ben had written rather more than the incidental music he was asked for,[122] Lennox dashed off a fan letter which could not resist another lash of self-mortification: 'I'm afraid that I go on liking your music better than my own. It just is better and though it rather annoys me to admit it, I am at the same time delighted because the music itself pleases and satisfies me so much.'[123]

A week later it was Lennox's turn to shine – or it should have been – when his oratorio *Jonah* was given a second performance at the Leeds Festival, with the boys' voices for which it was intended, and Lennox himself conducting. Along with his increasingly disturbed sister Geraldine, and his loyal fans John Greenidge and Gladys Bryans, Lennox invited Ben, who had heard it on the radio the first time round and had liked it. In his diary after the performance Ben wrote that Lennox 'conducts very well & has a good show'.[124] The audience warmed to it too, but the notices were 'frightful'[125] – Lennox's publishers said they attacked it 'with a wanton brutality of which English critics have seldom been guilty',[126] and Peter Dickinson suggests that this was prompted by the same kind of suspicious antagonism that the musical establishment felt for Ben.[127] (There is a hint here of the homophobia – much of it fomented by jealous composers within the BBC – that was to militate against both Ben and Lennox in the next few years.) H. C. Colles of *The Times* panned not only the performance and Lennox's conducting but the work itself, expressing incomprehension that the organizers should have expected anything else but failure after hearing the broadcast in 1936. This provoked Lennox to a rare and splendid little outburst – in a letter to Julian Herbage, of the BBC's music department:*

> I think that Colles's notice ... is absolutely monstrous, considering the reception it [the Leeds *Jonah*] got. And as for the performances – we only had one rehearsal of chorus and orchestra together which is really too little for a work of that length and difficulty. I hope you will forgive my writing like this, but I naturally believe in my work, and I am only asking you to stick to your opinion, if you think the work of interest, and not be influenced by these bloody critics.[128]

Neville Cardus of the *Manchester Guardian* – a trained singer (as well as one of the finest of all cricket writers) – was almost alone among the critics in liking the work. He even expressed the opinion that it bore the stamp of genius, and he called for another performance 'at once'. But *Jonah* had to wait fifty-three years before it got that third performance (in a reduction for organ),† though Herbage of the BBC did

*Julian Herbage (1904–1976) was Assistant Director of Music at the BBC 1940–6 , and founder and editor with Anna Instone (later his wife) of *Music Magazine* (which he himself presented from 1964) 1944 –1973.

†With Martyn Hill, David Wilson-Johnson, the St Michael's Singers and Matthew Morley (organ), conducted by Jonathan Rennert, at St. Michael's Church, Cornhill, on 31 March 1990 (SRC, pp. 59–60).

concede that the reviews had been unfair.[129] Later, though, Lennox withdrew *Jonah*, which he dismissed in 1953 as 'a very immature effort which I can't honestly say I want to see revived'.[130]

Back in London, a fortnight after the Leeds *Jonah*, Lennox spent a happy week watching Stravinsky rehearse the London Philharmonic Orchestra in the suite from his new ballet *Jeu de Cartes*. Lennox was bowled over by the work: 'What a marvellous thing,' he wrote enthusiastically to Nadia Boulanger (who did not need any persuading when it came to her beloved Stravinsky); there was so much to be learned, Lennox said, from 'this truly astonishing man'.[131] When a few years later Lennox heard and studied the *Mass for Mixed Chorus and Double Wind Quintet* he loved it, and told Nadia that it was not only the conception that was beautiful, but the extraordinary choice of notes. 'I find it's this quality of "choice" (in other words, taste) that is important, because it is taste, above all, that most composers, and nearly all the public, have lost. I often tell myself now – "Stravinsky doesn't have different notes, or superior notes, to use than I or anyone else. We all have the same notes to choose from. What matters is the use of that choice."'[132]

Lennox took Ben along to the British premiere of the *Jeu* suite conducted by the composer, at the Queen's Hall on 19 October,* and introduced him to Stravinsky afterwards. Ben found *Jeu* 'a charming & delightful work',[133] and, in congratulating Stravinsky, doubtless told him how much he had admired his 'really lovely' *Capriccio pour piano et orchestre*, which (again as Lennox's guest) he had heard Stravinsky's second son, Soulima, playing at the Proms a few weeks earlier.[134] (Ben had first heard the *Capriccio* in the spring of 1936, just before going to Barcelona, when Soulima played it with the Bournemouth Municipal Orchestra conducted by Igor at an all-Stravinsky concert in Bournemouth. 'A great man is Stravinsky – *sans doute*,' Ben had concluded on that occasion.[135])

At the Proms concert in September, when Soulima played his father's *Capriccio*, Lennox's party had also included the composer Sir Arnold Bax, and his mistress the pianist Harriet Cohen. In Bax's eyes, 'Tania', as he called her, was 'fantastic, volatile and delightful', a 'wonderful stray creature from the faery hills';[136] but Ben, cornered by Miss Cohen

*The same concert also included performances of symphonies by Schubert and Beethoven conducted by Dr Malcolm Sargent.

for most of the concert, found that 'she talks more unadulterated drivel than anyone I've ever met'.[137] Lennox was deaf to her effusions, seeing only the musician. In his view she was one of the few people who understood, and could interpret, modern music.[138]

If Lennox was broadening Ben's musical horizons with introductions to Stravinsky, Bax, Boulanger, and, soon, the princesse de Polignac and Aaron Copland, so Ben, in return, was introducing Lennox to fruitful contacts of his own. These included Ralph Hawkes (whose firm, Boosey & Hawkes, was to publish at least six of Lennox's works), the conductor Louis Boyd Neel (who later gave the premiere of what was to become one of Lennox's best-known works, the *Serenade for String Orchestra*), and the parson-patron, the Revd Walter Hussey, later Dean of Chichester (who was to commission three works from Lennox).

As part of the political re-education of his older friend, Ben the committed pacifist also brought Lennox together with the prominent left-wing poet and playwright Montagu Slater, with whom both composers were to collaborate on the music for some puppet plays for the Binyon sisters in 1938. (Ben wrote the music for *Old Spain*, Lennox for *The Seven Ages of Man* and *The Station Master*. All three scores, now lost, used singer, clarinet, violin, piano and dulcitone. The plays were performed by the puppeteers Helen and Margaret Binyon twice nightly for six nights from 22 June 1938 at the Mercury Theatre, Ladbroke Road, W11.[139])

Ben also reintroduced Lennox to the volatile dancer and director Rupert Doone (whom Lennox had first met in Paris, when Doone, a former protégé of Cocteau, was a soloist in the Rubinstein Ballet) and other members of the progressive Group Theatre. As a result, Lennox was invited to write incidental music for a Group Theatre production of Büchner's drama *Dantons Tod*, in a new translation by Stephen Spender, but war intervened and the project was abandoned.[140] A Group Theatre programme of 27 June 1939 announced that the company's next production was to be *Danton's Death*, in a new translation by Stephen Spender and Goronwy Rees, produced by Rupert Doone and Rollo Gamble with scenery and costumes by Robert Medley and John Piper, and music by Lennox and Brian Easdale.[141] But Ben's published diaries indicate that a year earlier Ben himself was planning to write the music.[142]

It was also Ben who introduced Lennox to the Workers' Music Association, founded in 1936 by the Marxist composer Alan Bush to bring socialism and music together as a 'means of attaining a brighter and better society'. Both Ben and Lennox remained members till at least 1950, and Ben served for a time as a vice-president.[143] They may even have contributed some 'unison songs with rousing (ideological) texts', which were among the specially-written compositions the WMA published* – though Lennox's passing interest in intellectual Communism, fed by little more than adoration of Ben, stopped short of a commitment as alien as this, since he believed that composers should never consciously deliver messages through their music.[144]

It was Peter Burra, not Ben, who introduced Lennox to another left-leaning musical association, the so-called Harley Mews Group. Formed by members of the New English Singers and the BBC Singers, this unofficial band of musical friends often gathered at 17 Harley Mews in London, home of the contralto Anne Wood and her friend Iris Holland-Rogers, in order to sing Elizabethan madrigals and English folk songs, and to practise and play and have fun. (During Burra's lifetime they had also met occasionally at his cottage at Bucklebury.) Foremost among them were Anne Wood and her brother, the baritone Richard Wood (who was a Communist at the time), the composer Mervyn Horder (who had been at school with Richard Wood), the conductor and bass Cuthbert Kelly, the tenor Steuart Wilson (a kinsman of Peter Pears),† Pears's lifelong friend Oliver Holt (an amateur bass who had sung in the Oxford University Opera Club with Pears and Burra, and later worked in publishing) and the conductor, harpsichordist and noted Handelian Arnold Goldsbrough, who was then a paid-up member of the Communist Party. Horder – later chairman of the publishers Duckworth – remembered Lennox attending these gatherings and 'making remarks about Bach's *Magnificat* and things like that'. Horder did not remember 'seeing Britten there very much'.[145]

There is no reason why Lennox and Ben should have liked one another's friends, and sometimes they did not. Lennox, for example, could not get on with the interfering Dodo Welford (Ben's sister's

*Alan Bush and the Communist poet Randall Swingler were the editors of *The Left Song Book* (Gollancz, 1938), which claimed that only socialism was 'capable of restoring to music a concrete social basis for its development and of utilising the power of music to the full'.

†Later Sir Steuart Wilson, music director of the Arts Council 1945–8, and Head of Music at the BBC 1948–9.

mother-in-law), who doted on Ben – or 'Fuzzy' as she called him.[146] And, much more seriously, because she was so important to Lennox, Ben did not really like Nadia Boulanger. According to Graham Johnson, he found her 'intimidating and pretentious' – and once tipped ice-cream all over her black velvet Lanvin evening dress at a dinner in London. 'She never forgave him, it seems, and the feeling was mutual.'[147] Nevertheless he thought her 'sweet' when Lennox brought her to hear the Boyd Neel Orchestra playing his *Variations on a Theme of Frank Bridge* at the BBC's Maida Vale studios in October 1937,[148] and when Lennox took Ben to the Queen's Hall four days later to hear Nadia conducting the Royal Philharmonic Orchestra in a repeat performance of the Fauré *Requiem* (which she had first brought to London the previous year) Ben described it as 'serenely beautiful'.[149] Lennox himself was again *bouleversé* by the *Requiem*, and in a letter he wrote the next day (and delivered to Claridge's Hotel where Nadia was staying with Princess Winnie), he urged her to do more conducting, so she could pass on to the whole world what she gave to her students.[150]

For the past few weeks Lennox had been working on a new version for chorus and orchestra of a Latin setting of Psalm 24, *Domini est terra*, which he seems to have composed while still a student in Paris. He intended to submit it to the selectors for the 1938 ISCM Festival in London. And just before Christmas he heard that it had been chosen – along with Britten's *Bridge Variations*, which had caused 'a major sensation' at its premiere at the Salzburg Festival in August.[151] Lennox was delighted for both of them, and there were some auspicious coincidences. It would be the second year running that they had both represented their country at this important festival of new music; both new works bore their composers' tenth opus number; and both were dedicated to, and inspired by, their respective teachers – Ben's *Variations* to Bridge, Lennox's *Psalm* to Boulanger. Fate seemed to be bringing them together.

18
Lennox and Ben, Snape, 1938

Full of hope – for his music, and for his new life with Ben – Lennox went off to France to spend Christmas 1937 in the quiet landscape of the Maine at the Benedictine monastery of Solesmes, then at the peak of its fame as the guardian of the Church's ancient liturgical tradition. There he attended as many of the eight daily offices as he could manage – the first two, Matins and Lauds, were well before dawn – rejoicing in the Latin liturgy and the Gregorian chant, for which Solesmes was then so well known.* After Mass he breakfasted in silence with other retreatants, but he took his lunch and dinner with the monks themselves in the Romantic splendour of the refectory – 'among colossal pillars, baronial chimney-pieces and heavy Norse vaults'[1] – listening in silence to the intoning of sacred texts, and the clatter of pewter food bowls. 'This must sound to you completely weird & extravagant!' he wrote to Ben, but it had all been so marvellous, and the monks' chanting so wonderful that he felt he 'should like to stay there altogether'.[2]

Lennox took with him to Solesmes, for quiet contemplation, a letter that Nadia Boulanger had written on the anniversary of his mother's death a few days earlier. He replied on the 29th to say that for him faith was all, since it brought the certainty of being one day reunited with his mother. Nothing short of this – and the love and understanding of true friends like Nadia – could make it possible to bear the pain of her death.[3]

*In recent years, perhaps because of the tourism which its famous chanting accidentally encouraged, the reputation of Solesmes has slipped. The current sources of the finest monastic chanting are to be found, not by coincidence, at two of the most vigorously flourishing and disciplined Benedictine houses in France, the 11th century abbey of Notre Dame at Fontgombault (in the diocese of Bourges), which was restored to Benedictine life by the monks of Solesmes in 1948, and the neo-Romanesque abbey of Ste Madeleine at Le Barroux (diocese of Avignon), founded as recently as 1970.

On his way back from the monastery to his flat in Paris, Lennox stopped at Le Mans and called in on his young friend Jean Françaix, about whom he had spoken so warmly to Ben in Cornwall eighteen months earlier (when he had urged him to catch a radio broadcast of the French composer's *Piano Concertino*). Françaix was really very nice, Lennox wrote now to Ben, 'quiet and modest' – but 'rather limited', in both his writing and his appreciation. For example he had never heard a note of Ben's music, and only liked music that sounded like his own. 'I feel that what he does is perfect of its kind, but that he will never have much variety.'[4] (This is very much what Ben himself had felt after listening to the *Piano Concertino* in the summer of 1936: 'very charming & ... makes a delicious effect. Perhaps too much like other works I know of his.'[5]) Lennox was touched by Françaix's unworldiness, and offered to accompany him on his first visit to England at the beginning of February, because 'he thinks he is going to feel rather lost, as he doesn't speak much English'.[6] And it was important that Françaix should have a bilingual friend to help him because he was going over to rehearse his ballet *Le roi nu* (based on Hans Andersen's *The Emperor's New Clothes*), which Serge Lifar had choreographed for the Paris Opéra in 1936 – and danced the role of the deluded emperor – and which Ninette de Valois was hastily re-working for Robert Helpmann and her Vic-Wells Ballet [later to become the Royal Ballet] to stage in April.*

Just as Lennox was writing to Ben from the flat in Cité Chaptal on 28 December, he read in the evening paper of the death that day of his early mentor Ravel. 'I feel it very much', he told Ben, 'because I had an absolute passion for his music at one time, and still love a great deal of it.'[7] For nearly ten years Ravel had been suffering from a degenerative cerebral disease – possibly Pick's Disease (lobar atrophy)[8] – caused by 'wear and tear after ... too much smoking, drinking and staying up all night',[9] and exacerbated by a head injury in a car accident in 1932, which had left him unable to compose. According to Lennox, in an article he wrote in 1978 (shortly before he himself suffered a similar

*de Valois's *Le roi nu* was staged on 7 April 1938 with Pearl Argyle as the Empress and Frederick Ashton, William Chappell and Claude Newman as the three Tailors. De Valois's version included the speaking line, 'But he has no clothes on!', which struck some of the critics at the time as discordant, vulgar and unnecessary (C. W. Beaumont, *Supplement to Complete Book of Ballets*, pp. 107–10).

cerebral collapse – but as a result of Alzheimer's disease), it was a 'strange and distressing' illness, which started with memory lapses, impaired concentration and loss of certain movements. 'As it went on he also became unable to write, finding that he could not remember how to shape the letters. The curious thing and perhaps the cruellest part of it was that he always remained perfectly conscious, understanding what was said to him but often not knowing how to summon the words he needed to reply.'[10]

Lennox remembered seeing Ravel at a concert during this time and being struck by the change in his expression: 'he seemed to be looking into the distance as though unaware of his immediate surroundings.' For the last three years of his life, unable to work, Ravel went travelling with his friend Léon Leyritz, which seemed, according to Lennox, 'the only way of diverting him'.[11] Eventually he agreed to have a brain operation, from which he recovered briefly before sinking into a coma.

Lennox believed that Ravel's true originality as a composer lay less in his power to evoke atmosphere than in his musical language itself.[12] Musicians everywhere should mourn Ravel's death, he told Nadia, because he had given to music something so personal – 'an indefinable quality' which Lennox loved so much.[13]

After Ravel's funeral on 30 December in Levallois-Perret, Lennox tried to get back to work. There was plenty on the stocks, including 'some rather voluptuous ballet-music',[14] but composing was getting harder and harder: the more he knew about music and life, he told Nadia, the less he was satisfied with himself. 'When I began I knew nothing – I thought I was doing very well (!) and I couldn't understand why everyone else didn't think so too; now it's the opposite – I have had lots of encouragement, yet I'm the one who's not satisfied. Ah well – it's always better to know what's good even if one can't achieve it.'[15]

Eased by this beating of his chest, Lennox went on to finish the piano score of his 'voluptuous' ballet *The Judgment of Paris* – a short piece based on the mythological beauty contest that led to the Trojan War. (As the handsomest man in the world, the shepherd Paris is given a golden apple and sent to Mount Ida to award it to the fairest goddess of all. Venus promises him the love of the world's most beautiful woman if he picks her. He does – and he wins Helen of Troy.) The scenario may have been influenced by Boris Kochno's ballet *Zéphire et Flore* (set on Mount Olympus) which Lennox saw with the Widow Lloyd when Diaghilev brought his Ballets russes to His Majesty's Theatre, London, in the summer of 1926, just before Lennox went to Paris. Musically the score is related to the neo-classicism of Stravinsky's *Apollon Musagète*, which Lennox saw in Paris during its European premiere run at the Ballets russes de Diaghilev in 1928. (It is interesting that Lennox was disappointed by *Apollon* at the time. 'I think I was expecting something like [the Russian Nationalist ballet-cantata] *Les Noces*,' he wrote years later, 'Stravinsky's neo-classic idiom being then quite new and rather disconcerting ...' But by the end of the Thirties he had already come to regard it as one of Stravinsky's best works: 'the scoring for string orchestra is quite wonderful, subtle and immensely effective.')[16]

Lennox seems to have written *The Judgment of Paris* on a whim – at any rate, without a commission – but as soon as he had completed the piano score he took it to Colonel de Basil's Ballets russes de Monte Carlo and played it through to the Polish dancer Leon Woizikovsky, who was then director of the second company. Woizikovsky was impressed and offered to stage it, on condition that Lennox changed the soft, slow ending, which he knew the dancers would hate, into something noisier and faster. Lennox insisted on a proper contract before he altered a note.[17] When it was clear that neither party would budge, he withdrew from negotiations and returned to work on the orchestration, drawing comfort from the possibility that even if *Paris* did not work as a ballet it might work as a concert suite – especially since Ralph Hawkes, with whom he had recently dined in Paris (and 'really is extraordinarily nice') had offered to publish it.[18]

But *The Judgment of Paris* was not yet lost to the theatre. When Lennox returned to London in February 1938, with Jean Françaix in tow, he discovered from the young Frenchman, who was soon plunged into rehearsals of *Le roi nu* at the Vic-Wells Ballet, that the company was looking for a new, short piece for the current season. In particular, the company needed a filler for a fund-raising gala in May – a *pièce d'occasion* that would serve as a showpiece for Pearl Argyle, one of the celebrated beauties of the age. From his Paris life Lennox already knew Frederick Ashton, who was now the chief choreographer of the Vic-Wells, and the dancer and designer William Chappell. He also knew Constant Lambert, the company's music director. When Lennox was a student of Nadia's, haunting the ballet, and hardly daring to hope for commissions, Lambert, though two years younger and already a celebrity, was at Diaghilev's right hand composing *Romeo and Juliet* and *Pomona*. They had all kept in touch, not least through the celebrated parties given by the painter Cedric Morris – another acquaintance from Paris – and his lover and manager, the artist Arthur Lett-Haines (always known as Lett Haines), at their studio at 32 Great Ormond Street, almost next door to Lennox and John Greenidge at No. 28. As well as Bells and Stracheys from the Bloomsbury Group, the parties drew an exotic coterie of Sadler's Wells characters including Lambert, Ashton, Chappell and Robert Helpmann. And usually there was an impromptu cabaret put on by Ashton and Chappell, including a deadpan version of the 'Black Bottom' dance, which Ashton later reworked as the 'Popular Song' in his ballet staging of the Walton/Sitwell *Façade*.*

Towards the end of February Lennox went up to Sadler's Wells to play his *Judgment of Paris* to Ashton, Lambert and the director of the Vic-Wells, Ninette de Valois. The verdict was positive, and agreement was soon reached on casting. Ashton himself was to create the choreography, Robert Helpmann was to be Paris, and Pearl Argyle Venus (sharing the role in repertory with Margot Fonteyn). Argyle had become Ashton's first English muse following her performance as a more pro-active Venus in his interlude piece *Mars and Venus* in 1929. Lambert himself would conduct, and Billy Chappell was to create the costumes and scenery. The premiere was set for 10 May, and *The Judgment of Paris* was to be given another performance on the last night of the season, with *Le roi nu* – a nice pairing of myth and fairytale; in the new season 1938/39 another three performances were scheduled.

A commission in the bag at last, Lennox quickly finished the orchestration and, as usual with a new work, he took the score around to Ben, who had just moved into a new flat in Earls Court with Peter Pears. Ben judged that it was 'very good', but could be even better – so he made, as his diary records, 'lots of orchestral suggestions which should improve it'.[19] It is likely that Ben's 'improvements' were connected with what he saw as deficiencies in construction. According to the guitarist Julian Bream, who later knew both composers well, Ben was 'a little irritated' by aspects of Lennox's music, particularly by weaknesses in form. Bream himself preferred to call these compositional imperfections 'Lennox's slight waywardness', which he himself regarded as part of the charm of his music – 'it's not music that has been construed'. Bream

*Berkeley and Lambert had been friends since Paris, and in 1934 they and Walton had stood with the Prommers at the Henry Wood Promenade Concerts in the Queen's Hall (H. Cohen, *A Bundle of Time*, p. 86 gives '1924', but Cohen and LB did not meet till 1934).

thought that, harmonically speaking, Lennox's music was more sumptuous and less austere than Ben's; for all his admiration of Ben's music, Lennox was 'his own man'.[20]

Come the big night (two days short of Lennox's thirty-fifth birthday), Ben caught the train up from Suffolk, José Raffalli came over from Paris, and Queen Elizabeth motored around from Buckingham Palace, with a posse of gentlewomen who had 'kindly consented to sell programmes'. The purpose of the gala was to raise the £24,000 still needed for essential additions to Sadler's Wells, in memory of Lilian Baylis, the theatre's founder. It was an almost entirely English programme put together by Ninette de Valois. In the first part, revivals of Bliss's *Checkmate* and Lambert's *Horoscope*; in the second part, Lennox's new *Judgment of Paris* and the Meyerbeer/Lambert *Les Patineurs*.[21] As the only premiere, *Paris* attracted most attention. Argyle looked 'divinely fair', 'condescended to do the splits', shed her skirt to reveal a fetching little undergarment and so upstaged the goddesses Juno and Minerva that Paris had no option but to give the golden apple to her.[22] The willowy Chappell, dancing Mercury, designed for himself a daringly brief tunic of white and gold, in which he posed provocatively on a flight of steps beside some classical columns. The choreography did not exactly bring the house down: the dancer and critic Fernau Hall described it as 'a completely conventional and pointless ballet, with no attempt at any characterisation, atmosphere or originality ...'.[23] Lennox's music fared better: according to *The Times*, it sounded 'like Rameau with modern harmonies'.[24] But when Julian Herbage suggested that the BBC should broadcast it, his colleague the composer Herbert Murrill (then a producer in the Music Department, later Head of Music) warned that 'like most of Berkeley's present writing, it is dry and arid ...'.[25] Murrill, whose own musical tastes were no less Francophile and Stravinskian than Lennox's, was to continue to snipe at Lennox, as a member of the powerful but anonymous BBC Music Advisory Panel. Meanwhile, despite him, *Judgment of Paris* was broadcast by the BBC in the winter of 1938/39.[26] Another colleague at the BBC, Basil Douglas, said, years later, that Murrill did not like anyone else's music: he was 'anti-queer and a disappointed composer'.[27]

Ben enjoyed the ballet, and thought the party afterwards 'very good too' – with Lennox and José, Ashton, Lambert and all the dancers, at Hanover Lodge, the magnificent Regency villa in Regent's Park, home of Ashton's admirer, the American heiress Mrs Raimund von

Hofmannsthal.[28] This was another useful contact for Ben. Alice von Hofmannsthal was, in his own words, 'fearfully rich (one of the Astors)'.* She was ten years old when her father drowned in the *Titanic* disaster, leaving her a fortune of five million dollars. A poor little rich girl, she had an unhappy childhood, neglected by her mother, and grew into what Ashton described as 'a hesitant gazelle ... an extraordinary creature; so elegant and sort of sad'.[29] She was also a generous patron of the arts, and Ben openly admitted to Sophie Wyss that he was angling for a commission,[30] but Mrs von Hofmannsthal 'did not respond in the way he had hoped, despite the fact that Ashton, still the focus of her attention, was then showing an interest in Britten's work'.[31]

For Lennox the collaboration with Ashton should have led to further work, because Ashton later intimated that he 'liked Lennox *above all other composers* ... even C. Lambert'.[32] And though Lennox was to be involved in at least five further ballet productions† – including two choreographed by Chappell – he never worked with Ashton again, though not for want of Ashton's trying. In the early 1980s Ashton asked him to write a full-length ballet for Covent Garden, but Lennox, struggling with his final (and never-completed) opera *Faldon Park*, could not commit to work that would involve 'even more notes than a symphony'.[33] Yet he wished very much that he had been able to write more ballet,[34] and once said he had been discouraged by Ben Britten's admission that he had been exhausted by the effort of composing his three-act ballet of 1957, *The Prince of the Pagodas*.[35]

While Lennox was rehearsing his ballet at Sadler's Wells and Ben and Peter Pears were flat-hunting in London, the Nazis marched into Austria and annexed it as part of the Reich. Ben's response was typical, and gives an idea of the sense of sheer frustration that every young man – even Lennox – must have felt at the time, if they had been honest

*Ava Alice Muriel, daughter of John Jacob Astor IV, was previously married to Prince Serge Obolensky, and was later to marry, successively, the British journalist Philip Harding and the New York architect David Pleydell-Bouverie. All four marriages ended in divorce. She died in New York City on 19 July 1956 at the age of 54. In 1939, following his divorce from Alice, Raimund von Hofmannsthal married Lady Elizabeth Paget, born 1916, daughter of the 6th Marquess of Anglesey

†In addition his *Serenade* was used by the Dutch choreographer Hans van Manen for his ballet *Variomatic*, premiered by the Nederland Dans Theater in Amsterdam on 6 July 1968.

enough to admit it: 'War within a month at least, I suppose,' he confided to his diary, 'end to all this pleasure – end of Snape, end of Concerts, friends, work, love – oh, blast, blast, damn ...'[36]

With a new sense of urgency, Ben moved into what was now to be called The Old Mill, even though the decorating was not quite finished – and the woodwork still crawling with grain weevils. His sister Beth remembered that bugs rained down from the beams while he was composing, and he used to swot them with a ruler.[37] Ben did not mind: this was home, his very first own home. 'O boy, o boy,' he wrote, 'the mill is grand.'[38]

On 19 April, two weeks after Ben had moved in, Lennox arrived at the Mill with some of the family furniture and silver he had inherited from his mother. His dining table and sideboard were a practical addition to the shared home, since Ben had neither. There was not time to stay and arrange all the other things, because he had to get back to Paris, but he offered to buy some beds and share the cost of a car, and he asked Ben to look out for a second-hand piano.[39] It was not till a month later that Lennox spent his first night at the Mill – and not with Ben, but with his former lover (and still his Paris flatmate) José, who had come over for the ballet gala and stayed on to help settle Lennox into the new home (from which he himself had been conspicuously excluded). Lennox had written in advance to ask Ben if it would be all right to bring him down to Snape to help sort out the furniture and put it all straight. José, he said, as though describing a gentleman's gentleman, had a talent for 'that sort of thing' – and as he was now without a job, he 'might just as well make himself useful'. Besides, Lennox added, José 'knows all the stuff I have got really better than I do myself'.[40] Ben tactfully left them to their domestic arrangements, and slipped away to the flat in Earls Court to entertain his young friend Francis Barton, while Peter Pears was singing in the chorus at Glyndebourne.[41]

If the stage seems confusingly full of boyfriends coming and going, it would be wrong to assume that this was free love. Wystan may have wished a wild debauch for Ben – or, at the very least, 'a passionate affair'[42] – but Ben was no more given to promiscuity than Lennox. Both were naturally private – and uncomfortable with their homosexuality. Lennox was much more concerned with music and his faith. Ben, essentially a narcissist, was obsessed with the mystical quest for lost innocence that drove both his life and his work. Whatever Lennox and José may have meant to one another – and it is difficult to imagine they were now anything but former lovers still sharing a Paris flat out of a mixture of convenience and habit – and whatever Ben and Peter may have meant to one another at this embryonic stage in their friendship, Lennox and Ben were simply close friends, flatmates and collaborators. Well, not quite 'simply': Ben needed companionship, rent and adoration, and hoped that Lennox would stick to the rules (which seem to have involved separate beds); Lennox needed a hero, a technical adviser and a faun to admire, and hoped that time might bring more.

The nature of this lop-sided relationship was caught in a striking photograph which the two men commissioned to mark the start of their professional collaboration at this time. It was taken by Howard Coster, the celebrated 'Photographer of Men' (and some women), most of them writers, musicians, actors and painters. Coster had a reputation for compositions of groups and creative partnerships – Auden-Isherwood-Spender, the Lehman siblings, Laurence Olivier and Vivien Leigh, John Gielgud and Peggy Ashcroft. Lennox and Ben made their bid for immortality at Coster's quirky but friendly studios in Essex Street, off the Strand, on the afternoon of 30 March 1938. It had to be late in the afternoon because from midday till three the Costers held a lunchtime salon, with Mrs Coster reading from the works of some of her favourite poets and mystics, Mr Coster leading a debate on the issues of the day, and Joe, the cockney servant, an ex-boxer, handing out sandwiches – ''am, beef or tongue?' – with coffee but never alcohol.[43] Howard Coster was an inveterate talker, who often quoted from the Bible, and though he was liable to fly off the handle if anything went wrong, he soon regained his usual cheerfulness. The novelist Angela Thirkell, recalling her visit to the studio that same year, described the photographer as 'a rum bird' who called her '"my dear" and (I think) "darling" ... and told me what he thought about things'.[44] Ben thought the session was 'most amusing'.[45]

Five of the black-and-white portraits that emerged from that day – shot with a single blue floodlight and a simple reflector[46] – are now at the National Portrait Gallery, where the better of the two double vignettes is available as a postcard (wrongly dated 1930). It shows Ben sitting on a desk facing the camera, while Lennox sits at the desk working, his head bent towards a score, his right hand correcting it with a pencil, his left hand grasping the curved arm of a very Thirties chair. There is no doubt about the star of the picture, since the spotlight picks out Ben's face while bothering with nothing more of Lennox's than the nape of his neck and his hand. The composer Nicholas Maw, who studied with Lennox years later, has perceptively analysed the composition and the body language:

> BB is looking somewhat coyly – and suggestively? – straight at the camera, as though he rather wishes to distance himself from the toiling figure of Lennox (who nevertheless manages to retain an aura of aristocratic elegance somewhat at variance with the tweedy, schoolmastery figure of BB!) in the background. Significant also, I think, that BB seems to have made quite sure Lennox is in the background – almost as though he were Ben's amanuensis.[47]

The other double portrait taken that afternoon is even more flattering to Ben's ego. This time Ben, still looking straight at the camera, is holding the score (there is no title on the cover, but it could be *Mont Juic*), while Lennox, sitting cross-legged slightly below him and almost lost in the shadowy background, flourishes a cigarette in his left hand while gazing across at the music with a look of sweet pleasure that is ten parts modest pride and ninety parts unbridled admiration. Lennox kept both these photos – indeed the whole set from that 1938 sitting – so he must have liked them. And he must have liked Coster's dramatic use of light and shade – not to mention his gifts as a flattering portraitist – because he returned for two more Coster treatments in the late Forties and early Fifties.

The first two weeks of June 1938 provided Lennox and Ben with a rare chance to be together at the Mill, mostly on their own, and for an extended period. They walked through cornfields along the banks of the Alde to the Maltings Quay, once the site of a thriving barley trade that plied the North Sea routes – and one day to become the centre of the Aldeburgh Festival. They explored the Sailors' Path that crosses the river over the narrow old hump-backed bridge at Snape. They inspected the church and its richly-carved font and saw the remains of a barrow where an Anglo-Saxon ship had been excavated seventy-five years earlier. They visited the Russian cellist Michel Cherniavsky who lived nearby, and played 'a little (appalling) tennis' with him,[48] they played more tennis with Kit Welford at Peasenhall, they swam from the shingle beach at Aldeburgh and they entertained Lennox's sister Gerry whom Ben described as 'a nice person – but embarrassingly flattering (& susceptable [*sic*]!)'.[49] However brief, it was a precious time which established an easy intimacy that brought them even closer than before,

18 Lennox and Ben, Snape, 1938

and seemed to offer – to Lennox anyway – the promise of a fuller and lasting relationship.

By the middle of June their time was up. They locked the house, and took the train back to London for the ISCM Festival. On the 17th the BBC Orchestra and the London Select Choir performed Lennox's psalm setting, *Domini est terra* (dedicated to Nadia Boulanger). Ben was very excited by the piece: 'It's the goods all right,' he told a friend – and Ben's approval of another composer's work was rare.[50] But his enthusiasm was not shared by all the critics. Though Philip Radcliffe of *The Criterion* thought it 'left an impression of quiet and individual beauty',[51] Alan Frank of the *Musical Times* said bluntly that it 'did not cut much ice ...'.[52] But Frank was not much happier with Britten's *Bridge Variations* which the Boyd Neel Strings played on the 20th. Whilst they were brilliantly written, he said, they did not wear well, and failed to achieve coherence.[53]

Lennox was not satisfied with the performance of his psalm (and did not know whether this was his fault or the players';[54] he re-orchestrated it later that summer and conducted it himself at the Three Choirs Festival in Worcester[55]). Predictably he 'adored' Ben's *Variations* which was 'head and shoulders above anything else in the programme'.[56] The Britten work and a few other pieces – fragments of the oratorio *Das Gesicht Jesajas* by the Swiss composer Willy Burkhard, a cantata by Ernst Krenek, and Aaron Copland's *El Salón México* – were the best things to be heard;[57] everything else, he said, was 'pretentious balderdash'.[5] Lennox was particularly impressed by the Copland piece: it was a grand piece and marvellously done, 'un véritable triomphe' – perhaps in some ways a little too realistic but 'so living', and 'I've learnt a lot from it'.[59] Ben thought it was 'the bright thing of the Festival', and its composer 'a winner'.[60] Since Lennox was an old friend from the Boulangerie it must have been he who introduced Copland to Ben. They took to one another straightaway, and Ben invited Copland down to Snape for what turned out to be a sweltering weekend at the end of July, which left 'a very deep impression' on the older and more established American composer, and forged a friendship that lasted till Ben's death.[61] Lennox himself could not join them at Snape, because he was staying with his sister at Falicon in the south of France, but he met Copland in Paris the week before and explained how to find Saxmundham (the nearest station to the Mill), when Copland pretended to think that the town was Sachsmundheim and that he would have to go to Germany.[62]

18 Lennox and Ben, Snape, 1938

As well as making a new musical friend at the ISCM Festival in London that June, Ben caught up with several old ones from previous festivals, in particular the German conductor Hermann Scherchen whom he had first met in Florence four years earlier. This turned out to be a critical encounter because it brought him back into contact with Scherchen's son Wolfgang, or 'Wulff', who had been fourteen when they first met in Italy four years earlier (and shared a mackintosh in a cloudburst in Siena – an intimate experience that neither of them ever forgot[63]). Wulff, it turned out, was now in England, living with his mother in Cambridge, and studying at the Perse School, from where he was hoping to get a scholarship to Christ's College, Cambridge.[64] The family had fled to Switzerland when the Nazis came to power in 1933, and Hermann and Gustel Scherchen were now separated. Ben wasted no time in inviting the young man to his 'windmill in Suffolk' for the weekend.[65] Wulff wasted no time in accepting. Together at the Mill for the weekend before Copland's visit, they reminisced about their first encounter in a Tuscan rainstorm, and Ben played a Beethoven sonata ('just for me', recalled Wulff, as a charming grandfather sixty-five years later, still affected – and even bewildered – by the mysterious power of that first love[66]). Ben was 'mesmerized' by the romantic young German, tall and blond;[67] Wulff, with his 'head full of Goethe and Schiller, of Verlaine and Baudelaire, Keats and Shelley etc', was 'enchanted' by the brilliant Ben – and by the Mill, which he described as a typically 'English sort of home ... well-ordered, well-organized and properly looked after'.[68] (And so it should have been with Mrs Hearn keeping house, Mr Hart looking after the garden and Vally the tomcat culling the vermin.) What particularly impressed him, apart from the location, the mill building itself, and the panoramic views from Ben's circular bedroom, were the showers in the boilerhouse between the mill proper and the converted cottages containing Lennox's quarters:

> There was enough space for two separate showerheads to have been fixed to the ceiling, making it possible for the two of us to wash in utter decorum whilst busily soaping and rinsing our bodies, all to the accompaniment of much joyful laughter. Clearly it was the most enjoyable way of starting the day bound in conviviality and I remember well how on a cold winter's day we would scamper back afterwards into the warmth of the Mill, making it a race to be in first.[69]

18 Lennox and Ben, Snape, 1938

Though Ben was twenty-four and Wulff eighteen, the two of them, in Wulff's words, 'just seemed to fit together'.[70] And when Wulff was invited to turn pages for Ben at rehearsals he thought it 'bliss!' Recalling it all as a grandfather in old age, he wrote: 'No wonder I was swept off my feet and was carried away into another existence altogether, where everyone called each other "Darling", and convention was thrown out of the window ... '[71]

It was the start of a complicated and powerful attachment that very quickly altered the chemistry of life at the Mill, as Ben pursued the still recognizable image of the fourteen-year-old boy he had first been drawn to, and Lennox was increasingly sidelined.

Meanwhile composition went on. Ben finished the full score of his *Piano Concerto* a few days after Copland went back to America, and on 18 August he himself gave the first performance with the BBC Symphony Orchestra, conducted by Sir Henry Wood, at the Proms in the Queen's Hall; as a consequence of the looming war it was the last Proms season to be sponsored by the BBC till 1942. Though he dedicated the new work to Lennox (and gave him the manuscript of the piano short score), Ben seems to have been thinking more of Wulff and the effect it would have on him. Both Mitchell and Carpenter argue that he saw the concerto as a means of seducing Wulff, along the lines of an elaborate campaign proposed by Wystan Auden, and that Lennox was in the know.[72] Wulff himself was not in England at the time of the premiere but heard the broadcast in Strasbourg and pleased Ben by writing to say that he recognized something of the Mill in it. Lennox was not there either, but he tuned in at Falicon. He had written to Ben beforehand to say he was sure it would be 'a terrific success', and, in what does look like a tacit understanding of the concerto's sub-plot – though it must have hurt to acknowledge it – he added, 'I hope that you will have a further success afterwards which I know you hope for. If music be indeed the food of love, I think you stand a very good chance.'[73] It seems generous of Lennox to hope that a concerto written and dedicated to him by the man he loved should win Wulff's heart, but he may not yet have seen Wulff as a serious rival.

At least he was busy. He had written a third piece, a *Capriccio* for two pianos (to join the *Polka* and *Nocturne* which Nadia and Clifford Curzon had played in Paris in January, and which Nadia and Jean Françaix were to play in America in 1939). Now he was working on his reciprocal gift to Ben, the *Introduction and Allegro for Two Pianos and Orchestra*, and chivvying the BBC for a fee for three works they had broadcast on the *National Programme*.[74] (Judging by the eight guineas the BBC paid Ben for playing his Concerto at the Proms that summer, Lennox is unlikely to have had much of a tax bill in 1938.)

Towards the end of the summer, Lennox returned to England – first to Worcester where he conducted his new psalm setting, then to the Mill where he joined Ben, not without misgivings, for it was fairly obvious that Ben was now obsessed with Wulff. One weekend in mid-September Wulff came over from Cambridge.[76] It cannot have been easy for any of them, particularly Lennox who had never met Wulff before and could now see plainly the competition he faced. Seventy years later, in his postwar persona of John Woolford, 'Wulff' recalled that Lennox's presence that weekend had made Ben 'somewhat peevish', so he and Lennox were left to walk around the garden together, 'to get to know each other', while Ben busied himself elsewhere. 'I think we both understood Ben's awkwardness and just made the best of things,' Wulff recalled. 'Lennox had such a warm personality we soon found ourselves enjoying an easy and comfortable relationship.'* For Lennox the relationship was not entirely comfortable, but he made the best of things, and, when the weekend was over, he probably expressed the polite wish that Wulff would come again. In a typed letter to 'Wulff, liebchen', Ben reported that 'Lennox approves of you & hopes you'll come here again!!!!!'[76] The five exclamation marks suggest amazement that the experiment had been such a success. But it had not: Lennox was determined to avoid a repeat of the weekend, and resolved to make sure he was out of the way for any repeat performance. Perhaps he hoped that if he ignored what he saw as Ben's little affair it would fizzle out. It was, however, far from being a little affair. For Wulff, eighteen and callow, the romantic friendship with Ben was so emotionally charged that he remembered it for the rest of his life:

> Best of all were the times at [the Mill at] Snape ... Just the two of us walking, talking, trying to add pieces to the huge jigsaw puzzle on the table by the entrance; stoking the boiler before

*In an email to TS (3 September 2008), from which this account is taken, WS suggests that this first meeting with Lennox happened over a weekend in March 1939, but a letter from BB to WS, dated 21 September 1938 (see extract below), confirms that it took place before then, and probably on 10 and 11 September 1938.

> showering in the morning in that little outhouse ... Weekends with Ben were always full of surprises. I don't think Ben was trying to make our weekends memorable but rather attempted to include me in his own life in his own house ... Above all he was always concerned to take care of me, to look after me, to be a sort of 'elder brother' ... [77]

In another, even later recollection, Wulff said his weekends at the Mill in the autumn and winter of 1938 culminated in a Christmas visit which extended to the New Year of 1939, with Christmas dinner every night at one or another of Ben's friends' houses nearby. 'It was a time when Ben and I cemented our relationship.'[78]

For Wulff and Ben and Lennox the world may have seemed to revolve around the Mill that September in 1938, but a wider drama was unfolding in Europe. The Prime Minister, Neville Chamberlain, had flown to Munich for face-to-face talks with Hitler on the 15th, and Ben and Lennox were not alone in heaving sighs of relief when he returned home on the 30th with the Munich Agreement promising 'peace for our time'. A terrible moment had passed, Lennox told Nadia Boulanger - but he sensed the danger was not yet over. 'One breathes again, but I have a real fear that we will not have peace as long as the actual regime still exists in Germany'.[79] Ben marked the Appeasement by going out to pick blackberries, and hoping, as he confided to Ralph Hawkes, that there might be a next year in which to eat the jam.[80]

Lennox spent the rest of the autumn of 1938 based at the Mill, showing his devotion to Ben by his commitment to their shared home. He supervised the removal of the 'hideous electric light poles' which disfigured the garden, and planted new trees and hedges. He also finished the *Introduction and Allegro for Two Pianos and Orchestra* which he had dedicated to Ben. In a letter to Wulff, Ben described it as Lennox's 'new masterpiece'.[81] Lennox found country life much easier for work, and much better for relationships too. He was well aware that it was 'dangerous' living with another composer, but he was able to tell Nadia, by letter at the end of September, that 'till now, by an inexplicable miracle, we haven't fallen out'.[82] On the contrary they had fallen into a happy harmony of composing, walking, playing tennis, making music, talking and entertaining friends. And Wulff notwithstanding, their relationship, at least as far as Lennox was concerned, grew even closer at that time – probably to the point of their sleeping together. Lennox's letters imply this, and a year later, he wrote fondly, and elegiacally, to Ben to say how much that period had meant: 'it was wonderful for me, and I shall never forget it.'[83]

On 22 November Ben turned twenty-five, and to celebrate both the birthday and their new intimacy, Lennox gave him a present he knew he would appreciate: a set of six old miniature scores of the complete Haydn String Quartets, beautifully bound with marbled endboards and white leather spines. They look, in John Bridcut's words, 'like little prayer books', and are now preserved at the Britten–Pears Library.[84]

From this time on Lennox's letters to Ben became distinctly more affectionate, as though he were suddenly confident of a new, and reciprocated, intensity. Indeed they are nothing short of love letters: 'Goodnight my sweet,' Lennox signs off in December,[85] writing again on Christmas Eve to 'Darling', and ending 'All my love Ben dear'.[86] It is no coincidence that this is the moment when they conceived the idea of going to America together the following winter – Ben to play his *Piano Concerto*, the pair of them to play Lennox's two-piano *Introduction and Allegro*, and possibly to share the conducting of the *Mont Juic* suite. Peter Pears had crossed the Atlantic, so had Bridge; Auden and Isherwood were about to go; Stravinsky was to follow in September 1939, and Boulanger in November 1940. What could be more natural than two collaborating composers, impatient with the old order in Europe, setting their sights on the New World, where anything was possible? As early as October 1937, just as Peter Pears was sailing away on his second trip across the Atlantic, Ben had said that going to America was 'one of the thousand and one things I'm going to do before long'.[87]

While Ralph Hawkes, of Boosey & Hawkes, was approaching American conductors on behalf of his two young protégés, Lennox wasted no time in writing to Nadia, now back in London for her third concert trip, to ask if she would put in a word for them during her trip to America in the spring. He was a little ashamed to ask such a favour, he said in his letter from Snape, 'but I know that a word from you counts for a lot'.[88] Nadia's word might well have counted, and she would have wanted to help, but she did not have much time to promote Lennox and Ben, with her gruelling schedule of 102 lectures in different cities in 118 days, conducting the New York Philharmonic, the Philadelphia, the National Symphony of Washington, and joining Jean Françaix for a performance of Mozart's double piano concerto. Just before Christmas Lennox also wrote to Aaron Copland seeking his help in rustling up American interest in the *Introduction and Allegro for Two Pianos and Orchestra*,* about which Lennox said – defensively as usual – that it was 'a good deal better than anything I have done so far', adding, in a way that suggested that he intended to go anyway, that an American date or two would provide a perfect excuse for crossing the Atlantic.[89]

Lennox wrote two new songs during the happy months at the Mill in late 1938: *The Beacon Barn*, setting a poem by Patrick O'Malley and dedicated to Ben's friend Ursula Nettleship (the singer and choir director, who owned the Cornish chalet where they had spent their holiday in the summer of 1936), and *Bells of Cordoba* (Lorca), dedicated to Peter Burra's patron Mary Behrend. At the end of his life Lennox reckoned that *Bells* was one of the best things he had ever done, 'because of the poetry and the feeling of bells'.[90] He finished it one Sunday morning in December 1938, and Peter Pears, who was staying with him at the Mill at the time, 'sang it beautifully almost straight off ...' It was wonderful, Lennox told Ben, who was in London, 'having a tame singer about to try things out with'.[91]

Lennox had first heard Peter's voice in Ben's religious programme, *The Company of Heaven*, on the BBC in September 1937, and he had been both impressed and surprised. Peter sang marvellously, Lennox had written to tell Ben – it was a surprise that he *could* sing so well. Peter's singing voice was unusually high – David Hemmings, the original Miles in *The Turn of the Screw*, described its quality as 'tenor sung like soprano'[92] – and, though no one denied Peter's acutely sensitive musicality, the shrill and tremulous quality of his voice was not to everyone's taste. Some critics accused it of wanting in body and steadiness.[93] Ben's closest childhood friend Basil Reeve, son of the vicar of Lowestoft and later a doctor, noticed that Peter's voice was 'fantastically similar' to Ben's mother's voice.[94] Whether Ben was consciously aware of this psychologically significant link, it is indisputable that Peter's distinctive voice was to become inseparable from Ben's music – inseparable even from Ben's well-being. When Peter was having difficulties with what Ben called his 'golden box' in 1943, Ben wrote to say, 'Something goes wrong with my life when that's not functioning properly.'[95]

*Published by J. & W. Chester this year (1938), but not performed till 6 September 1940.

18 Lennox and Ben, Snape, 1938

By the new year of 1939, it was still young Wulff, not yet Peter, who was occupying Ben's thoughts – and, unintentionally, distracting his attention from Lennox. When Wulff was not staying at the Mill, Ben was writing to him wishing he were – and encouraging him to write more poems. There seemed to be something at the back of that silly old head (Ben wrote in his bantering, St Custard's way) and poetry might help it out, *nicht wahr*? 'Damn it all – man – I'm writing you a bit of music – do the decent thing & reciprocate with something!'[96] The piece that Ben was writing for Wulff (or 'K. H. W. S.' as the dedicatee appears in the printed score) was 'Antique', No. 3b of his Rimbaud cycle *Les Illuminations*. It opens with the words 'O gracieux fils de Pan', and includes the lines 'Walk at night, softly moving this thigh, the other thigh, this left leg'.[97] Wulff, who had not yet seen it (and was somewhat taken aback when he did), set to, and within a week he had reciprocated with several poetical somethings, including one entitled 'To Benjamin Britten', a declaration of love decked out in the manner of Shakespeare and Keats.

> I love you, oh, beyond all comprehension.
> but should I not restrain and guide that love?
> for can I give you aught that you already not possess?
> your music calls and I become your slave
> yet linger I and dare not go, nor dare I stay.
> a friend, such as you are, is truly rare,
> but can I do honour to your friendship?
> for is't not you who has to give me help?
> how will you then find consolation and
> the recompense that is your due?
> therefore play on, play on and quench me with
> harmonious sound.[98]

What had started out as an adolescent crush, on both sides, was running out of control. And the high feelings were clearly mutual. In a letter to Ben, at about this time, Wulff signed himself, 'Your eternal pursuer (or pursued?)'.[99] Lennox, no less of a pursuer, but sadly unpursued, must by now have known for sure that he had been passed over.*

*See LB's letter to WS, 21 November 1938 (JWP), quoted below.

After the tense weekend at the Mill in September, the two 'rivals' did not actually meet again till 19 November when Lennox drove up to Cambridge for the last night of the Auden and Isherwood play *On the Frontier*. Ben had written the music and was directing the performance from the piano, and Peter Pears was playing the part of the Ostnian Announcer, who sings the linking passages between the scenes.* The play was not a great success, and the social gathering that preceded it at Wulff's mother's house was distinctly uncomfortable, as the perceptive Wulff was quick to pick up. For all his youth, Wulff was highly sensitive to the nuances of the complicated relationship they were all caught up in, and wrote to Lennox immediately afterwards to express his concern. In a generous but misguided attempt at Happy Families, Wulff even suggested they should all spend Christmas together at the Mill.[100] Lennox, who had only just recovered from a miserable drive home from Cambridge – in the pouring rain, and with broken windscreen wipers[101] – wrote back to scotch the plan:

> Dear Wulff, I'm sorry not to see you, but I am going away for Christmas, and in any case I don't think it would be any fun at all the three of us being here together. It's a pity, because, strangely enough, I like you. You mustn't worry yourself about me. That side of it is a matter between Ben and me, and so long as we have settled it, it is not your responsibility or even your concern. But it was uncommonly nice of you to think of it, and to feel what I saw you were feeling at Cambridge that week-end that I was there. So don't bother about all that ... [102]

This generous letter shows an uncharacteristic firmness in putting Wulff in his place, and a typical gentleness in recognizing his good intentions. It had been painful for Lennox to watch Ben flirting with Wulff in Cambridge that afternoon, and Wulff's sweetness in attempting to put things right both touched and embarrassed him. After all Lennox was not only the cuckold, but almost old enough to be his rival's father. But Wulff was still uncomfortable about the way Lennox had been displaced in Ben's affections, and, ignoring Lennox's implied rebuke ('it is not your ... concern'), he wrote to Ben criticizing his treatment of

*A Group Theatre production directed by Rupert Doone for the Arts Theatre, Cambridge; it played a single performance in London the following year on 12 February (LFAL, pp. 590–5).

Lennox. Ben could not see what all the fuss was about, and said so at the end of his next letter to Wulff: 'Lennox sends his love – really & truly he does! – & says no one could be nicer to him than I am – & he means it – so there! – you needn't be so angry with me or waste your sympathy on him! He was really touched by your niceness and kindness on Saturday! All my love as usual ...'[103]

To Ben, it was all perfectly straightforward, but to young Wulff, the reluctant observer, and to Lennox, the suffering victim, it was all part of what Rupert Christiansen has called 'the slippery game of emotional snakes and ladders in which Benjamin Britten involved his associates',[104] both then and, increasingly, later.

Worn out by the strain of his exams, and anxious about this unsatisfactory exchange of letters, Wulff was only too glad to be spending Christmas at the Mill, without Lennox, but with Ben, Peter and Ben's sister Barbara. When Peter and Barbara returned to London, Wulff stayed on alone with Ben till 2 January.[105] It must have been an intimate and highly-charged time, judging by the new intensity of their letters. Just before leaving for Snape, Wulff wrote to his 'Darling Ben', to say how much he was looking forward to their being together, and he concluded: 'Till Xmas dearest. All my love ... love, love, love ... oh my darling, I love you ... I'm feeling absolutely desolate. Don't ever leave me, darling xxxx.'[106]

The 'desolate' feeling and the fear of being abandoned are quite new in the correspondence, and may have come to Wulff as a result of observing how Ben had cast Lennox aside, and how Lennox was suffering. Wulff and Ben were now so close that there was no turning back, yet what lay ahead, as Wulff became a man and shed his boyish attractions? Wulff must have been fearful of the possibility of Ben's falling in love with someone younger and his having to play gooseberry to the new favourite. Ben tried to reassure him by writing to say, 'Remember I love you very, very much.'[107]

As a Christmas present for Ben, Wulff wrote an autobiographical poem, in which he stated that on his arrival in England, he had come to know again 'little Benny ... with whom then in love I fall, body, soul, and all and all'.[108] Alone with Ben at the Mill, after Peter and Barbara had gone, Wulff wrote another poem which he dedicated to Ben 'as part-payment of an unpayable gift: his friendship'. It was conceived in the small hours of the night of 30–31 December, and confirms a new and deeper phase in their friendship. It refers to two beings lying lost to

18 Lennox and Ben, Snape, 1938

their world: 'alone, yet one ... voluptuous, they love ... in their love / they know existence ...' Even music loses its charms 'in lover's frenzy'.[109] According to John Bridcut, 'Ben carried this poem with him for years afterwards'.[110]

Lennox's instincts were right. His relationship with Ben had gone rapidly downhill since the Cambridge episode, and he would have been *de trop* at Snape that Christmas. Instead he did what Lennox always did when he was hurt: he went to stay with old Gladys Bryans in Painswick. From there, on Christmas Eve, he poured his heart out to Ben:

> Darling, I must write because I can't think of anything but you, everything seems drab and uninteresting except you, and I cant [*sic*] give my mind to anything else, so I'm writing in dispair [*sic*], hoping to feel better after. It's a sort of illness which I suppose I shall recover from some day – I'm feeling its unpleasant and rather painful side just now, but the other side has made me marvellously happy and it's worth it a hundred times ... My love to ... Wulff though I can't feel quite so well disposed towards him at the moment as I shd like to. It *is* hell isn't it – not his fault, poor child. All my love Ben dear L.[111]

It is a measure of how very deeply Lennox had fallen in love that he should have confessed to Ben he had given up going to Mass for the time being, because he could not 'reconcile things' – though he said he would be going to midnight Mass at the Benedictine monastery at Prinknash, since Christmas would be meaningless otherwise.[112]

The moment Ben received this *cri de coeur* on the 27th, he put a call through to Painswick, but Lennox could not talk freely because Gladys's ears were flapping, so he wrote again to Ben that night to say he was bearing up, but feeling a bit depressed:

> It's almost impossible for me not to be haunted by the green-eyed monster when Wulff is with you, but still I keep saying to myself that you are happy and that it's only this mean and horrible jealousy that I can't quite get the better of that prevents me from being happy too ... I long to see you and wonder how I can live a whole month without you [Lennox was going on to Paris after Painswick] ... I feel an awful fool to have let myself fall in love so violently – I really ought to know better at my age ... Good night Darling ... Bless you, L. Love to Wulff; and I hope that Vally [the

tomcat] isn't pining on account of his uncle's absence. He's so fond of me (V not W). Could you make a supreme effort and write during the week-end? – to Paris ... [113]

Just after Christmas Ben went to Brussels, to play his *Piano Concerto* with the Belgian Radio Symphony Orchestra. He stayed with Auden and Isherwood (or 'Wys & Chrys', as he called them),[114] who had promised to introduce him to a sixteen-year-old 'something ... that will make you crazy ... Such eyes. O la la'.[115] This blind date, which Ben bragged about, only aggravated Lennox's despair – as he tried to explain to Ben.

> I hate to think of you doing – I mean – oh damn, well you know what I mean. It isn't jealousy this time, but a sort of respect for you and a really very deep kind of affection that makes me want you to be everything that's marvellous and good. It may seem absurd to you but I feel like what your Mother would have felt about that. It would shatter the little idealism that I still possess ...[116]

The reference to Ben's mother, a month before the first anniversary of her death, was a deliberate appeal to Ben's sense of guilt, since Lennox knew that Ben knew that Mrs Britten would have been appalled by the idea of sexual frolics in Brussels. It also indicates something of the nature of their new relationship. If mutual love were not possible, then Lennox could still offer a love that was nurturing, doting and protective: the love, in fact, of a mother. Lennox wrote this letter on the very day of the third anniversary of the death of his own mother. Thinking of Maman would have reminded him of his constant need to be worthy of her – and his despairing conviction that he never would be. 'I so much want to live as she'd have wished,' he had told his confessor, Nadia, in London before Christmas, 'and I fail ...'[117] Quite what Aline would have wished is never spelled out, but it probably amounted to leading a good Christian life, and keeping himself as 'clean' as Mrs Britten would have wished for her Ben.

If Lennox's letter to Ben sounds pious, or even sour grapes, it was not either: it was, quite simply, a loving Lennox trying to protect Ben from what he saw as moral danger. His adoration was connected to a belief that Ben's genius was divine. Perhaps it was – but Ben was also human, with ordinary human desires and a perfectly normal human need to let his hair down occasionally – a need, which, abnormally, he had tried hard to resist till now. The temptations offered by the 'complaisant boys with which Brussels apparently teemed' were just the medicine Wystan had been prescribing for his patient's chronic repression for two years.[118] Lennox, the devoted acolyte and faithful Catholic, truly felt that a loveless encounter (if the Brussels jaunt were ever actually to come to that) might somehow snuff out the divine spark.

Ben seems to have ignored Lennox's appeal for resistance to the sirens of Brussels, and, on Ben's return from Brussels, Wulff wrote him a letter in which he made a half-joking reference which implied that Ben had been unfaithful. Telling him he had invited his gay friend, the charming and handsome Ian Scott-Kilvert, to stay in Cambridge, Wulff wrote, '... you needn't be afraid, I'm not going to be the kind of whore you were.'[119] A fortnight later Wulff wrote again to thank Ben for 'two lovely days in London', during which he had attended a party given by Ben and Peter for Wystan and Christopher, on the eve of their departure for America.* Wulff told Ben how much he liked Peter Pears: 'I'm beginning to fall in love with Peter', he said, teasingly, 'in the way one falls in love with a friend and not a sex-maniac like you.'[120] The prudish Ben did not at all like this description – and punished Wulff with a barb of his own, sent from his lonely sitting room in Snape: 'Wish I had my spouse with me – ha! knew that'd make you angry ... I'm awfully glad that you *like* Peter ... the more you like my friends, the better I'm pleased. Certainly there is a limit – but I'm rather sure of my ground – hope I'm not too confident!! But, I *dislike* being called a s.-m. – even by *your* fairy lips. See? T'aint true – Oi'm a good boy, Oi am. Good-night, my darling ... .'[121] (Roger Nichols sees a possible link between Britten's use of 'Oi'm a good boy, Oi am' in this letter to Wulff, and the anguished cry of the possessed child, Miles, in *The Turn of the Screw*, 'You see, I am bad, I am bad, aren't I?', at the end of Act 1, when he has been discovered in the garden late at night, lured out by the corrupting spirits of Peter Quint and Miss Jessel.[122])

Ben's hyper-sensitivity to Wulff's playful provocation was connected to something he had heard from Wystan in Brussels earlier in the month – that his 'little friendship' with Wulff was being talked about all over the Continent. Apparently the source of the rumour was Wulff's father, the conductor Hermann Scherchen. Ben wrote primly to Wulff to warn

*The painter William Coldstream describes this 'slightly sticky' evening in Peter Parker, *Isherwood*, p. 412.

him not to forget that, as Fougasse's wartime posters were soon to say, walls have ears: '... be a little careful, my dear, in what you say. I personally don't care what people say – but it might react badly on you ... *I* should like to shout it to the skies – as you know.'[123]

Ben of course did care (a lot) what people said – otherwise he would not have ended the letter with the explicit instruction, '*Burn* this ...'[124]

Meanwhile, Lennox had retreated to Paris, and Ben, as bidden, had written to him there. But it was such a hearty, back-slapping sort of letter that it cannot have done much to console him:

> My dear Lennox, A *very* happy New Year to you! I'm sure you're feeling well now that you're in Paris and with José and all those friends of yours. I was going to say that you are now where you really belong, to cheer you up – but I'm not so sure about that – I think Snape is your spiritual home – whatever it is physically!! ... W[ulff] is with me for the week-end ... I'm afraid lunch is in – & I must post this. Much love, my dear; cheer up ... [125]

The following day, 2 January 1939, Wulff returned to his mother in Cambridge and wrote immediately to Ben: 'Dearest, thank you again for everything, & especially for last night. You mean more to me and matter more than anything else.'[126]

Wulff was now indisputably No. 1; Lennox's brief reign was over. Wulff knew it, Lennox instinctively felt it and Ben knew they both knew. Yet the Mill was Lennox's home. He had settled all his furniture there, he had paid a year's rent in advance, he was recognized by Mrs Hearn, Mr Hart and Vally as joint master, and furthermore his heart was still firmly lodged there. For better or for worse he returned to the Mill at the beginning of February. He knew the hopelessness of his situation, knew there was no place for him, yet he could not bear to think it was all over, and he may have tried to persuade Ben to give up Wulff. For a few days he made an effort to carry on as usual, and even wrote a friendly note to Wulff – in a complicit tone, playfully suggesting that they were both victims of the monster Britten – but the strain was too much and on the 6th he broke down. Ben did his best to console him, but he was powerless to change his feelings. On the 7th Ben wrote to Wulff, 'Sorry I couldn't write yesterday, but was abit [*sic*] occupied with LB. Why don't you write him a nice little note, saying "thank you for your nice letter – I agree with you that BB is a bloody nuisance in both our lives –" ...'[127] Wulff wrote back the next day to say he would write to Lennox as soon as he could 'find the guts', since he knew very well that Lennox had been dumped – and none too kindly.[128]

Everything had changed. Not only had Ben rejected Lennox in favour of Wulff, but he had dropped Lennox from his American plan too – and replaced him with Peter Pears. The first sign of this appears in a letter from Ben to Peter on March 16. But the plan must have been hatched well before then, perhaps in mid-February when Ben and Peter were away together in Oxford, for a concert at Balliol. There would have been plenty of opportunity to discuss it privately in their new flat in Hallam Street, and, given the worsening situation with Lennox back at the Mill, Ben spent as much time there as he could.

Lennox was now so distraught that he could not get anything right, and Ben was not kind about it. On 1 March he was supposed to meet Ben off the London train at Stowmarket, but got lost driving up from Snape and Ben had to wait on the station for forty minutes. Ben was beside himself with irritation, called Lennox a 'nitwit' and 'told him in a few brief sentences what I thought of him'.[129] They soon made it up, but Ben's impatience and unpleasantness will not have made these last few weeks any easier for Lennox.

At the height of all this turmoil, Lennox's new car arrived. He had ordered it well before Christmas - as much for Ben as for himself, and, knowing Ben's weakness for fast cars, he had chosen an Acedes Drop-head Coupé with a highly-tuned 16 h.p. engine, the smartest sports car of the day, hand-made to order by the Auto-carrier Car Company in Thames Ditton.[130] Ben told Wulff it was a twenty-fifth birthday present,[131] but it was a good three months late for that (and anyway Lennox had already given Ben the Haydn volumes). Perhaps Ben wanted to impress Wulff by boasting about an extravagant present given by an older admirer; if so, the attempt misfired, and seventy years later Wulff still remembered the episode with unease.[132]

Ben himself drove the new car down to the Mill with Lennox on Saturday 11 March,[133] and a couple of weeks later, while Lennox was away in Paris, he took her up to Cambridge to collect Wulff for the weekend. On the way back, on the 'nice & straight' Newmarket road the speedometer touched 85 mph ('just to show that the wheels were going round properly').[134] They made a detour via the seaside to collect a friend from Southwold – the conductor Trevor Harvey, assistant chorus master at the BBC (the man who had commissioned Ben's radio scores).[135] Harvey brought his ciné camera with him, to film the grand new car.* A few seconds of his movie survive at the Britten–Pears Library, in a print with handwritten captions. In the first sequence, entitled 'Arrival of Harvitone at Benjamin Britten's Mill', the AC roadster (registration number FLA 633) swings in the through the gates, with its grey leather-cloth hood down and Ben at the wheel.[136] In the second brief sequence, the youthful figure of Wulff, tall and straight-backed, in a long coat draped over his shoulders, strides from the front door towards the car. And in the final episode, a grinning Ben, now alone in the car, drives towards the camera held by Harvey, and mischievously pokes his tongue out as he passes.†

Ben was as besotted with the new car as he was with Wulff. It was 'a wonder', he told Peter Pears;[137] and to Enid Slater he wrote to say it was 'a heavenly thing' that 'goes like the wind'.[138] He generously permitted the legal owner to take the wheel on 14 March (judging later that Lennox's driving had not been '<u>too</u> bad'), he pulled the car to pieces at the garage the following day,[139] took her back to the garage for an overhaul a week later,[140] and he dazzled (and terrified) Wulff by touching ninety 'on the long straight stretch of the new Brighton Road' while staying with Wulff and his mother in Bognor Regis over the Easter weekend.[141]

If the AC had been intended as a love token at the time it was ordered before Christmas when the relationship seemed to be going so well, it was now too late: an embarrassment bordering on the grotesque. Only a week after the new car arrived at the Mill, there was 'a bit of a crisis' when Lennox seems to have attempted to restore the physical side of their relationship. Ben poured out all his feelings to Peter Pears: '... re. him [Lennox] ... I had the most fearful feeling of revulsion the other day – conscience and all that – just like the old days. He's very upset, poor dear – but that makes it worse.'[142]

What Ben did not reveal in the letter was that he had given Lennox his marching orders. Banished from Ben's heart, Lennox left England. Ben told Peter he was thankful they were going away to America.[142]

*According to WS (letter to MB, 14 August 2004, MBA), LB owned the camera and took the film, but John Bridcut and TS agree that since there is no evidence that LB was at the Mill that day and there is evidence that he was in Paris the following day, and since one of the film captions refers to 'Arrival of Harvitone', it is more likely that Trevor Harvey owned the camera and took the film.

†An ensuing scene is captioned 'Wulff Scherchen who was being tickled from below', but there is no more footage to explain it.

Wulff, when he heard about all this, was confused and upset – as he still remembered with discomfort in 2008:

> [Ben] admitted it [the car] had been a birthday present from Lennox, but explained that he had ended the relationship. All this was rather bewildering to me (who didn't really want to know what it was all about). I did receive a clear impression however of Lennox (who had given him the AC) having been given a definite and brutal brush off. This remains with me today as an unchanged and uncomfortable memory of a sudden cold shower down the back of the neck. My immediate reaction had been to query why Ben had not returned his present when making the break.[144]

Whatever he told Wulff, Ben knew that the car was not his – that he had only been lent it. Yet he continued to use it till his departure for America. 'It is grand to have such a car to drive!' he wrote to Lennox. 'But it's useless to say thank-you! you can't say thank you for a car – or should I say the permission to drive one ...'[145] Lennox was fond of the car too, and never forgot it, or the circumstances associated with it. But he did forget what happened to it, even though it had cost him £455 (or £22,000 by today's standards). He liked fine things, and was lucky enough to be able to afford them, but possession for its own sake was meaningless. That is one of the reasons why, throughout his life, he left a trail of objects behind him: not just the AC, but the family silver, his mother's jewels, a plot of land in the South of France.

After the row in Snape Lennox went first to Paris, where he started work on a cello concerto for the German-born American cellist Maurice Eisenberg (whom he had known in Paris ten years earlier), and then to his Aunt Annie d'Eppinghoven in Brussels. While he was in Paris he got a letter from Ben. It was not an apology, not did it offer sympathy or any kind of explanation. Instead it just blustered. Ben was enjoying the car, his sister Beth had had a baby boy, Vally the tomcat had been on the razzle, and he had given a recital at a girls' school but they were all terribly unattractive and he had not been converted. The letter ended with the breeziness Ben always adopted in tricky situations: 'Well – my dear – hope you're feeling better now – see *lots* of Marc (you dare!!) – & come back a new man – Love, Ben.'[146] ('Marc' was one of Lennox's young Paris friends – he may have been the Marc Chatellier to whom he dedicated the third of his *Four Concert Studies* in 1939.) Already badly hurt, Lennox now realized that Ben simply did not understand.

A fortnight later Ben and Peter finalized their travel plans. The idea was that they would leave Southampton on the Cunard White Star *Ausonia* on the 29th, arrive in Quebec on 9 May, Peter would return at the end of the summer, and Ben would go on down to the United States and stay away 'for at least six months'.[147] (Beth, though, was convinced that her brother had decided to make a new life on the other side of the Atlantic and that she would never see him again.[148]) On 16 April Ben wrote again to Lennox, who was now back in Paris after a week in Brussels, to say he hoped to see him to say goodbye before they left – and if he could not come, he must not fail to tune in to the BBC on the 21st for a broadcast of a complete programme of Britten, including some new Rimbaud settings (which were later to form part of *Les Illuminations*).[149] Since one of the settings – the 'orgiastically sexual' *Being Beauteous*[150] – was inspired by Wulff (though later dedicated to Peter),[151] this was, perhaps, tactless. Wulff was instructed to tune in too – and this was even more cruel, since it was only days since Wulff had learned that Ben was leaving him, to go to America with Peter. The news had come at one of a series of farewell parties in the Hallam Street flat. Wulff had not been comfortable there anyway – 'I didn't fit into this crowd,' he told Donald Mitchell years later[152] – and too much gin had made him tearful. But the discovery that he would soon be losing Ben, had come as 'a blow in the solar plexus'.[153] When Ben saw him sitting in a corner crying, he said he must 'get this kid out of here'. He had then driven the boy to Liverpool Street Station, and put him on the last train home to Cambridge.[154] Not surprisingly Wulff was in no mood to tune in to the Rimbaud settings on the 21st. Ben was furious that he had not 'taken the trouble to listen to my concert', and wrote to say to say how 'damn sick' he felt about it. 'Anyhow', he added, in a dig that was meant to sting, 'Lennox will have listened.'[155] Cast out as a lover, Lennox still had his uses as a fan.

On the night of the 28th Ben and Peter held the last of their farewell parties in the Hallam Street flat. Lennox may have attended, but Wulff did not. The following morning Ben and Peter caught the train to Southampton with Barbara Britten, Trevor Harvey and Ralph Hawkes, and on the quayside they found Frank and Ethel Bridge. As Ben and Peter were about to climb aboard the SS *Ausonia*, Bridge stepped forward and handed Ben his viola, as a farewell present.[156] Bridge was

18 Lennox and Ben, Snape, 1938

not the only one who feared they might be going for good. If Ben and Peter themselves were not already sure that war was coming, the introduction of conscription for all men of twenty and twenty-one just three days before their departure must have left them in no doubt of the fate they were escaping.*

Much has been written about why they went. Ben claimed the reasons were professional. He needed 'to do some really intensive thinking & for me personally to do somework [*sic*] to please *myself* & not necessarily the BBC or Basil Dean [the influential theatre and film producer]'.[157] And, judging by his letters to Wulff, he hoped he would make a fortune writing film music for Hollywood.[158] Peter said it was politics: 'Things weren't working awfully well in England ... we were both pacifists, and we didn't much see what we were going to do [when the war came]. Short of going to prison ... which didn't terribly appeal ... we decided – as Wystan had earlier – that the only thing to do was to go to America.'[159] It is clear from their letters at the time that Wulff assumed Ben was going for a holiday. But fifty years later he remembered it had looked like running away, and he had not been happy about it.[160] Yet Wulff himself was one of 'A thousand reasons – mostly "problems"' which had sent Ben to America.[161] Lennox was another. Ben had got too close to Wulff, Lennox had got too close to Ben, and Ben, 'nearly crazy with work' and the strain of all these emotional entanglements, needed to get away.[162] He had told Lennox that their relationship was over, and he had resolved with Wulff that they should try and forget one another too. Peter Pears may have been the broker of the pact, and, as he and Ben sailed away to America, perhaps only he saw into the future clearly enough to know that Ben would soon be his.

Graham Johnson has a theory that Ben and Peter, like Wystan and Isherwood before them – and, indeed, strongly under their influence – were consciously exchanging the sexual hypocrisy of England for the possibilities of erotic adventure in America.[163] The influence of the two young writers was powerful: Ben's steady friend Marjorie Fass claimed that he was 'bowled over with everything that Auden and Christopher Isherwood do'; dear Benjy, she said, was 'so young and *so* dazzled'.[164] The motivations were a combination of all these things,

*The Military Training Act, which required all men of 20 and 21 to undertake six months' military training, was introduced on 27 April 1939.

but it does seem that negative forces were at least as strong as positive ones.

'America takes us all!' Lennox had written to Nadia on April Fools' Day, halfway through her working tour of the States.[165] But he was wrong. At the last minute, America left him behind. Lennox was now out of that particular picture. And, for better or for worse, he was out of Ben's too.

19
Lennox and Wulff, London, 1939

Lennox was deeply hurt by Ben's departure for the New World in 1939. At a single stroke he had lost his lover, his musical collaborator, his house-mate and the dream of a joint trip to America. He had also lost his partner for the premiere of the two-piano piece he had written as a present for Ben. Lennox had been hoping that the two of them would play the *Introduction and Allegro* at the Proms in the summer of 1939, as a sort of public affirmation of their relationship, 'but as he [Ben] is going to be away for at least 6 months', he wrote to the BBC, 'that's a wash-out.'[1]* The irritation evident in his uncharacteristic use of the expression 'wash-out' shows how badly let down Lennox felt. All the plans they had made together were suddenly dashed. Ben had crossed the Atlantic without him – and with Peter Pears.

After saying goodbye on the last day of April 1939, Lennox went back to the flat in Bloomsbury that he shared with his old Oxford friend, the architect John Greenidge, now working in one of the wartime ministries. The very next day he drove down to Snape on his own, in the sports car he had bought for Ben's use. It was a mistake to go back so soon, but he must have felt an overpowering need to return to the scene of his recent happiness – if only to try to understand how everything could have gone so wrong. That first day in the empty Mill was, he told Ben in a letter addressed to Montreal to await his arrival there, 'absolutely bloody'.

*In the event the war postponed any plans for a Proms performance of the *Introduction and Allegro for Two Pianos and Orchestra*, and the piece had to wait for a premiere till 6 September 1940, though Ethel Bartlett and her husband Rae Robertson – 'the old gizzards' (BB to Beata Wachstein 6 June 1942, LFAL, p. 1062) – had hoped to play it with Barbirolli and the New York Philharmonic Orchestra in the winter of 1939/40 (LB to Ralph Hawkes, 22 October 1939, BFP).

> I wandered about the house feeling like a dog that's lost his master. After that I managed to pull myself together, and have been better since, but it still gives me a cold feeling in my tummy when I think of you being so far away. I love you far too much – I wish I hadn't let myself get like this. I'm paying for it now – and yet I can't really regret anything ... I need'nt [*sic*] say how much I miss you, Ben dear – I just have to try and keep off that subject. I hope you are happy anyhow, and enjoying it all. Love to Peter. Write soon. All my love, Lennox.[2]

The following day Lennox sought out Ben's abandoned pup, Wulff Scherchen, and had lunch with him in Cambridge, hoping, presumably, to share his grief with someone who would understand. But they were both too shy, or too proud – and anyway Frau Scherchen and Professor Dent* were there too – so the subject closest to their hearts remained unspoken.[3] Wulff subsequently reported to Ben that Lennox 'virtually invited me to the Mill sometimes when he's there', but nothing came of it – and not surprisingly, since they had little in common but Ben.[4]

A fortnight later Lennox had a letter from Ben. It was all about the rough journey, icebergs banging against the ship, too much food and not enough to do, friendship with 'a nice kid of 14', but most of the other passengers 'very dull colonials'. And it ended with an unconvincing sop for Lennox: 'I *do* hope that you're feeling OK, my dear. I think about you a great deal – really. Love B.'[5] What Ben did not say was that a photograph of Wulff stood on the cabin table in front of him as he was writing to Lennox in the middle of the Atlantic.[6] (The photo was taken by Enid Slater in the autumn of 1939.[7] Ben referred to it a lot in his later letters from America – and noted with pleasure that his cabin steward on the SS *Ausonia* asked if it was his brother.[8] But the photo he really wanted to have with him, he told Wulff, was one taken when Wulff was thirteen.[9]) Nor did he say that he had been inspired to transform his feelings for Wulff into a 'fanfare' for piano and orchestra called *Young Apollo*, based on the last lines of Keats's 'Hyperion', which describe the Young Apollo's 'golden tresses' and 'limbs/Celestial'.[10] Ben's resolution

*Professor of Music at Cambridge and President of the ISCM (which brought him close to the conductor Hermann Scherchen), Edward Dent was Wulff's mentor in Cambridge (LFAL, p. 564, note 4). Perhaps it was through him that Frau Scherchen found work as secretary to Dent's friend J. B. Trend, Professor of Spanish at Cambridge (LFAL, p. 612, note 3).

to forget Wulff had been undermined by the great distance that now separated them. 'I miss you pretty acutely, darling,' he wrote to Wulff from the Atlantic, only two days out of Southampton. 'The more I think of Snape & the visits to Cambridge and yours to Snape – the more I feel a fool to have left it all.'[11] In Toronto six weeks later, he was still missing Wulff: 'It's awful how much you mean to me – I had terrific resolutions when I left ... but I simply can't help thinking of you ...'.[12]

Wulff felt the same. Writing from Cambridge on his nineteenth birthday at the end of May, he told Ben he was beginning to feel he had lost something very important: 'I seem somehow shut off from the rest of the world ... The complete and sincere understanding that existed between us seems to have disappeared, and with it the full appreciation of life I had while with you ... everything seems emptier ... for all my resolutions I have not given you up.'[13]

In June Wulff wrote again – a very long typewritten letter, complaining bitterly that Ben had not written for three weeks: 'When will you write again? ... I'm waiting, pining away, slowly turning into a nervous wreck, rushing to the door ... because of the letter that never comes ... Darling, why did you ever have to go away anyway, can't you see how much I need you??'[14]

This exactly expresses how Lennox felt about the loss of Ben: wondering why he had gone, feeling lost without him, waiting anxiously for letters that did not come. But if Wulff had the consolation of knowing he was still, more or less, part of Ben's present, Lennox knew he was now firmly in the past. In late June he received his first letter from Ben in North America – 'Just a scribbled line', perky, patronizing and not a little boastful, quite out of tune with the mournful mood of Lennox, who had just lost a great love, and the nervy mood of Britain on the verge of war. Ben and Peter, the letter said, had had 'a terrific time' staying in Grand Rapids, Michigan, where they were 'fêted like Toscaninis', interviewed by the press and invited to house parties and luncheons; 'they think I'm pretty hot out here & I'm not trying to disillusion them.' Ben knew that Lennox was spending some time at the Mill with José Raffalli – it was 'honestly very nice' to think of him 'enjoying the combination of Snape & José!' – and he added an encouraging 'Atta boy!', before signing off with 'Much love to you both'.[15] But even in sunny June, Snape had very little appeal for Lennox without the company of Ben, and as José was now no more than a friend, the 'Atta boy!' was clumsy.

In a postscript to this breezy letter from Toronto, Ben asked Lennox to send Wulff ten shillings he owed him. This apparently innocent request verges on the duplicitous, since Ben knew very well that Wulff needed the money to buy a frame for a photograph of Ben.[16] (Ben was particularly proud of this picture, because it showed him, he thought, looking 'wonderfully tough'.[17]) Lennox did send the ten shillings, and Wulff wrote to Ben to offer his 'heart-alleviated thanks'.[18]

This seems to have been the last time the lives of Lennox and Wulff overlapped, apart from a brief exchange of (mainly musical) letters just after the war. But the correspondence between Wulff and Ben continued – increasingly desperately on Wulff's side, as the war began to turn his life upside down, and with diminishing enthusiasm on Ben's part, as Peter Pears slowly but decisively – and permanently – replaced the German boy in his affections. The tide seems to have turned in Grand Rapids, where, one night between 9 and 19 June, Ben had 'given himself' to Peter – to borrow Peter's own expression – at the home of a Congregationalist organist.[19] In view of Ben's complicated sexual nature, this surrender must have involved an accommodation of his real desires, but it worked so successfully that it lasted for the rest of their lives. It is significant that Ben's 'giving himself' to Peter did not prevent his continuing to hanker after the romantic ideal represented by Wulff. In September he wrote to the young German to say, 'How I wish I could get you out here',[20] and a couple of months later he wrote again: '... *if* you would come over here. *That*'s what I want most of all.'[21]

Ben's new piece, *Young Apollo*, makes a more or less open admission of his feelings for Wulff. He told Enid Slater that the piece was 'inspired by such sunshine as I've never seen before',[22] but to Wulff he was more explicit: 'You know whom that's written about.'[23] Lennox laughed when he heard about the literary source, thinking it might 'give rise to a certain amount of ribald comment' – but he admired Ben's nerve in choosing the title.[24]

To take his mind off Ben, Lennox threw himself into work: scoring the *Cello Concerto*, which he had written for Maurice Eisenberg to play in America,* writing a *Recorder Sonatina* for Manuel Jacobs and Carl

*In the event Eisenberg did not play it in America, and – astonishingly – Lennox completely forgot he had ever written a concerto for cello. Reminded of its existence in 1972 when PD was preparing a list of Berkeley's works for the *New Grove Dictionary of Music*, Lennox preferred not to include the *Cello Concerto*. Ten

Dolmetsch (which Lennox dedicated to his godmother Sybil Jackson), discussing some incidental music for a socialist film which Ben could not now do and Ralph Hawkes thought Lennox might take on (though he does not seem to have done so),[25] and mulling over some ideas for the piece that was to become his *Serenade for Strings*. In fact he was so busy that he had to farm out a two-piano arrangement of *Mont Juic* to a composer colleague who had fallen on hard times. In a letter to Ben at this time Lennox names the composer as 'Neeman'[26] (possibly Hans Neeman, a scholar who devoted much of his life to editing the music of Silvius Leopold Weiss, the early-eighteenth-century German lutenist and composer); nothing is known of any two-piano version of *Mont Juic*.

Despite his unhappiness, Lennox was working well. When the *Sonatina for Treble Recorder (or Flute) and Piano (or Harpsichord)* was played at the Wigmore Hall in London – by Dolmetsch and Christopher Wood (deputizing, on the harpsichord, for the pianist Joseph Saxby, who was on Civil Defence duties) – *The Times* reviewed it as 'a success both for the instrument and the composer'. Berkeley, the paper said, had taken some time to find himself stylistically, but his 'characteristic use of figuration sounded well on the crisp tones of the harpsichord' and the whole effect was 'neat, piquant and gay', something intrinsically charming in a modern idiom which gave new impetus to an eighteenth-century tradition that had lapsed.[27] That it was 'appallingly difficult' for the recorder Lennox well knew – indeed he thought Dolmetsch was the only player who could manage it[28] – but subsequent generations of recorder (and *flute*) players have retained a special affection for the Berkeley *Sonatina*.

Lennox considered the *Cello Concerto* was, in some ways, the best thing he had done, but – typically – it was 'still so far from what I hope some day to do'. Whether he would ever be able to do what he believed he could do remained to be seen, but, he told Ben, he felt 'rather frail and incompetent' about it.[29] Always short of confidence, Lennox was especially insecure just then – and the ominous rumblings from Europe did not help. As the government consolidated the Home Front, black-outs and air-raid precautions were tried out, and gas masks and

---

years later the work was rediscovered, in a bottom drawer, and given its belated premiere by Moray Welsh and the Hallé Orchestra conducted by James Loughran at the Cheltenham Festival on 17 July 1983 (MLB, pp. 33 and 42).

shelters put into production. War was no longer a question of If but of When. Till it actually happened, however, life went on in the same old way.

By mid-summer Lennox had finished his *Cello Concerto* and was feeling stronger, thanks to the support of John Greenidge, Gladys Bryans and José – all of whom, though never together, had occasionally kept him company at the Mill, when Beth and her new husband Kit Welford, or Barbara and her companion Helen Hurst, were not in residence. In August the weather was perfect and, putting the *Sonatina* aside, Lennox ventured outdoors – swimming in the sea at Aldeburgh ('almost warm'), playing in a tennis competition with Dodo Welford ('we got beaten in the 1st round'), motoring in the AC, and watching the corn being gathered in. 'I am glad you made me come and live here,' he wrote to Ben (who was now in New York). The countryside was looking lovely, and he could not help thinking what a pity it was that Ben had left it all, 'particularly as events look as though everything may blow up at any moment, and I wish you'd enjoyed this place more whilst you could'.[30]

The only bad news was that Vally, the amorous tomcat, had died – of pneumonia, after struggling back to the garden following a night on the tiles. For two hours he had fought for breath, till the vet arrived to put him out of his misery. Lennox had been 'awfully sick about it', and Mr Hart had dug a grave in the garden.[31]

Lennox had all sorts of planting plans for the garden in the autumn, but it was difficult to know how much was worth doing, with Ben away and the future so uncertain. He really thought Ben should come back in the winter 'and try to fix how and where you are going to live, and whether you really want to keep this place on or not'. Meanwhile Lennox admitted that he was missing Ben, though no longer so violently.[32] For his part, Ben was not at all keen to come home – in fact he was 'seriously thinking of staying over here permanently', he told his sister Beth from Canada.[33]

As Ben was drawn more deeply into his new American life his letters became scarcer and scarcer. His elder sister Barbara, always outspoken and teasing, ticked him off about his neglect of his family and loved ones, and took advantage of the chance to poke fun at Lennox's misery. 'I do not seem to have heard from you lately – & apparently neither has Lennox! Poor man, you *are* cruel & he is "keeping the home fires burning" so to speak! Are you coming home for Christmas? Or will you be married by then!!!? ... what would poor Lennox do then – poor thing!'[34]

On the subject of the 'poor thing' the letters between Ben and those who fanned the flames of his genius were to get considerably more spiteful than this. Like courtiers jockeying for position around a king, Ben's admirers – even his sisters – were acutely sensitive to signs that one of their number was falling from favour, and only too eager to speed an exit by putting in the bad word they knew Ben wanted to hear to justify a summary execution. This demonizing and dropping of friends was to become quite a trademark of Ben's social behaviour. Why he needed to employ what Rupert Christiansen has called the 'regal habit of cutting people dead' has never been satisfactorily explained. Christiansen observes that it later became 'the primary tactic in his strategy of creative self-preservation and protection', but it does seem strange that a master whose pre-eminence in music was universally recognized should have had so little self-confidence that he needed to behave so unkindly.[35] At all events as August rolled into September and war became increasingly inevitable, Ben's star continued to rise in America, and as it did, his sense of guilt at being absent from duties at home increased – and Lennox was made to take the blame.

By Thursday 31 August it was clear that Chamberlain's attempts to negotiate with Hitler over Poland had failed. Fearing the worst, the government began evacuating women and children from London to the countryside (even to Snape). On Friday Hitler invaded Poland, and on Sunday at eleven in the morning Britain went to war. Under the emergency British National Service (Armed Forces) Act, all men between the ages of eighteen and forty-one were put on alert for military service. Still only twenty-five, Ben was at his physical peak; Lennox, at thirty-six, was fit and well. But both were supposed to be pacifists, and Ben was in America. What should they do? At the Mill that Sunday, after hearing the news on the wireless, Lennox settled himself at his desk and picked up his pen to 'Dearest Ben':

> Well – we're for it this time, but everybody is very calm; it was becoming increasingly obvious that it would have to be war, and we were all ready. There can never be any real peace in the world until the Nazi regime is smashed – not very nice to have to do the smashing though. I've been in rather a dilemma about what I should do – moral dilemmas seem to be a chronic complaint with

> me – I've always been a pacifist at heart, how can one be anything else? But I think if there ever was a case where force has got to be used, this is it. ... Since I knew you, I've honestly felt that I understood and sympathized with the Left point of view; but since the Russian-German pact, the absurdity of the Communist and semi-Communist press has been enough to discourage anybody.[36]

For Ben in his safe haven on the other side of the Atlantic, this would not have made comfortable reading. Lennox's description of pacifism as unrealistic and of Soviet Communism as absurd will have seemed like personal criticisms, since, as Lennox knew, these were positions which Ben still held. If Ben was already feeling guilty about leaving England, Lennox's letter can only have rubbed it in. Lennox would not have intended to do this, but unconsciously he may have taken some pleasure in telling Ben he had rejected his views, just as he himself had been rejected. After a few more letters like this, Ben began to turn violently against Lennox, reading the worst into all that he wrote, and blackening his name to their friends. Lennox never knew about this *samizdat* campaign – if he had, he might have understood why when friendly relations were eventually restored the temperature never rose above tepid, with Ben firmly in control of the thermostat.

On the horns of another moral dilemma, Lennox could not decide whether to wait to be called up for national service, or to volunteer right away. If he were mobilized, he told Nadia, 'what'll be most irritating will be not being able to make music. That and also the idea of having to kill anyone, whoever they are.'[37] If he were not mobilized, he was keen to return to France, and he asked Nadia if she could arrange a performance of his *Polka, Nocturne and Capriccio for Two Pianos* (which she had played with Clifford Curzon in Paris in January and with Jean Françaix on her American tour in the spring) so that he would have a valid reason for crossing the Channel.[38]

There was plenty to do in Snape, with evacuees arriving by the trainload from London. Lennox told Ben he had been driving East End children from the village hall to their new billets ('thank God we kept the Morris'). It had been difficult sorting them all out – but at least he had been spared the 200 pregnant women, 'mostly in a semi-fainting condition', who had arrived at one reception centre. Two teachers in charge of the children were to be billeted at the Mill itself, in Ben's part of the house, and Lennox had been busy buying yards and yards of dark material (and, when that ran out, brown paper) for Mrs Hearn to black out the lighthouse windows of Ben's circular bedroom. Lennox did not think Ben would adapt well to an England at war – or that he should even have to, as he told Ben later in the letter he wrote on the day war was declared,

> Ben dear, for heaven's sake don't come back. It's going to be absolute hell. I want to see you again, I think more than anything in the world, but I'm glad you're not here now. You must be able to go on writing. I meant to say a lot about this but I can't find the right words – and anyhow only you can decide what you think the right thing to do ... The Proms have closed down along with all Cinemas and Theatres – so the performance of Mont Juic which was to have been on Tuesday is off ... Very much love B dearest – Lennox .[39]

Lennox's view, like Wilfred Owen's in the First World War, was that 'a live poet was worth more than a dead soldier'.[40] He told Ben he had spoken to Ralph Hawkes about the situation, and they both thought that 'only your own conscience can make you decide'. This was fair, even generous, but it did not go down at all well with Ben, who did not write again for four months. Instead he wrote to Beth, saying he sometimes felt 'pretty black' about Lennox: '... his letters to me are the only preachy ones I get ... all about conscience & that kind of thing – about *really* being a pacifist, but this being a just war – and that sort of nonsense! However it is easy to sit outside & criticize – it must be hell for him & his likes in the middle of this horrible thing.'[41]

The next letter Lennox received from Ben – via Beth, to whom it had been sent for passing on – was written on the same day as Lennox's, 3 September. It was brief, self-centred and irrelevant. Ben said he was working terribly hard – 'all in desperation, thinking that one may be stopped any moment'. Art was '*all-important* at this time – & [spiritual] faith, if you have it!' He was soaking himself in El Greco, Benvenuto Cellini and Buxtehude, who was 'absolutely astounding – so much better than Bach!!!' More and more he was being 'pushed off his old materialistic beliefs', and felt that at last he was growing up ('Don't laugh'). As for the Mill, 'Do what you like ... ,' he instructed Lennox, 'I hereby give you "carte blanche"!'[42]

By the end of September, when the immediate emergency had been succeeded by the inertia of the Phoney War, Lennox had a clearer picture of what was happening, both nationally and locally, and things were not as bad as he had expected. In fact, as Wulff told Ben, 'Everything continues as usual', except that police stations were now sandbagged, and 'little concrete Air Raid Warden's posts have sprung up all over the place'.[43]

As a German citizen, Wulff realized he was unlikely to remain unaffected by the war, but he felt so secure in Cambridge that he did not take the threat very seriously and pressed on with his life as best he could. Just before Christmas 1939 he was admitted to London University to study engineering at Queen Mary College.[44] At the same time his mother, unaccountably late, handed in their applications for naturalization as British subjects.[45] Wulff assumed that, with their clean record and their powerful friends, all would proceed satisfactorily, but he knew that once he was British he could be called up for National Service at any time.[46] In May 1940, the worst happened: he and his mother were arrested as enemy aliens and locked up in a detention camp in Cambridge. It was not pleasant sleeping on a concrete floor, but the local police were as helpful as they could be in the circumstances, and Wulff took comfort from being part of a distinguished company of German intellectuals. As he told Ben, 'When one looks at the kind of people that have been interned ... one begins to realize what Germany has lost in driving them out.'[47]

A week or two later Wulff was separated from his mother, and shipped out to Canada – to a prison camp for civilian internees, where he and the other aliens arrived sea sick and in a state of 'general neurosis and hysteria'.[48] For some time his mother did not know where he was, and Ben pulled as many strings as he could to locate Wulff and to put mother and son in touch again. Though the move to Canada had brought Wulff to the same continent as Ben, it did not feel as though it had brought them any closer because Ben either was not writing letters or his letters were not getting through the wartime restrictions. Like Lennox, who was feeling similarly neglected in England, Wulff was deeply frustrated and hurt, and from an unnamed military location in Canada (later identified as a camp near Ottawa[49]), in the summer of 1940, he wrote to Ben (who was staying with friends in Amityville, Long Island), pouring out his feelings – insofar as he was able in a letter scrutinized by the Canadian military censors: 'Please write immediately as I am suffering veritable agonies of suspense at the thought of being so close to you again ... I'm rather at a loss what to say since we are not allowed to criticize and that is a very hard thing not to do when you're on the wrong side of the barbed wire. It is hard not to be bitter when you have watched the rise of Naziism [and] gone into voluntary exile, but to be interned. You feel lost, hurt and disillusioned ...'[50]

Wulff and the other internees were cooped up in canvas tents on palliasses and groundsheets, they were cold and damp and muddy, and Wulff himself was exasperated by the noise in the canteen and the twanging of an out-of-tune piano.[51] He asked Ben for some gumboots size 11, money for a haircut, soap, toothpaste, Nivea cream and foot powder, Nestlé's chocolates, cigarettes and books (in particular Auden and Keats and Shakespeare).[52] He hated begging for favours, but explained that 'Our nerves and powers of resistance have been sapped, and must be replaced somehow.'[53] Some of the things he needed arrived – notably the boots and the Auden – but still no letter, and that is what Wulff most wanted: 'It is only here I am beginning to realize – painfully – what you once meant for me, and how these years of enforced separation have brought about not a dimming of those feelings; but a longing and a craving to see you again ... Love Wulff.'[54]

By December 1940 Wulff had enlisted in the Auxiliary Military Pioneer Camp in order to get back to England. He told Ben he could not stand by inactive while his friends at home were joining up to fight.[55] He had read in the Canadian papers of a 'relentless and barbarous destruction by air raids', of food queues and 'a hard-suffering England fighting a losing battle' and it had made him 'want to go and smash to pieces this force that was destroying everything'.[56] Once back in England, with the Pioneers, at a camp near Bristol, he wrote to Ben in the summer of 1941 to say he was reasonably happy in the Army, doing relatively little soldiering, still studying and writing poetry, convinced that one day he would be a poet. The air raid damage in Bristol, though terrible, was not as total as he had expected but it left a feeling of bitterness and impotence and 'makes one yearn for the battlefield and the gun'.[57]

At the start of the war Lennox talked to friends about joining up, but the blunt Barbara Britten, for one, told him 'not to be silly'[58] – and anyway no more volunteers were needed just then. The teacher lodgers he had been expecting at the Mill had been billeted somewhere else, so life at Snape was much the same, apart from what Mrs Hearn called 'excavated children', the unaccustomed sounds of cockney in the Suffolk countryside, 'v. drastic petrol rationing' and the blackout ('so dark that one kept bumping into people'). But it was a bit depressing living on his own at the Mill, so he decided to arrange for Beth and Kit Welford to move in temporarily, with Mrs Hearn running the house, while he himself went to stay with an old literary friend from Paris, John Davenport, at his large house in the West Country. As for Ben, Lennox thought it was better that he stayed in America, though, like Wulff, he still missed him terribly.[59] 'I feel just the same about you as I did the day you left, in a more interior sort of way. Nothing will ever change that, even if I were never to see you again in this life – but I hope it won't come to that.'[60]

By the same post Barbara, writing to Ben from her flat in London, voiced her concern about the Mill. If Beth and Kit had to move out, what would happen then? Should they let it? And if so, what about Ben's things? Barbara herself had no time to deal with these practical difficulties, and she clearly did not think that Lennox was up to it. 'Lennox is about as useful as a female fly! ... His money is the only thing that is useful about him. I'm sorry for him – poor dear – he doesn't know what to do with himself & feels he ought to be terribly brave & do something dashing.'[61]

In Barbara's defence it must be said that this cruel letter does not reflect her true feelings for Lennox. Only a month later she wrote again to Ben to say that Lennox was 'a dear & a good friend to you – & you must not lose touch with him'.[62] Like other mercurial people, Barbara was quite capable of saying one thing one day and the opposite the next (and anyway she was writing privately to her brother, little expecting to be quoted in a book about Lennox nearly seventy years later). But the sentiments are significant because they are couched in terms that seem to anticipate a sympathetic response from Ben, and may therefore reflect Ben's own feelings about Lennox at this turning-point in their relationship. Barbara was clearly exasperated by Lennox's chronic indecisiveness, and afraid that a responsibility she reckoned was his might by default pass to her. She does not seem to have realized that Lennox was actually doing all he possibly could to protect Ben's interests, not only at the Mill (where he was exercising the *carte blanche* Ben had expressly given him), but in a musical world that was far from sympathetic to Ben's American adventure. Things came to a head in June 1941 when the *Musical Times* published a letter from Pilot-Officer E. R. Lewis, suggesting that Britten had forfeited his right to the description 'British composer' and that the BBC should withdraw its particular favour. This unleashed a flood of correspondence reflecting the climate of hostility aroused by Britten and Pears, Auden and Isherwood and other absentee intellectuals.*

Furthermore Lennox was also doing his best to look after Peter Pears's flat in Hallam Street, which was not his responsibility, but which everyone seemed to expect him to sort out now that the caretaker-tenant, the hopelessly unreliable Jackie Hewit (Isherwood's abandoned boyfriend), had disappeared and was wanted by the police.[63] According to Ben, Hewit had robbed the gas meter and run away with a month's rent due, leaving the flat filthy and a pile of unpaid bills.[64]

Lennox reached a decision about the Mill sooner than he expected. His hand was forced by the emergency budget of September 27 which raised income tax to 7s. 6d. in the pound, thus making it economically impossible for him to keep the place on. Reluctantly he gave Mrs Hearn notice, and reduced Mr Hart's hours to a single day a week, to keep the garden from becoming a jungle. He considered shutting up the house and leaving it empty, but Beth was afraid that 'someone awful' would move in, so Lennox offered it for let.[65] First he asked Ralph Hawkes if he were still interested in renting it – Hawkes had asked about it some weeks before – then he went to see Ben's solicitor in Lowestoft, Arthur Nicholson, who probably told him what he later told Ben – that it would be easy to let 'if we had any serious air raids, but we have had nothing sufficiently worrying to make that likely' yet.[66] Meanwhile Nicholson thought that Hawkes was the best bet. But most of Lennox's interview with the solicitor was devoted to Nicholson's complaint that he had not had a single letter from Ben since he went to America.[67] Lennox himself had not heard from Ben for a month, and at the beginning of October, he wrote to Ben to pass on Nicholson's concerns,

> It's nothing to do with me, but I think you should be a little less casual – you can't expect the poor man to look after your interests if you won't answer his letters. Then there's a great hullabaloo going on about Jackie [Hewit, the absconded tenant of the Hallam St flat] – but I think that this is Peter's concern: Nicholson is afraid that they might pinch your piano, music etc. but is trying to disentangle you from any responsibility. Your family keeps asking me who is Jackie? – what does he do? If they're [not] careful I shall tell them.[68]

*This is the subject of an interesting account in LFAL, pp. 869–73.

The conventional Brittens would have winced if Lennox had been forced to reveal what Jackie did in fact do. 'People like me', Hewit himself said years later, 'were passed around' from man to man in a sort of gay freemasonry; 'I wasn't a trollop. Amoral perhaps ... .'[69] When Ben first met Hewit with Christopher Isherwood in Brussels in January, he thought he was a 'dear, nice creature' who was 'extraordinarily serene' despite 'one of the hardest lives anyone could possibly have had'.[70] Now he was forced to revise his opinion. On the rebound from Isherwood, who had gone to America and left him behind, Jackie Hewit had returned to his former lover, the spy Guy Burgess, and was soon to join the Army – and even MI5.[71]

Five weeks into the war, Lennox changed his view about Ben's predicament. Not only was wartime life in England less grim than he had feared, but there was a real risk, he told Ralph Hawkes, that if Ben got stuck in America for the whole war he might lose the commanding position in English music which he had worked so hard to achieve.[72] To Ben himself Lennox now wrote advising a return home – as well as chiding him for his 'infrequent and inadequate' letters.

> I don't think you would be interfered with by conscription, and if you have conscientious reasons for not taking part in the war, I think they would be respected – particularly in the case of somebody like you engaged in your kind of work. I can't make up my mind (as usual) about it. I don't see how a good end can be achieved by what everybody admits are bad means; and the thought that so many lives are being sacrificed, perhaps in vain, is awful. And yet what's the alternative? To acquiesce about Fascism – just give in and let it win, and control Europe. What I can't understand is that the very people who were the most violently opposed to Fascism, now that the fight is on, don't seem so keen about it. Of course, some are, and always have been, genuine pacifists and that's different.[73]

Ben was furious. He was already feeling quite bad enough about running away from England, abandoning two people who were in love with him, neglecting his correspondence, and leaving his friends to deal with his domestic problems at home. To be accused of bottling out 'now that the fight is on' was the last straw. That is not in fact what Lennox meant, but the ratty, guilt-ridden Ben decided to take it that way. Marjorie Fass, who adored Ben but not uncritically, had noticed two years earlier that he was spoilt, and could not take criticism: '... if one pricks his bubble', she wrote, 'he bleeds ...'[74] And lashes out. Seething with indignation, Ben scribbled a letter to his friend 'Howling' Hedli Anderson,* the cabaret singer who later married Louis MacNeice:

> My affairs are in the most awful muddle, because (i) letters take such ages to get to here and everything criss-crosses all the time ... (ii) the two tenants – [Lennox] at the Mill and [Hewit in] Hallam St – have proved such weak-kneed incompetent fools. Jackie has just gone off and paid nothing apparently – & Lennox frets and doesn't make decisions, writes letters about conscience & duty (King & Country etc) & complains about neglect – oh, Hedli, what a bloody fool I was about all that – one sees so much more clearly when one's away. He's just NO GOOD [*sic*].[75]

Ben let off more of the same kind of venomous steam in a letter to Enid Slater, wife of the left-wing playwright Montagu Slater (with whom Lennox and Ben had collaborated on the Binyon puppet plays in 1938),

> ... letters from the Mill have been dreadful. The only person who wrote to me about 'duty', 'conscience' – 'being a pacifist at heart, but this was a war, etc . . . – (sic, sic SIC!!!); was he of that noble ancestry. Besides too – the man (sic) has no sense. He now writes whiningly of his obligations to the Mill (as if anyone wouldn't adore to live at the Mill!) – & wants to let it; & what am I going to do? – Ralph Hawkes offered to rent it at the beginning of the war & L.B. couldn't make up his mind. Oh – this all sounds silly – but when letters take months to come, if they ever actually do come, complaints, & grumbles sound so ridiculous ... I got so ill at one time with these snarky, barky letters that now Peter opens my letters – I don't want to![76]

In a barbed reply Mrs Slater said the reason that Lennox 'yatters

*Hedli Anderson (1907–90) had an operatic training before joining the Group Theatre for Auden's *The Dance of Death* in 1934. Three years later she met BB, while both were involved in the Auden and Isherwood play *The Ascent of F6*. It was for her that BB wrote his setting of Auden's Four Cabaret Songs (LFAL, pp. 544–50).

about duty etc' was simply that he was missing Ben and wanting him home. 'Why carn't [*sic*] he be honest,' she wrote, 'he is at the moment muddled & miserable & I can't [help] feeling just a little sorry for him, if only he wouldn't talk about "my car"[;] if ever a car *wasn't* his[,] yours is it.' She herself did not think it was Ben's duty to come home (nor indeed did Lennox) but she agreed that he should return all the same: '... oh please do. You would not have to go to prison[;] no-one has to ...'[77] Enid Slater seems to have been a little in love with Ben, and may have regarded Lennox as a rival. In a letter five months later she fantasizes about driving down to Snape with Ben, once the war's over, going for a walk, having a drink in the pub, and tucking in to Mrs Hearn's queen's pudding, entirely *à deux*, 'I see you half sunk in a deep chair with an old polo jumper on. There would in this context be no *need* for Lennox or his curly furniture would there?'[78] *

Not content with winding up his women friends, Ben even had a go at Ralph Hawkes, suggesting that he should explain to Lennox the difficulty of replying to letters that had never been received: 'I am sorry to appear slightly bitter about this but when one receives day after day complaints and similar sour comments on one's behaviour, I think it is excusable, because I am trying to be a good boy.'[79]

Beth, to her credit, defended Lennox – even though she was bitterly opposed to his letting the Mill, which she had hoped would remain 'a haven of rest to go to, if necessary'.[80] She told Ben she felt 'rather sorry for the poor old thing ... everybody seems against him. He wasn't keeping the place up grudgingly[;] you misunderstood me. It's only that he was lonely living here by himself ... You are rather nasty to him aren't you? I don't think he means to preach to you, he's just made that way.'[81] And, like a big sister, she told Ben himself to 'buck up and try & take an interest in the muddles' he had left at home. 'We have all got enough to do & to think about without being bothered by them ... If you really

*By her reference to curly furniture, Mrs Slater may have had in mind a solid olive-wood dining table with unusual barley-sugar legs, which had been made for Lennox's parents in the South of France, had served LB and BB at the Mill, was moved to LB's bachelor flat in Warwick Square, moved again to Warwick Avenue at the start of LB's marriage, was later lent to their friend Robert Thomson in his flat at the top of Patrick Trevor-Roper's house in Park Square West, and has been in rustication in Hampshire with TS and LB's son Julian Berkeley for the past thirty-four years.

intend to stay out there for good you had better say so, & let the place be sold.'[82]

Beth was right – and courageous – to speak out, and Ben knew it. In his reply he admitted that Lennox really had no option but to let the Mill.[83] While it did not stop the Britten camp continuing to snipe at the hapless Lennox, Beth's intervention may have saved the relationship from total collapse, because it forced Ben to try to see the 'muddles' from Lennox's point of view.

But the Mill was not let. At the beginning of November Beth and Kit decided to move back in themselves, and cabled Ben to ask if they ought to pay Lennox some rent. Ben telegraphed back, 'Overjoyed hearing you are at Mill Dont consider leaving Dont pay Berkeley anything ...'[84] And in a letter twelve days later Ben confirmed his delight that they were living in the Mill. He wanted them to consider it as theirs and not to think of letting it to anyone else. There was no need to pay Lennox any money so long as they did not use his bedroom or his studio, but '*incase* [*sic*] he kicks up rough' Ben sent £50 to Barbara – '& £25 of that can be used for him (blast his eyes)'.[85]

Donald Mitchell argues that Ben's 'sometimes choleric letters from America' arose from 'the extraordinary anxieties and tensions of the period and difficulties of transatlantic communication'.[86] This is true, but it is no less true that Lennox experienced at least the same anxieties, tensions and difficulties – more so, back home in the firing line as it were – yet his letters never display anything more choleric than a mild impatience. Fortunately Lennox knew nothing of the bile exchanged behind his back, and, thanks to his natural sweetness and generosity – and, it must be said, to Ben's eventual appreciation of those qualities – their relationship, far from foundering, slowly changed down a gear into a new, less close but more workable and lasting friendship. Indeed, if it had not shed its uncomfortable intensity, Lennox – as he himself later realized – might never have been able to develop as a composer, or even as a man, because of the crippling sense of inferiority which his idolizing of Ben's genius induced. The break with Ben may have hurt him badly, but Lennox would never forget the debt he owed his younger friend for his vital help with the technical problems of composing, and in particular for weaning him from his unhealthy dependence on Nadia's approval. In a newspaper interview years later Lennox recalled how much Ben had helped him in the Thirties by telling him: 'If you want to do that, do it; don't think all the time about whether Nadia

Boulanger ... would approve.' And as a result of this encouragement 'my style somehow expanded.'[87]

Overwhelmed by his unhappiness and by the uncertainties of the Phoney War, Lennox needed a break and, in October 1939, despite emergency restrictions, he managed to obtain permission to escape to Paris for a month. Apart from anything else, he was anxious to spend some time with José Raffalli who had been mobilized but not yet called up. (By the beginning of April the following year José had joined the 3ième Régiment de Défense Passive at Montreuil-sous-bois, on the north-eastern outskirts of Paris.[88]) Lennox found the city 'pretty empty compared with normal times' and lax about air raid precautions ('a very dim lighting is allowed',[89] unlike London where blackout meant nothing but torches[90]). At home in Cité Chaptal, he made good progress on his *Serenade*, adding to the first three movements, which seem to reflect something of his brief happiness with Ben a year earlier, an unexpectedly slow and deep finale in which the opening melody of the first movement reappears but at half speed and the bass climbs rung by rung to the climax. This must have been influenced by his anxiety about the war and the fate of his friends – Ben stranded in America, José about to join the Army, Nadia still teaching in a beleaguered France.

While in Paris Lennox also worked on a new piano piece, a *Mazurka*, which he completed in Painswick, while spending Christmas with Gladys Bryans. In January 1940 he told Ben he had written a *Mazurka*, 'which I think you'd like'.[91] There is no record of any performance till the piece was re-used to form the first of the *Three Mazurkas* which Lennox assembled as a homage to Chopin in 1949, but there are manuscript scores at the British Library,[92] and the University of Sheffield; the Sheffield version is said to have belonged to Sir Thomas Beecham.[93] It is possible that the *Mazurka* was the new Berkeley piece which the novelist Eva Ibbotson remembered Myra Hess performing at one of her famous lunchtime concerts at the National Gallery during the war, [94] though she actually identified the piece as *Nocturne* (a work for *two* pianos, which Nadia Boulanger and Clifford Curzon had played for the first time, in Paris, in January 1938). * According to this source Myra Hess had such faith in the piece that she played it twice, in

*The *Nocturne* has been published on its own, in versions for two pianos and one piano, and together with two other pieces to form the *Polka*, dedicated to Ethel Bartlett and Rae Robertson (SRC, p. 60), *Nocturne and Capriccio* Op 5.

quick succession, to make it more familiar to her audience. 'That was the world premiere of Lennox Berkeley's *Nocturne*', Dame Myra is supposed to have announced – 'and now here it is again.' But Mrs Ibbotson may have been confusing Berkeley with the composer and editor Howard Ferguson, Myra Hess's assistant in the running of the daily National Gallery concerts, at one of which, in 1940, Hess gave the premiere of Ferguson's *F Minor Piano Sonata*.

After returning from Paris early in November 1939, Lennox went down to the Mill to collect his car and some other possessions. Then, in the AC, so intimately associated with Ben, he drove to his new home with the Davenports in the village of Marshfield on the edge of the Cotswolds, between Bath and Chippenham. The setting was Old England at her most traditional; the guest list was startlingly eccentric.

20
Lennox, Dylan Thomas and Co., Marshfield, 1940

Marshfield was once a centre of the malting industry, and the Davenports' house was built by a prosperous master maltster in the eighteenth century. A fine stone building, with fluted pilasters at the entrance, the Malting House stands in a terrace of substantial cottages on the main street. John Davenport bought the place in 1938,[1] partly with money inherited by his beautiful American wife Clement, a scene painter, and partly with his own lucrative earnings as a scriptwriter in Hollywood. An undergraduate with Dylan Thomas, Malcolm Lowry, Michael Redgrave and Jacob Bronowski at Cambridge, John was a man of letters who was now a critic and connoisseur rather than the poet he had once aspired to be. His friend the writer Constantine FitzGibbon, biographer of Dylan Thomas, described him as 'a generous, difficult, brilliant man with a very fine and profound knowledge of ... all the arts'.[2] The composer Humphrey Searle, who joined the Marshfield colony just before the Battle of Britain, said that John talked 'as if he had complete control of all contemporary artistic activities'.[3] If intellectually and emotionally John was complex, physically he was no less of a paradox: short, square and heavily built, he was still fit enough, at thirty-two, to coax his eighteen-stone bulk to impressive use at squash. Lennox described his performance on the Marshfield court as tremendously dignified – 'he hardly moves at all,' he told Ben, 'and yet gets most things back.'[4] At Cambridge John had won a blue as a heavyweight boxer, and though he was 'normally charming and affable', he had a 'terrible temper when roused'[5] and was 'inclined to be a bully'.[6] His daughter Natalie recalls that his need to brawl was so strong that when he was in London he used to trek out to rough pubs in the docks specifically to get drunk and pick a fight,* so that he could

*A pencil and wash drawing by Michael Ayrton showing Davenport in a bow tie and clutching a glass gives some idea of both his bulk and his pugnacity; the picture was sold by Bonhams, New Bond Street, on 3 October 2005.

stumble home 'covered in bruises – and feeling much better'.[7] FitzGibbon said he once had to restrain John Davenport from throttling Dylan Thomas, 'for the very simple and expressed reason that Dylan was a *poet* and John was not'.[8]

John Davenport was an accomplished pianist (with two grand pianos in the long drawing room upstairs) and a discerning collector of paintings by artists still then generally unknown. He was also a snob who loved 'playing the *grand seigneur*'.[9] His house was filled with pictures and books, babies (his and the Thomases'), animals, vintage wines and a tribe of artistic refugees still uncertain about their place in the war. If, like Lennox, they could afford it, they paid rent; if, like the Thomases, they could not, they did not. Apart from Dylan and Caitlin Thomas and Humphrey Searle, the resident ménage included Ben's friend the critic and composer Henry Boys, the composer Arnold Cooke (who had studied with Hindemith in Berlin) and the *Observer* music critic William Glock. To these were added a couple of regular visitors from the village: the Catholic novelist Antonia White, fresh from the annulment of her third marriage and another bout of mental illness, and the left-wing painter Robert Buhler,[10] who was working on a portrait of Lennox.[11] (Lennox sat to Buhler again, in London in the 1960s, and this portrait, showing him looking a little sad and wearing a yellow sweater, was acquired by the novelist Francis King following the death of Robert Buhler in 1989.)

Buhler, a 'pleasant, good-looking fellow',[12] was the son of Swiss parents who ran a restaurant in Soho much frequented by William Coldstream and other artists of the Euston Road School.[13] He trained in Switzerland and at St Martin's School of Art in London, and became 'the most painterly of painters'.[14] Buhler was a close friend of Stephen Spender, who had sat for him, and in 1939 the two of them printed poems and stories by unknown writers, on a letterpress which Spender had bought and set up in Buhler's flat.[15] By the end of 1939, when Buhler was still only twenty-three, Spender thought that both Buhler and his pregnant wife, Eve, had lost a little of their 'really shining quality'.[16] Enough shine remained in the summer of 1940 to charm Lennox, who thought young Buhler 'very nice',[17] but even the patient Lennox must have found that sitting for him was exhausting. Buhler required his subjects to sit still for up to two hours at a time for as many as ten sittings, while he first 'placed' his portrait with a drawing, then built it up with colour. It was only afterwards, and alone, that he worked on the setting – furniture, windows and so on.[18] John Davenport, the subject of 'his most telling portrait',[19] cannot have found the process comfortable, particularly since he was 'semi-intoxicated' at the time. No less than seven feet high, the painting shows him with a cigar in his hand, looking 'as if he was about to topple out of the frame'.[20]

Lennox first encountered Davenport in Paris in the early Thirties, and found him an 'extremely cultivated' man who 'knows music marvellously well'.[21] The two young men must have been reasonably close, because John later claimed that Lennox was the godfather of his daughter Natalie (though when Natalie jokingly reminded Lennox of his responsibilities at his seventieth birthday concert in London in 1973, 'he was terribly nice about it, and apologized for being so remiss – but actually', she said in 2003, 'I don't think he ever really was my godfather'.) Another luminary supposed to have been a godfather was Harold Acton, but no one ever told him either. According to the forbearing Natalie Davenport, her father began his career as a favourite of the aristocratic (and bisexual) travel-writer Norman Douglass* – 'and climbed from there'.[22]

There was no shortage of music at the Malting House that winter of 1939–40. Ben's friends the violinist Tony Brosa and the critic and composer Henry Boys played an arrangement of Ben's *Violin Concerto*; Lennox played his own *Polka, Nocturne and Capriccio* with William Glock (who had been a pupil of Artur Schnabel); Humphrey Searle played an arrangement of Liszt's *Les Préludes*; and, a little later in 1940, Dylan Thomas's wife, Caitlin, 'who looked like an Irish fairy with her long golden hair',[23] practised her 'dancing', alone in the chapel with a wind-up gramophone.

Lennox's letters make no mention of Caitlin, but they do refer, briefly, to Dylan ('most amusing and intelligent') and his poetry: '... I don't know what the hell he's talking about (in his poems I mean) but the rhythm and sound of the words are beautiful – much more beautiful than most of the modern poets who are often equally obscure.'[24] And Dylan claimed Lennox as one of the 'fine new friends' he had made that summer.[25]

*Douglass dropped his second 's' after divorcing his wife and moving to Capri to pursue, in a more tolerant Europe, his 'particular taste for the under-aged'. See the biographical sketch in Peter Parker (ed.), *The Reader's Companion to Twentieth Century Writers*, pp. 200–1.

Lennox was slightly in awe of William Glock. 'He's ... a terrifyingly severe critic', he told Ben, 'but it really means something with him – he's got a standard which is a real one ... .'[26] Lennox was not William's only admirer. Caitlin Thomas was so frustrated by the drudgery of looking after her wayward poet and their baby son that she determined to seduce him (even though beefy blonds of his type were not really to her taste). But her elaborate plan for a night of love in a Cardiff hotel turned out to be a disappointing flop when, perfumed and bedecked in her sexiest Isadora Duncan tunic, she emerged from the bathroom to find the virgin William lying in bed 'stretched out in his pyjamas like a stick'. Nothing ever happened: he just lay there, and she just lay beside him, 'looking at the ceiling and watching the shadows', all night long.[27] The next morning they slunk back to Marshfield, feeling slightly foolish. Dylan, himself no saint, was furiously jealous, threw a knife at Caitlin and for a while refused to sleep with her. In fact young William's real interest lay elsewhere in the Malting House, and when at last the household broke up in the late summer of 1940, he ran off with Mrs Davenport (and married her in May 1944).

The Marshfield ménage may sound highly charged – and Dylan Thomas's biographer Andrew Lycett describes it as a 'frenetic war-traumatised community'[28] – but it did not seem so to the participants at the time. Caitlin said of the others, 'They were all quiet, civilized people', though she admits that there were several discreet affairs going on. The fact that the mentally disturbed Antonia White admitted later that she had 'clung' for support to the famously unstable Thomases during this period[29] gives some idea of just how extremely odd everyone else must have seemed. Yet Lennox was as content at Marshfield as he had ever been anywhere. Perhaps he kept his head so deeply buried in his scores that he simply did not notice what was going on around him. He told his Paris friend Hélène Kahn-Casella that he was working as hard as he could. It was easier to compose in the country, and anyway, he said, London was 'vraiment lugubre en ce moment'.[30]

Marshfield, on the contrary, was far from *lugubre*. According to Caitlin Thomas's account, the mornings were devoted to 'quite a lot of pubbing', the afternoons were quiet, and in the evening 'we'd all get pretty jolly over dinner',[31] with the blackout curtains tightly drawn and the austerity menu jollied up with black-market extras. Alcohol notwithstanding, Caitlin managed to find time to choreograph her dances, Humphrey Searle went to work at the BBC Music Department in Bristol every day and even wrote a symphony (which Lennox later orchestrated for him),[32] Lennox wrote half a dozen new works, and John and Dylan locked themselves up in a room decorated as an olde-worlde pub and collaborated on – and even finished – a spoof thriller called *The Death of the King's Canary.*

No one is quite clear who wrote what in this bewildering novel. Set in a house called Dymmock Hall in Suffolk, it involves a huge cast of freakish characters, most of them artists, from all kinds of social backgrounds and of all kinds of sexual preference (including one who sleeps with horses). They flit in and out of the story without adding anything to the solution of the mysterious murder of the house's owner, the poet laureate, Hilary Byrd. If Dymmock is a parody of Marshfield the borrowed characters are not easily recognizable. There are six very small Mr Hartleys, a Julian Greensleaves, a hunchback, a nymphomaniac, 'a bloody shit' – and a frail Oxford aesthete called Berkeley, whose voice is 'all Balliol', whose head is neat and thin and whose nose twitches like a hare's.[33] The fictional Berkeley contributes nothing to the story, but puts in a single appearance to have his three features described.

Though occasionally brilliant, often funny and decidedly strong on sex and music and poems, the novel is impossible to follow as a narrative. The least opaque part is the opening sequence (presumably written by Dylan, though he always maintained that John was responsible), which describes the Prime Minister, on his way up to bed at Chequers, reading verses submitted by candidates for the Poet Laureateship. Because of these clever and possibly libellous pastiches of T. S. Eliot, Auden, Spender and Dylan Thomas himself – not to mention some saucy references to characters not a million miles removed from the Sitwells, Augustus John and Cyril Connolly – this surreal book could not be published till 1976.

The sympathetic company, if not the emotional ferment, of the Malting House seems to have been just what Lennox needed after his bruising at the Old Mill. It inspired some of his best and most virtuosic music for the piano, the *Four Concert Studies*, together with his *Quartet for Strings No. 2*, an arrangement of some music by Fauré for a new ballet and the first four of his haunting *Housman Songs*. Even though he had completed the *Serenade* just before moving to Marshfield, Lennox decided to dedicate that 'To John and Clement Davenport', as a gesture of thanks for their inspiring hospitality that summer.

The new ballet, *La Fête étrange*, was inspired and written by the music critic Ronald Crichton, and the commission probably came Lennox's way via Humphrey Searle, who was a friend of Crichton. The scenario is very loosely based on an episode in *Le grand Meaulnes*, Alain-Fournier's visionary novel about a lost world of youthful love. A country boy, wandering in a forest, suddenly finds himself at a château during a wedding party, and breaks the atmosphere of happy innocence by falling in love with the bride. Nothing happens: the party continues, as the boy returns to the forest – but somehow everything has changed. It is a delicate and touching story of a love that might have been. Crichton visualized *La Fête étrange* as 'the tragedy of sensitive adolescence, symbolized not only by the sequence of events [during a single short winter's day], but by the gradual though pronounced change of mood; anticipation leading through increasing happiness to ecstasy, which in its turn fades into sadness and disillusion'.[34] The choreographer was Andrée Howard, who had just returned from a brief spell with the newly-formed American Ballet Theatre in New York, and the designer was Sophie Fedorovitch, one of Ashton's closest friends and collaborators. Howard and Crichton were very specific about the music they wanted: a selection of nine short pieces by Fauré, most of them for piano but two of them songs, *Mandoline* and *Soir*.

Lennox, who had known Andrée Howard in France in 1933, when she was dancing with the new Ballets russes de Monte Carlo, and who was, of course, steeped in the French tradition, was thought to be the ideal man to provide a performing score. And since the Arts Theatre, where the London Ballet was planning to stage the new work, was very small, it was decided it should take the form of an arrangement for two pianos. Lennox relished the task, partly because he had always held that music and dancing were closely related, continually reacting on each other,[35] and partly because it gave him a chance to work with music of the kind he most admired: elegant, spare and restrained. His own music shares these qualities, so the textural transparency required by the subtleties of the story came quite naturally to him. But if he had needed any help he had only to look at the limpid orchestration which Fauré himself made of his own *F Sharp Ballade Op 19*. (It is interesting that Ravel, Faure's pupil – and Lennox's mentor – was very much taken by *Le grand Meaulnes* when he first read it in 1916, and even toyed with the idea of writing a fantasy piano concerto based on it.[36])

After *La Fête étrange*'s first performance at the Arts on 23 May

1940, the critic Cyril Beaumont, one of the most influential ballet writers of the period, claimed that the prime virtue of the piece was its power to establish and maintain 'a kind of re-living of a youthful experience, viewed vaguely, afar off, as though seen through the frosted window of a dream'.[37] According to the Canadian dancer and critic Fernau Hall, it had a 'considerable success', despite its 'vague drifting dances'.[38] The notices may not have resounded with superlatives, but *La Fête étrange* was far from dead. Once the war was over, Andrée Howard turned to it again – and Lennox was presented with a new challenge.

Meanwhile, in the warm security of the improbable family which the Davenports had assembled at Marshfield, Lennox was able at last to come to terms with the loss of Ben by putting his feelings into music. As a medium he chose song, and for words he turned to the romantic pessimism of A. E. Housman to express his suffering (while disguising its specific nature). One of the four poems he set (the third, 'He Would Not Stay for Me') expresses Housman's own passionate and permanent but utterly hopeless love for his unequivocally heterosexual Oxford friend, Moses Jackson. Lennox, like Housman, loved in vain because Ben, like Moses, was unable to return it. In both cases the lover was left abandoned and despairing.

> He would not stay for me; and who can wonder?
> He would not stay for me to stand and gaze.
> I shook his hand and tore my heart in sunder
> And went with half my life about my ways.[39]

All four of Lennox's Housman poems are about parting, all are bleak and final. The first is about the pain of unrequited love, and the second about a young soldier marching off to war; the fourth seems to suggest that the loved one is in love with himself, so he must not look in his lover's eye or he will see his own face and, like his lover, die. Lennox completed the settings in January 1940, but later in the year, he added a fifth song, 'Because I Like You Better'. Curiously he does not seem to have told Nadia about any of them, guessing, perhaps, that she would disapprove of their romantic mood of lyrical bitterness.

Once he had laid the ghost of his love for Ben, Lennox returned to piano music. The *Four Concert Studies* (and the music that inspired them: Beethoven's *Diabelli Variations* and the Chopin mazurkas)[40] had been an absorbing passion since late 1939. Now he wanted to create some modern music that was truly 'for piano',[41] and truly virtuosic, since there were so few pieces of this kind in the contemporary piano repertoire.[42] But these four pieces – later dedicated to friends he thought he had lost in Occupied France – were so fiendishly difficult that he himself could not play a bar of them.[43] 'They need Horowitz,' he told Nadia, 'they're absolutely made for him', though he was all too well aware that most virtuosi were not interested in new music.[44] The dedicatee of the first piece ('Presto'), David Ponsonby, lived till 1986; the Dutch composer Bep Geuer, dedicatee of the second piece ('Andante'), died in 1974; nothing is known of the third dedicatee, LB's Paris friend Marc Chatellier; and the dedicatee of the fourth piece (marked, like the third piece, 'Allegro') was his Geneva-based, Cambridge-educated, bilingual cousin Claude Berkeley, who was soon to become a secretary in the War Cabinet (and died in about 1976). Just after the war Lennox found his own Horowitz, the New Zealand pianist Colin Horsley; and, though too late for his own lifetime, a further Berkeley virtuoso emerged in the new century, when Margaret Fingerhut made a fine recording of a comprehensive Berkeley piano programme for Chandos.

Writing to Nadia from Marshfield on 28 December 1939, a day after the fourth anniversary of his mother's death, Lennox expressed 'the greatest need' to see his old teacher. He wanted to show her the new piano pieces which, though not extraordinary, would at least, he hoped, make her happy – and he wanted to talk about his Maman:

> What hurts when I think of her is not so much not having her with me any more – because I am so sure of finding her again one day, and her life here had become such a martyrdom – but of being so unworthy of her – of being so insubstantial, so weak. I am overcome with shame. If I could be worthy all the time and not just when I think of her that might be better. I must be less frivolous or I'll never be worth anything.[45]

It is not clear what Lennox can have meant by the 'moins frivole' in that last sentence, when so much of his life was manifestly occupied with entirely serious endeavour. It may have been that, like many gay men, he was ashamed of the amount of time he devoted to thinking about and occasionally pursuing desirable youths. And Lennox's Maman was not the only loved one occupying his thoughts at the beginning of 1940. There was still Ben, to whom he wrote, five days into the New Year, discussing the Mill, the war and music. He had just discovered Puccini's one-act opera *Gianni Schicchi*, and thought it 'the best thing of its kind I know, and perfectly done': 'You're the only person I can really share enthusiasm about that kind of music – most people are so infernally highbrow and inclined to turn up their noses at anything at all facile ... ' [46]

Ben was 'still the most thrilling person' he had ever known, and it had been awful to lose him so completely. [47] Referring to conscription registration which had now reached men aged twenty-eight, Lennox wondered about Ben's situation – Ben was twenty-seven, but was he immune by being in America? Lennox himself, at thirty-six, was still in the clear:

> For the first time in my life, I find an advantage in my advanced years; and though I am not a conscientious objector, I have no desire to embark on a military career for which I feel singularly ill-suited. I have thought a great deal about pacifism etc, but I've come to the conclusion that though the use of force can't be good, there are cases where it is better than the abandonment of certain principles.[48]

This further rejection of a pacifism which he had clung to all his life exasperated Ben. For him, pacifism could never be conditional. It is no coincidence that he does not seem to have written to Lennox for several months after this. But that did not stop Lennox from continuing to write his own letters of dogged devotion.

The next excuse for a fan letter was a concert at the London Contemporary Music Centre in a blizzard on 30 January, in the middle of the coldest winter for forty years. What with blocked roads, chaos on the railways, telephone wires down, and water mains burst, it is amazing anyone got there at all. Boyd Neel was conducting the premieres of Ben's Rimbaud cycle, *Les Illuminations*, sung by Sophie Wyss, and Lennox's own *Serenade.* As usual Lennox was ecstatic about Ben's work – 'marvellous ... grand music from beginning to end ... an absolute knock-out' – and self-deprecating about his own: though he conceded that his 'thing', as he called the *Serenade*, had gone well in a programme that also included works by Herbert Howells and Lord Berners. '... to be quite honest [he wrote to Ben] I must say I think it [the *Serenade*] was the best thing after yours ... so as I'm quite used to being eclipsed by you, I was quite happy.'[49]

Lennox admitted that he had felt 'very sentimental' when listening to Ben's songs. The whole cycle was so exactly like Ben himself that it had worked up in him 'all the old feelings!'[50] A few weeks later he bought the score and read it again and again. His favourite songs were the exciting *Villes* ('particularly all the part from 6 to the end is very much my cup of tea') and *Phrase* ('a dream of beauty').[51] He tried the new work on Nadia, but she did not like it, and they had 'a terrific argument'. She admired the string writing, but thought that Ben had not yet found his real musical language. Lennox sent Ben the score of his own *Serenade*, in the hope that he might be able to arrange a performance in America, 'as there is so little doing here',[52] and the first four of his *Housman Songs* for Peter Pears to try.* (The choice of the Housman texts and the pain apparent in the settings will have left neither of them in any doubt about the suffering that Lennox had gone through that Christmas of 1938; and, at some level, he must have wanted them to know.) He said he still felt 'pretty feeble' as a composer compared to Ben, but thought he had 'improved a bit'.[53]

Lennox really should not have been so modest about his scintillating *Serenade*, which is one of the most popular pieces of twentieth-century English string writing: much recorded, choreographed and used as a TV theme tune. Yet Ben's over-protective friends fed him negative reports in their transatlantic letters. Montagu Slater dismissed the *Serenade* as 'sixpennie five finger exercises' and said he had not realized 'Lennox could be so bad',[54] and Sophie Wyss (for whom Lennox was to write the song *Tant que mes yeux* in Paris a couple of months later) thought it was 'very attractive but still very thin'.[55] Beth Britten, who did not hear it – and does not seem to have minded missing it – was furious with Lennox because he had promised to tell her the date of the concert, and when he forgot she had missed Ben's song cycle, as she told her brother bitterly, 'Barbara heard of it just in time & went. He [Lennox] was there of course as something of his was done too. He really is a blighter, since he came & stayed the night here to fetch the AC we haven't heard a word from him. He's left all his silver & stuff lying about, he really deserves to lose it all. I hope he won't blame us if it gets pinched.'[56]

*In 1975 PP gave PD the MS of LB's still-unperformed *Housman Songs*, in the second, revised version, with the fifth song and the dedication to Peter Fraser (MLB, pp. 88–9). This MS is now at BPL; the MS of the first, four-song set, dated January 1940, is at the British Library.

Lennox seems to have forgotten about the silver, and though he took steps to protect his mother's jewellery, he managed to forget that too – till the manager of Lloyds Bank in Halesworth wrote to him some twenty years later to ask if he was the Lennox Berkeley whose diamonds had been discovered in the vaults.[57]

Silver and jewels were not uppermost in people's minds as the Nazis advanced through Europe that terrible spring. Between the invasions of Norway and Denmark on April 9 and Belgium a month later, Lennox wrote to Ben openly defending the war. The prospect of a Nazi triumph, he said, was so hideous that war was more than justified. Besides, his own personal life seemed so insignificant 'when all the things one loves most in life are threatened'. In the circumstances he was beginning to wonder whether he would ever see Ben again, but he was relieved that at least Ben was showing signs of missing England. 'I can't help feeling rather glad that you're homesick – I shd dispair [*sic*] of you altogether if you weren't. I should hold on to that feeling, even if it hurts. It's a very healthy one.'[58]

Despite the uncertainties of life in Paris, Nadia Boulanger had introduced Lennox's *Serenade* to its first French audience on 16 April. Among the audience, though not together, were a uniformed José, now serving with the Régiment de Défense Passive, and the fiercely patriotic French conductor Charles Münch, who was to remain in France conducting the Conservatoire Orchestra during the German occupation, protecting his musicians from the Gestapo and supporting the Resistance. Münch liked the *Serenade* and asked Boulanger to send him the score.[59] Nadia was warmly enthusiastic about the new work and must have written to Lennox to say so, though the letter is now lost. Lennox's reply said that her approval was more precious than any success. '... In my heart, all that I write is dedicated first and foremost to Maman and to you, because it's she who has given me life, and you who have shown me the use I must make of it.'[60]

It was not just Nadia's technical instruction that was so precious, he said, but the way she taught her students how to love music. So many musicians were more interested in career, fashion, theories or systems than in music itself. Yet only love could create what was good. Look at Mozart: part of the secret of his genius lay in his sheer love of music.[61]

Mozart had always been one of Lennox's favourite composers, and it would have excited him to know that his great-great-great-grandfather, Kenneth, Viscount Fortrose, actually made music with the boy Mozart.

It happened in 1770 when Fortrose, then twenty-six and already a widower, was living in Naples. His constant companion was a fellow Scot who shared his passion for music, painting, dancing, sport and Roman antiquities: the energetic Envoy to the Two Sicilies, William Hamilton (later Sir William; later still to marry Emma the Attitudiniste). With Hamilton's contacts, Fortrose drew around him a brilliant circle which included the music historian Charles Burney and the traveller Patrick Brydone, both touring Europe that year, the painters Pietro Fabris and Gabriele Ricciardelli, the celebrated castrato Gaetano Caffarelli who had sung with Handel in London, Italy's greatest violinist Emanuele Barbella, the harpsichordist Paolo Orgitano (Fortrose's teacher), and the composer Niccolò Jommelli. All admired Fortrose for the qualities recorded by Dr Burney:

> He really is a lively, sensible and accomplished young nobleman, in person very manly and pleasing[;] he has great talents and taste – he both draws and paints very well, understands perspective, rides, fences, dances, swims and plays on the harpsichord.... It is impossible for anyone to do the honours of his house better than Lord F. We are all at our ease and very cheerful and happy ...[62]

A typical morning, according to Brydone, began with nude sea-bathing from milord's 'large commodious boat', attended by ten private watermen, then 'an English breakfast' followed by 'a delightful little concert'.[63] Fabris made two charming paintings (now in the Scottish National Portrait Gallery) of the various activities in the fashionably neo-classical interiors of Fortrose's apartments. One shows the host presiding over a concert party, with Hamilton playing the viola, the composer Gaetano Pugnani, the violin, and none other than the visiting Mozarts providing keyboard accompaniment (Wolfgang, then fourteen, at the octave spinet, his father Leopold at the harpsichord). Fortrose's balletic stance (copied by one of his dogs) suggests he may have been conducting. The other picture is a fencing scene in the same room: the willowy Fortrose, stripped to his waistcoat, his foil temporarily at rest, watches two friends lunging, while the portly figure of Jommelli, seated at a table, scratches away with a quill at what may have been the score of his opera *Armida Abbandonata*, performed in Naples that May (with Mozart himself in attendance – and commenting that though the music was beautiful, the opera was old-fashioned.

Kenneth Fortrose was created Earl of Seaforth in 1771, and in gratitude raised a battalion of Seaforth Highlanders. Ten years later, on a long voyage to India, he and 247 of his soldiers lost their lives to scurvy. Lennox inherited some Neapolitan landscapes – and a genetic predisposition to music and Mozart.

In May 1940, the Phoney War suddenly came to an end when the German Panzers burst through the Ardennes, encircled the Allied armies in the north, and then advanced on Paris. On 12 May – Lennox's thirty-seventh birthday – Nadia closed down her school at Gargenville and motored south to the safety of a friend's villa at Uzerche. After a battle with her conscience, she decided she could do more for France as a free woman outside it than she could as an enemy of the collaborationist Vichy government within. In July she accepted a teaching post in America, and on 6 November she arrived in New York, safe for the rest of the war.

On 10 July the Germans began a full-scale, day and night air attack on south-eastern England, which was to culminate in the Battle of Britain a month later. Gradually the Marshfield party began to break up. In a very belated bread-and-butter letter, Dylan Thomas thanked the Davenports for a summer that had 'talked itself away'. Their jointly-written detective story was 'the Best of its Kind or unkind' and it had been amusing compiling their 'Club of Bad Books'. He had enjoyed Antonia White too:'... buttoned, unbuttoned, dame, flapper, [Antonia] was always a charmer and a caution.' It had been 'the nicest, fullest time for years', which is very much what the others felt too.[64]

Henry Boys and Humphrey Searle left to join the Army, William Glock, inspired by the skill and daring of the fighter pilots, chose the RAF (but not till he had played Lennox's *Introduction and Allegro* with Lennox himself at the 1940 Proms). Dylan who had got himself classified as unfit for military service (after 'mixing beer with sherry, whisky and gin' the night before his medical)[65] found a job as a scriptwriter with Strand Films in London. John Davenport joined the expanded BBC, and was soon appointed Head of the Belgian Section. And Lennox volunteered for the RAF, as he told Ben on 17 July, while German bombs rained down on England, '... we go on living in this nightmare which is likely to become a great deal more nightmarish very shortly. I have'nt [*sic*] been called up yet on account of my advanced years [he was now thirty-seven], but I have volunteered for the R.A.F. Volunteer Reserve for a ground job (I'm not proposing to become a pilot or air-gunner or anything like that!) ...'[66]

21
Freda, London, 1941

Freda decided she did not want to work for the pig farmer. What she really wanted was to move to London, where so many of her school friends were now working. But her guardian at the Public Trustee's office thought that wartime London was too dangerous. So she looked for another job locally.

At the outbreak of war some of the BBC's most interesting departments – Drama, Features, Monitoring, for example – had been evacuated to Wood Norton near Evesham. As Freda's lodgings in Harvington were only five miles north of Evesham, she tried her luck at the BBC. The passing-out certificate from Miss Kerr-Sander's Secretarial College – guaranteeing proficiency in shorthand and typing, and 'a good clear style and descriptive talent' – satisfied the personnel selectors, and Freda was offered a position as secretary to Lord Kingsale in the administration department of the Monitoring Service. It was the summer of 1941 and she was just eighteen.

Monitoring was accommodated in a colony of timber huts in the grounds of a Victorian house called Wood Norton Hall, once the home of a refugee Bourbon *duc*. Hundreds of linguists from all over the world now worked there, intercepting European radio stations, recording their broadcasts and transcribing the information which the Axis governments were feeding to the people of Germany, Italy and Occupied France. Most of the monitors were refugee academics; many were elderly and found it difficult to tune their wireless sets and operate the wax cylinder recording machines. With such a large and heterogeneous staff and so little space, listening positions were at a premium and had to be allotted on a strict shift system. Freda remembers Evesham as an extraordinarily exotic place – 'this market gardening town in the middle of England with all these Egyptians and Czechs and every sort of nationality'.[1]

Clare Lawson Dick, later to become Controller, Radio 4, spent the first two years of the war at Wood Norton, working in the Registry, filing letters. She loved the cosmopolitan atmosphere, which had brought out 'the dotty side of the BBC'. She recalled years later that there had even been a private siren at Wood Norton – not that they were expecting the enemy to drop paratroops into the Worcestershire countryside, but because of the IRA, which was carrying out bombing raids at the time. She remembered a siren instruction which read, 'If the alert is sounded, staff must run into the woods immediately and lie down. Preferably in pairs.'[2]

Freda travelled in on the bus each morning with Gilbert Harding, a Cambridge-educated former police constable and journalist who was now working in Monitoring as a sub-editor, and was later to become a national institution – and the world's first TV celebrity, as the famously bad-tempered panellist on BBC Television's long-running game show, *What's My Line?* Every week from 1951 till his early death in 1960, the combative Harding entertained – and sometimes outraged – viewers with his acid tongue. Known as the rudest man in Britain, he himself once admitted that his bad manners and ill temper were 'quite indefensible'. (This confession came in a TV interview with John Freeman on the BBC programme *Face to Face*, in the final year of his life. He said he was afraid of dying but would be glad to be dead, that he was unfit to live with and profoundly lonely.) In 1941, when he was still unknown, Gilbert Harding was billeted in Harvington with an elderly Catholic lady who adored him and encouraged him to befriend Freda, who remembers him as being 'very nice to me'.[3]

Freda liked her work and she liked her boss, Michael de Courcy, Lord Kingsale, 'a dear, kind old thing'.[4] His eldest son and heir had been killed in the war the previous summer, and he was evidently fond of Freda. An Indian Army colonel who had retired before the war, Kingsale was intensely proud of his ancient title, of which he was at least the 27th, and possibly even the 34th, holder (depending on which creation you started from). As Premier Baron of Ireland, he was entitled to the hereditary privilege of keeping his hat on in the presence of his monarch, but he told Freda that when his grandfather had put this to the test during an audience with Queen Victoria, she snapped at him, 'Don't be so silly. We are a lady. Remove your hat at once.'

Freda and her schoolfriend, Fay Boultbee, daughter of the rector of Harvington, the Revd Horace Boultbee, lived in the rectory with Fay's mother and sister. 'Pop' Boultbee was away most of the time, serving as an army chaplain on Salisbury Plain, so it was very much a female household, and they all looked forward to the rector's occasional leaves home, because he filled the house with fun. Without a resident parson, the church of St James the Great managed as best it could, the services being taken by laymen or visiting clergymen, and at one point by a Salvation Army captain, temporarily billeted with the ladies at the rectory, who galvanized the usually sedate Matins into a tambourine-bashing singalong.

Freda was especially close to the Braziers, a family of fruit farmers in Harvington. Both the handsome sons seem to have fallen for her, but she preferred their craggy father. 'We had a little dilly-dally', she recalls, 'and there was a bit of kissing among the Pershore plums. I think his wife knew probably.'[5] It was fun and flattering, but it was not what she really wanted – even though she did not yet know what she did want.

22
Lennox, London, 1941

Since the occupation of Paris on 14 June 1940 and France's capitulation on the 22nd, Lennox had abandoned all pretence of pacifism. Meanwhile, there had been no news from any of his French friends: José was supposed to be in Corsica, but he did not know what had happened to Nadia Boulanger or David Ponsonby, his cousin Claude Berkeley or Francis Poulenc and countless others. Music, at least, remained constant, as he told Ben:

> I've written a new *String Quartet* which I finished last month and which I really think is miles better than anything I've done yet. Our old friend the *Introduction and Allegro for 2 pianos and orchestra* is down for performance at a Prom on Sept 6th and I am supposed to be playing it with William Glock. Of course if I get into the RAF I probably shan't be able to play myself, but that won't matter much as it would [not] be difficult to find a more competant [*sic*] substitute. In any case one can't feel certain that the proms will come off at all – but Henry Wood seems determined to have them, war or no war ... Shall I ever see you again? If only this bloody war would stop. But still anything is better than for us to give in now, and meekly accept the annihilation of France and our own.[1]

Expanding on this theme to Nadia, when at last he got news of her from America, Lennox said he believed the drama was going to be long and disagreeable – but if the English had one quality it was tenacity, and 'what matters now is to hold firm'.[2] There were some principles for which it was necessary to fight, when all other means of resistance had been exhausted.[3] Nadia had come to the same conclusion. In the first week of May 1940, with the Germans pushing towards the Maginot Line, she had driven to Switzerland to give a series of talks, ostensibly about music but actually about the war. Lennox's friend David

Ponsonby accompanied her in her six-cylinder black Hotchkiss, and recalled the trip a few years later:

> I looked at her and felt that even if the world were going to crumble to pieces around us, this was a mind that held the secrets which give one courage to face things like danger and sacrifice ... The talks which she gave ... fully confirmed this impression. In that most poignant moment in the history of Europe ... she chose to quote simple, almost childlike phrases out of Rameau's treatise on composition, and from them she drew a profoundly moving picture of that steadfast faith in beauty, that certainty that no sacrifice is too great for the quest of an ideal ... By means of short musical examples, backed up by such sound and illuminating technical comments as, probably, she alone in Europe is capable of today, and by a few quotations from the letters of men like Rameau, Chausson, Fauré and Francis Poulenc, she performed the miracle of making her hearers feel that if we were all to be obliterated tomorrow, certain indestructible and eternal values would remain – something for which it would be hard to find a name – call it beauty, call it faith ... [4]

Lennox himself had every intention of playing his part in protecting Nadia's ideal. When his application for a commission in the Administrative and Special Duties Branch of the RAF Volunteer Reserve* was turned down – presumably for health reasons (and perhaps because of his colour blindness) – he volunteered to serve as a part-time, unpaid air-raid warden instead.[5] Following the first all-night raid on London at the end of August, Lennox was posted to an ARP station in Holborn, near his flat in Great Ormond Street. His job was night-patrolling during alerts, checking the air-raid shelters and calling out the rescue services when a bomb landed. He was on duty a night or two each week, till midnight, and during the day when needed.[6] It was exacting and sometimes distressing work, and he was constantly tired. 'The difficulty in London', he wrote to Ben, 'is to know where one can sleep with any degree of safety. I still sleep at Gt. Ormond Street when things are

*His friend Eddy Sackville-West was also rejected by the RAF (M. De-la-Noy, *Eddy*, pp. 174–5), but his older Oxford friend and London neighbour John 'the Widow' Lloyd was commissioned in the RAFVR in 1940 and his Paris friend Freddie Ashton served in the RAF during the war.

fairly quiet, but I generally try and take refuge elsewhere if it gets too hot, as it is a rickety old house, and there would be no hope if it was hit.'[7]

Enid Slater told Ben she had heard from a third party that Lennox had done 'wonderful work' dragging people out of the rubble when the big shelter at the end of his road was hit.[8] This was the occasion to which Lennox himself alluded in a letter to Nadia Boulanger in November, when he said he had attended to the wounded and the dead only once – 'it was frightful, and made me ill for three days.'[9] And in another letter to Boulanger two years later, he said he was in London throughout the air raids: it was 'a terrible time when they never stopped. How horrible it all is!'[10] To Ben – referring perhaps to the same incident in 1940 – Lennox said he had 'seen people crushed to death beneath a mass of masonry and tried to extract dead and dying *innocent* people', and the experience had changed his attitude to the war. 'Previous wars did'nt [*sic*] involve all this ... However, since I am here, I suppose the best thing is to try and do something to help – and the London people have really showed [*sic*] such unbelievable fortitude, that it makes one want to do something.'[11]

In his diary thirty-seven years later Lennox referred briefly to the Blitz. He had just been reading his friend James Lees-Milne's newly-published wartime diaries, *Prophesying Peace* – and, in particular, a passage about an air raid.[12] This vivid account brought back memories that were 'almost nostalgic ... because, although it was far from pleasant, the danger and excitement made one forget small worries ... One remembers too the joy of finding oneself still alive after the heavier raids, particularly if one had to be out in the streets on air-raid warden's duty to get people into shelters or the underground, occasionally lying down with one's face in the gutter when the whistle of a descending bomb seemed directly overhead.'[13]

Life in Britain was 'utterly bloody', he told Ben, and he was glad that Ben was away from it all in America. An artist's business was to get on with his work, and Ben's work was vital. There were not many people who could 'make something of lasting value' and those who could should do so – particularly 'now that the world seems to have nothing but destruction to offer as a solution.'[14] As Ben may have remembered, this was very much the line he himself had taken with Wystan when urging him not to go to Spain in 1937.

For the time being Lennox's business was to help his country as an

ARP warden and to get on with his music when he could, and even to combine the two, when the occasion rose – as it did eighteen months later. Through his connections at the Benedictine abbey of Prinknash, he was asked, in 1942, to write the music for a short documentary film about the contribution of Britain's three million Catholics to the war effort. Sponsored by the Ministry of Information, the film was designed to show that Catholics were just as patriotic as other Britons, even if they did owe their spiritual allegiance to Rome. But the fact that it was widely distributed in the American market, not long after the United States had been driven into the European war by the Japanese attack on Pearl Harbor in December 1941, suggests that it had another, more overtly political purpose: to persuade the 25 million Catholics in the USA to give their full support to President Roosevelt in the Allied assault on Germany and Italy. The film is entitled *The Sword of the Spirit*,* after the wartime movement founded by Cardinal Arthur Hinsley, Archbishop of Westminster (and a special friend of Prinknash), to provide 'A Catholic's Answer to Nazism'. The Sword of the Spirit crusade was intended for Catholics 'and all men of goodwill' who wanted 'to join in the defence of the natural law and go forward to a just victory and a just peace ...'.

The film shows Catholics attending Mass – in the old Latin Rite – at Westminster Cathedral and in the shell of Southwark Cathedral, which had recently been bombed. 'Our churches may be wrecked', says the commentary (written and spoken by Robert Speaight), 'but the spirit of Catholicism transcends material destruction.' There are dramatic re-enactments of the bombing of the chapel of a famous Catholic girls' school, when the Mother Superior plunges into the flames to rescue the tabernacle containing the blessed sacrament, and of a priest ARP warden climbing up into the ruins of a bombed house to give extreme unction to the dying victim of an air raid. There is also a roll call of Catholic war heroes, and footage of Catholic servicemen at Mass around the world – Polish airmen on land, British sailors at sea, Free French troops in the Western Desert. And in the middle of the film there is an address (with subtitles in Spanish – for the vast electorate of

*Directed by Henry Cass and produced by James Carr and Sydney Box of Verity Films for the Ministry of Information, with music direction by Muir Mathieson. No written score survives, and the only traceable prints of the film are at the British Film Institute in London and the Library of Congress in Washington DC. See also *Motion Picture Herald*, vol. 49, no. 8, 12 December 1942, p. 1055.

Hispanic Catholics) given by Cardinal Hinsley, who stresses the Church's uncompromising opposition to totalitarianism and the necessity for spiritual rather than material goals, 'if there is to be true freedom in victory'.

Lennox's musical contribution is small but significant. He provides a short and dramatic prelude to accompany a shot of tanks rolling across a theatre of war, an urgent section for strings as the priest clambers through the ruins to the dying woman, and a rousing closing piece, which develops and harmonizes the theme of the hymn, 'Hail Queen of Heaven, the Ocean Star!', sung by the sailors. Otherwise the sound effects are on-site recordings of Gregorian chant and polyphony (arranged by Henry Washington, later to become director of the Brompton Oratory Choir) and of the rumbles of bombers and anti-aircraft guns.

For Lennox this commission was particularly appropriate, since it gave him the threefold opportunity to play a part in propagating the prevailing spirit of patriotism, to honour his Church and to lay the ghosts of his harrowing experiences as an ARP warden in the Blitz.

Extraordinarily, despite the aerial battle raging over London, Henry Wood's Promenade Concert season started as planned that summer of 1940. The Proms were now sponsored privately, the BBC having pulled out at the beginning of the war. So the much-delayed premiere of Lennox's *Introduction and Allegro for 2 Pianos and Orchestra*, on 6 September 1940, was played not by the BBC Symphony Orchestra but by the Proms' new house orchestra, the London Symphony. Lennox himself and William Glock made their Proms débuts as soloists, in a Queen's Hall that was packed for the Beethoven on the programme. Sir Henry Wood conducted, and noted in his diary afterwards that the Berkeley work was 'Modern but interesting and good'.[15] Boosey & Hawkes, who had already brought out at least half a dozen of Lennox's scores, including the ballet *The Judgment of Paris,* sent along their editor Ernest Chapman to find out whether this new piece was worth publishing. On the whole, he thought not: though the *Introduction* included a 'subtle and beautiful *Adagio* with scoring of a very individual character', the *Allegro* suffered from a weak construction. All in all, 'rather disappointing'.[16]

Lennox was not much more positive himself. He wrote to tell Ben, to whom the work was dedicated, that he assumed he had over-scored it, since he had been told that the pianos could not be heard through the strings. As he had always had a tendency to score too thinly, he hoped he would get it right next time. The balance had been impossible to judge from the platform, because the players had been so squashed together that all he had heard was the oboe blowing into his right ear. As to his own playing, for once he was almost satisfied: 'I didn't play too badly considering my v. poor technical resources as a pianist.'[17] He gave much the same report to Nadia: his own playing had not been a catastrophe, and Glock's had been excellent.[18] It must have been disappointing for Lennox that this Prom was so long delayed, but as things turned out he was extremely lucky it happened at all. The very next day the Germans intensified their bombing raids over London and the Proms had to be closed down, a month early. Within the year the Queen's Hall itself was bombed and razed to the ground, in the same raid that practically destroyed the House of Commons. Lennox wondered how long he would be safe at home in Bloomsbury.

23
Freda, Weston-super-Mare, 1942

In the spring of 1942 Freda went down with appendicitis and was sent to convalesce at Weston-super-Mare, where the BBC had a hostel called Rozel, a former seaside hotel run by a large, eccentric and much-loved woman called Brownie. There she fell in with a group of radio actors from the BBC Repertory Company who had been evacuated from London to Bristol and were now billeted at Brownie's in Weston. To a shy orphan raised in country parsonages, Rozel was wonderfully Bohemian – and Freda's horizons were suddenly widened as she found herself in the middle of a new, extrovert and exciting circle of people. Most of them were older than her, most were men, and though many were gay, that did not stop them flirting with her – nor indeed did it diminish her enjoyment of their attentions. She was certainly a magnet in Weston-super-Mare. Despite her name, her looks were more Tartar than Hebrew: green eyes the shape of almonds, high cheek bones, wild black hair, fine skin, long legs, and a proud bearing.

The novelist John Keir Cross, a married Scot working for the Rep as a script editor, was instantly captivated.* Then there was the Casanova of the Rep, the tall and muscular Lancelot de Giberne Sieveking, who invited Freda on a tour of the underground air-raid shelters.† And the

*John Keir Cross (aka Stephen MacFarlane) adapted the Sherlock Holmes stories which Val Gielgud produced for the BBC in the 1950s, wrote nine novels and several short stories - mainly for children and often involving detectives and ghosts and creatures from outer space – and edited nine anthologies of horror stories. He died in 1967 aged fifty-six.

†Sieveking lived at The White House, Snape, which was hit by a flying bomb in October 1944 (LFAL, pp. 1230–1). The painter Edward Burra, who knew him in Paris in 1929, described him as 'jolly Lance Sieveking ... so picturesque the tall muscular form was in brown tweed trow[s]ers a biscuit shirt & a tie the tie arranged so romanesque' (Letter to William Chappell August 1929, Edward Burra, *Well, Dearie!,* p. 70).

actor Alan Wheatley – 'gay, much older than me,* very withdrawn, and I was rather taken with him – though he wasn't really interested'. There were also lots of other BBC admirers, including Teddy Wolfe, the billeting officer, Douglas Cleverdon (then the West Regional Features Producer), and the actors Charles Mason and Eric Lugg. 'Rozel was a real eye-opener,' Freda remembers, 'freedom, parties and drink – as much as one could in war-time. It was my coming-out, and I really did.'[1]

Apart from the air raids, Brownie's Rozel was non-stop fun, with play-readings in the hotel lounge on Monday nights, singing around the piano, films to be seen – *Dangerous Moonlight*, *The Day Will Dawn* – and, when the weather got warmer, swimming, for the hardy, in the Bristol Channel: down the front steps to the mud, 'shining like molten gold',[2] then a sticky hike to the water.

It was a long convalescence, longer than appendicitis required, but Freda's private life was demanding, and her boss Lord Kingsale was sympathetic. Even he, however, could not go on signing sick notes, and after six weeks Freda had to tear herself away from Weston and her new friends. Fully recovered, more confident and optimistic, she returned to Worcestershire in June and picked up the threads of home life with the Boultbees at Harvington, and of office life back at the Monitoring Unit at Wood Norton.

Without Freda, Rozel for the romantic John Keir Cross was 'quite deserted' and 'full of ghosts' – as he told her in a love letter which betrays that leaning towards the supernatural which was to characterize his later fiction:

> I come out of my room, and just for a moment I seem to see you against the light, leaning on the edge of the piano ... Oh my love it is so queerly, so fantastically empty! And it seems so strange that it is empty, that you are there & I am here and that it isn't possible merely by imagining ourselves together, merely by *thinking* it for us to *be* together in fact, touching each other ... I have a sort of quiet, suppressed, desperate longing for you now – nothing vehement or noisy, but only a sort of simple dull ache.[3]

But for Freda herself, Rozel was soon no more than a happy memory. Within a year of her return to Evesham, the BBC moved the Monitoring Unit closer to London, to premises with more room for the

*Alan Wheatley (1909–91).

expanding staff. The new home was Caversham Park, near Reading, once owned by the Crawshays, the iron masters of Merthyr Tydfil (the naturalized home of Freda's father, though she did not know of this connection at the time). Since 1922 it had been occupied by the Catholic public school The Oratory; now the school had gone to new premises at Woodcote on the other side of Reading (where Freda would one day send her own three sons), and in the spring of 1943 the BBC Monitoring Unit moved in. For a while she lived in a room in Reading, commuting out to Caversham by bus, but she hated her claustrophobic little home, and her friend Mildred Holland in Administration arranged for her to be transferred to a hostel further up the Thames at Goring (not far, in fact, from The Oratory's new home); and there she was much happier. (Poor Mildred was in love with a German professor at Monitoring called Baumgarten, who was soon to die.)

In her own search for security, and for an end, she hoped, to her recurring nightmares, Freda still hankered after a BBC job in London. Before the year was out, she got her wish, when the Corporation transferred her to the General Office, a sort of central typing pool cum in-house temping agency. The Public Trustee still would not allow her to live in central London, so she lodged with her uncle Alfred Nunney, an electrical retailer who had a house in Birchen Grove, Kingsbury, NW9, and commuted to Broadcasting House by bus. After three or four months there, Freda met a BBC widow called Nancy Gregory who offered her rooms at her home in the Hertfordshire town of Broxbourne. From there, Freda travelled in to work by train to Liverpool Street.

The GO was not perfect but at least it was London and a foot in the door. Freda reckoned she would be closer there to a better job. And that's what happened. Lent for a week to the pioneering Features and Drama, one of the most enterprising departments of the BBC at the time, she met up with some of her Rep friends from Rozel and was offered a job as assistant to the secretary of the newly-appointed Literary Editor, the humorist Stephen Potter. Soon to achieve fame as the inventor of *Gamesmanship* and *One-Upmanship*, Potter – and the secretaries – shared an office in Rothwell House, New Cavendish Street, with two other stars of Features, Edward Sackville-West, novelist, music critic and amateur pianist, and the producer Douglas Cleverdon, late of Rozel.*

*Douglas Cleverdon, born 1903, retired from the BBC in 1969, and died in 1987.

It could have been a wonderful break in a young woman's career, but it did not last. Though she liked Stephen Potter and the job – and was especially fond of the gentle Eddy Sackville-West, later to become a life-long friend – she could not bear the tyrannical senior secretary, the newly-divorced Betty Johnstone, who was 'a real dragon' and 'no one could stand her'.[4] Whenever Mrs Johnstone spoke to her, she felt like bursting into tears, but it was reassuring to know that the whole of Features and Drama was on her side.[5] Freda asked for another transfer and was sent to Light Music as secretary to the Dance Music Organizer, Douglas Lawrence. She started with Lawrence on the last day of January 1944, and recorded in her new, five-year diary: 'He is a nice little man but I know that I can't stay there long.'

The truth was that, the dragon notwithstanding, she missed her actor friends – and, in particular, the aloof and passionless Alan Wheatley, on whom she had become quite fixated. He was not only courtly, urbane and considerate, but undemanding, unresponsive and utterly unavailable: in every respect Freda's cup of tea. What she presumably wanted was to 'save' him from his homosexuality, but her complicated feelings for him made her wretched. In January 1944 she went to see him playing the Earl of Harpenden in Rattigan's *While the Sun Shines* – a romantic farce set in the Blitz – and wrote in her diary that though she had laughed a lot, she had felt 'horribly miserable afterwards – the theatre makes A so vivid.'[6] A couple of days later she saw him in Rothwell House after he had been rehearsing an anthology of poetry readings produced by Sackville-West. She was looking, she wrote in her diary later, 'an awful mess', while he was 'as immaculate as ever'. This left her feeling both inadequate and adoring and she could not understand why: it was 'something I can't explain to anyone'. That he was always so kind 'makes it all very much harder'.[7]

Alan Wheatley was by no means the only man in Freda's busy social life. There were also the painter Bill Redgrave; a gastroenterologist in Harley Street, Dr 'Perky' Perkins, and a radiographer, Dr John Sparkes; a Scot called Bill McCormack; a little dancing corporal she met at the Chevrons Club in Earls Court; an Irish army officer she met at a dance at the Regent Palace; an attractive, married Czech from Monitoring called Peter Heller; David Kendall who lived at the Mill in Broxbourne, and wrote poems; and the saxophonist Michael Krein, conductor of the BBC's London Light Concert Orchestra ('a strange, strange person with a bad inferiority complex').[8] She juggled these romantic friendships concurrently, once confusing the two Bills on the telephone.[9] Then there were elderly beaux, like her GP in Barons Court, Dr Gordon Ackland (who told her to look on him as 'an older brother'[10]), and not a few 'D.O.M.' as she called them: flashers and gropers like 'Old Hamilton', who invited her into his garden shed 'and started to get silly',[11] (though she was pleased when he signed her up as a lady member of the Surrey County Cricket Club at the Oval)[12] and Major O'Farrell who 'got all "confidential" in the train'.[13]

If her suitors were not dirty old men, they were married or gay or past it. With them all she felt safe; with gay men in particular she felt both safe and a vague desire, felt by many other women of the time, to 'rescue' them from a life which she imagined could only bring unhappiness. Lovers were not what she wanted, since sex was something she feared, and heterosexual men posed a threat. What she did want, and badly need, were affection, care, gentleness and appreciation. Intelligence and social ease were desirable too, and a certain malleability which would allow her to make the running. Marriage was clearly the objective, as her diary shows. In January 1944 she had lunch with Gwen Paine – 'lucky girl, she's getting married soon – & having such fun getting clothes!',[14] and in November she lunched with another friend, who is 'getting married soon – lucky girl'.[15]

Her eagerness to please left a trail of misunderstandings – not only for her admirers, but for Freda herself. 'I can't quite define my feelings about anyone at the minute,' she wrote on 11 February, and three days later: 'I don't know what's happened to me as far as my feelings are concerned.' Her diary is full of references to 'feeling desperately miserable' or 'horribly alone' with 'no one to understand'. She longed for 'someone to talk to who could really understand'. Apart from the diary itself, which provided a certain release, her hopes and fears remained 'bottled up inside'.[16]

Not surprisingly the strain took its toll on her health. And for most of April and May she was on sick leave, suffering from stomach pains and upsets caused by acute gastric ulcers – a condition which was to plague her for the rest of her life. Drs Ackland and Perkins prescribed rest and a diet of milk and eggs. But the air raids were not conducive to rest. One night a hundred German bombers flew over Broxbourne, and thirteen were shot down. When the alert sounded Freda leapt out of bed and hid under the stairs, shivering with cold and fear. Occasionally she would stay up in London and sleep with other BBC employees – on mattresses in the Concert Hall of Broadcasting House (women divided from men by a washing line hung with blankets), on pallets in the basements, or on bunks under the Peter Robinson department store on the north-eastern corner of Oxford Circus. This may have been uncomfortable, but there at least she had company and could rest. 'Slept at Oxford Street last night,' she recorded in January 1944, 'so didn't hear siren – being 40ft underground.'[17] (In the Concert Hall, not only the sirens but the bombs were so audible that nervous staff got up and wandered around the corridors in their pyjamas, as the Germans pounded Oxford Street and Broadcasting House rocked to the explosions.[18])

For all the camaraderie of the shelters, nothing could disguise the fact that Freda was alone, with no parents, no brothers or sisters, no lover, no special friend, no home of her own. She did have several surviving Nunney uncles and aunts, and two of the Canadian ones – Daisy Hughes in particular – had even offered to adopt her, but the Public Trustee would not allow it (presumably thinking them unsuitable).[19] Till she was twenty-one, she had no control over her money, no say over where she should live. There was no one to understand all the things that she herself could not understand, and no one to banish the nightmares.

24
Lennox and Peter, London, 1941

Lennox's private life took on a new dimension towards the end of 1940. Benjamin Britten had left him and gone to America with Peter Pears, José Raffalli had been called up, and John Greenidge was working in one of the wartime ministries. But Lennox now had a new friend, a Peter of his own, a clever and musical young airman: 'blond, plump and feminine',[1] with 'a sort of baby face, [and] rather pouting lips'.[2]

Like Jackie Hewit, Peter Fraser had been passed around from patron to patron, improving himself in the process. Unlike Jackie, Peter was highly intelligent and cultivated, thoroughly presentable – and Anglo-Catholic, if not actually Catholic. He was widely read – from the Catholic poets of the penal times (Thomas More, Robert Southwell and Ben Jonson) to Cocteau and T. S. Eliot – adventurous in his musical tastes (Bartók and Hindemith, as well as Bach), and unusually knowledgeable about painting. He was also something of a mystery. He claimed to have been educated at St Joseph's College, London SE19,[3] but the school has no record of his ever having been there. He claimed to be an orphan, but records show that his parents were alive and well at 7 Babington Road in Streatham. Both parents were professional musicians, and both Anglicans: the father, Leonard Fraser, a violinist, was the son of a skin merchant; the mother, Dorothy Gladys née Colin-Smith, was the daughter of the Deputy Registrar of the High Court at Allahabad in India (and distantly related to the Earls of Leven). And though he called himself Peter, his birth at Clapton Hospital was registered under the Christian names of Raymond Laurance [*sic*].[4] Unfortunately for Lennox, Peter Fraser was also manipulative, moody and serially promiscuous.[5]

The broker of this alliance was the High Sheriff of Montgomeryshire, aka the Widow Lloyd, bachelor landowner, late of Oxford, Lennox's friend and neighbour in Bloomsbury. The Widow seems to have inherited Peter Fraser from the music critic Desmond

Shawe-Taylor – when Shawe-Taylor joined the Royal Artillery in early 1940[6] – and the Widow passed him on to Lennox when he himself joined the RAF a month or two later (following a brief fling one weekend in York, where the Widow was training as a pilot officer in Intelligence.)[7] Peter Fraser was twenty when Lennox met him, and had just volunteered for a desk job at the Air Ministry in Monck Street, Victoria, having been turned down for active duty because he was diabetic and had a weak heart.*

Eager to show off his clever new friend, Lennox took him down to Painswick for a week with his English *in loco matris*, the adoring but strait-laced Gladys Bryans. The two men could not stay at Rudge House itself, because there were not enough bedrooms (which may have been Miss Bryans's way of keeping an unacceptable reality at bay), so they lodged nearby – in the place where Ben had stayed in the summer of 1937 – and went over to the house during the day. It was during this short respite from the Blitz, in the second week of November 1940, that Lennox first told Ben about Peter, without actually revealing his name. 'I have a friend with me ... Nobody you know. A very nice person aged 20, who is just going into the RAF. He's madly keen about music. Likes your music very much.'[8]

These few brief sentences seem designed both to crow and to whet the appetite. It is unlikely that Ben would have been able to resist the temptation of finding out more about the twenty-year-old who so admired his music, but there are no surviving letters from Ben to Lennox for the rest of Ben's stay in America; nor is there anything to show that Ben ever met Peter Fraser after returning to England in the spring of 1942.

The week in Painswick was just what Lennox needed after the trauma of the air raids. In the heart of the Cotswolds, locked in by a woodland valley, the war seemed a million miles away. Apart from the blackout, and fewer cars on the roads, Lennox told Ben that the place was more or less the same as it had been when they had stayed there together in 1937. Oxford, on the other hand, was so crammed with East End refugees that the High was more like Whitechapel. In 'a world gone mad' Lennox was drawn more than ever, he said, to music. He and Peter, who could read a score (and seems to have been able to play

*Fraser's death certificate lists amongst the causes of death ventricular failure, cardiomyopathy and diabetes.

the piano),* spent the week studying Bartók's eerie *Music for Strings, Percussion and Celesta*, and playing through some of the 'Progressive Pieces for Piano' in the same composer's earlier *Mikrokosmos*. On the whole, Lennox said, *Mikrokosmos* was a wonderful achievement, but Bartók produced some very ugly sounds when he was 'working out some experiment to its logical conclusion with an almost exasperating thoroughness'.[9] The two friends also listened to records of Mozart, especially the *String Quintet No. 4 in G Minor K 516*, which Lennox considered 'almost the greatest masterpiece in all music', and the *Clarinet Quintet* 'rottenly played by [the jazzman] Benny Goodman, who may be a good virtuoso but he's a poor musician'.[10]

The benefits of Painswick did not last long. Once back in London, with its wailing sirens, Lennox's revived spirits soon fell again. He had found a new friend, but almost immediately lost him to the RAF (Peter had enlisted on 30 September 1940,[11] and was now training on the Lancashire coast), and though Lennox himself had been rejected by the RAF, he was still eligible for Army service for another four years and could expect to be called up as soon as the military registrars reached his age group. He could not make up his mind what he should do while he waited. The options included staying in London doing more voluntary work for the ARP, finding a job in one of the reserved occupations, and moving out to the country and burying himself in his music. Nor could he make up his mind about Peter. The poor boy had nowhere of his own to escape to during his brief leaves from the RAF. Should Lennox give him a home? If he did, what would John Greenidge think? What would the Church think? What indeed would the law think? Blitz and all, it is hardly surprising that when Enid Slater saw Lennox in London in late November 1940 he had 'gone all jittery & odd'.[12]

No more than three weeks later Mrs Slater lunched with him in his flat in Great Ormond Street and found him a changed man, well and working again. He had decided to stay on in London, to continue with his ARP work and to concentrate on composition. He had freed himself from the problems of the Mill and Hallam Street at last, and he had

*During a visit to Bath in March 1941 Peter Fraser gave LB a copy of Busoni's piano transcription of Bach's *Chorale Preludes* for organ, and inscribed it: 'Lennox from Peter: In the hope that he may score it so that I can play it! March 1941.' This Busoni edition is in BFP.

given Peter Fraser a home in the Bloomsbury flat too.* Peter could not join him for more than the occasional weekend, but the commitment involved was cause for celebration. Perhaps that is why Lennox now wrote a final Housman song – though it is no less melancholy than the first four, and, like them, refers back to his break-up with Ben ('Because I liked you better / Than suits a man to say, / It irked you, and I promised / To throw the thought away').[13] He then dedicated the entire set of *Five Housman Songs* to Peter Fraser.

From the beginning of their relationship Peter seems to have bewitched Lennox into behaviour that was often untypical. Living together is one example: even in wartime London, when barriers blurred in the disorder of the emergency, a discreet bachelor of thirty-seven, rich and well-connected, sharing a flat with a penniless 'orphan' of twenty must have raised eyebrows. Then in March 1941 Lennox was persuaded to put Peter up for membership of his club, the Reform. Founded by radicals who had been denied entrance to Brooks's Club, the Reform was far from being a bastion of the Establishment. It was, on the contrary, proudly progressive – and even a little gay, in a discreet, upper-middle-class sort of way; but it cannot have been routine for members to recruit their young male lovers, nor can it have been comfortable for Lennox, so essentially conformist, to recall that this was the club to which his own father had belonged. But in 1941, at the height of the war, the blue uniform will have worked in Peter's favour when his name came before the membership committee. The nomination was seconded by Dr Sholto Mackenzie, a forty-one-year-old bachelor soon to succeed his father as Lord Amulree. And so, on 17 April 1941, Peter Fraser was elected to the Reform Club – as 'Ramond [*sic*] Frazer [*sic*]'.

At about the time he put Peter up for the Reform, Lennox received a summons from the past – an invitation to stay at Berkeley Castle. It did not come from his Uncle Randal, who had never forgotten the quarrel with Lennox's father over the golf course fence at Boar's Hill, but from Randal's American wife Molly. She knew all about the family row, felt badly about it and wanted to patch things up. Now that Randal was

*The first evidence that Fraser was living at Great Ormond Sreet with LB does not come till March 1941 when LB proposes Fraser for membership of the Reform, and Fraser gives his address as 'c/o Lennox Berkeley, Gt. Ormond St.'

too old and too ill to know what was going on, Molly thought it would be safe, and right, to have Lennox to stay. She herself was not there during the day, because she was looking after wounded soldiers in her cottage hospital and supervising the manufacture of pullovers for the 263rd Squadron stationed nearby. (Both the hospital and the knitting workshop had to be outside the castle, because 'Berkeley, being against war, would not allow any war work to be done in it'.[14]) So Lennox was left to his own devices.

It must have been curious – not to say, disturbing – to stay in a house which ought to have been his, with the husk of an uncle whose title was a constant reminder of family skeletons. We do not know what Lennox thought about all this at the time, but his diaries years later suggest that in his old age at least he was glad he had been spared from playing a role to which he was so unsuited. As Vita Sackville-West points out in the castle guide, the Berkeleys may once have been feudal lords, but essentially now they were 'country squires, looking after their estates and deeply concerned with their hounds and horses'.[15] This was not the life for Lennox. Not only was the castle gloomy, he recorded after visiting the place with the Lees-Milnes in 1968, but he had come away 'feeling no regrets and thankful that I did'nt [*sic*] have to live there'.[16] Seven years later he returned for Molly's funeral and was 'treated very much as representing the family which was gratifying as we had never been invited there before'. On that occasion, in the summer of 1975, he had wandered round the castle alone, 'thinking that it might have belonged to me, but I suspect that I'm better off, though not materially, as I am'.[17]

For at least a week at the end of March and the beginning of April 1941, Lennox was the guest of a senile host who did not know who he was – and an effusive hostess who was anxious the host should not find out. Since Randal was now in a world of his own, he was no longer able to bully people with his notorious 'exactitude', which so 'disconcerted small talk and woolly minds'. (One young visitor to Berkeley just before the war reported that nervous guests wondering what to talk about would often fall back on the weather, only to be challenged to explain themselves when they muttered, in desperation, 'It looks like clearing up.'[18]) But Randal's dementia was not the only change that had befallen Berkeley: the war had claimed most of the castle servants and the rooms were now under dust-sheets. Though the lavish standards which Molly had maintained till 1939 were no longer possible, dinner was still served in the banqueting hall, with the guests in evening dress, but now there was only the butler, Hedges, with Randal's personal servant, Lowe, and just two liveried footmen, and, instead of an Italian chef, a local woman cook. Randal still presided at one end of the huge table, with Molly at the other. But unlike the golden age of the Thirties, when the Italian chef used to make an ice-cream Rolls with motor and lights, which drove down the dining table from Molly to Randal, stopping to allow guests to slice off choice bits,[19] pudding now was Lady Sysonby's Tennis Balls (ground almonds, castor sugar, biscuit and egg whites mixed to a stiff paste and rolled into balls) or Stodge – a dark brown steamed pudding of bread-crumbs, chopped suet, sugar, jam and eggs. Lennox specially liked Stodge.[20]

Neither a scientist nor much of a golfer, Lennox did not hunt or shoot, or have any particular interest in the estate, so he used to take himself off to the Morning Room, formerly the Chapel of St Mary, and spread out his manuscript paper on the old refectory table. Beneath a timber ceiling painted with texts from Revelations in Norman French, Lennox worked hard on the symphony, which he had first conceived in 1937 under the influence of Peter Burra, and had recently sketched out at Marshfield.[21] He also started writing his first and only *Piano Sonata* – for Clifford Curzon, who not only knew and admired his music and shared his love of their teacher Nadia Boulanger, but was also a committed pacifist, which Lennox no longer was.

Uncharacteristically, Lennox seems to have poured into the *Sonata* much of his life at the time: all the feelings he had suppressed while working out his technical ideas for the piano in the *Four Concert Studies* of the previous year – his love for Peter, his hurt at the loss of Ben and the deaths of his parents, his homesickness for France, his fear of the war. It is a fiercely turbulent piece – 'passionate, wild and fiery, full of notes and melodies reflecting the turmoil of the war and perhaps of his own life at the time'.[22] It is not at all the kind of music you would expect from a composer known for moderation, subtlety and restraint – yet entirely Lennox for all that.

Just as Lennox was saying goodbye to Berkeley Castle, the Chancellor raised the standard rate of income tax to ten shillings in the pound. Faced with the loss of half his income, Lennox decided he would have to get a job. Since he had been turned down by the RAF and still had not been conscripted into the Army, he chose the so-called 'reserved occupation' of broadcasting and applied to the BBC. This was a popular option for many talented men who had been classified as unfit for anything but necessary jobs at home, since it guaranteed immunity from the call-up. But Lennox believed that it would give him a chance to make a contribution to the war effort.

If before the war the BBC had been a 'comfortable, cultured, leisured place',[23] where no true artist, according to the writer John Pudney, would waste his talent, now it was suddenly 'much favoured by the intelligentsia, a fashionable alternative to uniform'[24] (even though George Orwell, a BBC war correspondent, thought that, on the inside, it was 'halfway between a girls' school and a lunatic asylum'.[25]) Because of the war and the new, expanded role of the BBC, there were plenty of vacancies: in early 1939 staff numbers had been about 5,000, now, a year and a half into the war, the Corporation had more than doubled in size. But Lennox would not immediately commit himself to a full-time job: instead he eased himself in as a freelance.

That summer of 1941 he was commissioned to write two new pieces for Malcolm Baker-Smith, a producer friend in the Features and Drama Department. One was for a radio feature about Westminster Abbey, written by Louis MacNeice (who had joined Features earlier that year); this was broadcast on 7 September. The other was even more modest: an arrangement for military band of the Sarawak national anthem, for use in a programme called *White Rajah*, celebrating the centenary of the Malaysian state of Sarawak; this was broadcast on 23 September, and earned Lennox 2½ guineas.[26]

The prospects of further work providing incidental music for the expanding Features and Drama Department looked good as 1941 drew to a close. In an internal memo asking colleagues to recommend suitable composers for this purpose, the Overseas Music Director Kenneth Wright noted that he himself 'would rather try people like Rawsthorne and Berkeley first' (i.e. before the 'peculiarly pungent' – that is to say, Stalinist – Christian Darnton*), as he felt that they were 'inherently more musical'. Arthur Bliss, soon to take over as Director of Music, returned a list 'in order of practicality', which put Walter Leigh and Arnold Cooke at the top, followed by Berkeley, Rawsthorne and Darnton.[27]

Meanwhile, without his knowing, because its deliberations were confidential, the BBC Music Advisory Panel (which assessed new compositions submitted for broadcast) put a spoke in Lennox's works.

*Christian Darnton (1905–81) was subsequently banned from the BBC as a Communist.

At its meeting in September the panel rejected his new *String Quartet No. 2* as 'eccentric and laboured',[28] and the following month it found fault with the *Impromptu for Organ*, which he had just written for his flamboyant Oxford friend Fr Colin Gill, 'on the occasion of his translation from Holborn to Brighton'. (Fr Gill had been a priest at the Church of St Alban the Martyr, hotbed of Ritualism and spiritual home to generations of young men of aesthetic sensibilities, since 1931; his new parish was St Martin's, Brighton, of which he remained vicar till 1960.) Herbert Murrill, no friend of Lennox, thought the *Impromptu* was 'rather angular and crude', and the volatile Clarence Raybould did not accept it as music at all, but an 'effusion' with 'no redeeming merit'. Furthermore, wrote Raybould, 'If this rubbish is included [in a broadcast of English music] *despite* these reports, I hope I shall not be asked to give any more opinions.'[29]

Invited or not, Raybould continued to volunteer his controversial opinions, and in December 1941 he again questioned Lennox's competence as a composer when the *String Quartet No. 2* came before the panel for a second assessment. Recording that he had 'no patience for such note-spinning', Raybould added that he had never yet come across 'a single page of real music from the pen of this composer'. Murrill thought the *Quartet* was 'cerebral ... rather tortured & cranky at times', and in March 1942 the composer Edmund Rubbra added his objections. But three months later when Arthur Bliss became Director of Music he overruled them all and agreed to a broadcast.[30] Thanks to the 2008 recording by the Maggini Quartet, we can now hear what Bliss must have foreseen – that the *Second Quartet*, together with the first and third quartets, would become 'landmarks in 20th century British chamber music'.[31]The Magginis, clearly inspired by all three Berkeley quartets, find in them a Ravelian Frenchness, together with a classical elegance that is always present, whether the music is dramatic, jazzy or sad. The group's second violin David Angel believes that they are all beautifully crafted, with a texture that is light and transparent: 'Berkeley is a definite master.'[32] His music has survived the scorn of Clarence Raybould.

When the still incomplete *Symphony No. 1* came before the panel in January and February 1942, the composer Sydney Peine Waddington described it as 'dry, laboured, without any sort of charm', Murrill thought it was 'thin and brittle' and Raybould could not 'get up the slightest interest in this sort of stuff ... We have suffered far too much *before* the war from effusions like this.'[33] (Despite his reservations about the *Symphony*, Raybould had to conduct its first broadcast performance in Bedford on 20 March 1944.)

Recalling these covert but significant machinations years later, Basil Douglas, who joined the music staff of the BBC in 1936, told Peter Dickinson that the music panel was comprised of 'a lot of grey-suited figures' who disapproved of anything to do with Britten. Ben, he said, was considered 'very off-colour at the time', and Lennox's music 'suffered from that connection'. According to Basil Douglas, Britten and Pears 'weren't quite right' in the eyes of BBC 'Head Office', and he himself incurred the displeasure of his superiors when he tried to help Ben and Peter on their return to England in April 1942. Basil Douglas said that Lennox 'wasn't looked after well' by the BBC during the war (though 'he got his fair share once William Glock arrived [as Controller, Music, in 1959]').[34] At the root of the problem, which, even half a century later, the decent and fair-minded Basil Douglas could only refer to in confusing euphemisms, lay a deep-seated prejudice amongst some BBC staff against both conscientious objectors and gay men. Their particular targets were Britten and Pears, Auden and Isherwood and what Raybould called the 'gang of young people who are dodging the country's call'. Though Lennox was not of course one of these, he was tainted by association. To the prejudiced Raybould, 'conchies', 'commies' and 'queers' were all the same, and he had 'the utmost contempt' for the whole bang shoot of them. When, later in the war, the dedicated pacifist Michael Tippett registered as a conscientious objector and was sent to prison for refusing to do ARP work or even farm work, Raybould's blood rose to the boil again. And in an internal memo he repeated his disgust of '... the gang ... of Conscientious (!) Objectors and general slackers', and expressed the view that the 'unbalanced adulation of one or two of these people is enough to make a normal person rather sick'.[35]

Lennox was unaware of these undercurrents as he applied for a staff job. By the end of October 1941 he had got in to the BBC, though the exact nature of his work was still to be decided as the Corporation tried him out in various corners of its rapidly growing empire. For the first week or so he was sent to the Monitoring Service at Evesham (and probably – though without their noticing – passed through the Administration office where Freda was working as a secretary, and the Italian Section, where his cousin Vonnie was employed as a translator).* Seeking more appropriate means of exploiting his fluency in French, the BBC posted Lennox back to London at the beginning of November, to the Overseas Music Department, which does not seem to have regarded itself as 'the right place' for him,[36] and in the last week of November he spent a few days with Sir Adrian Boult's Home Service Music Section, which had been evacuated to the relative safety of Bedford after the bombing raids on Bristol. (The Home Service was the flagship of BBC radio: it came on the air in 1939 and became Radio 4 in 1967; Boult had been Director of Music at the BBC, and conductor of the BBC Symphony Orchestra, since 1930.) By 2 December Lennox was back in London – this time in the French Section of the European Service, where he joined the campaign to raise the spirits of French listeners and propagate the idea of Liberation. It was good to be in London again, he said in a letter, but he was sorry not to be involved with music.[37] His sympathetic mentor, Dr (later Sir) Reginald Thatcher, Deputy Director of Music, threw him a lifeline on 6 December: 'If you feel that music tugs hard at you at any time, let me know.'[38] Lennox did not forget.

Thatcher's letter reached Lennox's desk on the day the Japanese bombed Pearl Harbor. The following day Britain and America declared war on Japan, and on the 11th Germany and Italy declared war on the USA. As the hostilities took on an increasingly global perspective that Christmas of 1941, Lennox dug in at the European Service, glad to be doing something for his beloved France. He found it very difficult to do without France, he told Nadia. Writing to her (in English, for a change), at the Peabody Conservatory in Baltimore, Maryland, where she was then teaching, he said that France was 'a part of one's life that has suddenly ceased to exist'. What she herself must feel in America he could not think, but he hoped that things would soon begin to change.[39]

The new year of 1942 brought word from Berkeley Castle that his Uncle Randal, 8th and last of the Earls of Berkeley, had died; he was seventy-seven. 'In his sleep', Molly, his widow, wrote in her memoirs (attributing his demise to the wrong month), he 'quietly slipped away'. This left her, she recalled, 'with the wind howling around the Castle,

*Yvonne Berkeley left the Monitoring Unit soon afterwards and went to work for the Hungarian journalist and anti-Communist campaigner Judith, Countess of Listowel, on her new weekly paper, the anti-Soviet *East Europe*.

the bombs screeching overhead, and this great sorrow in my heart'.[40] But perhaps the sorrow was not so terribly great, since, at the end of her book, she writes that if Berkeley (his late lordship, her 'Dear Old Camembert'), were now 'ramping around' Purgatory, then she was 'certainly sorry for Purgatory'.[41] The funeral was held four days later, on 19 January, and Lennox joined the widow and Randal's stepdaughter Sybil Jackson in the procession behind the coffin, which was borne by six tenant farmers, on its short journey to the mortuary chapel at the side of the minster church adjoining the castle. Though Randal was an agnostic, he was buried by the Bishop of Tewkesbury according to the rites of the Church of England.

If Lennox had any expectations of his unpredictable uncle they will have evaporated in the castle after the committal, when Randal's solicitor and joint executor Arthur Borrer, of Boodle, Hatfield, & Co., read the will. In a document running to no fewer than thirty-seven pages, there was not one single mention of Lennox or his sister Geraldine, or their cousins Claude and Yvonne Berkeley. For the grudge-bearing Randal, these, his closest relations, the only living descendants of his parents, simply did not exist. Instead, his estate (valued at £361,877. 1s.[42] – nearly £15m by 2008 standards) provided, amongst other bequests, annuities for Molly and Sybil, and a year's wages for those of Randal's staff who had worked for him for at least three years. The castle and its contents and lands were entrusted for life to a distant kinsman, his thirteenth cousin Captain Robert Berkeley, who was well qualified to run an estate, since he already owned Spetchley Park, a large Palladian house near Worcester.* And to make absolutely certain that Berkeley Castle should never revert to his own line, Randal willed that if Robert Berkeley died without issue the place was to pass, in turn, to each of Robert Berkeley's brothers, then to the sons of each of Robert Berkeley's five uncles, and finally to the sons of Robert Berkeley's father's six male cousins and their issue. It was all very methodically drawn up to cause maximum hurt to the memory of his brother Hastings, with whom he had quarrelled over the height of a hedge thirty years before; it was also a deliberate rejection of his mother Cécile's dying appeal to his 'feelings of duty & justice' to 'help & protect your brothers'.[43] For Hastings's sake Lennox must have felt hurt; for his own, it is likely that he was no more than dismayed at such comprehensive vindictiveness. That the will also

*He was also a cricketer who played four first-class games for Worcestershire.

contained an instruction prohibiting any religious service anywhere in the castle except the Norman chapel for a period of twenty-one years from the death of any survivor of any issue then living of her late Majesty Queen Victoria, on forfeit of the castle itself, must have convinced Lennox that his uncle had long ago taken leave of his senses.[44]

Molly, left with nothing but a dowager's coronet, a generous annuity and several houses dotted about the world, took out her 'guts', she reveals alarmingly in her autobiography *Beaded Bubbles*, and 'started polishing them up'.[45] Within a month she had vacated the castle to make way for its new chatelaine, the Hon. Mrs (Myrtle) Berkeley, wife of the distant cousin Robert – just as Sybil Jackson had had to move out for Molly eighteen years earlier. For the rest of the war the Dowager Countess of Berkeley looked after wounded American soldiers as a sort of volunteer fairy godmother at the American Red Cross Club in Jermyn Street. There she converted to Catholicism, and after a vision of the Virgin Mary at the Cenacle Convent at Grayshott in Hampshire, she felt called to adopt twelve Italian shoeshine boys orphaned by the war. Advised that a dozen might be a bit of a handful for a woman in her sixties, she reduced her requisition to three, acquiring them from the Red Cross in Rome, 'rather as if ordering a brace of partridges from Harrods',[46] and bringing them up in an orphanage in the garden of her spectacular convent-villa on a hilltop above Assisi. (Nuns were still in occupation when she bought the place, as a half-ruin, before the war, but her architect, Cecil Pinsent, told her she could not possibly live there 'with these nuns hovering around', so she complained to the bishop and had them all evicted.[47]) One of the orphans, a hell-raiser called Vittorio Manunta, became the child star of the 1951 film classic *Never Take No for an Answer*, creating a winning urchin, but terrorizing the cast and crew with his sometimes violent tantrums. Molly admitted he was 'hard to handle', and sent him to be tamed at Downside, the Catholic public school in Somerset.[48]

Randal's calculated renunciation of his family not only created ill-will between Lennox and the new Berkeleys at the castle, but it also – so she claimed – bothered Molly. Often and emphatically in the years that followed, she promised Lennox that she intended to put right the wrongs that Randal had done. But she never quite got round to it. Following her death in Assisi in 1975, her will expressed the wish that her godson Julian Berkeley, Lennox's middle son, was to receive the income from her English properties – but only after her three orphan wards and their issue had enjoyed it for their lifetimes, which reduced the bequest to no more than a gesture. Molly's son Francis Lloyd Jr generously attempted to make amends by giving Julian the baroque Swiss house-organ in Molly's villa in Assisi – or, at any rate, what was left of it after years of depredation by the orphans.*

After the wayward will of his uncle, Lennox cannot have been surprised by the sting that Molly left in the tail of hers. At her specific request, the executors – Lennox among them – were to collect her body from Assisi and fly it back for burial beside Randal at Berkeley Castle. The family tomb was then to be permanently sealed, so that 'the body of no other person whomsoever shall thereafter be placed in that tomb'[49] – not even, when his time came, Lennox himself, the senior male Berkeley of the castle line. It is not clear why Molly left this high-handed instruction – or how, without being a Berkeley herself, she was able to – unless she were carrying out Randal's own private wishes. It certainly did not ease family tensions.

After the mixed emotions aroused by Randal's funeral, together with the malevolence of his will and the general gloom of the castle, Lennox was glad to get back to London in that January of 1942. But he was not happy at his new job as a talks producer in the BBC's French Section, based in Bush House at the bottom of Kingsway. He was proud to be part of a team that was playing an important part in rallying the French to resist the Nazis, and he knew the work was effective: Hitler's propaganda minister, Joseph Goebbels, was so daunted by the success of the BBC's overseas services that he referred to 'the intellectual invasion of the continent by British radio'.[50] But after only six weeks Lennox was finding that music was already tugging hard, as Dr Thatcher had anticipated. Not only was he missing the sounds and people of the musical world, but he began to realize that he could serve his country more usefully in a musical capacity. Convinced, like Kenneth Wright of the BBC, that 'Music can play such a role in this war as few people dream',[51] he saw the packed concert halls of wartime London as a sign that music was more important than ever,[52] and he was eager to help the BBC Music Department to meet the national need.

*This beautiful instrument, built by Josef Looser in 1786, was expertly restored, at Julian Berkeley's expense, by Edward Bennett of the Nottinghamshire organ builders, Goetze & Gwynn, in 1988, and is now in the safe-keeping of the Shrine to Music Museum at Vermillion, South Dakota.

Clutching at Thatcher's lifeline, Lennox wrote to ask if there might be a place for him in Music – based in London, if possible, so that he would not have to leave his flat in Bloomsbury. Since Sir Adrian Boult had been looking for someone to take over the administration of the BBC Symphony Orchestra, so that he himself could concentrate on conducting, Lennox's offer was snapped up.[53] He was offered a staff position, subject to satisfactory references and positive vetting, on a salary of about £12 a week,* and by the beginning of March he was settled in the new job. But it was not in London. Alerting his agent Douglas Gibson, of J. & W. Chester (by then his main publisher), in a letter from 16 St Andrew's Road, Bedford, Lennox wrote: 'As you see from the above address the very thing I feared has come to pass. However it is not too bad as the work is interesting.'[54]

Lennox's job was to plan orchestral concert programmes, with Herbert Murrill, in a big office in one of a pair of private hotels in Bushmead Avenue commandeered by Boult for the administration of the evacuated BBC Symphony Orchestra. With his wide knowledge of the repertoire, Lennox was invaluable, and, according to Boult's devoted secretary, Mrs Gwen Beckett, 'he quickly absorbed the work of running a great orchestra', attending all the rehearsals and concerts (which were held in the Great Hall of Bedford School, with the boys peeping down from the gallery, or in the Corn Exchange), and lifting 'much of a heavy burden from Sir Adrian's shoulders'.[55]

Despite Lennox's forebodings, Bedford was close enough to London for him to get home at weekends, so that he could catch up with his friends at the Reform on Saturday nights, and spend time with Aircraftman Peter Fraser on his occasional reappearances from various undisclosed air bases around the British Isles. 'In spite of everything', Lennox told Nadia, 'my life hasn't changed very much',[56] but the real problem with Bedford, he told Gibson of Chester's, was that all scores submitted for broadcast were sent to his office, and as the BBC was 'rather against giving things by people on the staff', he anticipated that it was going to be difficult to get his own work on the air.[57]

While Lennox was settling in to the new job in Bedford in the spring of 1942, Ben Britten and Peter Pears arrived back from America. They had been away for a little over three years, and Ben in particular had been

*These were the terms offered in May 1941 to Louis MacNeice (J. Stallworthy, *Louis MacNeice*, p. 297).

getting increasingly homesick. After registering as conscientious objectors in May, Peter was fully exempted from military service but Ben was required to serve in some non-combatant role. Ben appealed, on the grounds that his religious background made it as impossible to support a war as to fight it, and a second Tribunal granted him unconditional exemption. Having given up the lease on the flat in Hallam Street, Ben went to live at the Mill, which was still his, and Peter stayed with his parents in Barnes, while both attempted to pull their lives together.

On a visit to London in June, Ben re-established contact with Wulff Scherchen, who was also back in Britain, as a lance-corporal in the Auxiliary Military Pioneer Corps (for friendly aliens). He found that, after six months in an internment camp in Canada and another eighteen months of army life in Britain, Wulff was – not surprisingly – 'rather altered, I am afraid'. Quite apart from being twenty-two, and too old to interest Ben any longer, Wulff seemed to Ben's now cold eye, 'rather vindictive, and hard'.[58] He was forgetting that, unlike his own experience in America, Wulff had not had an easy three years of war. He had been arrested as an alien, shipped abroad and forced to live in a prison camp, his university career had been wrecked, he had been separated from his mother and abandoned by the one person he loved most. Perhaps Ben never realized what he meant to Wulff (or to Lennox, or to anyone else he had cast off). In letters from his Army base near Bristol in the summer of 1941, Wulff spelled out what he now felt. He still, sometimes, longed for Ben – 'not in terms of a marvellous past ... rather on a footing of myself as a different person, more grown-up, more secure and stripped of a number of illusions'.[59] Two months later, in a further letter, Wulff explained that though he had grown up at a tremendous rate, he was still in a 'very inchoate and amorphous state as far as myself is concerned', but he was slowly building up a personality of his own, and 'all of me wants to see you'. When he had lost Ben he had lost half of himself, 'for you were my first friend and the hours we spent together were and are the happiest and best of my life. I still feel that we are bound by a tie that is so lasting and deep nothing not even separation ... can depreciate its particular values.'[60]

Ben and Wulff met once or twice more that summer of 1942, but the intimacy had gone. To the fickle Ben, Wulff was now 'completely unbearable'. Though he had been through 'a hell of a time',[61] he was still 'an awfully sweet boy' underneath,[62] and 'looking very pretty', but Ben realized with a shock that he had 'grown completely away from him';[63] the best thing that could happen to Wulff, he thought, was to find the right girl and get married.[64] In fact Wulff had already found the right girl, Pauline Woolford, and on 10 October 1943 he married her: indeed she was so right that sixty-five years later, and living by then in Australia, they were still happily married.* Pauline had joined the WAAF at the outbreak of war and was now serving as a radio operator. Wulff had left the Pioneer Corps to join the Royal Engineers in bomb disposal and was required to change his German name in case he was captured by the Nazis,[65] so he adopted Pauline's surname and the new first name of John. The love affair with Ben was over, but John Woolford could never forget a friendship that had played such a significant role in his path to manhood, and, though he received only sporadic replies, he continued to write till Ben's death in 1976.

Once they had got through the ordeal of their Tribunal cases, Ben and Peter prepared to celebrate their return home – and, for those in the know, to celebrate their relationship – with the first public performance of Ben's *Seven Sonnets of Michelangelo*, at a Boosey & Hawkes chamber concert at the Wigmore Hall in London on 23 September. The two-year-old work was an immediate success. Edward Sackville-West, writing in the *New Statesman and Nation*, called it the finest collection of chamber songs England had produced since the seventeenth century. He praised Peter Pears too: it had been years since he had heard an English tenor with a voice 'at once so strong, so pure and so sweet'.[66] Julian Herbage of the BBC, who had heard the cycle in rehearsal, thought America had done Ben good: he had 'grown greatly in stature as a composer' and 'one looks for most important if not great things in the future'.[67] Lennox's old Marshfield friend John Davenport was 'rhapsodic', and Ben wondered, rather spitefully, whether this might have been 'a little to Lennox's disappointment??',[68] which could not have been further from the truth, since Lennox was still, and always would be, Britten's most ardent fan. Indeed he told Boulanger that the new songs were 'of the utmost beauty'. He knew she did not like all Britten's work, but she would find it impossible not to be moved by these.[69] And he told Ben, after listening to several more performances,

*On 10 October 2008, 'trundling along happily whilst coping with the challenges of daily life as best we can', John and Pauline Woolford celebrated their sixty-fifth wedding anniversary at home in Queensland with a party of twenty family and friends, including some of their four children, nine grandchildren and seven great-grandchildren (email, WS to TS, 9 October 2008).

that they sounded 'more beautiful every time. I shall never tire of them ...'[70] Inspired by the *Michelangelo Sonnets*, Lennox wrote a pair of new songs specially for Peter: one, *Lullaby*, with a text by Yeats, the other, *The Ecstatic*, a poem by C. Day Lewis.

On a personal level, the Wigmore concert will have left Lennox in no doubt not only that he and Ben were finished, but that Ben and Peter were now a firm, and public, partnership. Within six months they had moved into a flat in St John's Wood High Street, at the start of a 'marriage' that was to last till Ben's death in 1976. But, come what may, Lennox never veered from his belief in Ben. Behind the scenes he worked hard to get the *Michelangelo Sonnets* broadcast on the BBC, despite the powerful lobby opposed to Ben, and the following summer he was able to tell his old friend that he had succeeded: 'I've at last got them to fix a provisional date for the *Michelangelo Sonnets*, in the Home Service – you will be hearing about this soon, but don't say anything about it to anyone until you do, as technically it has nothing to do with me.'[71] (The broadcast took place on 20 July 1943.)

For his first couple of months in Bedford, Lennox had felt obliged to put his composing on one side, but then in April Arthur Bliss had replaced Boult as Director of Music and, regarding it as 'his national duty to present a bigger proportion of British music',[72] he had commissioned Lennox to write a new piece for Section C of the BBC Symphony Orchestra. 'Only a very small fee alas!' Lennox told his publisher, 'but at least it will be played! (If I have time to write it).'[73] What emerged, a year later, was the *Divertimento for Small Orchestra*, which was to prove one of his popular successes.

Despite the pressure of his BBC work, which now absorbed even his free time,[74] Lennox was able to complete his long-overdue *Symphony No. 1* in May 1942. Tautly-structured, sunny and fresh, this is no epic brow-beater of the Beethoven kind, but a happy symphony in the manner of Haydn.* The waltz of the second movement is particularly youthful and carefree, recalling happy times with Ben and Peter Burra in 1936 and 1937; the third, tragic movement must reflect the war, whatever Lennox later said; and the finale provides a brave note of what Kathleen Walker has identified as 'Churchillian defiance'.[75] Because of the

*In 2001 the BBC National Orchestra of Wales, conducted by Richard Hickox, produced a definitive recording of the *Symphony No. 1* – as vol. i, *The Berkeley Edition*, Chandos Records CHAN 9981.

war, the symphony had to wait a year for a performance, but the premiere was all the better for the delay. It was finally programmed in the 1943 Proms in the new venue of the Albert Hall (before it became Royal), in a concert that featured Benno Moiseiwitsch playing Rachmaninov's *Piano Concerto No. 3*. Lennox himself conducted the London Philharmonic Orchestra. Recalling the impact of that first performance, the critic Ronald Crichton wrote, forty-six years later, that the 'unassertive yet memorable opening [of the first movement] seemed in wartime like a shy assertion of faith in permanent values in danger of being overlooked'.[76] Roger Nichols believes the whole symphony is 'an outright success', containing 'many passages of great beauty', while the last movement is 'one of the best British symphony finales of the last [i.e. twentieth] century: tuneful, exciting and fun'.[77]

The Times welcomed the new *Symphony* as 'an enormous advance' on anything Lennox had written before, a really important turning-point in his career:

> The process of clarifying his style, which had been confused by his studies in the cosmopolitan school of Paris, has been going on for some time, and it now appears that he has absorbed what was good in it and has emerged with the typically French virtues of logic, lucidity, and a light touch ... Here [in the *Symphony*] was something new and original without the outlandishness, perversity or strain which sometimes marked the composer's earlier works ...[78]

The music critic Desmond Shawe-Taylor, who was probably the author of the *Times* notice, said a few years later that the aim of the new *Symphony* had been 'neither to impress nor to argue, but simply to give pleasure to the cultivated ear',[79] which pretty well sums up the modest but musicianly purpose of all Lennox's work for the concert hall – and the proudly elitist objective of Lord Reith's vision for the BBC. Yet the programme note for the 1943 premiere suggested the *Symphony* was 'recondite'. This amazed Lennox, who told Shawe-Taylor that the writer of the note, Scott Goddard, was 'quite crazy – I thought at first he must have mixed up my work with something else ... Those who, having read their programmes, had settled down to listen to something rather inscrutable must have been surprised!'[80]

For all the praise, Lennox himself was not altogether pleased with his first *Symphony*. He told Nadia that the Proms performance had gone quite well, but the work had been conceived two years ago and he thought he could do better now.[81] Perhaps Sir Henry Wood was disappointed too, because, in a note to the BBC about new commissions which he hoped to see in the following year's Proms, he listed five Bs – Bliss, Britten, Bantock, Bax and Bush – but no Berkeley.[82] Maybe Sir Henry thought that Lennox had had his turn. But then so had Ben. Just two nights after Lennox's *Symphony*, Ben and Clifford Curzon gave the British premiere of Britten's *Scottish Ballad for Two Pianos and Orchestra* and *The Times* panned it: 'Here for once Britten's fertility and resources have misguided him.'[83]

Later that same summer of 1943 Lennox completed the piece which Boult had commissioned in Bedford a year earlier, the four-movement *Divertimento*. As light and charming as a symphony by the boy Mozart, and as compact as Nadia Boulanger (to whom it is dedicated) could have wished,[84] the *Divertimento* is a work of such technical excellence that it is often used as a model of orchestral writing for composition students. As promised, the BBC broadcast it from Bedford on 1 October. A fortnight later it was given its first concert performance in another Boosey & Hawkes programme at the Wigmore Hall that also included Britten's *Serenade for Tenor, Horn and Strings*. The 'Orchestral Ensemble' was conducted by Walter Goehr, and Dennis Brain and Peter Pears were Ben's soloists (and dedicatees). A programme note explained that the title of Lennox's piece was 'to be taken in its literal or classical sense', and added, lest anyone in the audience might be tempted to slip away before the concert started: 'It is light and easy to listen to, which brings it into line with the Strings [*sic*] Serenade of 1940 rather than with the composer's more austere works.'[85]

The implicit defensiveness seems to suggest that the promoters feared the name Berkeley was still too closely associated with the disastrous *Jonah* of seven years earlier. With *Jonah* Lennox had tried to shake off a reputation for salon music – but the pendulum swung too far the other way, and ever since then Lennox had been regarded (in the BBC particularly) as a spiky modernist. Now at last he had found his feet, as *The Times* acknowledged in an unsigned notice on the 16th. Berkeley, it said, had now escaped from the influences which had begun to confuse Stravinsky's style. The new piece was 'deft and pretty in its carpentry and orchestration, and happy in many of its ideas'; it pleased with wit and ingenuity. Ben won the same sort of cordial reviews for his *Serenade*, and Lennox's old Marshfield friend William Glock, writing in *The Observer*, said Britten was a composer who offered visions as great as those of Brahms. The *Serenade* surpassed his previous works in strength and feeling. For this and the *Michelangelo Sonnets* the friendship of Pears and Britten should be blessed. Glock said the *Serenade* should be recorded without delay, and the BBC 'should see that the country is made aware of its new masterpiece'.[86]

This came as no surprise to Lennox, who had never had any doubts about Britten's abilities. When Ben's *String Quartet No. 1* was broadcast on the Home Service earlier in the year, Lennox had written a preview in *The Listener*, which gave him the opportunity not only to champion Ben's music in public, but take on their joint critics. While Ben's mastery of the technique of composition was now admitted by all, he wrote, the apparent ease with which he solved technical problems had been criticized, 'as though a high standard of professional competence were undesirable'. This, wrote Lennox, was based on the suspicion that Britten's astonishing technique was nothing more than slickness, and that his music lacked depth. Britten was an extremely traditional composer with a profound understanding of the classical masters. His music brought release from the outworn image, from every kind of cliché, from easy gestures that had become meaningless. 'The novelty of his music does not consist in any new discovery of musical language or form. He relies on the freshness and individuality of his musical thought rather than on deliberate innovation. True originality in an artist does not consist in his being peculiar, but in his being peculiar to himself.'[87]

If Lennox meant by 'peculiar to himself' being true to himself, that same honesty in Ben's music was a potent attraction for Eddy Sackville-West, who had formed a romantic passion for Ben after hearing the *Michelangelo Sonnets*, and was soon writing extravagantly lyrical letters. One of these began, 'My dear White Child', and ended, 'Good-night, my dear. A thousand blessings on your head ... My love as always, Eddy.'[88] In another letter Sackville-West told Britten he was 'a heavenly genius and potentially the greatest composer of the new era'.[89] His biographer Michael De-la-Noy suggests Sackville-West needed 'a new love object on which to focus his frustrated emotions' following the end of a masochistic affair with Sir Paul Latham, MP for Scarborough, who was now serving a prison sentence for 'sexually assaulting' his batman.[90] And presumably the more one-sided the better, since humiliation seems to have been Sackville-West's thing. In Berlin some years before, he had met a young man 'with more S.A. [sex appeal] than anyone I've ever seen', who had led him down a dark street on a dog-lead. It was so deliciously exciting, he told his friend, the critic Raymond Mortimer, that he had 'nearly expired with ecstasy'.[91]

Whether or not it was Lennox who brought Ben together with Eddy Sackville-West, whom he had met with Raymond Mortimer in Paris before the war, the association was to prove fruitful for all four men. In the early summer of 1943, Sackville-West and Stephen Potter were planning a radio anthology of modern French music and poetry, to be called *The Living Spirit of France*, and they invited Mortimer to choose the poems (which were read by Valentine Dyall and Peggy Ashcroft), Lennox to choose and arrange the music by Debussy and Poulenc, and Ben and Peter to perform it. Potter regarded the programme as part of his crusade to popularize the arts through the radio. He acknowledged that such a feature had only minority appeal, but he was keen to make the point that the minority he had in mind was not a highbrow one: he was not interested in 'Superior Man' or the 'Bloomsbury intelligentsia' – he hoped to reach 'the discriminating listener, who wants the best'. And the best, he boasted proudly in *Radio Times*, was there in *The Living Spirit of France*, created by specialists and 'connoisseurs' men'.[92]

The choice of singer and pianist did not meet with the approval of the Director of Music. At a meeting about the new feature a few weeks before it was broadcast, Arthur Bliss saw their names on a billing and threw up his arms in horror. 'Peter Pears and Benjamin Britten?' he queried dramatically, 'Really! This does *not* sound right.' And according to Potter's lively diary, Bliss was no less censorious about the music they were performing: Debussy and Poulenc? Les Six? Why, if these composers were not actually collaborationists, they were certainly old hat, hang-overs from the France of the Twenties – nothing but 'niggling, charming art-for-art-sakers'. These objections did not cut much ice with Laurence Gilliam, Head of Features, who reminded his colleague pretty sharply that he had seen the names coming up through all the preliminary discussions and had expressed no objection then. But that, according to Potter, was Bliss: his performance was not meant to be taken seriously – it was just 'a pretty piece of Blissing'.[93]

Sackville-West used Britten again – in November, as composer of background music, interludes and songs for his radio drama *The Rescue*, based on Homer's *Odyssey* – so he cannot have taken Bliss's criticism seriously either. A pianist himself, he recognized and revered Britten's worth as both performer and composer; and, as literary adviser, he helped him choose texts for the festival cantata, *Rejoice in the Lamb*, and the *Serenade for Tenor, Horn and Strings*. In return, Ben dedicated the beautiful *Serenade* to him. On 16 November 1942 Sackville-West and Ben collaborated as pianists to play Schubert and Chopin on two keyboards at a concert at Whistler's House in Chelsea. Peter sang the Schumann *Dichterliebe* and Ben's *Michelangelo Sonnets*, and James Lees-Milne reported in his diary that 'Everyone said what a good concert this was' (though he himself was 'so ignorant' he could only judge music emotionally).[94]

Ben was soon to lose not only his patience with Sackville-West's cloying devotion, but his faith in his literary usefulness. When looking for a librettist for *Peter Grimes* the following spring, he wrote to Peter Pears, 'Eddy[?] – well, perhaps; let's see how *The Rescue* turns out – I doubt whether he again [i.e. like Montagu Slater] is a good enough poet, whether he isn't too pretentious ...' And it was not only Sackville-West and Slater he criticized, he thought Auden was not right either, and he did not think he could work with MacNeice.*[95] Ben may have chopped and changed his friends and collaborators, but Lennox did not. Nor had he complained in early 1940 when his turn came and Ben dropped him too (by writing no more letters till he was back in England in 1942). He simply continued a one-way correspondence, clinging to what was left of the friendship, and accepting it gratefully. A little of Ben was better than none at all.

Ben was not the only composer whose cudgels Lennox took up in 1943, from his influential position as a BBC programme builder. In March he heard Louis Kentner and his wife Ilona Kabos playing the *Sonata for Two Pianos and Percussion* by Béla Bartók and wrote to Julian Herbage, then Assistant Director of Music, urging a broadcast. This, he said, was 'music of the first order, and one of the most important pieces of recent years.' Herbage begged to differ. Citing the *Sonata*'s ISCM performance in 1938 which had been considered 'pretty stiff going even by those without an antipathy to contemporary music,' Herbage took the view that a broadcast was likely to 'evoke rather more criticism than interest'.[96]

Lennox also – and courageously – lobbied for the maverick composer Michael Tippett. At the height of the BBC's unofficial campaign against conscientious objectors, he arranged a broadcast of the *Fantasia on a Theme of Handel* for July 1943. 'This is my third

*In the event, Britten stuck with Slater.

attempt to get it in,' he wrote to Tippett in early June, 'so I hope that nothing will go wrong.'[97] It did: Tippett was sent to prison for refusing to do even non-combatant war work. But, with Bliss's support, the *Handel Fantasia* was finally broadcast on 22 October, by which time the composer was a free man again. Lennox was much impressed and told Nadia that Tippett was 'doing very fine work – it is very original and you would be most interested.' Though Tippett was thirty-eight and had been writing for a long time, it was his recent work that Lennox thought so remarkable. ('I think it is in some ways a good sign to develop slowly in this way.'[98]) The following year Lennox and Ben attended the London premiere of Tippett's oratorio *A Child of Our Time*. Having already read the score, Ben knew that it was 'a grand work'. Lennox thought that it had 'much real beauty', but that it was 'not easy to assimilate from one hearing'. He had a feeling that it might lapse into hysteria at any moment, but this was only a first impression, and it was marvellous to find an English composer besides Ben who could write 'living music'.[99]

Ben had first met Tippett with Peter Pears at a concert at Morley College (for working men and women) in South London the previous year. Ben thought Tippett was 'an *excellent* composer, & [a] most delightful & intelligent man',[100] and Tippett thought Ben an astonishing pianist – 'the music simply spurted out of his fingers',[101] and he envied his technical fluency as a composer.[102] Tippett did not like everything Ben wrote or the subjects he wrote about, but he thought he was the only composer of the time who was 'worth watching'.[103] By the end of 1942 they were all good friends, and Ben had become a 'decisive and beloved personality in Tippett's life'.[104]

From the beginning of January 1943 Lennox had been back in London, doing the same job with the Home Service Music Section at 35 Marylebone High Street as he had been doing in Bedford, but working now with Basil Douglas rather than Herbert Murrill. He was so relieved to be away from Bedford that he told Ben he had been 'transformed – I mean transferred (genuine mistake!)'.[105] Basil Douglas, a 'dogged administrator',[106] who had known Lennox since before the war (when Douglas shared a flat with Trevor Harvey and Peter Pears), had not expected to find Lennox so practical in his approach to programme making. He knew that his 'knowledge was tremendous', but he was 'really very pleasantly surprised' at his efficiency. Lennox's catholic tastes led the orchestra down some unexpected paths – some 'underrated and under-performed French music', for example, and certain schools of music which might not have been featured if he had not been there – 'not Mahler, Bruckner or Schoenberg: Lennox's musical sympathies lay with clearer, less emotional writing.' (Lennox said years later that he had been allowed to programme contemporary music – 'but not too much or it would depress people'.)[107] As a singer himself, Basil Douglas often asked Lennox to play for him, and he was delighted to discover that he made a very good accompanist. As he got to know him better he grew to appreciate him as 'a very lovable person', modest and fun, with an infectious giggle that was often aimed 'at the powers that be and their foibles'.[108]

The child in Lennox enjoyed practical jokes, not only those of others, but his own too. Whatever the source, a good joke would set him chuckling, his appreciation showing first in a brightness of the eyes, then spreading to his tongue which pressed itself against his cheek, before the lips parted in a smile. He rarely laughed out loud, but giggled quietly to himself. It might only be something silly, like a funny-sounding word, or a rude noise, or a fruity chord of the kind that Poulenc liked. Poking fun at pomposity was what he enjoyed – nothing malicious, just a bit of mild sedition, something, as he would have said, 'a little naughty'. It seemed to suggest that he did not often break any rules, but would quite like to. Years later he became a fan of the BBC television programmes *Dad's Army* and *The Two Ronnies*. But in the spring of 1943 he created his own situation comedy. He started a rumour that the Marxist composer Alan Bush was writing an opera based on the newly-published Beveridge Report on Social Insurance (the famous blueprint for the welfare state, 'from the cradle to the grave').[109] Since Bush was a card-carrying member of the Communist Party whose music was more or less banned by the BBC (both then and till the end of Glock's time in 1972), and since the wartime BBC was controlled by a government which had commissioned the Beveridge Report, this was a well-judged piece of political subversion from the artistic sidelines, which must have caused a mild disturbance for a week or two, both at Broadcasting House and at 10 Downing Street, where Churchill's coalition cabinet was split over Beveridge's revolutionary plan. And if the rumour reached Bush himself, it may have raised a wry smile, as he filed away the index cards in the outpatients department at the military hospital at Millbank, where he was doing his war service as an army clerk.

25
Warwick Square, London, 1941–4

It was about this time that Lennox was bombed out of the flat he shared with Peter Fraser and John Greenidge in Great Ormond Street. It happened between the beginning of October 1942 and the middle of July 1943, probably in the raids that began on 18 January. None of the three was hurt and only John Greenidge lost any belongings, because Lennox's furniture was still at the Mill, and Peter did not have any. John moved out to his country cottage at Kettering in Northamptonshire, and commuted into London, where he continued to work for one of the government ministries; Lennox – with an occasional Peter, recently commissioned as a pilot officer, and soon to be promoted to flying officer[1] – was taken in by a sympathetic friend and admirer, Douglas Gordon, a parliamentary clerk, who had a house in Coulson Street, just off the King's Road.

From his new base in Chelsea, Lennox was able to catch up on the social life he had missed in Bedford. In particular he was a regular visitor at 55 Park Lane, where the exiled Princess Winnie was sharing a small flat in a block next door to the Dorchester with her latest and last young lover, the proud and beautiful Alvilde Chaplin (estranged wife of the zoologist, composer and former Boulanger pupil, Anthony Chaplin). The two women had been living together – first in Paris, then in exile in Devon and now in London – since Alvilde left her husband in the summer of 1939. But, for the sake of appearances, Anthony Chaplin (now a flight lieutenant in the RAF Volunteer Reserve) was still very much in evidence – along with his pet boa constrictor; by 1949 he had added to the household a toad in a chamber pot, a menagerie of lizards and frogs in cardboard boxes, and a mistress.[2]

Lennox was pleased to be reunited with an old friend from the rue Ballu. Chaplin, he thought, had behaved splendidly by joining RAF Bomber Command as a gunner, when he hated every minute of it and could so easily have done something less dangerous – but he was 'one of those who can only be content with what is best and finest'. The problem was that he did have rather extreme views about music, and though

Lennox, like Chaplin, was devoted to the sixteenth-century composers and Scarlatti, he did not see why that meant, as Chaplin held, that Beethoven and all the romantics should be consigned to the scrapheap.[3]

Another regular visitor at 55 Park Lane was James Lees-Milne, young Turk of the National Trust, who had just begun writing the brilliant diaries that were to make his name many years later. Jim was amused by Anthony Chaplin, with whom he delighted in talking 'arrant nonsense',[4] and much impressed by Alvilde, who was highly intelligent, decisive (even imperious), elegant and altogether redoubtable. On the down side, Alvilde was bossy and fussy, sensitive to criticism, and impatient with inefficiency, hesitancy and hopelessness – which tested both Lennox and Jim.[5] (When the latter fell in love with her ten years later, a mutual friend described her as 'that hard little thing'.[6]) Princess Winnie, now seventy-eight years old, looked to Jim 'rather like a large Buddha', and spoke in English laced with French. There was something godlike and 'very Faubourg Saint-Germain' about her, he said.[7] Terrified of the air-raids, she used to sit in the passage outside her flat on a milking stool till the bombers had gone.[8] According to Lennox, the old lady was suffering not only from acute angina but also from home-sickness for her family and possessions in France. She felt this separation very much, Lennox said: at her age it was a real trial.[9]

Princesse de Polignac had become as much of a celebrity for her early associations with Marcel Proust as for her generous and discerning support of modern music, and the young lions of London – Stephen Spender, Raymond Mortimer, James Pope-Hennessy – fought for invitations to meet her. But it was clear that she was now very ill. When Jim Lees-Milne dined with her on 24 November 1943, he recorded that she moved slowly and sedately, and her 'remarkable face, like some mountainous crag, was sunset pink' from shortness of breath.[10] The following night she had a heart attack at Sibyl Colefax's house on the King's Road, while listening to Ben's incidental music for Eddy Sackville-West's drama *The Rescue* on the BBC Home Service. She had another attack at home a few hours later, and died almost immediately, with Alvilde close at hand. A Requiem Mass was held at the Jesuit Church in Farm Street on 1 December, at which Peter Pears sang the 'Benedictus' from Bach's *B Minor Mass* and the 'In Paradisum' from Fauré's *Requiem*. (Peter had met the *princesse* with Ben at a luncheon at the Café Royal organized by Alvilde in 1942, at Lennox's suggestion.)

A week before the *princesse* died, Lennox had dined with John

Greenidge to celebrate John's election as a Fellow of the Royal Institute of British Architects, and on 22 November he may have attended Ben's thirtieth birthday party, with the Slaters and Clifford Curzon and a dozen other friends. But if he was invited, he was only an afterthought. Writing to Peter beforehand, with a list of proposed guests, Ben wrote: 'Any more? I can't remember. (Berkeley?).'[11] This seems to sum up Lennox's place in Ben's new life: more out than in.

Irked by his taking up politically incorrect causes and spreading subversive rumours, Lennox's bosses at the BBC seem to have taken much the same view of his attitude to work: less in than out. His annual confidential report, written by his immediate superior Julian Herbage, in the autumn of 1943, noted that his work 'tends to suffer as his private activities as a composer increase'.[12] There may have been some truth in this. The pianist Colin Horsley, who was to become one of Lennox's favourite interpreters, recalled that Lennox used to keep his own private work in the bottom drawer of his desk in the Music Department office in Marylebone High Street, so he could compose whenever the coast was clear.[13] Furthermore, it was felt that 'Berkeley does not seem to have settled down to office routine'.[14] Doubtless this was true too, because Lennox was not an office person, nor indeed a BBC person. But it is difficult not to read into these private memos a certain resentment of his private work as a composer. The Senior Arts Assistant, Music, H. Vowles, informed the Director of Music, Arthur Bliss, at the beginning of December, that even though Lennox had been notified of the contents of his report, 'I have discovered from ADM (Progs) [Julian Herbage] that things are not showing the signs of improvement that we had hoped.'[15]

It is possible that the stream of works Lennox was submitting to the BBC Music Advisory Panel for broadcast approval was giving the wrong impression. Not that it got him very far, but it was a bit tactless, since he was on the BBC staff, and even the more generous of his fellow composers on the panel did not really like it. When asked to assess Lennox's *Sonatina for Violin and Piano* in September 1943, William Walton hoped that other members of the music staff would not start sending in their compositions, 'as it is slightly embarrassing for us to be put in the position of turning them down, as is necessary in this case. No offence meant & I hope none taken!'[16] At this stage in the war Walton was working for the Ministry of Information, writing scores for patriotic films, such as *The First of the Few* and Laurence Olivier's version of *Henry V*. (He and Lennox had known one another since before the war and were to become closer friends later in their lives.) The older composer John Ireland agreed with Walton's point about staff composing: '... one is placed in rather an invidious position if one has to appraise works by members of the BBC programme builders. Without prejudice!'[17] Gordon Jacob thought that much of the *Sonatina* was needlessly perverse, with 'a depressing air of preciosity about it', but Herbert Howells liked it: 'much charm ... immediately attractive',[18] and when the piece came before the panel again in 1945 Mosco Carner recommended its 'spontaneous charm'.[19]*

The difficulties of getting his own work broadcast encouraged Lennox to look elsewhere for commissions, and, like Walton, but for different reasons, he now turned to films. Just before Christmas 1943 he was asked, at very short notice, to write the music for *Hotel Reserve*, based on Eric Ambler's thriller *Epitaph for a Spy*. It is about a shy Austrian medical student called Peter Vadassy (in the book, a 'Hungarian' language teacher called Josef Vadassy), whose holiday snaps of lizards print up to reveal hidden guns protecting the naval port of Toulon. Accused of spying for the Nazis, he manages to persuade the police that he is innocent, but unless he can unmask the real villain among the other guests at the luxurious Hotel Reserve where he is staying on the Riviera, he could face a death sentence. Victor Hanbury directed the film for RKO Radio Pictures, James Mason starred as the hero Vadassy, and the screenplay was by John Davenport, who may have had a hand in suggesting Lennox as composer.

It was a tough assignment: he had to write the full score – all forty-seven minutes of it – in three weeks. 'I don't think it is good to write as quickly regularly,' he told Nadia, 'but it does no harm – except make one very tired – to have to do it occasionally.' Lennox must have mentioned film music to Nadia in previous letters, and she had clearly expressed a certain disapproval, because in this letter, dated 25 January 1944, he went on to say that it was not necessary for a composer to lower his standards when writing film music, but merely to use an easier idiom – 'at least that is what I do.' It was, he said, like the difference between poetry and everyday speech: so long as the difference was acknowledged, 'we ourselves can keep the standard up.' Lennox added that the requirements of film composition – writing music that had to

*The violinist Max Rostal gave the first performance with Lennox himself in Hampstead in 1944.

be timed to the second, yet still satisfy the composer's sense of form – provided excellent discipline.[20]

Further discipline of the same kind followed too quickly for comfort. No sooner had he completed *Hotel Reserve* in mid-February 1944 than he was asked to write another piece of film music – and again in a matter of weeks. The commission came from one of Britain's first women directors, Jill Craigie, then only thirty-three. The film, called *Out of Chaos*, was a half-hour, black-and-white documentary, ostensibly about the work of British war artists, but actually a pioneering attempt to introduce the British public to modern art. Craigie wanted to show that out of the chaos of war had emerged not only order but enlightenment and inspiration.

Lennox was by no means her first choice for the music. She originally approached Vaughan Williams, who, she told Paul Nash, 'backed out', then Walton, who was busy with Laurence Olivier's film of *Henry V*, then Bliss, who was suddenly snapped up by the Hungarian director Gabriel Pascal to write a score for a film version of Shaw's *Caesar and Cleopatra* (though, in the event, he decided that in terms of music Pascal was 'a certified lunatic',[21] and pulled out); eventually Georges Auric wrote the music instead. Finally Craigie approached Britten, but he was too busy with *Peter Grimes*.[22] By the end of March Lennox was 'doing it & it is all signed and sealed', as Craigie wrote to the painter Paul Nash, one of the artists featured in her film. 'Did you hear his symphony the other night?[*] I think he's quite good & madly enthusiastic, but he's employed at the B.B.C. & isn't able to give his whole time to it, which is annoying. He reckons it'll take another three weeks.'[23]

By mid-May the music was written and recorded, and Jill Craigie was able to report that Lennox's score was 'very good & most effective' and included for Paul Nash's contribution 'a nice eerie slow movement'.[24] Lennox's vivid score weaves together some remarkably unselfconscious sequences showing Nash transforming the Battle of Britain into a rolling sea of twisted aircraft metal in his famous *Totes Meer* (Dead Sea), Stanley Spencer painting shipbuilders at work on the Clyde, Henry Moore sketching sleeping figures in the Tube shelters during the Blitz (and jotting down a memo to himself to remember the 'restlessness' of their sleep), and Graham Sutherland's black vision of the Cornish mines.

*It was played by the BBC Symphony Orchestra conducted by Clarence Raybould, and broadcast on the BBC in a concert relayed live from the Corn Exchange, Bedford, on 20 March 1944.

The film begins with a bustling scene in the National Gallery as ordinary men and women flock to see the new war paintings, then it flashes back to 1939 to show painters packing up their easels, art galleries and museums closing down and putting their valuables into storage, and Sir Kenneth (later Lord) Clark, wartime director of the National Gallery, explaining – with a foretaste of the flair he was to show in the BBC TV series *Civilization* years later – the purpose of the War Artists Committee. Next we meet some of the commissioned artists themselves, at work on site. The patrician Eric Newton analyses their work and offers a persuasive defence of 'modern art' to a group of hammy actors pretending to be Mr and Mrs Sceptical Man-on-the-street. Jill Craigie, later to become Mrs Michael Foot, not only directs but also narrates her own script. The music, played by the London Symphony Orchestra, conducted again by Muir Mathieson, reaches a dramatic climax with the Battle of Britain sequence and footage of aerial combat (changing mood as the battle dissolves into Nash's still and ghostly *Totes Meer)*; it ends with a rousingly patriotic, almost Elgarian, march, which filmgoers must have found themselves humming as they went home.

Craigie's backers, Two Cities Films, gave *Out of Chaos* 'a splash press show', but the distributors refused to put it on general release, in the belief that there was no market 'for this sort of film'.[25] Craigie complained to Nash that the internal politics of the film world were as involved as those of the House of Commons – 'though of course rather less than those of the art world'.[26] She started a campaign to press for wider showings of documentaries in mainstream cinemas, and even bearded the head of the Rank Organisation, the intimidating J. Arthur Rank himself, who did not change his mind about *Out of Chaos*, but did commission Craigie to make a feature film about the re-planning of the blitzed city of Plymouth.

Lennox told Jill Craigie that he was going to make an orchestral suite of his *Out of Chaos* music,[27] and there is some evidence, from a holograph preserved in the British Library, that he did assemble three sections of the music into a suite, but none that this was ever performed.[28]

That summer of 1944 the Allies invaded France. Without waiting for the liberation of Paris and the establishment of the Provisional Government under General de Gaulle, Lennox wrote a short piano piece for an album of ten works 'in honour of a redeemed France'. He called it *Paysage de France* and dedicated it to Raymond Mortimer, who had done so much for 'the diffusion of French criteria in England', to borrow Harold Acton's phrase.[29] As a reminder of a France Lennox longed for, Peter Fraser gave him a copy of the current best-seller, *Inoubliable France*, a book of evocative photographs of France with a text by Alice Jahier, a Frenchwoman who had unwillingly left her homeland in 1940 and had been an exile in England ever since. By way of thanks Lennox dedicated to Peter the beautiful anthem he had written for the BBC Chorus, a setting of *Lord, When the Sense of Thy Sweet Grace*, by the seventeenth-century Catholic convert Richard Crashaw. Lennox, who may have been introduced to the work of Crashaw by his Oxford mentor H. W. Garrod, would have identified with the poet's conversion to Rome on coming down from university, and with his fondness for the Spanish mystics – St Teresa in particular.

For Christmas 1944 Eddy Sackville-West invited Lennox and Ben and Michael Tippett to write something for a programme of words and music called *A Poet's Christmas*. Berkeley set a text by the contemporary nature poet Frances Cornford, *There Was Neither Grass Nor Corn* – and dedicated it to Eddy; Britten wrote two choral pieces to texts which Auden had hoped he would use for an oratorio; and Tippett set Edith Sitwell's *The Weeping Babe*.[30] The programme was broadcast on Christmas Eve, and the next day Eddy left the BBC to start a new job writing 'Radio Notes' for the *New Statesman*.

Arthur Bliss had recently left the BBC too, but his 'quiet, competent' secretary, Ursula Elliott,[31] was still there and looking around for a new boss – and possibly a husband. According to another young secretary, 'everybody was marrying everybody else in the BBC in those days'.[32] Bliss highly recommended his secretary: she was unflappable, equipped with a remarkable memory and her 'filing system was a work of art'.[33] It seems that she had had her eye on Lennox for some time,[34] and this Christmas she dropped a broad hint with a parcel containing the *Sonnets of Shakespeare*. Inside she wrote, with the confidence of a few walkings-out, and the hope, perhaps, of more to come, 'Lennox with love Ursula'. But further developments were impossible, because Ursula then sailed away to Canada – according to Bliss she belonged to a naval family with connections all over the world.[35] Maybe Lennox had indicated lack of interest and she fled abroad to get over him, but the spectre of Ursula Elliott and her possible return hovered over them both till she actually did come back in the spring of 1946.

If she really had been interested in marrying Lennox, Ursula Elliott would not have found the going easy, and most young women would not even have tried. Lennox had been together with Peter for four years, and the two were now living in a 'pretty fast' all-male ménage at 58 Warwick Square in Pimlico.[36] They had moved there on 4 November, with Lennox's French furniture which had arrived from the Mill the previous week.[37] They shared the top floor with two other young men – both intelligent, cultured and attractive, with a sense of humour that was 'subversive, and if not malicious, keen-eyed'.[38] Social equals, they were fellow spirits and high-flying men of the world. Through the Reform Club Lennox already slightly knew the quieter, steadier of the two, John Weyman. It was he, it seems, who conceived the idea that they should all live together (though the lease was in Lennox's name). Independently of Lennox, Peter had met the other man, the restless and engaging Richard Wyatt. Eleven years older than Wyatt, Weyman was a Marlborough-educated accountant who had recently been appointed finance director of the newly-formed Council for Industrial Design, forerunner of the Design Council. Wyatt, an Old Felstedian who spoke five languages including Russian, was a lieutenant-commander in the Navy. In July 1941 he had been posted to one of the most perilous missions of the war: escorting thirty-four Russian supply ships through the Nazi-patrolled Arctic Sea from Iceland to Archangel, to relieve the beleaguered people of Nazi-occupied Russia. After further dangerous missions in the Arctic, he was posted to the British Embassy in Constantinople, and now he was back in London, in a pivotal job at the Admiralty, heading the Russian section of the Intelligence Department.

Lieutenant-Commander Wyatt was not the only sailor at No. 58: in the basement and on the ground floor lived Commander David Magnay (occasionally with a soldier friend, Major George Greaves). Nor were the two naval officers the only maritime elements in the house, since the two middle floors were occupied by a 'Mrs Shipsteer'. Each man in the top flat had his own bedroom, and all were looked after by a housekeeper called Mrs Conway. She must have been unusually broad-minded, because the flat seems to have been as fast and loose as 'Liberty Hall', with a steady traffic of what the gay argot of the time called 'renters' and 'ruff' from pick-up places in Trafalgar Square, Birdcage Walk and St James's Park.[39]

A son of the distinguished diplomat Sir Stanley Wyatt, 'Dickie' Wyatt was driven by a 'positively dangerous need for excitement'.[40]

Flying Officer Fraser, now working in the Directorate of Intelligence at the Air Ministry, shared this drive and regularly exercised it by picking up guardsmen for one-night stands;[41] according to Wyatt, Fraser even once harboured a deserter.[42] Lennox and John Weyman were the sobersides, watching over their wayward charges like anxious nannies. For Weyman – not for nothing known as 'Matron' – this was ultimately a labour of love, in which reciprocal loyalties played a part. The glamorous Wyatt, despite his vagaries, was an inexhaustible source of interest and delight, and Weyman, once his lover, was now – and would remain until his death in 1975 – the admiring friend and protector, who supported Wyatt emotionally, and sometimes financially.* But for Lennox, the petulant and faithless Peter and his insatiable sex drive were the cause of real suffering. Lennox simply did not know how to cope with such dishonourable behaviour.[43]

Peter Fraser's chief at the Air Ministry, the art historian John Pope-Hennessy, knew Peter well (and met Lennox through him). Years later he said that Fraser had 'created a disastrous background against which no serious creative artist in any medium could have worked'. In his view it was a mistake for someone of Lennox's 'sensibility and refinement and essential orthodoxy' to have become involved with such a person. A highly respectable career man himself, Pope-Hennessy must have delivered this judgement with considerable feeling based on personal experience, since he suffered constantly from the similarly promiscuous behaviour of his brother James, who was eventually beaten to death by one of his male lovers in 1974. Not surprisingly, John Pope-Hennessy remembered Lennox in those war years as 'deeply unhappy'.[44]

Basil Douglas, who saw Lennox every day of the working week, recalled, with some understatement, that Lennox had not been 'secure about his private life' at this time, and, being so impressionable, his

*With Weyman's death in 1975, Wyatt – missing his support – began a downward spiral. His distinguished business career (he had been managing director of British Petroleum in Lisbon), and his successful social life, began to disintegrate, and he became a burden on his family. 'Wyatt was left', a friend said, 'to pursue unsatisfactory relationships that gave the partner all and Wyatt nothing.' In 1990 this once dazzling figure died a death that was as wretched and sad, if not as violent, as Pasolini's, in a rented apartment in Lisbon (Howard Davies, in a telephone conversation with TS, 27 June 2003, and Howard Davies and Joe de Freitas, in conversation with TS , London, 25 May 2004).

'domestic ... trouble' had spread to other areas of his life including his music. 'Dickie' Wyatt, who did not know Lennox so well – nor did he have very much in common with him – remembered him as 'highly neurotic, like a little sparrow', with a winning smile and a modesty of manner. In dress, he said, Lennox was impeccable – usually wearing a formal blue suit and spotted bow tie – but in his habits he was untidy. Wyatt was in no doubt that Peter Fraser, though 'enchanting', was 'very bad news'. Never one to be deterred by his friends' bad points – if the friends were young and pretty enough – Wyatt himself was aware of Peter's charms (and seconded his application for membership of the Travellers'). But he was realistic too, and he recognized Flying Officer Fraser as 'a terrific lady'. By this he may have meant that Peter was conspicuously effeminate, or that he was selfish, hysterical and demanding – possibly all these things. At any rate, he said, Lennox was 'scared stiff of him'.[45]

26
Freda, London, 1944

The war was nearing its end. As the Germans were driven first from Russia and then from Italy, the Allies began the liberation of France and Belgium. On the day before the Normandy landings, Freda noted in her diary, 'Planes go over by day and night – the roads are filled with convoys. We watch and pray.'[1] And on D Day itself, 'At 9.48 General Eisenhower announced that we have invaded France. Terrific tension – listened to all news. Churchill spoke in House. "Monty"* spoke on radio and the King at 9.0 p.m.'[2]

On 7 June Freda recorded that the invasion was going well, 'but there is hard fighting on the beaches'. If anyone thought the air raids might now be over, there was a shock in store the following week when Hitler launched his final assault on Britain with the V-1 flying bombs – the 'buzz bombs' or 'doodle-bugs'. These were pilotless aircraft, packed with high explosive, which droned menacingly towards their target, then fell silently to the ground, blowing up on impact. On 26 June the sirens in London wailed all afternoon, as Freda tried to type some programme announcements for her boss 'Dougie' Lawrence. 'Doodle-bugs falling around,' she wrote. 'Nerve-racking – felt horribly scared.'[3]

She made up for it by spoiling herself with real cream on holiday with her landlady and friend Nancy Gregory in Gorleston, joining long queues for luxuries like oranges, fish and brassieres. One day she really indulged herself: 'Bought a new suspender belt – a Utility *Caprice*, also got Walter de la Mare's Anthology *Love*.'

(If these wartime diary entries seem to lack resonance, it should be remembered that Freda was still an unsophisticated young woman, only twenty-one, recording the minutiae of her daily life, in so far as

*Field Marshal Bernard Montgomery (1887–1976), later Viscount Montgomery of Alamein. As C.-in-C. ground forces, Northern France, 1944, he commanded Operation Overlord, the Allied invasion of Occupied Normandy.

four short lines allowed, by way of therapy. In the absence of an intimate friend she was committing her thoughts to her diary, so she could share them with herself. She certainly never intended that anyone else should see the diary, let alone publish bits of it. Yet, for all its girlish effusiveness, the diary's honesty and vitality – and the discipline its author displays in refining the day's events – have their part to play.)

On 25 May Freda was twenty-one, and after opening her cards and parcels, she went out to lunch with Nancy, then returned to make tea for two friends. In later life she recalled a celebration party, but there is no mention of this in her diary which simply records: 'Everyone so kind. I've waited for this so long – and now?'[4]

For the time being, it was back to the old routine. Typing at the BBC – but never enough of it to keep her busy - lunching with chums, dancing at Chevron's Club, going to the theatre or the cinema: *Rookery Nook* ('heaps of laughs') and *Captains Courageous* ('wept buckets'). At weekends there were walks in the woods, hair to be washed, clothes to be mended, *ITMA* on the wireless, and rows with finicky Nancy (once, justifiably, because Freda had forgotten to turn out the bathroom light during the blackout).

On 8 July, after sixteen hours without an air-raid warning, she ventured out by bus from Oxford Circus to Queen's Park on a long-overdue visit to her grandparents. It was a warm and sunny day and she sat on the top deck admiring her mother's wedding ring, which the old people had recently given her as a twenty-first birthday present. She was pleased to see them, but found them much frailer than last time: Frederick Nunney was now nearly eighty, and Blanch seventy-seven. It was fourteen years since Freda had been part of their household, hiding from her nightmares at the top of the stairs and fetching jugs of mild-and-bitter from the pub opposite. Nothing could diminish her love for her grandparents, but she realized with a jolt how far she had grown away from 126 Lancefield Street, with its privy in the backyard. 'I can't believe that I once lived there!' she wrote on the journey home. (Three months later, when her grandfather celebrated his eightieth birthday, she went shopping with her grandmother to buy the old man a new shirt, and again she was struck by their poverty, noting in her diary, 'It's pathetic really how very hard up they are.'[5])

Freda was now legally her own mistress. Since her coming-of-age, the Public Trustee no longer had any control over her life – but neither would it willingly surrender control of her affairs. On the actual day of the birthday, she received a letter from her Trust Officer Mr Bowman, explaining that though the funds were now hers, she would be well advised to leave them in the care of the Public Trustee. She was, after all, a beautiful young woman with a small fortune which made her especially vulnerable.[6] Freda was touched by what she took to be his concern – though she might have been better advised to remove her funds from the Trustee and hand them over to her bank manager so they could be invested more imaginatively. The following day she went up to London for a meeting at the Public Trustee's, and agreed to everything that was proposed. As her guardian, she believed, the Trustee knew what was best for her. It never occurred to her to consult anyone else. If the long-term consequence was that she lost the full potential investment value of her money, the immediate consequence was a 'terrific fit of depression' back at Broxbourne that night – 'it's all rather overwhelming and I feel so alone.'[7]

A month later Mr Bowman took her to the offices of her late father's solicitors, Lewis & Lewis, in Ely Place, and guided her through the process of making a will and drawing up a new trust deed to protect her inheritance, which then stood at just over £21,000 (or about £633,000 by current values).[8] The settlement was a pretty restrictive document, which not only gave the Trustee the right to choose the way the money was invested, but also made it difficult for Freda herself to get at any of it.[9] The purpose, Mr Bowman said, was to fend off gold-diggers. But, as the years went by, Freda found it fended her off too. (When, in the 1980s, an opportunity arose to buy, at a sitting tenant's discount, the house which she and her family had been living in for forty years she discovered that a clause in her 1944 Settlement prevented her withdrawing more than £3,000 to buy a marital home. Advised that the only way to access the rest was to break the trust, she had to resort to the expensive instrument of an action before the Master of the Chancery Division in the High Court of Justice. Once it was done, she found that the money in her settlement fund had not even kept pace with inflation: there was barely enough to buy a car parking space in 1980s London. Defending its record, the Public Trustee explained that it was not its job to increase a ward's capital with uncertain investments, but to protect it with safe ones.) In 1944, however, Freda did not think to question Mr Bowman. On 22 August she signed both the settlement and her will, and the Public Trustee continued to pay her a small monthly allowance till she no longer needed it.

In September, just after the first V-2 ballistic missiles had fallen on London, the news from Europe improved again. Allied airborne troops had landed behind German lines at Arnhem: the blackout at home was to be reduced and fire guard duties brought to an end. It looked as though the war might soon be over. As though to cheer her up for the final push, a parcel arrived on the 21st from a cousin in Canada, with '2 prs stockings, lipstick, foundation, cleansing, rouge and powder'.[10]

In one of her lunch-hours the following week Freda and two BBC girlfriends from Light Music took the tube out to Earls Court to consult a fortune-teller they had heard about. Back home in Broxbourne that night Freda jotted down Mrs Atmore's conventional predictions with scepticism: '"Change in job, ring on finger within year – business man, travel a lot, v. happy!" Wot rot and bunkum!' But keeping her options open, since it had cost a guinea after all, she added, 'We shall see!'[11]

The job change came in mid-December. This time she did not seek it – it was thrust upon her. She was told she was to join the Music Department, in the orchestral programme builders' section based at 35 Marylebone High Street, working for Ronald Biggs, the conductor and eminent adjudicator who managed the section. Freda was very fed up, because she liked Light Music and did not want to move. Nevertheless she started the new job on December 18 and found there was practically nothing to do, because Biggs was at meetings all the time. 'Loathe music dept.,' she wrote in her diary the next day, '& all that therein is.'[12] Later that week Freda rang her friend Marie Dawson, the red-headed secretary who worked for the bandleader Fred Hartley back in Light Music, and suggested lunch in the canteen at Marylebone High Street to talk it all over.

As they sipped their coffee, a slim, elegant man in a dark suit and a bow tie walked past carrying a tray with his pudding on it. He was deep in thought and did not seem to notice what was going on around him.

'Don't look now', said Marie, 'but you know who that is, don't you?' assuming Freda must know, since they both worked in the same department.

'No,' said Freda. 'Who?'

In case he overheard, Marie whispered,'Lennox Berkeley.'[13]

27
Lennox and Freda, London, 1945

Freda's diary does not mention Lennox till the end of January 1945, when he makes his début as 'Lennox Berkeley rather sweet!'[1] Yet he was there at the time she joined the BBC Music Department at 35 Marylebone High Street in December 1944, so why did she not record that he occupied the small private office next to hers?

The fact is that Freda was preoccupied with the two other music producers who shared her office. One, because he was stalking her; the other, because she had developed a schoolgirl crush on him. Her boss Ronald Biggs, though married, had become infatuated with her from the very moment he saw her at the job interview. Uninvited, he met her off the Broxbourne train at Liverpool Street every morning, and in the office he sat staring at her through his thick spectacles, with a pencil in his mouth and his chin in his hand. But Freda herself had taken just as reckless a fancy to the other man in the office, Basil Douglas, even though she knew he was both gay and spoken for.

By the beginning of February Freda's curious passion for the unavailable Basil had so far eclipsed her earlier curious passion for the unavailable Alan Wheatley (the gay actor she had met in Weston-super-Mare) that when she bumped into Wheatley in a bookshop near the BBC and discovered he was about to leave the Corporation, she was 'strangely unmoved'.[2] But this cannot have come as such a surprise, since she had realized the previous summer that Alan Wheatley was utterly different from her,[3] and that pursuing him was like banging her head against a brick wall. So indeed it was, but it had not stopped her continuing to hope for a response from him throughout the autumn and winter of 1944. On 5 October she had seen Wheatley in the staff canteen, and 'felt ill with excitement'.[4] Six weeks later she still pined for him, and in mid-December she was wishing she could work for him.[5] Barely a week passed before she was moved across to Orchestral Music – and into the orbit of the handsome and sweet-natured Basil Douglas.

9a Freda with her grandparents, Blanch and Frederick Nunney, Herne Bay, *c.* 1929

9b Freda at St Helen's School, Abingdon, *c.* 1938

9c Freda at Weston-Super-Mare, 1942

10a Alan Searle, at the time he met Lennox, *c.* 1934

10b Lennox, golfing at Cap Ferrat, *c.* 1934

10c Arnold Cooke, Benjamin Britten and Lennox, Mont Juïc, 1936

11a Lennox working on *Five Short Pieces for Piano*, Crantock, Cornwall, 1936

11c Peter Burra, 1936

11b Benjamin Britten working on *Our Hunting Fathers*, Crantock, Cornwall, 1936

12a Lennox and Britten, 1938

12b The AC roadster which Lennox bought for Britten, with Wulff Scherchen in the passenger seat, 1939

12c Wulff Scherchen outside the Mill at Snape, 1938

13a Jim Lees-Milne

13b Peter Fraser, 1940

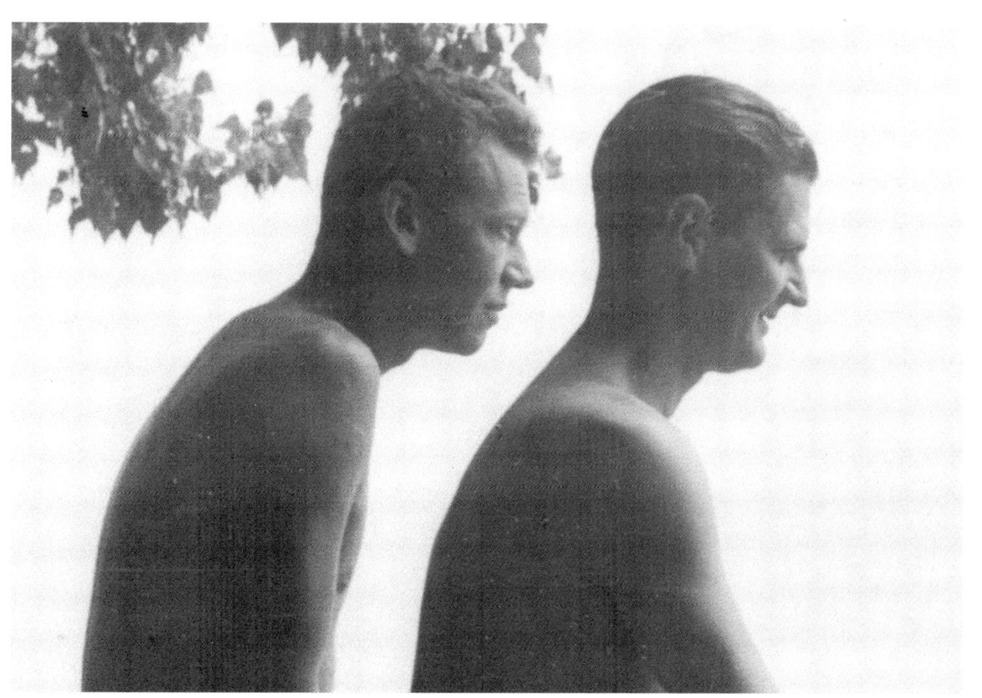

13b Lennox's wartime flatmates Lt.-Com. Richard Wyatt and John Weyman

14 Freda, 1946, the year of her marriage

15a Lennox and Freda with Michael and Julian at Julian's christening, St James's, Spanish Place, London, 1950

15b Numbers 10 (left, home of Lady Diana Cooper) and 8 (home of the Berkeleys) Warwick Avenue, Little Venice, London. Drawing by Stephen Pimbley.

16a Freda with (l to r) Desmond Shawe-Taylor, Lennox, Raymond Mortimer, Eddy Sackville-West and Eardley Knollys, Long Crichel, 1962

16b Ben Britten and Lennox with (l to r) Julian, Nicholas and Michael Berkeley, Blakeney Point, North Norfolk, 1961

16c Lennox at Warwick Avenue with his carer Bonnie McCallum O'Neil, and Tony Scotland, London, 1988

Just after the final meeting with Wheatley, in the bookshop, Freda recorded, with obvious pleasure, that Basil needed looking after.[6] This tug on her maternal instincts may explain the strong appeal which gay men had for Freda – in addition to their 'safety' and attentiveness. Douglas's needs, that first week of February 1945, were not quite pressing enough to warrant mothering: he simply had a septic toe, and his usual eczema.[7] Anyway his partner, the BBC drama producer Martyn C. Webster, provided a perfectly adequate nursing service for him at home in Primrose Hill.

Lennox Berkeley's needs, as Freda was to discover, were comprehensive, chronic and crippling. He was untidy, forgetful, vague, undomesticated, unsure of himself, often ill (coughs and colds, toothache, 'nerves', otitis, even scabies); a Little Johnny Head-in-Air lost in his music. Unable to manage everyday life, let alone the faithless Peter and the erotic comings and goings at Warwick Square, he was, in short, helpless. He needed not only a mother, but a secretary, a cook, a nurse and a housekeeper; possibly even a wife. Whether he knew it or not, he needed Freda. And Freda was in no doubt that she needed him – with his social connections, his celebrity, his polish, good looks, modesty, and gentleness. And it helped too that he was not sexually interested in her, because that meant that he could neither frighten nor control her.

The licence of the Warwick Square ménage had accentuated all the problems in Lennox's relationship with Peter by creating an atmosphere which seemed to accept Peter's promiscuity. Lennox was out of his depth, and his health, always weak, began to get worse. Shortly after St Valentine's Day he went to see his doctor, who told him what he already knew, that he was run-down and tired – and must take a fortnight off.

Before heeding the doctor's advice, Lennox gave a concert, accompanying Sophie Wyss in the first performance of two French songs he had written in 1940, *Ode du premier jour de mai* and *Tant que mes yeux*, and playing his *Paysage* for the first time, at Fyvie Hall in what is now the University of Westminster building in Upper Regent Street, near Broadcasting House. The next day, 21 February, he took off for Painswick, and some mothering from Gladys Bryans. 'The change is a God-send,' he told Chester's in a letter asking for a copy of Tippett's *String Quartet No. 2*, which he wanted to study while working on his own *Viola Sonata*.[8]

By 7 March he was back at the office, and, without either of them knowing it, he and Basil had become rivals for Freda's love. On the 13th, in the secrecy of her diary, Lennox was memorialized as 'a dear', but Douglas was 'my Basil'. On the 16th they were 'both sweet', with Lennox, additionally, 'a kind soul'. Douglas still had the edge: 'How very badly I've fallen,' Freda wrote on 19 March – though she wished he were not so moody.[9]

On the day after another V-2 rocket attack (which turned out to be the last), the sun came out and Lennox was suddenly reminded of spring. In a burst of spontaneous chivalry he presented Freda with a bunch of primroses and violets. A fortnight later he failed to appear at work one day, having taken what the BBC used to term a *bisque* (a day off that needs no explanation) because of a worrying dream the night before.[10] In an effort to ensure a good night's rest, he swallowed too many sleeping pills by mistake – and slept through the next morning.

With Lennox's unhappiness becoming increasingly apparent, it was now neck and neck in the race for Freda's heart, and her diary the following day records the turning point: 'Lennox sweet Basil sour.'[11]

As the pendulum began to swing in Lennox's direction, Douglas became no more than an adjunct – and even Freda was confused by her apparent inconstancy. For all her instinctive understanding and compassion, she was still only a schoolgirl and did not really know what she was doing, or why. 'I just don't understand myself at present,' she wrote on 25 April, 'all I know is that L is dear to me – very dear.' What Lennox felt we can only surmise. He was so used to male company – and so bound up with the problems at home at Warwick Square – that he never guessed the warmth of the feelings he had roused in Freda. He was just grateful that Freda was consistently kind and understanding, and never judgemental.

At the end of April Freda seems to have discovered that Lennox's private problems were more complicated than she can possibly have imagined. Without yet confessing that he was gay, or telling her directly about Peter, Lennox may have lodged in her mind the possibility that the 'friend' he lived with in Warwick Square, the young man who was always telephoning him at work, was more than a flatmate.

On 4 May, two days after it was announced that Hitler had committed suicide, Basil Douglas was transferred to Bedford. Freda was relieved. So was Ronald Biggs. Jealous of Douglas's superior position in Freda's estimation, Biggs had been constantly picking fault and bickering. Now, to use Freda's own expression, the 'bitchery' had ceased, and the two men were being civil once more. But the coast was no clearer for Biggs: his new rival, he began to grasp, with astonishment, was Lennox.

Meanwhile Mussolini had been killed by partisans, Fascist Venice had fallen, Berlin had surrendered to the Russians, and the Allies had entered Hamburg. On 7 May Nazi Germany surrendered unconditionally. The war in Europe was officially at an end, but the chaos it had created was to continue as millions of people started to move in all directions. On 8 May Britain celebrated VE Day: in London, flags and dancing in the streets; in Broxbourne, flags and bonfires; everywhere, parties. Freda and Lennox and Basil Douglas, independently, with their own friends, toasted the peace in champagne, that day and the next. All three had hangovers when they returned to work on the 10th.

Then came Lennox's forty-second birthday, and Peter Fraser gave him a new edition of André Gide's *l'Ecole des femmes*, three novels about the position of women in the modern world. Peter's tongue may have been in his cheek, since he had now realized that the modern young woman who answered the phone in the Music Department had fallen in love with Lennox – and furthermore, that Lennox was not discouraging her.

One day at the end of May, Lennox and Freda had lunch together, and, on the way to his bank afterwards, Lennox told her about his friendship the previous year with Bliss's secretary Ursula Elliott. In return for this confidence, which must have involved Lennox admitting that women were not his natural terrain, Freda told Lennox that she 'understood him physically'.[12] Freda now knew for certain that Lennox was gay – or 'not normal', as they both called it – and he knew she knew. But if she dared to imagine that his past form with Ursula Elliott offered her some kind of sporting chance, her hopes were dashed a fortnight later when, while walking in the lunch hour in Paddington Street Gardens, Lennox felt it necessary to emphasize that nothing could come of their relationship.[13] This did sink in, and on 1 June Freda recorded, in despair, 'I wish I'd never met him.' The next day, however, Lennox and Freda stayed on in the office after everyone else had gone home, and, in the suggestive words of Freda's later memory (though the reality was innocence itself), they 'ate tarts together'. This modest debauch only added to Freda's confusion. 'Very disturbed re L.,' she wrote in the diary, 'I felt elated, down and elated again'.

Despite all his office commitments and domestic problems, Lennox managed to keep up his composing.[14] He completed the *Piano Sonata* for Clifford Curzon, and the equally enduring *Viola Sonata* for Watson Forbes, and he wrote an orchestral suite called *Estérel*. He seems to have assembled this from one of his film scores – probably *Hotel Reserve*, which is set on the coast below the Estérel hills. In July the suite was recommended for broadcast by the reading panel. The composer Herbert Howells thought it was attractively varied, but a little long; Gordon Jacob, an authority on orchestral technique, said the scoring was effective, and that variety and colour carried the work along; and the conductor and critic Mosco Carner felt that since it was essentially film music the listener should be told what it illustrated.[15] That autumn three extracts from the original score of *Hotel Reserve* – 'Java', and 'On the Beach' parts 1 and 2, were played (and probably broadcast) by the BBC Northern Orchestra conducted by Muir Mathieson, who had been music director of the film.* These pieces may have constituted the *Estérel Suite*, which was considered for the 1945 Proms, but rejected; there is no record of *Estérel* in *The Times*'s daily preview of works to be heard at the Proms in the summer of 1945, and the score is now lost.

In the last few months of the war Lennox was offered an intriguing commission by the BBC. Research had shown that listeners were irritated by the beep tones (representing Bee-Bee-See), which were broadcast in the dead air between programmes and during under-runs, in order to keep the Home Service medium wavelength free of German interference. So the Music Department decided to commission some new music instead. The pieces had to be short and for a single instrument, and the idea was that they would be played live in the studio when needed. Several composers were approached. Herbert Howells wrote some pieces for harpsichord, and Lennox produced *Six Preludes* for piano, which he dedicated to Val Drewry, the self-styled 'Old Shark',[16] who worked in an office close to his, producing the Department's chamber music programmes. Influenced by Ravel, Mozart, Poulenc and Stravinsky, the six pieces are lyrical almost to the point of sensuality: Peter Dickinson describes them as 'the most indulgent music Berkeley had composed since his student days'.[17] Of the lyrical last one

*The performance was given on 28 October 1944 and a recording made by the BBC Transcription Service is preserved at the British Library Sound Archive.

– 'a cross between a *siciliano* and a blues' – Stephen Maddock has written that it is 'a kind of self-portrait with his own fingerprints in every bar'.*

In the event, Lennox's *Preludes* were never put to their intended purpose, because the war ended before they were completed. The first broadcast performance was not till the summer of 1947, when the Swiss pianist Albert Ferber played them in the Concert Hall of Broadcasting House, London, in a recital which went out live on the new Third Programme. The actual premiere, in the Wigmore Hall earlier that year, was to have been given by Eric Hope, but just as he was about to begin the third (and most difficult) prelude, he fainted over the keyboard. Though he soon recovered, he was not able to complete the performance, and Lennox, who was sitting in the auditorium with Freda, had to play them himself, without having prepared them, and with only limited proficiency as a performer.[18] Val Drewry's partner, the New Zealand pianist Colin Horsley, soon to become a close associate of Lennox, said years later that Lennox's playing 'was not exactly refined', but very capable.[19] The music critic Desmond Shawe-Taylor confirmed Lennox's deficiencies as a player. In an interview with Peter Dickinson, he said that Lennox 'wrote frightfully well for the piano – the *Four Concert Studies* [of 1939] are real virtuoso pieces – yet he was not a good pianist'.[20] Lennox himself regretted that he was not a better player. He even admitted to Peter Dickinson he wished he had Dickinson's own facility at the keyboard, to which his interviewer retorted graciously that he wished he could compose as well as Lennox, adding reassuringly that being a better pianist would not have made Lennox a better composer: look, he said, at Wagner, who could not play a note on any instrument.[21]

In 1949 Colin Horsley recorded the *Six Preludes* for HMV, as an afterthought in a set of 78s featuring works by Rachmaninov, Prokofiev and Szymanowski, and, to HMV's surprise, the Berkeley sold better that anything else.[22] By then Horsley had established a special working relationship with Lennox, which was to result in five other piano works, some of which were actually commissioned by Horsley, and

*Maddock knew Lennox for many years and described him as 'the most kindly and generous person you could ever meet' (Stephen Maddock, sleeve notes, 2007, for LB *Preludes 5 and 6*, and *Polka Op 5*, on Wigmore Hall Live – recorded 29 October 1993 – WHLIVE0014).

most of which are dedicated to him: the *Piano Concerto* of 1948, the *Scherzo* (1950), the *Trio for Horn, Violin and Piano* (1953), the *Concert Study* (1955) and the *Concerto for Piano and Double String Orchestra* (1958). Horsley remembers Lennox as 'a perfect gentleman ... exceedingly kind and charming' – too kind to offer any useful criticism. Pressed to reveal whether Lennox ever indicated how he wanted his piano music played, Horsley said he favoured 'a sort of classical way, because of his respect for Mozart', and, as with Ravel, Lennox did not like his work 'mucked about with'. In Horsley's estimation, Lennox was a genius as a miniaturist, producing 'elegant and beautiful phrases as well as subtle and pungent harmonies'.[23]

One of Lennox's most interesting musical tasks in 1945 was an anthem commissioned by the Revd Walter Hussey, vicar of St Matthew's, Northampton. The piece was to be performed at the church's patronal festival on St Matthew's Day in September that year. The choir of men and boys was only voluntary but had a high reputation, and the organ was a four-manual Walker of 1893.[24] (Roger Nichols, who played the organ in the 1960s, describes it as a fine instrument, but 'with an unbelievably heavy action'.[25])

Lennox was excited by the commission and originally planned to set a poem called *The Flower* by the early-seventeenth-century poet George Herbert, starting with the words, 'How fresh, O Lord, how sweet and clean'. But when he discovered that Hussey wanted something suitable for the Mass for St Matthew's Day, he decided on a combination of texts *à la* Vaughan Williams: just one verse of the Herbert, together with the medieval chant *Jerusalem et Sion filiae*, and the metaphysical *Easter Hymn* by Herbert's convert Henry Vaughan. 'I always find that the choice of a text for this sort of thing is more difficult than writing the work!' Lennox told Hussey.[26]

Choosing a title was no less of a challenge. He could not find anything in his selected texts that seemed appropriate, and he did not care for Hussey's suggestion of *His Own Inheritance*. In the end he called it, simply, *A Festival Anthem*, and added beneath the title a quotation from Donne, possibly taking it from his own copy of the Oxford Donne edited by his old tutor at Merton, H. W. Garrod: *Then turn, O pensive soul, to God*. Over the years this subsidiary title, which, as Lennox told Hussey, 'is such a beautiful line',[27] has been dropped, which is a pity in view of what it meant to Lennox, and what he hoped the work would mean to others. Indeed this one simple line contains the key to all Lennox's sacred writing. (At this very moment in 1945, Britten, who had explored the work of Donne under Auden's guidance while he was in America, had just finished his own setting of the *Holy Sonnets*, and though he had used nine of the nineteen in the collection, the one containing Lennox's favourite line – No. VIII – is not among them.) Lennox himself conducted the first performance of his new anthem at St Matthew's, Northampton, on 21 September 1945, which gave him a chance to admire another of the fruits of Hussey's enlightened patronage, Henry Moore's stone *Madonna and Child* (which was to be joined by Graham Sutherland's *Crucifixion* the following year).

Britten had already written for St Matthew's: his festival cantata *Rejoice in the Lamb* was performed at the patronal Mass during the church's jubilee year in 1943. It was Ben who had introduced Lennox to Walter Hussey, telling him how much he had enjoyed working for Hussey and how sympathetic he found the atmosphere at St Matthew's.[28] Perhaps it was Ben's way of thanking Lennox for his introduction to Francis Poulenc in January 1945,[29] which was to blossom into a warm friendship that lasted till Poulenc's death in 1963. Poulenc, who had been isolated in France since the beginning of the war, had flown over from Paris in a military aircraft to play his *Concerto for Two Pianos and Orchestra* with the LPO at the Albert Hall on 6 January, and Britten had provided the second pair of hands. On that same visit Poulenc had given a couple of recitals with his baritone partner Pierre Bernac, and made a BBC recording. Either then or in March when Poulenc returned to London for the premiere of his cantata *Figure humaine*, he had marked his long friendship with Lennox by presenting him with a copy of his ballet *Les animaux modèles* inscribed 'Pour mon cher Lennox avec vingt ans d'amitié'.*

By mid-1945 Ben was busy preparing the premiere of his new opera, *Peter Grimes*, which was to re-open Sadler's Wells on 7 June. Lennox had already heard the first act, which Ben had played to him from the piano sketch, in his flat over a grocer's shop in St John's Wood High Street, early in 1944. 'Though greatly excited' by that first introduction to *Grimes*, he recalled many years later, 'I was not astonished, because I knew already that he was capable of something like this; and was

*This inscribed score, along with others by Poulenc, is now at the BFP.

expecting it.' What he could not have foreseen, he wrote, was that success would come so quickly.[30] Lennox and Basil Douglas went to a dress rehearsal on 5 June, and returned for the big night on the 7th. Tension was high – not least because the score was extremely difficult and the orchestra worn out after years of provincial touring during the war. But the conductor Reginald Goodall, together with Joan Cross who sang Ellen Orford (and had worked tirelessly to get the production staged at all) and Peter Pears as Grimes, helped to make it the 'knock-out' Ben had predicted it would be.[31] The audience was ecstatic, and most of the reviews the next day hailed the new opera as a masterpiece.

Grimes remained one of Lennox's favourites of all Ben's works. When he saw it again at Sadler's Wells in 1963, he wrote in his diary that it was still a supreme achievement. Although Ben had by then gone far beyond *Grimes*, both musically and technically, Lennox believed that he would never surpass the deeply moving passage just before the storm interlude, at the end of the first scene, when the tormented Grimes wonders whether marrying Ellen might bring him the peace he longs for:

> What harbour shelters peace,
> Away from tidal waves, away from storms?
> What harbour can embrace
> Terrors and tragedies?

The huge, almost hysterical, leap of a major ninth from the E natural of 'What ...' to the high F# of 'har[bour] ...' is a searing metaphor for Grimes's tortured soul, which seems to find solace in a gentle cadence illustrating the harbour's safe embrace. But when the stage directions drench the lonely fisherman in the first wave of the storm, it is clear that no harbour will ever bring the peace he seeks. Lennox rated this brief but telling scene as one of the great moments of opera.[32] And even though he was never one to analyse emotions, particularly his own, the similarities with his own predicament cannot have escaped him by 1963, even if he had not consciously recognized the parallels in 1945.

Britten once said that *Peter Grimes* concerned 'a subject very close to my heart – the struggle of the individual against the masses'.[33] It is certainly about an outsider at odds with society, and in view of Ben's own complex psychology, and Grimes's abuse of his hapless boy apprentices (which is nothing short of sadism in the original poem by George Crabbe), it is possible to see this outsider as a gay man rejected by his community. Peter Pears, in a letter to Ben after an early run-through of part of *Grimes*, seemed to confirm this, if only by denying it: 'The more I hear of it, the more I feel that the queerness is unimportant & doesn't really exist in the music (or at any rate obtrude) so it mustn't do so in the words.'[34]

Lennox went back to Sadler's Wells to see *Grimes* for a third time in June 1945. Freda was there too that night, though they were not actually sitting together. She recorded her verdict as 'Strange, but enjoyed it.'[35] Lennox was again overwhelmed by the power of the piece, and could have written pages about it, as he told Ben in a brief fan letter a couple of days later:

> ... you have already fulfilled what I was certain you could do when I first saw a very early composition of yours, before I knew you; and [even] if my enthusiasm got mixed up with feelings that had very little to do with music, I think that nevertheless my original feeling was a very profound one! I loved Peter's singing too ...
> P.S. The effect of 1 Fog-Horn in Eb (off) is terrific![36]

The morning after the premiere of *Grimes*, Lennox drove down to Painswick for ten days' break from the dramas at home in Warwick Square. Freda missed him, but was not unhappy because she knew he needed a rest and it gave her the opportunity to write him her first letter, enclosing some music he wanted.[37] In return, Lennox sent her a postcard, saying that he was already feeling better. The card was addressed to 'Miss Bernstein', signed 'Yrs ever L. B.', and did not really say anything, except that it was pouring with rain.[38] Freda was delighted to get it at all: 'Bless him,' she wrote in her diary, 'very formal of course! What a dear ...'[39]

Only Lennox mattered now, and when, on a hot day in mid-June, he returned to the office, they walked around to the Gardens and lay down on the grass. 'I love him so much,' Freda wrote that night, 'I just want to shout for joy!'[40] But her happiness was short-lived. Two days later Lennox came into work in a thoroughly nervous state. Peter Fraser had moved a lover in to No. 58, and Lennox was so wretched he burst into tears. Freda cried too, because she realized that 'in comparison [to Peter] I mean nothing to L.' Ronald Biggs, watching the whole thing through Lennox's open door, drew the equally obvious conclusion that in comparison to Lennox, he meant nothing to Freda.

A fortnight later it all happened again. After a quarrel with Peter,

Lennox sat at his desk, sobbing uncontrollably. Freda offered comfort, and he told her she reminded him of his mother. This might not have won every girl's heart, but it hit the mark with Freda. After Lennox had gone home, Biggs, who had again witnessed the scene through the open door, tried to persuade Freda she was wasting her time with Lennox: he was not the marrying kind and would never be able to make her happy. The clear implication was that if Freda wanted consolation, Biggs was willing. But running down the beloved was no way to win Freda, and she told Biggs firmly that she was not interested.[41] In fact she was so sick of Biggs's attentions that she had applied for a transfer to Drama as secretary to the safer Old Shark.[42] (Nothing, as it happened, came of this – largely because Freda did not want to lose the daily contact with Lennox which the Music Department brought.)

Without knowing about Freda's plans, Lennox had reached a decision too: he had been to see the Director of Music to hand in his resignation with effect from October. He explained that he badly needed more time for his composing, and he planned to support himself with teaching work (to supplement a private income hard hit by income tax). His former boss Reginald Thatcher had left the BBC in 1943 to become Warden of the Royal Academy of Music (later its Principal), and he had offered Lennox a part-time post as a professor of composition. Privately, to Freda, Lennox said he liked the work in the Music Department, but could not get on with Biggs and some of the others in what he called 'that beastly office'. [43]

His decision cannot have come as a surprise to his superiors. The baritone George Baker, who had recently joined the BBC as Assistant Overseas Music Director, had known of Lennox's reputation before he joined the Corporation and was surprised that a composer of his potential should be 'sitting in an office, building programmes for other people to perform'.

> There he sat in a tiny cubby-hole ... poring over ledger-like books and odd bits of paper, racking his brains to concoct programmes for the delight of the musical connoisseur. When on rare occasions I went into his office I always thought he looked rather bewildered, and not a little bored. Knowing, as I do today [1954], the precise working of Lennox Berkeley's well-ordered and finely-poised brain, bewildered he could not have been, but bored he certainly was ... Office work is definitely not the ideal milieu for

creative musicians, and when one day I heard ... that Lennox was leaving, I received the news with the air of a man who might at any moment say, 'I told you so.'[44]

The BBC agreed to let him go, but not till January 1946.[45] Freda spent the rest of the year fretting, as 'the end' drew nearer.[46]

One Monday morning in July 1945 Lennox told Freda he had been thinking about her all weekend, and of 'how things wd. have been if he was normal'.[47] Freda's hopes were not much raised by Lennox's use of the conditional tense. But she bucked up a week later when Lennox said he had talked things over with his sister Geraldine and she had been sympathetic.[48]

Freda now began to resent Peter Fraser's hold over Lennox. The fact that she had recently met Peter and liked him only made things harder.[49] Overcome with despair, she spent the whole of 12 July following Lennox around the office like a dog, and feeling wretched and cross. On the 29th, after another 'Cloudburst in rehearsal room', when Lennox announced that he was going home early to be with Peter, Freda took a fortnight's holiday, and escaped to Bude, the surfing resort on the north coast of Cornwall.

On one of the following two days Lennox had an unexpected visit from an old friend, who called around at 35 Marylebone High Street. To Lennox's astonishment it was David Ponsonby, whom he had given up for dead after the occupation of Paris in June 1940. Lennox wrote to tell Nadia Boulanger that their mutual friend had turned up out of the blue and given a potted version of his adventures, telling of 'things that could only happen to him!' and recounting them 'with that modesty – never taking himself seriously – and that humour which is so characteristic, and so unique'.[50]

When he was turned down for military service in England, David had stayed on in Paris, coaching piano pupils for Alfred Cortot and Nadia. Finding himself trapped at the time of the Nazi invasion, he had fled south with the column of refugees, in Nadia's 6-cylinder Hotchkiss. He took with him a startling carload: three elderly ladies and their maid, a French friend and his schnautzer dog, two Swiss friends and the Polish girlfriend of one of them, and a mountain of luggage on the roof. David left a vivid description of their escape from the 'abandoned ship' of Paris on 12 June 1940: '... a strange black mist ... came up during the lovely summer afternoon, something like a London fog accompanied by great heat. Many people thought the city was on fire, others that it was partly dispersed smoke-screen, but I have never heard it explained yet.' [51]

For a while he had lived a clandestine existence in Vichy France, assuming a false identity to escape internment, and narrowly escaping arrest by the Nazis. Hiding in the hilly forests of the Lozère massif, on the edge of what is now the Parc national des Cevennes, he had been recruited into the Resistance and finally he had joined the French Third Army as its only serving British officer, acting as a translator with the rank of sub-lieutenant, and the welcome services of a sergeant-batman. When the war in Europe was over, he was demobilized and awarded the Croix de Guerre (in recognition of bravery in the face of the enemy). Pinning the medal on David's chest, the commander of the Third Army, General Edgard de Larminat,* read out a citation which acknowledged David's devotion to his comrades – 'parce qu'il ne voulait pas quitter ses amis'. Since then David had been repatriated, with the help of his friends, the Duff Coopers, at the British Embassy in Paris, and their Second Secretary, David's cousin 'Eric' Duncannon. His intention now was to return to France to live.†

After listening to these adventures – so different from his own, prosaic war in England – Lennox took down a volume of music from the bookshelf above his desk and, handing it to David, explained that it was his *Four Concert Studies* which he had dedicated to friends presumed to have been lost in the war.[52] The first of the four virtuoso studies, marked *Presto*, was dedicated 'To David Ponsonby'. Taking up his pen, Lennox now added a personal inscription, 'To David – At last – four years late! Lennox, London July 1945.'‡

When David arrived back in Paris, he learned and memorized his Berkeley piece, together with the second Study (dedicated to the Dutch composer Bep Geuer), and in the winter of 1946–7 he included them both in a lecture-recital entitled 'England's Place in Keyboard Music', which he took on a tour of all the towns in France which he had known

*Born 29 November 1895, Acting Governor-General of French Equatorial Africa 1940–1, author of *Chroniques Irrévérencieuses* (Paris, Librairie Plon, 1962) about the setting up of the constitution for a free French African state in 1940, committed suicide 1 July 1962.

†For this summary of Ponsonby's French war I am indebted to Howard Davies.

‡The inscribed volume is now in the possession of Howard Davies.

during the war, to show the French that 'English music did exist, for all their doubts'.[53]

Meanwhile, if Freda was hoping to get away from it all in Bude, she was in for a surprise. Her hosts there were her Broxbourne friends, the Kendalls, who had taken a house called The Balconies at Downs View. Fond as she was of them all, living *en famille* was a strain, because the son, David, was a little too fond of her. At best he was 'vague and infuriating', at worst 'foolish and difficult'.* However the weather was fine, and Freda was able to surf and sunbathe and explore the rocky coast up to Morwenstow and down to Dizzard Point; and in the evenings there were parlour games like the Prince of Wales's Hat, card games, books to be read, letters to be written. All went reasonably smoothly till 7 August when the telephone rang and a familiar voice announced that Ronald Biggs was in town – with his wife, Cécile.

The Head of Orchestral Programming had come to lay siege to his secretary, out of sight of Lennox and Basil Douglas. With Mrs Biggs in tow, he could not very well declare his love, so he opened his campaign by attacking the enemy. On the morning of the 8th, as the USSR was invading the Japanese puppet state of Manchukuo in one of the last offensives of the war, Biggs took Freda down to the beach for a long walk, during which he revealed some important news. He told her he had heard from 'D. P.' (perhaps the BBC's Director of Publicity, Kenneth Adam) that Lennox was not a bachelor at all, but a married man – who was now divorced (and therefore, in the society of the 1940s, beyond the pale). If Ronald Biggs had been hoping that Freda would be shocked, he did not know Freda. Even if she had believed him, she would not have minded, but she was so used to Biggs's improbable denunciations of anyone she liked that she made no comment, beyond adding an exclamation mark at the end of her account of the episode in her diary.[54] Freda seems to have accepted Ronald Biggs's presence in Bude with the same detached amusement (only occasionally rising to irritation) that she had shown when he took

*(FB, Diary, 16 and 17 August 1945, BFP). David Kendall emigrated to Canada in 1957, with his wife Nancy and three children, became a paediatrician specializing in brain damage,. He also taught at the University of British Columbia in Vancouver, and continued to write, and publish, poetry. In 2005, suffering from Alzheimer's Disease, he was living at a home on Vancouver Island (Letter from Stephen Watson, of Cowichan Station, Duncan, British Columbia, to FB, 18 March 2005, BFP).

her up to Regent's Park for a picnic lunch earlier in the summer, holding her hand and calling her 'my little Freda'.[55]

On 14 August, after the Americans had dropped their second atomic bomb, Japan surrendered unconditionally, and the new Labour Prime Minister Clement Attlee announced in a late-night radio broadcast that the Second World War was over. The next day, with her arm in a sling, following a surfing accident in which she had pulled a chest muscle, Freda went round to the Biggses' boarding house in Waterloo Road and celebrated V. J. Day with 'cocoa – searchlights – tea!'[56]

28
Lennox, Peter, Freda and Hans, London, 1945

Lennox was away in Painswick while all this was going on – taking it easy with Gladys Bryans, and on retreat with the Benedictine monks at Prinknash Abbey. He had hoped to spend some time at Prinknash at Whitsun in 1944 but had left the arrangements so late that the guests rooms were all booked. A year later his need for quiet contemplation and the community's prayers was more pressing than ever. We know that Lennox had wanted to talk to the abbot in April 1944, so it is unlikely that he missed the opportunity to try again now. Since his domestic problems were uppermost in his mind at this time, it is not impossible that, in the broadest terms, these – and their relationship to his faith – formed the substance of any discussions that took place between them. Lennox needed to unload his conflicts, and he knew that, though obliged to condemn his situation, the Roman priesthood, with its 'vast knowledge of the human heart',[1] would at least understand. But love and faith would not have monopolized their conversation: there would have been room too for the British movie business in general, and *Hotel Reserve* and James Mason in particular, since Abbot Wilfrid Upson was a keen film buff (who was to make a pilgrimage to the United States in 1947 to visit other Benedictine houses, and to meet some of his screen heroes. Three years later he published an account of his trip, under the title *Movies and Monasteries in USA*, which includes a photo of the author 'discussing religious films with Cecil B. de Mille'.[2])

Lennox was not well when he got back to London, and came to work for only a few hours a day. Freda, who had been so keenly looking forward to seeing him again, was upset by his constant absences and 'bad heads', and took it all personally.[3] But his abstraction was nothing to do with her. The thing was that Peter Fraser had brought another pick-up home to Warwick Square – and kept him there for a week. On 23 August Lennox could not tolerate it any longer, and moved out to Primrose Hill to stay with Basil Douglas and Martyn Webster. This rattled Peter, who suddenly woke up to the real possibility that he might lose Lennox (and his monthly allowance) if he did not change his ways. The next morning Peter rang the office, and promised Lennox it would never happen again. Freda was wrenched by these seesaw dramas, which she could not fail to overhear, and Lennox told her all about anyway.[4]

Peter's good intentions were short-lived. On 1 September he brought another man back to stay at Warwick Square. Lennox took it badly, and he – and Freda – burst into tears in the office. Perhaps as a result of something she suggested, Lennox rang Peter at his desk at the Air Ministry in the afternoon and told him he had decided to move out of Warwick Square and find a place of his own. Predictably a *rapprochement* followed, and within forty-eight hours all was forgiven.[5] Till next time.

There was consolation for Freda at home that week. Her admirer from the Monitoring Unit, the married Czech translator Peter Heller, came down to Broxbourne for the day. It was blazing hot and they went for a walk, then had tea in the garden. Freda knew that Heller was fond of her, and she enjoyed seeing him again, but whereas a year ago she might have cared, now nobody but Lennox meant anything to her.[6]

The more she felt for Lennox, the more it hurt when things went wrong. A week after Heller's visit, she was having lunch in the office with Lennox when Peter Fraser turned up. Instead of asking him to come back later, Lennox meekly allowed him to join them, whispering to Freda that he would make up for it at teatime.[7] Understandably Freda was unhappy and jealous – but no less determined to maintain her war of attrition. A few days later she bought Lennox some 'sandwiches, tobacco & cigs' to take to Northampton for a rehearsal of his new anthem at St Matthew's.[8] On his return to London, he showed his appreciation of her constant care and thoughtfulness by taking her out on their first date together, to hear his *Viola Sonata* at the National Gallery (presumably played by Watson Forbes, to whom it is dedicated; he and the pianist Denise Lassimonne gave another performance at the Contemporary Music Centre, London, on 3 May 1946).[9] Freda found the new work 'terribly moving', because, she wrote in her diary, it was 'so like him'[10] – an interesting response to a *Sonata* that's 'gloomy and pessimistic, with patches of dark brooding', according to the critic Edward Lockspeiser, who argued that this despondent mood reflected the Brahmsian, emotional side of Lennox's musical personality. Of the lighter, French side – the dry wit and intellectual elegance he learned from Boulanger – the *Sonata* showed no sign.[11]

Lennox may have been forty-two, established, successful and apparently secure, but to Freda he was a little boy lost. His modesty and gentleness, his absent-mindedness and impracticality conveyed the impression of a man too sensitive for the bumps of life, a man in need of looking after. It was not only women who wanted to mother him – or to exercise the authority that mothering involves. Peter Fraser loved Lennox, presumably as much for himself as for the benefits that came with him: absolute devotion, access to a smarter social world, and financial security. An instinct had told him, when they first met in 1940, that the habits of the biddable Lennox could be forged to make their life together work to Peter's advantage. Lennox returned Peter's love, but it was not a balanced relationship, because Peter was controlling and Lennox was afraid of him – of his unpredictability and his tantrums. As the years had passed, Peter had taken increasing advantage of Lennox's sweet nature, knowing that however wayward his own behaviour, Lennox would always forgive him. But Lennox was not without his own faults, even if many of them were simply another way of looking at his virtues. He was stubborn and secretive, undomesticated, slow and indecisive – and so deeply absorbed in his music, and the interior life that fed it, that he may not have had enough time for Peter. Still a boy at twenty-one, Peter wanted sensation and gratification; Lennox wanted peace.

Peter had come into Lennox's life with a history of promiscuity, so no one can have been surprised when it continued. But his behaviour was now so intrusive that Lennox dreaded going home, for fear of finding him in bed with another stranger. It may be that Peter was provoked by Lennox's apparent unresponsiveness, but it is more likely that he had now become addicted to the thrill of casual sex and, quite apart from any moral considerations, no longer felt any obligation even to be discreet. This, in turn, had thrown Lennox into the arms of Freda, which made Peter jealous and angry and determined to punish Lennox – thus further sorties into the night, more strangers at breakfast, and increased unhappiness for all concerned.

Lennox was not used to unreasonableness and did not know how to react. He had tried appeals, confrontation, tears and threats. Nothing had any lasting effect. Unable to understand Peter – let alone manage him – he seems finally to have decided that, though they were still nominally lovers, Peter's faithlessness had forfeited any claim on Lennox's own fidelity. If Peter could break the unwritten rules, then so could he. Though Lennox may have persuaded himself of the logic of this argument, he did not find its practical consequences easy. For one thing, 'sleeping around' betrayed his ideals. For another, the process was entirely alien to his character: he did not have the compulsiveness or the single-mindedness which promiscuity requires – and he did have the scruples which it does not. His weakness, if that is what it amounted to, was for deeper emotional entanglements; and to Peter these may well have seemed more threatening to their relationship than his own brief peccadilloes. Freda's diaries show that, unlike Peter's one-night stands, Lennox's consolations were short affairs. There were at least two of them – one in the autumn of 1945, the other in the summer of 1946. Apart from making Peter jealous and providing some comfort for himself, these relationships may have been designed to throw Freda off the scent, to prove that he really was gay, that it was not just his relationship with Peter that made a full relationship with her impossible.

The first new friend was a sailor called Pat. Lennox met him one evening in October, and brought him back to the flat, where he stayed for the next five weeks. Freda was upset when Lennox told her about this man.[12] She decided she must try to give Lennox up, but she found she could not.

On Saturday 13 October Lennox invited her up to the flat for the first time. Freda made them some lunch, then they settled down for an afternoon by the fire. Just when everything seemed to be going well, Lennox spoiled it all by announcing that Pat the sailor was coming round later on. Freda ought to have been hurt and angry, but her diary entry that night suggests she was no more than miffed. Despite the sailor, she was still convinced that Lennox was her man.[13]

Nevertheless it was a strain loving someone who was actually so unattainable, despite the signals he sent out, and later that month, during a difficult morning at the BBC, Freda lost her composure and told Lennox he was 'completely callous'.[14] One only wonders why she had never said so before, because, although Lennox would never have consciously hurt anyone, his behaviour to Freda was, to say the least, confusing. Perhaps he took the view that as she had chosen to fall in love with a man she knew to be gay and physically unable to respond to her, then any hurt was her own fault. It is more likely, however, that he was so involved with his own domestic troubles that he never gave a thought to his effect on Freda; he just assumed she knew how grateful he was for her friendship. Her unaccustomed show of mettle on 25 October seems to have worked. That very afternoon Lennox extended his usual theme of 'If only ...' to talk of actual marriage, and in Freda's presence he wrote a firm letter to Peter.

But nothing changed. Still Lennox went home to Peter, still Peter dragged back his 'rough trade', still Lennox invited Freda to lunch and spoke wistfully of marriage and children, still Peter barged in to claim Lennox as his, and still Lennox let him.

Peter's telephone calls to Lennox at the office – whispered, secretive and excluding – began to loom as a real threat to Freda. She thought she would go mad if he rang again. One day in November, in the new office (formerly Julian Herbage's) which they had just moved into, Peter spoke to Lennox on the phone for an unprecedented twenty minutes, while Freda pretended not to listen, and Ronald Biggs pretended not to watch her pretending not to listen. When Lennox eventually went home, Biggs looked up from his desk and told Freda he could not help being jealous of Lennox. 'Oh hell,' she wrote that night, 'I just can't bear it much longer.'[15]

Over the next fortnight the lovesick Biggs became so overwrought that his health suffered, which left Freda feeling nothing but disgust. On 29 November they had a blazing row. Two days later they had words again, but this time Biggs changed his tack: instead of disparaging Lennox, he defended him, warning Freda that she would end up hurting Lennox if she continued to chase him. 'Feel I loathe R. B.,' she wrote.[16]

Freda was caught in an extraordinary quadrangular relationship. She loved Lennox, who loved and feared Peter, who was jealous of Freda, who was loved by the married Biggs, who was bitter that Freda did not return his feelings and jealous of Lennox. But Freda's dogged devotion was beginning to make a positive impact on Lennox. On 23 November she noted that he was getting fonder of her; furthermore, he had told her that Peter was so very difficult that he would not be able to go on living with him for much longer.[17] When, a month later, Lennox was ill again and in some pain, Freda gave him all her sympathy and attention. Lennox was deeply grateful, and told her that no one had ever been so kind to him; he even talked, so her diary claims, of 'our imaginary babe'.[18]

Freda had achieved what no other marriageable woman had ever managed to achieve in Lennox's life before. In a courtship of patient attrition, she had won, successively, his interest, his admiration, his trust, and now his love. It helped that she was beautiful, charming and physically desirable (flirtatious too), but what tipped the scales were a kind heart, an uncritical mind, and a magnetic appeal that engendered mystery and attracted confidences.[19] Like her diary Freda seemed to be an open book – open, indeed, to the point of recklessness (since she was ready to accept anyone who was nice to her). But beneath the surface she was surprisingly strong and determined, so that she usually got her way. Lennox was not the first man to have found her irresistible – nor, by a long chalk, the last. Many of her fans have been homosexual, or bisexual, men, and some of them have found her sexually attractive. All turned to her with their troubles. Jim Lees-Milne once wrote, 'Never could I imagine a better friend or greater consolation in unhappiness than she.'[20]

If Freda was an extrovert, Lennox was the elusive opposite that strongly attracted: private, modest and absorbed in his own interior world. He was also absent-minded, impractical and indecisive, but he may have exaggerated these characteristics to create a shield behind which he could retreat into his inner life. His faith ran deep, giving him a foundation that was much firmer than the appearance of the structure above. A devout Catholic of the Continental kind, he believed intensely with the heart as well as the mind. In essence, his faith combined something of the passionate mysticism of St Teresa of Avila (and a lot of her wit) with the serenity of a contemplative monk. This feeling for the spiritual was partly a legacy from his mother, and partly the result of devotional meditation. From his mother too he had acquired, and with the latter he had honed, an intellectual discipline which is as characteristic of his music as its well-known 'Gallic charm': indeed it provides a check on the charm, preventing its becoming sentimental, though never disallowing the bittersweetness which gives the music such an engaging edge. The consequence of these paradoxes was that Lennox moved through life, as perhaps he moves through these pages, like a wraith, enhancing the vividness of those around him, while remaining indistinct himself. He seemed almost to have a foot in the next world, which may explain the 'saintliness' that was later ascribed to him. When Lennox died, Jim Lees-Milne wrote in his diary that he and his wife Alvilde felt unmoved by his departure, because they 'never quite got through to him'. Perhaps, he speculated, 'all saints are intangible.'[21] But to Freda who did get through to Lennox, instinctively and immediately, he was neither intangible nor a saint but the man she wanted to marry.

In December 1945 she may have felt he was getting closer to her emotionally, but geographically he was slipping off her map: in less than a fortnight he would be leaving the BBC to become a full-time composer. To make matters worse for Freda, she had just heard that Ursula Elliot, the secretary who had set her cap at Lennox during the war, was on her way back to England, and might want Lennox back. Freda would have to make some kind of move, and soon.

On 14 December she and Lennox met for a drink after work, then went on to a concert given by the oboist Evelyn Rothwell, wife of John Barbirolli. On the 17th they were going to have lunch together, but at the last minute Lennox put her off – in favour of Pat the sailor. On the Friday before Christmas they exchanged presents: he gave her a book and promised a proper present later, she gave him a leather dispatch case for his music. On Boxing Day Lennox came up to Broxbourne for a party – and at last, according to Freda's diary, he told her what she had been waiting so long to hear. 'Glorious few hours – he told me he loved me – and I knew it – if only ... The party was a success and for me it was more than that.'[22]

They both went back to work the following day, and in the lunch hour they caught a bus down to the National Gallery for a concert at which the viola d'amore player Karl Haas and his London Baroque Ensemble played some of Lennox's music. On the 28th they had a final teatime together, and the next day, Lennox's last at the BBC, they had a snack lunch followed by an intimate talk in the office. Freda made Lennox promise that if he could not survive on his freelance earnings as a composer and teacher, he would not be too proud to ask for her help. Perhaps with this in mind, a clause had been written into her 1944 Settlement, which permitted the loan of up to £2,000 'to any husband ... for the purpose of his profession'.[23] But Lennox was unlikely to need Freda's money. Commissions for new works were then so plentiful that a month after going freelance, he was able to report, 'If I can go on doing as well as I have since leaving I should more than make up for my former salary.'[24]

On 30 December 1945 Lennox went into the London Clinic to have a minor operation. The nature of the surgery was of no interest to

Freda: all she cared about was that it should not hurt, and that Lennox would be more comfortable afterwards. That same day she wrote in her diary, 'And so ends the happiest, unhappiest year of my life!' On a blank page at the end of the diary she expanded on this riddle, '1945. Without doubt the most eventful year of my life because in it I met my darling Lennox. How all this happened, neither of us know; we can neither of us remember the beginning of it all; it had no beginning – it just seemed to happen.'

Freda was convinced their paths had crossed for a purpose, but even she could not quite see what fate was going to do about it. Meanwhile she continued her hospital visits. She bought Lennox yellow chrysanthemums (yellow was the only colour he could recognize) at the wildly extravagant price of 8/6d each bloom (or £11.61 at today's values), she got him some new pyjamas, she went round to the flat and made lunch for Peter, and on the evening of 5 January she spent two and a quarter hours with Lennox at the London Clinic. He read Yeats to her, she read Dickens to him. Then she slipped into his bed.

On 12 January Lennox left hospital. The following day, a Sunday, Freda took the train up from Broxbourne to see him at home in Warwick Square, and he played Chopin and Bach for her. Her pleasure must have been marred by the presence of Peter who joined them for tea. Then on the Monday Lennox went off to Painswick for ten days' recuperation with Gladys Bryans. Peter put him on the train at Paddington.

The next day the weather suddenly got very cold, and Freda posted off a mercy parcel for Lennox at Painswick – 'cigs, tobacco & chocolate'.[25] What with these luxuries and the combination of breakfast in bed, country walks, and good home cooking, Lennox was soon feeling a different man – and his work was going well too. He was writing some incidental music for Louis MacNeice's radio feature about Guy de Maupassant, *A Glutton for Life* (for which the BBC paid him 35 guineas),[26] and a new piece for the 1946 Proms, *Nocturne for Orchestra*, which he dedicated to Peter Fraser.

Back in London, there had been two further developments. Peter had gone into hospital for an operation to correct a chronic nasal problem – his fourth operation since they had been together.[27] And Lennox's sister Geraldine had been sectioned under the 1930 Mental Health Act, and was now confined to the old Royal Lunatic Asylum in Manchester, one of the dreaded water-tower asylums of Victorian England. She had been found wandering in Ireland, giving her money away to strangers – or, what was left of her money after the depredations of an unknown religious sect whose leader she is said to have become involved with. It was not the first time that she had been picked up by the police, and it was clear that she now needed the protection of full-time psychiatric care.

Freda remembers Geraldine Berkeley – or Margaret, as she preferred to be called – as a gentle eccentric, who used to visit the Warwick Square flat, sitting in a corner, darning her stockings with brightly-coloured cottons, and talking quietly to herself. [28] Miss Berkeley was not the only person Miss Berkeley talked to: while Lennox was in the London Clinic, she had an intimate, and highly indiscreet, chat with Mrs Farrell, the daily at No. 58, during which she revealed the sleeping arrangements of the entire household.[29]

To Lennox's 'inexpressible relief', Geraldine wrote to Painswick to say she had settled down well in hospital, 'and no difficulties have arisen'.[30] By the summer of 1946 she had been discharged. In 1949 she was living in Belsize Park,[31] and the following year she had an address in Eastbourne, but it was not long before she was returned to Cheadle. She was to find institutional life less threatening than the outside world, into which she made one or two unsatisfactory return forays, for short periods, before being re-admitted in 1953 to what was by then called the Cheadle Royal Infirmary.That same year her affairs were put in the hands of the Court of Protection. Geraldine was to remain at the Cheadle Infirmary for the thirty-five years left of her life; she died there on 6 June 1988, aged ninety-one.

The diaries and letters of this time – January 1946 – suggest that Lennox hoped he could maintain the *status quo* of his private life – Peter as lover, 'son' and flatmate, Freda as girlfriend, 'mother' and *confidante*. To persuade him it was all working fine, Freda kept saying how nice Peter was. She was afraid that the alternative would be no Lennox in her life at all. Lennox was delighted: 'I can't tell you how happy I am that you and he get on so well together,' he wrote to Freda from Painswick.[32] When Freda tentatively proposed a private meeting with Lennox on his return to London, Lennox explained that he had to spend some time with Peter – because of his recent operation – but hoped he might be able to see her for part of an evening.[33]

Aware that 'part of an evening together' might well be as much as she would ever get, unless she changed her tactics, Freda decided to tell Lennox some home truths about Peter. While he was still at Painswick, she wrote to say she had called round at the flat and found 'a v. sulky, petulant, spoilt Peter'.[34] Lennox was less upset than amused by her account, and, like an indulgent parent, said he was glad that 'these "spoilt child" moments' were becoming less frequent.

> Though in the past I gave in to him far too much, I don't any more. He was in a very black mood when I arrived [back in London] on Saturday, but I paid no attention and after about 20 minutes he brightened up, and was quite cheerful when I left. He must grow out of this, and as I say I think he is much better. What a strange mixture of things people's characters are made up of – we have these contradictions, most people learn to disguise them.[35]

It was clear that Lennox was content with Peter just as he was. Freda, who was not, decided she had had enough. What was the point of 'constantly longing for the impossible?' she asked herself, not for the first time.[36] Determined to try to forget Lennox, she applied for a job in Austria, with the British Element of the Control Commission. This was the civilian organization set up by the Allies at the end of the war to supervise the restoration of normal life in the defeated states of Europe. She was not sure what exactly she would be expected to do once she got to Austria, but she was sure that she did not want to be in London any more. Secretly she hoped that Lennox would talk her out of it, and during his brief break in London, he had given her lunch at Canuto's and told her he had missed her more than he had expected and that he did not want her to go to Austria.[37] But when he was back in Painswick he was able to take a more objective view of her plan, and he wrote to say he did not think he should stand in her way, '... on the one hand I should hate you to disappear for a year, but on the other you must lead your own life and not neglect opportunities ... The head and the heart are so often in opposition.'[38]

By the beginning of February Lennox was even more certain that she should go to Austria, and wrote to tell her so. This was not at all what Freda wanted to hear. 'I love him so & can't can't have him,' she wrote, in bewildered frustration.[39] Then on the 17th something happened that seems to have ruled out Austria. It was the night of the broadcast of MacNeice's Maupassant feature, *A Glutton for Life*, and Lennox was not feeling well so Freda went into the studio with him, holding his hand while Walter Goehr conducted an *ad hoc* orchestra in a live performance of Lennox's incidental music. Afterwards he was feeling so out of sorts that they skipped dinner and took a taxi straight back to Warwick Square, where Lennox allowed Freda to put him to bed. Feeling a little better the next day, he invited Freda to lunch at the flat – with Peter. That was hardly what she had hoped for, after the advance of the night before, but she took it bravely and went along, ever hopeful. 'What a strange strange situation,' her diary reports.[40] 'If only L was normal and we could marry.'[41]

And so it went on, the ups and downs of a relationship which made no one happy – and everyone ill. No sooner had Peter left hospital after his nose operation than Freda got a poisoned leg and had to have it lanced, then Lennox got otitis and had to have his ear-drum pierced. To make matters worse, he had also caught scabies, a highly infectious infestation of tiny parasitic mites, which caused intense itching all over his body. The treatment involved coating himself with petroleum jelly mixed with sulphur for three nights in a row, and wearing gloves to blunt the effects of scratching.

With Lennox needing her so badly, Freda's feelings for him only increased. She could not bear the thought of leaving him, and gave up any idea of escape – to Austria or anywhere else. Instead she applied for a job at Sotheby's, the fine-art auctioneers, as secretary to Lennox's old Oxford friend Vere Pilkington, who was now a director (and soon to be chairman). Freda's diary makes no bones about her reasons for choosing Sotheby's: because she thought it would retain her closeness with Lennox.[42] Perhaps, too, she sensed that Vere might be an ally in her fight for Lennox, since he himself, though formerly gay, was now happily married – to Honor Philipps, a daughter of the controversial Welsh shipowner Lord Kylsant (and the divorced wife of another gay man, Lord Faringdon). Freda was offered the job at Sotheby's on 23 March, and resigned from the BBC on the same day.[43] Whether she knew it or not – and Lennox did not – the office was thick with gossip that she was leaving to marry Lennox.[44]

A few days later Freda found herself even closer to Lennox than the new job could possibly have brought her. Mrs Conway, the housekeeper at Warwick Square, was ill and could not come to work, so Lennox rang Freda and asked if she would come round to make the beds and rustle up some lunch. This was just the sort of mercy errand that Freda loved. And she was well rewarded when, after lunch, Lennox hinted vaguely that 'things might come right ultimately'.[45] She herself still did not dare hope that they would, or even could, come right,[46] but on 28 March, when they were alone together, after dinner with Peter at the flat, Lennox said he thought that marriage really was on the cards.

One of the obstacles, though Lennox did not discuss it with Freda, was the difficulty of breaking free of the dependent and volatile Peter, but this was a decision which, ultimately, would need only courage and resolve. There was another obstacle that was much more complicated. If Lennox was going to commit himself to marriage, he had to be sure not only that he really loved Freda, but that he could make her as happy, in every possible way, as she had the right to expect of a husband. Whilst he was sure he did love her, he was sufficiently realistic to realize that as a middle-aged gay man he was unlikely to make a satisfactory lover – however optimistic, generous and skilful she might be. The problem was not that he was gay (she already knew that), but that he always would be gay, that he could not change: this she was too young to know, or, at any rate, to accept. In this one respect, their marriage was bound to be incomplete, inadequate for both of them. It might flower in other ways – and he hoped (and she knew instinctively) that it would. But it would always be more platonic than erotic. Maybe, though, that did not matter; maybe, if honestly faced, it might even provide a securer basis for marriage.

Lennox needed to get away for a while, and a British Council concert of his *Symphony No. 1* in Strasbourg offered the perfect opportunity. On 17 April, three days before he was appointed a professor of composition at the Royal Academy of Music, and four before Freda started her new job at Sotheby's, he crossed the Channel for the first time since the beginning of the war. Nadia, now back in France after her exile in America, was very much in his thoughts. 'I am so happy to know you are back,' he had written to her, before he set off – 'it's the best news for a long time!'[47] He invited her to join him for the weekend at Le Mé Chaplin, the romantic property in a wood on a hill at Jouy-en-Josas near Versailles, where he was staying with Alvilde Chaplin, who had inherited the house from the princesse de Polignac. Ma'moiselle could not stay the weekend, but she did come over for a long lunch. Lennox was overjoyed to see her again – and to find she had hardly changed at all.[48]

Recounting it all in a letter to 'My dear Freda' on Easter Day, Lennox said he longed to bring her together with Nadia. He was sure she would immediately appreciate Nadia's special qualities, since they shared the same capacity for recognizing true values in people.[49]

Lennox explained that he was leaving for Paris that evening, to play in a private performance of his *Sonatina for Treble Recorder*, and the following day he was travelling on to Strasbourg to conduct his *Symphony*. He signed the letter 'All love, Lennox'.

On his way home from Strasbourg, Lennox stopped in Paris for dinner with Nadia, and a more private talk than he had been able to have at Le Mé. It is reasonable to assume that he might have wanted to tell her about Freda, but there is no evidence that he talked of anything but music, so perhaps he felt that it would be inappropriate. He talked of Britten, trying, again, to win Nadia over to his music – and failing again, because, although she conceded that Britten wrote 'with meticulous care', she found his language too romantic.[50] But at least he was able to recharge his musical batteries. Back home in London he wrote to tell Nadia how wonderful it had been to see her after so long, and how badly he had needed re-exposure to her 'attitude towards music':

> I feel that I can now 'get away' with things rather too easily, mainly because my music happens to be more pleasing to the ear and more easily understood than most contemporary music, and because of this I am perhaps more tempted to think that it is good than I would be if it were written in a more difficult idiom. But you bring me back to reality in a moment! And I find myself already looking at my work with a more critical eye since I have seen you. I think that certain natures easily confuse beauty with pleasure and have to make a continual effort to keep them apart – I think that Poulenc for instance is apt to do this, but though it is dangerous to people like him and me it is perhaps a good thing that the element of pleasure should return to music after all the grim and false austerity ... [51]

This is precisely what alarmed Lennox's admirers about Nadia Boulanger's influence – the danger that her dislike of the merely pleasing in music would lead to the 'grim and false austerity', which, in the guise of his oratorio *Jonah,* had been branded 'Stravinskian dessication', and had 'nearly wrecked' Lennox's chances as a composer.[52] But the letter seems to show a newly independent Lennox welcoming the return of pleasure to his music.

Nadia was not unaware that part of the letter – the reference to the poles of 'beauty' (or restraint and order) and 'pleasure' (or abandon and chaos) – was as much about Lennox himself as his music. In Lennox's view, Poulenc made the mistake of confusing the two – of trying to mix what Rostand called the 'monk' side of his nature, his Catholicism, with the 'guttersnipe' side, his homosexuality.[53] Watching Poulenc straining at the leash of these contradictions, Lennox seems now to have come to the conclusion that beauty and pleasure should be kept apart. Since he is writing at the height of his dilemma over Freda and Peter, 'beauty' could be said to represent his spiritual love for Freda, and 'pleasure' his sexual love for Peter. If he had hoped he could run the two concurrently, he now saw the danger; perhaps he was even ready to replace one with the other.

Freda was so excited to have Lennox back in London that she may have pushed things a little too far after dinner on their first evening together. It is not clear what went wrong, but in some way she must have presumed the relationship was further advanced than suited Lennox, and he must have shown his displeasure. Whatever happened, it left Freda wretched for a week. 'Sheer and utter misery,' she entered in her diary for May Day. She got home to Broxbourne very late and, alone in her room, she 'howled' into her pillow. At breakfast she vowed she would never see him again. But once in the office, she only just resisted the temptation to phone him, and at lunch she went out to Alfred Dunhill's smart pipe shop in Duke Street to buy him a silver lighter for his birthday. (Later she resolved to hang on to it till he had offered an olive branch – but when peace was made, she decided the lighter was not 'nice enough', so she gave it to someone else, and chose a better one – 'v. expensive but awfully nice' – which she finally handed over on 10 July.[54]) For three weeks they saw nothing of one another, but on 21 May Lennox broke the ice by proposing they should go together to watch a matinée showing of *Hotel Reserve*, for which he had written the music.

Nine days later there was a significant development. After dining alone with Freda at No. 58, Lennox gave her a specially warm hug, sat her down with him in the big chair they often shared on such intimate evenings, talked to her of her recent birthday, of their feelings for one another, and of the absent Peter. He then explained gently and kindly how he regretted that he could not feel anything physical for her. Freda had heard this before, and did not take it too seriously. Nor, it seems, did Lennox, because the evening ended in some kind of sexual contact.[55] A fortnight later, the same thing happened again, but without the contradictory warning beforehand, and with a much more positive conclusion: '... another *very* wonderful evening with my darling L ... We talked of our children – how we both wished ... He wants everything to happen & it's going to.'[56]

Lennox then lost his nerve, fearing that he was leading Freda on – or encouraging her to lead him on – towards an inevitably unhappy ending, and on 26 June he told her their intimate meetings had to stop. She was hurt, assuming he meant they should part for ever. The next day they put it all straight again, but the *détente* seems to have involved maintaining a certain distance, and for nearly three months they saw very much less of one another, though they continued to exchange affectionate letters.

That they had been able to meet privately in the flat suggests that Lennox and Peter may have reached an understanding, granting each the latitude that Peter had previously taken unilaterally. Now that he had forbidden himself Freda's company in the evenings, and Pat the sailor had gone (while Peter, a *stratophile*, who liked 'a bit of scarlet', was still working his way through the Brigade of Guards), Lennox suddenly found himself alone. Driven by a combination of loneliness and temptation, he picked up a new young man, Fred, who was to spend occasional nights at Warwick Square throughout July.[57]

It was not long before Freda got wind of Fred. Needing a shoulder to cry on in these curious circumstances, she found herself confiding in a senior colleague at Sotheby's, the art historian Hans-Dietrich Gronau. The son of the eminent author of standard texts on Bellini and Correggio, Dr Gronau had studied in Göttingen with the scholar of the Dutch baroque Wolfgang Stechow, and, while there, he had met and married Carmen Joachim von Wogau, a student of Nikolaus Pevsner. In the mid-thirties, with Hitler as Chancellor and the Nazis ruthlessly crushing all opposition, the young Gronaus had fled to Britain – to the safety of Carmen's Feilding cousins at Beckley Park in Oxfordshire. When war broke out, Gronau was interned as an enemy alien, but later released into the Pioneer Corps (in which Wulff Scherchen was also serving – along with 10,000 other British aliens) for war work within the UK. At the end of the war he was recruited by Vere Pilkington as cataloguer, to help build up Sotheby's picture department, as a direct challenge to Christie's. By mid-1946 Gronau was head of the Old Masters Department (a position to which his widow succeeded after his early death, of a congenital heart condition, in 1951).*

Hans Gronau, then aged forty-two, was captivated by the beautiful secretary in Vere Pilkington's office, and he and Freda were soon meeting for long talks in his office in the basement. By way of thanks he presented Freda with his own, much-treasured, copy of *The Drawings of Leonardo da Vinci*, in which, at her request, he wrote, 'F. B. In gratitude. H. D. G. Whitsun 1946.'[58] This modest inscription hardly does justice to the intense feelings which Freda had stirred up. The truth was that he had fallen in love with her, and she cannot have done much to discourage him since, a week letter, she confesses in her diary, 'Like Dr G. so much – he attracts me very much physically ... tho I wish L felt as he does about me.'[59] There are no photos of Gronau in Freda's extensive collection of family photos. When asked why, she explains that they never exchanged photographs, since they both felt it necessary to keep their friendship secret. She remembers him as broad-shouldered, with dark brown crinkly hair, spectacles and a kind face.[60]

On 17 June Gronau invited her out to dinner, and afterwards they walked up to Regent's Park and sat and talked under the trees. By the following day, promoted in Freda's diary from 'Dr G.' to 'Hans', he took her out for a drink after work. One day they had tea, and afterwards sat together in St James's Park; on another day he gave her fifty cigarettes, and she gave him some home-grown tomatoes. Once they were having lunch together at Sotheby's when Lennox suddenly arrived to look at the paintings: Freda introduced her two admirers and was delighted that they seemed to like one another.[61] Inevitably the day came when Gronau came into Freda's office to announce that his wife had guessed about them.[62]

Torn by this newly-complicated twist in her life, Freda was glad to escape to Cornwall with the Kendalls for her summer holidays at the beginning of August. But Bude was not any safer. While looking for a place to sunbathe on the Atlantic beach of Crooklets on the sunny morning of the 4th, Freda bumped into the bathing-trunked Head of Orchestral Planning, Ronald Biggs. The combination of her panting

*The same heart condition was to cause the early deaths of both his sons. In 1958 Carmen Gronau was appointed the first woman director of Sotheby's, to form a powerful leadership with the chairman Peter Wilson.. She died in Florence at her father-in-law's villa on 15 February 1999, aged 88 (Obituary, *The Times*, 11 March 1999).

former boss and the temperamental David Kendall, whose interest in Freda manifested itself in constant arguments, did nothing to contribute to the rest she needed. She hoped that the week still to come with the Boultbees at Harvington might cheer her up. But Harvington was no better. While picking plums in Pershore she ran into another old admirer, Brian Brazier, elder son of the market gardener with whom she had had the dalliance in 1942. Like his father, young Brian still had eyes for Freda – but time had moved on, and for Freda now there was no one but Lennox.

Back in London in the middle of August she took up with Hans Gronau again, even visiting his mansion flat near the Albert Hall, and, on one occasion, looking after his baby son Philip. But Gronau knew that his feelings for Freda were putting a strain on them all, particularly his wife, Carmen, and since he also knew that Freda's heart lay elsewhere, he wrote to her on 9 September to say 'All this must cease.' Not that there was much to cease, beyond what Freda calls 'kisses and cuddles in the the basement'.[63] For a week or two things were difficult at work, till Hans Gronau managed to steady his feelings and to steer the relationship back into the stiller waters of platonic friendship.

29
Lennox and Freda, London, 1946

Lennox was having a busy and successful summer. It started with the premiere of his *Piano Sonata*, given by its dedicatee Clifford Curzon, at a widely-noticed and well-attended recital at the Wigmore Hall on 22 July 1946. Hearing Curzon at rehearsals, Lennox was inspired to write to Desmond Shawe-Taylor, urging him to come to the recital, and to bring Eddy Sackville-West with him. Curzon, he said, 'plays my Sonata wonderfully, and I think it's really my best effort so far'.[1]

The new piece came between Schubert's *B Flat Sonata* and Liszt's *B Minor Sonata*. *The Times*, whilst noting that Curzon was 'among the most musicianly of our pianists' and had given a 'most beautiful performance' of the Schubert, was only grudgingly appreciative of Lennox's work. Trying to overcome a first impression of 'patent eclecticism', the anonymous critic thought the opening movement lacked direction. The inner movements were 'more successful', and the finale had some 'fine bravura writing ... and an impressive coda'. At least', the review concluded, Berkeley was 'not afraid to indulge in showy passage work'.[2] This lukewarm notice contrasts oddly with the verdict of the Australian composer Malcolm Williamson, Master of the Queen's Music, who hailed the work in 1991 as 'an absolutely faultless, stupefying masterpiece'.[3] Perhaps the fact that the difficult *Sonata* has survived sixty years and is still a favourite of discerning pianists (at least four of whom have recorded it),* seems to support Dr Williamson's judgement.

*The Berkeley *Piano Sonata* has been recorded by Colin Horsley (in 1959 – on Lyrita RCS 9), Christopher Headington (1988 – on Kingdom Records KCI CD 2012), Raphael Terroni (1993 – on British Music Society Records BMS 416 CD), and Margaret Fingerhut (2004 – on Chandos Digital CHAN 10247), and it can be heard online in a performance by the Japanese pianist the late Kumiko Ida (formerly a committee member of the Lennox Berkeley Society) in her British Piano Series with Schatzgraber on www.schatz.co.jp/british/sonatae.html.

Freda went to the concert with Lennox, Peter, John Weyman and John Pope-Hennessy, having made lunch for them all at the flat beforehand. Lennox placed Freda on his right, with Peter on her other side, then Weyman and finally Pope-Hennessy on Lennox's left. Afterwards they all went back to the flat for dinner.[4]

A month later Lennox's *Nocturne* was played at the Proms (by the BBC Symphony Orchestra, conducted by Sir Adrian Boult). Freda was there, and reported loyally that it 'went down very well'. *The Times* liked it too ('first-rate', with a 'nice sense of orchestral colour' and a 'most beautiful' climax.)[5] The next day Freda rang Lennox to congratulate him, and was touched that he seemed so pleased.[6] That morning he was already back at the keyboard, completing a sketch of a new, shorter orchestral piece – *Overture* – which he had started some months earlier but had abandoned because he got stuck. 'It's very light and rather gay,' he told Freda – 'in complete contrast to the *Nocturne*'[7] (which Peter Dickinson describes as 'a nightmarish piece').[8] The *Overture* was written for Anthony Bernard and his chamber orchestra, but shortly after its first performance in Canterbury Cathedral in June 1947 Lennox disowned the piece, and the music is now lost, so it is impossible to say for sure, but, if the anguished intervals and dramatic arguments of the *Nocturne* reflect something of the tension of Lennox's life with Peter (to whom it is dedicated), the *Overture* may have represented a glimpse of happier times with Freda.

Lennox had also written five new song settings, to poems by Walter de la Mare, for Pierre Bernac and Francis Poulenc (who performed them on their London tour the following winter), and some incidental music for a Shakespeare play at Stratford-upon-Avon and a Greek drama on the radio. He had also made an orchestration of the Fauré pieces which he had arranged for two pianos in 1940, for a grand new production of the *Le grand Meaulnes* ballet, *La Fête étrange*, planned for the much bigger stage of Sadler's Wells.[9]

In the midst of all this activity Wulff Scherchen, now renamed John Woolford, had suddenly reappeared – by letter from Germany, where he was working as Assistant Musical Director of the British Forces Network radio station in Hamburg.* He was keen to broadcast some of

*Later in 1946, after an office 'intrigue', John Woolford was released from the broadcasting section of BFN, Hamburg (Pauline Woolford to BB, 18 November 1946, LFAL, p. 183). In 1947 Woolford left the Army and became a civil servant in Cambridge (John Woolford to BB, 13 April 1948, JWP). In 1965 he was

Lennox's new music, and wanted some advice about what to choose.[10] In reply, Lennox sent a list of the nine 'more important things' he had written since the beginning of the war: *Serenade for Strings* (1939), *String Quartet No. 2* (1940), *Symphony* (1941), *Sonatina for Violin and Piano* (1942), *Divertimento for Orchestra* (1942), *Sonata for Piano* (1943), *String Trio* (1944), *Sonata for Violin and Piano* (1945), and *Nocturne for Orchestra* (1946). He also said he had recently seen Ben Britten who 'seemed all right', but was 'having to pay the usual price for success – lack of quiet, and time for things outside work'.[11]

A week after writing to Wulff, Lennox went down to Glyndebourne for the premiere of Ben's new opera, *Lucretia*, with Peter Pears, Joan Cross and Kathleen Ferrier in the leading roles, and Ansermet conducting. He liked it so much that he went again on 15 July (and, for a third time, with Freda, on 3 September). One or two musical moments, he told Desmond Shawe-Taylor, were so beautiful that he found himself subconsciously thinking about them the whole time.[12] And it was not just the music, but the singing too – in particular the voice, and the character, of Kathleen Ferrier, who was to provide an important inspiration for Lennox himself just six months later.

That summer of 1946 Lennox was invited to join the BBC Music Advisory Panel, and not long afterwards he also became a music adjudicator for the BBC. But he was so generous in his judgement of artists auditioning for radio broadcasts that the BBC had to instruct him to raise his standards and 'ruthlessly reject all border-line cases', in order to reduce the number of artists on the books.[13] In his reply, Lennox admitted that he was inclined to be too lenient, and undertook to try to raise the standard. Though always fair, Lennox was not a pushover: as a score reader on the advisory panel he recorded that one particular composer's violin sonata was 'hopelessly banal'.[14] The man in question was the organist and composer Allan Biggs, brother of Lennox's unlamented former boss Ronald Biggs.

By now Peter had been transferred to Reading, for a final brief posting before his discharge from the RAF. There Lennox stayed with him, in his billet, in mid-August, after returning from a happy week with the Harrises in Jersey. The two had an eventful twenty-four hours, visiting

---

working for the Ministry of Technology (John Woolford to BB, 1 December 1965, JWP). He later emigrated to Australia, where he was still living with his wife Pauline in 2009.

Caversham House, where Freda had worked earlier in the war, and going to see the Ealing Studios spy drama *The Captive Heart*, set (and actually filmed) in a German POW camp. Produced by Michael Balcon and directed by Basil Dearden, the film stars Michael Redgrave as a Czech patriot who pretends to be a dead British officer in order to avoid being shot by the Nazis. When he is captured and interned, the British prisoners think he is a spy – till he shows his colours during a daring escape. Redgrave's wife Rachel Kempson plays the dead officer's widow, with whom the Czech eventually falls in love. Lennox thought it a very good film, but 'rather harrowing'.[15] There is no record of what he thought about the score by Alan Rawsthorne, a composer he much admired.

Peter, who had recently been been ill with 'a liver attack', was now quite recovered, and the weekend after the Reading reunion with Lennox he had returned to London – where Lennox, by then in peaceful Painswick with Gladys Bryans, thought he was probably having 'a high old time in my absence!'[16]

Come September, Lennox and Freda were both back in London. Responding to Lennox's warm letters, Freda invited him to Broxbourne for the day, to see where she lived and to meet her friend and landlady Nancy Gregory. He agreed and they fixed a date for Sunday the 22nd. But then he forgot – or was barred by Peter. Freda was furious, and hurt – and that night she got 'horribly drunk'. The sequel, however, was positive. Lennox had a row with Peter and gave him his marching orders.[17] Not that Freda set much store by Lennox's resolve, having heard it all before – so she simply reassured him that he had done the right thing, and noted in her diary: 'How ludicrous it all is!'[18] Then she locked away the diary, put on her favourite little black dress from Dickins and Jones, and caught the bus to Hertford for a cocktail party in aid of the Conservatives.

The following weekend she found herself in the middle of a family drama. Her aunt Lilian Nunney – wife of Alfred, the eldest of the Nunney sons – rang on the Saturday to say that Grandmother Nunney had suffered another stroke, six weeks short of her eightieth birthday, and was not expected to survive. Freda rushed up to town, and managed to reach the house in Lancefield Street just before the old lady died – without, though, regaining consciousness, so Freda was not able to say a proper goodbye. It consoled her that she had looked so calm and peaceful, but she was sad that her grandfather was completely broken.[19] On the day of the funeral, four days later, Freda watched her grandfather stretch out a hand to stroke his wife's face before the coffin was sealed, and noted that this gesture left him much more composed. After the funeral, the family followed the horse-drawn hearse up to Willesden Lane, Kilburn, for the committal at Paddington Old Cemetery, where Blanch Nunney was laid to rest in the grave of her father-in-law. Freda, who had long ago grown apart from her Nunney relations, felt disconcertingly remote from it all, and was relieved when the day was over.[20]

'Completely and utterly alone & wretched', Freda realized that Lennox mattered more than ever, and decided to risk a second invitation to Broxbourne. Lennox was quick to accept this time. But first Freda had to check with Nancy Gregory if it was all right – the house was hers, after all. Nancy decided it was not all right, and they had a frightful row.[21] By the next morning Nancy had changed her mind – Lennox could come after all.[22]

He arrived after dinner on the Saturday night. They had a long talk, sitting together on the sofa, then 'after intense emotion', they went to bed – not in Freda's room, but, for Nancy's sake, in the spare room. The bed was a bit small for both, but 'everything happened', just as she had always prayed it would. In the morning they went for a walk, then lunch, then a talk in Freda's room, then another longer walk. In the evening they lay on Freda's bed, and at nine Lennox caught the train back to London.[23]

In retrospect the weekend seemed no more real than a dream, and Freda was 'outrageously, gloriously, blissfully happy'. She had found what she called 'a new Lennox' – a Lennox 'as normal as I am'. It was, she wrote in her diary, a miracle.[24] Lennox was, of course, no more or less 'normal' than he had been on the Saturday morning. Freda can be forgiven for thinking it was a miracle, because Lennox had so often told her that, whatever else their relationship might involve, there could never be any love-making. But he had not changed, he had simply responded to the heat of the moment. He loved her and he was glad he had made her happy: it was not a miracle, but a caprice of human nature. In so far as it opened the way to marriage, it was going to make a tremendous difference to his life, he told Freda. It would make no less of a difference to Freda's life too – and to Peter's, for he depended on Lennox, socially and economically as well as emotionally. Conscious of all his responsibilities, Lennox still could not bring himself to make the decision that would commit him to marriage, though he rang Freda every day.

A fortnight after the Broxbourne weekend, Lennox and Freda

lunched together at Warwick Square, and Lennox expressed misgivings about marriage. Freda left for home in such deep despair that Lennox was worried and made her promise she would ring from Broxbourne to say she had got back all right. But she was not all right, so she ignored her promise. Later that night he rang her. Freda would have been more than mollified by this gesture, but Nancy Gregory, who was in the room at the time and had had enough of Lennox's dithering, snatched the phone and gave him a lecture about his responsibilities.[25] Perhaps Nancy had guessed what Freda was to realize five days later.[26]

Freda's first response to the reality that she might be pregnant was to make an appointment with her doctor, Gordon Ackland. She was not sure what she felt about it, but she did know very clearly that she wanted to keep the news from Lennox.[27] She was fearful it would force him into a marriage he did not really want – and that Peter would think she had planned it all.

The next day, after work, Freda set off to see the doctor. She was, her diary records, 'feeling desperate'. Somehow she 'mustn't have the child – and Lennox must never know.' At 6 pm on 11 November she left the office at Sotheby's in George Street, intending to walk down to Piccadilly to catch a bus to Barons Court. As she was turning the corner into New Bond Street, Hans Gronau caught her up and asked her why she had not said goodbye. His kindness made her cry, and, there and then, she told him everything. Gronau bundled her into a passing taxi, got in with her, and, on the way to Barons Court, he made her understand that whatever happened she had to have the baby.

She arrived at the surgery feeling more at peace. Gronau then left, taking the taxi back to his mansion flat in Kensington Court Place. Dr Ackland, like Gronau, urged Freda to tell Lennox immediately, and invited her to use the telephone on his desk. When she got through to Lennox (who was practising some song accompaniments), he told her to call round at nine that evening. Then she left the surgery, returned to the West End, found a Lyons' Corner House and struggled through a fry-up till the appointed time.[28]

It might reasonably be expected that when at last nine o'clock came, Freda burst into tears and asked Lennox to make a respectable woman of her, but this would be wide of the mark. What actually happened in the drawing room of No. 58 that winter's night was that she and the father of her unborn baby just sat and laughed. Faced with a domestic crisis that threatened to throw their lives into confusion – and despite having 'very mingled feelings' – Freda found Lennox neither angry nor repentant; simply happy.

Actually there was not much time for any talk, because at ten Lennox had to be in Chelsea to take part in a musical evening at the home of Alvilde Chaplin's bachelor cousin, the decorator Angus Menzies. So he suggested they should walk round there together, talking on the way. At the door of Angus's house they parted. Freda made her way back to Barons Court, where she was spending the night with her friend Margaret Brazell. Lennox went on in, to play the piano for two amateur singers: Menzies himself and the young writer and broadcaster Barbara Ward, a governor of the BBC and Assistant Editor of *The Economist*. Jim Lees-Milne who was there with Alvilde and her estranged husband Anthony Chaplin recorded that Barbara Ward sang 'in a very missish voice which no one applauded', and that Menzies's voice was 'deep and mellifluous'. He could not resist adding that the 'seductive' Menzies had 'glossy black hair and a Michelangelo mouth and eyes'.[29] What Jim did not know – and would have had something to say if he had – was that the pianist, a Catholic bachelor of forty-three, had learned that very night that he was about to become a father.

For the rest of the week Lennox and Freda were up and down with 'constant telephonings'.[30] On the 19th Freda got a letter from Dr Ackland confirming that her tests were positive: there was no doubt that she was pregnant. That night she and Lennox dined at a restaurant, then went on to a party at the Gronaus' and they both ended up in Barons Court at Freda's friend's flat. The next day all Lennox's old fears returned and he rang Freda at Sotheby's to say he did not see how he could tell Peter. Twenty-four hours later he was talking of buying a house for himself and Freda and the baby. On the 22nd Lennox's flatmate, John Weyman, told Freda that Lennox had confided the night before that he was definitely going to marry her. But when Freda came up to Paddington to see Lennox off to Reading, where he was going to stay with Peter, Lennox said nothing, so Freda spent the rest of the day wandering around London feeling miserable. The following day Lennox rang to say that at last he really had told Peter. Freda went straight to Warwick Square, and both of them wept with relief that it was all over.

And there Freda's diary ends. Yet the drama was far from over. Lennox may have spoken to Peter, but all he had told him was that Freda was pregnant and that he was the father. He still had not told him they were getting married. Nor had he told Freda – because he still had not decided. The diary was abandoned not because the last obstacle had been cleared, but because its clearance suddenly revealed all the other obstacles – and Freda, now ill and anxious, was in no state to waste time scribbling.

Lennox was in the tightest corner of his life. A middle-aged Catholic, living with a possessive, temperamental and unreliable young man in a relationship that was both destructive and illegal, he had fallen in love with an orphaned half-Jewish girl young enough to be his daughter – and made her pregnant. Ever since moving into Warwick Square, his private life had become more open, more complicated and more bohemian – and his essentially conventional nature had been tested to the limit. Now his life seemed to be running out of control, and he was paralysed with indecision. If he did not marry Freda, what did the future promise? Did he really want to go on living with a hysterical, mercenary young man who only made him miserable? And if it were not Peter, was it not likely to be more of the same? If he did marry Freda, he would gain a beautiful and devoted wife, a family, social respectability, the blessing of his Church, and, perhaps, a sense of fulfilment he had never yet experienced. But by nature he would still be homosexual, subject to all the old feelings and desires. Was this fair to Freda? Was it fair to himself?

The social and legal pressures on gay men in the late 1940s were almost overwhelmingly hostile. Society expected men to marry and father children, particularly in 1946 as a victorious but economically crippled Britain gathered together all her strength for the rebuilding effort after the losses of six years at war. Furthermore the law still punished active homosexuality, even in the privacy of the bedroom. In such an atmosphere, bachelors were considered at worst suspect and at best inadequate, and blackmail was rife. Not all gay men could cope. Some denied their nature, even to themselves, and entered into marriages that could not possibly work (for example, Lennox's friends Gavin Faringdon and Patrick Kinross, and both the husbands of the rich and beautiful painter Primrose Harley, John Codrington and Lanning Roper).*

*Daughter of the heart specialist Dr Vaughan Harley, Primrose Harley married first, at the Royal Military Chapel, Wellington Barracks, on 21 December 1936, Major John Codrington, Coldstream Guards, but the couple divorced in 1942. Codrington left the Army as a lieutenant-colonel and went into MI5, then films, and finally (like his successor as Prim's second husband, Lanning Roper) landscape gardening.

Some still preferred the independence of the single life, despite society's disapproval. Some, like Peter Fraser, positively thrived on the sense of danger. A few brave souls – by no means all of them protected by the tolerance of an artistic circle – formed their own domestic arrangements, which, like Ben and Peter's, were marriages in all but the eyes of the law and the Church.* But in whatever way they chose to live out their lives, gay men formed a distinctive underworld.

Lennox enjoyed the camaraderie, even the excitement, of this exclusive underworld, but he was never really comfortable about actually being gay: he was not, as the French say, *bien dans sa peau* (comfortable in his skin). And he was not comfortable living with Peter. Lennox knew well enough what he was, and knew he could not change it even if he wanted to. Like many other unhappy homosexual men in those intolerant and proscriptive years, he saw marriage as a possible way out. His contemporary, and fellow Catholic convert, the writer Michael Burn, wrestling with a similar problem in the late Thirties, saw marriage as a distinct way in. Burn wanted to learn about women and to discover what his emotions towards them really were, but he was caught in a sexual relationship with the manipulative Guy Burgess – later to be unmasked as a Soviet spy – and felt himself to be 'falling under a dangerous spell'. In his autobiography he writes that he 'imagined, so far theoretically, a profound experience with a woman, and finally life with a woman, to be one of the immortal openings into life which, the more time I spent with Guy, became that much the more obstructed.'[31]

Lennox may have recognized something of this in his trap-like relationship with Peter, though, nearly ten years older than Michael Burn, entrenched in the gay scene and the father of Freda's unborn child, he had passed the point of wondering what a woman was like. In his case he wanted to extract himself from a pernicious relationship, and marriage seemed the only possible escape. Certainly it would bring a number of practical advantages, but his strict moral code required that any such marriage would have to be absolutely honest and open. If Freda's sexual expectations were to be reduced by marrying a gay man,

*In Britain, since 2006, there has been a further enlightened option for gay men: under the system of state-sanctioned civil partnerships, introduced by Tony Blair's New Labour Government, domestic partners of the same sex may register their relationships and acquire the same legal status and rights (and obligations) as married couples.

then he would have to deny the physical needs of his own nature – or, at least, to relinquish the freedom to express them. This might no longer be so very difficult, since one of the compensations of advancing years was that one was less prone to what he later called 'the violent emotions that beset one in youth'.[32] But there could be no half measures: marriage had to mean no more young men, ever. He would have his religious faith to inspire him, and a disciplined will to support him. And, if he were able to keep his resolution, there would be the rewards of a purer, higher, truer, deeper love to sustain the marriage – and peace with God and the Church.

Five years later Lennox gave a hint of the dilemma he was facing as a devout Roman Catholic, when he advised his bisexual friend Jim Lees-Milne about *his* marriage to Alvilde Chaplin. Though Alvilde's husband Anthony Chaplin (described by James Pope-Hennessy as 'a thoroughly selfish, if charming, cad'[33]) was happy enough to agree to a divorce, since it freed him to marry his young mistress Rosemary Lyttelton,* the Church refused to grant a papal annulment. This was a blow to Jim's faith (since, like Lennox, he was a convert to Catholicism), but he and Alvilde married nonetheless, at Chelsea Register Office in November 1951, witnessed by Jim's former lover, Harold Nicolson, and Alvilde's later lover, Vita Sackville-West, Mrs Harold Nicolson.[34] The ceremony lasted no more than five minutes, and Harold Nicolson found it 'embarrassing & sad'.[35] Jim himself described it as 'rather strained and uneasy'.[36] Yet the marriage lasted, mostly happily, till Alvilde's death in 1994.

Vita Sackville-West had been one of many friends who had urged Jim to marry, regardless of the Church's objections. It was nonsense, she said, for the Catholic Church to discountenance a Catholic marrying a divorced Protestant, whose previous marriage it had not regarded as a sacrament.[37] Perplexed and exasperated by the Church's obstinate adherence to its rules, which left him feeling guilty about his civil marriage to Alvilde, Jim Lees-Milne raised the whole question of the demands of faith in a conversation with Lennox at a dinner party a few days before his civil wedding. Writing back the next day, Lennox gave an indication of what might have been his own response to the similar

*Hon Rosemary Lyttelton, born 1922, daughter of 1st Viscount Chandos, married, in 1951, as his second wife, Anthony 3rd Viscount Chaplin, who died in 1981. She died in 2003.

problem, before his own marriage, of being gay in a Church that forbids all physical expressions of sexuality outside marriage.

> I know what a struggle it must have been for you to come to a decision. I feel sure that in the circumstances I should have acted as you have. As we were saying last night, the Church has to have these very strict rules, but I can't help feeling that there are cases where the only sensible solution involves breaking with strict observance. I think there may have been many Catholics who have found themselves obliged to lead their religious lives *en marge* for reasons similar to yours, but remaining true Catholics at heart.[38]

It is possible that Lennox similarly 'marginalized' himself from the Church over issues with which he found it impossible to come to terms: first of all his sexuality, and, much later, the loss of the Latin liturgy under the 'reforms' of the Second Vatican Council. But, like the speculative rebels he mentions in his letter, he remained a true Catholic at heart. In the autumn of 1946 the opportunity to turn himself into a true Catholic in practice played a major part in his decision to marry Freda.

Lennox may have been able to contemplate relinquishing the physical side of his former life, but he did not at all want to lose his gay friends and a *milieu* he was used to, liked and needed. Nor was he happy about abandoning Peter, with whom he had been intimately involved for six tumultuous years. Without Lennox – and Lennox's money – what would happen to Peter, who had shown himself to be not only dependent but unstable?

Lennox's friends were no less divided on the question of whether or not he should marry: they were even running a book on who would 'get' Lennox – the boy or the girl.[39] The married friends, especially the Pilkingtons, Primrose Roper,* the Heywood Hills,† the

*Following the collapse of her marriage to LB's Oxford friend John Codrington, Primrose Harley, untiringly attracted to sexually ambiguous men, had married the American landscape architect Lanning Roper. That too was to break up, but her own unhappy experience of marriage did nothing to discourage Prim Roper from encouraging her friends to try it.

†The bookseller Heywood Hill (died 1986), proprietor of the famous shop in Curzon Street, Mayfair, married in 1938 Lady Anne Gathorne-Hardy (1911–2006), daughter of the 3rd Earl of Cranbrook.

Chaplins and the Francis Watsons* – all of whom had gone through more or less what he and Freda were going through now – were strongly in favour; the bachelors – especially the Warwick Square set – were dead against, and their opposition was not moderated by a barrage of anonymous letters (sent by a misguided woman friend of Lennox's) accusing them of hypocrisy. In the bachelors' view, Lennox was immutably gay and Freda 'a little scheming Jewess'[40] who wanted to change him – a woman who would transform 'his free and secret self into something ordinary, domesticated, resentful' (like the heroine in Rosamond Lehmann's novel *Dusty Answer*, who falls in love with a gay man and, confronted with the dilemma of stealing him from his boyfriend, sees herself as a 'creature of evil design, dangerous to him ...'[41]).

Yet Freda had no intention of changing Lennox, or of dropping his friends. Even at twenty-three she was far too realistic to see herself as the good woman who was going to convert the errant homosexual. Nothing if not practical, she hoped only to change her own lonely existence, without exposing herself to sexual threats. Her plan for Lennox, if such a thing existed, was to give him the life he had always had – his friends, his music, his club, the Church – against a new, and perhaps more rewarding, background of wife and children and family home. In that way they would all have what they wanted.

Lennox was in torment, and, as usual when indecision got the better of him, he became ill. (In fact he had come to the conclusion that just being in London was bad for him. He really ought to live in the country, he told Freda, but did not see how it could be done at present.[42]) The doctor ordered him to go to the country and rest, so he went to Montgomeryshire to stay with his old Oxford friend the Widow Lloyd, and to consult him about his problems at the same time.[43] The Widow had sown his wild oats, and was now happily settled at home in Wales, committed to a life of scholarship as an

*The art historian Francis Watson (1907–92), then Deputy Director of the Wallace Collection (later, Director; and Surveyor of the Queen's Works of Art; knighted 1973), married in 1941 a cat fancier, Mary 'Jane' Rosalie Gray née Strong (1904–69). After her death he adopted a Chinese son, Ch'eng Huan, whom he and his wife had known as a Cambridge law student. In 1933, as a young man with a fondness for skipping and dressing up, Watson was very close to the Widow Lloyd (JDK Lloyd Photo Album 5 (1933), [Llyfr Ffoto Album 156], National Library of Wales).

antiquary, and of public service as an officer of numerous associations and committees. He had become as eminently respectable, even distinguished, as once he had been so extravagantly disreputable. Shortly before he had finally cast off boys and booze, he had been Mayor of Montgomery (from 1932 to 1938), and was to be so again twice in the Sixties; he had been High Sheriff of the county in 1940, and was to be appointed a Deputy Lieutenant in 1960; and, since 1934, he had been a magistrate. He was also a county councillor (later an alderman), a churchwarden and lay reader, and soon he was to be honoured with an OBE. Lennox could not have found a sounder, more experienced or more sympathetic friend to guide him through the most difficult time of his life. The Widow, no longer a Bright Young Thing, still 'brightened everything', was 'wonderful company, witty with a touch of malice, but fundamentally tolerant and understanding'.[44] He lived comfortably in a country house called Bryn Cadwrfa (for which John Greenidge had designed an extension in 1933).* Lennox promised Freda he would reach a decision while he was there, and that he would send her a signal as soon as he had.

The Widow was too wise to advise Lennox how to resolve his dilemma. Instead he listened. Then he asked Lennox what he himself thought he ought to do. When Lennox said, 'Get married', the Widow said, simply, 'Good.'[45] And the matter was done.

On the evening of 1 December, as promised, Lennox sent a postcard to Freda, addressed to Sotheby's. Its businesslike tone does not seem to offer much reassurance, but Freda confirms that this was indeed the signal she had been waiting for, and that it came as a colossal relief.

> Montgomery – Sunday. Could you come to Warwick Square at 6.30 tomorrow evening? and perhaps you could reserve a table for dinner later at Speranza (or somewhere). I'm coming up by the afternoon train, as the only other one leaves at an uncomfortably early hour and makes difficulties here. Love – L.[46]

The fact is that although Lennox had, in principle, decided to marry Freda he still could not quite bring himself to put the plan into practice

*Lloyd probably bought the house with money raised from the sale of Castell Forwyn, Co. Montgomery, which he had inherited from his uncle in 1925. His bachelor brother Dr Wyndham Lloyd lived in the family house, Plas Trefaldwyn, Montgomery.

– and indeed he did not take action for another week, but he gave Freda his word that her waiting would be over by the 9th.

On the eve of the deadline, Freda received a letter from Hans Gronau, whom she had precipitately asked to be a witness at the wedding. It offered just the counsel she so badly needed: well-judged, firm but kind – and incredibly generous (since he himself was still in love with Freda, and doing his best to keep it under control). It was Gronau's belief that she should stand as firm as possible, ignoring the cross-currents that might distract but would never divert Lennox.

> ... by showing distress and doubts you can only increase his own unhappiness. I know it is much to ask of you *not* to be influenced or even distracted to something very near despair. But this surely is your only course – to be firm and as radiantly sure of the final happiness that will be yours as you can ... But should Lennox still waver and be undecided, surely it is far better that you – and he – find out before you are actually married ... If you will really have me as a witness, you know I could not, in my heart, refuse. I will say a prayer for you tomorrow [the day of Lennox's deadline], for all it may be worth. Yours as ever, Hans.[47]

Freda did not have to stand firm for very much longer. The next day Lennox asked her to marry him. Hans Gronau, her truest friend, was the first to offer his congratulations, in a letter that arrived on the 11th:

> ... I rejoice in the knowledge that everything is so wonderfully well now ... You know I mean that with all my heart, just as you know how worried I have been about you this last fortnight – so much more than I have been able to show you or cared letting you know. I wish you all the happiness in the world, dearest Freda. The past will live in me for ever. There is no bitterness. Nothing will, or shall, ever alter that ... [48]

On Friday the 13th Freda remembered that she ought to inform the Public Trustee, so she rang Mr Bowman and announced she was getting married the next morning. Taken aback, he asked why she had not let him know earlier. Freda explained that it had all happened suddenly. Was she sure, Mr Bowman wanted to know, that the man wasn't marrying her for her money? Freda was quite sure – the man had got his own money. 'Well I hope you're doing the right thing,' he said. 'I know I am,' she replied.[49]

On Saturday morning, in the thick fog and deep snow of one of the coldest winters on record, Lennox and Freda were married in a Nissen hut in Claverton Street on the site of the Church of the Holy Apostles which had been flattened by a Nazi bomb. The wedding service (not a full nuptial Mass, because Freda was not a Catholic) was conducted by the parish priest, Fr Edmund Hadfield, and the witnesses were Hans Gronau (for Freda), who also gave her away, and John Greenidge (for Lennox), who doubled as best man. The only others present were Nancy Gregory, Peter Fraser and John Weyman; Wyatt was abroad. (It may seem odd that Peter, the loser, should have turned up in church to see his lover marrying his rival, but he had accepted what he had long guessed was inevitable, and he had been persuaded, probably by John Weyman, to behave in a dignified way.)

For the special day Freda wore 'a deep-blue two-piece costume from Dickins and Jones, quite pretty, with a black velvet hat and matching court shoes'.[50] Lennox wore his standard uniform of dark suit and bow tie. John, as the senior man, opened the champagne back at the flat. The battles were over, but the celebration could not be anything but muted, as Lennox and Freda and Peter contemplated the shifting balance of their relationships. Afterwards, at Peter's insistence, the couple spent their wedding night at Claridge's, in a welter of flowers arranged by Peter himself. By then Mr and Mrs Berkeley were so exhausted they fell asleep.

The following morning, Sunday the 15th, after Mass, Lennox went back to 58 Warwick Square, and Freda returned home to Broxbourne, with her wedding bouquet and a second-hand gold ring on her finger. She was 'anxious', she admits now, because it was 'a horrid sort of parting' at the hotel.[51]

Back at work at Sotheby's on the Monday Freda suddenly felt faint and started to lose blood. She telephoned Lennox, who rushed her into a nursing home in Avenue Road, St John's Wood. Within a few hours she had had a miscarriage and lost their first baby.

Not long afterwards Peter Fraser invited them out to dinner. Sensing they needed to talk alone, and eager to show her trust in Lennox, Freda suggested they should go without her; she could always join them on another occasion. Lennox failed to return home that night, and Freda thought she had lost him. But in the morning he came back, contrite, apologetic and promising it would never happen again. And it did not – with Peter, or with anyone else.

'It was a terrible time,' Freda recalls now. 'All Lennox's men friends were convinced I'd tricked him into marriage. I don't think anyone thought it would last. Except me. I knew it would work out in the end.'[52]

30
Lennox and Freda Berkeley, London, 1946

Just after Christmas 1946, with the snow still thick on the ground and the temperature never rising above freezing, Lennox and Freda moved into their first home together, a long, single-storey Regency villa (once a farmhouse) with a huge studio, hidden away in South Kensington. Approached by an archway and a hedge-lined lane, Park House was set in an acre of romantic garden on a triangle bounded by Onslow Square, Pelham Street and the Fulham Road. This magical place belonged to their friend Primrose Codrington, who had divorced her husband John in 1942 and spent the war as a volunteer artist, designing camouflage, and painting murals for rescue centres, hospitals and schools.* Though her marriage had been 'only briefly happy',† (and her next marriage, to the American landscape architect Lanning Roper, was destined to be no more successful‡), the gallant 'Prim' was a staunch advocate of the institution and did all she could to promote it. To give the Berkeleys a helping hand at the unpropitious start of their marriage, she offered them the use of Park House rent-free for six months while she was away in Madeira. 'Prim' suffered from chronic bronchitis, and every winter she left England in search of the healing sun: this year she had gone to Funchal to stay with her gardening friends the Blandys, founders of the Madeira Wine Company and owners of Reid's Hotel. All she asked of Lennox and Freda while she was away was that they should look after her black and white cat Rubus.

It was, as Freda recalls, 'a dream house to start married life in', and

*The gardening writer and biographer Jane Brown, in an entry on 'Primrose Roper' [1908–78] in the *Oxford Dictionary of National Biography*, OUP, 2004, notes that 'as all this work was unpaid, it is also largely unrecorded'.
†*Ibid.*
‡FB, a close friend and executrix of Primrose Roper, told TS, 26 October 2001, that 'Lanning was obviously gay but loved grand ladies and [...] used to drag Prim off for grand weekends in country houses when all she wanted to do was to stay at home. The marriage was a disaster.'

they were very contented. But the weather was not on their side. It was not only arctic – 'colder than ever this morning, Madam,' Mrs Harrison, the daily, used to say, in a lugubrious voice that relished bad news – but the winds were so strong and gusty that the powdery snow was driven under the door of the studio where Lennox composed (and where Augustus John had painted at the beginning of the war); and the only way he could keep warm was to pull the grand piano almost on top of the stove.[1] But Lennox was so grateful for the unaccustomed quiet, and the calm which Freda generated – not to mention her devoted management of him – that he happily tolerated the bitter cold and the snowdrifts around his feet, and embarked on what was to be one of his finest works, the *Four Poems of St Teresa of Avila* for contralto and strings.

It is no coincidence that he should have turned to a religious – and profoundly mystical – text at this critical moment in his life. He could not have done it at 58 Warwick Square, with all the comings and goings, dramas and rows. Yet he had wanted to write for his Church ever since he had converted to Catholicism. Music, to Lennox, was an integral part of the spiritual world, and 'the best music', he believed, was 'that which communicates the most strongly and the most urgently on that level'.[2] But, as a traditionalist Catholic in a gay relationship, he had felt inhibited about offering his music to his Church. As a married man – and therefore, in his own strictly orthodox view, a more complete Catholic – he was no longer under any such constraint, though he still did not venture near the actual liturgy of the Catholic Church till 1960, when he wrote his *Missa brevis* for the Westminster Cathedral Choir. His *Mass for Five Voices*, also written for Westminster Cathedral, followed in 1964, and the *Magnificat* in 1968. (Lennox's musical association with the Cathedral began in the early Fifties when he met the harpsichordist and conductor George Malcolm, who, as Master of Music from 1947 to 1959, developed the vigorous physicality of the tone-quality which gave such passionate conviction to both the chant and the Italianate polyphony for which the Westminster Cathedral Choir became – and still is – so celebrated.)

It may seem odd that a composer-convert should wait some twenty years before writing his own settings of a liturgy he revered, and to which he must have been longing to make his own contribution. He had first encountered Gregorian chant at school, and since then he had sought it out wherever he could – at Oxford, in Paris, at the monasteries of Solemnes and Prinknash, and at Westminster Cathedral (a stone's throw from the Warwick Square flat) where it was still then in use as part of the daily Mass. At the BBC he had often discussed the chant with an acknowledged authority, his friend Fr Alec Robertson (chief producer of music talks, who had been a chaplain at the Cathedral before the war.)* And about now Lennox acquired his own *Graduale*, to follow – and to study – the chants of the Mass.† Eighteen years may have elapsed since he became a Catholic, but that just showed that conversion was not 'a once and for all event but a process' that lay in incubation.[3] The incubation had continued till marriage, when at last the process found the right climate and the right soil to take root and grow. Now, like Francis Poulenc after his conversion experience at Rocamadour in 1936, Lennox could give birth to all the semi-formed works which had lain dormant within him, locked in what Poulenc himself had called 'the limbo of ... creative imagination'.[4]

In the liturgical works he was inspired to write for George Malcolm and the Westminster Cathedral choir Lennox plumbed the wellspring of his faith, investing his music with some of the most profound feelings he was ever to express. The choral conductor and composer Colin Mawby, a former Master of Music at Westminster Cathedral, has aptly described these works as set against 'the background of eternity', which gives them 'a feeling of radiance, reflection and serenity'.[5]

When Gerald Cooper, the Purcell scholar whose chamber concerts at the Wigmore Hall in London had famously defied the flying bombs,[6] suggested that Lennox should set St Teresa, he was absolutely ready to take this step nearer the actual liturgy. For one thing, Lennox was keen to do more word-setting – Ben Britten's *Grimes* and *Donne Sonnets* had fired him up, and his own Northampton anthem had whetted his appetite for more. (One critic suggested that Lennox's post-war passion for word-setting had played a part in 'modifying the asperity of his dissonant harmony'.[7]) He already knew St Teresa's poems, in the translations of Arthur Symons, and he was acutely responsive to their mood of religious ecstasy. The first and third of the verses he chose, *If, Lord, Thy love for me is strong* and *Let mine eyes see Thee*, are passionate love-songs addressed to God – yearning and lilting, respectively; the

*It was Fr Robertson (1892–1982) who provided Britten with the plainsong 'Hodie Christus natus est' for *A Ceremony of Carols.*

†This 1945 edition is now in the possession of Julian Berkeley, who uses it, in conjunction with an original Flemish edition of 1598, for his chant groups.

other two are shepherd songs – a *musette* and a lively dance. Apart from the texts, Lennox's other inspiration was the contralto Kathleen Ferrier. Ever since hearing her as Britten's Lucretia the previous summer, he had wanted to write something for her. It was not just the depth and clarity and warmth of her darkly beautiful voice, or her natural musicality, but what Ben's librettist Ronald Duncan called 'the true innocence and purity of her character'.[8] As her records continue to prove, Ferrier's voice expressed the spirit of what she was singing – whether it was ecstatic, compassionate, humorous or serene; and the emotional bond she forged with her audience shines through all the technical distortions of the many live recordings that survive. Inspired by Kathleen Ferrier, Lennox created a musical language that is strong, lean and mellifluous – and, as always with his religious music, but perhaps most particularly in these St Teresa songs, 'one can hear the deep conviction ... coming from "the one thing needful"', as the composer (and Berkeley student) Sir John Tavener has put it.[9]

By April he had finished the vocal score; a month later he had completed the orchestration, and added a dedication to his old friend John Greenidge; and on his forty-fourth birthday, to celebrate the arrival of an important new score, Freda gave him *The Complete Works of St Teresa*, which had just been published in a newly-translated three-volume edition.* It was a year before Lennox's *Four Poems of St Teresa* were first performed, in a live broadcast from the Concert Hall of Broadcasting House, London, on 4 April 1948, with Kathleen Ferrier and the Goldsbrough String Orchestra conducted by Arnold Goldsbrough. The first concert performance had to wait another fifteen months, when Ferrier sang them at the Edinburgh Festival, with the Jacques Orchestra under Reginald Jacques, at the Freemasons' Hall, Edinburgh, on 5 September 1949;[10] and later that autumn Ferrier gave a further, memorably dramatic, performance at the Albert Hall in Manchester, with the strings of the Hallé Orchestra conducted by Sir John Barbirolli – this too was broadcast by the BBC, on 23 November 1949.†

In a sleeve note accompanying another powerful recording, by Pamela

*Translated and edited by E. Allison Peers and published by Sheed & Ward, 1946.
†This performance is now available on Pavilion Records CD GEM 0229. Ferrier's first broadcast with the Goldsbrough Strings has been released on BBC Records REGL 368, and a third BBC broadcast recording, with the former jazz violinist Hugo Rignold conducting the strings of the London Symphony Orchestra in 1952, is also available.

Bowden, made in 1960, Andrew Porter wrote that the *St Teresa Poems* show every facet of Lennox's musical personality at its finest: 'his melodic invention; the sheer prettiness of his writing; its elegance and unaffected distinction; his unerring sense of form ... [and] a quiet passion and intensity'.[11] The 'quiet passion and intensity' had always been there in his music, but now they were matched with words which expressed his faith. The French composer Alexis Roland-Manuel – pupil, friend and biographer of Ravel – hearing the work for the first time, in the Bowden recording, hailed it as 'a masterpiece of lyricism',[12], which was both 'very beautiful and very moving'.[13] Eager to introduce the work to France, to promote Lennox's music there, Roland-Manuel programmed the *St Teresa Poems* in the series *Plaisir de la Musique* on RTF radio in February 1966, with Jeannine Collard as the soloist and the ORTF Chamber Orchestra conducted by André Girard. A month later Roland-Manuel told Lennox he was still receiving letters from listeners who had been profoundly affected by the four songs – and surprised to discover a work which they felt they ought to have known about before.[14]

The *St Teresa Poems* were a natural vehicle – both in the their tessitura and their spiritual conviction – for the English mezzo-soprano Janet Baker, who performed them at the 1960 Aldeburgh Festival, at a concert conducted by Britten in Blythburgh church. Writing in the August number of the *Musical Times* that year, Noël Goodwin said the work's 'elegance of thought and style' made a deeper impression with each hearing, and Baker had sung 'most beautifully'; he regretted that performances were 'all too infrequent'. Lennox appreciated Baker's performance too and acknowledged it in an inscription in her copy of the score. Nearly half a century later Dame Janet recalled the day in the summer of 1960 when Lennox had attended the orchestral rehearsals. It could have been intimidating and stressful for an inexperienced singer, she said, but 'what I remember of that day, so long ago, was his quiet manner, kindness, encouragement and sweetness of character.' English was often thought to be a difficult language to sing, but in the hands of a superb composer, it was just as beautiful as any other. 'The way Lennox set English was a gift to a singer, music and words always a perfect expressive match.' Dame Janet said she had sung the *St Teresa Poems* several times since then (and Berkeley's *Five Poems by W. H. Auden*);* the last of the *St*

*A 1983 recording by Janet Baker and the pianist Geoffrey Parsons is available on the BBC Legends label (BBCL41172).

Teresa Poems, 'Let mine eyes see thee', was so 'sublimely written' that singing it was 'an unforgettable experience'.[15] Baker's rich and eloquent voice, searching musical intelligence and warm personality affected Lennox deeply, and in 1977 he wrote a set of three songs especially for her.*

Lennox's new spirit of confidence also found expression in music for the theatre. When the choreographer Andrée Howard had the chance to revive her haunting ballet, *La Fête étrange*, on the cavernous stage of Sadler's Wells Theatre in March 1947, she asked Lennox if he would write a suitably amplified score for full orchestra. Whether the role of arranger/orchestrator of Fauré provided him with a shield behind which he could release his inhibitions, or whether he was so flush with the success of his Teresa songs, or so newly self-assured as a happily-married man, Lennox produced a masterpiece of musical 'impressionism'.

Nearly sixty years after the premiere of Lennox's Fauré orchestration, the conductor Richard Bernas, eager to find the orchestral parts for a revival of *La Fête étrange* at the Royal Ballet, precipitated the rediscovery of Lennox's 'lost' score in the archives of the Royal Opera House. The moment he saw it, he recognized not only the transparent textures he had hoped for, but the sound world of Fauré's own orchestral works. In his view, Lennox's 'ambitious' arrangements showed a deep knowledge of French orchestral writing. 'Many passages are delightfully light in tone,' he wrote, 'while the outer numbers have a deep seriousness and grandeur.'[16] Bernas conducted the Berkeley orchestration for the Royal Ballet's revival of the 1947 production – choreography Howard, designs Sophie Fedorovitch, whom Lennox had known in Paris in the early Thirties – with Darcey Bussell as the Bride and Ricardo Cervera as the Boy, at the Royal Opera House, Covent Garden, on 17 October 2005. And Lennox's score proved itself to be so perfectly French, so finely tuned to the subtle nuances of the story, so romantic and yet so elegantly restrained, that the *Daily Telegraph*, hailing 'a jewel of a ballet', spoke of Lennox's orchestration as 'a rich Fauré score that ought to break the heart'.[17] No orchestrator could hope for a higher accolade than to be mistaken for the composer of the original score.

* *Another Spring* sets texts by Walter de la Mare. Janet Baker and Geoffrey Pratley gave the first performance in Chichester Cathedral on 20 July 1977, as part of a tribute to the retiring Dean, the Very Revd Walter Hussey.

To show his gratitude to Freda for her inspiration, Lennox decided to give her a surprise holiday – not exactly a honeymoon (that was planned for July), but a break from the grim weather, from her work at Sotheby's, from the sadness of her miscarriage. Halfway through the composition of the *St Teresa Poems*, and just after the premiere of *La Fête étrange*, Lennox took Freda to Jersey to stay with his uncle Arthur Harris. They flew from Northolt in an hour and a half – and though it was Freda's first experience of flying (her first time 'abroad' too), she was, according to Lennox, 'very self-possessed'.[18] And at this point in their lives, Freda's diary starts again, but only for a few entries, and most of them in Lennox's own hand, as though he wanted to emphasize their intimacy by this personal appearance in his wife's private diary. On the 11th, after dinner, they went for a walk by the farm above Beaumont, and Lennox recorded: 'Wonderful feeling of happiness and peace.' He was referring specifically to Jersey, at that moment, with Freda, but he could have been writing about the whole new direction his life had taken. A studio photograph of Freda, taken by Germaine Kanova at about this time, suggests that marriage had been as beneficial for her. She is seen as a young, healthy, beautiful woman, laughing and bright-eyed, brimming with confidence and optimism.

It is ironic that the same photographer should have taken two distinctly solemn photographs of Lennox and Peter Fraser the previous year (also, and separately, at her studio at 60 Baker Street, London). Both these earlier photos were intended to convey the artistic temperament, but both are too posed to be convincing: the one of Lennox (for Chester's) shows him looking wistful if not melancholy, and the one of Peter is rather self-consciously reflective. (Shortly before the Lennox and Peter sessions, Kanova had been in Germany with the French army of liberation, photographing survivors of the Nazi concentration camp Wiesengrund, at Vaihingen near Stuttgart.)

On their return to Park House they wondered where they were going to live when Primrose Roper got back from Madeira. Lennox told Freda he quite liked the idea of Little Venice in West London, overlooking the waterways and houseboats where the Regent's Canal connects with the Paddington arm of the Grand Union Canal to form a pool with an island in the centre (now known as Browning's Pool and Browning's Island, after the poet who lived at 19 Warwick Crescent from 1862 to 1887). One summer evening at a cocktail party in the Pilkingtons' garden they learned from the Heywood Hills that No. 8

Warwick Avenue, directly overlooking Browning's Pool, was about to become vacant, and they went to have a look.

No. 8 was perfect for the Berkeleys: a handsome, stuccoed semi-detached house of 'withdrawn distinction',[19] with pilasters and tall windows, on four floors: a large drawing room above a long, quiet garden, a study for Lennox overlooking Browning's Island, an extensive basement with cellars, and lots of room for an expanding family. Plus, of course, Heywood and Anne next door at No. 10 (later to be occupied by Lady Diana Cooper), Lennox's old Oxford friend Patrick Balfour (by now Lord Kinross) up the road at No. 4, and Heywood's sister and brother-in-law, the John Hills, around the corner in Maida Avenue: a veritable colony of artists and writers and sympathetic souls. Lennox applied to the Church Commissioners, who owned the whole of the Maida Vale Estate, and secured a long lease for a starting rent of £38 per year. In June he and Freda – with a Bechstein grand piano lent by Hans Gronau – moved in, little expecting that they would spend the rest of their married life in the same house.

There was not much work to be done. People did not then tinker with the structure of houses – they fitted their lives into whatever was there. The Berkeleys did, however, repair the roof, and spruce up the interiors. The previous tenant, the decorator Morrough Barnard, had been too free with the cream paint for Freda's taste. So she replaced this with wallpapers supplied by John Hill, who ran the smart interior-decorators Green and Abbott. But she left the cloakroom and first-floor lavatory, which Barnard had lined with a hand-printed paper of Chinese birds. It did not take long to fill the empty rooms with Lennox's French furniture and family pictures, rescued from the bachelors' flat in Pimlico, the flat in Paris (which had been empty since the death of José Raffalli) and the country house on the Riviera; pieces given by the Pilkingtons, 'Prim' Roper, Alvilde Chaplin and other friends, a painting by Evie Hone of a sturdy old tree in her garden in Ireland (a wedding present from Peter Fraser), and things bought by Freda herself. She had an eye for spotting bargains in antique shops and sale rooms, and found, in those early days, a Victorian bird's-eye maple sofa-table, a Wedgwood dinner service in Napoleon Ivy, and paintings by Duncan Grant of his tabby cat Puss, of trees in a ravine by John Craxton, a cottage by Rowland Suddaby, a Paris street scene by Christopher Wood, a bird in winter foliage by Cedric Morris and a still life with roses by Vanessa Bell.

Freda was soon pregnant again – but, for a second time, she lost the baby. And the nervous collapse that caused the first two miscarriages was responsible for a third the following year. These were increasingly bitter blows, but Freda was assured by her doctors that there was nothing technically wrong, so she and Lennox bravely continued trying for a family.

Apart from fathering children, Lennox was not able to help much with practical arrangements at No. 8 – even if he had been of a mind to. Ever since moving into Warwick Avenue he had been working on an important commission from Britten: a thirty-minute work for the newly-formed English Opera Group to take on tour abroad with Britten's own recent operas, *The Rape of Lucretia* and *Albert Herring*. Lennox turned again to a religious text – this time a Latin one: *Stabat Mater*, the ancient hymn describing the sorrows of the mother of Christ on the Cross. To suit the EOG's touring forces, he set the ten verses for six solo voices and eleven instruments with percussion. It was quite a task, and there was not much time: the piece was wanted for performance in Zurich in August. By the end of July it was finished, and Lennox wrote on the manuscript 'To Benjamin Britten'.*

In mid-June Lennox took time off from the new composition to attend rehearsals of Frederick Ashton's production of *Albert Herring* at Glyndebourne, partly because he never missed a new work of Ben's, and partly because he wanted to hear the musicians and singers who would be performing his *Stabat Mater*. Freda went with him, and, at lunch, the famous Ben of whom she had heard so much, introduced himself. 'He came over to our table', Freda recalls, 'and kissed me. He was terribly nice and said he was so pleased about what had happened to us.'[20] On the 20th they returned to Glyndebourne, with the Pilkingtons, for the premiere of *Herring*. For this significant occasion, Freda made a rare return to diary-keeping: '1st perf of Albert Herring. Both enjoyed it. Rotten dinner. Returned by train with Barbara Britten.'†

Eight days later they were back at Glyndebourne again, so that Lennox could show what he had written of the *Stabat Mater*. This time

*The MS, in the British Library (LOAN 101.74), is dated 'London June–July 1947'.

†Although this diary entry is written on the page for 1 July, the Glyndebourne premiere of *Albert Herring* was actually on 20 June.

they lunched with Ben and Peter, Eric Crozier, the librettist of *Herring* (and later of Lennox's religious opera *Ruth*) and Nancy Evans, the mezzo-soprano who created the roles of Nancy in *Herring* and Lucretia, and was to become Crozier's wife. That evening they saw *Herring* for the third time 'and enjoyed it even more'.[21]

On 14 July, leaving Ben to conduct preliminary rehearsals of the *Stabat Mater*, Lennox turned his back on music and home, in order to take Freda on a late honeymoon. They caught the train at Victoria, crossed the Channel to Boulogne and were met in Paris by the Chaplins, who then drove them out to Jouy for a few days. 'Such a luxurious house and wonderful position,' wrote Freda in the diary, 'Lazed and read: absolute peace – and luscious food!' [22] Then they headed south on the Train Bleu, so Lennox could show Freda the scenes of his childhood in Nice, Falicon and Cap Ferrat. On the way back they made a long diversion northwards to Amsterdam for a rehearsal of the *Stabat Mater* by the English Opera Group, who were in Holland performing *Lucretia* and *Herring*.

After only a fortnight back in London, during which No. 8 was thrown into chaos by the arrival of lorryloads of furniture from John Greenidge's old house in Kettering (John having decided to move back to Great Ormond Street), Lennox and Freda set off on their travels once more, bound this time for Zurich and the world premiere of the *Stabat Mater*. En route they stopped in Lucerne, for performances of Britten's two operas, as part of the festival programme. Ben himself had travelled over in his open-top Rolls with Peter Pears and their driver, George Behrend, the twenty-five-year-old son of Peter Burra's patrons. Freda and Lennox went by train. It was Freda's first experience of a night sleeper: 'What a wonderful life I have now. Dinner on train: all v. exciting!'[23]

Lennox himself conducted his *Stabat Mater* in the Zurich Tonhalle on 19 August, the soloists including Peter Pears. It formed part of a programme of English music from Morley to Britten. The following month Ben took the baton for the English premiere at the Friends' Meeting House in Euston Road, London, and the next day, 27 September 1947, the new work was played again in Broadcasting House for a live broadcast on the Third Programme.[24] Ben conducted the *Stabat Mater* for a further performance in 1953, at the music festival which he and Peter had by then established in Aldeburgh, but the work was not repeated till twenty-five years later, when Nicholas Braithwaite conducted a performance using a version re-scored for standard chamber orchestra by Michael Berkeley. From the beginning the critics regarded Lennox's powerful *Stabat Mater* as one of his finest achievements – yet the work is now almost forgotten, and long overdue for a revival, and a recording.

If the *Teresa Poems* and the *Stabat Mater* represent the newly-married Lennox celebrating his faith, the next work he wrote in 1947, the *Concerto for Piano and Orchestra*, reflects the new sense of optimism which his marriage had brought. It is an exciting piece, full of dash and high spirits, with a fresh and sunny quality, and a sublimely spiritual slow movement. The work was conceived as a chamber concerto in the spirit of Mozart, and the central movement was inspired by the unison passages of Mozart's *C Major Piano Concerto K 503*.[25] The concerto was a further product of the close rapport between Lennox and the pianist Colin Horsley, who commissioned it with his friend Val Drewry (still working as a producer in the BBC Music Department). Horsley, to whom the concerto is dedicated, gave the first performance with the London Symphony Orchestra conducted by Basil Cameron, at a Promenade Concert in the Royal Albert Hall on 31 August 1948. *The Times* said that Horsley had 'carefully struck the right balance between classical and romantic playing'. Of the work itself, the paper could find little to say beyond the impenetrable judgement that 'Mr Berkeley's ordered mind has seen to it that there are no inconsequentialities of formal incident or balance about the logical often charming flow of the work'.[26] The audience, on the other hand, manifestly enjoyed the new piece, and the ISCM selectors were so impressed that they chose it to represent British music at the 23rd ISCM Festival in Palermo in 1949, when Horsley was again the soloist, with the Rome Radio Orchestra conducted by Constant Lambert.[27]

Horsley gave a further twenty-six performances in Britain, Australia, New Zealand, Belgium and northern Holland, including at least one performance conducted by Lennox himself. 'It was a joy to work with Lennox,' he commented years later, '... I felt free and not on tenterhooks as you can be with an indifferent conductor. He conducted beautifully.'[28] Unfortunately they never recorded it, and since then the work has been strangely neglected – possibly, Horsley speculates, because it requires a lot of study and rehearsal.[29] But a recent, dynamic recording by Howard Shelley and the BBC National Orchestra of Wales conducted by Richard Hickox* may persuade artists and managements to have another look at this blithe and sparkling work.

Right at the end of 1947 Lennox was asked to write a film score for a costume drama called *The First Gentleman*, starring Cecil Parker as the Prince Regent, who tries to force his daughter into a popular marriage. The music was ready by Christmas and recorded by the Royal Philharmonic Orchestra in London on 19 January 1948, with Sir Thomas Beecham conducting. After the session Lennox told his publisher that 'everyone seems delighted with the music', the great man had 'behaved like a lamb', and apart from one or two places where Lennox's timing had not been quite accurate, there had been no musical hitches. There were, however, some 'technical mishaps' (nothing to do with Lennox), including one in which the film stock caught fire – 'appropriately enough just after the music to one of the love scenes!'[30]

But the Berkeleys' big news of late 1947 was domestic. After the tragedy of three consecutive miscarriages, Freda was pregnant again and praying for a successful delivery the following May. Lennox lost no time in telling Nadia Boulanger. This time, he wrote, 'it looks as though all is going well and we are very happy about it.' (The same letter says that Soulima Stravinsky has written 'a very beautiful sonata' and Lennox was trying to persuade the BBC to 'to get him over to play it'.[31]) Full of confidence Lennox asked Ben if he would be a godfather. Ben's charming reply must have reassured him that their friendship was back on course again: 'I'd be honoured & delighted to be godfather to the infant when it arrives. Please give my love to Freda & tell her how pleased I am ... How superb it must feel to be creating a real *live* symphony! Lucky things. Love as ever Ben.'[32]

The doctors were not taking any chances with Freda. To make quite sure her fourth pregnancy went the full term, she was ordered to rest in bed for a week every month of the pregnancy.[33] It is significant that during this time Freda chose to convert to the Catholic faith. She took instruction from Fr Richard Mangan, S. J., at the Jesuit Church in Farm Street, and chose Veronica as her baptismal name, because she liked the legend of the holy woman of Jerusalem who took pity on Christ as he made his way to Calvary, and wiped his brow with her

*This recording, with Catherine Wyn-Rogers singing the *Four Poems of St Teresa of Avila*, together with MB's *Gethsemane Fragment* and *Tristessa,* is available in the fifth volume of Chandos Records' definitive Berkeley Edition, CHAN 10265.

head-cloth.* Lennox put no pressure on Freda to become a Catholic, but he was pleased when she did finally convert – and glad it happened before the birth of the baby.

Freda went into labour, in a private nursing home in Weymouth Street, not far from her old haunts at the BBC, on the morning of Saturday 29 May, and, though assured by a leading gynaecologist that she was perfectly constructed for child-bearing and had nothing to worry about, the delivery was in fact long, hard and risky. When at last the baby appeared, he was dangerously blue and not expected to live; Freda remained unconscious for the rest of the night.

Fathers in those days were not expected to take any part in the business of childbirth: they waited till mother and child came home. So Lennox occupied himself with rehearsals for a new ballet, *The Lovers' Gallery* (set to his orchestral *Divertimento*), and the first person to see his son and heir was Nadia Boulanger, who had come over to London for a concert with the Boyd Neel Strings at the Wigmore on Thursday and had stayed on specially.† Nadia called at the nursing home after Mass on Sunday, and saw the baby, though not Freda. It was not till the next morning that Freda came round from the anaesthetic. That evening, while Lennox was attending the première of his film *The First Gentleman*, she was allowed to hold the child for the first time. On Tuesday morning *The Times* carried a notice of the birth of a nameless Berkeley son. This conventionally anonymous formula suited them both, since they had been unable to agree on the name which Lennox had registered, Richard (possibly after the metaphysical poet and Catholic convert Richard Crashaw, whose writing he so much admired). Later that day, between rehearsals for his ballet, Lennox was permitted to visit his wife – and to meet his son. By Wednesday morning Freda had recovered sufficient strength to write to Lennox, with firm resolve:

*According to the Christian story, after its contact with Christ's face, Veronica's headcloth bore a miraculous imprint of Christ's features. The fabric, preserved in St Peter's Basilica, is venerated as a holy relic, and Veronica's act of charity is commemorated in the Stations of the Cross. While she is not included in the Roman Martyrology, she does have her own feast day, July 12.

†Boulanger had been conducting a section of the Boyd Neel Orchestra in concertos for two harpsichords by J. S. and C. P. E. Bach (in which the soloists were Lucille Wallace and Clifford Curzon), a new concertino by the Polish composer Antoni Szałowski (a pupil of Boulanger 1931–6) and Hindemith's *Eight Little Pieces for Strings* (*The Times*, 31 May 1948).

30 Lennox and Freda Berkeley, London, 1946

> My beloved darling, I have now definitely decided – he is to be Michael FitzHardinge Berkeley! Ever since I first set eyes on the wee scrap I've had my doubts about Richard – too big a name for such a very small boy! This being so my pet, perhaps you'd call in at Marylebone Town Hall, on your way to the R.A.M. [the Royal Academy of Music, where Lennox was teaching composition] in the morning and ask them to scrap the first one [i.e. birth certificate], and fill in the necessary for the right one, and pay another 3/9d! ... My darling I'm so wonderfully happy; how lovely to have our son – we did want him so badly didn't we? I love you with all my heart dearest Lennox ... I do hope sweetheart that your ballet was a great success.[34]

Actually the ballet had still not quite happened – it was due to launch the new Metropolitan Ballet company at the Scala Theatre in Charlotte Street on the very evening of the day on which Freda wrote the letter. And it was not a great success. The scenario is built around the idea of pictures in a gallery that come to life and disconcert two lovers (a storyline that closely resembles that of Lennox's last and unfinished opera, *Faldon Park*). According to *The Times*, the piece 'fell between the two stools of fantasy and comedy'. The plot had possibilities, but the choreography by Frank Staff was 'too laboured and the pace too slow to save the piece from seeming silly'. In *The Times*'s view, 'only Lennox Berkeley's music had any distinction'.[35]

With Freda and Michael still so ill, it was some weeks before they were allowed home – with a copy of the manual of the day, Dr John Gibbens's *The Care of Young Babies*. Even four months later, Freda was still wearing an elastic abdominal support. On the morning of 12 July the baby was christened by Fr Mangan at St James's, Spanish Place, in the presence of two of his godparents, John Greenidge and Gladys Bryans.[36] Curiously, Ben Britten, the third godparent, was not actually present.[37] He was certainly in London that day, but his diary shows a very heavy programme.[38] Judging by the further muddles over the next baby's christening, when the day was changed half a dozen times and all the wrong godparents turned up, it is not at all unlikely that Lennox and Freda forgot to tell him till it was too late for him to change his plans. There is no doubt, however, that Ben was keenly interested in his godson, and remained so till his death. For the baby's first Christmas, he sent a toy dog. In a thank-you letter, Lennox pointed out that Michael's natural reaction to inanimate objects was to eat them – but 'as this would spoil the dog, & be very bad for Michael's inside, we're not letting him have it just yet'.[39]

Years later when Michael was emerging as a composer and going through a difficult period of illness and personal problems, he sent Ben one of his first pieces, *De profundis clamavi* for brass ensemble, explaining that he felt an emotional affinity with the words. Ben paid him the compliment of analysing the piece, and writing back with an affectionate letter which was not only encouraging ('lots of good things ... really conceived for the medium ... plan is quite clear ... form is well balanced ... certainly no amateur affair'), but also practical ('... hear it properly played – you'd learn so much ... rehearsals would go more easily if you marked & phrased it more fully'). Referring to the words '*Out of the depths have I cried unto Thee, O Lord*', he revealed something of his own philosophy (put to such telling effect in the *War Requiem*):

> I am entirely sympathetic to your approach to the 'programme' – certainly artists can, most usefully, & generally do, just call attention to the problems of life rather than suggest handy solutions to them (we often come a terrible cropper if we do the latter!).[40]

For some months following the birth, No. 8 was so preoccupied with the baby that Lennox could not concentrate on his latest work, a *Concerto for Two Pianos and Orchestra*, commissioned by the Henry Wood Concert Society. Indeed he could not even sleep properly, with little Michael waking twice and sometimes three times a night, and screaming.[41] In September he went to Painswick for three days' quiet work, and a rest, at Gladys's. While there he wrote to Freda, to say, tactfully, that Gladys was most impressed that he had been allowed out on his own, and, tactlessly, that Gladys was surprised that Michael had not yet been weaned. Fortunately Gladys's meddling did not extend to her pet composer, so he was making good progress with the concerto – though he found '2 pianos & orchestra rather a cumbersome medium' which made it difficult to keep the textures clear. But the real reason for his letter was to say how much he was missing his new wife:

> My darling ... It was really worth coming away to feel how strongly we are united. I didn't need to discover that, but one takes these things for a matter of course, and sometimes if you remove yourself a little way from something, you see it much more clearly. I feel all the more strongly that what we have between us is something

beyond price, and that very few are lucky enough to have it. Most human relationships are so fragile, and I don't feel that ours is ...[42]

Judging by the letter Freda wrote the next day, she felt the same. 'When you first went on Friday I felt rather like I did when I was at Broxbourne for the weekends before we were married ... It's wonderful to ... realise again, what I've always told you, that I love you, if possible, more than before.'[43]

The sheer happiness which Lennox and Freda now felt in their life together is unmistakably present in the *Concerto for Two Pianos and Orchestra*, which was heard for the first time at the Royal Albert Hall on 13 December. The soloists were its dedicatees, Phyllis Sellick and Cyril Smith, with the London Symphony Orchestra conducted by the newly-knighted Sir Malcolm Sargent.[44] The veteran concert-goer Lady (Charlotte) Bonham-Carter, a lifelong champion of Lennox's music, took Jim Lees-Milne to the premiere in a party that also included Freda, the Pilkingtons and Patrick Kinross. Jim noted in his diary that night that the new piece was 'enjoyable, full of melodies and vigour'. Romantic in expression, classical in form, it is indeed all that he claimed for it. The first of the two movements, marked *Molto moderato*, ends with a most beautiful *lento* section; and the second is a *Theme* with eleven brilliant *Variations*, including an impressionist one, a Poulencian one and a classical one in which the two pianos chase each other antiphonally in continuous semi-quavers. Each of the variations runs into the next, and the concerto ends with a Stravinskian variation full of tension and drama.[45] Jim's keen eye watched Lennox listening to that first performance in 1948, 'with his long nose turned to the orchestra like a serious salmon, in his tense, shy, modest manner'. At the end of the piece, the diarist recorded, there was much applause, and the 'child-like' Lennox 'appeared on the platform three times and bowed sweetly as though wondering why he was there'.[46]

The Times was much more appreciative of the double concerto than of its predecessor, calling it 'attractive, ingenious and concentrated', and praising the playing as 'brilliant'.[47] But Lennox was not entirely satisfied with it, as he confided to Nadia when she told him at Christmas that she wanted to conduct the new work in Paris in the New Year. He was proud of the confidence she had shown in him by booking it sight unseen, but he worried that it was not worthy of her, and was 'still so far from what I want to do!' However, it was at least pointing in the right direction – and there was not, he added wryly, much new music one could say that about.[48]

31
Lennox, Freda and Family

A month after Nadia Boulanger had given the French premiere of his *Concerto for Two Pianos and Orchestra*, on 27 February 1949, Lennox himself was in France. The British Council sent him on a lecture tour to promote modern British music, with piano and gramophone illustrations. He was away for ten days, starting in Roubaix near Lille on 21 March, continuing in Nancy and Strasbourg, and ending in Paris on the 30th – and, though absence could not have made his heart any fonder, it made him aware of just how fond it had grown. He wrote to Freda to say he was feeling 'rather lost', missing home, and would never go anywhere without his wife and son again, if he could help it – 'I don't like it at all!'[1] Never having had a home before, Freda understood exactly, and wrote back, 'It is a wonderful feeling to have roots somewhere isn't it? – to know that there's always someone waiting for you and wanting you.'[2]

The same letter from Freda bore the good news that the Berkeley [Castle] Estate, of which Lennox was now a Trustee, had sent a cheque for £702. 15s., which would help with Michael's education, when the time came. Lennox replied from Lille with other, more immediate plans for the windfall: 'I think we might buy anything we still need for the house – I'll use it anyway to pay the roof repairs ... and the rest we can always put to ... the future.'[3]

They wrote to one another daily during that French tour, and Freda's letters brim with domestic snippets: she had had her 'firkin put in order!' [her hair done]; she had dined with Lennox's erratic student, John Prideaux-Brune, who had paid her more attention than he ought (though 'Your Mouse', she assures Lennox, 'is a very one man little creature'[4]); there had been a fork supper at Charlotte Bonham-Carter's with the Stephen Spenders, a French Embassy couple and the novelist L. P. Hartley; the chimneypiece was covered with further invitations from the Harewoods, Topolskis, Pilkingtons and Hills; and she had been to a concert of music by Britten, Purcell and Ben's young protégé Arthur Oldham, given by the Boyd Neel String Orchestra with Peter

Pears and Dennis Brain at Chelsea Town Hall – followed by a reception, which had given her a big lift:

> ... darling, I was so happy! First Ben kissed me – then Joan Cross came and was charming – offered to give me a lift home – then Peter saw me, excused himself to someone he was talking to and came over & kissed me, and Barbara Britten and I talked for a long time ... And then Basil [Douglas] offered to take me home! ... You see, before [this party,] I knew they were all nice to me but I rather felt it was because of you – but last night I knew they liked me for myself. And it made me feel quite ridiculously elated![5]

For Freda all these social kisses meant more than Lennox can possibly have known; they showed she had been accepted in his world, not just as Mrs Berkeley but as Freda too. Always unconfident, always needing proof of love, she was reaping some of the rewards she had hoped that marriage would bring.

Lennox could hardly bear to read Freda's letters because they made him feel so homesick. From the 'very un-beautiful town' of Lille, where he was 'getting rather tired of hanging about with nothing to do' (even though the food was good), he wrote back to say he was missing Mikey (the 'dear little man'), and to suggest that Freda should ask the Gronaus and John Pope-Hennessy to dinner – but not during Holy Week, which would not be very suitable for entertaining.[6]

While Lennox was in France, Freda had received a letter from Peter Fraser in Ireland. He had left the flat in Warwick Square (though Weyman and Wyatt were still there) and had attached himself to Lennox's Merton friend Billy Clonmore, now Lord Wicklow. Once a Church of England curate, now a Catholic businessman, Clonmore had succeeded to his father's earldom in 1946 and was running a hotel at the family seat, Shelton Abbey in Co. Wicklow.* He was still a bachelor (though he was to marry a few years later), and no less susceptible to decorative young men than he had been at Oxford, but he had no money. Nor, indeed, had the feckless Peter – beyond

*Within two years the estate was declared bankrupt, and Lord Wicklow retired to the seaside at Sandycove, Co. Dublin. In 1959 he married, and in 1978 he died childless; his titles are now extinct. Since 1973 Shelton Abbey has been a men's prison.

the monthly allowance that Lennox was still paying him – so Freda wondered who was paying the bills? In Lennox's absence, she took the liberty of calling in at the bank and asking them to keep a weather eye on Peter's account. She had little doubt that 'further debts are inevitable'.[7] Perhaps Peter had already served the prison sentence for theft, about which John Pope-Hennessy later told Roger Nichols.[8]

Peter Fraser does not feature again in the Berkeley story till the summer of 1973, when Lennox paid a surprise call at his digs in North London overlooking Highgate Ponds – while walking the dog.* It was the day of Peter's fifty-third birthday,[9] and Lennox must have been intending to wish him happy birthday, and, at the same time, to satisfy his curiosity about what Peter was doing now, what he looked like, where and how (and possibly with whom) he was living, whether he was happy. But Peter was out, so Lennox posted a note through the door. The following day a postcard arrived with an N6 postmark and a reproduction of Ptolemy's map of the British Isles. 'Dear Lennox,' it said, 'Thanks for yr note. You have the address correctly – pity you had to journey up here to confirm it! And without even a drink as a consolation. Peter.'[10]

This brief but friendly message, matching the tone of Lennox's, contained no suggestion that they should meet. And why should it? What could they have in common, twenty-seven years after Lennox had left Peter to marry Freda? This was the last Lennox heard from the man with whom he had shared so much of the war. Over the next three years Peter Fraser developed a variety of heart conditions, culminating in acute pulmonary oedema, which, combined with his diabetes, proved fatal, and on 5 March 1976 he died in Guy's Hospital, London. The death certificate describes him as a journalist. He left no family and no property – just a few letters, and a kind landlady, Miss Alice Shavelson, of Millfield Lane, Highgate, still wondering who he was and where he came from, and what she should do with his few possessions.[11]

*Dog-walking was an important part of LB's new regime, and always came after lunch. The dog in question was not his much-loved Labrador, Black Prince, who had been killed in a road accident three years earlier, but it may have been his son MB's first dog, a fine black-and-tan crossbreed called Trout, often to be seen, in the 1970s, attached to a parking meter outside Broadcasting House, while his master was broadcasting from the Radio Three continuity studio.

Lennox learned of Peter's death from a notice in *The Times* on 11 March, which requested friends and relatives to contact Miss Shavelson at home. The funeral was at Golders Green Crematorium that same morning, so it is unlikely that he would have been able to attend at such short notice. The following May Miss Shavelson wrote to the only person she knew had been a friend of Peter, the Widow Lloyd, enclosing some photos of Peter taken outside her house in Highgate in about 1973. A few days later the Widow forwarded these and Miss Shavelson's letter, to Lennox, together with two photos which he himself had taken of Peter when they first met in 1940, while both were serving in the RAF in Yorkshire, the Widow as an Intelligence officer.* Not having seen Peter for thirty years, the Widow was surprised how well he had aged: he was not 'nearly so *dégringolé*' [disintegrated] as might have been expected. Miss Shavelson's snaps show Peter wearing a light raincoat and a confidential smile. He has not gone to the dogs at all – on the contrary he looks fit and confident, even smug – and the landlady appears to be rather proud of him. According to the Widow, Miss Shavelson was 'madly keen to find out about his origins', but Peter's provenance was likely to remain, the Widow thought, 'for ever a mystery. Perhaps as well!'[12]

The other men friends from Lennox's wartime bachelor days were still very much part of his new married life, despite the cynical predictions of most of them. Freda had been determined that Lennox should not lose touch with them, and now they had become her friends too. She and Lennox still saw John Weyman and Dickie Wyatt, who remained together at Warwick Square till at least 1954, when Wyatt went to Lisbon as managing director of BP Portugal (Weyman did not join him till his retirement from the Design Council in 1958, and for some years after that they retained a base in London).[13] And Lennox still went to the Reform Club for Saturday night revels in the upstairs Committee Room which had been commandeered as a dining club by a clique of distinguished professionals, who had nowhere else to meet in that last decade before Wolfenden, when gay men, living in an

*During his time in the RAF (1940–3) Lloyd acquired some interesting photographs – aerial shots of German targets, British POWs in Germany, individual airmen at work and at play, squadron groups, etc – which he assembled into two albums, now in the safekeeping of the National Library of Wales – Llyfr Ffoto Album 161 and 162 (JDK Lloyd Photo Albums 10 [1941–3] and 11 [1943–8]).

atmosphere of fear and guilt, had to be immensely guarded about revealing themselves.*

It was not just that homosexuality was still illegal, but since the war it had become increasingly linked in the popular mind with communism and moral corruption. This attitude was not tempered by the virulently homophobic views of the new Home Secretary, Sir David Maxwell Fyfe, and the new Commissioner of Police at Scotland Yard, Sir John Nott-Bower – the one promising 'a new drive against male vice' that would 'rid England of this plague',[14] the other promising to prosecute homosexuals 'with ferocious zeal'.[15] It was an ugly time, and many homosexual men went further underground. But the voices of the Saturday-night Reformers rang out more shrilly than ever. Not everyone liked them. Sir Michael Howard (then a history don at King's College, London)† still shudders, fifty years on, when he recalls 'that coven at the Reform Club!' They were, he says, 'an *awful* lot'.[16] A fellow member of the Reform remembered them as a 'gaggle of geese'. Freda joined Lennox for the Reform Saturdays – by popular demand: the only woman in an otherwise exclusively male club, their pin-up, their mascot, their cover. Howard believes she was a civilizing influence. 'In fact her presence must have done them all a world of good.' He had always noticed how 'they stopped their bitchy gossip' when there was a woman around, 'and started behaving like quite intelligent beings!'[17] Freda herself recalls that what she did not want to hear she did not listen to; and when she sensed it was time to leave the men on their own, she used to retire to the library and read *Queen* magazine and the *Tatler*, or talk about horse-racing with her two favourite waiters, 'Phyllis', a 'peroxide queen', and Austin, 'married, but sympathetic'.

*According to Patrick Trevor-Roper (interviewed by Michael Bloch for his biography of the Liberal leader Jeremy Thorpe), the gay clique remained at the Reform until the mid-1960s when, 'frightened off by a new and less sympathetic Secretary, they all resigned and joined Harold Nicolson and Raymond Mortimer at the Travellers' Club' (Michael Bloch, in a telephone conversation with TS, 27 July 2004).

†Sir Michael Howard (born 1922) was Regius Professor of Modern History at Oxford 1980–9, and later Robert A. Lovett Professor of Military and Naval History at Yale University. During the Second World War he was commissioned in the Coldstream Guards and fought in the Italian Campaign. He was twice wounded and won a Military Cross at Salerno. In 2002 he was appointed CH and in 2005 OM. His revealing autobiography, *Captain Professor: A Life in War and Peace*, was published by Continuum in 2006.

If Freda had any lingering doubts about the rightness of steering Lennox off his earlier course, they were finally dispelled by a letter she received in the autumn of 1952, at the very height of the government's witch-hunt against homosexual men. It came from Lennox's admirer and wartime landlord Douglas Gordon, who was still working in the Clerk's Office at the House of Commons, as an adviser on protocol and precedence. On House of Commons paper he wrote to Freda, whom he barely knew, to say he had recently seen Lennox and had been 'wholly *delighted*' to find him so 'refurbished and rejuvenated'.

> He and I are very different types of animal; but in the war years I grew to hold very much of a feeling for him, and to appreciate his gentle and direct outlook. At times I hated to see how worried and tired he looked ... And now I see him ten years younger; far more spry; sleek (? *fat*!); and looking happy. And I am so very pleased to see it. You have done a miraculous job ... I was in at the beginning of it; and I thought it quite inauspicious; and I was quite wrong. I'll say in my defence that I didn't think it inauspicious for very long; and, in gratitude, that you have been such a friendly creature all the way that you've never reminded me even indirectly that I did think so! It is (widely) thought to be a thumping success – and your success ... [18]

Freda was so greatly touched by this 'recantation' that she scribbled on the back of the envelope 'From Douglas Gordon ... who was dead against L marrying!' and locked it away with her other treasures, as a sort of testimonial.

John Greenidge may have been Lennox's oldest and closest friend, but Ben was still the friend whose opinion mattered most. We do not know directly what Ben really felt about Lennox's marriage, but we do know he had told Freda he was pleased and we can assume that, having chosen a form of marriage himself, he would have understood Lennox's more orthodox arrangement. Ben was not part of the Reform coterie, and Lennox did not see as much of him as he did of the Reformers, but by 1949 the friendship was so secure, within its post-Mill limits, and so important, that when Lennox made a new will that year it was Ben who figured in a key role. He was not an executor or a primary benefactor but, in the event of the simultaneous deaths of Lennox and Freda, Ben – then living with Peter Pears at Crag House on the Aldeburgh sea-front – was named as guardian of baby Michael.[19] This was an unusual arrangement to have made in those unenlightened days when child-rearing was still very strictly conventional. Quite apart from the qualms that some parents might have had about Ben's reputation, the idea of entrusting a baby boy to a couple of musical bachelors would have seemed utterly impractical, however much Ben and Peter might have enjoyed being parents. Ben would probably have welcomed the role. Three times already he had attempted to adopt, or at least foster, a boy (an East London child in 1937, the Basque refugee in 1938 and, in this same year of 1949, a wild Aldeburgh twelve-year-old known as the Nipper).[20] And it did not stop there. In 1952 Ben considered adopting two children from a displaced persons camp in Germany, according to his friend Imogen Holst:

> He said he'd been thinking about it for ages because he realised that it was unlikely that he'd ever marry and have children of his own, and he'd got such an immense instinct of love for them that it spilled over and was wasted. Also that he felt that otherwise he might get more selfish. That he'd try and find the right school for them and then would arrange all his concert tours in the term time so as to be free for them in the holidays. He said he'd probably spoil them ...[21]

In 1955, still feeling the urge to adopt, Ben approached the poet Ronald Duncan and asked if he would allow him to share his twelve-year-old son Roger.[22] Duncan agreed, and Ben was so astonished and delighted that he looked, in Duncan's words, as if he had been given three opera houses. For the next ten years Ben was a second father to Roger Duncan, giving him affection and advice as he grew up, writing one and sometimes two letters a week, visiting him at school and keeping a room for him in the house at Aldeburgh.[23]

To prove that the guardianship plan was not just a gesture, Lennox repeated his intentions when he updated his will in 1961, appointing Ben as 'the Guardian of my infant children'.[24] By this time there were three Berkeley boys: Michael was at the difficult age of thirteen, Julian was eleven, and Nicholas five. For all that John Betjeman considered them 'three perfectly beautiful boys',* they were a wild tribe, and

*In a poem he wrote for Lennox and Freda's silver wedding, copied into the flyleaf of his *Collected Poems* as an anniversary present, and read aloud at a party at 8 Warwick Avenue on 14 December 1971. Three years younger than Lennox, John Betjeman had missed him at the Dragon School and had then gone on to Marlborough, but they caught up at Oxford in 1926 and remained friends. Betjeman became Poet Laureate in 1972.

would have intimidated the most experienced parents, let alone the fastidious and childless masters of the Red House, Aldeburgh (to which Ben and Peter had moved from Crag House in 1957). Presumably Ben was consulted about his putative role as foster father, and presumably he talked about it to Peter, but there is no record in the surviving correspondence of what they felt about the plan, and they must have hoped – as, surely, Lennox and Freda did too – that providence would let them all off the hook (which, with Ben's death, it did in 1976). Lennox's intentions speak volumes for the warmth of feeling that continued to exist between Little Venice and Aldeburgh, for the Berkeleys' absolute trust in Ben's integrity – and for Ben's generosity.

Freda was not above making her own unlikely domestic decisions. When she realized she was pregnant again, in November 1949, she decided she needed extra help at home, and hired – of all people – 'Ma' Watson, the parson's wife who had beaten her as a little girl at Aldworth in the Thirties. Always generous, trusting and eager to please, Freda seems to have been more concerned about what to pay Mrs Watson for her baby-sitting at No. 8, than about whether her old tormenter was a fit person to care for her children. Ostensibly she wanted to help a widow who had fallen on hard times, but at some deeper level she was trying to disarm a foe and lay a ghost of the past.

Still desperately unsure of herself, Freda was not yet free of her nightmares. They were now less frequent, but no less vivid and terrifying – and when she had them, she woke shrieking, to the consternation of Lennox. When he was away, it was worse. Then she was so frightened, alone in the big house with the baby that she had to sleep with the lights on. Sometimes she asked the Italian *au pair*, Virginia Santos, to sleep with her – for example while Lennox was cruising the Mediterranean on the aircraft carrier HMS *Vengeance*, gathering local colour for his new opera *Nelson*.

This was in the winter of 1950 when Lennox was the guest of the Flag Officer commanding the 3rd Aircraft Carrier Squadron, Rear-Admiral Charles Lambe (later Admiral of the Fleet Sir Charles Lambe, First Sea Lord). An accomplished amateur pianist, and a lifelong member of the Bach Choir, Admiral Lambe had installed two grand pianos in his day-cabin so they could play duets by Mozart and Schubert for an hour or two every evening. When they reached Cape St

Vincent the admiral slowed the squadron so that Lennox would have time to absorb the atmosphere of the place where Nelson fought the French and Spanish fleets in the Battle of Trafalgar. Then, in accordance with naval tradition, a wreath was cast on the waters where Nelson lost his life at the moment of victory.[25] For Lennox, born under the White Ensign – his father was a naval captain, his Harris great-grandfather a commander, and his Berkeley great-great-grandfather an admiral – the voyage was a consolation prize for a thwarted ambition. If it had not been for his colour blindness (and poor mathematics) he too might have joined the Navy. The trip also provided him with material he was to use in the last act of *Nelson*, set in the cockpit of HMS *Victory* during the decisive battle. This is where Lennox's thoughts still lingered when the squadron put in at Gibraltar at the beginning of February. He had just arranged a lift home in a battleship,[26] when Her Majesty's Governor handed him a letter. Imagining it must be official business, he did not immediately look at it. Later, alone, he recognized the writing as Freda's, and read a letter which took him right back into Warwick Avenue and domesticity. Pregnant, lonely and still haunted by nightmares, Freda had asked the *au pair* to sleep with her in their big bed.

> I would try and go through with it [i.e. sleeping alone and risking nightmares] only I do feel it's not very good for our new baby ... I went to 12 o'clock Mass at Lisson Grove today, and said prayers and lit a candle for you from Mikie and me. We both love you so much my darling and long to have you with us again ... Ben has just 'phoned to ask us out to lunch: I couldn't go as Ma Watson was coming! He was very impressed about your trip ... . [27]

The new baby was born on 6 July – with no delivery difficulties this time. Another boy, he was christened Julian Lennox on 13 October. It has always been assumed – not least by themselves – that his godparents were Nadia Boulanger; his great-aunt Molly, Countess of Berkeley, then living in her converted convent above Assisi (and inevitably more concerned with the problems of her increasingly aggressive war orphans); the interior decorator John Hill; and Anthony Chaplin (who was busy at the time divorcing Alvilde and marrying Rosemary Lyttelton). But the baptismal register at the Catholic Church of St James's, Spanish Place,[28] shows that Hill and Lord Chaplin were the only ones of these friends actually present – and, as non-Catholics, they were listed not as 'godparents' but as 'witnesses'. The other witness was Lavinia Baker-Smith, a Catholic neighbour of the Berkeleys, who stood proxy for Nadia and Molly Berkeley (who were unable to attend because of several changes of the date).[29] By their unavoidable absences, which prevented their making the necessary vows, neither was properly a godparent. Nevertheless Nadia, though the strictest of Catholics herself, took no notice of this procedural irregularity and played the part devotedly, remembering every anniversary in Julian's life till the very end of hers, often sending esoteric musical offerings to her godson's brothers as well.

To help with the growing family Freda now took on a full-time housekeeper, an Ulsterwoman called Babs McKeever, who lived in the spare room at No. 8 with her husband Dick and was to remain with the Berkeleys, devoted and faithful, for nearly forty years. But Freda was not good at managing staff or children, and Lennox began to find it seriously difficult to concentrate on his work, against a background of 'the noise and interruptions of family life'. While staying with the William Waltons on Ischia, in 1970, he confided to his diary: 'I felt envious of the ideal conditions in which he [Walton] can compose, so different from mine – and yet I thought I might easily do nothing in such perfect surroundings, having been accustomed to struggle against the noise and interruptions of family life, I might well be unable to concentrate in such complete calm!'[30]

At Easter 1953, needing peace and quiet to finish a six-movement orchestral *Suite* which had been commissioned by the Third Programme for Coronation Week, Lennox decided to escape to the south of France, to stay with Alvilde and Jim Lees-Milne, now married, in Alvilde's picturesque cottage, La Méridienne, on the edge of the remote mountain village of Roquebrune in the Alpes Maritimes. Jim hated Roquebrune – 'the isolation, the pent-upness of our doll-like house and the claustrophobia of the village'[31] – but the region was full of memories for Lennox: he had first been there when he was four, on a visit to his Aunt and Uncle d'Eppinghoven at their villa in Menton. He had got to know it well when his parents settled there for part of the final decade of their lives, and he had taken Freda there as part of the honeymoon tour in 1947, when they stayed at the Voile d'Or (the *pension* – now a grand hotel – overlooking the harbour of St Jean-Cap Ferrat, and owned then by the film director Michael

Powell). At the end of his life Lennox was to return to this same coast every spring as a member of the jury of the Prince Pierre of Monaco Music Prize (with Nadia, Georges Auric, Roland-Manuel and other old Paris friends). 'It's odd the way I always seem to have come back ... to this point,' he wrote in his diary in 1968, 'not really from choice, though I've always liked it and felt at home here, but by the force of circumstances.'[32]

At Roquebrune, Alvilde put Lennox in a small, detached guest-room nicknamed the Wagon-lit, overlooking some orange and lemon trees.[33] Separated from the house, and with the use of a grand piano, Lennox was able to work 'at any time of the day or night undisturbed'.[34] He had never had so much freedom, he told Freda, and he lapped it up, not only for composing but for walks – and religious observance too: 'On Friday evening we watched the Good Friday procession through the village – they make little lights out of snail shells and decorate their houses ... I went to confession on Sat: evening and to communion this morning – I thought it would be a good thing as it seems so difficult to fit in in London. There seems so much time for everything when the children are not with one!'[35]

Jim Lees-Milne, himself a Catholic convert, noted in his diary that Lennox followed the Stations of the Cross 'with a sort of dumb reverence'. He admired Lennox's 'exceptionally good and utterly childlike nature', his 'humility and simplicity of heart', but felt excluded by an earnest devotion that locked Lennox in a private world 'which is not mine and into which I cannot penetrate'. Nor did Jim care for Lennox's 'chill' music, in particular the *Suite* undergoing construction in the Wagon-lit, from which he complained he heard 'occasional dissonant noises, but nothing consecutive'.[36]

While Lennox was in France, Freda and the boys were on holiday with the Harrises at Beaumont in Jersey. Nellie Harris was still grieving for her husband, the good Arthur, who had died eighteen months earlier – at almost the same time as Hans Gronau too had suddenly died. Nellie and Arthur had been married for forty-one years, and after the funeral in December 1951 Nellie had said she had a presentiment that Freda and Lennox would have the same long and happy life together.[37]

Reunited at the end of April, the Berkeleys attended the premieres of Lennox's *Suite*, played by the BBC Symphony Orchestra conducted by Sir Malcolm Sargent at the BBC on 6 June, and of his *Concerto for Flute and Chamber Orchestra* played by John Francis and the BBC

Symphony Orchestra, again conducted by Sargent, at the Proms seven weeks later.

That autumn they lost another friend, the enigmatic John Greenidge, whom Lennox had known since they were boys in North Oxford. His brother Terence rang to say that John had died of a coronary thrombosis in the Homoeopathic Hospital in Great Ormond Street, a few doors away from the flat which he and Lennox used to share. He was only fifty-four.[38] Under the terms of his will he left £200 of his small estate to Prinknash Abbey for their building fund and the rest in trust for Terence and Terence's daughter, Althea.[39]

Dismayed by the loss of such a dear friend, Lennox threw himself into finishing his epic *Nelson*, the greatest challenge of his composing career, a real, old-fashioned grand opera. He had started it in the spring of 1949 and only now, four and a half years later, had he reached the scoring stage. Musically inspired by *Peter Grimes*, the plot came from Carola Oman's 1947 biography of Nelson, which debunks the myths and establishes the real man.[40] The librettist was Alan Pryce-Jones, a friend from France in the early Thirties, who had been editor of the *Times Literary Supplement* since 1948, and their idea was to show a national hero as an ordinary man at war with himself in a blistering love triangle.

A run-through with piano at the Wigmore Hall on 14 February 1954 went so well that Sadler's Wells was persuaded (by Basil Douglas) to mount a full-scale staged production, directed by George Devine and conducted by Vilem Tausky. The opera then generated such a fever of publicity that the BBC decided to broadcast the opening night performance (on 22 September) live on the radio – not on the minority Third Programme, but on the popular Home Service. But the opera was not the unqualified hit that its supporters had hoped for. Over the course of the following week the reviews were only mixed: 'a singers' opera' (*Daily Telegraph*), 'many qualities likely to ensure it permanence' (*Observer*), 'generous expanses of subtle music' (*News Chronicle*); *The Times* passed the withering but ultimately meaningless judgement that, while Berkeley had 'long outgrown his dry-as-a-biscuit manner', his music could 'never be other than aristocratic'. Some critics blamed the male singers, some the production. But the truth is that Horatio Nelson was not really Lennox's kind of hero, and grand opera was not his *métier*. As a later critic pointed out, Lennox was too modest a man to be able to tackle such a heroic theme, and on such a scale.[41] The opera's musical invention, as *The Times* said, was 'copious, fresh and symphonically delightful', but lacked – though only just – 'dramatic flight'. And Pryce-Jones, a brilliant journalist, did not have the necessary practical experience to construct a dramatic opera – even if his libretto did have the makings of a gripping novel.

The piece might have worked as a cantata, or as a tone poem – and Lennox did make two concert versions for timpani, percussion, harp and strings (a *Suite* of sixteen minutes, with the addition of celesta, and an *Interlude* of five minutes). But he had not been able to resist trying to do what Ben had done so effectively in *Grimes*, even though he was well aware of the pitfalls. From the very beginning he anticipated 'all sorts of difficulties',[42] and it is interesting that this time the new Lennox, husband of Freda, grappled with these technical problems on his own – as he revealed in a letter to Ben, just after he had started work, 'How often I've wished you were at hand to give me advice, but one can only learn by making mistakes, and I have to forget about you or I would never dare do it at all!'[43]

Years later Lennox admitted that though *Nelson* had some good things in it, he was not satisfied with it as a whole.[44] Michael Berkeley, who has composed three highly theatrical operas himself,* has a more positive opinion of his father's *Nelson*. He is convinced the score could still work with a condensation of the slow first act, a tweak or two to develop and extend the rousing choral motif and a beefing-up of the battle interlude. But he concedes that the libretto needs surgery too.

The year 1954 was one of the busiest periods in Lennox's life. At the very same time that he was writing *Nelson* – and four or five other pieces too – he was also working on another opera, a comic one-acter, inspired by *Albert Herring*. For words he turned to his friend Paul Dehn, poet and screenwriter, who produced a hilarious libretto loosely based on a disastrous dinner party at No. 8, when the main course caught fire. *A Dinner Engagement* is about a retired and penniless diplomatic couple, Lord and Lady Dunmow, seeking a smart match for their daughter. They invite the Grand Duchess of Monteblanco, whom they know from their last posting, to bring her eligible son to dinner. But just as the guests arrive, the hired help Mrs Kneebone burns the

**Baa Baa Black Sheep* (based on Kipling; 1993), and *Jane Eyre* (2000), both to libretti by the Australian novelist David Malouf, and *For You* (2008) to a libretto by the novelist Ian McEwan.

entrée. It is left to the daughter herself to save the day – and win the prince, with her modern ways, and his favourite dish, cold cherry soup.*

This charming, light, little opera would have been as beyond the capabilities of the withdrawn bachelor Lennox – the 'dry-as-a-biscuit' Lennox – as the epic *Nelson*, or the ecstatic *Teresa Songs* or the powerful *Stabat Mater*. Marriage had released him to be the composer his talents, his temperament, his background and his faith meant him to be. George Baker, Lennox's friend and former BBC colleague, was as surprised by news of the marriage as everyone else – but, unlike the others, he had had a hunch it would work. Freda, he said, was unusually intelligent, capable and charming, and he was convinced that 'the happiness she has brought into her husband's life has ... more than anything else enabled him to bring to full bloom his abundant gifts as a composer'.[45]

In middle age Lennox had found his identity as a composer, as a man and as a Catholic. His music was more confident, more uniquely his: its originality set free to reveal an individual new composer (just as the perceptive critic had foreseen in *The Times* in 1929).[46] As a result, commissions were more abundant – nearly twenty-five from the time of his marriage till 1956. His social life, as a married man, was flourishing, with invitations which had never come his way as a bachelor. In his faith he was surer and more relaxed. He was freer of the 'various forms of insecurity ... that beset one in youth', his individuality was more firmly established and he no longer cared what other people thought of him.[47] In his person – as photos show – he was fuller, taller, more assured, more often smiling than not.

Lennox himself recognized that in every way he was stronger and more fulfilled. He knew why, even if he still did not quite know how, and he was grateful – as he wrote on a scrap of paper in November 1966: 'Next month will be the 20th anniversary of our marriage. I can still hardly believe what happened 20 yrs ago and that I shd have had

*The English Opera Group gave the first performance at the Jubilee Hall in Aldeburgh on 17 June 1954, in a production conducted by Vilem Tausky and directed by LB's Paris friend, the dancer and designer William Chappell. In LB's centenary year, 2003, Richard Hickox and the City of London Sinfonia with the singers Roderick Williams, Yvonne Kenny, Claire Rutter, Jean Rigby, Anne Collins, Robin Leggate and Blake Fischer performed the work at the Cheltenham Festival (recorded by Chandos on CHAN 10219).

the good fortune to marry someone who is not merely adored by me but I think really loved by all who know her.' Five years later, on his silver wedding anniversary, he wrote in his diary, 'I can't imagine what my life can have been without Freda – perhaps I just prefer not to remember it.'[48] Typically unembellished, this sentence forms as ringing an endorsement of his marriage, and as clear a rejection of his confused life before 1946, as someone of Lennox's diffident nature could ever have made. Indeed to have committed it to paper at all is an indication of how deeply he believed it, and, perhaps, of how much he wanted others to know it. Marriage had not made him heterosexual – it could not have done, and neither he nor Freda had ever expected it to. His sexuality remained unchanged. The only difference was that now, deflected, subdued, it was not a disturbance any more. Through marriage to Freda he had found the confidence to be the man he had been waiting and wanting and needing to be. And though he would remain reticent and vague and forgetful, he had become a devoted husband, a firm and loving father, and a sensitive teacher.

That his students would span the entire range of musical personalities – from the luminously simple John Tavener to the fearsomely complex Brian Ferneyhough – and that all revered and loved him is an indication of his extraordinary gifts. He never forced his personality or his technique or his musical ideas on any of his students: instead he sought out their own individual talents and strove to develop them with warm encouragement. Like Nadia's lessons in Paris, Lennox's would often involve an analysis of a Bach cantata, or even a visit to Vespers at Westminster Cathedral – the spiritual dimension being no less important than the musical. When he specially enjoyed a concert or an opera, he would play to his students – and to his sons – favourite bits of the score, partly to savour them again and partly to examine the construction and scoring. The lessons always ended, as Nadia's had done, with tea and cakes.[49] This ritual was preceded, in Richard Stoker's case, by a smoggy smoke-up, the master filling his pipe with Black Sobranie, while young Stoker, to Lennox's delight, stuffed his with shreds of a tobacco called Baby's Bottom.[50]

In his teaching and his family life, as in his music, Lennox now knew clearly who he was and what he was doing – and at last he was content. His country soon recognized his contribution to its musical life and rewarded him with a CBE and eventually a knighthood (and from the Vatican came a papal Knighthood of St Gregory), but he never rested on his laurels. As soon as he had finished one piece, which he usually thought was the best thing he had done till then, he would press on to the next, experimenting with new techniques and new ideas. Incongruously for such a tonal composer, he even ventured into his own brand of serialism (in, for example, the *Violin Concerto*, the *Sonatina for Oboe and Piano*, the *Symphony No. 3* and 'Aria 1' from the *Concertino*); if nothing else, he said, it was useful as a means of developing musical ideas.[51] And for Lennox this was what composition was. Whilst he regarded music as an act of communication, he never thought about an audience when he was writing. His only concern was how best to present the musical ideas that came to him.[52]

Till the onset of his final illness, Lennox was to continue working to a rigid routine: composing from nine till lunchtime, walking the dog in the afternoon (quite often in Regent's Park, so he could watch the animals in the Zoo), scoring sketches till dinner, playing duets and writing letters afterwards.[53] It was no use complaining that you could not get on with a piece, he told his students, if you did not actually sit down and just get on with it. The daily grind of sitting at the keyboard with a sheet of manuscript paper and writing, writing anything, was the only way to engage the muse.

This regimen, instilled by Nadia Boulanger in the rue Ballu, enabled Lennox to write far more music than his naturally slow pace would otherwise have permitted. His complete list runs to nearly 230 individual works. They all bear the unmistakable stamp of his character: restraint, elegance, spareness and a hidden strength. All that Lennox might have said about himself, his life and his faith, he says in his music – if only unconsciously, since it was his firm belief that music was an intellectual abstraction, no less real than life, but entirely separate from it. The raw material springs from a profound and mysterious source – from, if you like, the soul. But the voice is always recognizably Lennox's own. Its defining qualities are partly a legacy of his French ancestry and partly learned from Fauré, via Boulanger and Ravel. Like his teachers, Lennox was influenced by Fauré's Romantic sensibilities, and the sense of classical form which kept them so discreetly in check. Like Fauré, Lennox was a musician's musician, a composer whose elusive depths are well worth exploring. This is why he is admired by so many younger composers, why his chamber music and songs are increasingly performed, why his liturgical music (especially the *Missa Brevis*) is part of the repertoire of every cathedral choir, and why his guitar music – among the greatest of the twentieth century – is in constant demand around the world.* A list of Berkeley masterpieces would include the *Recorder Sonatina* (often played on the flute), the *Horn Trio*, the piano *Preludes* and *Sonata*, many of the songs, the orchestral *Serenade* and *Divertimento*, the joyous *First Symphony* and the tougher *Third Symphony*, the single and double *Piano Concertos*, the *St Teresa Poems*, the *Stabat Mater* and *A Dinner Engagement*. † All these works share an enduring quality that transcends period, and will for ever reward rediscovery.

In 1955 Ben offered Lennox the chance to write another opera for the English Opera Group. Lennox was ready. To express his gratitude to the remarkable woman who had changed his life, he decided to set a subtle love story from the Old Testament book of *Ruth*. The sacred drama he created is indicative of more than Lennox's lyrical gifts – it is a tribute to the steadfastness of Freda (who was to produce their third son, Nicholas Eadnoth, while *Ruth* was in process of composition).

The librettist was Eric Crozier, who had already shown his mastery of stagecraft as director of *Peter Grimes* and the *Rape of Lucretia* and librettist of four of Britten's works, including *Albert Herring* and (with E. M. Forster) *Billy Budd*. It was not an easy job to dramatize such static material. In contrast to the blood and thunder of so many of the other stories of the old kingdom of Israel, *Ruth* is a pastoral episode, quiet and peaceful and happy – a parable of outsiderness and virtue rewarded.

Although Lennox recognized that 'events ... can produce feelings that might cause one to write music', he did not believe in composers 'consciously delivering a message'.[54] But when an artist is as secretive about his personal life as Lennox was, we are forced, like the painter Clea, exploring the psychology of the writer Pursewarden in *The*

*The Australian-born guitarist Craig Ogden has recorded the *Guitar Concerto* with the Northern Sinfonia conducted by Richard Hickox, on Chandos CHAN 9963, and a number of pieces by LB and MB, on Chandos CHAN 10261.

†Richard Hickox and the BBC National Orchestra of Wales recorded many of these works for the Chandos label – the *Serenade* and the *Symphony No. 1* are on CHAN 9981, the *Symphony No. 3* is on CHAN 10022, the *Piano Concerto* (soloist Howard Shelley) and the *St Teresa Poems* (soloist Catherine Wyn-Rogers) are on CHAN 10265, the *Concerto for Two Pianos* (soloists Howard Shelley and Kathryn Stott) is on CHAN 10408, and *the Six Preludes* and other piano pieces by LB and MB are played by Margaret Fingerhut on CHAN 10247.

Alexandria Quartet, 'to go to his books if we want to touch the true source of his feelings'.[55] And in Lennox's *Ruth*, as transparent in significance as in musical texture, it is impossible not to recognize elements of the story of his marriage in the gentle and touching account of the beautiful young Ruth, a foreigner, alone and homesick 'amid the alien corn',[56] who proposes to the landowner Boaz, rich, mature and wifeless.

According to Crozier's version of the Bible story, when Ruth's husband dies in the land of Moab, her mother-in-law Naomi, a native Israelite with no surviving male relatives, decides to return to Bethlehem, and Ruth, though a Moabite and an enemy of the Israelites, generously offers to accompany her. Once there, Ruth tries to support Naomi by gleaning spilled corn from fields owned by Boaz, a rich and influential connection of Naomi's late husband. But the harvest workers turn on her, complaining to the Head Reaper that she is a stranger, not one of them – why should they feed an enemy? 'Drive her away!' they cry, 'Cast her out! Stone her!'(anticipating the hostile crowd in the Gospels, who call on Pontius Pilate to crucify Jesus). The Head Reaper tells Boaz that the workers are afraid of Ruth because she is different – a foreigner (just as Lennox's gay friends had been afraid of Freda because she was different – a woman, and half Jewish). But Boaz is impressed by Ruth's devotion to Naomi and her loyalty to God, and he tells his workers to drop some corn deliberately so that Ruth will have plenty to collect; he also gives her access to water, and orders the men not to molest her. As the harvest progresses, old Boaz grows increasingly fond of the young Moabite, and one day he presents her with a basket of corn. 'O noble-hearted maiden of a foreign race!' he says, 'fair art thou, and young, and full of grace: yet fairer still I find the steadfast courage of thy mind, thy generosity of soul, thy noble spirit.'

At the end of the harvest, after all the corn has been gathered and threshed, Boaz gives a party for his workers, and when everyone has gone home, tipsy and happy, Ruth approaches the place where Boaz is sleeping. She kneels beside him and whispers 'Master!' Marvelling at this vision of youth and innocence that has come to him in the stillness of the night, as once the angels came to Jacob, Boaz asks what she wants. Ruth says she wants him to 'spread his cloak' over her, in the name of her dead husband, his kinsman. But why? Boaz asks, and Ruth answers, 'That I may be thy wife, and bring up sons unto Naomi lest her name perish from the land and be forgotten.' Boaz is so touched by Ruth's devotion to Naomi (greater than that of seven sons, he says in Crozier's libretto) and so amazed and grateful that she should choose him rather than a younger man, that he readily does as she asks, and spreads his cloak over her. In the morning he presents Ruth to his people as his wife, and she is honoured throughout Israel. (But there the parallels end, since Ruth and Boaz go on to fulfil the theological purpose of the Bible story by producing a son who begets Obed who begets Jesse who begets David, the ancestor of Jesus himself.)

Ironically it was Lennox's successor in the affections of Ben, the tenor Peter Pears, who sang the role of Boaz/Lennox, with Anna Pollak as Ruth/Freda,* in the first performance of *Ruth* conducted by Charles Mackerras (then principal conductor, BBC Concert Orchestra) at the Scala Theatre in London on 2 October 1956; Peter Potter was the director and the Welsh painter Ceri Richards created some memorably evocative designs. Ben liked the new work, and when he wanted to revive it at the Aldeburgh Festival in 1957 he asked Lennox to add an overture and lengthen the introductions to the later scenes,[57] but Lennox was his own man by now,† and decided to leave the score unchanged.[58]‡ Regardless of what Ben or Crozier or the critics may have felt about *Ruth*, he himself believed that it was 'in many ways the best thing I have done'. The Britten scholar Donald Mitchell agreed: it was 'a distinguished work' and both composer and librettist were 'surprisingly successful' in making such 'improbable, though undeniably very beautiful, material' work on stage.[59] Lennox urged Chester's to publish it for concert performance,[60] and added on the vocal score, above the title, the dedication, 'To Freda'.

With this simple inscription Lennox acknowledged his debt to the outsider whose courage, constancy and love had brought him, at last, a sense of equilibrium. It may have seemed an unlikely match – and

*Anna Pollak (1912–96) had created the role of Lady Nelson in LB's *Nelson* at Sadler's Wells in 1954.

†He was also a CBE (*The Times*, 1 January 1957), the first of many honours that were to come, culminating in a papal knighthood in 1973 and a KBE the following year.

‡At the Cheltenham Festival in LB's centenary year, 2003, Richard Hickox conducted a performance of *Ruth* (with Jean Rigby in the title role, Yvonne Kenny as Naomi, and Mark Tucker as Boaz, the Joyful Company of Singers and the City of London Sinfonia), which was later released by Chandos on CHAN 10301.

indeed it did involve physical compromises – but together they had found their place in life. With their three sons, they remained at 8 Warwick Avenue for nearly half a century, their personalities matched, balanced and fused, their weaknesses accepted, strengths shared. Domestically, emotionally and spiritually, the marriage was as close to the ideal of a perfect union as any two people are able to achieve. Lennox and Freda loved one another with a trust, respect and understanding that deepened as the years passed, and a need that never diminished.* Like Robert Herrick, they could not explain how their love came in: it just took root in their hearts and minds, and, unlike Herrick's, it never left.

*For their silver wedding at 8 Warwick Avenue in 1971 their friend the screenwriter Paul Dehn, who wrote the libretti for two of Berkeley's one-act operas, *A Dinner Engagement* and *Castaway*, composed an *Acrostic Sonnet* in celebration of 'Lennox-and-Freda – ever-hyphenated'.

Epilogue

Not long after his eightieth birthday in 1983 Lennox began to lose his powers of concentration. He was working on a full-length opera, *Faldon Park*, for English National Opera, and he kept going back to what he had written, deleting and recasting, rather than pushing on to the end. He did the same in his diary: crossing out and rewriting, often without making any significant changes. It seemed that, like Ravel at the end of his life, Lennox could not express on paper, either through music or words, what was clear in his mind.

In truth he had never been wholly committed to the opera. The libretto was written by a friend, the Handel scholar Winton Dean, who had invited him to turn it into an opera as early as 1971. But Lennox was not persuaded by the plot, and kept stalling. In 1976 when Lord Harewood asked him if he would like to write a new opera for the London Coliseum, Lennox felt obliged to suggest *Faldon Park*. But it was a struggle to conjure and juggle a grand opera so late in his working life – particularly when his heart was not in it. And increasingly his mind was not either. Walking with Jim Lees-Milne in Badminton Park in the summer of 1982, he admitted that he had days when he could not write and feared he might never compose again – 'and it's awful, awful'. Afterwards Jim recorded in his diary that Lennox 'lives in a cloud'.[1]

By 1983 he still had not reached the end of the first act of *Faldon Park*, and before the year was out he made the decision to abandon the project. He also resolved to refuse other new commissions, and gave up all his work on committees and charities. We hoped that this would free him to focus his failing powers on the smaller tasks that he still wanted to complete. But it did not. Instead he became increasingly confused and fretful, worrying not only about composition but about imaginary appointments.

One summer evening in 1985 I knocked at Lennox's study door to call him for dinner, and found him at the piano, leaning forward with a pencil in his hand scribbling on a sheet of manuscript paper. He was agitated, which was unlike him, and crying. 'I don't know what's happening,' he said, 'I can't understand it.' Neither could we. But worse was to come, and, within a year, Lennox was diagnosed with Alzheimer's.

Despite our best efforts to protect him – and there were several of us in the Warwick Avenue house in those years – Lennox disappeared from time to time, often taking his diaries, which did not always come back, and usually intent on fulfilling some non-existent engagement. Once I found him at the BBC's Maida Vale studios, gate-crashing an orchestral rehearsal; when I tried to take him home he hid behind the double basses. On another occasion he was rescued from the Westway flyover during the evening rush hour. Later still he disappeared for two days and was found by the police lying on a pavement near Oxford Circus. At first he was mistaken for a down-and-out, till someone suggested he might be the composer whose disappearance had been reported on the news that morning. From then on Freda employed professional carers to look after him day and night.

Throughout this time, though all his other senses were fading, Lennox still clearly responded to the Mass (which he attended every Sunday at the Catholic Church in Lisson Grove) and to music. He became obsessed with a piece of Poulenc's, the *Nocturne No. 4 in C Minor*, sub-titled 'Le bal fantôme',* which he played over and over again till his fingers could no longer follow his mind's instructions. The piece illustrates a passage in the novel *Le Visionnaire* by Julian Green, in which a bed-ridden invalid listens to the sound of dance-music floating up from a party below and dreams of the happy days of his youth.* Perhaps Lennox knew what was happening to him.

To keep him in touch with music, kind friends used to call at 8 Warwick Avenue to talk or play or sing. Roger Nichols, the author of a biography of Ravel, recalls that on one such occasion he was talking about Ravel 'and Lennox was barely responding, when he suddenly got up, sat on the piano stool and played sixteen bars of *La Valse* note-perfect'.[2]

Peter Dickinson often came to play for his old teacher and friend.

*Lennox had been introduced to the work by his friend Burnet Pavitt (1908–2002), who was similarly enthralled by the piece during his own last few months of piano-playing. Managing director of the British subsidiary of the Swiss pharmaceuticals company Hoffmann–La Roche, Pavitt was a fine amateur pianist who was chairman of the English Opera Group and a board member of the Royal Opera House, Covent Garden. It was he who commissioned the piano duet version of LB's *Palm Court Waltz*, which shares a similar bitter-sweetness with Poulenc's *Nocturne No. 4*.

Lennox listened attentively and always recognized his own music – even the *Three Piano Pieces* of 1927, which he cannot have heard for over fifty years.[3]

In the summer of 1988 another P. Dickinson reappeared in Lennox's life. It was twenty-four years since Patric Dickinson, then a thirteen-year-old schoolboy, had fallen under the spell of Berkeley Castle and begun a comprehensive study of its history. For seventeen months he haunted the libraries and public records offices of Gloucester, Cheltenham, Bristol and Stroud, before committing his research to an elegant treatise on the Berkeleys' ancient origins. (They owed their name, he discovered, to the nature of the land they occupied near the River Severn after the departure of the Romans in the fifth century: 'berke' coming from 'beorce', the Saxon for birch trees, and 'ley' coming from 'lau' or pasture.) But Dickinson was also musical, and at least one puzzle remained: where did the composer Sir Lennox Berkeley fit into the family history? Unable to find any reference to Lennox or his parents in any of the standard genealogical reference works, yet suspecting, from the repeated pattern of their given names, that they were closely connected to the last earl, young Dickinson wrote to Lennox in 1964 asking for information. In a warm, frank reply Lennox explained that 'my grandfather was in fact seventh Earl of Berkeley, but was not legitimately married to my Grandmother at the time of my Father's birth, he therefore (my Father) was unable to inherit the title which passed to the younger of his two brothers ...'[4] The dogged Dickinson bounced back with a further inquiry about Lennox's relationship to Sir Ernest Berkeley, at which Lennox, having confirmed that Ernest was his uncle, the younger of the two illegitimate brothers, brought the correspondence to a gentle close with, 'I think you've now got the whole rather unfortunate picture!'[5] By 1988 this same Patric Dickinson had metamorphosed into Rouge Dragon Pursuivant of Arms and wrote again requesting current genealogical data for a record of the collateral family of the last earl in a new entry under the Berkeley barony in the next edition of *Debrett's Peerage*.[6] When the proofs of the 1990 *Debrett's** arrived we showed them to Lennox, trying to explain what they meant. He may or may not have understood, but his eyes brightened, and he smiled.

*Charles Kidd and (the late) David Williamson (eds.), *Debrett's Peerage and Baronetage*, Macmillan, 1990. For an account of the Berkeley Peerage Case, see Appendix 3, pp. 452–5.

In the summer of 1989 Freda realized she could no longer keep Lennox at home, and in July he was admitted to St Charles's Hospital, Ladbroke Grove. It was only reluctantly that we abandoned him to what seemed the bedlam of a mixed ward in the geriatric wing. But it turned out to be the best place for him: the nurses were wonderful, and Lennox seemed to enjoy the constant distractions.

He was always pleased to see visitors, and, though he could no longer talk coherently, he could still relate to music. Julian made a tape of some of his favourite pieces, including the Poulenc *Nocturne*, Britten's *Sea Interludes*, Lennox's own setting of *The Lord Is My Shepherd* and the piece he valued above all others, Mozart's *G Minor String Quintet*. He would respond by beating time, humming, or just closing his eyes and smiling; occasionally he wept.

Once we arrived late at night when the other patients were asleep. The lights were dimmed but the ward sounded more like a battlefield than a hospital, with snores like machine-gun fire, mutters and groans (and Lennox's legless friend in the next bed repeating the alphabet, 'to stop me going mad'). In the centre of the large ward, illuminated by a lamp, four nurses were gathered around a table as their shift changed. Propped up on his pillows, Lennox watched the four young heads intently. Seeing us approach, he put a finger to his lips. 'Shhh! Quartet.'

At eight on Boxing Day morning 1989, he died, with the family gathered around his bed. He was eighty-six.

As a good Catholic he had been prepared for death; as a man he had been thinking about it ever since he felt himself slipping into old age. Jotting some notes in an exercise book in about 1974, for an essay he had been asked to write about old age, he said he could not claim to have no fear of death – 'that would hardly be human' – but he was convinced that there would be little happiness in continuing life indefinitely. Besides, he wrote, 'even the un-Christian can believe, as did Socrates, that the better part of man can live on after death.'[7]

After a Latin Requiem Mass, with Gregorian chant, at his parish church, Our Lady, Lisson Grove, on 4 January,* Lennox's remains were

*The Mass was celebrated by Fr Michael Hollings, parish priest of St Mary of the Angels, Bayswater, assisted by the parish priest of Our Lady, Fr Charles McGowan, and the High Anglican vicar of St Mary's Paddington Green, the Revd Prebendary John Foster. The *schola* was formed of men from the choir of Westminster Cathedral.

cremated at Golders Green, in a brief ceremony during which the cellist Lowri Blake played a movement from one of the unaccompanied suites by Bach. On 20 March there was a memorial Requiem Mass at Westminster Cathedral,* celebrated by the Archbishop, Cardinal Basil Hume, and broadcast live on BBC Radio 3, with a commentary by a former Radio 3 chief announcer, Fr Cormac Rigby.

Quite soon after Lennox's death Freda left the house in Warwick Avenue, and moved into a large flat in a mansion block in Notting Hill Gate, with most of the furniture, pictures, books and music she and Lennox had accumulated during forty-two years of marriage. Uncertain what to do with his ashes, she left them in Little Venice, in a jar under the altar of the eighteenth-century church of St Mary's, Paddington Green, in the safekeeping of her old friend Fr John Foster.† It was a typically capricious arrangement, which came to an unexpected end. Following the Church of England's decision, in 1992, to ordain women priests, Fr Foster himself converted to Catholicism, later becoming a priest. Concerned about the propriety of handing over St Mary's with a Catholic under the altar, Fr Foster returned the ashes to Freda, who then placed them in an oriental urn on Sybil Jackson's Bechstein piano in the dining room.

In 1994 Jim Lees-Milne proposed a nostalgic trip to Menton (which he still called by its old Italian name, Mentone), and Freda seized on the chance to scatter some of Lennox's ashes on his parents' graves in Nice. Jim has left a touching, and at times hilarious, account of this unconventional pilgrimage which he and Freda made in March 1995 with two other old friends, 'Coote' Heber-Percy and 'Billa' Harrod.[8] Unable to find the right graveyard, and with time running out, they sprinkled Lennox's ashes in the wrong place, and the wind blew them over Jim's shoes. Freda decided to bring the rest home, to the urn on the piano, where they remain to this day.

Two months after the Menton trip I took Freda on another journey into the past. It was her seventy-second birthday, and I thought she would like to visit some of the places associated with her father and his family

*The music included not only LB's *Mass for Five Voices* and 'Oh that I once past changing were' from his *A Festival Anthem*, but also MB's motet *Qui me dignatus est*, of which LB was especially fond.
†See the asterisked note p. 439.

in South Wales – places she had never been to, or even known about, because she had never met any Bernsteins except her father, and even he was no more than a shadowy memory.

In Newport I showed her the site of Isaac Bernstein's boot business in St John's Road and his three properties in Chepstow Road; in Rhymney, his terrace of twelve houses. In Merthyr Tydfil, in a commanding position at the top end of Church Street, overlooking shuttered shops – this was six years before EU money revitalized the economic black spots of South Wales – we saw the Ruritanian synagogue which Isaac endowed on his death.

Two miles outside the town, on the mountain road to Brecon, I stopped the car at Cefn Coed y Cymmer to explore Merthyr's Jewish graveyard on the hill above the Christian graveyard that falls down to the river on the other side of the road. Beneath lichened granite slabs carved with Jewish texts are the mortal remains of several hundred long-dead Jews of Merthyr and Tredegar – including Freda's Litvak grandparents, Hyman Joseph and Fradel Bernstein. These are the relics of the Jewish emigrants who fled persecution in eastern Europe to make new and better lives for their descendants in the Welsh valleys. Freda was visibly moved as she wandered through the grazing sheep, looking at alien headstones in the spring sunshine, thinking of a family she never knew and an exotic community she could only imagine.

Afterwards we had tea in Merthyr with the keeper of the graveyard, George Black, the son of a Polish tailor. Himself a retired barber, he claimed to be the last Jew in Merthyr.*

In 1996 I took Freda on another surprise outing. Once again it was her birthday, and again our destination was her past: this time her mother's family in west London. Driving north over the Paddington railway line to Queen's Park, I looked for the house where her Nunney grandparents used to live. The street was easy to find – down the Harrow Road and into First Avenue which becomes Lancefield Street. But 126 was not there – nor was the rest of the top end of the street. In Freda's day Lancefield Street used to run all the way up to Kilburn Lane, now it ends at a new housing estate just after Mozart Street. Even St Jude's

*A few weeks later he and his wife Lilian retired to Manchester to live with their daughter. In 1998 Mr Black died, and his family brought him home to Merthyr, to rest in peace with his parents on the Hebrew hillside at Cefn Coed y Cymmer.

Church has gone. But we did see the pub where she used to refill the beer jug with mild-and-bitter for her grandparents.

We then drove on up Willesden Lane to locate her grandmother's grave in Old Paddington Cemetery. (Grandfather Nunney, for some reason, was buried separately in Golders Green.) We soon found the plot, but there was no longer any headstone or anything indicating the presence of a grave.

Heading next for Child's Hill, we turned across Kilburn High Road into Finchley Road to look for the house where Freda was born. She recognized No. 613 straightaway, even though two pine trees that used to stand in the front garden had gone, revealing just a tall, white, stuccoed, semi-detached house. She had not seen it for sixty-eight years. We did not linger because a girl was watching us from behind the curtains.

Our final stop was just around the corner in Hampstead Cemetery. It is a lovely open space – twenty-six acres of trees and grass and wildlife, more parkland than graveyard – with an exhilarating sense of being high above the busy city spread below like a rippling carpet. It seemed a perfect resting place: light, high, green and quiet, yet still part of a living world.

The Bernstein grave was easy to pinpoint on the undertaker's map, but hard to find in reality, because the headstone, a plain granite cross, was obscured by brambles and a holly bush. Freda had never seen the grave before, did not even know it was there. Hanging her coat, scarf and bag on a headstone nearby, she set to work with a fork borrowed from a plant stall at the gate, and, letter by letter, the words on the stone tablet revealed themselves. She gazed in silence at the place where the remains of a mother and father she could not remember lay buried.

Back at the mansion flat in Notting Hill Gate, sitting in her Chippendale armchair, she told me it had been 'strange and wonderful' to discover her parents' grave. 'When my turn comes,' she said, 'I'd like to join them there.' She paused, and looked across at one of Ceri Richards's costume designs for *Ruth*. 'I think it would be right in Hampstead. That's what I'd like. With Lennox's ashes. Never having known my parents properly in life, it'd be rather nice to be with them in death. I think Lennox would like that too.'

It was sad that Freda had never met any of her Bernstein relatives. I had tried to trace them but without success, though her father Isaac's brother Lewis had at least eleven children. One day in February 2006, on impulse, I placed an advertisement online in the Manchester *Jewish Telegraph*, seeking surviving Bernsteins of Merthyr and Tredegar. Late at night on 11 April, the phone rang. A warm, strong voice identified itself as that of Harry Ellis, a retired solicitor, aged ninety, living in Bournemouth. He said he had seen the ad, and thought I might be interested to know that his mother's cousin had married a Moses Bernstein, who was a draper in Tredegar. Was there, perhaps, a connection, he wondered? There certainly was: Moses Bernstein was one of the eleven children of Lewis, brother of Isaac and a first cousin of Freda. I asked Mr Ellis if he could put me in touch with the family. 'You're in luck,' he said, 'Moses Bernstein's son Lewis is a lawyer who lives in North America, but he also has a house in Regent's Park – and he just happens to be in London tonight.' I rang immediately, and a fortnight later Lewis Bernstein and his musical wife Ernestine came round to the flat in Notting Hill Gate for lunch with Freda. It was an emotional occasion for the first cousins once removed. As children, both, for different reasons, had been encouraged to keep their Bernstein relations at bay – Freda's Nunney grandparents feared they wanted her money, Lewis's Samson mother thought they were not good enough. Not only had they never met before, but neither had even known of the other's existence. With the wheels oiled by the writer Michael Bloch – like Lewis a barrister, like Freda the special friend of Jim Lees-Milne, like both the descendant of central European Jews – the meeting marked the start of an important friendship. Freda woke the next morning sensing that something significant had happened. 'I feel I've known Lewis all my life', she said, 'and I wish I had.'

At the time this book goes to press Freda is still living in her sunny flat in Notting Hill Gate – though the Chippendale chair has been replaced by a rise-and-recline electric chair and a team of full-time carers; and Lennox's ashes are still in the urn on the piano. She often dreams of him, but cannot remember what happens in the dreams – 'he's just with me, usually in Norfolk.' (In 1957 Lennox and Freda had bought a holiday cottage at Morston on the wild coast of North Norfolk. The house was called Coldblow, which was no more than true, and the boys loved it – playing on the marshes and dunes, and sailing up and down the tidal creek, while Lennox composed and Freda cooked mackerel from Mr Breeze, the mobile fishmonger, and samphire gathered fresh from the mudflats. Many happy holidays were spent at Coldblow, and many long lasting friendships struck. But as the boys grew up the place became impracticable, and in the late Sixties the Berkeleys sold up. Freda instantly regretted it, for Norfolk had cast on her and her sons the same spell that had enchanted Lennox as a schoolboy during the First World War.) In view of the memories, her recurring dreams of Lennox and Norfolk might upset her – but no, she says, 'Not at all.' Nor is she surprised. 'I just take it for granted; we're always very happy together.'

Meanwhile she leads a busy life, with visits and telephone calls from friends and family, a balcony full of plants and birds (for a time a duck took up residence on a pot of geraniums, and hatched eight chicks), and occasional outings in her wheelchair, sometimes to events organized by the Lennox Berkeley Society.

On 12 June 2008 we took her back to 8 Warwick Avenue for the first time since she left eighteen years ago, to witness the unveiling of a Westminster City Council Green Plaque commemorating Lennox's occupation of the house from 1947 to 1989. Dame Janet Baker, a patron of the Berkeley Society (and an old friend of the Berkeleys), and the Lord Mayor of Westminster, Councillor Louise Hyams, pulled a curtain to reveal the plaque. Many friends of Lennox and Freda were there to watch, with members of the Berkeley Society, led by the chairman, the radio presenter Petroc Trelawny, who organized it all. The occasion was made possible by the hospitality of the present owners of the house, the actress Louise Bangay and her husband James Rowsell, who said they had felt a special connection with No. 8 from the moment they first walked in. 'To have found this wonderful history is a delight,' Louise wrote, 'and somehow not surprising. There is a great atmosphere in this beautiful building.'[9]

Freda is sure that something of Lennox's gentle spirit still lingers in the house where he lived and worked and thought for almost half his life. No less than Herrick, she believes in the soul and its survival – and, if the soul is the vital inner force, intangible but not imaginary, she seems to have a way of reaching it. So she was particularly receptive to the contents of a letter she received a day or two after Lennox's death, from one of the psychotherapists who had cared for him at St Charles's Hospital, Michaela von Britzke. It was prompted, the writer said, by an obituary which had described Lennox as 'a saintly figure passing on the love of music as a spiritual imperative in a foreign, material age'.[10] Ms von Britzke told Freda she had been deeply moved by this observation, which corresponded with her own experience of Lennox. Alzheimer's disease may have dulled his mind and body, but his spirit had transcended the confusion and the indignity. Nothing had been able to destroy what she termed his 'angelic energy'. This had touched all those around him – and indicated that there was more to human nature than just the intellect. 'Meeting Lennox was a lesson in knowing that the spirit is eternal.'[11]

APPENDIX 1
Lennox Berkeley and the Tridentine Rite

The Tridentine (or Roman) Rite, promulgated by Pope Pius V in 1570, was the standard and mandatory liturgy of the Catholic Church till the Second Vatican Council introduced a new vernacular liturgy in 1964. The Latin of its language was not only beautiful in itself but a particularly mellifluous vehicle for singing; it also had the advantages of being as other-worldly as its subject and universally familiar to Catholics everywhere.

The Latin Mass, and the strict and unchanging formularies of its celebration, were a strong attraction of the pre-Conciliar Church – and one of the reasons that Lennox himself converted in 1929. Writing about it at the time of the changes, Lennox said the old Rite had become an integral part of his life, and, as a composer, he wanted to bring to it all that he had to offer. It is a significant reflection of the depth of his religious feelings that in composing for his Church he should have sought to make his music more impersonal, 'so that it would merge into the liturgy, and not ... cause too much distraction'.[1]

By the time Lennox came to write his *Missa Brevis* for four voices and organ (1959), his two elder sons had become choristers at Westminster Cathedral, and Lennox's new *Mass*, dedicated to 'To Michael and Julian and the boys of Westminster Cathedral Choir', received its first performance in 1960. Julian recalled, in an article in *The Tablet*, 'the tension of trying to learn and pitch some tricky intervals while at the same time being rather nervously conscious of the reactions of my fellow chorister to this "modern music"'.[2] In the same article he wrote about his father's Faith and its effect on his music:

> The intention of Cardinal Vaughan in founding the Cathedral was that the full Divine Office should be sung daily in public in the centre of the capital city. To carry out this plan he had hoped to recreate what had existed down the road at the Abbey – a Benedictine foundation. His dream was not to be fulfilled in its entirety,

but the choir did sing High Mass and Vespers each day, with the addition of Compline on Sundays (and of course Tenebrae in Holy Week).

By the Fifties and Sixties with Monsignor Gordon Wheeler as Administrator and George Malcolm directing the choir, the liturgy and music achieved an amazing standard of perfection; ceremonies were carefully choreographed with solemnity and precision in the most dramatic of ecclesiastical settings. Visitors to the Cathedral spoke of being drawn into an almost overwhelmingly powerful spiritual atmosphere.

In 1964 Cardinal Heenan commissioned Lennox to write a new unaccompanied *Five-part Mass* which received its first performance by the choir under the direction of the new Master of Music, Colin Mawby, a former Malcolm protégé.

Like so many who were brought up in, or converted to, the preconciliar Church, Lennox was bewildered and dismayed that a consequence of the Council should be the brutal destruction of a liturgy which was at the core of his being. Although he wrote plenty of church music to fine English texts for Anglican choirs, when he was asked to compose a vernacular setting for the new Mass, the sheer banality and impermanence of the texts proposed at that time did not appeal and so he declined. He was horrified by the Cromwellian iconoclasm which he witnessed. 'Reformers easily become destroyers, as we, in this country should hardly need to be told,' he wrote. 'It would be a pity if, this time, destruction were wrought, not by the Church's enemies, but by those in authority within it.'[3]

Sadly, Lennox did not live to see the extraordinary seeds of Catholic revival emerging from the husks of the modernist Church. Whereas he would have been saddened that diocesan seminaries are struggling for their existence through lack of vocations, he would have been delighted that traditionalist seminaries are now over-subscribed. He would have lamented those monastic establishments which, having abandoned or betrayed the ideals of their foundation, are slowly withering away – but he would have rejoiced that new monasteries, seeking to be faithful to the Church's liturgical tradition, are growing and attracting young people in pursuit of the contemplative life.

Julian Berkeley concluded his article by making the point that in religion, as in music, extreme reactions tend to provoke counter-reactions. When a composer had achieved total abstraction in music the only way forward was to re-explore traditional techniques. Such cyclic patterns were the very image of life.[4]

APPENDIX 2
The Greenidge Brothers

John Greenidge was a friend of Lennox from their time at school at Lynam's in Oxford, and they remained close till Greenidge's death in 1953. His ancestors were Somerset Puritans who fled to the West Indies to escape from Judge Jeffreys's Bloody Assizes after the Battle of Sedgemoor.[1] John's father Abel Greenidge was a brilliant don at Oxford – a lecturer in ancient history at two colleges, Hertford and Brasenose. As the author of meticulously-researched works on Roman history and Roman law, he was widely thought to be 'one of the best and most conscientious' scholars in England at the time.[2] John's mother was Edith Lucy, youngest daughter of an Oxford iron founder related to the Warwickshire squires of Charlecote near Stratford-upon-Avon. When John was seven his father suddenly died of a heart attack brought on by years of worry about his financial hardships. (These problems were caused by his having to surrender his bachelor Fellowship at Hertford, when he married.*) Sixteen months later John's broken-hearted mother died too,[3] leaving him and his younger brother Terence as orphans in the care of a guardian, their father's friend the Revd H. H. Williams, then tutor and lecturer in philosophy at Hertford College.

In his diaries, Evelyn Waugh, who relished discomforting his friends (and family) quite as much as he enjoyed persecuting his unfortunate enemies, refers to John Greenidge as 'the Bastard'. The diaries' editor Michael Davie marks the reference with a footnote, identifying 'the Bastard' as 'Terence Greenidge's illegitimate brother John'.[4] Since John's birth certificate of 27 May 1899 shows Abel and Edith as his parents (and Terence, therefore, his full blood brother), and a marriage

*[R. W. Lee and the Revd Mark Pottle, 'Greenidge, Abel Hendy Jones (1865–1906)', *Oxford Dictionary of National Biography*, Oxford University Press, 2004.] The same article states that in 1907 a civil list pension of £75 p.a. was granted to Mrs Abel Greenidge, in consideration of her late husband's services to the study of Roman law and history – yet it also reveals that, following his death, Greenidge's wealth was valued for probate at £3,762. 4s. 1d, or a quarter of a million pounds at 2008 values.

certificate of 29 June 1895 confirms the legitimacy of his parents' marriage, the nickname was probably a typical Waugh joke. According to Waugh's grandson Alexander, Evelyn and his Oxford boyfriend Alastair Graham invented a private vocabulary which called all brothers 'bastards'. (By the same code mending was 'masturbating', and talking to someone 'lying with them'.[5])

It is possible that Dr Greenidge had to pretend not to be married (and to disown the baby John) in order to retain his Oxford lectureships, though he had already had to resign his Hertford Fellowship which was more strictly conditional on the status of bachelorhood. The 1901 Census returns for Oxford show some odd Greenidge data: Dr Greenidge and his cook and sixteen-year-old housemaid are the only occupants of his house at 4 Blackhall Road, St Giles, on the day the Census was taken, 31 March 1901, while Edith's parents' home at 107 Woodstock Road contains only her widowed mother and two servants. There is no mention at either address of John, who was nearly three by then, or of his mother, and neither name is recorded at any other address in Britain on that day in 1901.

Both the Greenidge boys were sent to Rugby, where John showed an early interest in architecture (and meteorology) and Terence revealed an original turn of mind when, in a debate about Britain's wartime relationship with Russia, he illustrated a point 'by references to a colonel and strawberry ices'.[6]

From Rugby John went up to St Edmund Hall, where his guardian, the Revd H. H. Williams (later Bishop of Carlisle), was then the Principal, and Terence followed him to Oxford in 1920 with a scholarship to his father's old college, Hertford, as 'Founder's Kin' (i.e. a descendant of the Revd William Lucy, who had endowed Hertford).[7] It is curious that John, the elder brother, did not also take advantage of this scholarship, but perhaps Dr Williams wanted to keep an eye on him at his own college.

Photographs of John as an undergraduate show him as unsmiling, with a troubled expression bordering on defiance, and a penchant for bow ties and Fair Isle socks. He seems to have been fond of gadgets and tricks: Waugh recalled that John once taught him how to short-circuit a telephone and make it sing.[8] Other friends remembered him as clever and musical, quiet and secretive, 'buttoned-up', careful with his money.[9] The sadness of John Greenidge's childhood – orphaned at eight – would have struck a chord with Lennox, whose own family background was so blighted by lies and misbehaviour. Lennox's writings say next to nothing of John, but in his diary he does credit his friend with opening his eyes to a wider artistic world: 'I had very little visual sense in my young days, perhaps owing to my obsession with music. It was only later that I learned to see as far as pictures and architecture were concerned and in this I learnt much from John Greenidge.'[10]

A successful architect, John Greenidge later designed buildings for both his old schools (Lynam's and Rugby), various country houses, including the Widow Lloyd's Bryn Cadwrfa in Montgomery in 1932, and the Benedictine monastery at Prinknash, where Lennox so often went on retreats in later life, and to whose building fund John left £200 in his will (though he might not have liked the modernist box that eventually went up in 1972). He died, unmarried, in London in 1953, leaving the rest of his small estate to his brother Terence, and his niece Althea.[11]

The quietly and benignly eccentric John Greenidge could not have been less like the darkly eccentric Terence whose extreme oddness was calculated to offend and subvert. Grubby, drunken and exhibitionistic, Terence used to declaim Greek choruses loudly in the middle of the night, stuff his pockets with rubbish (which he later dumped on Evelyn Waugh's floor), steal hairbrushes and keys and inkpots (which he later hid behind the books in the library), and lick the backs of his hands. He was a man of short-lived passions – at one moment he was identifying with Lionel Barrymore and dressing up like one of his film characters in a short black jacket with astrakhan collar and cuffs, at the next he was obsessed with Dostoievsky or cross-country running or cinematography. He made up vivid nicknames (Philbrick the Flagellant, Midnight Badger, Hotlunch) and invented cruel practical jokes. It was Terence who encouraged Waugh in the merciless baiting of C. R. M. F. Cruttwell, Waugh's tutor at Hertford. Fantasizing that Cruttwell enjoyed improper relations with dogs, Terence bought a stuffed one and placed it in the quad beneath the tutor's window, then, hiding, he and Waugh barked all night.[12] In the opinion of Harold Acton, Terence Greenidge was 'very mad. A dear charming loony.'[13] Forty years later, he turned up at a party for the Oxford University Railway Club – trains (and actresses) then being his current passions – and, though he had had 'large parts of his brain removed by a surgeon', he was still 'very talkative'.[14] For a while he worked as an actor with the Royal Shakespeare Company, but resigned in about 1968 and died in a mental asylum the following year.[15]

APPENDIX 3
The Berkeley Peerage Case

Lennox's great-great-great uncle, Frederick Berkeley, 5th Earl of Berkeley, married his wife, Mary Cole, too late to legitimize the first seven of his thirteen children.* In an attempt to put this right, the earl fiddled the books, making a fraudulent entry in the Berkeley parish records, to try to prove that he had married his wife before the birth of the first child. After his death the validity of this alleged marriage was tested by the Committee for Privileges of the House of Lords – and found wanting: in the opinion of their Lordships, the parish register entry was a blatant forgery.

As a consequence, the castle and estates passed to the 5th earl's eldest son, while the title went to the sixth (and eldest legitimate) son Moreton. The eldest son, Colonel William Berkeley, was a rotter as vicious and stupid as his father and as cunning as his mother[1] (a London newspaper memorialized him as 'a tenth-rate Rochester'[2]). In due course Colonel Berkeley tried to claim his father's title, on the ancient grounds that as he lived in a castle he deserved to be a peer. The House of Lords rejected this argument, but, because he was politically powerful, their lordships gave him the consolation prize of a newly-created title all his own, Earl FitzHardinge. When he died his second brother Admiral Sir Maurice Berkeley inherited the castle and he too pressed for a peerage on the same grounds – and was similarly refused, but, being no less politically useful, he was fobbed off with another freshly-minted title, Baron FitzHardinge.

There was much amusement to be had at the expense of the Berkeley family's endless claims for peerages in the nineteenth century. In 1861 the satirical magazine *Punch* published a parody of the Berkeley Peerage Case, in which it quoted the Lord Chancellor, Lord St Leonards, as saying that Admiral Sir Maurice Berkeley's claim had been turned down because '... he had failed to show the discontinuance of the

*The story is told in full in Hope Costley-White, *Mary Cole, Countess of Berkeley: A Biography*.

outstanding term contingent upon the enfeoffment of the non-entailed *cessio bonorum pour autre vie* after the *conveyance de droit* under the charter-party of Edward the Third had merged the laches in a general tenancy by the courtesy with cross remainders over.' And it quoted Admiral Berkeley as having replied 'that it made a fellow's lee-scuppers run over, to hear a cove coil and belay such High Dutch lingo'.[3]

In 1811 the House of Lords ruled that the five eldest sons of the 5th earl (including Francis who had died in the year of his birth) were all illegitimate, and that the title therefore devolved upon the sixth son Moreton. Overwhelmed with shame and guilt, and cowed by the bullying of his elder brothers, Moreton never used his legal title of Earl of Berkeley, and, remaining unmarried, he left no heirs when he died in 1882. There had been two younger brothers, both legitimate, and therefore both potential heirs, but the elder one, George, had died the previous year, leaving no surviving sons, and the younger, Craven, had died without sons in 1855. According to the family's twentieth-century biographer Bernard Falk, a 'sinister fatalism' and 'malignant hereditary forces' seem to have pursued the Berkeleys through the nineteenth century. 'One by one, as though in obedience to the decree of inescapable destiny, the threads by which hung the permanence of the Berkeley direct male line snapped.'[4] And so, with the extinction of all the legitimate male descendants of the 5th earl, the succession turned to his only brother Admiral Sir George Cranfield Berkeley and his sons and heirs. And thus, in August 1882, Moreton Berkeley's title passed to his first cousin once removed, the admiral's grandson George Berkeley; and Lennox's grandfather suddenly found himself 7th Earl of Berkeley.

If the new Lord Berkeley's two elder sons – Lennox's father Hastings and his Uncle Ernest – had not till then known anything about their illegitimate origins, their younger brother's jubilant rattling of his new coronet would have given them a pretty rude shock. For Randal, who was then a seventeen-year-old midshipman in the Channel Squadron, lost no time in instructing the editors of the *Navy List* to note his social advancement from Mr Berkeley to Viscount Dursley (the courtesy title of the Earl of Berkeley's eldest son) – and this was how he appeared in the fourth edition of the 1882 *List*, as a midshipman aboard the corvette HMS *Curacao* in the South China Sea. *Burke's Peerage*, *Debrett's Peerage*, the *Royal Kalendar* and the *Royal Blue Book* soon followed suit, casting Hastings and Ernest into the social twilight. As far as the published registers of the Upper Ten Thousand were concerned, Randal was his parents' only son – Hastings and Ernest and their families simply did not exist.

Six years later George the 7th earl died, and the title – though not yet the castle and the huge estates – passed to his only legal son, Randal. But there was still a flicker of doubt hanging over the validity of Randal's succession, at least at Berkeley Castle. And, in a final attempt to legitimize – very retrospectively – the five elder sons of the 5th earl, Randal's second cousin Francis, Lord FitzHardinge* challenged Randal's claim to the title and petitioned the House of Lords to recognize him, Lord FitzHardinge, as 8th Earl of Berkeley. Over the course of three months in the spring and summer of 1891 the Committee for Privileges considered the Berkeley Peerage Case (for the umpteenth time), and on 1 August it found against Lord FitzHardinge, and in favour of Randal.

Lord FitzHardinge had taken the same stubborn line as his father and his uncle earlier in the century that the first marriage of the 5th earl had certainly taken place – the parish register proved it – and that all thirteen children were therefore legitimate. Tired of these Berkeley claims, the House did not even bother to re-examine the facts: as far as their lordships were concerned the register had already been proved a forgery, and, in the absence of any other evidence, they could only conclude that this first marriage had been nothing but wishful thinking.

Randal's defence revolved around two propositions: that the legitimate male issue of the 5th earl was extinct, and that he was the legitimate male heir of the 4th earl. To support the second proposition, Randal argued that his parents, George and Cécile, had legally married in Brussels in 1860 (nothing was said of their first marriage the previous year). This was accepted, and Randal was recognized as 'the first and only son of the marriage', and the only surviving male heir of the 4th earl. No mention was made of Hastings and Ernest, who had been born before him – but out of wedlock.

Reading the lengthy reports in *The Times* that year must have been painful for Cécile. She had been through it all before, and must have wondered why Randal was exposing the family to further pain. But at stake were the castle and the huge Berkeley estates, including, in London, Berkeley Square and a swathe of Mayfair. It was one of the most extensive landed properties in England. If Lord FitzHardinge had won, he could have reunited the castle with its title and passed both on

*Elder son of Admiral Sir Maurice Berkeley, 2nd Baron FitzHardinge.

to his brother. For Randal the victory meant not only that he could retain the title, but that he would eventually inherit, by right of the earldom (under a settlement made earlier in the century), the castle and its estates. This was some plum – and in 1891 only two old men, both childless, stood between him and it. Exactly a quarter of a century later the survivor of these two brothers, Charles, 3rd (and last) Baron FitzHardinge, died, without issue, and the Berkeley Castle estates passed at last to Randal, 7th Earl of Berkeley.

APPENDIX 4
The Writings of Hastings Berkeley

Hastings Berkeley's studies were unusually arcane. In 1889 and 1890 he was working on ideas for the reform of the currency, in particular what was then called 'bi-metallism'– the ratio between gold and silver – which he believed should be fixed naturally by the market. It might all seem 'very stiff and dry,' Hastings told his future wife Aline Harris, but 'next to love [it] has driven more men mad than anything else'[1], and he wrote long letters on the subject to *The Times*, initiating a heated debate in the year before the Berkeley peerage case. The Thunderer accused Hastings of devoting too much effort to demolishing his opponents and not enough to overcoming the 'prevailing malady of puzzle-headedness'.[2] (This rebuff did not stop Hastings from returning to the fray, on the subject of free trade, a couple of years later; nor did it stop *The Times* from turning its great guns on him again. This time it is difficult not to reach the conclusion that Hastings enjoyed the fight for the sheer fun of the thing.[3])

Commander Berkeley* was a most persistent correspondent, but he wrote so well and on such serious – if dry – topics that *The Times* seems to have been happy to give him space. In September 1887, in an entire column – from the top of the broadsheet page to the bottom – he had a go at the disparity between Britain's falling exports and her growing imports; in August 1890 it was trade concessions in Liberia; and in October 1889 he argued that the recent London dock strike had been caused by 'demagogues, socialistic agitators and irresponsible chatterers'.[4]

Throughout this period Hastings was also working on a book about modern European life as observed by a liberated young Japanese on the Grand Tour, in letters addressed to a conservative old philosopher at home in Tokyo. This curious – and, it must be said, laboured – formula gave him an opportunity to let off steam on some of his favourite subjects, including Protestantism, which protects its believers from

*He was not promoted to captain till his second retirement from the Navy, in 1918.

'blind obedience to authority' and the 'tyranny of the priestly caste',[5] and, rightly in his view, always puts 'business first, and other matters, religion included, afterwards'.[6] On the subject of Jews (who had 'put to an ignominious death the founder of the Christian religion, and were therefore long regarded as the natural enemies of all Christians') Hastings noted, with approval, that in England at least Jewish people had gradually emerged from a position of 'social and political degradation' to one of 'absolute equality with the Christians'. He attributed this improvement in their status to the growth of tolerance, and especially the spread of 'all those ideas which are associated with industry and commerce'.[7] For the same reason, tailors too had been emancipated from 'the bond of good-natured popular contempt'.[8]

In a chapter on the 'Differences between the French and the English', his Japanese traveller claimed the English were uniformly, genuinely and frankly dull, while the French had 'a consuming desire to please, to charm, to entertain' – why? because the Englishman made an idol of his self-esteem, and the Frenchman worshipped, in the enchanted mirror of flattery, what appeared there as his own image.[9]

There is also a chapter entitled 'Talent & Class & Primogeniture', about the last of which Hastings might have had some pretty acid things to say, but restricted himself to pointing out that the sole distinction remaining in England, now that talent was regarded with such suspicion, was 'birth within the aristocratic order ... a system by no means easy to apply'.[10] And he should know.

The reviews of the book generally acknowledged that it was a clever satire, and its author a shrewd and hard thinker with an elegant pen.

In 1910 Commander Berkeley brought out another book. The new one comprised 264 dense pages of polemic on current mathematical teaching, entitled *The Mysticism of Modern Mathematics*. Rejected by John Murray, it was finally published by Oxford University Press, and it was not well received. One reviewer dismissed the author as 'a Cook's tourist in mathematical territory'.[11] Another delivered the devastating judgement that Berkeley had failed fully to understand the theories he was trying to demolish. However the same reviewer did admit that he was an independent thinker and that 'his book should therefore he interesting even to those who find themselves unable to agree with him'.[12]

APPENDIX 5
Sir James Harris and Nice, 1884–1901

The Harrises dominated Riviera society from the 1860s, when the pleasure-loving diplomat Sir Horace Rumbold remembered Nice as 'a lively French town, in rapid course of transformation into the Brighton of the South'. Sir Horace recalled that he found himself '*en plein cousinage*' with the Harrises and, through them, milords Rokeby, Portarlington, Loughborough, Camden and Ashburton and miscellaneous German princelings. Together they formed 'an extremely pleasant and almost inseparable coterie' and a very good time they had of it in Nice – with 'little dances, and picnic luncheon parties all about the neighbourhood'; also on one occasion some successful *tableaux vivants* (which were much to the taste of the actress in Mrs Harris). And when at the beginning of April their cosy little winter set broke up, they all set off for Genoa where they started partying all over again at the Harrises' summer house, a renaissance palazzo overlooking the harbour.[1] The new Mrs Harris – Gerhardine von Gall, daughter of the German theatre director Ferdinand, Freiherr von Gall (Lord Chamberlain to William I, King of Württemberg), and niece of the novelist and playwright, Louise Freiin von Gall – had inherited a love of theatricals which made her the star of their set. But, by her own reckoning, she flirted perhaps a little too outrageously. In that brilliant season of 1862, as she confided to her diary, 'I amused myself imensly [*sic*], turning people's heads and then being sorry for it all in the most inocent [*sic*] way'. (But she soon 'learnt to think more seriously about the matter and see clearly that ... it is playing with fire'.[2])

Flammability notwithstanding, Lady Harris had increasing recourse to these amorous diversions as her husband and his rich young friend Prince Albert of Monaco disappeared on long sailing trips around the Mediterranean aboard the royal yacht *Princess Alice*, [3] Sir James with his sketchbooks and Prince Albert with his mobile oceanographic laboratory.

On James Harris's death in 1904, by which time he had been knighted, the local paper ran a gushing *nécrologie* in which it said that

Queen Victoria could not but have been flattered that amidst the greenery and the flowers of Nice – justly called the salon of France – the place to which '*l'élite aristocratique*' had flocked with such alacrity for upwards of thirty years – was none other than the home of her own personal representative. In throwing open their villa, the epicentre of that radiant society so agreeable to Her Majesty, Sir James and Lady Harris had promoted the trajectory of the star that had given Nice such dazzle. And so forth.[4]

Source Notes

CHAPTER ONE

1 BB to his mother, postmarked 21 April 1936, BPL.
2 PB to his sister 18 April 1936, B–MA.
3 PB, 'Music Festival at Barcelona', *The Times*, 21 April 1936.
4 E. M. Forster to Mrs Ella Burra, 29 April 1937, B–MA , and Richard Thompson, The Burra–Moody Archive, unpublished MS, 2002, B–MA.
5 Peter Burra, *Van Gogh*, London, Duckworth, 1934; 'Virginia Woolf' in *The Nineteenth Century and After*, vol. CXV, January 1934, pp. 112–25; 'The Novels of E.M. Forster' in *The Nineteenth Century and After*, vol. CXVI, November 1934; *Wordsworth*, London, Duckworth, 1936.
6 David Gilmour, *Cities of Spain*, p. 154.
7 BB on himself, in the Mentorn TV film *Britten's Children* (director John Bridcut), first shown on BBC 2, 5 June 2004.
8 Donald Mitchell, Introduction, LFAL, p. 18.
9 *Ibid.*, pp. 6–7.
10 BB, Diary, 13 November 1928, BPL.
11 W. H. Auden, 'Night covers up the rigid land', *W. H. Auden Collected Shorter Poems*.
12 *A Manual of Plainsong for Divine Service Containing the Canticles Noted, The Psalter Noted to Gregorian Tones ...* was one of the two music books used in the chapel at Gresham's (LFAL, p. 95).
13 Richard Stoker recalled [letter to TS 14 July 2003] that the American composer Virgil Thomson had revealed this in 1962 at an evening at Nadia Boulanger's (where Stoker was studying at the time).
14 LB to Alan Searle, n.d. [about autumn 1934], Somerset Maugham Archive, Howard Gotlieb Archival Research Center, Boston University.
15 Louis MacNeice, *The Strings Are False: an Unfinished Autobiography*, p. 102.
16 James Lees-Milne (abridged and introduced by Michael Bloch), *Diaries 1971–83*, John Murray, 2007, p. 220.
17 LB to NB (TS translation from French), 19 January 1936, FSNB.
18 *Ibid.*

19 *Ibid.*, 1 April 1939, FSNB.
20 Frances Partridge, *Diaries 1939–72*, in an entry for 1 February 1946, p. 140.
21 E. M Forster, *A Passage to India*, with an introduction by PB and some notes by the author, London, J. M. Dent & Sons, 1942.
22 BB, Diary, 29 April 1937, BPL.
23 BB, Diary, 14 March 1937, BPL.
24 LB to BB 30 June 1945, BPL.
25 LB, Diary, n.d., probably late 1970s, BFP.
26 BB, Diary, 17 March 1931, LFAL, pp. 167–8.
27 BB to his parents, 19 January 1930, quoted LFAL, p. 119. For the 'friction' between BB and his teachers see LFAL, pp. 29–30.
28 BB, Diary, 1 February 1930, BPL.
29 JDK Lloyd Photo Albums 2 (1923–8) and 4 (1931–2), [Llyfr Ffoto Albums 153 and 155, National Library of Wales].
30 The two are 'Willi' and Hans Raab. See photo of Raab in Nazi uniform in Papers of Edward Dent GBR/0272/PP/EJD/5/2/17–20, King's College Archive Centre, Cambridge; and PB to Edward Dent, 22 February 1937, and E.M. Forster to Christopher Isherwood, 28 January 1937, The Papers of Edward Dent GBR/0272/PP/EJD, Ibid; and email Richard Thompson to TS, 17 May 2007.
31 PB, 'The Barcelona Festival' in *The Monthly Musical Record*, June 1936, p. 107, and Dr Richard Thompson's revealing – and unpublished – account of the Barcelona Festival, drawn from letters by Britten, Berkeley and Burra in his important collection, B–MA.
32 *Ibid.*
33 John Langdon-Davies, *Dancing Catalans*.
34 *Ibid.*, *Gatherings from Catalonia*, pp. 137–45.
35 LB, Diary, n.d., probably late 1970s, BFP.
36 John Langdon-Davies, *Gatherings from Catalonia*, pp. 137–45.
37 PB, 'The Barcelona Festival' in *The Monthly Musical Record*, June 1936, p. 107.
38 *Ibid.*
39 BB to Grace Williams, 26 April 1936, LFAL, p. 425.
40 LB, Diary, n.d., probably late 1970s, BFP.
41 Julian Symons, *The Thirties*, p. 55.
42 LB to PB 2 August 1936, B–MA.
43 LB, Diary, n.d., probably late 1970s, BFP.
44 James Lees-Milne, *Through Wood and Dale*, p. 135.
45 PB to his mother, n.d., but probably 25 April 1936, B–MA.
46 BB, Diary, 19 April 1936, BPL.
47 LB, Diary, n.d., probably late 1970s, BFP.

48 *The Monthly Musical Record*, June 1936.
49 LB, Diary, n.d., probably late 1970s, BFP.
50 *Ibid.*
51 BB to his mother, 21 April 1936, BPL.
52 *News Chronicle*, *The Times*, *Morning Post*, 2 October 1935.
53 Peter Burra, 'The Barcelona Festival' in *The Monthly Musical Record*, June 1936, p. 108.
54 LB, Diary, n.d., probably late 1970s, BFP.
55 Peter Burra, 'The Barcelona Festival' in *The Monthly Musical Record*, June 1936, p. 108.
56 LB to PB, n.d., but must be about 20 July 1936, B–MA.
57 PB, 'The Barcelona Festival' in *The Monthly Musical Record*, June 1936, p. 108.
58 Donald Mitchell, 'Introduction', LFAL, p. 29.
59 LB, 'Britten and His String Quartet', *The Listener*, 27 May 1943.
60 *London Evening News*, 2 October 1935.
61 PB, 'The Barcelona Festival', *The Monthly Musical Record*, June 1936, p. 108.
62 Richard Stoker, in a long interview with John France published on Classical Music Web at www.musicweb.uk.net.
63 BB, Diary, 26 April 1936, BPL.
64 *Ibid.*, 24 April 1936, BPL.
65 According to PP, quoted HC, pp. 112 and 113.
66 BB Diary, 24 April 1936, BPL; LFAL, p. 425; and HC, pp. 79 and 80 (though this gives date as 25 April).
67 The tenor John Elwes, quoting George Malcolm, Master of Music at Westminster Cathedral at the time, in John Bridcut, *Britten's Children*, pp. 129–30.
68 PB to his mother, 30 April 1936, B–MA.
69 *Ibid.*, n.d. but probably 25 April 1936, B–MA.
70 John Langdon-Davies, *Gatherings from Catalonia*, p. 169.
71 Clover de Pertinez in William Chappell, *Edward Burra*, p. 75, quoted Jane Stevenson, *Edward Burra*, p. 195.
72 Jean Genêt, *The Thief's Journal*, Paris, The Olympia Press, 1954, pp. 27, 39 and 75.
73 *Time Out–Barcelona*, London, Penguin Books, 2002, pp. 80–1.
74 BB, Diary, 22 April 1936, BPL.
75 Carlos Soldevila, *Guia de Barcelona*, Barcelona, Ediciones Destina, 1952.
76 LB to PB, 1 May 1936, B–MA.
77 LB to PB, n.d. [30 April 1936], B–MA.
78 PB to his mother, 4 May 1936, B–MA.
79 BB, Diary, 27 April 1936, BPL.

80 LB to PB, n.d. [early May 1936], B–MA.
81 *Ibid.*, 8 May 1936, B–MA.
82 PB to PP, 1 May 1936, B–MA.

CHAPTER TWO

1 See Bibliography and Appendix 4.
2 In a letter to FB, LB lists these qualities as belonging to his Uncle Arthur, who was, he writes, very like his mother (LB to FB, 10 August 1946, BFP).
3 Gerhardine Harris née von Gall, Diary, 21 September 1858, BFP.
4 J. C. Harris, *Décadence de Nice comme Station d'Hiver*, publisher unknown, 1884. See also Appendix 5, pp. 458–9.
5 John Smyth, *Lives of the Berkeleys*, compiled *c.* 1618, published 1885, quoted Hope Costley-White, *Mary Cole*, p. 25.
6 LB, Diary, n.d., c. late 1970s, BFP.
7 LB to FB 10 August 1946, BFP.
8 Harold Hartley, *Obituary Notice of Randal Earl of Berkeley*, p. 167.
9 Unpublished memoirs of Yvonne Berkeley, *c.* 1968, BFP.
10 Harold Hartley, *Obituary Notice of Randal Earl of Berkeley*, p. 167.
11 MLB, p. 3.
12 See the Exmouth family website at http://www.pellew.com.
13 The rest of this account of the marriage and divorce of Cécile and the admiral comes from the report of the Pellew v. Pellew divorce case, *The Times*, 9 July 1859.
14 The Revd Edward Pellew to *The Times*, 14 January 1854.
15 From the obituary of Admiral Pellew, *The Times*, 1 August 1861.
16 Henry Newbolt, *The Book of the Blue Sea*, chapter 4.
17 According to Charles Berkeley, of Berkeley Castle, in letters to TS dated 20 June and 1 August 2002.
18 Molly [Countess of] Berkeley, *Beaded Bubbles*, p. 63.
19 Army List, 1855.
20 *The Times*, 28 December 1853, and the Revd Edward Pellew, letter to *The Times*, 14 January 1854.
21 Rupert Christiansen, *Tales of the New Babylon*, p. 17.
22 Baptismal certificate of Hastings Berkeley, 1 January 1856, gives his parents' address as Bains de Tivoli, Paris, BFP. (In Hachette Paris 1902 'Grands Bains de Tivoli' are shown at 32 Blvd des Batignolles.)
23 Unpublished memoirs of Yvonne Berkeley, *c.* 1968, BFP. (The expression 'the husband' is used, because Lennox's eccentric cousin Vonnie did not know his name and thought he was a Frenchman.)

24 *The Times*, 15 July 1872.
25 Will of George Rawdon Lennox Berkeley, dated 5 March 1884, proved 15 November 1888.
26 Will of General Randal Rumley, dated 25 July 1883, proved 8 November 1884.
27 Molly [Countess of] Berkeley, *Beaded Bubbles*, p. 63.
28 Peter Parker, *The Old Lie*, p. 99.
29 Henry John Coke, *Tracks of a Rolling Stone*.
30 Royal Navy's website at http://www.royal-navy.mod.uk.
31 See Appendix 3, pp. 452–5.
32 Harold Hartley, *Obituary Notices*, pp. 167–9.
33 Molly [Countess of] Berkeley, *Beaded Bubbles*, 130.
34 See letters from Cécile Countess of Berkeley to Randal Earl of Berkeley, 1906 and 1909, BFP.
35 Molly [Countess of] Berkeley, *Beaded Bubbles*, pp. 62 and 64.
36 Harold Hartley, *Obituary Notices*, p. 177. (The portrait is now hanging in the Dining Room at Berkeley Castle.)
37 *Ibid.*, quoting L. P. Hartley, p. 180.
38 Molly [Countess of] Berkeley, *Beaded Bubbles*, p. 62.
39 Birth Certificate of Kate Brand, born Bedford Street, Cheetham, 15 April 1854.
40 Death Certificate of Arthur Herbert Jackson, of 11 Oxford & Cambridge Mansions, London, 27 September 1881.
41 *Musical Times,* 1 November 1881. Arthur Jackson was the third son of a Brighton piano-tuner (1861 Census).
42 According to her first husband's great-nephew Neville Jackson, piano-tuner, of London; information, 3 November 2005, via the counter-tenor Tay Cheng-Jim (for whom LB wrote the song *i carry your heart with me*, to words by e. e. cummings, in 1972).
43 Cdr Hastings Berkeley to Aline Harris, 15 November 1889, BFP.
44 Death certificate of Kate, Countess of Berkeley, at Wootton, 29 March 1898.
45 Cdr Hastings Berkeley to Aline Harris, 4 November 1916, BFP.
46 *Ibid.*, 20 March1890, BFP.
47 *Ibid.*, 12 December and 19 November 1890, respectively, BFP.
48 Hastings Berkeley to Aline Harris, March/April 1890, BFP.
49 *Ibid.*, 5 December 1890, BFP.
50 *Ibid.*, 12 November 1890, BFP,
51 Marriage certificate, BFP, and *The Times*, 29 January 1891,
52 Kanigel, Robert, *High Season in Nice*, pp. 128–9 quoting J. C. Harris, *Décadence de Nice comme Station d'Hiver*.

53 R. T. Günther, *The Oxford Country*, London, John Murray, 1912, pp. 39–41.
54 Evelyn Waugh, *Brideshead Revisited*, London, Chapman & Hall, 1960, p. 35 (quoting a Berkeley deed of 1927), and Foxcombe Hall, The Open University, 1994.
55 For much of this paragraph TS is indebted to the architect Philip J. Stewart, who gathered this research to support his 1995 case for the official listing of what then remained of Foxcombe Hall, as it was later known (see note 95); his correspondence with Freda Berkeley is in BFP.
56 Margaret Aldiss and Patricia Simms (eds.), *A Boars Hill Anthology*, p. 63.
57 Stephen Salter, architect, postcard to H. B. Cooper, postmarked 19 December 1906, www.headington.org.uk/oxon/postcards/boars.hill.
58 Margaret Aldiss and Patricia Simms (eds.), *A Boars Hill Anthology*, p. 54.
59 Sybil Jackson, interview in the *Oxford Mail*, 3 August 1973.
60 *Ibid.*
61 Beatrice Playne, a niece of Lennox's elderly admirer Gladys Bryans, in an interview with RN, Malvern, 4 December 1986, RNA.
62 Harold Hartley, *Obituary Notice of Randal Earl of Berkeley*, p. 175.
63 Hastings at Boars Hill to Aline, n.d. [?1899], BFP.
64 In 2007 the house was offered for sale by John D. Wood for £1,750,000.

CHAPTER THREE

1 'History of the Jews in Russian and the Soviet Union', *Wikipedia* online encyclopaedia, http://en.wikipedia.org.
2 This link, first suggested by Prof. Aubrey Newman, was recorded in Wendy Bellany, 'The Jews of Merthyr Tydfil', *Shemot* [journal of the Jewish Genealogical Society of Great Britain], vol. 6, no. 3, September 1998, pp. 11–13.
3 Mr Ben Hamilton [Himmelstein], lawyer, in Wendy Bellany, 'The Jews of Merthyr Tydfil', *Shemot* [journal of the Jewish Genealogical Society of Great Britain], vol. 6, no. 3, September 1998, p. 4.
4 Michael Wallach, 'How "Greeners" Came to the Valley', *Jewish Chronicle*, 28 November 1975.
5 Mr Joe Price, a retired businessman from Cardiff, who was born in Merthyr, of a tinker father who emigrated from Poland in the 1880s, quoted in TS, 'The Last Jew in Merthyr', *The Sunday Telegraph*, 6 July 1997.
6 Leo Abse, 'A tale of collaboration not conflict with the "People of the

Book"' [a highly critical review of Ursula R. Q. Henriques (ed.), *The Jews of South Wales: Historical Studies*, Cardiff, University of Wales Press, 1993], *The New Welsh Review*, no. 22, Autumn 1993.

7 Wendy I. Bellany, 'The Jews of Merthyr Tydfil', *Shemot* [journal of the Jewish Genealogical Society of Great Britain], vol. 6, no. 3, September 1998, p. 11.

8 Leo Abse, 'A tale of collaboration not conflict with the "People of the Book"', *The New Welsh Review*, no. 22, Autumn 1993.

9 *Ibid.*

10 This, and all the other biographical information about Bernsteins in this chapter, is drawn from certificates of birth, death and marriage; wills; census returns; trade directories; valuation lists; naturalization papers; registers of electors; Companies House; genealogical data available on the invaluable JewishGen.org website; and memorial stones in the Jewish cemetery at Cefn-coed-y-cymmer just outside Merthyr Tydfil.

11 Speculations of the late Leo Abse, in conversation with TS, 17 May 2006.

12 Quoted in Wendy I. Bellany, 'The Jews of Merthyr Tydfil', *Shemot* [journal of the Jewish Genealogical Society of Great Britain], vol. 6, no. 3, September 1998, p. 2.

13 Aviva Neeman, 'Coupling Cousins', *Shemot* [journal of the Jewish Genealogical Society of Great Britain], vol. 6, no. 3, September 1998, pp. 23–4.

14 Mr George Black, one of the trustees of the synagogue and caretaker of the cemetery, quoted in TS, 'The Last Jew in Merthyr', *The Sunday Telegraph*, 6 July 1997. In 1998 Mr Black retired to Manchester, and handed over responsibility for the Cefn-Coed Jewish Cemetery to Mrs Nettie Whitlen, of Cardiff; he died later the same year.

15 Wendy Bellany, 'The Jews of Merthyr Tydfil', *Shemot* [journal of the Jewish Genealogical Society of Great Britain], vol. 6, no. 3, September 1998, p. 12.

16 *The Times*, 20 August 1911.

17 Leo Abse, 'A tale of collaboration not conflict with the "People of the Book"', *The New Welsh Review*, no. 22, Autumn 1993.

18 *The Times*, 24 August 1911.

19 Leo Abse, 'A tale of collaboration not conflict with the "People of the Book"', *The New Welsh Review*, no. 22, Autumn 1993; and Tam Dalyell, obituary, Leo Abse, *The Independent*, 21 August 2008.

20 Ursula R. Q. Henriques (ed.), *The Jews of South Wales: Historical Studies*, Cardiff, University of Wales Press, 1993, p. 169.

21 Marie Davies, 'Childhood Memories', in *Gwent Local History*, vol. 63, autumn 1987, p. 32.

22 *Ibid.*, p. 33.
23 Ursula R. Q. Henriques (ed.), *The Jews of South Wales: Historical Studies*, Cardiff, University of Wales Press, 1993, p. 171.
24 Michael Wallach, 'How "Greeners" Came to the Valley', *Jewish Chronicle*, 28 November 1975.
25 Deposition in Isaac Bernstein's Naturalization Papers HO 144/709/108479, Public Record Office, London.
26 *Ibid.*
27 Ursula R. Q. Henriques (ed.), *The Jews of South Wales: Historical Studies*, Cardiff, University of Wales Press, 1993, p. 171.
28 Letters of Administration of the Estate, proved 29 December 1919, of his brother Lewis Bernstein who died intestate at 27 Bridge Street, Tredegar, on 28 November 1918.
29 Leo Abse, 'A tale of collaboration not conflict with the "People of the Book"', *The New Welsh Review*, no. 22, Autumn 1993.

CHAPTER FOUR

1 FB, in a telephone conversation with TS, 8 August 2003.
2 Cdr Hastings Berkeley to his wife Aline, n.d. [post-1903, pre-April 1908] (BFP).
3 Cécile Countess of Berkeley to her son, Randal Earl of Berkeley, Nice, 8 April 1906, BFP.
4 *Ibid.*
5 Cdr Hastings Berkeley to his wife Aline, 5 January 1912, BFP.
6 Death Certificate of Kate, Countess of Berkeley, at Wootton, 29 March 1870, 1898.
7 Unpublished memoirs of Yvonne Berkeley (1899–post 1984), completed about 1968, BFP.
8 Harold Hartley, *Obituary Notice of Randal Earl of Berkeley*, p. 169.
9 From information provided by the architect Philip J. Stewart, in letters to FB, 1995, BFP.
10 Harold Hartley, *Obituary Notice of Randal Earl of Berkeley*, p. 175.
11 *Ibid.*
12 Deeds etc in the possession of the Oxford Preservation Trust, and information provided by David S. Carter, of Boars Hill, to TS 2 September 2003.
13 Harold Hartley, *Obituary Notice of Randal Earl of Berkeley*, p. 180.
14 Cdr Hastings Berkeley to Aline, 13 November 1916, BFP.
15 A. Wood, 'Lennox Berkeley, 70, hits the high point of his career', *Oxford Mail*, 3 August 1973.
16 Silvia [*sic*] Hartley, daughter of Major Ernald Hartley, Lord Berkeley's

research collaborator at Foxcombe 1902–16, to FB, 8 August 1989, BFP. The school was run by Miss Sainsbury and her friend Miss Zimmeren.

17 Postcard from Aline Berkeley to her daughter Geraldine, February 1907, BFP.

18 J. Lees-Milne, writing of his own childhood, in his Diary, 30 July 1997, in J. Lees-Milne (ed. M. Bloch), *The Milk of Paradise*, p. 285.

19 LB, in an interview with C. B. Cox, Allan Young and Michael Schmidt in *Poetry Nation*, no. 2, 1974.

20 Cdr Hastings Berkeley to his wife Aline, January 1913, BFP.

21 *Hampton's Scholastic Directory*, 1905–6.

22 Dragon School records.

23 Cdr Hastings Berkeley to his wife Aline, 5 January 1912, BFP.

24 Sale particulars published by Knight Frank, Oxford, March 2003.

25 Cdr Hastings Berkeley to his wife Aline, 6 November 1916, BFP.

26 Title Number ON227916, Gloucester District Land Registry.

27 LB, Diary, 30 August 1968, BFP.

28 *Oxford Mail*, 3 August 1973.

29 Captain Berkeley is listed as a member of Mind Association, in *Mind*, 1916, XXV (1), 141.

30 Cdr Hastings Berkeley to his wife Aline, 14 January 1912, BFP.

31 *Ibid.*

32 Cdr Hastings Berkeley to his wife Aline, 18 January 1913, BFP.

CHAPTER FIVE

1 S. Smart, *When Heroes Die*, p. 13.

2 Cdr Hastings Berkeley to his wife Aline, 22 January 1913, BFP.

3 *Hampton's Scholastic Directory*, 1913–14.

4 J. Thomas and T. Baldwin (eds.), *Lippincott's Geographical Dictionary of the World*, p. 865.

5 A. Mee, *Norfolk*, p. 189.

6 *Ibid.*

7 G. Howson, Speech Day 28 July 1918, quoted Smart, *When Heroes Die*, p. 151.

8 J. Gathorne-Hardy, *The Public School Phenomenon*, pp, 296, 319–20.

9 Edward Mendelson (ed.), *The English Auden*, p. 325.

10 BB Diary, 6 December 1929.

11 S. Smart, *When Heroes Die*, p. 165 (quoting a memoir of Howson in *The Gresham*).

12 J. Pudney, *Home and Away*, p. 49.

13 LFAL, p. 223.

14 W. H. Auden, 'Honour', *The Old School, Essays by Diverse Hands* edited by Graham Greene, London, Cape, 1934, pp. 5–6.
15 Stephen Spender, 'Greatorex' in *Grasshopper*, Holt, Gresham's, 1955, quoted LFAL, p. 223.
16 BB, Diary, 1 February 1930 and 22 May 1930, BPL.
17 Bishop John Daly to RN, 7 July 1989, RNA.
18 Roy Daniell to RN, 15 May 1989, RNA.
19 LB, Diary, 16 November 1977, BFP.
20 LFAL, p. 95.
21 Henry Kemeys Bagnall-Oakeley to RN, 11 May 1989, RNA.
22 LB, 'The Sound of Words', *The Times*, 28 June 1962.
23 Cdr Hastings Berkeley to his wife Aline, 19 November 1916, BFP.
24 Henry Kemeys Bagnall-Oakeley to RN, 11 May 1989, RNA.
25 *Ibid.*
26 Richard Higham to RN, 9 May 1989, RNA.
27 Henry Kemeys Bagnall-Oakeley to RN, 11 May 1989, RNA.
28 Richard Higham to RN, 9 May 1989, RNA.
29 Henry Kemeys Bagnall-Oakeley to RN, 11 May 1989, RNA.
30 Cdr Hastings Berkeley to his wife Aline, 12 November 1916, BFP.
31 *Ibid.*, 1916–17, BFP.
32 *Ibid.*, 22 October 1916, BFP.
33 *Ibid.*, 14 January 1917, BFP.
34 *Ibid.*, 13 January 1917, BFP.
35 *Ibid.*, 28 October 1916, BFP.
36 *Ibid.*,14 January 1913, BFP.
37 *Ibid.*, 29 November 1916, BFP.
38 S. Smart, *When Heroes Die*, p. 166.
39 *Ibid.*, pp. 163 and 166 (quoting Edith, Duchess of Hamilton).
40 *Ibid.*, p. 34.
41 *Ibid.*, pp. 34–36.
42 Unpublished memoirs of Yvonne Berkeley (1899–post 1984), completed about 1968, BFP.
43 Information provided by Grant of Probate, 24 April 1915.
44 Sir Ernest Berkeley to his brother Randal, Earl of Berkeley, 6 February 1922, BFP.
45 Will of Cécile, Countess of Berkeley, dated 23 December 1909, proved by Capt Hastings Berkeley, 24 April 1915, BFP.
46 Cdr Hastings Berkeley to his wife Aline, from Nice, January 1913, BFP.
47 Will of Charles, 2nd Lord FitzHardinge, proved 23 February 1917.
48 Cdr Hastings Berkeley to his wife Aline, from Nice, 20 December 1916, BFP.
49 *Ibid.*, 21 December 1916, BFP.

50 Obituary, Randal, Earl of Berkeley, *The Times*, 16 January 1942.
51 David S. Carter of Boars Hill to TS, 2 September 2003; and *The Times*, 6 September 1927.
52 *A Full History of St George's V. A. School*, www.stgeorges.herts.sch.uk.
53 Louis MacNeice, *The Strings Are False*, p. 104.
54 Romain Rolland, *Jean Christophe*, vol. 1, New York, Henry Holt, 1913.
55 R. L. Stevenson, 'The Vagabond' (lines 4–8, verse 2) from *Songs of Travel*, London, Chatto & Windus, 1905.

CHAPTER SIX

1 D. Mackenzie (ed.), *Holborn Old and New*, London, The Princeton Press (for the First Avenue Hotel), n.d., pp. ii–iv.
2 Information provided by Jane Norman after a visit to Canada in 1997 when she spoke to Mrs Kathleen ('Kay') Lampard, daughter of Grace's elder sister Mabel.
3 Information conveyed to TS by Anthony Nunney, by telephone, 21 March 2006, following a telephone conversation with his Canadian cousin Kathleen Lampard a few days earlier.
4 D. Mackenzie, *Holborn Old and New,* London, The First Avenue Hotel, n.d., pp. ii–iv, Camden Archives Centre, London.
5 Both quotations are given, unsourced, in an article on Childs Hill in *Wikipedia*, en.wikipedia.org/wiki/Childs_Hill.
6 C. R. Elrington (ed.), *A History of the County of Middlesex*, vol. ix (Hampstead and Paddington), 1989, pp. 73–5.
7 Bernice Rubens, *Brothers*, p. 188.
8 Information from Mrs Irene Hughes.

CHAPTER SEVEN

1 Merton College Boat Club records (2nd VIII, 1923), Merton College Library.
2 Reginald Ellison, a neighbour in Little Venice, to FB, 27 December 1989, BFP.
3 Reginald Ellison interviewed by RN, 9 February 1989, RNA.
4 Judy Pearce, 'A cox's job', Letter to the Editor, *The Spectator*, 8 April 2006.
5 E. Waugh, *A Little Learning*, p. 213.
6 H. Green, *Pack My Bag*, London, The Hogarth Press, 1979, p. 220.
7 Alec Waugh, *Island in the Sun*, p. 124.
8 T. Driberg, *Ruling Passions*, p. 55.
9 Barbara Key-Seymer, in Kavanagh, *Secret Muses*, p. 83.

10 Edith Olivier, *op. cit.*, p. 84.
11 William Chappel, *op. cit.*, 85.
12 Alec Waugh, *Island in the Sun*, p. 123.
13 Lord Clonmore to David Talbot Rice, 3 March 1925, in James Knox, *Robert Byron*, p. 75.
14 E. Waugh, *A Little Learning*, p. 204.
15 Harold Acton to Evelyn Waugh, 25 September 1964, quoted in Stannard, *Evelyn Waugh*, vol. ii, p. 481.
16 O. Lancaster, *With an Eye to the Future*, pp. 80–1.
17 L. MacNeice, *The Strings Are False*, pp. 102–6.
18 Terence Greenidge, *Degenerate Oxford?*, pp. 106–7.
19 *Ibid.*, p. 94.
20 M. Stannard, *Evelyn Waugh*, vol. i, p. 92.
21 H. Green, *Pack My Bag*, London, The Hogarth Press, 1979, p. 218.
22 C. Sykes, 'Robert Byron', *Four Studies in Loyalty*, London, Collins, 1946, pp. 80–1.
23 Evelyn Waugh to Tom Driberg [1922], Mark Amory (ed.), *The Letters of Evelyn Waugh*, p. 10.
24 C. Day Lewis, *The Buried Day*, p. 157.
25 A paraphrase of both Harold Acton and James Knox from J. Knox, *Robert Byron*, pp. 28 and 29.
26 E. Waugh., *A Little Learning*, pp. 199–200.
27 R. Byron (ed. L. Butler), *Robert Byron Letters Home*, p. 18.
28 LB, Diary, 16 August 1968, BFP.
29 *Oxford Mail*, 3 August 1973.
30 LB, 'The Sound of Words', *The Times*, 28 June 1962.
31 J.-K. Huysmans, *A Rebours*, quoted in 'Modern Mysticism', *The Quarterly Review*, vol. 190, January–December 1899.
32 LB, Diary, 28 June 1962, BFP.
33 LB, Diary, 1 December 1973, BFP.
34 Obituary, Julien [*sic*] Green, *The Daily Telegraph*, 19 August 1998.
35 E. Waugh, *The Life of Ronald Knox*, p. 14.
36 Obituary, H. W. Garrod, *The Times*, 28 December 1960.
37 H. W. Garrod (ed.), *List of The Writings of H. W. Garrod*, Oxford, The University Press [*c.* 1947].
38 Obituary, H. W. Garrod, *The Times*, 28 December 1960.
39 Martin and Highfield, *A History of Merton College*, p. 332.
40 MLB, pp. 4–5.
41 Gordon Bryan, 'The Younger English Composers, part V: Lennox Berkeley', *Monthly Music Record*, vol. 59, June 1929, 161–2.
42 Jill Balcon, 'Introduction', *The Complete Poems of C. Day Lewis*, Sinclair-Stevenson, p. xii.

43 Sean Day-Lewis, *Cecil Day-Lewis: An English Literary Life*, p. 42.
44 *Ibid.*
45 Charles Osborne, *W. H. Auden*, pp. 45–6.
46 *Ibid.*, p. 47, quoting from Christopher Isherwood, *Christopher and His Kind.*
47 *Ibid.*, p. 45, quoting C. Day-Lewis, *The Buried Day: A Personal Memoir.*
48 Charles Plumb and W. H. Auden (eds.), *Oxford Poetry 1926*, Oxford, Basil Blackwell, 1926, p. v.
49 Peter Parker (ed.), *The Reader's Companion to Twentieth Century Writers*, pp. 216–17.
50 W. H. Auden, 'Cinders', *Oxford Poetry 1926*, pp. 6–7.
51 Charles Osborne, *W. H. Auden*, p. 46.
52 W. H. Auden to LB, 9 June [1957], BFP.
53 LB, Diary, 23 October 1967 [after the first performance of *Signs in the Dark* (setting four poems by Laurie Lee), at Stroud], BFP.
54 J .F. Waterhouse, *Composer and Librettist*, in the series 'World of Music', *Birmingham Post,* n.d. [probably September 1954].
55 SRC, p. 51, and MLB, pp. 6–7.
56 The MS is in BFP.
57 Warden Bowman's successor Geoffrey Mure, quoted in Martin & Highfield, *A History of Merton College*, p. 327.
58 Julian Potter, *Stephen Potter at the BBC*, p. 26.
59 Obituary, H. W. Garrod, *The Times*, 28 December 1960.
60 George Mallaby, *From My Level*, Hutchinson, 1965, p. 211.
61 Item 14, Nicol Smith Collection, Merton College Library.
62 George Mallaby, *From My Level*, Hutchinson, 1965, p. 211.
63 L. MacNeice, *The Strings Are False*, p. 104.
64 Reginald Ellison interviewed by RN, 9 February1989, RNA.
65 Myrmidon Club Minutes, 28 November 1925, Merton College Library.
66 A rule introduced by the President, Lord Elmley [E. Waugh, *A Little Learning*, p. 180].
67 The name he and Terence Greenidge gave to their coterie, whose assemblies Greenidge dubbed 'offal' [*ibid.*, pp. 178–9].
68 Terence Greenidge in conversation with Christopher Sykes, transcript of a recording made 25 January 1967, Georgetown University Library.
69 Evelyn Waugh to Tom Driberg, n. d. [1922], in Evelyn Waugh (ed. Mark Amory), *The Letters of Evelyn Waugh*, p. 9.
70 J. Fothergill, *An Innkeeper's Diary*, pp. 22–4 and 47, and the photograph pasted in the back of the book of signatures on the Heights Wall, also E. Waugh (ed. Michael Davie), *The Diaries of Evelyn Waugh*, p. 273.
71 E. Waugh, *A Little Learning*, p. 200.

72 Maurice Bowra, quoted De-la-Noy, *Eddy*, p. 78.
73 See Appendix 2, pp. 446–8.
74 LB to Alan Searle, n.d. [January 1935], Somerset Maugham Archive, Howard Gotlieb Archival Research Center, Boston University.
75 J. Lees-Milne, *Through Wood and Dale*, p. 205.
76 Advertisement, *Cornell Alumni News*, 21 June 1902.
77 Trinity College Admissions Register, 18 January 1919.
78 Anthony Powell, *Infants of the Spring*, p. 71, quoted in James Knox, *Robert Byron*, p. 66.
79 See LB's letters to Alan Searle 1933–6, Somerset Maugham Archive, Howard Gotlieb Archival Research Center, Boston University.
80 O. Lancaster, *With an Eye to the Future*, p. 81.
81 J. Knox, Obituary, Tamara Talbot Rice, *The Times*, 29 September 1993.
82 See Appendix 2, pp. 446–8.
83 Charles E. Linck, Jr, 'Waugh-Greenidge Film *The Scarlet Woman*, *Evelyn Waugh Newsletter,* vol. 3 no. 2, Autumn 1969. See also John Howard Wilson, '*The Scarlet Woman:* An Appreciation', *Evelyn Waugh Newsletter,* vol. 33, no. 2, Autumn 2002.
84 *Ibid.*
85 C. Sykes, *Evelyn Waugh*, p. 56.
86 M. Stannard, *Evelyn Waugh*, vol. i, p. 84. Pares later became Professor History at Edinburgh University, and an expert in the 18th-century sugar trade.
87 C. Sykes, *Evelyn Waugh*, p. 48.
88 C. Hollis, *Oxford in the Twenties*, p. 85.
89 E. Waugh (ed. Michael Davie), *The Diaries of Evelyn Waugh*, p. 170.
90 See photographs in J. D. K. Lloyd's Photo Album 2 (1923–8), Llyfr Ffoto Album153, National Library of Wales.
91 From a carbon copy of a typed memoir about Evelyn Waugh by Patrick Kinross, in the possession of TS.
92 Terence Greenidge to Charles Linck, 8 October 1961, photocopy, Harry Ransom Humanities Research Center, University of Texas at Austin.
93 Alec Waugh, *Island in the Sun*, p. 124.

CHAPTER EIGHT

1 14th edition, 1921. This book, inscribed with his name, is with BFP.
2 'Modern Mysticism', *The Quarterly Review*, vol. 190, January–December 1899.
3 D. Hibberd, *Wilfred Owen – A New Biography*, p. 136.
4 R. D. E. Burton, *Francis Poulenc*, p. 45.
5 W. R. Inge, *Light, Life and Love*, 1904.

6 LB, Music List for his Mother, 1925, in Aline Berkeley, Diary, 1925–6, BFP.
7 MB, in conversation with TS, 21 September 2005. John Francis Bentley, 1839–1902, a convert to Rome, designed and built Westminster Cathedral, which was opened a year after his death.
8 Pope Benedict XVI, *Motu Proprio* [Apostolic Letter], Summorum Pontificum, Vatican City, 7 July 2007.
9 This paragraph draws on W. L. Sumner, 'Some Oxford Organs', *The Organ*, vol. xxvi, no. 104, April 1947, and the experience of Julian Berkeley.
10 Letters of 1904–41 from Henry Ley to TS's maiden great-aunts, Frances Cecilia Troyte Dunn and Joanna Dyke Dunn.
11 LB, 'Igor Stravinsky – A Centenary Tribute', *Musical Times*, June 1982.
12 John Codrington to RN, 4 September 1989, RNA.
13 LB, n.d. handwritten notes of *c.* 1969 inspired by recollections of his *Second String Quartet*, BFP.
14 H. Ley to Joanna Dunn, 27 December 1908. In 1941, by which time Henry Ley was Precentor at Eton, Miss Dunn, no longer playing the violin, presented her instrument to Eton, where it was played-in by King George VI at a family concert in Windsor Castle on 22 July.
15 Handwritten notes for an article on Ravel published by *Adam International Review,* vol. xli, nos. 404–6, 1978.
16 Annotated typescript of a talk given by LB on Ravel, BBC Radio 3, 3 March 1975, BFP.
17 *Ibid.*
18 LB, 'Maurice Ravel', *Adam International Review*, vol. xli, nos. 404–6, 1978, p. 15.
19 LB, handwritten notes for an article or talk on 'Modern French Ballet', n.d. but probably 1945/6, BFP.
20 Deduced from LB's own written recollections (*op. cit.*); Charles Harding to FB, 10 March 1990 (BFP); the pianist Gordon Bryan quoted in N. Demuth, *Ravel*, pp. 40–1; Larner, *Maurice Ravel*, p. 190; an interview in Danish in *Berlinske Tidende*, 30 January 1926, in Arbie Orenstein, *A Ravel Reader*, p. 439 , and RN, *Ravel*, p. 131.
21 LB, annotated typescript of a talk about Ravel [Radio 3, 3 March 1975], BFP.
22 Massimo Freccia, *The Sounds of Memory*, pp. 91–2.
23 According to the pianist Gordon Bryan quoted in N. Demuth, *Ravel*, p. 40.
24 LB, Diary, 28 December 1978, BFP.
25 LB to Desmond Shawe-Taylor, 14 February 1956, BFP.
26 M. Berkeley, Note, Lennox Berkeley *Quatre Pièces pour la Guitare*, Ancona, Bèrben Edizioni musicali, 2002.

27 Annotated typescript of a talk given by LB on Ravel [Radio 3, 3 March 1975], BFP.
28 LB, in an interview with C. B. Cox, Allan Young and Michael Schmidt, *Poetry Nation*, no. 2, 1974.
29 LB lecture, 'Paris and Boulanger', British Institute of Recorded Sound, 7 January 1972, T 581 W, National Sound Archive.
30 H. C. Colles (ed.), *Grove's Dictionary of Music and Musicians*, vol. 5, 3rd edition, 1928, p. 460.
31 L. Rosenstiel, *Nadia Boulanger*, pp. 114, 224, 251–2.
32 LB, in an interview with Carolyn Scott, 'Portrait of a very cultivated person', *Catholic Herald* [December 1976], BFP.
33 Interview with Roy Plomley, *Desert Island Discs*, BBC Radio 4, 13 May 1978.
34 LB, in an interview with Paul Dobson, *Kensington News and Post*, 27 July 1973.
35 LB to NB (TS translation from French), 19 January 1936, FSNB.
36 Carolyn Scott, 'Portrait of a very cultivated person' [Lennox Berkeley], the *Catholic Herald* (December 1976), BFP.
37 Jessica Douglas-Home, *Violet*, p. 190.
38 Edward Marsh and Christopher Hassal, *Ambrosia and Small Beer*, p. 337.
39 Jessica Douglas-Home, *Violet*, p. 190.
40 ADD MS 63847.
41 Mary Bernard to FB, 28 June 1986, BFP, quoting from a lecture given by Anthony Bernard on Ravel at Morley College .
42 E. Junge, *Anthony Bernard*, p. 28.
43 Mary Bernard to FB, 28 June 1986, BFP.
44 James Knox, *Robert Byron*, p. 92.
45 William Boyd, *Any Human Heart*, p. 140.
46 Alexander Waugh, *Fathers and Sons*, p. 164.
47 H. Hartley, *Obituary Notice of Randal Earl of Berkeley*, pp. 176–7.
48 Molly Berkeley, *Beaded Bubbles*, p. 98, and L. P. Hartley, Foreword, *ibid*, p. xi.
49 *Ibid.*, p. 66.
50 Adrian Wright, *Foreign Country*, p. 120.
51 *Ibid.*, p. 178, quoting John Calmann.
52 M. Berkeley, *Beaded Bubbles*, p. 98.
53 *Ibid.*, p. 68.
54 *Ibid.*, p. 78.
55 *Ibid.*, p. 67.
56 *Ibid.*, p. 61.
57 LB, *Monthly Musical Record*, vol. 61, 1 December 1931.

58 DPM.
59 See Christopher J. Walker, 'The Margravine of Ansbach', *Journal of The Lennox Berkeley Society*, 2009.
60 H. Acton, *Memoirs of an Aesthete*, p. 149.
61 The composer Richard Stoker (a student of both LB and NB), recalling a conversation with LB in 1962, in an email letter to TS, 17 March 2004.
62 LB, Diary, 13 November 1966, BFP.

CHAPTER NINE

1 FB, in conversation with TS, 26 March 2005, said that her Nunney grandparents often emphasized how much Isaac Bernstein loved his wife.
2 Memories of FB's cousin, Irene Syme née Hughes, in conversation with FB and TS at 8 Warwick Avenue, in 1974.
3 All FB's memories quoted in this chapter – apart from those otherwise sourced – are based on a series of taped interviews between FB and TS at Hereford Mansions, W2, in January 1997, 17 June 1998, 24 October 2001, and 25 and 26 December 2001, together with further memories recalled by FB in a telephone conversation with TS on 26 July 2004.
4 *Hampstead and Highgate Express*, 21 January 1928, p. 6.
5 *Ibid.*
6 Grave no. 32, Section o/12.
7 Government Legal Service at www.gls.gov.uk/about/departments/offsol.htm.

CHAPTER TEN

1 Richard Stoker, recalling a conversation with NB in 1962, in an email letter to TS, 17 March 2004.
2 LB, 'Boulanger the Dedicated', *Sunday Telegraph*, 4 June 1961.
3 *Ibid.*
4 H. Cuénod, in a taped interview with TS, 8–10 July 1994.
5 DPM.
6 V. Thomson, *Virgil Thomson*, p. 54.
7 DPM.
8 *Ibid.*
9 L. Rosenstiel, *Nadia Boulanger*, p. 22.
10 *Ibid.*, p. 53.
11 DPM.
12 *Ibid.*
13 *Ibid.*

14 Christopher Ford, profile of LB, 'Berkeley square', in *The Guardian*, 3 August 1973.
15 LB, transcript of a lecture on Boulanger at the British Institute of Recorded Sound, London, 7 January 1972, National Sound Archive, London.
16 LB, 'Boulanger the Dedicated', *Sunday Telegraph*, 4 June 1961.
17 LB, 'Nadia Boulanger as Teacher', *The Monthly Musical Record*, 1 January 1931.
18 LB, transcript of a lecture on Boulanger at the British Institute of Recorded Sound, London, 7 January 1972, National Sound Archive, London.
19 *Ibid.*
20 DPM.
21 LB, interview with C. B. Cox, Allan Young and Michael Schmidt, *Poetry Nation*, no. 2, 1974.
22 LB, 'Modern French Ballet Music', autograph notes for an illustrated talk, n.d. [soon after March 1945], BFP.
23 Review of S. M. I. concert, Salle Gaveau, 1 June 1927, in *Le Ménestrel*, 10 June 1927, pp. 259–60; see also Allan Clive Jones, 'Lennox Berkeley's *Quatre Pièces pour la Guitare* – Part 1', Classical Guitar, vol. 21, no. 6, February 2003. 'Elitist' is RN's adjective in *The Harlequin Years*, p. 257.
24 In a performance by Sophie Wyss and the London Chamber Orchestra conducted by Anthony Bernard [SRC, 52, and Gordon Bryan, 'The Younger English Composers, part V: Lennox Berkeley', *Monthly Music Record*, vol. 59, June 1929, 161–2]. On 10 February 1931 the same conductor and orchestra gave the first concert performance of this orchestral version with the soprano Jeanne Dusseau, in the Aeolian Hall in London (MLB, p. 10, and SRC, p. 52).
25 LB, 'Music in Paris', *Monthly Musical Record*, vol. 61, December 1931, p. 360.
26 MLB, 10–11.
27 Sir Arthur Bliss, on 2 July 1943, quoted by Stephen Potter in Julian Potter, *Stephen Potter at the BBC*, p. 151.
28 LB, 'Modern French Ballet Music', handwritten notes for an illustrated radio talk, n. d. [but soon after March 1945], BFP.
29 See J. Lees-Milne (ed. M. Bloch), *The Milk of Paradise, Diaries 1993–97*, p. 161, 15 March 1995.
30 Jean Hugo, *Le regard de la mémoire*, p. 212 – quoted in R. D. E. Burton, *Francis Poulenc*, p. 29.
31 R. D. E. Burton, *Francis Poulenc*, p. 31.
32 *Ibid.*, p. 29.
33 Virgil Thomson, *Virgil Thomson*, pp. 56–7.

34 R. D. E. Burton, *Francis Poulenc*, p. 62.
35 RN to TS, email, 5 September 2007.
36 Jean-Charles Hoffelé, 'Les intrus dans le sanctuaire', notes for a 2-CD set of 38 of Wiéner and Doucet's recordings of the 1920s and '30s, *Les Rarissimes de Jean Wiéner & Clément Doucet – Les Années Folles*, EMI Classics 7243 5 86480 2 7. See also: G. Larner, *Maurice Ravel*, p. 178, and RN, *The Harlequin Years*, p. 117.
37 Arthur Bliss, *As I Remember*, p. 56.
38 LB, transcript of a lecture on Boulanger at the British Institute of Recorded Sound, London, 7 January 1972, National Sound Archive, London.
39 Ravel was an habitué, and took Lennox to Le Boeuf in November 1928 (Talbot Rice, *Tamara*, p. 196).
40 LB, in Arbie Orenstein (ed.), *A Ravel Reader*, p. 15.
41 LB, 'Maurice Ravel', *Adam International Review*, nos. 404–6, 1978, p. 13.
42 Léon-Paul Fargue, quoted in Arbie Orenstein (ed.), *A Ravel Reader*, p. 15.
43 LB, annotated typescript of a talk about Ravel (BBC Radio 3, 3 March 1975), BFP.
44 RN, quoting a recollection he himself garnered from Manuel Rosenthal – RN, email to TS, 5 September 2007.
45 LB, annotated typescript of a talk about Ravel for BBC Radio 3, 3 March 1975, BFP.
46 G. Larner, *Maurice Ravel*, p. 178.
47 DPM.
48 LB, annotated typescript of a talk about Ravel (Radio 3, 3 March 1975), BFP.
49 Tamara Talbot Rice, *Tamara,* p. 196.
50 LB, handwritten notes for a talk on his life as a composer [possibly for 'A composer speaks – 2', *Composer,* no. 43 (Spring 1972), 17–19], BFP.
51 LB, annotated typescript based on his 'Maurice Ravel', *Adam International Review*, nos. 404–6, 1978, BFP.
52 LB, in N. Demuth, *Ravel*, p. 177.
53 LB, annotated typescript of a talk about Ravel (BBC Radio 3, 3 March 1975), BFP.
54 LB, in Arbie Orenstein (ed.), *A Ravel Reader*, p. 15.
55 LB, in N. Demuth, *Ravel*, p. 177.
56 *Ibid.*
57 LB, 'Maurice Ravel', *Adam International Review*, nos. 404–6, 1978, p. 17.
58 LB, in N. Demuth, *Ravel*, p. 177.

59 G. Larner, *Maurice Ravel*, p. 221.
60 See RN on Ravel's 'Personality, Aesthetic, Technique', the final chapter of his Master Musicians biography of Ravel, pp. 152–9.
61 G. Larner, *Maurice Ravel*, p.219.
62 LB, annotated typescript, n.d., of a talk about Ravel [BBC Radio 3, 3 March 1975], BFP.
63 MLB, p. 24.
64 A collection of 19 letters and one postcard which LB wrote to Hélène Kahn-Casella 1926–40, was acquired by FB from the dealer Thierry Bodin in Paris in 2004, and this is now part of the BFP at BPL.
65 RN, *The Harlequin Years*, p. 48.
66 Allan Clive Jones, 'Lennox Berkeley's *Quatre Pièces*', Pt 1, *Classical Guitar*, vol. 21, no. 6, February 2003.
67 LB to Mme Kahn-Casella, 1 November 1926, BFP.
68 LB pays tribute to Segovia in 'Music in Paris', *Monthly Musical Record*, vol. 61, 1 July 1931, p. 210.
69 These observations based on MB's Note in the published edition of the *Quatre Pièces* (see note below).
70 Julian Bream, in a personal communication with MB, May 2002.
71 Joseph Baruzi, review of a concert on 27 January 1928, *Le Ménéstrel*, 3 February 1928, p. 49 (with thanks to Allan Clive Jones for finding it); translation TS.
72 LB, 'Boulanger the Dedicated', *Sunday Telegraph*, 4 June 1961.
73 LB, n.d. typescript, with pencil annotations in LB's hand, of an illustrated talk about NB, BFP.
74 Alan Kendall, *The Tender Tyrant*, p. 60.
75 LB, 'Boulanger the Dedicated', *Sunday Telegraph*, 4 June 1961.
76 Alan Kendall, *The Tender Tyrant*, p. 95.
77 L. Rosenstiel, *Nadia Boulanger*, p. 226.
78 LB, 'Boulanger the Dedicated', *Sunday Telegraph*, 4 June 1961.
79 Aaron Copland, 'Intro of NB as Teacher', handwritten notes, The Aaron Copland Collection, Aaron Copland Fund for Music, New York.
80 DPM.
81 *Ibid.*
82 Aaron Copland, 'Intro of NB as Teacher', handwritten notes, The Aaron Copland Collection, Aaron Copland Fund for Music, New York.
83 DPM.
84 Alan Kendall, *The Tender Tyrant*, p. 57.
85 DPM.
86 *Ibid.*
87 *Ibid.*

88 LB, 'Nadia Boulanger as Teacher', *The Monthly Musical Record*, 1 January 1931.
89 L. Rosenstiel, *Nadia Boulanger*, p. 355.
90 DPM.
91 *Ibid.*
92 LB, in a interview with Carolyn Scott, 'Portrait of a very cultivated person', *Catholic Herald* (December 1976), BFP.
93 LB, n.d. typescript, with pencil annotations in LB's hand, of an illustrated talk about NB, BFP. LB used the large, 1860 Bach Gesellschaft editions, which he bought in a secondhand bookshop in Paris, and are now in the possession of his son Julian; Cantata 42, *Am Abende aber desselbigen Sabbats*, has been so well used that one of the pages has been torn.
94 DPM.
95 I. Markevitch, *Être et avoir été*, p. 133 (translation TS).
96 L. Rosenstiel, *Nadia Boulanger*, p. 263.
97 I. Markevitch, *Être et avoir été*, p. 134 (translation TS).
98 RN, obituary, 'Sir Lennox Berkeley', *The Independent*, 27 December 1989.
99 I. Markevitch, *Être et avoir été*, p. 70 (translation TS).
100 LB, 'Music in Paris', *Monthly Musical Record*, vol. 61, March 1931, p. 82.
101 LB, Diary, 16 April 1972, BFP.
102 I. Markevitch, *Être et avoir été*, p. 161 (translation TS).
103 *Ibid*, p. 162 (translation TS).
104 *Ibid.*
105 LB, 'A Centenary Tribute' [to Igor Stravinsky], *The Musical Times*, June 1982.
106 PD discusses this ballet in MLB, pp. 21–4. See also SRC, pp. 57 and 132–3.
107 *The Times*, 13 September 1929.
108 LB to BBC, 15 April 1929, BBCWAC.
109 K. A. Wright to LB, 23 April 1929, BBCWAC.
110 LB to BBC, June 1929 [received by the BBC on 28 June], BBCWAC.
111 BBC to LB, 29 June 1929, BBCWAC.
112 LB to BBC, 2 September 1929, BBCWAC.
113 BBC to LB, 3 September 1929, BBCWAC.
114 *Ibid*, 7 September.
115 Typewritten scripts on foolscap and quarto for articles on Ravel in *Composer*, no. 43, Spring 1972, and [annotated in LB's own hand] in *Adam International Review*, nos. 404–6, 1978, pp. 13–17.
116 According to the pianist Gordon Bryan, quoted in Demuth, *Ravel*, p. 41.

117 *Ibid*, pp. 40–1.
118 Obituary, 'Gordon Bryan', *The Times*, 22 November 1957.
119 According to the pianist Gordon Bryan, quoted in Demuth, *Ravel*, p. 41; and *The Times*, 20 October 1928.
120 *Manchester Guardian*, 11 October 1928.
121 Colin Mawby, former Master of Music at Westminster Cathedral, in a n.d. and unidentified newspaper article [probably *Catholic Herald*, 1978], BFP.
122 RN, *The Harlequin Years*, 105–6.
123 According to the pianist Gordon Bryan, quoted in Demuth, *Ravel*, p. 41.
124 *The Times*, 24 October 1928.

CHAPTER ELEVEN

1 G. Larner, *Maurice Ravel*, p. 203. Henri Prunières, editor of *La revue musicale*, described it as 'a picture in the manner of Goya' (RN, *The Harlequin Years*, p. 171).
2 G. Larner., *Maurice Ravel*, p. 203.
3 Alan Riding, 'The Secret Pan', a review of Benjamin Ivry's biography of Ravel, *New York Times*, 3 December 2000.
4 G. Larner, *Maurice Ravel*, p. 207.
5 *The Guardian*, 25 April 2001.
6 LB, Diary, 4 February 1969.
7 RN, *The Harlequin Years*, pp. 169–72.
8 Tamara Talbot Rice, *Tamara*, pp. 195–6.
9 G. Larner, *Maurice Ravel*, p. 34.
10 LB, 'Music in Paris', *Monthly Musical Record*, vol. 63, June 1933, p. 112.
11 D. Vaughan, *Frederick Ashton*, p. 26.
12 Julie Kavanagh, *Secret Muses*, pp. 102–3; obituary, Ida Rubinstein, *The Times*, 21 October 1960.
13 *Ibid.*, p. 109.
14 *Ibid.*, pp. 103–5.
15 According to RN, to whom he spoke about it (RN, email to TS, 5 September 2007).
16 *Ibid.*, and Edward Burra to Barbara Ker-Seymer, 9 October 1928, quoted in Julie Kavanagh, *Secret Muses*, pp. 92–3 (and I am indebted to Mrs Kathleen Walker for drawing my attention to this reference).
17 J. D. K Lloyd Photo Album 2 (1923–8) [Llyfr Ffoto Album 153, National Library of Wales].
18 Julie Kavanagh, *Secret Muses*, p. 92.
19 Edward Burra to Barbara Ker-Seymer, 9 October 1928, *ibid.*

20 LB to BBC, 2 September 1929, BBCWAC.
21 Holborn electoral roll, 1925, and *Kelly's Directory,* 1925.
22 Anthony Powell, *Messengers of Day*, p. 85, and *Faces in My Time*, p. 16.
23 Tamara Talbot Rice, *Tamara*, pp. 195–6.
24 J. D. K. Lloyd Photo Album 2 (1923–8), [Llyfr Ffoto Album 153, National Library of Wales].
25 FB to TS, 20 November 2005.
26 LB, in a taped interview with PD, 8 March 1985, PDA.
27 Tamara Talbot Rice, *Tamara*, p. 196.
28 LB, Music List, 1925, in Aline Berkeley, Diary, 1925–6, BFP.
29 Obituary, 'Gordon Bryan', *The Times*, 22 November 1957. Bryan died on 19 November 1957, aged 62.
30 Eric Fenby, *Delius*, p. 15.
31 *Ibid.*, p. 27.
32 *Ibid.*, p. 79.
33 Gordon Bryan, 'The Younger English Composers Part V: Lennox Berkeley', *Monthly Musical Record*, vol. 59, June 1929, pp. 161–2.
34 *Ibid.*
35 SRC, p. 255.
36 Graham Parlett, *A Catalogue of the Works of Sir Arnold Bax.*
37 This review is contained in a scrapbook of cuttings preserved at BFP.
38 Gordon Bryan, 'The Younger English Composers Part V: Lennox Berkeley', *Monthly Musical Record*, vol. 59, June 1929, pp. 161–2.
39 Obituary, Gordon Bryan, *The Times*, 22 November 1957.
40 MLB, pp. 20–1.
41 LB, 'Letter from Paris', *Monthly Musical Record*, 1 June 1929.
42 From an interview with Igor Stravinsky by Janet Flanner in 1934, quoted in Vera Stravinsky and Robert Craft, *Stravinsky in Pictures and Documents*, Hutchinson, 1979, p. 323.
43 LB, Diary, 5 January 1973 and 12 December 1978, BFP; and LB, lecture on Paris and Boulanger at the British Institute of Recorded Sound, London, 7 January 1972 (recording preserved, T 581 W, National Sound Archive, British Library).
44 LB, Diary, 12 December 1978, BFP.
45 LB, 'Igor Stravinsky – A Centenary Tribute', *Musical Times*, June 1982.
46 From an interview with Igor Stravinsky by Janet Flanner in 1934, quoted in Vera Stravinsky and Robert Craft, *Stravinsky in Pictures and Documents*, Hutchinson, 1979, p. 323.
47 MB in telephone conversation with TS, 29 October 2005, recalling conversations with his father, in which LB had told him about his Paris encounters with Stravinsky.

48 LB, interview with PD, in MLB, pp. 18–19.
49 LB, *Monthly Musical Record*, vol. 62, March–April 1932, p. 63.
50 LB to NB (TS translation from French), 14 March 1935, FSNB.
51 *The Times*, 13 March 1933; the concert that same night does not seem to have been reviewed in *The Times*.
52 BFP.
53 LB, 'Music in Paris', *Monthly Musical Record*, vol. 59, June 1929, p. 174.
54 L. Rosenstiel, *Nadia Boulanger*, p. 212.
55 B. Ivry, *Francis Poulenc*, p. 80.
56 *Ibid.*, pp. 8 and 156; R. D. E. Burton, *Francis Poulenc*, pp. 61–2, 123.
57 R. D. E. Burton, *Francis Poulenc*, p. 123.
58 LB, Diary, 1 December 1972 (commenting on a 'very good article' about the songs by the accompanist Graham Johnson, in the Royal Academy of Music magazine), BFP.
59 LB, 'Francis Poulenc 1899–1963', *The Musical Times*, March 1963.
60 LB, Address at a Memorial Concert for Poulenc, Arts Council, London, 7 May 1963 (at which BB and PP performed some of Poulenc's songs - *The Times*, 8 May 1963, pays BB, the pianist, rather a back-handed compliment) – annotated typescript, BFP.
61 R. D. E. Burton, *Francis Poulenc*, pp. 46–7.

CHAPTER TWELVE

1 FB, in a taped interview with TS, January 1997.
2 TS, in conversations with FB and Anthony Nunney, at a family gathering at FB's flat in Hereford Mansions on 9 February 2006, and on the telephone on 12 February 2006.
3 Additional information about Frederick Nunney kindly provided by his grandson Anthony Nunney, in conversation with TS, 9 February 2006.
4 FB, on the telephone to TS, 9 January 2006.
5 FB, in conversation with TS at Hereford Mansions, 8 March 2005.
6 Mrs Joy Stibbe née Thornton, a pupil, with FB, 1930–9, in a telephone conversation with TS, 27 October 2001.
7 *Ibid.*

CHAPTER THIRTEEN

1 LB, Diary, 18 August 1978, BFP. See also Paul Johnson, 'Thank God for a wise, truth-telling Pope', *The Spectator*, 14 April 2007.
2 The Revd Arthur Wollaston, 'Cardinal Newman', *The Encyclopaedia Britannica*, vol. xix, Cambridge at the University Press, 1911, p. 519.

3 Evelyn Waugh to E. Sackville-West, 6 August 1949, quoted M. De-la-Noy, *Eddy*, p. 227.
4 Obituary, Tamara Talbot Rice, *The Independent*, 29 September 1993.
5 LB, Diary, 21 April 1975, BFP. See also Appendix 1.
6 LB in an interview with Carolyn Scott, 'Portrait of a very cultivated person', *Catholic Herald* [December 1976], BFP.
7 LB, 'The Old Mass and the New', *Pax – a Benedictine Review*, vol. lxi, Gloucester, Prinknash Abbey, Autumn/Winter 1971.
8 Evelyn Waugh to Julian Jebb – M. Stannard, *Evelyn Waugh*, vol. i, p. 228.
9 Reginald Ellison, a Catholic friend and Oxford contemporary, in an interview with RN, 9 February1989, RNA – though LB told the *Catholic Herald*, in an interview with Carolyn Scott [December 1976], that both his parents were Anglican.
10 Hastings Berkeley, *Japanese Letters: Eastern impressions of western men and manners, as contained in the correspondence of Tokiwara, and Yashiri*, John Murray, 1891, p. 173.
11 Evelyn Waugh, after his conversion on 29 September 1930 – quoted in M. Stannard, *Evelyn Waugh*, vol. i, p. 222.
12 Baptismal Certificate of François Berkeley, 16 October 1929; copy, Diocese of Paris.
13 Feeling a divine call to imitate Christ's life and to preach, St Francis gathered about him a small group of followers and drew up, in about 1209, the rules of life for the monastic order called the Friars Minor, later known as the Franciscans. He died on 3 October 1226 and is commemorated by the Church on 4 October.
14 FB, fragment of a handwritten memo, n.d., BFP.
15 Richard Stoker to TS, 14 July 2003, BFP.
16 LB, Diary, 9–10 November 1968, BFP.
17 DPM.
18 From a taped interview, 22 February1991, PDA.
19 LB, Diary, 1978, BFP.
20 R. D. E. Burton, *Francis Poulenc*, p. 54.
21 LB to James Lees-Milne, 18 November 1951, James Lees-Milne Papers, Beinecke Rare Book and Manuscript Library, Yale University.
22 R. D. E. Burton, *Francis Poulenc*, p. 48.
23 LB to NB, 3 January 1934 (TS translation from French), FSNB.
24 RN, Obituary, 'Lennox Berkeley', *The Independent*, 27 December 1989.
25 Hugues Cuénod, recorded interview with TS, Switzerland, 8–10 July 1994.
26 LB, interview with Christopher Ford, *The Guardian*, 3 August 1973.

27 RN, in conversation with Paul Guinery, 'Choir Works', BBC Radio Three, 11 May 2003.
28 L. Rosenstiel, *Nadia Boulanger*, pp. 217–18 and 240.
29 A. Copland, *The Teacher: Nadia Boulanger*, The Aaron Copland Collection *c*.1900–90, The Library of Congress.
30 L. Rosenstiel, *Nadia Boulanger*, p. 198.
31 *Ibid.*, p. 199.
32 LB to NB, 14 April 1933 (TS translation from French), FSNB.
33 LB to Hélène Kahn-Casella, 16 September and 13 November, 1932, BFP.
34 LB to NB, 5 October 1932 (TS translation from French), FSNB.
35 *Ibid.*, 13 and 18 November 1932.
36 LB to NB, 14 April 1933 (TS translation from French), FSNB.
37 *New York Herald*, Paris, 19 June 1933, LB cuttings album, BFP.
38 LB to Hélène Kahn-Casella, n.d. [June 1933], BFP.
39 Michael Bloch, *James Lees-Milne: The Life*, John Murray, 2009.
40 Robert Calder, *Willie*, p. 209.
41 LB to Alan Searle, n.d. [October/November 1934], W. Somerset Maugham Collection, Howard Gotlieb Archival Research Center, Boston University.

CHAPTER FOURTEEN

1 Somerset Maugham, *Strictly Personal*, p. 2.
2 T. Morgan, *Somerset Maugham*, p. 355.
3 *Ibid.*, and p. 315.
4 Beverley Nichols, *A Case of Human Bondage*, pp. 18–19, 146.
5 Somerset Maugham, *Strictly Personal*, pp. 17–18, 44.
6 Somerset Maugham, *The Summing Up*.
7 Frederic Raphael, 'William Somerset Maugham', *Dictionary of National Biography* 1961–1970, p. 743.
8 Letter from 'George Egerton' (real name Mary Chavelita Dunne Bright, 1859–1945), 10 February 1930, quoted Ted Morgan, *Somerset Maugham*, p. 329.
9 According to FB, who occasionally lunched at the Mauresque in the 1950s and '60s – in conversation with TS, 4 April 2007.
10 Beverley Nichols, *A Case of Human Bondage*, pp. 20, 30, 146.
11 B. Connon, *Somerset Maugham*, p. 93.
12 *Ibid.*; and T. Morgan, *Somerset Maugham*, pp. 314 and 495.
13 Beverley Nichols, *A Case of Human Bondage*, pp. 31, 32, 149.
14 LB to Alan Searle, n.d. [1934], Somerset Maugham Archive, Howard Gotlieb Archival Research Center, Boston University.

15 *Ibid.*, n.d. [? September 1934].
16 *Ibid.*, 1 September [1934].
17 *Ibid.*, n.d. [? September 1934].
18 Guy Little to Alan Searle, 10 May 1934, Somerset Maugham Archive, Howard Gotlieb Archival Research Center, Boston University.
19 *Ibid.*
20 *Ibid.*, n.d. [Spring 1934].
21 *Ibid.*, 16 January 1934.
22 *Ibid.*, 15 April 1934.
23 LB to Alan Searle, n.d. [1934], Somerset Maugham Archive, Howard Gotlieb Archival Research Center, Boston University.
24 Postcard Aline Berkeley to Alan Searle, n.d. [21 December 1934], Somerset Maugham Archive, Howard Gotlieb Archival Research Center, Boston University.
25 According to Arthur Marshall, quoted in Ted Morgan, *Somerset Maugham*, p. 316.
26 LB to Alan Searle, 24 December [1934], Somerset Maugham Archive, Howard Gotlieb Archival Research Center, Boston University.
27 *Ibid.*, 1 September [1934], Somerset Maugham Archive, Howard Gotlieb Archival Research Center, Boston University.
28 Paul Bailey, *Three Queer Lives*, p. 188
29 LB to Alan Searle, n.d. [January 1935], Somerset Maugham Archive, Howard Gotlieb Archival Research Center, Boston University.
30 *Who's Who 1966*, p. 2816.
31 L. P. Hartley to Marie Belloc Lowndes, quoted Adrian Wright, *Foreign Country*, p. 103.
32 LB to Alan Searle, n.d. [September 1934], Somerset Maugham Archive, Howard Gotlieb Archival Research Center, Boston University.
33 Adrian Wright, *Foreign Country*, p. 104.
34 Moura Budberg (1892–1974): see Nina Berberova (trans. from Russian by Marian Schwartz and Richard D. Sylvester), 'Moura – The Dangerous Life of the Baroness Budberg', *New York Review*, 2005.
35 Ted Morgan, *Somerset Maugham*, p. 382.
36 Beverley Nichols, *A Case of Human Bondage*, pp. 95–9.
37 Ted Morgan, *Somerset Maugham*, p. 368.
38 LB to Alan Searle, 24 December [1934], Somerset Maugham Archive, Howard Gotlieb Archival Research Center, Boston University.
39 Richard Davenport-Hines, *A Night at the Majestic*, pp. 63 and 264–5.
40 LB to Alan Searle, n.d. [late summer 1934], Somerset Maugham Archive, Howard Gotlieb Archival Research Center, Boston University.
41 *Ibid.*, 1 September [1934].
42 *Ibid.*, 30 September [1934].

43 *Ibid.*, n.d. [Summer 1934].
44 *Ibid.,* 7 January [1935].
45 *Ibid.*, 24 December 1934.
46 *Ibid.*, 30 September [1934].
47 *Ibid.*, n.d. [January 1935].
48 *Ibid.*, 1 September [1934].
49 *Ibid.*, n.d. [September 1934].
50 *Ibid.*, September 1 [1934].
51 *Ibid.*
52 *Ibid.*, n.d. [September 1934].
53 *Ibid*, 24 December [1934].
54 *Ibid*, n.d. [September 1934].
55 *Ibid*, n.d.
56 Somerset Maugham to Alan Searle, n.d. [?August 1935], Somerset Maugham Archive, Howard Gotlieb Archival Research Center, Boston University; with thanks to Selina Hastings for drawing it to my attention.
57 Frederic Raphael, 'William Somerset Maugham', *Dictionary of National Biography* 1961–1970, p. 743.
58 Robert Calder, *Willie*, p. 247.
59 LB to Alan Searle, n.d. [January 1935] , Somerset Maugham Archive, Howard Gotlieb Archival Research Center, Boston University.
60 *Ibid.*
61 LB, interview with C.B. Cox, Allan Young and Michael Schmidt, *Poetry Nation*, no. 2 , 1974.
62 Mrs Pauline Challoner, solicitor, Nice, to FB, 18 April 1995, BFP.
63 Edward Lockspeiser, 'The Music of Lennox Berkeley', *The Listener*, 10 July 1947.
64 LB, interview on BBC World Service, 11 June 1969, transcript in BFP.
65 LB to Alan Searle, n.d. [September 1934], Somerset Maugham Archive, Howard Gotlieb Archival Research Center, Boston University.
66 *Ibid.* [October/November 1934] and 7 January [1934], Somerset Maugham Archive, Howard Gotlieb Archival Research Center, Boston University.
67 SRC, 251.
68 LB to Alan Pryce-Jones, 24 September, no year [?1933 or 4], Beinecke Rare Book and Manuscript Library, Yale University.
69 *The Chesterian*, vol. xv, no. 114, April 1934, J. & W. Chester.
70 LB to Alan Searle, n.d. [summer, 1934], Somerset Maugham Archive, Howard Gotlieb Archival Research Center, Boston University.
71 *Ibid.* [Autumn 1934].
72 *Ibid.* [October 1934].

73 *Ibid.* [September 1934].
74 *Ibid.* [October 1934].
75 Harriet Cohen, *A Bundle of Time*, p. 179.
76 LB, interview with C.B. Cox, Allan Young and Michael Schmidt, *Poetry Nation*, no. 2 , 1974.
77 *Ibid.*
78 LB to Alan Searle, n.d. [2 December 1934], Somerset Maugham Archive, Howard Gotlieb Archival Research Center, Boston University.
79 LB, *Monthly Musical Record*, vol. 64, June 1934, p. 110.
80 *The Times*, 29 November 1934.
81 *Ibid.*
82 LB to Alan Searle, n.d. [2 December 1934], Somerset Maugham Archive, Howard Gotlieb Archival Research Center, Boston University.
83 *Ibid.*
84 *Ibid.*, n.d. [December 1934].
85 *Ibid.* [August 1934].
86 *Ibid.* [December 1934].
87 *Evening News*, 2 October 1935, goes for Prague; *The Star*, 2 October 1935, goes for Carlsbad (LB cuttings book, BFP). See also *The Musical Times*, vol. 76, no. 1104 (February 1935), p. 121.
88 LB to Alan Searle, 24 December [1934], Somerset Maugham Archive, Howard Gotlieb Archival Research Center, Boston University.
89 Harriet Cohen, *A Bundle of Time*, p. 247.
90 *Ibid.*
91 *News Chronicle*, 2 October 1935.
92 *The Times*, 2 October 1935.
93 *Sunday Times*, 6 October 1935.
94 J. A. Forsyth, *The Star*, 2 October 1935.
95 *London Evening News*, 2 October 1935.
96 *Bristol Evening World*, 15 October 1935.
97 Richard Amey, reviewing a performance of LB's *String Quartet No. 1* by the Maggini Quartet, in Hove on 3 December 2006, *Worthing Today*, December 2006.
98 Aline Berkeley to her sister Annie, Baroness d'Eppinghoven, n.d. [15 November 1935], BFP; and LB to NB (TS translation from French), 19 January 1936, FSNB.
99 *The Times*, 22 November 1935.
100 *The Lady*, 28 November 1935.
101 *Liverpool Daily Post*, 20 November 1935.
102 *The Times*, 21 November 1935.
103 LB to NB (TS translation from French), 19 January 1936, FSNB.
104 *Ibid.*

105 *Ibid.*
106 LB to his Aunt Annie, Baroness d'Eppinghoven, 1 January 1936, BFP.
107 *Ibid.*
108 LB to the BBC, 13 August 1938, BBCWAC.
109 LB to NB (TS translation from French), 19 January 1936, FSNB.
110 *Ibid.*
111 *Ibid.*

CHAPTER FIFTEEEN

1 FB in conversation with TS, 23 June 2004.
2 Stephen Watson to FB, 18 March 2005, BFP.
3 FB, in conversation with TS, 26 March 2005.
4 *Ibid.*, 9 March 2005.
5 *St Helen's School Magazine*, Autumn Term 1935, pp. 1, 10, 11, 16, 18, BFP.
6 *Ibid.*, Summer Term 1936, pp. 4, 5, 11, 24.
7 FB, in conversation with TS, 23 November 2006.
8 *St Helen's School Magazine*, Summer Term 1937, pp. 1, 4, 19.

CHAPTER SIXTEEN

1 According to the date '1933' inscribed, with nothing else, after the closing bar of the final chorus on p. 164 of the MS (SRC, p. 189).
2 From a notice of 'New and Important Issues', published by J. & W. Chester Ltd, in *The Musical Quarterly*, Oxford, *c.* 1936 – see mq.oxfordjournals.org/cgi/issue_pdf.
3 LB to BBC, 3 May 1936, BBCWAC.
4 *Ibid.*
5 LB to PB, n.d. but probably 15 June 1936, B–MA.
6 *Ibid.*
7 See MLB, 40–4.
8 BB to PB 22 June 1936, BPL.
9 BB, Diary, 19 June 1936, BPL.
10 This letter from BB to LB, written some time between 19 and 23 June 1936, is lost, but LB refers to it in his reply, 23 June 1936, BPL.
11 LB to BB 23 June 1936, BPL.
12 LB, Diary, n.d. but about 1969, BFP.
13 Basil Douglas, Diary, 16 June 1936, B–MA.
14 *Ibid.*, 19 June 1936, B–MA.
15 *Ibid.*, interview with PD, 28 November 1990, PDA.

16 Our Music Critic, 'The Career of Lennox Berkeley', *The Times*, 19 October 1956.
17 MLB, p. 33.
18 LFAL, p. 923.
19 Graham Johnson, *Britten, Voice & Piano*, pp. 54–5.
20 LB to BB, 22 October 1936, BPL.
21 *Ibid.*, 21 April 1940, BPL.
22 Profile LB by Christopher Ford, *The Guardian*, 3 August 1973.
23 LB to NB (TS translation from French), 4 January 1937, FSNB.
24 See Copland's account of 'A Visit to Snape' – and his MS notes for this account – in The Aaron Copland Collection, The Library of Congress, online at http://memory.loc.gov.
25 MLB, p. 33.
26 R. Stradling, *History and Legend*, pp. 76–7.
27 LFAL, pp. 383–4.
28 John Fuller, *W. H. Auden: A Commentary*, p. 171
29 BB to John Pounder, 23 June 1936, LFAL, p. 429. For biographical note on Pounder see LFAL, p. 84.
30 Graham Johnson, *Britten, Voice and Pianio – Lectures on the Vocal Music of Benjamin Britten.*
31 BB, Diary, 1 December 1936, BPL.
32 This was the opinion of Elizabeth Sweeting of Glyndebourne Festival Opera, based on her observation of BB during the production of *Albert Herring* in 1947 (HC, p. 261).
33 LB to BB, 27 December 1937, BPL.
34 EFB Diary, 6 July 1945, BFP.
35 BB to PB, 16 July 1936, B–MA.
36 BB to his sister Beth Britten, 9 July 1936.
37 *Ibid.*
38 Email Dr Richard Thompson to TS, 13 May 2006.
39 LB to BB, 25 August 1935 [actually 1936], BFP.
40 LB to PB, 16 July 1936, B–MA.
41 LB to BB, 18 July 1936, BPL.
42 BB to his mother, [28 July 1936], BPL.
43 LB to BB, 22 October 1936, BPL.
44 LB, 'Reflections on Old Age and Death', in R. Ricketts (ed.), *Bid the World Goodnight*, London Search Press, 1981, pp. 19–21.
45 PP, talking about BB at the time he first met him, in an interview with Donald Mitchell in Tony Palmer's 1980 London Weekend Television film *A Time There Was: A Profile of Benjamin Britten*, quoted in HC, pp. 112–13.
46 BB Diary, 19 January 1937, BPL.

47 *Ibid.*
48 BB to his sister Beth, 9 July 1936, LFAL.
49 BB, Diary, 16 July 1936, BPL.
50 BB to his mother, 28 July 1936, BPL.
51 BB, Diary, 26 July 1936, BPL.
52 BB to his mother, 28 July 1936, BPL.
53 LB to BB 25 August 1936 [though letter mistakenly gives 1935], BPL.
54 BB Diary, 19 July 1936, BPL.
55 *Ibid.*, 28 July 1936, BPL.
56 HC, p. 261.
57 LB to FB, 10 August 1946, BFP.
58 BB Diary, LFAL, p. 439, BPL.
59 LFAL, p. 434.
60 LB to BB, 25 August 1936 [though letter mistakenly gives 1935], BPL.
61 BB to his mother 28 July 1936, BPL.
62 LB to PB, 2 August 1936, B–MA.
63 HC, pp. 200–3, quoting first the librettist and director Eric Crozier, then the composer Colin Matthews.
64 From an interview with Michael Berkeley in the ATV Network film *Composers* made in the summer of 1980 and broadcast on 14 May 1981; director Richie Stewart, producer J. B. J. Berrow (copy in BFP).
65 LB, interview with PD, London, 8 March 1985, PDA.
66 LB, Diary, 14 October 1976, quoting the French-Rumanian composer Marcel Mihalovici, BFP.
67 BB, Diary, 29 July 1936, BPL.
68 A. Copland, 'A visit to Snape' in MS (for Anthony Gishford (ed.), *Tribute to Benjamin Britten on his Fiftieth Birthday*, London, Faber & Faber, 1963), The Aaron Copland Collection ca 1900–90, The Library of Congress.
69 HC, p. 78.
70 LB to PB 13 October 1936, B–MA.
71 BB, Diary, 28 July 1936, BPL.
72 *Ibid.*, 28 July 1937, BPL.
73 LB, interview with C.B. Cox, Allan Young and Michael Schmidt, Poetry Nation 2, 1974.
74 BB, Diary, 26 July 193, BPL.
75 LB to BB, 17 July 1940, BFP.
76 BB, Diary 29 July 1936, BPL.
77 *Ibid.*, 30 July, BPL.
78 C. Headington, *Britten*, pp. 34–6.
79 Edward Mendelson, *Early Auden*, p. 211.
80 LFAL, p. 402.

81 *Ibid.*, p. 404.
82 J. Bridcut, *Britten's Children*, p. 52. For the whole Morris story see *Ibid.*, pp. 46–54.
83 Donald Mitchell, 'Introduction: Happy Families?', LFAL, vol. 3, pp. 3–52.
84 R. Christiansen, 'Protecting the flames of genius', *The Spectator*, 16 October 2004, p. 70.
85 J. Bridcut, *Britten's Children*, pp. 6–7.
86 *Ibid.*, p. 2.
87 See David Hemmings' rather sad account of this phenomenon in John Bridcut, *Britten's Children*, p. 210.
88 Peter Parker, 'Only an old-fashioned schoolboy', *Daily Telegraph*, 10 June 2006.
89 BB to Enid Slater 7 November 1939, quoted LFAL, pp. 724–5.
90 BB to his mother, 28 July 1936.
91 BB, Diary, 30 July 1936, BPL.
92 LB to PB, 2 August 1936, B–MA.
93 Colin Mason, 'The Progress of Lennox Berkeley', *The Listener*, 27 September 1956, p. 485.
94 BB, Diary, 30 July 1936, BPL.
95 BB to his mother, 28 July 1936.
96 Donald Mitchell, Introduction, LFAL, p. 18.
97 Beatrice Playne, niece of LB's elderly admirer Gladys Bryans, in conversation with RN, Malvern, 4 December 1986, RNA, and FB, in conversation with TS, 26 February 2004.

CHAPTER SEVENTEEN

1 LB to PB, 2 August 1936, B–MA.
2 *Ibid*, 13 October 1936, B–MA.
3 LB, in an interview with C. B. Cox, Allan Young and Michael Schmidt, *Poetry Nation,* no. 2, 1974.
4 LB to NB, 25 January 1944, in English, FSNB.
5 LB to BB, 22 October 1936, BPL.
6 BB, Diary, 10 November 1936, BPL.
7 *Ibid.*, 20 November 1936, BPL.
8 Sylvia Kahan, *Music's Modern Muse*, p. 337. *Deux Poèmes* had not been added to the programme when *The Times* announced the concert on 18 December 1936.
9 LFAL 457.
10 BB, Diary, 19 November 1936, BPL.
11 L. Rosenstiel, *Nadia Boulanger*, p. 268.

12 LB to NB (TS translated from French), dated 'Mardi' [17 November 1936], FSNB.
13 *The Times*, 25 November 1936.
14 *Ibid.*
15 See HC, pp. 163–5.
16 Marjorie Fass to Daphne Oliver, December 1937, LFAL, p. 19.
17 BB, Diary, 15 March 1937, LFAL, p. 483.
18 Edward Mendelson, *The English Auden*, p. xix.
19 BB, Diary, 5 November 1936, BPL.
20 BB, Diary, 1 December 1936, BPL.
21 LFAL, p. 461.
22 BB, Diary, 10 December 1936, BPL.
23 LB to BB, 19 May 1937, BPL.
24 BB, Diary, 10 December 1936, BPL.
25 *Ibid.*
26 BB, Diary, 29 November 1936, BPL.
27 BB, Diary, 8 January 1937, BPL.
28 *Ibid.*, 12 January 1937.
29 *Ibid.*
30 This copy is now in the possession of the B–MA (email Richard Thompson to TS, 28 February 2006).
31 BB, Diary, 31 January 1937, BPL.
32 LB to NB, 4 January 1937, FSNB.
33 HC, p. 97.
34 BB, Diary, 5 March 1937, BPL.
35 BB, Diary, 12 February 1937, BPL.
36 *Ibid.*, 14 March 1937.
37 *Ibid.*, 13 March 1937.
38 C. Headington, *Peter Pears*, p. 64.
39 Richard Thompson, email to TS, 19 February 2006.
40 BB, quoted by C. Headington, *Peter Pears*, p. 64. See also email from Dr Richard Thompson, owner of the Burra–Moody Archive, to TS 7 July 2002.
41 BB, Diary, 14 March 1937, BPL.
42 E. M. Forster to Christopher Isherwood, 28 January 1937, The Papers of Edward Morgan Forster GBR/0272/PP/EMF, King's College Archive Centre, Cambridge.
43 PB to Edward Dent, 22 February 1937 (The Papers of Edward Dent GBR/0272/PP/EJD, King's College Archive Centre, Cambridge).
44 From information in a letter from E. M. Forster to Christopher Isherwood, 28 January 1937 (The Papers of Edward Dent GBR/0272/PP/EJD, King's College Archive Centre, Cambridge) and in

an email from the owner of the Burra-Moody Archive, Richard Thompson, to TS, 17 May 2007.

45 PB to Edward Dent, 22 February 1937 (The Papers of Edward Dent GBR/0272/PP/EJD, King's College Archive Centre, Cambridge).
46 BB, Diary, 14 March 1937, BPL.
47 *Ibid.*, 13 March 1937.
48 BB, Diary, 24 March 1937, BPL.
49 *Ibid.* , 8, 9 and 11 April 1937, BPL.
50 Postcard LB to PB, 7 April 1937, B–MA.
51 Rosamunde Strode, former Keeper of MSS at BPL, to Stewart Craggs, 26 September 1986, SRC, p. 62.
52 BB, Diary, 6 April 1937.
53 LB to BB, 11 January 1938, BFP.
54 *Ibid.*, 19 April 1938, BFP.
55 MLB, p. 35.
56 LB, 'Note', Lennox Berkeley and Benjamin Britten, *Mont Juic*, Boosey & Hawkes (HPS [Hawkes Pocket Scores] no. 951), [1979].
57 MB, in a telephone conversation with TS, 21 June 2004.
58 *Ibid.*, 21 September 2005.
59 BB, Diary, 11 April 1937, BPL.
60 *Ibid.*, 4 April 1937.
61 *Ibid.*, 12, 19, 21 and 23–5 April 1937, BPL. LB to Burra, n.d. [?20 April 1937], confirms the plan to visit the house for sale, B–MA.
62 Former Aircraftman Tony Headon, in Don Belt, 'Lawrence of Arabia', *National Geographic*, January 1999.
63 R. Thompson, 'Peter Burra' and 'Air Smash' [an account not only of the death of PB but of his interlinking friendships with LB, BB and PP], unpublished MSS, 2002; and R. Thompson, 'The Anderson–Burra Flying Accident 27/4/37', unpublished MS, February 2006, B–MA.
64 Simon Nowell Smith to Mrs Ella Burra, 28 April 1937, B–MA.
65 PB to his mother, 25 April 1937, B–MA.
66 R. Thompson, 'Air Smash' , unpublished MS, 2002; and 'The Anderson–Burra Flying Accident 27/4/37, unpublished MS, February 2006, B–MA.
67 *Ibid.*, 'The Anderson-Burra Flying Accident 27/4/37', unpublished MS, February 2006, B–MA.
68 *Newbury Weekly News*, 29 April 1937.
69 Former Aircraftman Tony Headon, in Don Belt, 'Lawrence of Arabia', *National Geographic*, January 1999.
70 *Newbury Weekly News*, 29 April 1937.
71 R. Thompson, 'Air Smash', unpublished MS, 2002, B–MA; and *Newbury Weekly News*, 29 April and 20 May 1937; and letter to TS, 13 May 2006.

72 *Ibid.*, 'The Anderson–Burra Flying Accident 27/4/37, unpublished MS, February 2006, B–MA; email to TS, 19 February 2006; and telephone conversation with TS, 17 February 2006.
73 *Newbury Weekly News*, 20 May 1937.
74 R. Thompson, *The Anderson–Burra Flying Accident 27/4/37*, unpublished MS, February 2006, B–MA.
75 J. R. Ackerley to Mrs Burra, 5 May 1937, B–MA.
76 PB (ed. R. Thompson), 'Spencer's Oratory', an essay on Stanley Spencer's First World War murals at the Sandham Memorial Chapel at Burghclere in Hampshire, MS, n.d. [?1934], B–MA.
77 BB, Diary, 27 April 1937, BPL.
78 R. Thompson, 'Air Smash', unpublished MS, 2002, B–MA.
79 LB to BB, 8 May 1937, BPL.
80 HC, p. 98.
81 R. Thompson, 'Air Smash', unpublished MS, 2002, B–MA; and email Dr Thompson to TS, 7 July 2002.
82 R. Stradling, *History and Legend – Writing the International Brigades*, p. 34.
83 PP in *The Tenor Man's Story*, a Central Television documentary film by Donald Mitchell and Barrie Gavin, 1985, quoted by C. Headington, *Peter Pears*, p. 64.
84 Richard Thompson to TS, 13 May 2006.
85 BB, Diary, 7 May 1937, LFAL, p. 490.
86 BB, Diary, 7 May 1937, BPL.
87 *Ibid.*, 29 April 1937, BPL.
88 LB, Diary, 6 September 1973, BFP.
89 Their daughter Harriet Frazer, in conversation with TS, 22 April 2002.
90 LB to BB, 8 May 1937, BPL.
91 *Ibid.*, 19 May 1937, BPL.
92 BB, Diary, 18 May 1937, BPL.
93 *Ibid.*, 3 July and 29 June 1937, BPL; BB to Nell Burra, 14 July 1937, BPL; and WS to BB, 13 July 1941, JWP.
94 *Ibid.*, 8 July 1937, BPL.
95 LFAL, pp. 495–6, and HC, p. 117.
96 BB, Diary, 8 September 1937, BPL.
97 LB to BB, 19 May 1937, BPL.
98 Auden's phrase: J. Bridcut, *Britten's Children*, p. 6.
99 *Ibid.*
100 BB, Diary, 26 June 1937, BPL; J. Bridcut, *Britten's Children*, p. 47.
101 *Ibid.*, 11 October 1937; J. Bridcut, *Britten's Children*, p. 53.
102 *Ibid.*, 3 July 1937.
103 G. Johnson, 'Beginnings (Auden) and Ends (Eliot)' from *Britten, Voice*

and Piano - Lectures on the Vocal Music of Benjamin Britten, p. 166. See also Donald Mitchell's Note on Auden and Britten, LFAL, pp. 379–84.

104 W. H. Auden, 'Underneath the abject willow', *The English Auden.*
105 G. Johnson, *Britten, Voice and Piano*, p. 150.
106 BB, Diary, 15 October 1937, BPL.
107 LB to BB, n.d. (probably 20 November 1937), BPL.
108 BB, Diary, 8 January 1937, BPL.
109 G. Johnson, *Britten, Voice and Piano*, p. 160.
110 W. H. Auden (ed. Edward Mendelson), Poem XXXII (For Benjamin Britten), 'Poems 1931–6', *The English Auden*, Faber & Faber, 1977.
111 *Five Poems* [of W. H. Auden, 1958].
112 LB, in an interview with C. B. Cox, Allan Young and Michael Schmidt, *Poetry Nation*, no. 2, 1974.
113 W. H. Auden to LB, 9 June [1957], BFP.
114 LB, 'Music as it was', MS notes, *c.* 1974, BFP.
115 An observation by the composer Nicholas Maw, passed on to TS by MB, 21 September 2005.
116 MLB, pp. 37–40.
117 BB, Diary, 28 April 1937, BPL.
118 PB to BB, n.d., but must be July 1936, BPL.
119 LB to BB, 11 January 1938, BFP.
120 Donald Mitchell and Hans Keller (eds.), *Benjamin Britten: A Commentary on His Works from a Group of Specialists*, Rockliff, 1952, p. 288.
121 *Ibid.*
122 See LFAL, pp. 498–500.
123 LB to BB, 30 September 1937, BPL.
124 BB, Diary, 7 October 1937, BPL.
125 LB (TS translation from French) to NB, 18 October 1937, FSNB.
126 Robin Hull, 'The Style of Lennox Berkeley', *Chesterian*, April 1950, pp. 84–7; MLB, pp. 28–9.
127 MLB, p. 29.
128 LB to Julian Herbage, 14 October 1937, BBCWAC.
129 Julian Herbage to LB, 15 October 1937, BBCWAC.
130 LB to Christopher [? Headington], 15 March 1953, CMA.
131 LB (TS translation from French) to NB, 18 October 1937, FSNB; and, for details of the concert: D. Bayes, 'Notes of the Term 1938' [at Sir George Monoux College, Walthamstow], http://www.oldmonovians.com/text2/notesofterm1938.htm.
132 LB to NB, 26 October 1951, in French, FSNB.
133 BB, Diary, 19 October 1937, BPL.
134 *Ibid.*, 23 September 1937, BPL.

135 *Ibid.*, 27 March 1936.
136 Richard Wigmore, 'A Composer Writes', *BBC Music Magazine*, August 2003.
137 BB, Diary, 23 September 1937, BPL.
138 Harriet Cohen, *A Bundle of Time*, p. 247.
139 'Puppet Show 1938' flyer, BFP; LFAL, pp. 477–9; SRC, 64; correspondence Edmund Gray and FB, 2001, BFP; and R. Morphet, 'Introduction', from Binyon, *Eric Ravilious*, pp. 14–16.
140 Footnote, LFAL, p. 1334. Group Theatre's biographer Michael Sidnell makes no reference to the production (M. Sidnell, *Dances of Death*).
141 Group Theatre programme, 27 June 1939, in the possession of Dr Richard Thompson, B–MA.
142 BB to Spender, 26 May 1938, BPL.
143 Judith LeGrove and others, *The Darkened World - Catalogue* [of an exhibition exploring artists' responses to war], Aldeburgh, BPL, 2002, p. 36.
144 LB, in an interview with C. B. Cox, Allan Young and Michael Schmidt, *Poetry Nation* , no. 2, 1974.
145 Mervyn Horder (1910–97), in a taped conversation with Dr Richard Thompson, mid-1990s, B–MA.
146 LB to BB, n.d. [December 1938], BPL.
147 G. Johnson, *Britten, Voice and Piano*, p. 55.
148 BB, Diary, 31 October 1937, BPL.
149 *Ibid.*, 4 November 1937, BPL.
150 LB to NB (TS translation from French), n.d. [5 November 1937], FSNB.
151 Boyd Neel, 'The String Orchestra', in Mitchell and Keller, *Benjamin Britten*, LFAL, pp. 501–2.

CHAPTER EIGHTEEN

1 P. Leigh Fermor, *A Time to Keep Silence*, p. 53.
2 LB to BB, 28 December 1937, BPL.
3 LB to NB, 29 December 1937, FSNB.
4 LB to BB, 28 December 1937, BPL.
5 BB, Diary, 20 July 1936, BPL.
6 LB to BB 23 January 1938, BPL.
7 BB, Diary, 20 July 1936, BPL.
8 D. Kerner, 'Ravels Tod', *Münchener medizinische Wochenschrift*, no. 117 (4), 4 April 1975, pp. 591–6.
9 Benjamin Ivry, *Maurice Ravel*, quotiong an eminent neurologist.
10 LB, 'Maurice Ravel', *Adam International Review*, vol. xli, 1978, pp. 16–17
11 *Ibid.*, p. 17.

12 *Ibid.*
13 LB to NB (TS translation from French), 29 December 1937, FSNB.
14 LB to BB, 28 December 1937, BPL.
15 LB to NB (TS translation from French), 10 January 1938, FSNB.
16 LB, Diary, 2 November 1973 (after visiting his former pupil Christopher Headington in Oxford, and reading with him the score of *Apollon Musagète*), BFP.
17 LB to BB, 11 January 1938, BPL.
18 *Ibid.*, 23 January 1938, BPL, and SRC, p. 19.
19 H. Cohen, *A Bundle of Time*, p. 86 (she refers to 1924 but means 1934).
20 BB, Diary, 26 March 1938, BPL.
21 MLB, p. 49.
22 Programme, Gala Performance of Ballet, Sadler's Wells Theatre, 10 May 1938, Archives, Royal Opera House, Covent Garden.
23 Horace Horsnell, *The Observer*, 15 May 1938.
24 F. Hall, *Modern English Ballet*, p. 96.
25 *The Times*, 11 May 1938. The score was rediscovered in 2004 and recorded by the Royal Ballet Sinfonia conducted by Barry Wordsworth on the CD *Sir Frederick Ashton Ballets* (Dutton Digital CDLX 7149). For a fuller description of the ballet see Vaughan, D., *Frederick Ashton and his Ballets*, pp. 164–5. Two months after the premiere of Berkeley's *The Judgment of Paris*, another ballet with the same name was given its first performance in London by the Ballet Club, Mercury Theatre, with music adapted from Kurt Weill's *Die Dreigroschenoper* and choreography by Antony Tudor.
26 Memo H. Murrill to J. Herbage, 29 July 1938, BBCWAC.
27 LB to BB, 21 November 1939, BFP.
28 Basil Douglas, interview with RN, RNA.
29 BB, Diary, 10 May 1938, BPL.
30 Julie Kavanagh, *Secret Muses*, p. 192.
31 BB to Sophie Wyss, 26 June 1938, BPL.
32 Julie Kavanagh, *Secret Muses*, pp. 236–7.
33 Richard Stoker to TS, 23 March 2004.
34 FB, in a telephone conversation with TS, 16 April 2008.
35 LB, interview with PD, London, 8 March 1985, PDA.
36 LB, 'The Musician Talks', *The Times*, n.d. [Spring, 1959], BFP.
37 BB, Diary, 12 March 1938, BPL.
38 Beth Britten, *My Brother Benjamin*, p. 106.
39 BB to Henry Boys, n.d. [between 26 February and before 2 March 1938], LFAL 551.
40 LB to BB, 19 April 1938, BPL.
41 *Ibid.*, and BB, Diary, 21 May 1938, BPL.

42 HC, pp. 117–18.
43 W. H. Auden, 'Last Will and Testament', *Letters from Iceland*, p. 238.
44 Simon Tait, 'Focusing on the Thirties', *Telegraph Sunday Magazine*, 16 June 1985; Terence Pepper, 'Introduction', and Arthur Strong, 'Working with Howard Coster', *Howard Coster's Celebrity Portraits*.
45 Terence Pepper, 'Introduction', *Howard Coster's Celebrity Portraits*, p. x.
46 BB, Diary, 30 March 1938, BPL.
47 Arthur Strong, 'Working with Howard Coster', *Howard Coster's Celebrity Portraits*, p. xiv.
48 Nicholas Maw to RN, 13 October 1991, RNA.
49 BB, Diary, 12 June 1938, BPL.
50 *Ibid.*, 14 June 1938, BPL.
51 Julian Bream, MLB, p. 49.
52 MLB, p. 41.
53 LFAL, p. 561.
54 *Ibid.*
55 LB to NB, in French, 25 June 1938, FSNB.
56 LB to Hélène Kahn-Casella, 28 August 1938 (TS translation from French), BFP.
57 LB to BB, n.d. [*c.* 21 June 1938], BPL.
58 LB to NB, 25 June 1938 (TS translation from French), FSNB, and LB to Hélène Kahn-Casella, 28 August 1938 (TS translation from French), BFP.
59 LB to BB, 5 January 1940, BFP.
60 *Ibid.* and LB to NB 25 June 1938 (TS translation from French), FSNB.
61 BB to Ralph Hawkes, 28 June 1938, BPL.
62 See Copland's account of 'A Visit to Snape' – and his MS notes for this account – in The Aaron Copland Collection, The Library of Congress, online at http://memory.loc.gov.
63 LB to BB, 21 July 1938, BPL.
64 LFAL, pp. 563 and 568; J.Bridcut, *Britten's Children*, pp. 56–7.
65 Gustel Scherchen was the secretary of J. B. Trend, who was the Professor of Spanish at Cambridge (LFAL, p. 612).
66 BB to WS, n.d. [25 June 1938], BPL.
67 From the Mentorn TV film *Britten's Children* (director John Bridcut), first shown on BBC 2, 5 June 2004.
68 J. Bridcut, *Britten's Children*, p. 61 – but a small black-and-white photo (showing Wulff wearing round gold-rimmed spectacles), which WS sent to BB in a letter, 5 April 1940 [JWP] suggests he was dark-haired, not blond.
69 Transcript of a taped interview between WS and Donald Mitchell, London 15 September 1989, BPL.

70 WS, email to TS, 3 September 2008.
71 From the Mentorn TV film *Britten's Children* (director John Bridcut), first shown on BBC 2, 5 June 1004.
72 WS, email to Tina Morrow, 9 June 2004, JWP.
73 See LFAL, note 1, pp. 574–5, and HC, p. 121.
74 LB to BB, 21 July 1938, BPL.
75 LB to BBC, 13 August [?1938], BBCWAC.
76 BB to Wulff Scherchen, 1 August 1938, LFAL, p. 573.
77 BB to WS, 21 September 1938, JWP.
78 WS to Donald Mitchell, email, 9 June 2004, JWP.
79 WS to TS, email, 3 September 2008.
80 LB to NB, 30 September 1938 (TS translation from French), FSNB.
81 BB to Ralph Hawkes, 29 September 1938.
82 BB to WS, 10 October 1938, JWP.
83 LB to NB, 30 September 1938 (TS translation from French), FSNB.
84 LB to BB, 21 November 1939, BFP.
85 John Bridcut, by telephone to TS, 11 August 2008.
86 LB to BB, n.d. [4, 11 or 18 December 1938], BFP.
87 *Ibid.*, 24 December 1938.
88 BB to PP, 24 October 1937, LFAL, p. 518.
89 LB to NB, 10 November [1938] (TS translation from French), FSNB.
90 LB to Aaron Copland, 20 December 1938, BPL.
91 LB interview with PD, London, 8 March 1985, PDA.
92 LB to BB, n.d. [4, 11 or 18 December 1938], BFP.
93 David Hemmings, talking in the Mentorn TV film *Britten's Children* (director John Bridcut), shown on BBC 2, 5 June 2004.
94 J. B. Steane, *The Grand Tradition*, pp. 506–7.
95 Dr Basil Reeve, interview with Donald Mitchell, London, 3 October 1986, LFAL, p. 14.
96 BB to PP, n.d. [18 November 1943], LFAL, p. 1165, and see p. 14.
97 BB to WS, 3 October 1938, LFAL, p. 589.
98 Translation by Helen Rootham, used by BB in the vocal score, and quoted HC, p. 137.
99 K. H. W. S. [Wulff Scherchen], To Benjamin Britten [...], 30 October 1938, JWP.
100 WS to BB, 29 January 1939, JWP.
101 This letter no longer exists, but its contents are implied by LB's letter to WS, n.d. [last week of September 1938], JWP.
102 BB to WS, 21 November 1938, JWP.
103 LB to WS, n.d. [last week of September 1938], JWP.
104 BB to WS, 21 November 1938, JWP.
105 Rupert Christiansen, 'The Ben and Basil Story' [a review of Maureen

Garnham, *As I Saw It: Basil Douglas, Benjamin Britten and the English Opera Group, 1955–7*], *The Spectator*, 18 July 1998.

106 BB to LB, 1 January 1939, LFAL, p. 605.
107 WS to BB, 6 December 1938, JWP.
108 BB to WS, n.d. [pre-Christmas 1938], BPL.
109 WS, a poem entitled, *For B. Happy Xmas (to be read aloud)* [...], 12 December 1938, JWP.
110 Wulff Scherchen, *A Madrigal* – Bridcut, J., *Britten's Children*, p. 75.
111 *Ibid.*
112 LB to BB, 24 December 1938, BFP.
113 *Ibid.*
114 *Ibid.*, 27 December 1938.
115 BB to PP, n.d. [5 January 1939], LFAL, vol. iii, p. 78.
116 W. H. Auden to BB, n.d. [August 1938], BPL.
117 LB to BB, 27 December 1938, BFP.
118 LB to NB, 10 November [1938] (TS translation from French), FSNB.
119 P. Parker, *Isherwood*, p. 411.
120 WS to BB, 5 January 1939, JWP.
121 *Ibid.*, 19 January 1939, JWP.
122 BB to WS, 22 January 1939, JWP.
123 RN email to TS, 5 September 2007.
124 BB to WS, 11 January 1939, JWP.
125 *Ibid.*
126 BB to LB, 1 January 1939, BPL.
127 WS to BB, 2 January 1939, JWP.
128 BB to WS, 7 February 1939, JWP.
129 WS to BB, 8 February 1939, JWP; and WS email to TS, 3 September 2008.
130 BB to WS, 1 March 1939, JWP.
131 LFAL vol. 1, pp. 611 and 614.
132 WS, letter to MB, August 2004 (MBA); and WS, email to TS, 3 September 2008.
133 WS, email to TS, 3 September 2008.
134 BB to Enid Slater, 13 March 1939, BPL.
135 BB to LB, 30 March 1939, BFP.
136 LFAL, p. 632.
137 WS to MB, 14 August 2004, MBA.
138 BB to PP, 16 March 1939, BPL.
139 BB to Enid Slater, 13 March 1939, BPL.
140 BB to PP, 16 March 1939, BPL.
141 BB to LB, 30 March 1939, BFP.
142 WS, interview with Donald Mitchell, London, 15 September 1989, BPL;

LFAL note 5, p. 614; HC, pp. 121–2; and WS to BB, 16 March and 9 April 1939, JWP.

143 BB to PP, 16 March 1939, BPL

144 BB to PP, 16 March 1939, BPL.

145 WS, email to TS, 3 September 2008.

146 BB to LB, 20 March 1939, BPL.

147 BB to LB, 30 March 1939, BFP.

148 LB to Julian Herbage, 27 April 1939, BBCWAC; and BB to Mary Behrend, 17 April, 1939, LFAL, p. 618.

149 Beth Britten, *My Brother Benjamin*, p. 109, and HC, p. 126.

150 BB to LB, 16 April 1939, BFP; and LFAL, pp. 617–18.

151 HC, p. 138.

152 J. Bridcut, *Britten's Children*, p. 102.

153 HC, p. 128.

154 J. Bridcut, *Britten's Children*, p. 85.

155 WS, interviewed by John Bridcut – *ibid.*

156 BB to WS, n.d. [postmarked 22 April 1939], JWP.

157 *Ibid.*

158 BB to Mary Behrend, 17 April 1939, BPL.

159 BB to Wulff Scherchen [17 February 1939], BPL.

160 PP in *A Time There Was: A Profile of Benjamin Britten*, film directed by Tony Palmer, London Weekend Television, 1980 (HC, pp. 127–8).

161 WS, interview with Donald Mitchell, London, 15 September 1989, BPL.

162 BB to Aaron Copland, 8 May 1939, BPL.

163 *Ibid.*

164 G. Johnson, *Britten, Voice and Piano*, pp. 150 and 156–7.

165 Marjorie Fass to Daphne Oliver, December 1937, quoted in LFAL, p. 19.

166 LB to NB, 1 April 1939, translated from French, FSNB.

CHAPTER NINETEEN

1 LB to Julian Herbage, 27 April 1939, BBCWAC.

2 LB to BB, 4 May 1939, BFP.

3 *Ibid.*

4 WS to BB, 19 May 1939, JWP/BPL.

5 BB to LB, 3 May 1939, BPL.

6 HC, p. 129.

7 BB to WS, September 1939, JWP/BPL.

8 *Ibid.*, 1 May 1939.

9 *Ibid.*, 8 December 1939.

10 HC, p. 133.

11 BB to WS, 1 May 1939, JWP/BPL.

12 *Ibid.*, 9 June 1939.
13 WS to BB, 30 May 1939, JWP/BPL.
14 *Ibid.*, 15 June 1939.
15 BB to LB, 4 June 1939, BPL.
16 BB to LB, 30 May 1939.
17 BB to WS, n.d. [postmarked 12 February 1939], JWP/BPL.
18 WS to BB, 6 July 1939, JWP/BPL.
19 PP to BB, n.d. [9 January1940], BPL.
20 BB to WS, n.d. [post-marked 29 September 1939], JWP/BPL.
21 *Ibid.*, 8 December 1939, JWP/BPL.
22 BB to Enid Slater, 29 July 1939, BPL.
23 BB to WS, 8 December 1939, BPL.
24 LB to BB, 21 August 1939, BFP.
25 LFAL, p. 568.
26 LB to BB, 4 May 1939, BFP,
27 *The Times*, 20 November 1939. (The Sonatina was first performed by Carl Dolmetsch, treble recorder, and Joseph Saxby, piano, at a meeting of the London Contemporary Music Centre on 17 June 1939 [Andrew Mayes, *Carl Dolmetsch*].)
28 LB to Carl Dolmetsch, 8 August 1939 (A. Mayes, *Carl Dolmetsch*).
29 LB to BB, 5 January 1940, BFP.
30 *Ibid.*, 21 August 1939, BFP.
31 *Ibid.*
32 *Ibid.*
33 BB to Beth Britten, 25 June 1939, BPL.
34 Barbara Britten to BB, 20 August 1939, BPL.
35 Rupert Christiansen, 'Protecting the Flames of Genius', *The Spectator*, 16 October 2004, p. 70.
36 LB to BB, 3 September 1939, BFP.
37 LB to NB, n.d. [*c.* September 1939] (TS translation from French), FSNB.
38 *Ibid.*
39 LB to BB, 3 September 1939, BFP.
40 D. Hibberd, *Wilfred Owen – A New Biography*, p. 133.
41 BB to Beth Welford, 19 October 1939, BPL.
42 BB to LB, no date [3 September 1939], BFP. The opening sentence notes that it has been enclosed in a letter addressed to Barbara. LFAL, p. 752, dates it as 1 January 1940, i.e. as having been enclosed in the letter to Barbara Britten of that date, but a) the last sentence of that letter, which asks Barbara to forward the enclosed letters, does not mention one to LB, and b) the undated letter to LB makes reference to Buxtehude, to which LB replies on 24 September, suggesting that this BB letter was enclosed in the letter to Barbara dated 3 September 1939.

43 WS to BB, 1 September 1939, JWP/BPL.
44 *Ibid.*, 5 December 1939.
45 *Ibid.*, 5 December 1939.
46 *Ibid.*, 22 January 1940.
47 *Ibid.*, 13 May 1940.
48 *Ibid.*, 6 September 1940.
49 HC, p. 143.
50 WS to BB, n.d. [? summer 1940], JWP/BPL.
51 *Ibid.*, 27 August and 10 September 1940.
52 *Ibid.*, 3, 10, 20, 24 September, 1 October and 10 November 1940.
53 *Ibid.*, 1 October 1940.
54 *Ibid.*, 24 November.
55 *Ibid.*, 3 December 1940.
56 *Ibid.*, 13 July 1941.
57 *Ibid.*
58 Barbara Britten to BB, 14 September 1939, BPL.
59 LB to BB, 24 September 1939, BFP.
60 *Ibid.*
61 Barbara Britten to BB, 24 September 1939, BPL.
62 *Ibid*, 28 October 1939, BPL.
63 Arthur Nicholson to BB, 6 November 1939, BPL.
64 BB to WS, 8 December 1939, JWP/BPL.
65 Beth Welford to BB, 1 October 1939, BPL.
66 Arthur Nicholson to BB, 6 November 1939, BPL.
67 LB to BB, 8 October 1939, BFP.
68 *Ibid.*
69 LFAL, p. 606, quoting Hewit's own account of his early life, in Penrose and Freeman, *Conspiracy of Silence*, pp. 200–6.
70 BB to WS, 11 January 1939, JWP/BPL .
71 LFAL, vol. iii, p.78, n. 4.
72 LB to Ralph Hawkes, 22 October 1939, BFP.
73 LB to BB, 8 October 1939, BFP.
74 Marjorie Fass to Daphne Oliver, December 1937.
75 BB to Hedli Anderson, n.d. [October 1939], BPL.
76 BB to Enid Slater, 7 November 1939, BPL.
77 Enid Slater to BB, 4 December 1939, BPL.
78 *Ibid.*, 23 May 1940, BPL.
79 BB to Ralph Hawkes, 27 October, 1939, BFP.
80 Beth Welford to BB, 1 October 1939, BPL.
81 *Ibid*, 19 November 1939, BPL.
82 *Ibid*, 9 October 1939, BPL.
83 BB to Beth Welford, 19 October 1939, BPL.

84 Telegram BB to Beth Welford, 16 November 1939, BPL.
85 BB to Beth Welford, 28 November 1939, BPL.
86 D. Mitchell, 'Introduction', LFAL, p. 40.
87 'The Musician Talks', n.d., unidentified cutting (?*The Times*) post February 1959, BFP.
88 LB to NB 2 April 1940 (TS translation from French), FSNB.
89 LB to Ralph Hawkes 22 October 1939, BFP.
90 LB to BB, 24 September 1939, BFP.
91 *Ibid.*, 5 January 1940, BFP.
92 British Library, LOAN 101.89b.
93 MLB, p. 64.
94 Eva Ibbotson, *Front Row*, BBC Radio 4, 6 September 2006.

CHAPTER TWENTY

1 D. Thomas (ed. P. Ferris), *The Collected Letters of Dylan Thomas*, p. 337.
2 Constantine FitzGibbon, 'Introduction', Thomas and Davenport, *The Death of the King's Canary*, p. ix.
3 H. Searle, *Quadrille with a Raven*, ch. 7.
4 LB to BB, 5 January 1940, BFP.
5 H. Searle, *Quadrille with a Raven*, ch. 7.
6 Paul Ferris, *Caitlin*.
7 Natalie Davenport, in conversation with TS at a Bath Festival concert at Marshfield on 26 May 2003.
8 Constantine Fitzgibbon, 'Introduction', Thomas and Davenport, *The Death of the King's Canary*, p. ix.
9 Caitlin Thomas, *Caitlin: A Warring Absence*, p. 73.
10 J. A. Sutherland, *Stephen Spender*, p. 251.
11 LB to BB, 17 July 1940, BFP..
12 John Lewis, *Such Things Happen*, p. 148.
13 C. FitzGibbon, *The Life of Dylan Thomas*, p. 164.
14 John Lewis, *Such Things Happen*, p. 149.
15 Stephen Spender, Journal, 26 September 1939, in S. Spender, *Journals*, p. 41.
16 Stephen Spender to Christopher Isherwood, 26 October 1939, in S. Spender, *Letters to Christopher*, p. 202.
17 LB to BB, 17 July 1940, BFP.
18 According to Sir John Rothenstein, quoted by the London art gallery Offer Waterman & Co (at www.waterman.co.uk).
19 John Lewis, *Such Things Happen*, p. 149.
20 *Ibid.*
21 LB to BB, 28 December 1939, BFP.

22 Natalie Davenport, in conversation with TS at a Bath Festival concert at Marshfield on 26 May 2003.
23 H. Searle, *Quadrille with a Raven*, ch. 7.
24 LB to BB, 17 July 1940, BFP.
25 Dylan Thomas to John Davenport, 8 January 1941, D. Thomas, *Collected Letters*, p. 472.
26 LB to BB, 5 January 1940, BFP.
27 Caitlin Thomas, *Caitlin: A Warring Absence*, pp. 74–5.
28 A. Lycett, *Dylan Thomas*, p. 187.
29 *Ibid.*
30 LB to Hélène Kahn-Casella, 10 December 1939 (TS translation from French), BFP.
31 Caitlin Thomas, *Caitlin: A Warring Absence*, p. 73.
32 H. Searle, *Quadrille with a Raven*, ch 7.
33 D. Thomas and J. Davenport, *The Death of the King's Canary*, p. 85.
34 C. W. Beaumont, *Supplement to Complete Book of Ballets*, pp. 143–6.
35 LB, 'Modern French Ballet Music', autograph notes for an illustrated talk, n.d. [soon after March 1945], BFP.
36 G. Larner, *Maurice Ravel*, pp. 157 and 204.
37 C. W. Beaumont, *Supplement to Complete Book of Ballets*, pp. 143–6.
38 F. Hall, *Modern English Ballet*, p. 122.
39 A. E. Housman, 'Additional Poems (1939)', VII, from *The Collected Poems of A. E. Housman*, reproduced by permission of The Society of Authors.
40 LB to BB, 17 July 1940, BFP.
41 LB to NB, 28 December 1939 (TS translation from French), FSNB.
42 LB to Hélène Kahn-Casella, 15 February 1940 (TS translation from French), BFP.
43 LB to BB, 5 January 1940, BFP.
44 LB to NB, 28 December 1939 (TS translation from French), FSNB.
45 *Ibid*, 28 December 1939 (TS translation from French), FSNB.
46 LB to BB, 5 January 1940, BFP.
47 *Ibid.*
48 *Ibid.*
49 *Ibid.*, 4 February 1940, BFP.
50 *Ibid.*
51 *Ibid.*, 17 July 1940, BFP.
52 *Ibid.*
53 *Ibid.*
54 Enid Slater to BB, 3 February 1940, BPL.
55 Sophie Wyss to BB, 1 February 1940.
56 Beth Welford to BB, n.d. [February 1940], BPL.

57 FB to TS, 8 November 2004.
58 LB to BB, 21 April 1940, BFP.
59 LB to NB, 2 and 12 April 1940 (TS translation from French), FSNB.
60 *Ibid.*, 25 April 1940 (TS translation from French), FSNB.
61 *Ibid.*
62 Burney, Charles (ed. H. Edmund Poole), *Music, Men and Manners 1770*, p. 182.
63 Patrick Brydone, *A Tour through Sicily and Malta*, p. 8.
64 Dylan Thomas to John Davenport, 8 January 1941, in D. Thomas, *Collected Letters*, p. 472.
65 Caitlin Thomas, *Caitlin: A Warring Absence*, p. 72.
66 LB to BB, 17 July 1940, BFP.

CHAPTER TWENTY-ONE

1 FB, in a taped conversation with TS, Hereford Mansions, January 1997.
2 Clare Lawson Dick, in an interview with WW2 People's War, bbc.co.uk/dna/ww2/A3651527.
3 FB, in a taped conversation with TS, Hereford Mansions, January 1997.
4 *Ibid.*
5 *Ibid.*

CHAPTER TWENTY-TWO

1 LB to BB, 17 July 1940, BFP,
2 LB to NB, 21 November 1940 (TS translation from French), FSNB,
3 *Ibid.*, 28 December 1939 (TS translation from French), FSNB,
4 David Ponsonby, untitled essay in typescript, unpublished, n.d. but late 1940s, DPM.
5 LB to BB, 9 November 1940, BFP.
6 LB to NB, 21 November 1940 (TS translation from French), FSNB.
7 LB to BB, 9 November 1940, BFP.
8 Enid Slater to BB, 12 December 1940, BPL.
9 LB to NB, 21 November 1940 (TS translation from French), FSNB.
10 *Ibid.*, 6 October 1942, in English, FSNB.
11 LB to BB, 9 November 1940, BFP.
12 James Lees-Milne, Diary, 18 February 1944, *Prophesying Peace*, p. 25.
13 LB, Diary, 25 October 1977, BFP.
14 LB to BB, 9 November 1940, BFP.
15 R. Pound, *Sir Henry Wood*, p. 264.
16 Ernest Chapman to Erwin Stein, 18 September 1940, L. Foreman, *From Parry to Britten*, p. 236.

17 LB to BB, 9 November 1940, BFP.
18 LB to NB, 21 November 1940 (TS translation from French), FSNB.

CHAPTER TWENTY-THREE

1 FB, in a a taped conversation with TS, Hereford Mansions, January 1997, and a further conversation with TS on 8 March 2005.
2 John Keir Cross to FB, 5 July 1942, BFP.
3 *Ibid.*
4 FB, in a taped conversation with TS, Hereford Mansions, January 1997.
5 FB Diary, 21 and 25 January 1944, BFP.
6 *Ibid.*, 4 January 1944.
7 *Ibid.*, 6 and 7 January 1944.
8 *Ibid.*, 21 November 1944.
9 *Ibid.*, 13 March 1944.
10 *Ibid.*, 27 June 1944.
11 *Ibid.*, 14 May 1944.
12 FB, in a conversation with TS at Hereford Mansions, 8 March 2005.
13 FB Diary, 21 July 1944, BFP.
14 *Ibid.*, 27 January 1944.
15 *Ibid.*, 28 November 1944.
16 *Ibid.*, 4 May 1944.
17 *Ibid.*, 5 January 1944.
18 Clare Lawson Dick, in an interview with WW2 People's War, bbc.co.uk/dna/ww2/A3651527.
19 FB, in conversation with TS at Hereford Mansions, 8 March 2005.

CHAPTER TWENTY-FOUR

1 John Pope-Hennessy to RN, 6 December 1990, RNA.
2 FB in conversation with TS, 15 June 2003; FB, in taped interview with TS, London, 17 June 1998.
3 Peter Fraser's London landlady Mrs Alice Shavelson to John Lloyd, 6 May 1976, BFP.
4 Birth certificate of 'Peter' Fraser, Clapton, 17 August 1920, and marriage certificate of his parents, Leonard Patrick Fraser and Dorothy Gladys Colin-Smith, Brighton, 22 April 1918. There is no record at the General Register Office of the death of either of his parents from the date of his birth till 1950.
5 FB, in taped interview with TS, London, 17 June 1998.
6 Postcard from Peter Fraser and LB at 28 Great Ormond Street, London

WCI., to Gunner Desmond Shawe-Taylor, c/o Brooks's Club, 2 October [1940], BFP.

7 John Lloyd to LB, 11 May 1976, BFP.
8 LB to BB, 9 November 1940, BFP.
9 *Ibid.*
10 *Ibid.*
11 RAF Personnel Management Agency, RAF Innsworth, Gloucester, to TS, 16 February 2002.
12 Enid Slater to BB, 12 December 1940, BPL.
13 A. E. Housman, 'More Poems 1936', XXX, from *The Collected Poems of A. E. Housman*, reproduced by permission of The Society of Authors.
14 Molly Berkeley, *Beaded Bubbles*, p. 99.
15 V. Sackville West [*sic*], *Berkeley Castle*, p. 32.
16 LB, Diary, 19 August 1968, BFP.
17 *Ibid.*, 24 August 1975, BFP.
18 Michael Burn, *Turned Towards the Sun*, p. 67.
19 *Ibid.*
20 TS in conversation with FB, 12 January 2008.
21 LB to Douglas Gibson, Chester's, 31 March 1941, CMA.
22 The Romanian pianist Anda Anastasescu, who played the *Sonata* at the Wigmore Hall in London in LB's centenary year, in conversation with TS on the telephone, 15 May 2002.
23 J. Pudney, *Thank Goodness for Cake*, pp. 64–5.
24 *Ibid.*
25 Asa Briggs, *The BBC: The First Fifty Years*, p. 194.
26 Memo by Malcolm Baker-Smith, 10 September 1941, Copyright File, BBCWAC.
27 Lewis Foreman, *From Parry to Britten – British Music in Letters 1900–1945*, p. 244.
28 Music Reports 1928–1954, R27/552 (September 1941), BBCWAC.
29 *Ibid.* (October 1941), BBCWAC.
30 *Ibid.* (10 December 1941, 18 March 1942, June 1942), BBCWAC.
31 PD, reviewing the Maggini Quartet's CD of the three Berkeley Quartets [Naxos 8 570415] , *The Gramophone*, February 2008.
32 David Angel, interview accompanying Peter Dickinson's review of the Maggini Quartet's CD of the three Berkeley Quartets [Naxos 8 570415], *The Gramophone*, February 2008.
33 Music Reports 1928–1954, R27/552 (20 January 1942), BBCWAC.
34 Basil Douglas, in an interview with PD, recorded 28 November 1990, PDA.
35 Martin Cotton, 'Michael Tippett', *BBC Music Magazine*, January 2002, pp. 38–9.

36 Kenneth Wright to R. S. Thatcher, 18 November 1941, BBCWAC.
37 LB to R. S. Thatcher, 2 December 1941, BBCWAC.
38 R. S. Thatcher to LB, 6 December 1941, BBCWAC.
39 LB to NB, 6 October 1942, FSNB.
40 Molly Berkeley, *Beaded Bubbles*, pp. 99–100.
41 *Ibid., p.* 145.
42 John Shorter, 'Berkeley, Randal Thomas Mowbray Rawdon, eighth earl of Berkeley (1865–1942)', *Oxford Dictionary of National Biography*, Oxford University Press, 2004.
43 Cécile Countess of Berkeley to her son Randal Earl of Berkeley, 8 April 1906, BFP.
44 Will of the Rt. Hon. Randal Thomas Mowbray, Earl of Berkeley, dated 10 November 1936, proved 4 May 1942.
45 Molly Berkeley, *Beaded Bubbles*, p. 100.
46 J. Holmstrom, *The Moving Picture Boy*, p. 228.
47 Molly Berkeley, *Beaded Bubbles*, p. 96.
48 *Ibid.*, pp. 121, 126.
49 The will of Mary Emlen Berkeley, Countess of Berkeley, dated 1 October 1966.
50 'The BBC at War – Overseas Programming' - http://www.bbc.co.uk/heritage/story/ww2/overseas.shtml.
51 Kenneth Wright to Trudy Bliss, thanking her for releasing husband Arthur to work for BBC (A. Bliss, *As I Remember*, p. 140).
52 LB to NB, 6 October 1942 (this second section of the letter in English), FSNB.
53 Mrs Gwen Becket to RN, 12 December 1990, RNA.
54 LB to R. Douglas Gibson, Chester Music, 3 March 1942, CMA.
55 Mrs Gwen Becket to RN, 12 December 1990, RNA.
56 LB to NB, 6 October 1942 (TS translation from French), FSNB.
57 LB to R. Douglas Gibson, 3 March 1942, CMA.
58 BB to Elizabeth Mayer, 5 June 1942, BPL.
59 WS to BB, 13 July 1941, JWP.
60 *Ibid.*, 29 September 1941.
61 BB to PP, 1 June 1942. (J. Bridcut, *Britten's Children*, p. 123.)
62 BB to Elizabeth Mayer, 5 June 1942. (J. Bridcut, *Britten's Children*, p. 124.)
63 BB to PP, 1 June 1942. (J. Bridcut, *Britten's Children*, p. 123.)
64 BB to Elizabeth Mayer, 5 June 1942. (J. Bridcut, *Britten's Children*, p. 124.)
65 J. Bridcut, *Britten's Children*, p. 125.
66 LFAL, pp. 1077–8.
67 Julian Herbage to Sir Adrian Boult, 23 April 1942.
68 BB to PP, 25 September 1942, BPL.
69 LB to NB, 6 October 1942, in English, FSNB.

70 LB to BB [? March/April 1943], BPL.
71 *Ibid.*, 6 June 1943.
72 A. Briggs, *The BBC: The First Fifty Years*, p. 213.
73 LB to R. Douglas Gibson, 29 May 1942, CMA.
74 LB to NB, 6 October 1942, translated from French, FSNB.
75 Kathleen Walker, 'The Best of Berkeley', *Lennox Berkeley Society Journal*, 2009.
76 Ronald Crichton, 'Obituary – Sir Lennox Berkeley', *Financial Times*, 28 December 1989.
77 RN, 'Composer of the Month – Lennox Berkeley', *BBC Music Magazine*, June 2003.
78 *The Times*, 9 July 1943.
79 D. Shawe-Taylor, 'Music', *The New Statesman and Nation* [probably April 1948].
80 LB to Desmond Shawe-Taylor, 14 October 1943, Shawe-Taylor MSS, Lilly Library, Indiana University.
81 LB to NB, 10 August 1943, in English, FSNB.
82 Quoted by RN, 'Berkeley Evening', BBC Radio Three, 21 May 2003, marking the centenary of LB's birth.
83 *The Times*, 12 July 1943.
84 MLB, pp. 61–2.
85 Programme note by Edwin Evans, Concert, Wigmore Hall, 15 October 1943 – LFAL, p. 1179.
86 *The Observer*, 24 October 1943; LFAL, pp. 1175–6.
87 LB, 'Britten and his String Quartet', *The Listener*, 27 May 1943.
88 Edward Sackville-West to BB, December 1942 – M. De-la-Noy, *Eddy*, p. 196.
89 *Ibid.*, n.d. [1943], M. De-la-Noy, *Eddy*, p. 197.
90 M. De-la-Noy, *Eddy*, p. 195.
91 Edward Sackville-West to Raymond Mortimer, 5 November 1928 – M. De-la-Noy, *Eddy*, 126.
92 From an article by Stephen Potter in *Radio Times*, August 1943, paraphrased in J. Potter, *Stephen Potter at the BBC*, pp. 110 and 111.
93 J. Potter, *Stephen Potter at the BBC*, p. 151.
94 J. Lees-Milne, *Ancestral Voices*, p. 125.
95 BB to PP, 11 March 1943, BPL.
96 Misha Donat, 'Béla Bartók', *BBC Music Magazine*, August 2002, pp. 52–3.
97 Martin Cotton, 'Michael Tippett', *BBC Music Magazine*, January 2002, pp. 38–9.
98 LB to NB, 10 August 1943 (in English), FSNB.
99 LB to BB [soon after 19 March 1944], BFP.

100 BB to Elizabeth Mayer, 22 May 1943, BPL.
101 Michael Tippett, interviewed by Humphrey Carpenter, HC, p. 192.
102 HC, p. 196.
103 *Ibid.*
104 Meirion Bowen (ed.), *Music of the Angels: Essays and Sketchbooks of Michael Tippett*, Eulenberg Books, 1980, p. 77.
105 LB to BB, 31 December 1942, BPL.
106 Rupert Christiansen, 'The Ben and Basil Story' [a review of Maureen Garnham, *As I Saw It: Basil Douglas, Benjamin Britten and the English Opera Group, 1955–7*], *The Spectator*, 18 July 1998.
107 RN, 'Composer of the Month–Lennox Berkeley', *BBC Music Magazine*, June 2003.
108 Basil Douglas, in a taped conversation with PD, 28 November 1990, PDA.
109 LB to BB [? March/April 1943], BPL.

CHAPTER TWENTY-FIVE

1 'Granted commission [as Pilot Officer] for the emergency', 1 October 1942; promoted to Flying Officer, 1 June 1943 (RAF Personnel Management Agency to TS, 16 February 2002.)
2 J. Lees-Milne (abridged and introduced by Michael Bloch), *Diaries, 1942–1954*, p. 385.
3 LB to NB, 10 August 1943, in English, FSNB.
4 J. Lees-Milne, *Caves of Ice*, p. 242.
5 *Ibid.* (abridged and introduced by Michael Bloch), *Diaries, 1942–1954*, pp. 407 and 414.
6 Anne, Countess of Rosse, quoted in J. Lees-Milne (abridged and introduced by Michael Bloch), *Diaries, 1942–1954*, p. 401.
7 J. Lees-Milne, *Ancestral Voices*, p. 195.
8 *Ibid., Ancestral Voices*, p. 264.
9 LB to NB, 10 August 1943, in English, FSNB.
10 J. Lees-Milne, *Ancestral Voices*, p. 272.
11 BB to PP, (18 November 1943), BPL.
12 BBCWAC.
13 Colin Horsley, in a taped conversation with PD, 30 November 1990, PDA.
14 BBCWAC.
15 Vowles's sepulchral memo of 1 December 1943 was cited by RN during the Berkeley Evening on BBC Radio Three on 21 May 2003.
16 Music Reports 1928–1954, R27/552 (September 1943), BBCWAC.
17 *Ibid.*
18 *Ibid.*

19 *Ibid*, March 1945.
20 LB to NB, 25 January 1944, in English, FSNB.
21 Stephen Lloyd, *The Film Music of Sir Arthur Bliss*, www.musicweb-international.
22 Jill Craigie to Paul Nash, 26 March 1944, TGA 7050/463/114, Hyman Kreitman Research Centre, Tate Britain.
23 *Ibid.*, and 29 May 1944, TGA 7050/463/114, Hyman Kreitman Research Centre, Tate Britain.
24 *Ibid.*, 26 March 1944.
25 *Ibid.*, 11 May 1944.
26 *Ibid.*, 24 January 1945.
27 *Ibid.*, 11 May 1944.
28 The holograph, entitled *Out of Chaos*, contains three movements (I Moderato, II Allegro 'Shipyard Sequence', and III Allegro 'Battle of Britain' and Andante 'Totes Meer') – British Library SRC, 71, 217.
29 Harold Acton, *Memoirs of an Aesthete*, p. 149.
30 Other poets represented included Laurie Lee and C. Day Lewis (whose wife Jill Balcon also took part).
31 A. Bliss, *As I Remember*, p. 140.
32 FB, in a taped interview with TS, 17 June 1998.
33 A. Bliss, *As I Remember*, p. 140.
34 FB, Diary, 15 May 1945, BFP; and FB, in a telephone conversation with TS, 30 January 2005.
35 A. Bliss, *As I Remember*, p. 147.
36 Howard Davies, in a telephone conversation with TS, 27 June 2003.
37 BB to PP ['after 28 October and before 2 November 1944'].
38 Howard Davies to TS, 24 January 2005.
39 Bentley Bridgewater [1911–96], Secretary of the British Museum, in conversation with TS, 1971.
40 Howard Davies, in conversation with TS, 25 February 2004.
41 FB, in a taped conversation with TS, 17 June 1998.
42 R. D. Wyatt, in telephone conversation with RN, early September 1989, RNA.
43 FB, in a conversation with TS, 22 February 2006.
44 John Pope-Hennessy to RN, 6 December 1990, RNA.
45 R. D.Wyatt, in a telephone conversation with RN, early September 1989, RNA.

CHAPTER TWENTY-SIX

1 FB, Diary, 5 June 1944, BFP.
2 *Ibid.*, 6 June 1944.

3 *Ibid.*, 26 June 1944.
4 *Ibid.*, 25 May 1944.
5 *Ibid.*, 14 October 1944.
6 FB, on the telephone to TS, 14 January 2005.
7 FB, Diary, 26 May 1944, BFP.
8 *Ibid.*, 21 June 1944.
9 Settlement dated 22 August 1944 between FB and Public Trustee.
10 FB, Diary, 21 September 1944, BFP.
11 *Ibid.*, 9 June 1945 and 28 September 1944; and FB, on the telephone to TS, 12 January 2005.
12 *Ibid.*, 19 December 1944.
13 FB, in a taped conversation with TS, Hereford Mansions, January 1997.

CHAPTER TWENTY-SEVEN

1 FB, Diary, 29 January 1945, BFP.
2 *Ibid.*, 2 February. In the 1950s Wheatley gained wide notice as the Sheriff of Nottingham in the film series *The Adventures of Robin Hood*. He also appeared in episodes of the TV series *Dr Who*, *Danger Man*, *The Protectors* and *Department S*. He died in 1991.
3 FB, Diary, 3 July 1944, BFP.
4 *Ibid.*, 5 October 1944.
5 *Ibid.*, 12 December 1944.
6 *Ibid.*, 5 February 1945.
7 *Ibid.*, 10 February and 23 March.
8 LB to Douglas Gibson of Chester's, 22 February 1945, CMA.
9 FB, Diary, 4 April 1945, BFP.
10 *Ibid.*, 10 April.
11 *Ibid.*, 12 April.
12 *Ibid.*, 15 May.
13 FB, Diary, 30 May 1945, BFP.
14 LB to the Revd Walter Hussey, 19 May 1945, W. Hussey, *Patron of Art*, pp. 94–6.
15 Music Reports 1928–1954, R27/552 (6 July 1945), BBCWAC.
16 FB to LB, 2 February 1950, BFP.
17 MLB, p. 70 (PD examines the *Six Preludes* in detail on pp. 64–73).
18 Colin Horsley, in a telephone conversation with TS, 7 February 2006; confirmed by FB, by phone to TS, 7 February 2006.
19 *Ibid.*, in a taped interview with PD, 30 November 1990, PDA.
20 Desmond Shawe-Taylor, in a taped interview with PD, 28 November 1990, PDA.
21 LB, in a taped interview with PD, 8 March 1985, PDA.

22 Colin Horsley, in a telephone conversation with TS, 7 February 2006.
23 *Ibid.*
24 The Revd Walter Hussey to BB, 22 March 1943, BPL; LFAL, 1139–40.
25 Email to TS, 5 September 2007.
26 LB to the Revd Walter Hussey, 24 May 1945, W. Hussey, *Patron of Art*, pp. 94–6.
27 *Ibid.*, 14 August 1945.
28 LB to the Revd Walter Hussey, Christmas Day 1944, W. Hussey, *Patron of Art*, pp. 94–6.
29 Philip Reed, 'Poulenc, Britten, Aldeburgh: A Chronicle', in Sidney Buckland and Myriam Chimènes (eds.), *Francis Poulenc. Music, Art and Literature*, pp. 348–50.
30 LB, Diary, 16 June 1968, BFP.
31 BB to PP, 10 January 1944, in Paul Banks (ed.), *The Making of Peter Grimes*, p. 32.
32 LB, Diary, 16 June1968, BFP.
33 Clifford Hindley, 'Peter Grimes', in J. Guinn, and L. Stone (eds.), *The St. James Opera Encyclopaedia*, Detroit, Visible Ink Press, 1997, p. 620.
34 PP to BB, [1 March] 1944, BPL; Paul Banks (ed.), *The Making of Peter Grimes*, pp. 32–3.
35 FB, Diary, 24 June 1945, BFP.
36 LB to BB, 30 June 1945, BFP.
37 FB, Diary, 8 June 1945, BFP.
38 LB to FB, 11 June 1945, BFP.
39 FB, Diary, 12 June 1945, BFP.
40 *Ibid.*, 18 June.
41 *Ibid.*, 6 July.
42 *Ibid.*, 23 and 25 June .
43 LB to FB, n.d. [17 January 1946], BFP.
44 George Baker, 'Lennox Berkeley', the sixth in the series, 'What are they like at home?', *Music Teacher and Piano Student*, September 1954.
45 FB, Diary, 4 July 1945, BFP.
46 *Ibid.*, 14 and 17 September.
47 *Ibid.*, 2 July.
48 *Ibid.*, 9 July.
49 *Ibid.*, 11 May.
50 LB to NB, 18 November 1945 (TS translation from French), FSNB.
51 DPM.
52 *Ibid.*
53 *Ibid.* and concert programme, 'England's Place in Keyboard Music: A Piano Recital with Comments by David Ponsonby', Wigmore Hall, 14 October, 1947.

54 FB, Diary, 8 August 1945, BFP.
55 *Ibid.*, 18 July.
56 *Ibid.*, 15 August.

CHAPTER TWENTY-EIGHT

1 Michael Burn, *Turned towards the* Sun, paperback edition (2007), p. 119.
2 Abbot Wilfrid Upson, *Movies and Monasteries in USA*, Prinknash Abbey, 1950.
3 FB, Diary, 22 August 1945, BFP.
4 *Ibid.*, 23 and 24 August.
5 *Ibid.*, 3 September.
6 *Ibid.*, 2 September.
7 *Ibid.*, 7 September.
8 *Ibid.*, 12 September.
9 SRC, p. 73.
10 FB, Diary, 26 September 1945, BFP.
11 Edward Lockspeiser, 'The Music of Lennox Berkeley', *The Listener*, 10 July 1947.
12 FB, Diary, 10 October 1945, BFP.
13 *Ibid.*, 13 and 15 October.
14 *Ibid.*, 25 October.
15 *Ibid.*, 9 November.
16 *Ibid.*, 4 December.
17 *Ibid.*, 15 and 17 November.
18 *Ibid.*, 11 December.
19 James Lees-Milne, Diary, 6 November 1971, *A Mingled Measure*, p. 157.
20 *Ibid.*, 3 April 1992, *Ceaseless Turmoil*, p. 292.
21 *Ibid.*, 28 December 1989, *Ceaseless Turmoil*, pp. 138–9.
22 FB, Diary, 26 December 1945, BFP.
23 Settlement dated 22 August 1944 between FB and Public Trustee.
24 LB to FB, n.d. [29 January 1946], BFP.
25 FB, Diary, 16 January 1946, BFP.
26 LB to FB, n.d. [29 January 1946], BFP.
27 *Ibid.*, 22 January 1946.
28 FB, in conversation with TS, 26 February 2004.
29 FB, Diary, 11January 1946, BFP.
30 LB to FB, 22 January [1946], BFP.
31 LB, Will, unsigned, 9 September 1949, BFP.
32 LB to FB, 22 January [1946], BFP.
33 *Ibid.*, n.d. [17 January 1946], BFP.

34 FB, Diary, 26 January 1946, BFP.
35 LB to FB, n.d. [29 January 1946], copy in the possession of RN; location of original unknown.
36 FB, Diary, 27 January 1946, BFP.
37 *Ibid.*, 24 January 1946, BFP.
38 LB to FB, n.d. [29 January 1946], BFP.
39 FB, Diary, 2 February 1946, BFP.
40 *Ibid.*, 18 February.
41 *Ibid.*, 6 March.
42 *Ibid.*, 21 March.
43 *Ibid.*, 23 and 30 March.
44 George Baker, 'Lennox Berkeley', the sixth in the series, 'What are they like at home?', *Music Teacher and Piano Student*, September 1954.
45 FB, Diary, 26 March, BFP.
46 *Ibid.*, 27 March.
47 LB to NB, 12 April 1946 (TS translation from French), BFP.
48 LB to FB, 21 April 1946, BFP.
49 *Ibid.*
50 LB to NB, 5 May 1946, in English, FSNB.
51 *Ibid.*
52 Our Music Critic, 'The Career of Lennox Berkeley', *The Times*, 19 October 1956.
53 B. Ivry, *Francis Poulenc*, 8 and 156; R. D. E. Burton, *Francis Poulenc*, pp. 61–2, 123.
54 FB, Diary, 1 and 2 May, 9 and 10 July 1946, BFP. The lighter is now in the safe-keeping of Julian Berkeley.
55 *Ibid.*, 30 May 1946, BFP. A page in the Memoranda at the back of the Diary fills in the details.
56 *Ibid.*, 11 June (and note in Memoranda at back of the Diary).
57 *Ibid.*, 29 July.
58 *Ibid.*, 5 and 6 June 1946, BFP. In October 2003 FB gave this book to TS.
59 *Ibid.*, 12 and 17 June.
60 FB to TS by telephone, 7 July 2008.
61 FB, Diary, 15 July 1946, BFP.
62 *Ibid.*, 4 July.
63 FB to TS by telephone, 11 May 2008.

CHAPTER TWENTY-NINE

1 LB to Desmond Shawe-Taylor , 18 July 1946, Shawe-Taylor MSS, Lilly Library, Indiana University.
2 *The Times*, 24 July 1946.

3 Malcolm Williamson, Master of the Queen's Music, in an interview with PD, 22 February 1991 – MLB, p. 73.
4 FB, Diary, 22 July 1946, BFP.
5 *The Times*, 30 August 1946, p. 7.
6 FB, Diary, 28 and 29 August, BFP.
7 LB to FB, 19 August 1946, BFP.
8 MLB, p. 89.
9 LB to FB, 10 August 1946, BFP.
10 WS to MFB, 14 August 2004, MBA.
11 LB to WS, 6 July 1946, MBA.
12 LB to Desmond Shawe-Taylor, 18 July 1946, Shawe-Taylor MSS, Lilly Library, Indiana University.
13 Head of Music Programmes (Sound), Maurice Johnstone, to LB, 28 May 1953, Artist File 2 Lennox Berkeley 53–9, BBCWAC.
14 LB to HMP(S), 22 June 1949, Music Reports 1928–54, BBCWAC.
15 LB to FB, 19 August 1946, BFP.
16 *Ibid.,* 10 and 19 August.
17 FB, Diary, 24 September 1946, BFP.
18 *Ibid.*
19 *Ibid.*, 28 September.
20 *Ibid.*, 2 October.
21 *Ibid.*, 16 October.
22 *Ibid.*, 17 October.
23 *Ibid.*, 19–21 October.
24 *Ibid.*, 30 May, 30 September, 1 and 21 October, and a page in the Memoranda at the back of the Diary.
25 *Ibid.*, 4 November.
26 FB, in a taped interview with TS, 17 June 1998.
27 FB, Diary, 9 and 10 November 1946, BFP.
28 *Ibid.*, 11 November 1946, and a longer note in the Memoranda at the back of the Diary, BFP.
29 J. Lees-Milne, *Caves of Ice*, pp. 11, 106 and 133.
30 FB, Diary, 11 November 1946, and a longer note in the Memoranda at the back of the Diary, BFP.
31 Michael Burn, *Turned towards the Sun*, paperback edn (2007), p. 98.
32 LB, 'Reflections on Old Age and Death', in R. Ricketts (ed.), *Bid the World Goodnight*, pp. 19–21.
33 J. Lees-Milne (abridged and introduced by Michael Bloch), *Diaries, 1942–1954*, p. 402.
34 From a monograph by Michael Bloch, James Lees-Milne's literary heir, editor and biographer, published on the official James Lees-Milne website, www.jamesleesmilne.com .

35 Harold Nicolson, Diary, 19 November 1951, from the typescript of Michael's Bloch's biography of James Lees-Milne.
36 James Lees-Milne, Diary, 19 November 1991, from the typescript of Michael's Bloch's biography of James Lees-Milne.
37 James Lees-Milne, abridged and introduced by Michael Bloch), *Diaries, 1942–1954*, p. 405.
38 LB to James Lees-Milne, 18 November 1951, James Lees-Milne Papers, Beinecke Rare Book and Manuscript Library, Yale University.
39 So Francis Watson told RN (RN to TS, email 18 August 2008).
40 'Dickie' Wyatt, in a telephone conversation with RN, autumn 1989, RNA.
41 Virago edition, p. 150.
42 LB to FB, 10 August 1946, BFP.
43 FB, in a taped conversation with TS, Christmas 1993. See also LB to Desmond Shawe-Taylor, postcard, n.d. [postmark 29 November 1946], Shawe-Taylor MSS, Lilly Library, Indiana University.
44 LB, Diary, 1 December 1972, BFP.
45 FB, in a taped conversation with TS, Christmas 1993.
46 LB to FB, postcard, n.d. [postmark 1 December 1946], BFP.
47 Hans Gronau to FB, n.d. [postmark 7 December 1946], BFP.
48 *Ibid.*, [10 December 1946].
49 FB, in a taped conversation with TS, 17 June 1998.
50 *Ibid.*
51 *Ibid.*
52 FB, in a conversation with TS, 10 December 2001.

CHAPTER THIRTY

1 FB, telephone conversations with TS, 25 October 2001, and 26 & 29 March 2005.
2 LB, BBC radio talk, quoted MLB, p. 101.
3 R. D. E. Burton, *Poulenc*, p. 75.
4 *Ibid.*, pp. 75–6.
5 Colin Mawby, in a n.d., unidentified newspaper article [probably *Catholic Herald*, 1978], BFP.
6 J. MacRae, *Wigmore Hall*, p. 56.
7 Unsigned feature, *The Times*, 19 October 1956.
8 LFAL, vol. 3, p. 147.
9 Sir John Tavener, 'A Note', *Lennox Berkeley Society Newsletter*, no. 16, September 2004, p. 3.
10 According to Dr John Reay, who attended rehearsals as a young music student, 'During the rehearsal of the Poems I recall Dr Jacques making a

change in tempo or dynamics and saying to the players that composers did not always know what was best for the works in performance.' (Dr John Reay to PD, Christmas 2005).

11 Andrew Porter, sleeve-note for Pamela Bowden's 1960 recording of *Four Poems of St Teresa of Avila*, EMI DLP 1209.
12 Roland-Manuel to LB, 14 November 1965, BFP.
13 *Ibid.*, 8 March 1966, BFP.
14 *Ibid.*
15 Dame Janet Baker was speaking on 12 June 2008, before unveiling a Westminster City Council Green Plaque at 8 Warwick Avenue, London W2.
16 Richard Bernas, notes for a press release, Royal Ballet, 18 October 2005.
17 Mark Monahan, reviewing *La Fête étrange*, in the *Daily Telegraph*, 19 October 2005.
18 FB, Diary, entry in LB's hand, 8 April 1947, BFP.
19 David Piper, *Companion Guide to London*, p. 404.
20 FB, in a telephone conversation with TS, 30 May 2003.
21 FB, Diary, 9 July 1947, BFP.
22 *Ibid.*, 15 July 1947.
23 *Ibid.*, 15 August 1947.
24 LFAL, vol. 3, pp. 306–8, and SRC, p. 78.
25 Colin Horsley, in a telephone conversation with TS, 7 February 2006 (as his piano tuner was working on the two Steinways at his home in the Isle of Man, preparatory to a Mozart recital he was about to give, in his 86th year).
26 *The Times*, 1 September 1948.
27 SRC, 79.
28 Colin Horsley, in MLB, p. 78.
29 *Ibid.*, p. 77.
30 LB to Douglas Gibson of Chester Music, 19 January 1948, CMA.
31 LB to NB, 30 November 1947, (TS translation from French), FSNB.
32 BB to LB, n.d. [but LFAL, vol. III, p. 335 gives '*c.* 15 November 1947'], BPL.
33 FB, in a taped conversation with TS, 17 June 1998.
34 FB to LB, Wednesday evening [2 June 1948], BFP.
35 *The Times*, 3 June 1947.
36 Baptismal Certificate, 12 July 1949, MBA.
37 *Ibid.*
38 BB, Diary, 12 July 1949, BPL
39 LB to BB, 2 January 1949, BPL.
40 BB to MB, 30 August 1970, MBA.
41 FB to LB, Sunday [? September 1948, after the n.d. letter LB at Painswick to FB], BFP.

42 LB to FB, Saturday [? September 1948], BFP.
43 FB to LB, Saturday [? September 1948], BFP.
44 SRC, 80.
45 The work was given an exciting performance by Howard Shelley and Kathryn Stott, with the BBC National Orchestra of Wales, conducted by Richard Hickox, in the Brangwyn Hall, Swansea, in January 2006. The performance was recorded and released in 2007, with Michael Berkeley's *Gregorian Variations* and *Concerto for Orchestra*, in the *Berkeley Father and Son* series on Chandos Digital CHAN 10408.
46 Diary entry for 13 December 1948, J. Lees-Milne, *Midway on the Waves*, p. 135.
47 *The Times*, 14 December 1948.
48 LB to NB, 19 January 1947, (TS translation from French), FSNB.

CHAPTER THIRTY-ONE

1 LB to FB, 22 and 24 March 1949, BFP.
2 FB to LB, 23 March 1948 [but she means 1949. Throughout 1949, when she remembers to date her letters at all, FB persists in calling 1949 1948, and when 1950 arrives that becomes 1949 – and February becomes January], BFP.
3 LB to FB, n.d. [25 March 1949], BFP.
4 FB to LB, 29 March 1948 [1949], BFP.
5 *Ibid.*
6 LB to FB, n.d., [24 November 1949], BFP.
7 FB to LB, 23 March 1948 [1949], BFP.
8 John Pope-Hennessy to RN, 6 December 1990, RNA.
9 17 August 1973.
10 Peter Fraser to LB, postcard, 17 August 1973, BFP.
11 Peter Raymond Lawrence Fraser [*sic*], Death certificate, 5 March 1976; and letter from Mrs Alice Shavelson, of 3 West Hill Court, Millfield Lane, N6, to J. D. K. Lloyd, 6 May 1976, BFP.
12 J. D. K. Lloyd to FB, 11 May 1976, BFP.
13 Howard Davies to TS, 24 January 2005 and 21 February 2006; and [Joe de Freitas], Obituary of R. D. Wyatt, *Anglo-Portuguese News*, 9 August 1990.
14 *Mail on Sunday*, 15 June 2008.
15 Wendy E. Everett, *Terence Davies*, Manchester University Press, 2004, p. 17.
16 Sir Michael Howard to TS, 11 September 2007.
17 *Ibid.*

18 Douglas Gordon to FB, 12 October 1952, BFP.
19 LB, Copy Will, 9 September 1949, unsigned, BFP.
20 HC, pp. 111, 116–17, and 285–6.
21 *Ibid.*, pp. 353–4.
22 *Ibid.*, pp. 366–7.
23 *Ibid.*, p. 367.
24 LB, Copy Will, 1961, unsigned, BFP.
25 Edward Thomas, letter to *The Independent*, 30 December 1989.
26 WS to TS, email, 3 September 2008.
27 FB to LB, 'Friday 3.1.'49' [actually 3 February 1950], BFP.
28 This information kindly provided by the Rector, Fr Terence Phipps.
29 This must explain why the gold medallion she gave to Julian bears just the month and the year, no day.
30 LB, Diary, 13 May 1970, BFP.
31 J. Lees-Milne, Diary, 6 December 1980, from J. Lees-Milne (abridged by Michael Bloch), *Diaries, 1971–1983*, p. 353.
32 LB, Diary, 5 May 1968, BFP.
33 FB, in a telephone conversation with TS, 2 August 2005.
34 LB to FB, n.d. [2 April 1953], BFP; and J. Lees-Milne, Diary, 3 April 1953, in J. Lees-Milne, *A Mingled Measure*, p. 18.
35 LB to FB, Easter Day [7 April 1953], BFP.
36 J. Lees-Milne, Diary, 3 April 1953, in J. Lees-Milne, *A Mingled Measure*, p. 18.
37 FB to LB, n.d., 13 December 1951], BFP.
38 Death Certificate, John Theodore Waterman Greenidge, died 1 October 1953.
39 Will, J. T. W. Greenidge, proved 18 January 1954.
40 *The Times*, August 30 1954.
41 S. Banfield, 'The Cultivated Ear', *Musical Times*, January 1991, p. 709, quoted by MLB, 139, in an analysis of *Nelson,* pp. 128–40.
42 LB to FB, n.d. [25 March 1949], BFP.
43 LB to BB, 18 June 1950, BPL.
44 MLB, p. 140.
45 George Baker, 'Lennox Berkeley', the sixth in the series, 'What are they like at home?', *Music Teacher and Piano Student*, September 1954.
46 *The Times*, 13 September 1929.
47 LB, 'Reflections on Old Age and Death', in R. Ricketts, *Bid the World Goodnight*, pp. 19–21.
48 LB, Diary, 14 December [1971], BFP.
49 MB, in conversation with TS, 20 September 2005.
50 Richard Stoker, in a long interview with John France published on Classical Music Web, 2003, at www.musicweb.uk.net.

51 MB, in conversation with TS, 13 October 2005.
52 LB in an interview with C. B. Cox, Allan Young and Michael Schmidt, *Poetry Nation*, no. 2, 1974.
53 MB, in conversation with TS, 20 September 2005.
54 LB, in an interview with C. B. Cox, Allan Young and Michael Schmidt, *Poetry Nation*, no. 2, 1974.
55 L. Durrell, *Justine, p.* 94.
56 J. Keats, *Ode to a Nightingale.*
57 BB to LB, 21 January 1957, BFP.
58 LB to BB, 7 June 1957, BPL.
59 D. Mitchell, 'London Concerts and Opera', *The Musical Times*, November 1956.
60 LB to Douglas Gibson, 25 June 1957, CMA.

EPILOGUE

1 James Lees-Milne (ed. Michael Bloch), *Holy Dread: Diaries 1982–1984*, pp. 35–6.
2 RN to TS, email, 7 September 2007.
3 PD to TS, email, 26 April 2008.
4 LB to Patric Dickinson, 23 August 1964.
5 *Ibid.*, n.d. [postmarked 14 September 1964].
6 Patric Dickinson to TS, 5 August 1988.
7 LB, notes in a blue exercise book, n.d., but *c.* 1974 (BFP), for an article 'Reflections on Old Age and Death', in R. Ricketts (ed.), *Bid the World Goodnight*, pp. 19–21.
8 J. Lees-Milne (ed. Michael Bloch), *The Milk of Paradise*, pp. 158–63.
9 Postcard, Louise Bangay to TS, n.d. [July 2008].
10 Peter Dickinson, Obituary, 'Sir Lennox Berkeley', *The Independent*, 27 December 1989.
11 Michaela von Britzke to FB, 27 December 1989, BFP.

APPENDIX ONE

1 LB, 'Truth in Music', the second in the series 'Religion and the Arts', *Times Literary Supplement*, 3 March 1966.
2 Julian Berkeley, 'A Modern Magnificat', *The Tablet*, 30 August 2003.
3 LB, 'The Old Mass and the New', *Pax: A Benedictine Review*, vol. LXI, Gloucester, Prinknash Abbey, Autumn/Winter 1971.
4 Julian Berkeley, 'A Modern Magnificat', *The Tablet*, 30 August 2003; and *The Lennox Berkeley Society* Journal, 2008.

APPENDIX TWO

1 This theory was kindly suggested by Martin Scott of Bridport, whose aunt was an Oxford friend of Mrs Abel Greenidge – postcard to TS, 1 February 2002.
2 G. B. Grundy, *Fifty-five Years at Oxford: An Unconventional Autobiography*, p. 80.
3 *Ibid.*
4 E. Waugh (ed. Michael Davie), *The Diaries of Evelyn Waugh*, p. 166.
5 Alexander Waugh, *Fathers and Sons*, p. 183.
6 Rugby School magazine, *The Meteor*, 3 April 1917, p. 39.
7 *Oxford University Calendar*, 1921, pp. 496–7.
8 E. Waugh (ed. Michael Davie), *The Diaries of Evelyn Waugh*, p. 169.
9 FB to TS, 24 March 2004.
10 LB, Diary, 16 August 1968, BFP.
11 Will of J. T. W. Greenidge dated 13 June 1951, proved 18 January 1954.
12 E. Waugh, *A Little Learning*, pp. 176–9; and T. Greenidge, *Degenerate Oxford?*, p. 4.
13 M. Stannard, *Evelyn Waugh*, vol. i, p. 74.
14 E. Waugh (ed. Michael Davie), *The Diaries of Evelyn Waugh*, p. 792.
15 Charles E. Linck, Jr, 'Waugh-Greenidge Film *The Scarlet Woman*, *Evelyn Waugh Newsletter,* vol. 3, no. 2, Autumn 1969; and email Prof. John H. Wilson to TS, 23 March 2004.

APPENDIX THREE

1 B. Falk, *The Berkeleys of Berkeley Square*, p. 233.
2 *Morning Leader*, 17 October, 1857 – quoted in B. Falk, *The Berkeleys of Berkeley Square*, p. 233.
3 *Punch,* 9 March 1861.
4 B. Falk, *The Berkeleys of Berkeley Square*, pp. 265–7.

APPENDIX FOUR

1 Commander Hastings Berkeley to Aline Harris, 30 December 1889, BFP.
2 *The Times*, 2, 4, 7 and 23 January 1890.
3 *Ibid.*, 22, 24, 27 and 29 September 1892.
4 *Ibid.*, 9 September 1887.
5 Hastings George FitzHardinge Berkeley, *Japanese Letters: Eastern Impressions of Western Men and Manners, as Contained in the Correspondence of Tokiwara and Yashiri*, p. 173.

6 *Ibid.*, p. 172.
7 *Ibid.*, p. 61
8 *Ibid.*, p. 62.
9 *Ibid.*, p. 125.
10 *Ibid.*, p. 129.
11 G. H. H[ardy], *The Cambridge Review*, 26 May 1910.
12 *Manchester Guardian*, 28 June 1910.

APPENDIX FIVE

1 Horace Rumbold, *Recollections of a Diplomatist*, vol. ii, pp. 89–91.
2 Gerhardine Harris [née von Gall], unpublished 'Recollections', 1862, BFP.
3 Gerhardine Harris, Diary for 20 July 1873, and the unpublished memoirs of Yvonne Berkeley, BFP; also the Revd H. N. Hutchinson, *The Living Rulers of Mankind*, p. 229.
4 Obituary, 'Sir James Harris', *l'Elaireur de Nice*, 9 November 1904.

Bibliography

(NB Place of publication is London unless otherwise stated)

Abse, Leo, 'A tale of collaboration not conflict with the "People of the Book"' [a review of Ursula R. Q. Henriques (ed.), *The Jews of South Wales: Historical Studies*, Cardiff, University of Wales Press, 1993], *The New Welsh Review*, Aberystwyth, no. 22, Autumn 1993, pp. 16–21

Acton, Harold, *Memoirs of an Aesthete*, Methuen, 1970

Addis, W. E., and Thomas Arnold, *A Catholic Dictionary*, Virtue & Co., 1954

Aldiss, Margaret, and Patricia Simms, *A Boars Hill Anthology*, Oxford, Thornton's, on behalf of the Boars Hill Association, 1998

Allen, Walter, *As I Walked Down New Grub Street: Memories of a Writing Life*, Heinemann, 1981

Les Anglais dans le Comté de Nice et en Provence depuis le XVIIIe Siècle, Nice, Editions des Amis du Musée Masséna, 1934

Auden, W. H., *W. H. Auden Collected Shorter Poems*, Faber & Faber, 1969

—— (ed. Edward Mendelson), *The English Auden*, Faber & Faber, 1977

——, 'Honour', *The Old School: Essays by Diverse Hands* (ed. Graham Greene), Cape, 1934

——, and Louis MacNeice, *Letters from Iceland*, Faber & Faber, 1937

Bailey, Paul, *Three Queer Lives: An Alternative Biography of Fred Barnes, Naomi Jacob and Arthur Marshall*, Hamish Hamilton, 2001

Banks, Philip (ed.), *The Making of Peter Grimes*, 2 vols., Woodbridge, The Britten Estate Ltd and The Boydell Press, 1996

Barbedette, Gilles, and Michel Carassou (eds.), *Gay Paris 1925*, Paris, Presses de la Renaissance, 1981

Baring-Gould, Sabine, *A Book of the Riviera*, Methuen & Co., 1905

Bartholomew, J. G., *Handy Reference Atlas of London and Suburbs*, Edinburgh, John Bartholomew & Son, 1921

Beaumont, Cyril W., *Supplement to Complete Book of Ballets*, C. W. Beaumont, 75 Charing Cross Road, 1942

Benét, William Rose, *The Reader's Encyclopaedia*, Book Club Associates, 1974

Berkeley, Grantley FitzHardinge, *My Life and Recollections*, 4 vols., Hurst & Blackett, 1865–6

——, *Anecdotes of the Upper Ten Thousand*, 1868

Berkeley, Hastings George FitzHardinge, *Wealth and Welfare; or, Our National Trade Policy and its Cost*, John Murray, 1887

——, *Japanese Letters: Eastern Impressions of Western Men and Manners, as Contained in the Correspondence of Tokiwara and Yashiri*, John Murray, 1891

——, *Mysticism in Modern Mathematics*, Oxford, Oxford University Press, 1910

Berkeley, Molly [Dowager Countess of Berkeley], *Beaded Bubbles*, Hamish Hamilton, 1967

Berkeley, Randal [Earl of Berkeley], 'Berkeley Castle', *Transactions of the Bristol & Gloucestershire Archaeological Society*, vol. 49, 1927, pp. 183–93

——, *Sound Golf by Applying Principles to Practice*, Seeley, Service & Co., 1936

Bermant, Chaim, *What's the Joke? A Study of Jewish Humour through the Ages*, Weidenfeld & Nicolson, 1986

Betham-Edwards, Matilda, *Holidays in Eastern France*, Hurst & Blackett, 1879

Betjeman, John, *Summoned by Bells*, John Murray, 1960

Bliss, Arthur, *As I Remember*, Faber & Faber, 1970

Bloch, Michael, *James Lees-Milne: The Life*, John Murray, 2009

Blyth, Alan, *Remembering Britten*, Hutchinson, 1981

Blythe, Ronald (ed.), *Aldeburgh Anthology*, Snape Maltings Foundation/ Faber Music, 1972

Boyd, Malcolm, 'Benjamin Britten and Grace Williams: Chronicle of a Friendship', *Welsh Music, 6/6*, Winter 1980–1

——, *Grace Williams,* University of Wales, Welsh Arts Council, 1980

Boyd, William, *Any Human Heart: The Intimate Journals of Logan Mountstuart*, Penguin, 2002

Bridcut, John, *Britten's Children*, Faber & Faber, 2006

Briggs, Asa, *The BBC: The First Fifty Years,* OUP, 1985

Britten, Beth, *My Brother Benjamin*, The Kensal Press, 1986

Brooks, J., 'Nadia Boulanger and the Salon of the Princesse de Polignac' in *Journal of the American Musicological Society*, vol. 476, no. 3, University of Chicago Press, 1993

Bryan, G., 'The Younger English Composers – Lennox Berkeley', in *Monthly Musical Record*, 59, Augener, June 1929, pp. 161–2

Brydone, Patrick, *A Tour through Sicily and Malta*, R. Marchbank for the Company of Booksellers, 1780

Buckland, Sidney (ed. and trans.), *Francis Poulenc: 'Echo and Source': Selected Correspondence 1915–1963*, Fayard, 1994

Buckland, Sidney, and Myriam Chimènes (eds.), *Francis Poulenc: Music, Art and Literature*, Aldershot, Ashgate, 1999

Buckle, Richard, *Nijinsky*, Penguin, 1980

Burn, Michael, *Turned towards the Sun: An Autobiography*, Norwich, Michael Russell, 2003

Burnel, Auguste, *Étude sur Nice,* Nice, Société typographique, 1856

Burney, Charles (ed. H. Edmund Poole), *Music, Men, and Manners in France and Italy 1770, Being the Journal Written by Charles Burney, Mus. D., during a Tour through Those Countries Undertaken to Collect Material for 'A General History of Music'*, The Folio Society, 1969

Burra, Edward (ed. William Chappell), *Well, Dearie! The Letters of Edward Burra*, Gordon Fraser, 1985

Burra, Peter, *Wordsworth*, Duckworth, 1936

Burton, Richard D. E., *Francis Poulenc*, Bath, Absolute Press, 2002

Byron, Robert (with an Introduction by David Talbot Rice), *The Road to Oxiana,* John Lehmann, 1950

Byron, Robert (ed. Lucy Butler), *Robert Byron: Letters Home*, John Murray, 1991

Calder, Robert, *Willie: The Life of W. Somerset Maugham*, Heinemann, 1989

Campion, Paul, *Ferrier: A Career Recorded*, 2nd edn, Thames Publishing, 2005

Carpenter, Humphrey, *W. H. Auden: A Biography*, George Allen and Unwin, 1981

——, *Benjamin Britten A Biography*, Faber & Faber, 1992

——, *The Brideshead Generation: Evelyn Waugh and His Friends*, Weidenfeld & Nicolson, 1989

—— (with research by Jennifer Doctor), *The Envy of the World: Fifty Years of the BBC Third Programme and Radio Three 1946–1996*, Weidenfeld & Nicolson, 1996

Chappell, William (ed.), *Edward Burra: A Painter Remembered by his Friends ...* , André Deutsch in association with the Lefevre Gallery, 1982

Chimènes, Myriam, 'Poulenc and his Patrons: Social Convergences' in Sidney Buckland and Myriam Chimènes (eds.), *Francis Poulenc: Music, Art and Literature*, Aldershot, Ashgate, 1999

Christiansen, Rupert, *Tales of the New Babylon: Paris in the Mid-19th Century*, Minerva, 1995

Clark, J. W., and Margot Heinemann, etc (eds.), *Culture and Crisis in Britain in the Thirties*, Lawrence and Wishart, 1979

Cohen, Harriet, *A Bundle of Time: the Memoirs of Harriet Cohen*, Faber & Faber, 1969

——, *Music's Handmaid*, Faber & Faber, 1936

Coke, Henry John, *Tracks of a Rolling Stone*, Smith, Elder & Co., 1905

Connon, Bryan, *Somerset Maugham and the Maugham Dynasty*, Sinclair-Stevenson, 1997

Cooke, James Herbert, *A Sketch of the History of Berkeley: its Castle, Church and the Berkeley Family*, Gloucester, John Bellows, *c.* 1871

Copland, Aaron, and Vivian Perlis, *Copland 1900 through 1942*, Faber & Faber, 1984

Cornford, John, *Collected Writings*, Manchester, Carcanet, 1986

Costley-White, Hope, *Mary Cole, Countess of Berkeley – A Biography*, George Harrap & Co, 1961

Coton, A. V., *Writings on Dance 1938–68*, Dance Books, 1975

Coulton, Barbara, *Louis MacNeice in the BBC*, Faber & Faber, 1980

Craggs, Stewart R., *Lennox Berkeley: A Source Book*, Aldershot, Ashgate, 2000

Curtis, Anthony, *Somerset Maugham*, Weidenfeld & Nicolson, 1977

Cuthbert, Caroline, 'From William Coldstream's Notebooks', in Lawrence Gowing and David Sylvester, *The Paintings of William Coldstream 1908–1987*, Tate Gallery, 1990

Davenport-Hines, Richard, *A Night at the Majestic: Proust and the Great Modernist Dinner Party of 1922*, Faber & Faber, 2006

Davies, Marie, 'Childhood Memories', *Gwent Local History*, vol. 63, autumn 1987, pp. 30–7

Day Lewis, C. *The Buried Day: A Personal Memoir*, Chatto & Windus, 1960

—— [ed. Jill Balcon], *The Complete Poems of C. Day Lewis*, Sinclair-Stevenson, 1992

Day-Lewis, Sean, *C. Day-Lewis: An English Literary Life*, Weidenfeld, 1980

Dean, Basil, *Mind's Eye: An Autobiography 1927–1972*, Hutchinson, 1973

de Cossart, Michael, *The Food of Love: Princesse Edmond de Polignac (1865–1943) and Her Salon*, Hamish Hamilton, 1978

De-la-Noy, Michael, *Eddy: The Life of Edward Sackville-West*, Arcadia Books, 1999

Delius, Frederick, and Peter Warlock [pseudonym of Philip Heseltine] (ed. Barry Smith), *Frederick Delius and Peter Warlock: A Friendship Revealed*, Oxford, Oxford University Press, 2000

Dickinson, Peter, *Lord Berners: Composer, Writer, Painter*, Woodbridge, Boydell & Brewer, 2008

——, *The Music of Lennox Berkeley*, Thames Publishing, 1988; Second (revised and expanded) edition, Woodbridge, The Boydell Press, 2003

——, 'Interview with Sir Lennox Berkeley', in P. Dickinson (ed.), *Twenty British Composers*, J. & W. Chester for the Feeney Trust, 1975, pp. 23–9

Douglas-Home, Jessica, *Violet: The Life and Loves of Violet Gordon Woodhouse*, Harvill Press, 1996

Driberg, T., *Ruling Passions*, Jonathan Cape, 1977

Droescher, Werner, 'Towards an Alternative Society' in *Thr@ll magazine: Anarchist news and Views from Aotearoa, New Zealand*, no. 16, November/December 2000

Duff, David, *Victoria Travels: Journeys of Queen Victoria between 1830 and 1900, with Extracts from Her Journal*, Frederick Muller, 1970

Duncan, Ronald, *Working with Britten: A Personal Memoir*, Rebel Press, 1981

Dyer, Colin, 'Hivernants et habitants sur la Riviera Française' in *Recherches régionales Alpes-Maritimes*, no. 143, Nice, 1998

Evans, John, Philip Reed and Paul Wilson (compilers), *A Britten Source Book*, Aldeburgh, Britten–Pears Library, 1987

Falk, Bernard, *The Berkeleys of Berkeley Square and Some of Their Kinfolk*, Hutchinson, 1944

Farnan, Dorothy J., *Auden in Love*, Faber & Faber, 1985

Fenby, Eric, *Delius as I Knew Him*, G. Bell & Sons, 1936

Ferris, Paul, *Caitlin*, Hutchinson, 1993

FitzGibbon, Constantine, *The Life of Dylan Thomas*, J. M. Dent & Sons

Flanner, Janet [Genêt] (ed. Irving Drutman), *Paris Was Yesterday: 1925–39*, Angus and Robertson, 1973

Foreman, Lewis, *From Parry to Britten: British Music in Letters 1900–1945*, Batsford, 1987

Forster, E. M., *A Passage to India* with an introduction by Peter Burra and some notes by the author, Everyman's Library 972, J. M. Dent & Sons Ltd., 1942

Fothergill, John, *An Innkeeper's Diary*, Chatto & Windus, 1931

Frost, Stella (ed.), *A Tribute to Evie Hone and Mainie Jellett*, Dublin, Browne and Nolan, 1957

Fuller, *W. H. Auden: A Commentary*, Faber & Faber, 1998

Fryer, Jonathan, *Isherwood: A Biography of Christopher Isherwood*, New English Library, 1977

Garafola, Lynn, *Diaghilev's Ballets Russes*, OUP, 1989

Gardiner, James, *A Class Apart: The Private Pictures of Montague Glover*, Serpent's Tail, 1993

Garnham, Maureen, *As I Saw It: Basil Douglas, Benjamin Britten and the English Opera Group, 1955–7*, St George's Publications, 1998

Gathorne-Hardy, Jonathan, *The Public School Phenomenon, 597–1977*, Hodder & Stoughton, 1977

——, *Half an Arch*, Timewell Press, 2004

Genêt, Jean (trans. Bernard Frechtman), *The Thief's Journal*, Paris, The Olympia Press, 1954

Gilmour, David, *Cities of Spain*, John Murray, 1992.

Gishford, Anthony (ed.), *Tribute to Benjamin Britten on His Fiftieth Birthday*, Faber & Faber, 1963
Glock, William, *Notes in Advance*, Oxford, Oxford University Press, 1991
Golding, Robin, Programme Notes for a concert of works by Mozart and Lennox Berkeley given by Dennis Brain Wind Ensemble, V & A Museum, 28 March 1954
Green, Henry, *Pack My Bag: A Self Portrait*, The Hogarth Press, 1979
Green, Julien, *Jeunesse*, Plon, 1974
—— (translated by Jocelyn Godefroi), *Personal Record 1928–1939*, Harper & Brothers, 1939
Green, Martin, *Children of the Sun: A Narrative of Decadence in England after 1918*, New York, Basic Books, 1976
Green, V. H. H., *A History of Oxford University*, B. T. Batsford, 1974
Greene, Graham, *The Heart of the Matter*, Heinemann, 1948
Greenidge, Terence Lucy, *Degenerate Oxford? A Critical Study of Modern University Life*, Chapman & Hall, 1930
—— (ed. Charles Linck), *Evelyn Waugh in Letters by Terence Greenidge*, Commerce, Texas, Cow Hill Press, *c.* 1994
Gresham's School Register, Gresham's School, Holt
Grogan, Christopher (ed.), *Imogen Holst: A Life in Music*, Woodbridge, The Boydell Press, 2007
Gyseghem, André van, 'British Theatre in the Thirties: An Autobiographical Record', in *Culture and Crisis in the Thirties* (eds. Jon Clark, Margot Heinemann, David Margolies and Carol Snee), Lawrence & Wishart, 1979
Guide Pratique de Nice, Lyon, Société des Guides Pol, n.d.
Günther, R.T., *The Oxford Country*, John Murray, 1912
Hall, Fernau, *Modern English Ballet,* Andrew Melrose, 1950
Hampton's Scholastic Directory for London and the Provinces, J. W. Clarke, 1913–14
Harding, James, *The Ox on the Roof: Scenes from Musical Life in Paris in the Twenties*, Macdonald, 1972
Hare, Augustus J. C., *Days near Paris,* George Allen, n.d..
——, *Paris*, 2 vols., George Allen, 1900
——, *The Rivieras*, 1897
——, *South-Eastern France*, 1890
Harris, J. C., *Décadence de Nice comme Station d'Hiver*; pamphlet, no publisher, 1884
Harrod, Wilhelmine, *The Norfolk Guide*, Bury St Edmunds, The Alastair Press, 1988
Hartley, Harold, 'Randal Thomas Mowbray Rawdon Berkeley Earl of Berkeley', *Obituary Notices of Fellows of the Royal Society*, vol. 4, November 1942

Hastings, Selina, *Evelyn Waugh: A Biography*, Sinclair-Stevenson, 1994
——, *Rosamond Lehmann*, Chatto & Windus, 2002
——, *The Secret Lives of Somerset Maugham*, John Murray, 2009
Haug, C. James, *Leisure & Urbanism in Nineteenth-Century Nice*, The Regents Press of Kansas, Lawrence, 1982
Headington, Christopher, *Britten*, Eyre Methuen, 1981
——, *Peter Pears: A Biography*, Faber & Faber, 1992
Henriques, Ursula R. Q. (ed.), *The Jews of South Wales: Historical Studies*, Cardiff, University of Wales Press, 1993
Hibberd, Dominic, *Wilfred Owen: A New Biography*, Chicago, Ivan R. Dee, 2003
Hollis, Christopher, *Oxford in the Twenties: Recollections of Five Friends*, Heinemann, 1976
——, *The Seven Ages: Their Exits and Their Entrances*, Heinemann, 1974
Holroyd, Michael, *Augustus John*, 2 vols, Heinemann, 1974
Holmstrom, John, *The Moving Picture Boy – An International Encyclopaedia: 1895–1995*, Norwich, Michael Russell, 1996
Horniman, Roy, *Israel Rank*, Eyre and Spottiswoode, 1907
Howard, Michael, *Captain Professor: A Life in War and Peace*, Continuum, 2006
Howarth, Patrick, *When the Riviera Was Ours*, Routledge & Kegan Paul, 1977
Hussey, Walter, *Patron of Art: The Revival of a Great Tradition among Modern Artists*, Weidenfeld & Nicolson, 1985
Hutchings, Arthur, *Delius*, Macmillan, 1948
Hutchinson, the Revd H. N., *The Living Rulers of Mankind*, George Allen, 1902
Isherwood, Christopher, *Christopher and His Kind 1929–1939*, Eyre Methuen, 1977
Isnard, Roger, 'Les Anglais à Nice' in *Nice Historique*, October–December 1985, Nice, Acadèmia Nissarda, 1985, pp. 103–19
Ivry, Benjamin, *Francis Poulenc*, Phaidon Press, 1996
——, *Maurice Ravel: A Life*, New York, Welcome Rain Publishers, 2000
Johnson, Graham, *Britten, Voice and Piano: Lectures on the Vocal Music of Benjamin Britten*, The Guildhall School of Music & Drama and Ashgate Publishing, Aldershot, 2003
Jordan, Mark D., *The Silence of Sodom: Homosexuality in Modern Catholicism*, University of Chicago Press, 2000
Junge, Ewald, *Anthony Bernard: A Life in Music*, Tunbridge Wells, 1992
Kahan, Sylvia, *Music's Modern Muse: A Life of Winnaretta Singer, Princesse de Polignac*, Rochester NY, University of Rochester Press, 2003

Kanigel, Robert, *High Season in Nice: How One French Riviera Town Has Seduced Travellers for Two Thousand Years*, Little, Brown, 2002
Kavanagh, Julie, *Secret Muses: The Life of Frederick Ashton*, Faber, 1996
Kendall, Alan, *The Tender Tyrant: Nadia Boulanger – A Life Devoted to Music*, Macdonald & Jane's, 1976
Kidd, Charles, and David Williamson (eds.), *Debrett's Peerage and Baronetage*, Macmillan, 1990
Knox, James, *Robert Byron*, John Murray, 2003
Lancaster, Osbert, *With an Eye to the Future*, John Murray, 1967
Langdon-Davies, John, *Gatherings from Catalonia*, Cassell & Company, 1953
——, *Dancing Catalans*, Jonathan Cape, 1929
Larner, Gerald, *Maurice Ravel*, Phaidon Press, 1996
Latouche, Robert, *Histoire de Nice*, 3 vols., Nice, 1951–65
Leeming, David, *Stephen Spender – A Life in Modernism*, Duckworth, 1999
Lees-Milne, James, *Another Self*, Hamish Hamilton, 1970
——, *Ancestral Voices* [Diaries, 1942–43], Chatto & Windus, 1975
——, *Prophesying Peace* [Diaries, 1944–45], Chatto & Windus, 1977
——, *Caves of Ice* [Diaries, 1946–1947], Chatto & Windus, The Hogarth Press, 1983
——, *Midway on the Waves* [Diaries, 1948–1949], John Murray, 1985
——, *A Mingled Measure: Diaries, 1953–1972*, John Murray, 1994
——, *Ancient as the Hills: Diaries, 1973–1974*, John Murray, 1997
——, *Through Wood and Dale: Diaries, 1975–1978*, John Murray, 1998
—— (ed. Michael Bloch), *Deep Romantic Chasm – Diaries, 1979–1981*, John Murray, 2000
—— ——, *Holy Dread: Diaries, 1982 –1984*, John Murray, 2001
—— ——, *Beneath a Waning Moon: Diaries, 1985–1987*, John Murray, 2003
—— ——, *Ceaseless Turmoil: Diaries, 1988–1992*, John Murray 2004
—— ——, *The Milk of Paradise: Diaries 1993–1997*, John Murray, 2005
——, *Diaries, 1942–1954*, abridged and introduced by Michael Bloch, John Murray, 2006
——, *Diaries, 1971–1983*, abridged and introduced by Michael Bloch, John Murray, 2007
——, *Diaries, 1984–1997*, abridged and introduced by Michael Bloch, John Murray, 2008
——, *Fourteen Friends*, John Murray, 1996
Lehmann, Rosamond, *Dusty Answer*, Virago Press, 2000 [first published Chatto & Windus, 1927]
Leigh Fermor, Patrick, *A Time to Keep Silence*, John Murray, 1957

Leneman, Helen, *The Performed Bible: The Story of Ruth in Opera and Oratorio*, Sheffield, Sheffield Phoenix Press, 2007

Lewis, John, *Such Things Happen: The Life of a Typographer*, Stowmarket, Unicorn Press, 1994

Linck, Charles E., Jr (ed.), 'Waugh–Greenidge Film – *The Scarlet Woman*', *Evelyn Waugh Newsletter*, vol. 3, no. 2, Lock Haven University of Pennsylvania, 1969, pp. 1–7

Lloyd, Stephen, *H. Balfour Gardiner*, Cambridge University Press, 1984

Lowinsky, Ruth, *Food for Pleasure*, Rupert Hart-Davis, 1950

Lycett, Andrew, *Dylan Thomas: A New Life*, Weidenfeld & Nicolson, 2003

Mackenzie, D. (ed.), *Holborn Old and New*, The Princeton Press (for the First Avenue Hotel), n.d.

MacNeice, Louis, *The Strings Are False: An Unfinished Autobiography*, Faber & Faber, 1965

MacRae, Julia (ed.), *Wigmore Hall 1901–2001*, Wigmore Hall Trust, 2001

Mallaby, George, *From My Level*, Hutchinson & Co., 1965.

Markevitch, Igor, *Être et avoir été – mémoires*, Paris, Gallimard, 1980

Marsh, Edward, and Christopher Hassall, *Ambrosia and Small Beer: The Record of a Correspondence between Edward Marsh and Christopher Hassall*, Longmans, 1964

Marshall, Arthur, *Girls Will Be Girls*, Hamish Hamilton, 1974

Martin, G. H., and J. R. L. Highfield, *A History of Merton College*, Oxford, Oxford University Press, 1997

Matthews, David, *Britten*, Haus Publishing, 2003

Maugham, Robin, *Escape from the Shadows*, Hodder & Stoughton, 1972

Maugham, W. Somerset, *The Summing Up*, Heinemann, 1938

——, *Strictly Personal*, Heinemann, 1942

Mayes, Andrew C. D., *Carl Dolmetsch and the Recorder Repertoire of the 20th Century*, Aldershot, Ashgate, 2003

Medley, Robert, 'The Group Theatre 1932–9: Rupert Doone and Wystan Auden', *London Magazine*, January 1981

Mee, Arthur (ed.), *Norfolk: Green Pastures and Still Waters*, Hodder and Stoughton, 1940

Mellers, Wilfred, *Francis Poulenc*, Oxford Univerity Press, 1993

Mendelson, Edward, *Early Auden*, Faber & Faber, 1981

Merton College Register, 1900–1964, Oxford, Blackwell, 1964

Mitchell, D., *Britten and Auden in the Thirties*, Faber & Faber, 1981

—— and J. Evans (compilers), *Benjamin Britten: Pictures from a Life 1913–76*, Faber & Faber, 1978

—— and Hans Keller (eds.), *Benjamin Britten: A Commentary on His Works from a Group of Specialists*, Rockliff, 1952

—— and P. Reed, *Letters from a Life: Selected Letters and Diaries of Benjamin Britten* vol. 1, 1930–39, vol. 2, 1939–45, Faber & Faber, 1991
—— —— and Mervyn Cooke, *Letters from a Life: The Selected Letters and Diaries of Benjamin Britten*, vol. 3, 1946–51, Faber & Faber 2004
—— and P. Reed and Mervyn Cooke, *Letters from a Life: The Selected Letters of Benjamin Britten*, vol. 4, 1952–57, Woodbridge, The Boydell Press in association with The Britten–Pears Foundation, 2008
Mitchell, Michael, and Susan Wightman, *House Rules: A Practical Manual of Book Typography*, Marlborough, Libanus Press, 2005
Morgan, Ted, *Somerset Maugham*, Jonathan Cape, 1980
Morphet, Richard, 'Introduction' [and biographical sketch of Helen Binyon] in Binyon, Helen, *Eric Ravilious: Memoir of an Artist*, Guildford, Lutterworth Press, 1983
Murray's Handbook for Travellers, France, part II, John Murray, 1892
Nash, James, *The Royal Guide to Nice*, Nice, Bensa, 1896
Nelson, Michael, *Queen Victoria and the Discovery of the Riviera*, I. B. Tauris, 2001
Newbolt, Henry, *The Book of the Blue Sea*, Longmans, Green, 1914
Nice Historique, 'Centenaire 1898–1998', nos. 1 and 2/1998, Nice, Académia Nissarda, 1998
Nichols, Beverley, *A Case of Human Bondage*, Secker & Warburg, 1966
Nichols, Roger, *The Harlequin Years: Music in Paris 1917–1929*, Thames and Hudson, 2002
——, *Ravel*, Dent, 1977
—— (ed.), *Ravel Remembered*, Faber, 1987
Nicolson, Harold (ed. Nigel Nicolson), *Diaries and Letters 1930–62*, 3 vols., Collins, 1969–71
Oman, Carola, *Nelson*, Hodder & Stoughton, 1947
Orenstein, A., (ed.), *A Ravel Reader*, New York and Oxford, Columbia University Press, 1990
Orwell, George, *Homage to Catalonia*, Secker & Warburg, 1938
Osborne, Charles, *W. H. Auden: The Life of a Poet,* Eyre Methuen, 1979
Oxford Dictionary of National Biography, Oxford University Press, 2004
Palmer, Christopher (ed.), *The Britten Companion*, Faber & Faber, 1984
Parker, Peter, *Ackerley: A Life of J. R. Ackerley*, Constable, 1989
——, *Isherwood: A Life*, Picador, 2004
——, *The Old Lie: The Great War and the Public School Ethos*, Constable, 1987
—— (ed.), *The Reader's Companion to Twentieth Century Writers*, Fourth Estate and Helicon, 1995
Parlett, Graham, *A Catalogue of the Works of Sir Arnold Bax* , Oxford, Clarendon Press, 1999

Partridge, Frances, *Diaries 1939–72* [including *A Pacifist's War: Diaries 1939–45*], Orion Publishing, 2000
Penrose, Barrie, and Simon Freeman, *Conspiracy of Silence: The Secret Life of Anthony Blunt*, Grafton Books, 1986
Pepper, Terence, *Howard Coster's Celebrity Portraits: 101 Photographs of Personalities in Literature and the Arts*, National Portrait Gallery, in association with Dover Publications, New York, 1985
Petit, Edgar, 'Carabacel', in *Nice Historique*, no. 1/2001, Nice, Académia Nissarda, 2001
Piper, David, *The Companion Guide to London*, Collins, 1964
Potter, Julian, *Stephen Potter at the BBC: 'Features' in War and Peace*, Orford, Orford Books, 2004
Pound, Reginald, *Sir Henry Wood*, Cassell, 1969
Powell, Anthony, *Infants of the Spring* [vol.1 of *To Keep the Ball Rolling: The Memoirs of Anthony Powell*], Heinemann, 1976
——, *Messengers of Day* [vol. 2], 1978
——, *Faces in My Time* [vol. 3], 1980
——, *The Strangers Are All Gone* [vol. 4], 1982
Provence, 'Les Guides Bleus', Paris, Librairie Hachette, 1922
Pryce-Jones, Alan, *The Bonus of Laughter*, Hamish Hamilton, 1987
Pryce-Jones, David (ed.), *Evelyn Waugh and His World*, Weidenfeld & Nicolson, 1973
Pudney, John, *Home and Away: An Autobiographical Gambit*, Michael Joseph, 1960
——, *Thank Goodness for Cake*, Michael Joseph, 1978
Raphael, Frederic, *W. Somerset Maugham and His World*, Thames & Hudson, 1977
Ravel, Maurice (ed. Arbie Orenstein), *A Ravel Reader*, Columbia University Press, 1990
Redding, Joan, *A Descriptive List of the Musical Manuscripts of Sir Lennox Berkeley*, MSc. (Library Science) Thesis, University of North Carolina at Chapel Hill, 1988
Reed, Philip, 'Poulenc, Britten, Aldeburgh: A Chronicle', in Sidney Buckland and Myriam Chimènes (eds.), *Francis Poulenc: Music, Art and Literature*, Aldershot, Ashgate, 1999
Ricketts, Ralph (ed.), *Bid the World Goodnight*, Search Press, 1981
Rosenstiel, Léonie, *Nadia Boulanger: A Life in Music*, NewYork, W. W. Norton & Co, 1982
Rogal, Samuel J. (ed.), *A William Somerset Maugham Encyclopaedia*, Connecticut, Greenwood Press, 1997
Roth, Ernst, *Reflections of a Music Publisher*, Cassell, 1966
Rubens, Bernice, *Brothers*, Abacus, 1984

Rumbold, Horace, *Recollections of a Diplomatist,* 2 vols., Edward Arnold, 1902

Sackville West [*sic*], V., *Berkeley Castle*, Derby, English Life Publications, 1978

St Aubyn, Giles, *Queen Victoria*, Sinclair-Stevenson, 1991

Saumarez Smith, John, *The Bookshop at 10 Curzon Street: Letters between Nancy Mitford and Heywood Hill 1952–73*, Frances Lincoln, 2004

Schmidt, Carl B., *The Music of Francis Poulenc*, Oxford, OUP, 1995

Scholes, Percy (ed.), *The Great Dr. Burney – His Life, His Travels, His Works, His Family and His Friends*, 2 vols, Oxford, Geoffrey Cumberledge, Oxford University Press, 1948

Searle, Humphrey, *Quadrille with a Raven: Memoirs*, Classical Music on the Web, 1998, at http://www.musicweb-international.com/ searle/titlepg.htm

Sidnell, Michael, *Dances of Death: The Group Theatre of London in the Thirties*, Faber & Faber, 1984

Smart, Sue, *When Heroes Die: A Forgotten Archive Reveals the Last Days of the School Friends who Died for Britain*, Derby, Breedon Books Publishing Co., 2001

Smith, William Clifford (ed. F. E. A. Yates), *Tredegar My Town: The Collected Jottings of W. C. Smith*, Risca, The Starling Press, 1976

Smyth, John (ed. Sir John Maclean, 1883–85), *Lives of the Berkeleys*, compiled *c.* 1618, printed for the Bristol and Gloucestershire Archaeology Society by John Bellows, Gloucester, 1885

Soldevila, Carlos, *Guia de Barcelona*, Barcelona, Ediciones Destino, 1952

Spender, Stephen (ed. John Goldsmith), *Journals 1939–1983*, Faber & Faber, 1985

—— (ed. Lee Bartlett), *Letters to Christopher [Isherwood, 1929–39]*, Black Sparrow Press, Santa Rosa, California, 1980

——, *World Within World: The Autobiography of Stephen Spender*, Hamish Hamilton, 1952

Spycket, Jérôme, *Nadia Boulanger*, Lausanne, Lattès, 1987

Stallworthy, Jon, *Louis MacNeice*, Faber & Faber, 1995

Stancioff, Ivan D., *Diplomat and Gardener: Memoirs*, Sofia, Petrikov Publishers, 1998

Stanford, Peter, *C. Day-Lewis: A Life*, Continuum, 2007

Stannard, Martin, *Evelyn Waugh: The Early Years 1903–1939*, J.M. Dent and Sons, 1986

——, *Evelyn Waugh: No Abiding City 1939–66*, J. M. Dent and Sons, 1992

Steane, J. B., *The Grand Tradition: Seventy Years of Singing on Record 1900 to 1970*, Duckworth, 1974

Steegmuller, Francis, *Cocteau: A Biography*, Constable, 1986

Steve, Michel, 'L'architecture dans le quartier Carabacel', in *Nice Historique*, no. 1/2001, Nice, Académia Nissarda, 2001

Stevenson, Jane, *Edward Burra: Twentieth-Century Eye*, Jonathan Cape, 2007

Stoker, Richard (interviewed by John France), *Lennox Berkeley*, Classical Music on the Web, classicallink.com, 2003

Stradling, Rob, *History and Legend: Writing the International Brigades*, Cardiff, University of Wales Press, 2003

Summers, Julie, *Fearless on Everest: The Quest for Sandy Irvine*, Weidenfeld & Nicolson, 2000

Sutherland, J. A., *Stephen Spender: The Authorized Biography*, Viking, 2004

Sykes, Christopher, *Evelyn Waugh – A Biography*, Collins, 1975

——, *Four Studies in Loyalty*, Collins, 1946

Symons, Julian, *The Thirties: A Dream Revolved*, Faber & Faber, 2nd edn, 1975

Talbot Rice, Tamara (ed. Elizabeth Talbot Rice), *Tamara: Memoirs of St Petersburg, Paris, Oxford and Byzantium*, John Murray, 1996

Teed, Roy, 'A Birthday Tribute to Sir Lennox Berkeley', *The Royal Academy of Music Magazine*, no. 232, Summer 1983.

Thomas, Caitlin, with George Tremlett, *Caitlin: A Warring Absence*, Secker & Warburg, 1986

Thomas, Dylan (ed. Paul Ferris), *The Collected Letters of Dylan Thomas*, J. M. Dent & Sons, 1985

Thomas, Dylan, and John Davenport, *The Death of the King's Canary*, Hutchinson, 1976

Thomas, J., and T. Baldwin (eds.), *Lippincott's Geographical Dictionary of the World*, Philadelphia, J. B. Lippincott, 1862

Thomson, Virgil, *Virgil Thomson*, Weidenfeld & Nicolson, 1967

Tierney, Neil, *William Walton: His Life and Music*, Robert Hale, 1984

Time Out – Barcelona, Penguin Books, 2002

Tippett, Michael (ed. Thomas Schuttenhelm), *Selected Letters of Michael Tippett*, Faber & Faber, 2005

——, *Those Twentieth Century Blues*, Hutchinson, 1991

Tóibín, Colm, *Homage to Barcelona*, Picador, 2002

Treves, Sir Frederick, *The Riviera of the Corniche Road,* Cassell, 1921

Vaughan, David, *Frederick Ashton and His Ballets*, A. & C. Black, 1977

Walsh, Stephen, *Igor Stravinsky: A Creative Spring – Russia and France, 1882–1934*, Jonathan Cape, 1999

——, *Stravinsky: The Second Exile; France and America, 1934–1971*, Jonathan Cape, 2006

Waugh, Alec, *The Loom of Youth*, Grant Richards, 1917

——, *Island in the Sun*, Cassell & Co., 1956
——, *The Early Years of Alec Waugh*, Cassell & Co., 1962
——, *My Brother Evelyn and Other Profiles*, Cassell & Co., 1967
Waugh, Alexander, *Fathers and Sons*, Headline, 2004
Waugh, Evelyn, *The Life of Ronald Knox*, Chapman & Hall, 1959
——, *Brideshead Revisited: The Sacred and Profane Memories of Captain Charles Ryder*, a revised edition with a new preface, Chapman & Hall, 1960
——, *A Little Learning: The First Volume of an Autobiography*, Chapman & Hall, 1964
——, '*The Scarlet Woman*: An Ecclesiastical Melodrama', *Evelyn Waugh Newsletter*, vol. 3, no. 2, Lock Haven University of Pennsylvania, 1969, pp. 2–7
—— (ed. Michael Davie), *The Diaries of Evelyn Waugh*, Book Club Associates, 1976
—— (ed. Mark Amory), *The Letters of Evelyn Waugh*, Phoenix, 1995
Weisbord, Albert, 'Two Visits to Barcelona' published in the Internet Archives of Albert & Vera Weisbord, www.weisbord.org
Wheen, Francis, *Tom Driberg: His Life and Indiscretions*, Chatto & Windus, 1990
White, Edmund, *The Flâneur: A Stroll through the Paradoxes of Paris*, Bloomsbury, 2001
Wilcox, Michael, *Benjamin Britten's Operas*, Absolute Press, 1997
Wildeblood, Peter, *Against the Law*, Weidenfeld & Nicolson, 1955
Wilson, John Howard, *Evelyn Waugh: A Literary Biography 1903–1924*, Fairleigh Dickinson University Press, Teaneck, New Jersey, 1996
Wright, Adrian, *Foreign Country: The Life of L. P. Hartley*, André Deutsch, 1996

Index

v camp – was not choosey at

the women he lunged at ch 174

LB changes of mind ab pacifism 274
(reproach to BB?)

Freda - in love w/ old (gay) married men - scared of sex, wanted to save gay men 312
LB v needy - she liked neediness 353
F's view of L - little boy 369
She weeps him down w/ attention - kindness 372
LB will always be gay ✱ 378
but they have sex 388
She's pregnant 389
3 miscarriages; 4th pregnancy - converts to Catholicism 411

? reading about his own birth? 413